THE ROUTLEDGE COMPANION
AND HUMAN RIGHTS

The Routledge Companion to Media and Human Rights offers a comprehensive and contemporary survey of the key themes, approaches and debates in the field of media and human rights.

The *Companion* is the first collection to bring together two distinct ways of thinking about human rights and media, including scholarship that examines media as a human right alongside that which looks at media coverage of human rights issues. This international collection of 49 newly written pieces thus provides a unique overview of current research in the field, while also providing historical context to help students and scholars appreciate how such developments depart from past practices.

The volume examines the universal principals of freedom of expression, legal instruments, the right to know, media as a human right, and the role of media organisations and journalistic work. It is organised thematically in five parts:

- Communication, Expression and Human Rights
- Media Performance and Human Rights: Political Processes
- Media Performance and Human Rights: News and Journalism
- Digital Activism, Witnessing and Human Rights
- Media Representation of Human Rights: Cultural, Social and Political.

Individual essays cover an array of topics, including mass-surveillance, LGBT advocacy, press law, freedom of information and children's rights in the digital age. With contributions from both leading scholars and emerging scholars, the *Companion* offers an interdisciplinary and multidisciplinary approach to media and human rights allowing for international comparisons and varying perspectives.

The Routledge Companion to Media and Human Rights provides a comprehensive introduction to the current field useful for both students and researchers, and defines the agenda for future research.

Howard Tumber is Professor of Journalism at City, University of London, UK. He is a founder and co-editor-in-chief of *Journalism: Theory, Practice and Criticism*. He has published widely in the field of the sociology of news and journalism.

Silvio Waisbord is Professor in the School of Media and Public Affairs at George Washington University, USA. He is the editor-in-chief of *The Journal of Communication*, and he has published widely about news, politics and social change.

Contributors: Stuart Allan, Kari Andén-Papadopoulos, Amelia H. Arsenault, Vian Bakir, Ekaterina Balabanova, Guy Berger, Emma Briant, Michael Bromley, Lisa Brooten, Bart Cammaerts, Cynthia Carter, Martin Conboy, Glenda Cooper, Giovanna Dell'Orto, Helen Fenwick, Divina Frau-Meigs, Barbara M. Freeman, Celeste González de Bustamante, Beth A. Haller, Mark Hampton, Summer Harlow, Kari Karppinen, Diana Lemberg, Libby Lester, Steven Livingston, Sonia Livingstone, Paul Mason, Ella McPherson, Stefania Milan, Jolyon Mitchell, Kerry Moore, Brigitte L. Nacos, Eve Ng, Julian Petley, Matthew Powers, Jeannine E. Relly, Joshua Rey, Sandra Ristovska, Beatrice Santa-Wood, Anya Schiffrin, Mehdi Semati, Jan Servaes, Ibrahim Seaga Shaw, Gavin J.D. Smith, Meghan Sobel, Dominik Stecula, Sebastian Stier, Trevor Thrall, Judith Townend, Melissa Wall, Stephen J. A. Ward, Sonja Wolf and Ben Worthy.

THE ROUTLEDGE COMPANION TO MEDIA AND HUMAN RIGHTS

*Edited by Howard Tumber
and Silvio Waisbord*

LONDON AND NEW YORK

First published 2017
by Routledge
2 Park Square, Milton Park, Abingdon, Oxon OX14 4RN

and by Routledge
52 Vanderbilt Avenue, New York, NY 10017

First issued in paperback 2020

Routledge is an imprint of the Taylor & Francis Group, an informa business

British Library Cataloguing-in-Publication Data
A catalogue record for this book is available from the British Library

Library of Congress Cataloging-in-Publication Data
Names: Tumber, Howard editor. | Waisbord, Silvio R. (Silvio Ricardo), 1961– editor.
Title: The Routledge companion to media and human rights /
edited by Howard Tumber and Silvio Waisbord.
Description: London; New York : Routledge, 2017.
Identifiers: LCCN 2016054861| ISBN 9781138665545
(hardback : alk. paper) | ISBN 9781315619835 (e-book)
Subjects: LCSH: Human rights in mass media. | Human rights–Press coverage. |
Television broadcasting of news–Political aspects. |
Human rights advocacy.
Classification: LCC P96.H85 R57 2017 | DDC 323–dc23
LC record available at https://lccn.loc.gov/2016054861

ISBN 13: 978-0-367-58122-0 (pbk)
ISBN 13: 978-1-138-66554-5 (hbk)

Typeset in Bembo
by Deanta Global Publishing Services, Chennai, India

CONTENTS

Contents

FIGURES

TABLES

CONTRIBUTORS

Stuart Allan is professor and head of the School of Journalism, Media and Cultural Studies (JOMEC) at Cardiff University, UK. He is the author of *Citizen Witnessing: Revisioning Journalism in Times of Crisis* (2013) and his current research focuses on the evolving ecology of photojournalism in a digital age, particularly in war, conflict and crisis situations.

Kari Andén-Papadopoulos is professor at the Department of Media Studies, Stockholm University. She has published internationally on photojournalism in times of crisis and war. Her current research concerns digital media activism in the Middle East, with a specific focus on emergent modes of civic expression and engagement connected to digital and networked cameras.

Amelia H. Arsenault is assistant professor of communication at Georgia State University. Her scholarly work has appeared in the *International Journal of Communication*, *International Sociology*, *The ANNALS of the American Academy of Political and Social Science* and *Information, Communication, and Society*.

Vian Bakir is professor in political communication and journalism at Bangor University, Wales, UK. She is author of *Torture, Intelligence and Sousveillance in the War on Terror: Agenda-Building Struggles* (2013) and *Sousveillance, Media and Strategic Political Communication: Iraq, USA, UK* (2010).

Ekaterina Balabanova is senior lecturer in political communication at the University of Liverpool, UK. Her research interests lie at the intersection of international politics and international communication. Her latest book *The Media and Human Rights: The Cosmopolitan Promise* was published in 2014 by Routledge.

Guy Berger was formerly an editor and thereafter head of the School of Journalism and Media Studies at Rhodes University, South Africa. Between 1980 and 1983, he was imprisoned for breaking censorship laws in apartheid South Africa. Berger is currently director for freedom of expression and media development at UNESCO.

Emma L. Briant is an academic specialist in political communication at University of Sheffield, Department of Journalism Studies and her main research interests are in propaganda, particularly in US and British governmental adaptation to a changing media and conflict environment. She is the author of *Propaganda and Counter-terrorism* and co-author of *Bad News for Refugees* (2013).

Michael Bromley is professor of international journalism at City, University of London, where he was previously head of the Department of Journalism. He has also been head of the School of Journalism and Communication at the University of Queensland (Australia). He has taught in universities in the US as well as the UK and Australia.

Lisa Brooten is associate professor in the Department of Radio, Television and Digital Media at Southern Illinois University Carbondale, USA. She is a Fulbright Research Fellowship recipient and a member of the Fulbright Specialist Roster, has consulted for Freedom House and PEN American Center, and published widely in the areas of media, human rights, media reform and democratization of media.

Bart Cammaerts is associate professor in the Department of Media and Communications at the London School of Economics and Political Science (LSE). He is co-editor of *Mediation and Protest Movements* (2013) and co-author of *Youth Participation in Democratic Life: Stories of Hope and Disillusion* (2015).

Cynthia Carter is reader in the School of Journalism, Media and Cultural Studies, Cardiff University, UK. Her recent books include *Current Perspectives in Feminist Media Studies* (2013) and the *Routledge Companion to Media and Gender* (2014). She is a founding co-editor of *Feminist Media Studies* and serves on the editorial board of various journals.

Martin Conboy is professor of journalism history in the Department of Journalism Studies at the University of Sheffield where he is also the co-director of the Centre for the Study of Journalism and History. He has produced ten books on the language and history of journalism including *The Language of the News* (2007) and *Journalism Studies: The Basics* (2012).

Glenda Cooper is lecturer in journalism at City, University of London. She is editor of *The Future of Humanitarian Reporting* (2014) and the co-editor of *Humanitarianism, Communications and Change* (2015). Before that, she was the Guardian Research Fellow at Nuffield College, Oxford and a staff journalist at places including the BBC, the *Independent*, *Daily Mail*, *Washington Post* and the *Daily Telegraph*.

Giovanna Dell'Orto is associate professor at the University of Minnesota's School of Journalism and Mass Communication. She is the author of *AP Foreign Correspondents in Action* (2013) and *American Journalism and International Relations* (2015). She is also co-editor of *Reporting at the Southern Borders* (Routledge 2013).

Helen Fenwick is professor of law at Durham University and a human rights consultant to Doughty Street Chambers. She is the author of *Civil Rights: New Labour, Freedom and the Human Rights Act* (2000) and *Civil Liberties and Human Rights* (5th ed. 2016), co-author of *Media Freedom under the Human Rights Act* (2006) and contributor to *Halsbury's Laws*, 5th Edition (2013) Volume 88A Parts 1 and 2.

Divina Frau-Meigs is professor of media and ICT sociology at the Université Sorbonne Nouvelle, France. She is a specialist in cultural diversity, Internet governance, media and information literacy (MIL) and the media uses and practices of young people. She holds the UNESCO chair "Savoir-devenir in sustainable digital development" she lead projects TRANSLIT, ECO and ECFOLI and is currently the head of the European Chapter of GAPMIL, the Global Alliance for Partnerships on MIL.

Barbara M. Freeman is an adjunct research professor in the School of Journalism and Communication, Carleton University, Ottawa. Her current project examines the working lives of Canada's female journalists, 1945–2000. She has published three books examining the role of women in the news media – Kit's Kingdom (1989), The Satellite Sex (2001) and Beyond Bylines (2011).

Celeste González de Bustamante is associate professor in the School of Journalism at The University of Arizona. Her research interests include the history of news media in Mexico and Brazil, and the US-Mexico borderlands. She is the author of *'Muy buenas noches,' Mexico, Television and the Cold War* (2012) and co-editor of *Arizona Firestorm: Global Immigration Realities, National Media, and Provincial Politics* (2012).

Beth A. Haller is professor of mass communication at Towson University, Maryland. She is the author of *Representing Disability in an Ableist World: Essays on Mass Media* (2010) and *Byline of Hope: Collected Newspaper and Magazine Writings of Helen Keller* (2015). She is the former co-editor of the Society for Disability Studies' scholarly journal, *Disability Studies Quarterly*, (2003–06).

Mark Hampton is associate professor of history at Lingnan University, Hong Kong, where he is also associate dean of the Faculty of Arts. He is author of *Visions of the Press in Britain, 1850–1950* (2004) and *Hong Kong and British Culture, 1945–1997* (2016), and co-editor of *Anglo-American Media Interactions, 1850–2000* (2007) and *The Cultural Construction of the British World* (2016).

Summer Harlow is Assistant Professor in the Jack J. Valenti School of Communication at the University of Houston. She is the author of *Liberation Technology in El Salvador: Re-appropriating Social Media Among Alternative Media Projects* (2017). Her recent research has been published in the *Journal of Communication*.

Kari Karppinen is a postdoctoral researcher in Media and Communication Studies at the University of Helsinki, Finland. His research focuses on the guiding principles and ideologies of media and communication policy. He is the author of the book *Rethinking Media Pluralism* (2013) and a number of journal articles and book chapters.

Diana Lemberg is assistant professor of history at Lingnan University in Hong Kong. A specialist in twentieth-century US international history and Euro-American relations, she is broadly interested in the cultural, intellectual and technological dimensions of human-rights history. Her book *Barriers Down: Freedom of Information and American Power* is forthcoming from Columbia University Press.

Libby Lester is professor and head of journalism, media and communications at the University of Tasmania, Australia. She is the author and co-editor of four books on media and environmental politics, and her recent research, funded by the Australian Research Council, investigates transnational environmental politics and trade in the Asia-Australia region.

Steven Livingston is professor of media and public affairs and international affairs at George Washington University. He studies the role of advanced technology in governance and the provisioning of public goods, including human security and rights. He is currently working on a book about the use of commercial remote sensing satellites, DNA sequencing technology and digital networks by human rights organisations.

Sonia Livingstone, OBE, is the professor of media and communications, London School of Economics and Political Science, and has published 20 books, including most recently *The Class: Living and Learning in the Digital Age* (with Julian Sefton-Green 2016). A fellow of the British Psychological Society, Royal Society for the Arts, and fellow and past president of the International Communication Association, she leads the projects Global Kids Online and Preparing for a Digital Future.

Paul Mason is a barrister at Doughty Street Chambers in London. He was previously senior lecturer in the School for Journalism, Media and Cultural Studies at Cardiff University. He is widely published, including *Captured by the Media: Prison Discourse in Media Culture* (ed. 2006), *Criminal Visions: Media Representations of Crime and Justice* (ed. 2003) and *Policing and the Media: Facts, Fiction and Faction* (2003 with Frank Leishman).

Ella McPherson is the University of Cambridge's lecturer in the sociology of new media and digital technology. Ella is currently researching the use of social media in the pursuit of human rights accountability. She has previously published on mediated human rights, including in the *International Journal of Communication, American Behavioral Scientist* and the *Journal of Human Rights*.

Stefania Milan is assistant professor of new media and digital culture at the University of Amsterdam and Associate Professor (II) of Media Innovation at the University of Oslo. Her work explores the intersection of digital technology, activism and governance, with a particular attention to radical internet practices. She is the author of *Social Movements and Their Technologies: Wiring Social Change* (2013) and co-author of *Media/Society* (2011).

Jolyon Mitchell is Professor at the University of Edinburgh where he specialises in Religion, Violence and Peacebuilding, with special reference to the arts and media. A former BBC World Service Producer and Journalist, his recent books include *Promoting Peace, Inciting Violence: The Role of Religion and Media* (Routledge, 2012) and *Martyrdom: A Very Short Introduction* (2012).

Kerry Moore is lecturer at Cardiff University School of Journalism, Media and Cultural Studies. Her research focuses on cultural theory and politics, and particularly on racism in news media and political discourse. She is co-editor of *Migrations and the Media* (2013) and editor of the special journal issue *The Meaning of Migration* (Jomec Journal 2015).

Brigitte L. Nacos is a journalist, author and adjunct professor of political science at Columbia University. Her terrorism/counterterrorism-related books are *Terrorism and the Media* (1996); *Mass-Mediated Terrorism* (2007), now in its third edition, and *Terrorism and Counterterrorism* (Routledge 2016), now in its fifth edition.

Eve Ng is assistant professor in the School of Media Arts and Studies and the Women's, Gender, and Sexuality Program at Ohio University. Her research has examined class and taste, digital media and participation, popular media fandoms, LGBT cultural production, and LGBT activism in Southeast Asia. She has been published in venues including *Communication, Culture, and Critique, Feminist Media Studies, Flow TV*, and *Popular Communication*.

Julian Petley is professor of journalism and screen media in the Department of Social Sciences, Media and Communications at Brunel University London. He is the editor of *Media and Public Shaming: Drawing the Boundaries of Disclosure* (2013), a member on the advisory board of Index on Censorship and of the national council of the Campaign for Press and Broadcasting Freedom.

Matthew Powers is assistant professor in the Department of Communication at the University of Washington in Seattle, and the associate director of the Centre for Communication and Civic Engagement. His academic writings have been published in *Journal of Communication, Media, Culture and Society* and the *International Journal of Press/Politics*, among others.

Jeannine E. Relly is associate professor in the School of Journalism at The University of Arizona and has a courtesy appointment with the School of Government and Public Policy. Her research focuses on influences on news media systems, press–state relations, democratic institutions and freedom of expression and information access in countries in conflict and political transition.

Joshua Rey is a clergyman in the Church of England, currently working as Chaplain to the Bishop of Southwark. Prior to ordination his career included field postings as an aid worker in situations where religion, human rights and media all played a significant role: Afghanistan under the Taliban, Albania during the Kosovo war, Central Sudan during the Sudanese Civil War.

Sandra Ristovska is the George Gerbner Postdoctoral Fellow at the Annenberg School for Communication at the University of Pennsylvania and a fellow at the Information Society Project at the Yale Law School, where she helps manage the Visual Law Project. Her work has been published in Media Culture and Society, Journal of Human Rights, Communication Review and other venues.

Beatrice Santa-Wood graduated from Beloit College with a bachelor's in political science. She was a Fulbright ETA in Gaziantep, Turkey and is currently pursuing a master's in international affairs from Columbia University School of International and Public Affairs.

Anya Schiffrin is lecturer and director of the media, advocacy and communications department at Columbia University's School of International and Public Affairs. Her most recent book is *Global Muckraking: 100 years of Investigative Journalism from Around the World*.

Mehdi Semati is professor of communication at Northern Illinois University. His writings on Iranian culture and media and international communication have appeared in various scholarly journals. His books include *Media, Culture and Society in Iran: Living with Globalization and the Islamic State* (2008), and *New Frontiers in International Communication Theory* (2004).

Jan Servaes is editor-in-chief of the journal *Telematics and Informatics: An Interdisciplinary Journal on the Social Impacts of New Technologies* and editor of the series Communication, Globalization and Cultural Identity and Communication, Culture and Change in Asia. He has taught international communication and communication for social change in 55 countries and is known for his 'multiplicity paradigm' in *Communication for Development. One World, Multiple Cultures* (1999).

Ibrahim Seaga Shaw is senior lecturer in media and politics at Northumbria University, UK. He is author of four books, including two monographs: *Human Rights Journalism* (2012) and *Business Journalism: A Critical Political Economy Approach* (Routledge, 2016). He has a background in journalism spanning 20 years, having worked in Sierra Leone, Britain and France.

Gavin J.D. Smith is senior lecturer in the ANU's Research School of Social Sciences and Deputy Head of the ANU School of Sociology. His research explores the impacts of digital technologies and datafication processes on social relations, specifically examining how social factors mediate practices of watching and being watched. His recent book, *Opening the Black Box: The Work of Watching* (Routledge 2015) provides an ethnographic account of CCTV camera operation. He was previously an editor of *Surveillance and Society*.

Meghan Sobel is assistant professor in the Department of Communication at Regis University. Dr. Sobel's professional experience includes work with anti-human trafficking organizations in Thailand and the United States Department of State in Malawi. Her research interests focus on international communication, public diplomacy and the role of media in combatting human rights abuses and humanitarian crises.

Dominik Stecula is a PhD candidate in political science at the University of British Columbia. His research primarily focuses on the role that the changing media environment plays in politics, primarily in the United States but also in a comparative context, as well as on research methods, primarily the analysis of text as data.

Sebastian Stier is a postdoctoral researcher at GESIS – Leibniz Institute for the Social Sciences in Cologne. He analyses the relationship between political institutions and political communication in the mass media and on the Internet. Furthermore, he studies the political use of social media like Twitter and Facebook using the methods of comparative politics and computational social science.

Trevor Thrall is associate professor of international security at the Schar School of Policy and Government at George Mason University. His research and teaching focus on the intersection of political communication and international affairs. Thrall is co-editor of *American Foreign Policy and the Politics of Fear* (Routledge 2009) and *Why Did the United States Invade Iraq?* (2011).

Judith Townend is lecturer in media and information law at the University of Sussex. She is co-editor of *Media Power and Plurality* (2015) and her interdisciplinary research focuses on access to information and, more broadly, the development of media and information law and policy in society.

Melissa Wall is professor of journalism at California State University – Northridge where she studies the intersections of mobile and social media with journalism, particularly within international contexts. She is the editor of *Citizen Journalism: Valuable, Useless or Dangerous* and a former Fulbright Scholar to Lebanon and an Open Society Academic Scholar to Ukraine.

Stephen J. A. Ward is distinguished lecturer in ethics at the University of British Columbia, and founding director of the Centre for Journalism Ethics at the University of Wisconsin. He is the author of the award-winning *The Invention of Journalism Ethics* (2005) and *Radical Media Ethics: A Global Approach* (2015).

Sonja Wolf is a CONACYT research fellow with the Drug Policy Program at the Centro de Investigación y Docencia Económicas, Mexico. Her research focuses on violence, street gangs, migration and displacement as well as on security and drug policies. She is the author of *Mano Dura: The Politics of Gang Control in El Salvador* (2017)

Ben Worthy is lecturer in Politics at Birkbeck College, University of London. He has written extensively on issues around transparency and freedom of information. He is co-author of *Does FOI Work? The Impact of the Freedom of Information Act 2000 on British Central Government* (2010) and author of *The Politics of Freedom of Information: How and Why Governments Pass Laws That Threaten Their Power* (2017).

PREFACE

The Companion to Media and Human Rights consists of contributions, through a variety of perspectives, methodologies and historical comparisons, that examine universal principals of freedom of expression, legal instruments, the right to know, media as a human right, digital activism, witnessing and the media representation of human rights including the role of media organisations and journalistic work.

The Companion will be the first collection to examine all these various aspects in one volume. The distinctiveness of the companion is that it encompasses a variety of subject areas: communication, journalism, law, human rights, sociology, cultural studies, international politics and criminology. The chapters are theoretically pluralist and take various historical and critical approaches to provide an understanding of the media as a human right and in the context of human rights. The companion is therefore both interdisciplinary and multidisciplinary and also provides culturally specific ideas allowing for international comparisons and varying perspectives. The Companion sets out to chart the field and define the agenda for future research. It is impossible even in 49 chapters to cover every single dimension of the topic of media and human rights. We had some difficult choices to make in what to include and what to leave out. But we hope that this Companion provides a resource for scholars in all the disciplines connected to this field of enquiry and opens up avenues for future research

The Companion to Media and Human Rights project has been in incubation for some time and we are grateful to Natalie Foster, senior publisher at Routledge, for her encouragement and persistence in seeing this project to fruition. We would like to take this opportunity to express our gratitude to all authors for their excellent contributions to the Companion. We would also like to thank Sheni Kruger, Jamie Askew and the production staff at Routledge. We also offer thanks to Zoey Lichtenheld and Eissa Saeed for their assistance in preparing the manuscript.

Editing this collection has been an enjoyable task and we hope that scholars and students will enjoy a similar experience whilst reading it.

Howard Tumber – City, University of London and
Silvio Waisbord – George Washington University
Autumn 2016

1

MEDIA AND HUMAN RIGHTS
Mapping the field

Howard Tumber and Silvio Waisbord

A rich academic literature has examined the relationship between the media and human rights. A simple online search for 'media' and 'human rights' yields a long list of citations about a diversity of topics – from the globalisation of the right of expression to news coverage about the situation of particular rights, from the communication rights of specific groups to citizens' uses of digital platforms to demand government protection, from visual depictions of suffering and barbarism in the news to the application of technologies in order to monitor and document abuses, or from the vulnerability of reporters' rights to the utilisation of news photos in recovery from traumatic experiences in war and conflict.

This vast scope of themes and questions can be attributed to several factors. First, both concepts – 'the media' and 'human rights' – have multiple semantic dimensions. 'The media' refers to the institutions, industries and technologies for the large-scale production of content. The digital revolution has expanded traditional notions of 'the media' originally coined at the heyday of print and broadcast media in the first half of the twentieth century. Today, 'the media' include digital platforms and companies whose structures, characteristics, technological affordances and performance are considerably different from the modern 'mass' media. Consequently, media analysis of human rights has included a broad set of issues, forms, content, technologies and industries.

'Human rights' is a multifaceted concept, too (Minogue 1979). It refers to universal rights, rights of specific populations, historical evolution and philosophical debates, legal agreements and processes, governments and mobilised citizens. Rights belong to individuals and communities. They set the obligations of governments to protect citizens and enforce laws. Rights provide a language to define human dignity and personhood, frame political and social demands and examine issues. Rights crystallise a wide range of shared international norms. It is not exaggerated to say that virtually any topic can be understood as a question of human rights – the right to housing and education, land ownership, equality, privacy, safety, food, safe water and sanitation, association, decent wages and impartial justice.

Second, growing interest in media and rights reflects the global ascendancy of human rights since the end of the Second World War. Human rights as a subject has a long and convoluted intellectual and political history (Clapham 2015; Hunt 2007) punctuated by the evolution of rights-claiming movements and legal achievements. It gained unprecedented international relevance as both a political framework and normative horizon with the 1948 Universal Declaration of Human Rights by the United Nations. Subsequently, surging grassroots activism, particularly in the context of authoritarianism and consequent large-scale violations of rights in different regions of the world, and the signing of numerous treaties and international declarations further elevated the prominence of human rights.

During the past decades, remarkable gains have been made in rights, notwithstanding slow, gradual and imperfect advances (Donnelly 2003). The proliferation of legal frameworks that define a range of universal rights as well as rights for specific populations (such as children, ethnic and linguistic minorities, immigrants, women and people with disabilities) has no precedent in human history (Elliot 2011). Simultaneously, the number of national and international organizations in charge of institutionalising norms and monitoring the state of human rights has multiplied. The vibrant citizen mobilisation at local, national and global levels to demand the adoption and enforcement of rights is remarkable, too. These processes have been responsible for the global spread of rights-based language and norms that infuse international legislation and political discourse.

Still, there is a yawning gap between legal, policy-based and institutional progress and the many 'pathologies of human rights' (Beitz 2011) in contemporary societies. The transition 'from commitment to compliance' (Risse, Ropp, and Sikkink 2013) has suffered from false starts, contradictions and plain failures. If human rights are premised on the 'sacredness of the person' (Joas 2013), the persistence of dire conditions is a painful reminder of the unfulfilled promises of the project of universal human rights. The regular violations of political and civil rights coupled with the persistence of crushing poverty contradict the foundational idea of human rights that all humans should 'live in dignity' (Benhabib 2011). The ambitious ideals that laid down the legal foundations of human rights remain relevant despite the troubling record of governments and international bodies in enforcing protections and sanctions.

Human rights are unevenly observed across countries and specific areas. Formal doctrines and regulations are not consistently translated into effective practices. Myriad international conventions, regular attention and mobilization have not prevented or stopped grave abuses or brought justice. Governments have failed to show consistent and unfailing commitment to enforcing the very same conventions they signed. The international community has often held ambiguous positions and weak determination in relation to the scrutiny of conditions and ensuring rights.

A sophisticated legal architecture, soaring rhetoric, spirited debates and buoyant hopes contrast with dire conditions around the globe. Disappointment with the promise of human rights is warranted given persistent violations of rights in recent years, including torture, slavery and the death penalty; genocide and ethnic cleansing; the discrimination of individuals and groups based on religion, race, gender, sex and other factors; the imposition of restriction on mobility and association; environmental degradation; child labour; and entrenched poverty and social inequality. Addressing unmet demands, preventing violations and bringing justice are part of the full and complex international agenda of human rights.

Continued failure to address problems and guarantee rights for the vast majority of the world's population might prove sceptics right. Critics point at the chasm between hope and reality as evidence that lofty proclamations become hollow rhetoric, legal frameworks are toothless tools, governments are hypocritical and international bodies tasked with monitoring enforcement and prosecuting violators are systematically ineffective (Hopgood 2013).[1]

Third, the 'mediatisation' of global societies also explains significant scholarly interest in media and human rights. *Mediatization* refers to a 'double-sided process' in which the media have become one 'independent institution with a logic of its own that other social institutions have to accommodate to' as well as an integrated part of other institutions like politics, work, family and religion as more and more of these institutional activities are performed through both interactive and mass media (Hjarvard 2008).

Just as in other realms of politics and society, key aspects of contemporary human rights are intertwined with the role of the media. It is not an exaggeration to say that the way societies come to understand and experience the situation of 'human rights' is largely shaped by mediated communication. Considering that human rights are socially constructed (Nash 2015), communication and persuasion are central processes by which societies come to define, understand and implement rights-based policies. They underpin the processes by which activists petition authorities to act, and to demand laws, active monitoring, and enforcement; by which governments aim to convince various publics about policies and decisions; and the way publics react to denunciations of human rights violations, develop empathy with victims and the manner in which affected communities tell stories and seek justice,

The media play critical roles in large-scale communication and persuasion (Bob 2005; Brysk 2013). Without addressing the media can we think about the globalization of human rights and the rise of transnational networks of activists in recent decades? Can we explain the dynamics of campaigns intended to raise public awareness, advocate for legal reforms and 'name and shame' the perpetrators of atrocities? Or can we understand the public outrage and support for humanitarian interventions?

The media constitute a central source of information about global conditions. It is hard to imagine how large publics would come to know about unspeakable tragedies and the impact of violations on people's lives without the presence of the media. The media are the purveyors of information via in-depth investigations, harrowing testimonies, gruesome pictures and images of empowerment and struggle. The media are witnesses to barbarism and acts of justice. The media present daily perpetrators of hate, bigotry and other forms of anti-rights discourse as well as committed actors that denounce abuses and demand justice. The media are arenas where political and social actors battle over the definition of public perception and actions about human rights. The media convey a sense of actions being taken to address and prevent abuses. The media magnify the presence of certain human rights problems whilst minimising the relevance of others.

Media coverage may prompt officials to conduct hearings, investigate conditions, pass legislation, set up programs, earmark funding and take policy-related actions – from sanctions against governments to the deployment of troops. Governments try to influence news coverage through news management. Monitoring bodies closely follow media reports to assess conditions, produce information and recommend actions. Activists utilise media technologies and platforms to call attention to conditions, document situations and make demands. News reports about rights affect public perception about situations, influence opinion and stimulate people into action. Human rights organizations design news-making tactics to bring visibility to specific conditions. Humanitarian actions are often sparked by intense, emotional media coverage. Single media images become symbolic of humanitarian tragedies, global compassion or negligence, power and struggle.

Needless to say, the mediated reality of 'human rights' conditions does not perfectly mirror actual conditions. Several factors affect the selection process through which the media approach human rights. Media coverage does not have a similar, predictable influence on the overall enterprise of human rights. There are many dimensions to the way the media have affected the way societies comprehend, develop attitudes and positions towards, and support actions to tackle human rights.

The media are also connected to another key aspect of communication and persuasion about human rights: the mobilization of rights-based discourse to define issues and problems and justify actions. By understanding any given question as a matter of rights, governments and activists deliberately set out to identify it as a basic matter of human dignity. 'Human rights' is quite a malleable trope used to frame quite different political causes and actions. It provides a vocabulary to understand conditions based on the premise that all citizens have equal rights that need to be respected and observed.

Human rights has become a master interpretive framework to understand human life and makes calls to pay attention and take action. The discursive power of 'human rights' represents the broadening of human rights as a fundamental, all-encompassing perspective that is not limited exclusively to particular issues. The expansion of the agenda of human rights can be attributed to the flexibility and the moral power of the narrative of human rights (Freeman 2011).

New challenges, such as humanitarian crises driven by war, cross-border migration, climate change and natural disasters, have been redefined as assaults on basic rights. Public health activists define access to reproductive services or HIV/AIDS care and treatment as a question of rights. Children's advocates defend educational and family policies as the fulfilment of basic children's rights. Refugee and immigrant groups similarly invoke human rights to appeal to human solidarity and to pressure policymakers to take actions. Governments utilize rights-based discourse to legitimise decisions, too. With the hope of persuading legislators and the public, they tap into rights language to justify a range of actions: from supporting parliamentary bills to authorising military actions 'to protect and safeguard the human rights' of specific populations.

The growing complexity of the right to expression and communication also explains interest in media and human rights. The media are the subjects of the freedom of expression: a fundamental, emblematic democratic right. Historically, this has never been a simple, straightforward issue with clear definitions and legal and practical implications. Rather, it has been a matter of constant debate and controversy.

Recent developments in public communication have added additional dimensions to the global spread of democracy, old and new threats, the recognition of particular speech rights for certain populations, and the compatibility with other human rights in a multicultural, globally connected world. The digitalisation of public life has introduced a new plethora of questions related to the right of free expression on the Internet. Public expression in digital spaces takes place on the same platforms used for multiple purposes: sociability, commerce, political participation, entertainment and other activities. It is embedded in networks created and controlled by private intermediaries whose operations and decisions affecting speech are opaque and primarily driven by commercial objectives. The same digital platforms that provide opportunities for expression are used for marketing as well as commercial and political surveillance.

In summary, the multiple semantic dimensions of 'media' and 'human rights', the preeminent presence of human rights in the global scene, the 'mediatization' of global societies and the increased complexity of the right of expression explain the intensity of interest in media and human rights. Underlying this interest lies the belief in the significance and urgency of human rights in the contemporary world and the role of scholarly work in helping to understand and act upon both the challenges and solutions. The result of this combination of factors is a copious, thematically diverse and scattered body of research.

Why this companion

In our own work, we have long been interested in various aspects of the relationship between the media and human rights: the intersection between journalism, conflict, war; the press and freedom of expression; debates over media policies; and the definition of expression and communication rights in contemporary democracies. We noticed not only that communication and media research on human rights covered a wide range of issues, but also that there was a lack of any attempt to make sense of the dispersed lines of research and arguments.

Our interest in this Companion is to delineate key themes, questions and debates in the field of media and human rights, with the hope that it provides analytical connecting threads and encourages further research. Our belief is that media studies has continued to make important contributions to the study of human rights. Together with recent attention from public policy, sociology, political science and international relations, the growth of media research reflects ongoing movements to broaden academic perspectives in the analysis of human rights beyond legal studies. By presenting a comprehensive survey of topics and sketching out clusters of research interests, we argue that media studies offers unique and multiple perspectives on central aspects of contemporary human rights.

We decided to cast a wide analytical net to identify fundamental themes, arguments and debates. With this goal in mind, we asked scholars to provide critical and thorough assessments of particular subjects linking media and human rights – analytical foci, positions and research trends. We do not pretend to cover every possible topic that falls under the subjects of media and human rights. That would be virtually impossible even within the space of this Companion given the multidimensional nature of 'the media' and human rights.

We propose to organise the study of the media and human rights into four clusters grounded in distinct streams of research within the domain of media studies. The cluster of 'Communication, Expression and Human Rights' (Part 1) places media and human rights within the study of media policies, law and regulation, and the right of expression and communication. The cluster on 'Media Performance and Processes' (Parts 2 and 3) brings together studies concerned with human rights regarding political processes, journalistic practice, the dynamics of news-making, and the relationship between the news media and other social institutions. The cluster on 'digital activism and witnessing' (Part 4) looks at how the right of expression has evolved through the digitisation of media bringing novel ways of witnessing, agitating and purveying information. 'Media Representation of Human Rights' (Part 5) addresses the characteristics of the news coverage of human rights and the roles of the media in providing information, visibility and legitimacy, fostering accountability and monitoring, channelling demands and mobilization, shaping public attitudes and prompting public response and policy actions.

Communication, Expression and Human Rights (Part 1)

One set of issues focuses on the media as the subject of the basic and inalienable right of expression and communication. Article 19 of the Universal Declaration of Human Rights establishes that 'everyone has the right to freedom of opinion and expression; this right includes freedom to hold opinions without interference and to seek, receive and impart information and ideas through any media and regardless of frontiers'. It lays down the foundation for the contemporary right of expression that largely reflects the sense of possibility in the aftermath of the devastation of the Second World War and the emergent ideological conflict of the Cold War. It has been the source of inspiration for national and regional media regulation and the intellectual beacon for free speech movements worldwide.

What happened during the past 60 years, however, was not quite the resplendent trajectory some imagined, even as democracy consolidated in the West and made significant strides globally. The post-war era confirms that the history of freedom of expression is not one of a straightforward unfolding and inevitable triumph. Rather, it has been a long, conflictive, and sinuous process. In the West, the intellectual and political cradle of modern human rights, there is no single and predetermined path to complete freedom of expression. Reversals have threatened or swept gains, especially in the context of war, internal conflict and authoritarianism. In the global South, the right of expression has experienced a bumpy ride given the spotty record of democracy. In recent decades, however, democratic consolidation has allowed for better conditions for public expression in Asia, Africa, the Middle East and South America, notwithstanding deep-seated problems and the questionable quality of democracy in much of the global South. The recent passing of legislation protecting speech, guaranteeing access to public information and curbing discretionary intervention by governments are auspicious signs.

The right to expression remains in constant tension with other democratic values. How should free speech be reconciled with other rights and concerns such as privacy, hate speech and national interest? These questions remain at the centre of public debates over the limitations of public expression. For example, harmonising the right of expression with tolerance is deemed necessary for civic life, particularly in the context of global multiculturalism and constant migration flows. Tinderbox-like political conditions, shaped by historical patterns of the social exclusion of minorities and the growing recognition of cultural and social diversity, have made this a salient issue in recent years.

The digitalization of public communication has brought new questions to the fore. On the one hand, it offers unprecedented opportunities for individual and collective expression, even as the 'digital divide' in many countries persists. On the other hand, it has raised ushered in concerns about the safeguarding of privacy, the untrammelled power of private technology conglomerates, online harassment and blackmailing, national sovereignty and control in digital communication, and the surveillance power of both governments and commercial companies. Digital public expression takes place in the same connected platforms used for multiple uses by individuals, groups, corporations and governments. It is the common space for sociability, work, commerce and political participation. Unsurprisingly then, public expression is intertwined with new issues such as personal data ownership, the utilization of digital data by governments and private providers, and the opacity of private companies that control popular social media and search engines. Everyday uses of digital platforms are intertwined with massive and sophisticated surveillance apparatuses controlled by governments and private operators. It is within this context that demands for a new set of rights (including the right to privacy, the right to be forgotten and the right to Internet access) need to be understood.

In the first chapter of Part 1: Communication, Expression and Human Rights, Guy Berger (Chapter 2) looks at the changes to free expression brought about by social media and traces the history of how UNESCO has interpreted the media and human rights through its various actions and policies. The historical theme is continued by Mark Hampton and Diana Lemberg (Chapter 3). Their chapter demonstrates, through the lenses of historical cases, the emergence and development of media protection from state control, and the conception of access to media as a human right. Free expression is examined in a more contemporary scenario in Europe by Helen Fenwick (Chapter 4). She examines the Strasbourg Court and the contrast in media freedom jurisprudence between political and non-political speech. As she points out, protecting freedom of expression in many cases usually refers to media freedom of expression rather than non-media bodies, or individuals. Many of the issues surrounding media and human rights involve a dichotomy, at times unresolvable. Using historical and contemporary examples, Bart Cammaerts (Chapter 5) illustrates the normative conflict between the protection of press freedom and the advocating of communication rights and media regulation. As he points out 'overcoming this gridlock is not straightforward as press freedom and communication rights are both part of a human rights agenda'. Extending the idea of freedom of expression to include the right to access information is taken up by Ben Worthy (Chapter 6). As he says, 'there is growing legal argument that internationally access to information now represents a fundamental human right'. He traces the development and spread of the freedom of information (FOI) showing how its increased use by non-media sources—NGOs and individual citizens – brings a new culture and ecosystem to the idea of transparency. Judith Townend (Chapter 7) examines the way freedom of expression may be 'chilled' whether it is through 'overt censorship by governments or more subtle controls such as ambiguous legislation, high legal costs and surveillance laws that provoke uncertainty, fear and self-censorship among writers and journalists'. The legal position of the freedom of expression is also taken up by Julian Petley (Chapter 8). He examines the impact on media, and the press in particular, of the European Convention on Human Rights and the UK Human Rights Act 1998, demonstrating how their introduction has protected 'responsible' journalism whilst at the same time restraining intrusion and privacy invasion by sections of the press. Kari Karppinen (Chapter 9) takes up the issue of communicative rights in the digital era. He maps various approaches to digital rights 'highlighting differences in terms of normative assumptions, interpretation of relevant rights and the means by which they can be realised'. Childrens' rights in the digital age are examined by Sonia Livingstone (Chapter 10). She argues that long-established rights to identity or education or freedom from abuse, albeit now differently instantiated and regulated in a digital age must remain a focus alongside new rights to digital identity, e-learning and protection from online abuse. Children's voices and experiences must be included in any global process of dialogue and deliberation regarding rights in the digital era. The digital transition is a theme taken up by Divina Frau-Meigs (Chapter 11), she examines the transformation of media and information literacy (MIL) and human rights in terms of the digital social and smart turn and shows how they are impacted by the Internet, social networks and big data. The question of new regulation and governance in the digital era is discussed in many of the pieces in the companion and in Chapter 12 Gavin Smith examines whether traditional privacy frameworks are 'an adequate or indeed desirable legal and moral device for regulating and protecting the flows of personal information being leaked into the surrounding 'digital enclosure' or whether a more fruitful regulatory and rights approach might focus on revealing the fallibilities, of data flows, and breaking up state-corporate monopolies of digital infrastructure. Jan Servaes closes this first section (Chapter 13) by looking at the connection between human rights and communication in terms of development and social change. He argues that 'a communication rights-based approach needs to be explicitly built into development plans and social change projects to ensure that a mutual sharing/learning process is facilitated. Such communicative sharing is deemed the best guarantee for creating successful transformations'.

Media Performance and Human Rights: Political Processes (Part 2)

A second set of studies are concerned with media performance and political processes indicating the conditions of the right of expression and communication in specific contexts. Remarkable legal and policy advances that support the media's right of expression have not always been matched by on-the-ground realities.

The reality of press performance is messy. It cannot be captured simply by examining legislation and policies. Reporters and organizations strive to balance different values amid changing circumstances and pressures. Responsible journalism coexists with irresponsible actions that, in the name of free speech, blatantly step on individual privacy. The legal protections enjoyed by the press are used to pursue the public interest as well as private gain. Authorities gag the press when they use (or threaten to use) legislation to stifle free speech by invoking matters of national security and public safety. The current state of media performance and mediated processes present well-entrenched problems as well as novel opportunities to expand expression.

Sebastian Stier (Chapter 14) opens Part 2 by showing that 'the degree of freedom in the reporting of print and broadcast media crucially depends on political context'. He argues that 'the presence of democratic institutions is a necessary but not a sufficient condition for the emergence and preservation of a free media system'. In the digital era 'increasingly obscure violations of media freedom not only limit the role of the media as a public watchdog but endanger human rights in general'. Questions of universalism and relativism figure in Mehdi Semati's (Chapter 15) analysis of the discourse of human rights. In writing about human rights how does one avoid being either an apologist for the forces of empire or an apologist for authoritarian regimes. 'Writing about human rights and communication media presents its own set of challenges'. Limits to media and citizen rights are taken up in the next two chapters. Emma Briant (Chapter 16) tackles the prescient issue of surveillance, rights and media, recently brought to the fore by the Edward Snowden revelations. Like many of the issues and themes arising out of this Companion, debates about surveillance and human rights highlight another problematic. In this case, one of 'security versus liberty'. Vian Bakir (Chapter 17) demonstrates how political-intelligence elites can manipulate the public through the media under the guise of national security. Where that policy also contravenes non-derogable human rights, the domestic mainstream press is activated to shape public attitudes and act as a conduit for political-intelligence-elite-sourced propaganda. The following two chapters show how the media are crucial to both historical and current discourses in shaping other areas of politics, namely foreign policy and public diplomacy. Ekaterina Balabanova (Chapter 18) examines 'the debate over humanitarian intervention and the role of the media in foreign policy' and analyses the 'new claims for a revolutionary role for the media in the context of shifts in international relations and communications technologies in the 21st century'. Similarly Amelia Arsenault (Chapter 19) looks at public diplomacy, and shows how 'media and communication systems are both the conduits for public diplomacy and the object of debates and initiatives about human rights'.

The news media confront multiple threats around the world. The type, intensity and urgency of the problems vary across countries. Old and new forms of censorship persist from the blatant suppression and persecution of dissidents to subtle forms of political and economic censorship. Market concentration stifles expression and cements inequalities in public access to the media. Anti-press violence in the form of physical and verbal abuses, generally by governments and parastate actors, undermines the right of expression. This is particularly tangible in contexts of statelessness and armed conflict. Violence silences reporters who dare to scrutinise power and disciplines newsrooms to comply with power and naked force. Also, officials continue to utilize 'gagging' laws to chill expression on the grounds that certain forms of speech 'threaten' social welfare, domestic peace and national security.

These challenges make free speech an elusive goal. News organizations are cowed into submission. Self-censorship is common. The right to expression enshrined in national and global legislation is too distant a protection for journalists and citizens who are the targets of persecution or fear retaliation for exercising the right of expression. Global conventions are insufficient to protect media workers who exercise the legitimate right to free speech.

Part 3, Media Performance and Human Rights: News and Journalism, brings media performance and human rights issues concerning news and journalism to the fore. Stephen J. A. Ward (Chapter 20) advocates for a global media ethics for contemporary journalism, to advance human rights. To do this he suggests that journalists should eschew the parochial and 'adopt the notions of moral globalism, cosmopolitan values and global human flourishing'. Michael Bromley (Chapter 21) looks at one form of Journalism: investigative. Its status as an idealised form of Journalism has historically made it 'intimately connected with the recognition, promotion and protection of human rights, acting as a form of "private regulator" of public actions but without a legally sanctioned mandate'. Another form of journalism – international reporting – is documented by Giovanna Dell'Orto (Chapter 22). She traces the history of aspects of foreign reporting and illustrates both the decline and the challenges facing international reporting particularly for foreign news bureaus, which have long been the source of most human rights coverage. International flows are important for exposing human rights violations so the protection of newsgathering and transmission from interference becomes paramount. This theme is continued by Jeannine E. Relly And Celeste González De Bustamente (Chapter 23) in their historical examination of violence against journalists and the initiatives, including resolutions and declarations to end impunity for those responsible for anti-press violence. NGO's play a crucial role in any discussion about the discourse of news and human rights. The next two chapters tackle the relationship between NGOs, news media and human rights. Matthew Powers (Chapter 24) traces the increase in human rights news frames which now embrace social issues and not solely war crimes. The vacuum left by the demise of broadcast foreign news outlets has been filled by a growing 'professional' advocacy sector using the 'proliferation of digital technologies to increase and diversify their content offerings'. Who retains prominence in shaping human rights news becomes a key question. Glenda Cooper (Chapter 25) poses a further question surrounding namely the way citizen journalists, who are nowadays often the creators of disaster and crisis-event-related content, operate. Whilst this is seen as democratising communication, there are concerns that citizen journalists who tweet and blog on various platforms do not treat victims and survivors in the same 'regulated' way that legacy media operate. Cooper examines how the voices of victims are mediated and mediatised and discusses the legal issues of the rights to privacy, intellectual property and freedom of expression which inevitably arise. We return to the problem of violence against journalists in the final piece of this section. Libby Lester (Chapter 26) acknowledges the dissolution of the distinction between journalism and activism within the context of transnational flows of trade and information concerned with natural resources, environmental harm and human rights violations. She demonstrates the increase in the risk of violence against the journalists and activists working in the environmental area.

It is important to recognise that digital media has facilitated novel opportunities to exercise the right of expression. Social movements, non-government organizations and individual citizens have used a variety of digital tools to bring attention to the problems related to free speech. For rights activists and journalists, the media offer unique opportunities to bring attention to existing conditions and disseminate information. Part 4: Digital Activism, Witnessing and Human Rights, offers various perspectives on advocacy and social media. Ella McPherson (Chapter 27) shows how social media has enabled transparency and participation. It has also 'heightened uncertainty and inequality'. She argues that 'the better-resourced actors in the human rights NGO field are able to understand social media logics and the opportunities and risks they create for advocates – while the less resourced are potentially left further and further behind'.

The enticing subject of celebrity advocacy for human rights is analysed by Trevor Thrall and Dominik Stecula (Chapter 28). They argue that despite the widespread assumption that celebrity advocacy can assist issues, victims and NGOs in getting attention there is little data beyond anecdotes to support this conventional wisdom. However they show that celebrity humanitarians are a vital and growing part of global human rights networks, their effectiveness though split between the optimists who suggest that they operate as 'moral entrepreneurs' thanks to their more personal and emotional approach to human rights issues, as interpreters and intermediaries between their audiences and distant victims and tragedies, and as critical elements of the broader transnational advocacy network. The pessimists accuse celebrities of being 'unelected and untrained elites of society, and should not be the ones deciding which human rights issues get attention and which do not'. A more fundamental criticism, 'is that rather than producing real social change, celebrity advocacy is in fact turning human rights into a shopping experience'. Beth A. Haller (Chapter 29) shows how social media has 'reinvigorated disability rights activism, as well as fostering more interaction within the international disability rights community regardless of age, ethnicity, gender, disability or geography'. Social media is allowing disability activists to use global networks to promote relevant human rights issues. She argues that 'the Internet truly has become a form of "liberating technology" for disabled people around the world'. Eve Ng (Chapter 30) in her discussion of LGBT rights shows that digital media provide LGBT activists with a variety of ways to advance their goals although privileged segments of LGBT communities are more likely to shape the agendas. In addition, 'visibility has complex implications for LGBT advocacy; being "out" cannot be assumed to be an unproblematic, universal goal'. Summer Harlow (Chapter 31) offers a critique of how digital technologies offer an unfiltered voice to advocates, activists and victims of human rights. Social networking sites provide an opportunity for mobilising protest activity in the fight for social justice. Stefania Milan (Chapter 32) explores what she calls the media/protest assemblage from a human rights perspective and looks at the sociological processes triggered by engagement with communicative action. She speculates how the human rights discourse will unfold in the near future in relation to this protest/media assemblage, as citizens become aware of the threats to their privacy.

The importance of visual media to human rights advocacy is documented by the following three pieces. Camera-mediated imagery is analysed by Kari Andén-Papadopoulos (Chapter 33). She poses the ethical questions surrounding the making and watching of images of suffering others arguing 'that the current embrace of digital (mobile) cameras as perhaps the most power-shifting device for local human rights subjects urges us to attend also to the practices of creating, mobilizing and looking at images in the contexts where injustice or violence occurs'. Witnessing can become a contested terrain and Stuart Allan (Chapter 34) looks in detail at the work of WITNESS, posing questions about the re-mediation of imagery relating to human rights and social justice. Whilst acknowledging the ethical obligations to those represented (as also discussed in Chapter 33), advocacy videos also expose the 'experiences of those otherwise likely to be ignored, marginalised or trivialised in (traditional) media representations'. Sandra Ristovska (Chapter 35) shows how witnessing has been operationalised for use by the International Criminal Tribunal for Yugoslavia. Video can both capture and disseminate human rights abuses, and mediate the work of the courts. 'The employment of video to perform these roles shows how the wider cultural significance of witnessing is entering into the law'. How human rights advocates can alter the balance in bringing abuses to attention is discussed in the final piece in this section, Steven Livingston (Chapter 36) shows how scientific and technical tools and expertise that are now available can alter the 'framing contests between human rights advocates and those suspected of violating human rights and committing war crimes'. Forensic scientists can assist first in establishing the existence of war crimes followed by the construction of 'a scientifically grounded narrative as to what happened'.

Media and the state of human rights

Part 5 of the Companion examines the Media Representation of Human Rights: Cultural, Social, and Political.

The media are public, collective resources used to cultivate public understanding about the conditions and the complexity of human rights. No other institution matches the power of the media to publicise and prompt debates about the state of human rights. Evidence suggests growing news interest in human rights in past decades. Human rights as a news subject has gained presence as it became the matter of policy debates. Conventions covering the rights of various populations were discussed and signed, and populations mobilized to demand rights and denounce abuses.

The news media play many roles. They raise awareness about particular situations across several domains – political, social, cultural and economic – document conditions, spotlight abuses, generate understanding and empathy, mobilise public opinion, influence governments and international organizations and provide visibility to the actions of human rights activists: conditions that otherwise may remain unknown to large segments of the public.

The literature has been generally critical of the way the media typically cover human rights and concludes that media coverage is generally fraught with numerous problems. Human rights generally make news when several conditions are present. They are more likely to get coverage when they affect individual political and legal rights; they are related to open, armed conflicts; when large-scale abuses have taken place; when reporters have relatively easy access to sources and victims; when powerful sources and geopolitics have calculated interest in attracting news attention; when they primarily affect better-off and urban populations; and when grassroots and international organizations successfully mobilize to gain media attention. Consequently, a range of human rights issues are likely to be absent, misrepresented or to have received brief and superficial attention from the news media. This includes socioeconomic rights, the rights of socially excluded populations, abuses committed by the military as well as those committed by powerful political and economic interests, and/or geographically located in hard-to-access sites for journalists.

It remains an open question whether the digital revolution has considerably changed traditional patterns in the way the media cover human rights. In principle, the popularity of social media and the flattening of news production and distribution provide new opportunities for documenting human rights conditions and articulating demands and proposals. It is far from obvious, however, that journalistic performance has completely changed even as more information is easily available on digital platforms outside traditional media organizations.

The media are also important when they raise questions about human rights. The definition and interpretation of human rights remain contested (Dembour 2010). When are rights made effective? Are rights granted or demanded? Are there universal rights? How can the defence of particularistic rights grounded in cultural mores be reconciled with cosmopolitan ambitions for shared principles and goals? Are rights a Trojan horse of Western colonialism? Who defines rights? Who is responsible for defining, monitoring and enforcing rights? How are universal individual rights viable amid power inequalities? The media are also sites for collective action aimed at defining and claiming rights. Media coverage and images provide public legitimacy to demands whilst actors are symbolic markers of struggles, successes and failures.

Finally, the media contribute to bringing human rights into the public sphere by using a rights-based interpretative frame in the coverage of social conditions. Talking about specific issues as human rights – for example, access to quality education, housing, and healthcare – builds a sense that populations are rights holders. By doing so, the media rearticulates rights as collective issues (rather than only as individual prerogatives). Furthermore, this language has other important consequences. It directs attention to the role of governments in fulfilling basic rights, and places citizens as actors that may legitimately demand policies to deliver common public goods and hold authorities accountable.

Ibrahim Seaga Shaw (Chapter 37) in the opening chapter in Part 5 takes a critical gaze at the intersections between culture, media and human rights. Tracing the literature, particularly in relation to cultural violence, he argues that 'an intercultural communication approach informed by human rights journalism is needed in reporting cultural differences if a clash of cultures is to be avoided or minimised'. Barbara M. Freeman (Chapter 38) provides a critical review of news media representation of women and their rights. She portends that in the media coverage of the female voice in politics and public life, violence and oppression against women especially in conflict zones is often limited or prejudiced. Meghan Sobel (Chapter 39) using a cross-country content analysis presents the findings of the relationship between news media coverage and female genital cutting (FGC). The results of the analysis highlight the opposing views of the subject. 'FGC was predominantly reported on as a cultural practice with negative/harmful implications, furthering the argument of anti-FGC advocates'. Whilst 'advocates of the opposing position would no doubt maintain their criticism that coverage perpetuates narratives which oversimplify the array of complexities that accompany the practice and the cultures within which it occurs'. Religion has a unique relationship with human rights. Jolyon Mitchell and Joshua Rey (Chapter 40) argue that human rights and religion offer competing frames for various interpretations of events with historically the human rights frame often predominating, leading to the over-simplifying of religious issues. Cynthia Carter (Chapter 41) stresses 'the importance of news to children's citizenship' with the news media being 'central to the advancement of children's civic inclusion in democratic societies'. She argues for paying more attention to the importance of children's information and communication rights and the part 'news media can play in deepening children's understanding of social justice and human rights'. Language is an important variable in any discussion of the representation of human rights. Martin Conboy (Chapter 42) assesses how the language of the news can exclude vulnerable outsider communities as part of the process of media-audience construction. Using the British press as a case study, he illustrates the linguistic devices that newspapers from all aspects of the political spectrum regularly deploy in substantiating their support or opposition to contemporary legislation regarding human rights. On the issue of human rights, 'all newspapers consider themselves and the British to be squarely within a discourse of Western superiority with different newspapers qualifying their support depending on where they stand on broader issues'. Lisa Brooten (Chapter 43) examines the intersection of human rights, media and political discourse. Drawing on critical rights scholarship she presents an overview of the emergence and pervasiveness of the politics of rights and the impact on political discourse as a result of the increasing pervasiveness of rights. She analyses the 'efficacy of human rights discourse as a tool for addressing fundamental global problems', paying 'special attention to its impact on immigration and citizenship, war and humanitarian disasters, and media reform'. Human rights discourse is further analysed by Kerry Moore (Chapter 44) in looking at the representation of asylum and immigration. Taking examples from the British press she reviews 'the conditions of possibility underlying public discourse positioning human rights as antagonistic to social order and threatening to national security'. This challenges 'the assumption that the dominant media discourse in liberal democratic states will be pro-human rights'. Labour reporting is the theme of Anya Schiffrin and Beatrice Santa-Wood's piece (Chapter 45). Looking at two stories, one domestic (US) and one foreign but with a home connection, they highlight 'essential differences in the way that labor reporting media can bring about social change'. In both instances, NGOs and journalists, using social media and legacy media, targeted elite policymakers and public opinion, providing information about a problem that needed fixing. Sonja Wolf (Chapter 46) examines the media coverage of public safety issues and their human rights implications. She argues that 'the prevalence of commercial media, with their reliance on certain news production styles and routines, results in mostly decontextualised news content that distorts the social reality of crime, helps increase audiences' fear of crime, and elicits preferences for punitive strategies'. To make the news treatment of public safety issues more rigorous and comprehensive she suggests more use of data journalism 'to tell more compelling stories about the nature and impact of crime and violence in society, and the professionalisation of the advocacy journalism of civil society groups. Crime is a theme continued in Paul Mason's (Chapter 47) analysis of the media discourse of prison and prisoners. In the UK he finds that the dominant representation of prisoners is a 'partial and misleading one of danger, fear and risk' leading to the further media construction of prisoners as 'undeserving of the same rights as the rest of the population, or as possessing too many rights'. The outcome is that 'media discourses of prison and prisoners' rights therefore become a potent opinion shaper for the public' reflected inevitably in government policies on prisoners' rights. The final two chapters of this section and indeed the Companion bring us back to the notions of freedom of expression and a free press. Melissa Wall (Chapter 48) surveys the way war-making, human rights and the media have separately and collectively evolved in the 21st century creating new patterns and practices. She shows the manner in which 'human rights have historically been both a mediatized justification for war and an information strategy in carrying out war'. New actors and technologies have entered the field complicating the 'growing ethical questions about audience spectatorship for human rights media content'. Brigitte L. Nacos (Chapter 49) shows how terrorism crystallises many of the key issues surrounding media and human rights. Social media in particular has enabled terrorist groups to disseminate their propaganda. Whilst authoritarian regimes have no compunction in censoring terrorist voices. Often suppressing opposition under the guise of counterterrorism, liberal democracies have to navigate between restraints on the media often included in anti-terrorism laws and refrain from curbing fundamental human rights and civil liberties.

This Companion offers a comprehensive and updated survey of key lines of research, theoretical approaches and debates in media and human rights. Without a doubt, media and human rights is a rich area of inquiry that addresses multiple questions – from the right to expression and communication, to media contributions, to shaping public awareness and public debates. Just as with the field of human rights in general, research on media and human rights has expanded, too, in recent years. As a result of growing interest coupled with a broad analytical lens, media studies suggest that despite notable gains in human rights, tough challenges remain to affirm multiple generations of communication and expression rights as well as to foster public knowledge and understanding about the present conditions of the rights of various populations. Basic matters about human rights remain contested even as the discourse of rights infuses public life in the contemporary global society. Not all rights regularly receive similar media attention as news organizations generally cover rights in specific circumstances. The explosion of digital media has ushered in new opportunities for documenting and monitoring rights, including citizen actions intended to hold governments accountable.

We hope that the volume provides an analytical platform for future research, sparks new ideas and debates, and inspires action.

Note

1   For a recent discussion on changing perspectives on human rights, see *Debating The Endtimes of Human Rights Activism and Institutions in a Neo-Westphalian World*, edited by Doutje Lettinga and Lars van Troost, Amnesty International Netherlands, 2014.

References

Beitz, C. (2011). *The Idea of Human Rights*. New York: Oxford University Press.
Benhabib, S. (2011). *Dignity in Adversity: Human Rights in Troubled Times*. Cambridge, UK: Polity.
Bob, C. (2005). *The Marketing of Rebellion: Insurgents, Media and International Activism*. Cambridge: Cambridge University Press.
Brysk, A. (2013). *Speaking Rights to Power; Constructing Political Will*. Oxford: Oxford University Press.
Clapham, A. (2015). *Human Rights: A Very Short Introduction*. New York: Oxford University Press.
Dembour, M. (2010). 'What Are Human Rights? Four Schools of Thought', *Human Rights Quarterly*, 32(1), pp. 1–20.

Donnelly, J. (1989). *Universal Human Rights in Theory and Practice*. Ithaca: Cornell University Press.

Elliott, M. A. (2011). 'The Institutional Expansion of Human Rights, 1863–2003: A Comprehensive Dataset of International Instruments', *Journal of Peace Research*, 48(4), pp. 537–46.

Freeman, M. (2011). *Human Rights*. Cambridge: Polity.

Hjarvard, S. (2008). 'The Mediatization of Society: A Theory of the Media as Agents of Social and Cultural Change', *Nordicom Review*, 29(2), pp. 105–34.

Hopgood, S. (2013). *The Endtimes of Human Rights*. Ithaca: Cornell University Press.

Hunt, L. (2007). *Inventing Human Rights: A History*. New York: W. W. Norton.

Joas, H. (2013). *The Sacredness of the Person: A New Genealogy of Human Rights*. Washington, DC: Georgetown University Press.

Nash, K. (2015). *The Political Sociology of Human Rights*. Cambridge: Cambridge University Press.

Risse, T., Ropp, S. C. and Sikkink, K., eds. (2013). *The Persistent Power of Human Rights: From Commitment to Compliance*. Cambridge: Cambridge University Press.

PART I

Communication, expression and human rights

2

EXPRESSING THE CHANGES

International perspectives on evolutions in the right to free expression

Guy Berger

Introduction

Freedom of expression has historically been seen as the right most relevant to 'media'. That sounds obvious, yet what this means has not stayed static over time. Changes have impacted upon the notion of 'media' and the relevance to media of other rights (e.g. privacy and participation). The conceptualisation of the 'freedom of expression' itself continues to evolve. This chapter unpacks some of the developments and the response of UNESCO, the lead UN agency dealing with the right to free expression.

Concerning 'rights', since the Universal Declaration of Human Rights set these out as principles in 1948, there has been a strengthening of their significance as internationally agreed standards. This trend was reinforced by the International Convention on Civil and Political Rights (ICCPR) as agreed at the UN General Assembly in 1966. A 'right to development' was agreed in 1986 and potentially has renewed resonance with the UN's sustainable development goals (SDGs) agreed in 2015, and to the significance of media therein.[1] However, ideas for other new rights, such as a right to communication, or to internet access, or to anonymity or encryption, have not won endorsement at the UN. Instead, their normative status – to the extent that it exists – depends on them being cast as derivatives and/or enablers of already agreed fundamental rights (to free expression, participation, privacy, etc). The basics set out initially in 1948 continue to be seen in many UN resolutions as maintaining their relevance – as being as appropriate to the 'digital age' as to its prehistorical 'analogue'.[2]

In contrast, the concept of 'media' appears to have undergone far more evolution.[3] The primary historical use has been to conflate media with '*the* media' – in the sense of the media industry. This dominant sense of 'media' has not precluded other expressions such as fashion, architecture and video games. However, it has particularly put the emphasis on information disseminated in word and image. In this sense, the 'media' was what converted individual expressions into what Habermas (1989) designated as the modern public sphere. In this way, 'media' has therefore been historically distinct from the private use of expression. 'Media' in this mode is integrally bound up with the word 'mass', and it was for many years envisaged as the industrial-scale production and one-way dissemination of meaning by newspapers, magazines, book publishers, radio, television and film. Within this, from a genre point of view, information was equated to news – which in turn was seen as being based upon journalism produced by specialised workers identified as journalists.

For many, this specific genre has occupied an elevated place in a hierarchy of the functions of media, for example above those of education and entertainment, and it has been particularly relevant to the issues of rights and democracy. In this context, freedom of expression in general was less significant than was press freedom in particular, albeit that the latter depends on the former.

What continues today is that the ownership and control of the means of communication – which have historically done so much to shape the production, distribution and consumption of public expression – are still dominated by private ownership and terms of service, as well as commercial dynamics. However, access to digital means of communication, even within the limits established by platform owners, is unprecedented. This vastly expands the range of direct stakeholders in the 'media' and in freedom of expression, and it also tilts power away from governments and media companies towards a handful of technology companies that operate transnationally.[4]

This new environment has expanded the institutional and individual sources who make use of digital platforms for imparting meaning to various publics, and access is being used for both public and private, that is, interpersonal, communications as well as for hybrids between these realms. The term 'social media' came into use in the 21st century to capture this new development. Since then, the mass media industry, in both old and new formations, has increasingly spawned integrations with this sphere. The result has blurred many public-private distinctions.

Combined with increased commercialisation of media institutions and communications more broadly, distinctions between information, education and entertainment on digital media are less exclusive than previously. Nevertheless, it can be argued that, at least in terms of idealised aspiration, journalism in essence retains its character as a realist endeavour which differs from fictional and purely creative expression in types of knowledge outcomes. But it is no longer confined to news media institutions.

One of the changes has been disintermediation of earlier media business models in which single companies or the state had controlled integrated value chains across all stages of production and distribution. Today, access to publish and to receive content is free' to the (connected) user. It is funded by data-driven models, including advertising, which replace the old method of horizontal ownership of platforms, content production processes and dissemination. The effect has been severe advertising competition with old-model media organisations, with an adverse economic impact on journalism.

There are also nowadays new powerful functions in communications such as curation, listings (search engines) and discovery – often by automated algorithmic recommendations that serve up specific content. Gatekeeping has become a more complex phenomenon – more responsive to ratings and page views, and sometimes involving crowd-based decisions, while agenda setting nowadays is also today less a function of ideology or conscious decision making than of considerations about what captures attention and clicks.

The rise and fall of corporate actors is increasingly conditioned by network effects, entrenching key actors such as Facebook, Google and Amazon in many countries. However, new issues such as continuous innovation, choice, privacy concerns amongst users, and unintended effects also make monopolisation unpredictable.

This relative cornucopia of communications possibilities is certainly uneven around the world, reflecting political, economic, ideological, gender and linguistic factors amongst others. Even so, the overall shifts are also part of wider changes – for instance, in how elections are contested; commerce is operated; cultural hegemonies are challenged; cities are run; identities are constructed, etc.

These developments raise many new questions about how human rights relate to this fast-moving panorama of communicative activity – and not least to the issue of 'journalism'. It is therefore appropriate to turn now to changes in the realm of 'rights' and the international institutions that deal with them.

UNESCO's positions and policies on media and human rights

In the UN system, the specialised body dealing with human rights has been the Human Rights Council, comprised of 47 states elected by the UN General Assembly, and which appoints the Human Rights Committee to provide authoritative interpretations of rights.[5] The HRC is also responsible for appointing a special rapporteur on freedom of opinion and expression, and in 2015 it also introduced a new special rapporteur on the right to privacy. These actors all impact in important ways on the subject matter of this book.[6] Nevertheless, the focus in this chapter is on UNESCO, a 195-member-state UN agency, which has a dedicated focus on the right to freedom of expression.

UNESCO's constitution says the Organization is set up to promote the 'free exchange of ideas and knowledge'. This predates, but has since been interpreted in the light of, the famous Article 19 of the Universal Declaration of Human Rights,[7] taken forward into the ICCPR, which sets out that the fundamental right of freedom of expression encompasses the freedom to 'to seek, receive and impart information and ideas through any media and regardless of frontiers'.

What merits immediate attention is that the reference to 'any media' is broad enough as to be applied to an emerging world of multiple producers and consumers of meaning. While the right emerged in a world when only certain actors could speak, and the rest were positioned as listeners, nowadays the freedom to *impart* information (while still constrained in varying degrees) is decreasingly the prerogative of a select group. On the other side of the coin, the freedom to *seek and receive* was conceived in a context limited by a scarcity of information entering the public sphere (a scarcity that was technically, economically and politically determined). Today, there is, relatively, a growing abundance.

In the history of this dual-dimensioned freedom, the 'media' was operated by a relative few although with some broader public benefit. Still the 'media' was a preserve linked to politics, class, colony, gender, language and similar dimensions of power and inequality. This impacted on how the right to free expression was used with regard to imparting and receiving information. In this context, the right to *impart* information and ideas came to be known as the subsidiary right to 'press freedom' – reflecting the historical character of the key communications industry at the time. On the other hand, freedom of expression from 1948 onward was never intrinsically the right of a particular industry, but of human beings in general.

It is also from this historical context, that the right to *seek and receive* came to be seen (relatively belatedly) as the foundation of a subsidiary 'right to information' – sometimes called 'freedom of information' or the 'right of access to information'. Historically, this right was first legislated in 1766 in the territory of current-day Sweden and Finland. However, it was not developed historically as a counterpart to ending the censorship of imparted expression; that is, an approach whereby censorship – when seen from the consumption side – is experienced as depriving those who seek information.[8] Instead, the right to information has had a particular sense of access not to all information but specifically to state holdings. In turn, this interpretation has spurred the development of transparency as a virtue, and encouraged the evolution of 'open governance'. In a sense then, the right to information has been linked to the right to participation and democratic accountability.

As will be further discussed in this chapter, even though 'media' has changed, the degree to which a society has a rich and open information environment nevertheless continues to depend on the conditions for freedom of expression in both sender and receiver dimensions – that is, press freedom and the right to information, and this combination retains relevance. This analytical framework provides a context for understanding how freedom of expression (in its two dimensions) has evolved within UNESCO.

The Organisation's 1945 constitutional reference to the 'free flow of ideas by word and image' has direct relevance both for imparting and for seeking/receiving information. Starting in the mid-1970s, a debate emerged around a 'New World Information and Communication Order'. This reflected criticism at the time that cross-border information flows were not equitable, and that 'free flow' justified 'media imperialism'. Inequalities in imparting information meant imbalances in receiving information. This focus ended after the USA and the UK resigned from UNESCO in the mid-1980s. By the time they returned almost 15 years later, the 'flow' realities themselves were changing. Several countries in the South were becoming, in varying degrees, regional media powers in some fields (e.g. Mexico, the Republic of Korea, Kenya and Nigeria). At the same time, Canada and France had resisted 'free flow' in global trade agreements in terms of their cultural industries. Satellite broadcasting was emerging as a transnational platform for actors outside the West's traditional media industry. In time, the Internet was to further dilute the content imbalance problem.

After the Cold War ended, neoliberal thinking came to the fore as a perspective. In parallel, Western international aid to media in developing countries (including that channelled through UNESCO) began to move in the 1990s from supporting national news agencies and state-owned broadcasting, to backing community media (informed by the right to participation and the notion of 'communication for development') as well as to private media institutions.

In this context, UNESCO began to emphasise 'free flow' and press freedom within individual countries. The milestone in this new phase was the 1991 Windhoek Conference of African journalists, convened by UNESCO, which focused on the right to press freedom in particular, and elaborated it in terms of three fundamental preconditions: media freedom (legal level), pluralism (ownership, media sectors and diversity of content) and independence (editorial and institutional autonomy). (See further elaboration below). Subsequently, the UNESCO Member States endorsed the Windhoek Declaration, and the UN General Assembly agreed to recognize the date of the Declaration, 3 May, as 'World Press Freedom Day'.

One outcome of the Windhoek framework was UNESCO's conceptualisation of 'media development' as designating the development of free, pluralistic and independent media. In this regard, the UNESCO Media Development Indicators (MDIs) research framework (UNESCO 2008), was adopted in 2008 by the 39 governments represented on UNESCO's International Programme for the Development of Communication (IPDC). While the Windhoek Declaration had been newspaper-centric, the MDIs included the importance to pluralism of public service broadcasting and community broadcasting, and they also touched on Internet infrastructure issues.

Significantly, the MDIs also included the 'safety of journalists', reflecting an earlier concern about the killing of correspondents. As an indication of the importance of this, in 1997 UNESCO Member States passed Resolution 29, as a result of which UNESCO's Director General publicly condemns each killing of a journalist or media worker (and since 2012 also covers cases of social media producers who generate a significant amount of journalism[9]). Since 2008, the Director General, has also presented a biannual official report on the subject, which includes Member States' responses concerning judicial follow-up to killings of journalists. In 2011, UNESCO initiated the United Nations Plan of Action on the Safety of Journalists and the Issue of Impunity, as a global framework for stakeholder co-operation. The same year, the Organisation's General Conference mandated ongoing monitoring on trends of press freedom and safety which was manifested in 2014 and 2015 in two consecutive studies titled *World Trends in Freedom of Expression and Media Development* (UNESCO 2014, 2015a; see below). In 2013, UNESCO elaborated specialized Journalists' Safety Indicators which include digital safety issues.

Also relevant to UNESCO in the post-Windhoek period has been the acknowledgement of gender equality between men and women. This is a cross-cutting issue for media freedom, pluralism, independence and safety. In 2012, the Gender Sensitive Indicators for Media were launched. Additional intellectual development at UNESCO since Windhoek is the composite concept of Media and Information Literacy (see 'Reflecting on the range of the Right to Information'), promoted since 2010. This concept complements the media–centric focus of other work at UNESCO by focusing on the user's side. It has gained enhanced significance with regard to the competencies needed for consuming and producing information in regard to the Internet.

Rethinking and unpacking 'press freedom'

Building on these developments, UNESCO has developed its thinking about the right to freedom of expression in contemporary times. In this regard, the Organisation has begun interpreting: (i) *press freedom* as the right to make information public, and (ii) *the right to information* as the situation of transparency as regards the exercise of public power (which power is wider than that wielded by governments).

In UNESCO's 2014 *World Trends* report (UNESCO 2014), it is recognised that although journalists are among the greatest users of press freedom, the space that this right affords (or should afford) is not limited to the news media. In this sense, each individual using social media is seen as having a direct stake in press freedom. The *World Trends* report elaborates this conception of press freedom as follows:

> *Media freedom* designates the importance of a protective legal and statutory environment in which media institutions and platforms operate, including a right to information law. *Pluralism* is designated as an additional condition of press freedom, helping to give substance to freedom 'for', not only freedom 'from'. A register of pluralism is the existence of viable and distinctive public, private and community media online and offline. *Independence* refers to an absence of external political or commercial interference, and to the existence of self-regulatory mechanisms (and their autonomy in regard to statutory regulation). It includes the degree of professional standards of journalists or other people doing journalism. An ecology of organisations that supports autonomous journalism through advocacy, training, etc. is also a factor impacting on independence.

This does raise the issue of the continued evolution of the changing meaning of 'journalism' over history, with the *World Trends* conceptualising it as the production and circulation of verifiable information and informed comment and analysis for the purpose of public interest.

For UNESCO, the press freedom framework evolved on the Windhoek foundation retains relevance to the digital era. Freedom of expression – whether online and offline – continues to need legal protection and those doing journalism may incur attacks and thus specifically need both legal as well as digital protection (see Henrichsen, Betz and Lisosky, 2015). Pluralism requires open opportunities and net neutrality, and a role for public, private and community media types on the Internet. Independence entails voluntary setting of public interest standards for journalism on all platforms. The right to gender equality in and through media needs continued attention, and online misogyny has to be resisted.

Reflecting on the range of the Right to Information

In unpacking the second dimension of freedom of expression, that is, the right to seek and receive information, UNESCO has recognised two complementary aspects – the rights dimension, and the issues of practical access. Each aspect is stunted if considered without the other. This is the essence of the new International Day for Universal Access to Information, every 28 September, agreed by UNESCO Member States in December 2015. This development partly echoes the historical Windhoek process, in that the initiative tracks back to a UNESCO-sponsored conference of African stakeholders in 2011.[10] The organisations involved, known as the African Platform for Access to Information, subsequently brought their perspective to UNESCO Member States who agreed to the proclamation of the Day – thereby adding UN weight to an occasion hitherto marked by the civil society group called Freedom of Information Advocates Network (FOIAnet) and other supporters.

A key dimension of this approach is that the direct stakeholders of the right to information are seen as society in general, and not specifically the news media. The right is thus seen as directly relevant to environmental activists, anti-corruption campaigners, human rights defenders, etc. – and not only journalists.

In addition, a proactive disclosure dimension is highlighted by UNESCO in broad terms, especially via the Internet. The Organisation thus interprets 'access' as access to information and knowledge. This entails promoting policies for online multilingualism, digital preservation, open education resources, disability-friendly policies for the Web, and the use of ICT-enhanced public information management policies (see UNESCO 2004).

Also in this picture, is the dimension which UNESCO calls 'media and information literacy', which reflects the Organisation's interlinkage of the fields of media literacy and information literacy. Within this umbrella notion, are new sub-literacies – which reflect both media production and consumption competencies (imparting, seeking and receiving public information in the online environment), as well as issues such as 'netiquette', digital security and engaging with online racism, sexism, bullying and incitement.

More broadly, the Open Government Partnership, the Open Data movement, and the Global Alliance for Partnerships on Media and Information Literacy (initiated by UNESCO), reveal the breadth of interest in a composite conception of the right to seek and receive which fuses issues of right and access. These aspects are further elaborated in UNESCO's comprehensive Internet Study, published in 2015 as *Keystones to Foster Knowledge Societies. Access to Information and Knowledge, Freedom of Expression, Privacy, and Ethics on a Global Internet* (UNESCO 2015b). The instrumental value of this interpretation of the right to information for sustainable development was stressed in the Finlandia Declaration[11] that was adopted at UNESCO's World Press Freedom Day global conference in Helsinki in May 2016.

One aspect of the Finlandia Declaration is a call for a UN process to explicitly recognise the right to information as a right to public documents, on the basis that the historic right to 'seek and receive' does not expressly call for state transparency. The Declaration further stated that the right encompasses access to information 'held by or on behalf of public authorities, or which public authorities are entitled to access by law, as well as access to information that is held by private bodies in respect of the exercise of public functions'. This latter part thus extends the earlier widespread view which had limited the scope of the right to official information, turning it more towards a conception of a 'right to know' – which would include, for example, a right to information held by private companies which may have environmental impact.

A new study under way at UNESCO at the time of writing by UNESCO (UNESCO 2016) raises further issues around interpreting the right to information and transparency in the digital age. This recognises first that huge advances in transparency are enabled by digital technologies, as regards both public and particularly private institutions. Second, it recognises that more and more information is not just being expressed, but is being also collected, stored and processed. Third, the point is made that information provided for communicative purposes is increasingly dwarfed by meta- and other data (e.g. Spatial movements) being collected for business or surveillance purposes. This also has a bearing on the universe of data which may be the object of seeking and receiving information. For instance, it raises whether the right to information extends to matters such as algorithms – including those that impact on information searching and receiving. This further implicates private ownership and intellectual property issues for the continued evolution of this realm.

In short, the right to information today begs the question of whether the right includes a right to data, including that held by Internet intermediary companies, and even transportation companies like Uber. This goes beyond the voluntary transparency reports (of varying breadth and depth) by companies about their responses to governmental requests, to encompass their internal practices of data curation and policy development. These developments mean that the right to information and data protection issues increasingly have significant intersections. UNESCO is currently grappling with these issues, which are likely to intensify as the 'Internet of Things' unfolds.

Debating freedom of expression and in relation to other rights

For UNESCO, where rights have to be balanced, each should be preserved as much as possible, with limitations being exceptional, and also congruent with international standards for legitimacy. Furthermore, UNESCO works with the established UN notion of avoiding an either/or prioritisation paradigm, accepting that human rights are indivisible. The different rights are thus seen not as being in a hierarchy, or in opposition to each other, but rather as a venn diagram. The challenge is to draw the line to avoid one intruding too far on the other, and also to enlarge the sweet spot of central overlap. The framing is more one of reconciling than a zero-sum balancing of rights.

For UNESCO, in order to keep press freedom and the right to access information as intact as possible, restrictions based on privacy, security, reputation or other concerns need to respect the internationally established conditions of legitimate purpose along with necessity, proportionality and redress opportunity. However, it is evident that much ongoing work is required to see such standards being applied in practice in many instances.

The two interdependent and changing dimensions of freedom of expression – press freedom and the right to information - are prominently intertwined with the right to privacy in the digital age, with potential synergies as well as tensions. As an indication of UNESCO's increased attention to privacy, the Organisation published in 2012, the *Global Survey on Internet Privacy and Freedom of Expression* (Mendel, T. et al 2012). The subject was also one of four components of the aforementioned *Keystones* study. There was recognition that privacy was becoming an issue for journalistic expression in a resolution at the UNESCO General Conference in 2013: '…*Privacy is essential to protect journalistic sources, which enable a society to benefit from investigative journalism, to strengthen good governance and the rule of law, and…such privacy should not be subject to arbitrary or unlawful interference…*' (Resolution on internet-related issues, November 2013).[12]

In the aforementioned UNESCO studies, there is recognition that strong privacy can strengthen the ability of journalism to draw on confidential sources for public interest information, but also that it can also weaken transparency and conceal information in which there could be legitimate public interest. Further, it is acknowledged that weak privacy can lead to journalistic sources withholding information or practising self-censorship, because of a fear of being arbitrarily monitored. Weak privacy may also enable an overreach which amounts to an unjustified intrusion into people's personal lives – such as in the tabloid phone-hacking scandal.

While space limitations preclude substantive commentary on changing understandings of the right to privacy (a right that is widely seen as lacking detail), there have been significant developments not only in the prominence of this right, but also its scope. The senses relevant to this book are that of the confidentiality of communications and the control of personal data, and seclusion in the sense of limiting intrusion. In this context, disentangling public-private realms in media becomes complex.

Until the Snowden surveillance revelations, most attention was given to data protection as a mechanism for ensuring that individuals' data in the private sector's hands were subject to limits on collection, storage, use and accuracy. Now privacy is seen as a much bigger issue. UN resolutions on the 'right to privacy in the digital age' have urged review, transparency and independent oversight of surveillance in order to protect the right to privacy. Civil society groups have produced the necessaryandproportionate.org principles. The UN Special Rapporteurs have published influential reports on anonymity, encryption and the free development of personality. Privacy now extends to issues such as the European Court of Justice 'right to be forgotten' which curtails the right to seek information where such is decided to be irrelevant, outdated or inaccurate by 'data-controllers' such as Google. All this highlights that it is certainly no longer possible to consider freedom of expression in isolation of the right to privacy.

Beyond privacy, other rights also have a growing bearing on the freedom of expression. Already in the predigital age, freedom of expression has often come up against governments using national security or rule of law arguments - to the effect that people's right to safety ('life, liberty and security of person') trumps the right to free speech. These arguments are sometimes legitimate, but also often overly broad – such as in responding to so-called 'online radicalisation'. In terms of international standards, incitement to hostility, discrimination and violence is a case where free expression faces legitimate limits. At the same time, newer frames of 'dangerous speech' and 'fear speech', as well as the Rabat Plan of Action (to which UNESCO contributed), as well as the Johannesburg Principles and the Tshwane Principles, have provided much greater nuance for when restrictions to curtail incitement to defined harm can be considered legitimate.

A further longstanding example of restricting the freedom of expression is defamation, which applies today both online or offline. This is generally seen, in principle, as a legitimate limit to the exercise of expression, in the interests of the right to reputation. However, many argue that criminal sanctions should be scrapped as 'unnecessary', because there are less intrusive remedies (e.g. civil actions, fines, apologies). Dignity and equality are also seen as important rights to privilege in the face of racist and/or misogynistic 'hate' speech, something that has become a greater concern in relation to such expression on the Internet (Gagliadone et al, 2015). Evidently, different countries and cultures give different interpretations in regulating this particular interface of rights.

Another evolution in reconciling rights relevant to media is one that addresses the power of private actors. In the perspective of the UN's Guiding Principles on Business and Human Rights[13], it is the responsibility of state actors to protect all rights, but at the same time, it is the responsibility of the private sector to respect these rights. This perspective has informed relevant civil society initiatives such as the Manila Principles and the Ranking Digital Rights project which spell out human rights implications for Internet intermediaries. As is argued in the UNESCO research study by MacKinnon et al. (2014), *Fostering Freedom Online: The Role of Internet Intermediaries*, a strong case can also be made that intermediaries' own terms of service should align with international standards. To be legitimate, the limitations imposed by companies should be transparent and rule-based terms of service, rather than being arbitrary (i.e. this is analogous to the role played by law). Finally, protection of rights requires opportunities for redress. To avoid privitisation of censorship, where governments can seek to dodge direct responsibility for violations, users should also always be able to appeal to courts. Although, private actors have the right to enforce their 'community standards', these practices should not become a substitute for unaccountable censorship on behalf of authorities, which is extralegal in nature.

Another issue that has arisen in the digital age concerns systems of licensing and registration for online publishing, such as for bloggers. Such systems do not easily square with international standards for free expression, where identification and prior restraint are justifiable only in highly exceptional circumstances and only for legitimate purpose.

It is evident that limiting online publishing can also be achieved in regard to the demand side – such as via online filtering and blocking. Here the imparting of information is not suppressed (for various reasons – often jurisdictional), but where receipt is prevented. There can indeed be cases for such limitations, but often these steps do not measure up to international standards – they are not exceptional, and they are disproportionate (such as blocking a whole site rather than offending subsections, or filtering which excludes wholly legitimate use of targeted words). Further, these steps are frequently opaque, implemented for purposes outside of those specified in the international standards (such as for narrow political reasons), indeterminate in duration, and lacking in any mechanism of appeal. Another concern is the 'notice and take down' (aka 'cease and desist') procedure, which – as the UNESCO (2015b) *Keystones* study recognises – tends to predispose intermediaries to remove or block content without giving due consideration to its possible legitimacy.

Finally, UNESCO takes the view that online blocking when motivated as a 'protection' of people from speech deemed to be problematic, misses out on the need to empower users to manage their own access to information. In this regard, Media and Information Literacy, signalled earlier, is an alternative to blocking and filtering strategies.

Upcoming dynamics and debates

UNESCO's work on human rights and media issues that interface with digital matters is partly grounded in UN mandates from the 2003 and 2005 World Summits on the Information Society (WSIS). UNESCO further coined its own concept of 'Knowledge Societies' which highlights issues of access, education, diversity and, significantly, freedom of expression.[14] The Organisation has amongst the 'action lines' assigned to it by WSIS, one that concerns 'media'. Follow-up work has included regular involvements at the WSIS fora and the Internet Governance Forum, promoting the importance of free, pluralistic and independent media online and offline. In February 2013, UNESCO hosted a WSIS review conference. The multistakeholder-developed Final Statement and Final Recommendations, later endorsed by UNESCO Member States, strongly underlined the importance of freedom of expression on the Internet (UNESCO, 2013a, 2013b). This was informed by delegates debating a report on the significance of media mutations (Frau-Meigs, 2013). Subsequently, as a result in part of UNESCO advocacy, the final statement of the UN's 10-year review of WSIS, which was agreed at the UN General Assembly in December 2015, recognised – in addition to a general statement on the importance of human rights – the need for journalistic safety in the information society. This part of the statement signals how media and rights issues are increasingly being located within a wider focus relating to the Internet.

However, the issue of what is 'media' in the online environment has also become of legal significance in regulatory questions. Internet intermediaries invariably prefer not to be recognized as 'media', on the grounds that they are platforms for others, and do not generally make editorial decisions. The distinction means that they can in many countries claim limited legal liability for content on or via their platforms, and that they can operate with individual terms of service and avoid an industry-wide shared code of ethics such as is sometimes imposed by broadcast regulators or agreed by voluntary press councils. The Council of Europe has wrestled with this issue,[15] and the European Court of Human Rights has held one intermediary liable for content deemed to be incitement (known as the Delfi case), though upheld limited liability in another case.[16] Facebook in May 2016 admitted to editing its 'trending topics', while still denying that its services counted as 'media'. This is clearly an issue in evolution and something for UNESCO and others to further explore.

That the Internet has widened UNESCO's focus on media and freedom of expression is also reflected in the resolution by Member States in November 2013 requiring UNESCO to conduct the *Keystones* study cited previously. The resulting 18-month consultative research process investigated the areas of freedom of expression as well as access to information and knowledge, privacy and ethical dimensions of the Internet, and the intersections between these.[17] Importantly, the resolution behind this study followed substantial debate sparked by the Snowden disclosures. Unlike the NWICO period, this saw compromise on all sides in the interests of a common position.[18] The 2015 General Conference of UNESCO Member States endorsed the outcomes of the study, including a concept of 'Internet universality', which identifies four 'ROAM' principles that underpin the 'norms' for a singular Internet:[19]

- Rights-respecting values and behaviours (including freedom of expression rights, as well as other rights including privacy, participation, dignity and safety).
- Openness (technologically open, and open in terms of economic opportunities).
- Accessibility (as regards connections, costs, language, media and information literacy, etc).
- Multi-stakeholder mode (the participation of multiple stakeholders in developing and deciding on the Internet).

Overall, in the universality of the Internet, conceived in this way, is embedded a Windhoek Declaration sense of freedom, pluralism, independence (with self-regulation and professional standards) and safety. Gender, and media and information literacy, are also integral to Internet universality. What this signals is that, in the face of the multidimensionality of the Internet, a vantage point centred on freedom of expression has to be interlinked with the breadth and interdependence of issues in this sphere. One example is encryption – which is not just an issue for confidentiality of journalistic research, but part of wider policy that impacts ecommerce, law enforcement and the Internet of Things.

What the Internet universality concept means at national and international levels is that any governmental or intergovernmental regulation should be guided by the wider normative framework of the integrated four R.O.A.M. principles. In cases where regulation is either not desirable or is not viable, the norms themselves can provide some guidance to both users and intermediaries as they take part in 'free flow' internationally. It is by promoting these norms universally that the historic freedom of expression provision, 'regardless of frontiers', can be striven for. In addition, in terms of reconciling rights, the ROAM framework suggests that in addition to the generic international tests of legality, necessity and legitimate purpose, consideration should be given to how any resolution might impact on Openness and on Accessibility, and whether a multi-stakeholder process is involved. The complexity of the Internet, in other words, requires an approach that is tailored to the nature of the platform on which free expression is exercised.

Conclusion

UNESCO in 2016 began to focus its work within the 2030 Development Agenda, which is based on 17 sustainable development goals agreed at the UN General Assembly in 2015. At the same time, UNESCO has also continued to highlight the complementary role of the WSIS processes for these sustainable development goals.

In general, the right to development intersects with varying roles of media sectors (public, private and community) which can enable participation, agenda setting, framing, holding power to account, etc. From the point of view of the right to free expression, the directly relevant part of the SDGs is goal 16, which aims to 'promote peaceful and inclusive societies for sustainable development, provide access to justice for all and build effective, accountable and inclusive institutions at all levels'. There is direct resonance in development target 16.10: 'public access to information and protect fundamental freedoms, in accordance with national legislation and international agreements'. This is an important acknowledgement that has direct media relevance.

For UNESCO, it is clear that public access to information ties directly to the right to information and press freedom, and thence to the fundamental freedom of expression. UNESCO thus argues that this target 16.10 is not only an end in itself, but also an important means to Goal 16 as a whole, and to the rest of the SDG goals – such as those on gender equality and addressing climate change. For the Organisation and other stakeholders, the task ahead is to monitor progress, stasis or regress on 16.10 in terms of two global indicators agreed by the UN Statistical Commission after much lobbying.[20] One indicator incorporates the safety of journalists, and the other refers to public guarantees of access to information.

What this means in sum is that freedom of expression in all its dimensions, and media in various dimensions, are integral parts of two interrelated international agendas: WSIS and the SDGs. This contemporary framing can be developed to incorporate specific reference to the importance of journalism.[21] As media and rights continue to evolve, UNESCO can be expected to elaborate these further on the foundations of the original right to freedom of expression, and the Windhoek and *World Trends* conceptualisations.

Notes

1 Office of the High Commissioner on Human Rights. 2016. 'Frequently Asked Questions on the Right to Development'. http://www.ohchr.org/Documents/Publications/FSheet37_RtD_EN.pdf

2 One early linkage was the declaration on '21st Century Media: New Frontiers, New Barriers' adopted at the UNESCO World Press Freedom Day conference in Washington, DC in 2011. This declaration called on UNESCO Member States to 'recognize and ensure that the same principles of freedom of expression apply equally to the Internet and other new information technologies, as they apply to traditional forms of media'. It further called on UNESCO itself to 'sensitize Member States, public authorities, civil society and individuals about exercising freedom of expression through new media, and the importance of such media in democratic societies', and to support 'an open and unrestricted Internet'.

3 An interesting analysis here is that by Richter (2016).

4 UNESCO. 2014. *World Trends in Freedom of Expression and Media Development.* http://www.unesco.org/new/en/world-media-trends

5 Most relevant here is UN Human Rights Committee's General Comment 34 on Article 19 of the International Covenant on Civil and Political Rights (ICCPR).

6 So too do other Rapporteurs, such as the OSCE Representative on the Freedom of the Media, the African Union's Special Rapporteur Freedom of Expression and Access to Information in Africa, and the Inter-American Rapporteur for Freedom of Expression.

7 Adopted by the United Nations on 10 December, 1948.

8 See Riekkinen and Suksi (2016).

9 The 39 Member State of UNESCO's IPDC Council used the formulation in its Decision of 23 March, 2012.

10 See http://www.africanplatform.org/. Disclosure: the author organised this conference before joining UNESCO.

11 https://en.unesco.org/sites/default/files/finlandia_declaration_3_may_2016.pdf
12 For a study on this topic, see the chapter by Posetti, J. in UNESCO (2015a).
13 http://www.ohchr.org/documents/publications/GuidingprinciplesBusinesshr_en.pdf
14 http://unesdoc.unesco.org/images/0014/001418/141843e.pdf
15 Recommendation CM/Rec(2011)7 of the Committee of Ministers to member states on a new notion of media. (Adopted by the Committee of Ministers on 21 September, 2011 at the 1121st Meeting of the Ministers' Deputies.) http://www.osce.org/odihr/101403
16 Judgment Magyar Tartalomszolgaltatok Egyesulete and Index.hu Zrt v. Hungary.pdf, http://hudoc. echr.coe.int/eng#{%22fulltext%22:[%22Magyar%20Tartalomszolgaltatok%22],%22languageisocode% 22:[%22ENG%22],%22documentcollectionid2%22:[%22GRANDCHAMBER%22,%22CHAMBE R%22],%22itemid%22:[%22001-160314%22]}
17 http://www.unesco.org/new/en/internetstudy
18 http://www.unesco.org/new/en/communication-and-information/resources/news-and-in-focus-articles/all-news/news/resolution_on_internet_related_issues_adopted_by_unesco_general_confer-ence_at_its_37th_session/#.UySQ92dOVMt
19 See 'Internet Universality: A Means Towards Building Knowledge Societies and the Post-2015 Sustainable Development Agenda', http://www.unesco.org/new/en/communication-and-informa-tion/crosscutting-priorities/unesco-internet-study/internet-universality/
20 UN Economic and Social Council, Statistics Commission (2016). *Report of the Inter-Agency and Expert Group on Sustainable Development Goal Indicators (Revised)* E/CN.3/2016/2/Rev.1. http://unstats. un.org/unsd/statcom/47th-session/documents/2016-2-IAEG-SDGs-Rev1-E.pdf
21 The World Editors Forum has proposed five principles to 'distinguish professional journalism and secure greater public recognition of its relevance'. World Editors Forum urges editors to adopt new principles to build trust in journalism. http://www.wan-ifra.org/press-releases/2016/06/14/world-editors-forum-urges-editors-to-adopt-new-principles-to-build-trust-i

References

Frau-Meigs, D. (2013). *Exploring the Evolving Mediascape: Towards Updating Strategies to Face Challenges and Seize Opportunities.* Available at: https://www.unesco-ci.org/cmscore/28/28-exploring-evolving-mediascape-towards-updating-strategies-face-challenges-and-seize [Accessed 4 Aug. 2016].

Gagliardone, I., Gal, D., Alves, T. and Martinez, G. (2015). *Countering Online Hate Speech.* Paris: UNESCO. Available at: http://unesdoc.unesco.org/images/0023/002332/233231e.pdf [Accessed 4 Aug. 2016].

Habermas, J. (1989). *The Structural Transformation of the Public Sphere.* Trans. Burger, T. Cambridge: MIT Press.

Henrichsen, J. R; Betz, M. and Lisosky, J. M. (2015). *Building Digital Safety for Journalists: A Survey of Selected Issues.* Paris: UNESCO. Available at: http://unesdoc.unesco.org/images/0023/002323/232358e.pdf [Accessed 4 Aug. 2016].

MacKinnon J., Hickok, E., Bar, A. and Hae-in, L. (2014). *Fostering Freedom Online: the Role of Internet Intermediaries.* Paris: UNESCO/Internet Society. Available at: http://unesdoc.unesco.org/images/ 0023/002311/231162e.pdf [Accessed 4 Aug. 2016].

Mendel, T., Puddephatt, A., Wagner, B., Hawtin, D. and Torres, N. (2012). *Global Survey on Internet Privacy and Freedom of Expression.* Paris: UNESCO. Available at: http://unesdoc.unesco.org/images/ 0021/002182/218273e.pdf [Accessed 4 Aug. 2016].

Richter, A. (2016). *'Defining Media Freedom in International Policy Debates'. Global Media and Communication.* 1–16. Available at: http://gmc.sagepub.com/content/early/2016/06/08/1742766516652164.full.pdf+ html [Accessed 4 Aug. 2016].

Riekkinen, M. and Suksi, M. (2016). *Access to Information and Documents as a Human Right.* Turku/Abo: Institute for Human Rights, Abo Akademi University.

UNESCO (2004). *Policy Guidelines for the Development and Promotion of Governmental Public Domain Information.* Available at: http://unesdoc.unesco.org/images/0013/001373/137363eo.pdf [Accessed 4 Aug. 2016].

UNESCO (2008). *Media Development Indicators: Framework for Assessing Media Development.* Paris: UNESCO. Available at: http://unesdoc.unesco.org/images/0016/001631/163102e.pdf [Accessed 4 Aug. 2016].

UNESCO (2013a). Recommendations from the First WSIS+10 Review Event, *Towards Knowledge Societies for Peace and Sustainable Development,* Paris 25–27 February, 2013. Available at: http://www.unesco.org/ new/fileadmin/MULTIMEDIA/HQ/CI/CI/pdf/wsis/WSIS_10_Event/wsis10_recommendations_ en.pdf [Accessed 4 Aug. 2016].

UNESCO (2013b). Final statement from the First WSIS+10 Review Event, *Towards Knowledge Societies for Peace and Sustainable Development*, Paris 25–27 February, 2013. Available at: http://www.unesco.org/new/fileadmin/MULTIMEDIA/HQ/CI/CI/pdf/wsis/WSIS_10_Event/wsis10_final_statement_en.pdf [Accessed 4 Aug. 2016].

UNESCO (2014). World Trends in Freedom of Expression and Media Development. Paris: UNESCO. Available at: http://www.unesco.org/new/en/world-media-trends [Accessed 4 Aug. 2016].

UNESCO (2015a). *World Trends in Freedom of Expression and Media Development, Selected Digital Trends*. Paris: UNESCO. Available at: https://unesdoc.unesco.org/images/0023/002349/234933e.pdf [Accessed 4 Aug. 2016].

UNESCO (2015b). *Keystones to Foster Knowledge Societies. Access to Information and Knowledge, Freedom of Expression, Privacy, and Ethics on a Global Internet*. Paris: UNESCO. Available at: http://unesdoc.unesco.org/images/0023/002325/232563E.pdf [Accessed 4 Aug. 2016].

UNESCO (2016). Privacy, free expression and transparence. Redefining their new boundaries in the digital age. Authors: Cannataci J.A, Zhao B, Torres Vives G, Monteleone S, Mifsud Bonnici J, Moyakine E. Paris: UNESCO. (Available at: http://unesdoc.unesco.org/images/0024/002466/246610e.pdf [Accessed 28 Mar. 2017].

3

HISTORY OF MEDIA AND HUMAN RIGHTS

Mark Hampton and Diana Lemberg

This chapter traces the emergence and development of two distinct phenomena: the idea that media should be legally protected from state interference; and the conception of access to media as a human right. Although it treats primarily discourses about media, the chapter also addresses historical episodes during which media were mobilized in campaigns for press freedoms, human rights and humanitarian causes. Finally, before we begin our survey of how human rights and media have intersected historically, a note on historiography: In the past decade, a recurrent tension has emerged in scholarship on the history of human rights, between a quest for origins (as early as the 17th century) on one hand and, on the other, an emphasis on the quite recent emergence (as late as the 1970s) of the contemporary human-rights regime. While this chapter does not attempt to adjudicate definitively between these competing approaches, it does aim to point readers towards major references in the scholarly debates.

Origins

The historical relationship between human rights and media in the modern world can be traced to the eighteenth-century Enlightenment 'rights of man' discourse, nineteenth-century discourses of 'humanitarianism', and the earliest articulations of the 'liberty of the press', though we should be careful in all three cases to avoid anachronism. As Samuel Moyn has argued, neither the rights of man nor humanitarianism, in their pre-twentieth-century manifestations, carried with them implications central to the post-1970s idea of 'human rights', that is that rights are inherent in all humans and transcend state sovereignty. A similar comparison can be made about post-1945 claims to media access as a human right. As David Copeland has pointed out, the earliest advocates of press freedom, including John Milton in *Aereopagitica* (1644), did not assert a general 'right' to a free press, but rather advocated it for instrumental religious reasons, and were motivated chiefly by concern for their own freedom to practice a dissenting Christianity.[1] At the same time, what we would today call the 'mass media' was limited to books, pamphlets, broadsides and fairly rudimentary newspapers and magazines. Censorship was general in Europe, while even in a relatively freer England, which had seen pre-publication censorship eliminated in 1695, extensive licensing requirements and the threat of post-publication punishments constituted a significant barrier to press freedom until the early 19th century.

Eighteenth- and early nineteenth-century demands for 'liberty of the press', even when expressed in secular rather than religious terms, usually remained instrumental in focus, and did not articulate a universal 'human right'. The Declaration of the Rights of Man and the Citizen, issued in 1789 during the French Revolution's constitutional monarchy phase, exceptionally included in Article XI a robust defence of freedom of expression, including speech, writing and printing, as 'one of the most precious rights of man', though during the subsequent radical phase of the Revolution, press controls were reintroduced.[2] More importantly for present purposes, most eighteenth- and nineteenth-century advocates of press freedom focused less on abstract universal rights to a free press than on more tangible and practical goals. The United States famously enshrined press freedom in its constitution's First Amendment, and its political elites regarded a properly functioning press as sufficiently important for facilitating republican political discourse that they used public money to subsidise the distribution of news, chiefly through the Post Office.[3] For Britain's Whig reformers, campaigning less against overt censorship than against licensing requirements and 'taxes on knowledge' that kept newspapers' prices deliberately high, the press was cast alternatively as a vehicle for educating both the restricted political nation and the working classes who in principle could join it, and as a vehicle for exposing tyranny and corruption on the part of the state.[4]

If 'liberty of the press' was rarely cast in the eighteenth and nineteenth centuries in terms of access to media as a human right, media were arguably central to the development of concepts of the 'rights of man' and humanitarianism. According to Lynn Hunt, human rights claims – that is, the articulation of rights that are 'natural (inherent in human beings); equal (the same for everyone); and universal (applicable everywhere)' – entered European discourse in the late 18th century, specifically in the contexts of the American and French Revolutions. For Hunt, the emergence of the very concept of 'human rights' depended upon a change in mentalities, indeed to the physical composition of the brain as a result of reading epistolary novels and descriptions of torture. In her words, 'New kinds of reading (and viewing and listening) created new individual experiences (empathy), which in turn made possible new social and political concepts (human rights)'.[5]

The rise of humanitarianism in the long 19th century

Hunt has focused on explaining why 'human rights' discourse retreated in the 19th century, but similar links can be found between media and the development of humanitarianism. Michael Barnett notes that 'for many students of humanitarianism and human rights, it all began with the antislavery movement', and highlights the role of pamphlets (and lecture tours) in spreading the anti-slavery message in the early 19th century.[6] The slave trade was abolished in the British Empire in 1807 and slavery itself in 1837. Across the Atlantic, newspapers were central to the Abolitionist campaign in the United States, with Elijah Lovejoy's *St. Louis Observer* (later relocated to Illinois) and William Lloyd Garrison's *Liberator* as two key examples.[7]

As Barnett defines it, humanitarianism, like 'human rights', focuses on individuals beyond the borders of one's own country, and in this regard, key examples of media promotion of humanitarianism include W. T. Stead's 'Bulgarian atrocities' campaign in the *Darlington Northern Echo* (1876) and E. D. Morel's journalistic campaign in the early 20th century against forced labour in the Belgian Congo. The former case centred on the brutal response by the Ottoman Empire to an uprising by its Bulgarian subjects, and the Disraeli government's continued support of Britain's traditional Ottoman ally. Though this campaign often invoked universal liberal values against tyranny, the campaign simultaneously highlighted the Christian character of Britain and the Christian identity of the Bulgarian victims, as opposed to the tyrannical character of an

Islamic government; in much of the press, Disraeli's supposed indifference to the plight of the Bulgarian Christians was linked to his Jewish origins. In this campaign, not only the editorials of Stead, but also the London comic press's use of caricature, contributed to the articulation of a humanitarian cause.[8]

Morel's campaign against the Belgian King Leopold's Congo began when Morel, a clerk for the Liverpool-based Elder Dempster company who had long been writing articles critical of the treatment of African colonial subjects, observed the discrepancy between the flow of weapons on ships from Belgium to the Congo and valuable commodities (ivory and rubber) on ships going the other direction, and inferred an exploitative labour regime tantamount to slavery. In 1902 he quit his position with the company, becoming a full-time journalist and founding the *West African Mail* in 1903. Over the next several years, Morel worked with the Congo Reform Association, whose members published several books and pamphlets exposing the atrocities committed by Leopold's regime, and with missionaries who provided photographic evidence (including images of maimed Congolese). This campaign helped lead to the Belgian government's formal incorporation of the Congo (i.e. removing it from King Leopold's personal control).[9]

All of these campaigns occurred in the context of media environments in which basic press freedoms were legally guaranteed, albeit within certain constraints such as laws pertaining to indecency or libel. At the same time, as already noted, the language of 'human rights' retreated significantly in the post-revolutionary period in the face of nationalist claims. When humanitarian advocacy groups, above all the International Committee of the Red Cross (established in 1863), focused on abuses overseas, moreover, they concentrated on the immediate 'emergency' more than the underlying causes (as a later type of humanitarianism, one that Michael Barnett calls the 'alchemical' branch, would highlight). In large part this reflected an attempt to remain 'apolitical' so that they could have access to enemy territories or territories controlled by absolutist governments. For these reasons, discourse on the press focusing domestically did not typically centre on the language of human rights, while nineteenth-century humanitarian engagements with territories beyond Western Europe and North America typically did not address the lack of press freedoms in such territories.

Transformations and threats, 1914–39

The outbreak of the First World War in the summer of 1914 would mark the beginning of three decades of profound uncertainty as to the role of press freedoms in the modern world, and ultimately those of liberalism and democracy *tout court*. The war would usher in an era of restrictions on the media even in the relatively liberal United States and United Kingdom, exemplified by Britain's Defence of the Realm Act (1914) and the U.S. Supreme Court's 1919 decision articulating a 'clear and present danger' test for justifying limitations to the First Amendment. The British government's pioneering approach to information management during the war raised uncomfortable questions about the fate of liberal press freedoms. So, too, did the interwar arguments of influential American intellectuals such as Walter Lippmann and Harold Lasswell, who contended that ordinary people were easily manipulated by propaganda and that governments should therefore pursue the enlightened management of public opinion.[10] The repressive post-war atmosphere was typified by the red scare that swept the United States in 1919 and 1920, following the Russian Revolution. Yet the aftermath of the First World War also saw the birth of the American Civil Liberties Union (created in 1920), devoted to protecting civil liberties against governmental abuses within the United States. On the international plane, new institutions were meanwhile emerging to address the unprecedented upheaval occasioned by the global conflict. The historian Keith David Watenpaugh has called the League of Nations' efforts to locate and resettle survivors of the Armenian Genocide of 1915 an early instance of 'modern humanitarianism', based on secular principles of scientific management and ostensibly permanent administrative structures. Humanitarian organizations' use of mass-circulation advertisements and posters to reach far-flung audiences during this episode would foreshadow the ways in which later human-rights organizations sought to publicize their causes.[11]

But by the 1930s, both internationalism and liberal democracy were in retreat, in the face of worldwide economic depression and rising fascist and Stalinist alternatives. Many predicted the definitive eclipse of older notions of individual rights and liberties, as Mussolini and then Hitler shrewdly manipulated the 'new media' of the interwar era – film and especially radio – in the service of their exclusionary and expansionist programs. It was only with Hitler's attack on Poland and the abandonment of appeasement in the fall of 1939 that Allied leaders would begin to offer a more robust defence of the individual against the state.

The institutionalisation of human rights in the 1940s

The depredations of the Axis powers would spur widespread – if belated – recognition of the need to reinvigorate individual liberties and democratic values in the 1940s. In the United States, President Franklin Roosevelt emphasised 'freedom of speech and expression – everywhere in the world' as one of the essential 'Four Freedoms' in his 1941 State of the Union address, as he advocated for US intervention in the war. The progressive cast of much Allied wartime propaganda – which in Britain stressed the theme of the 'people's war', and in the United States highlighted interethnic and interracial cooperation – amounted to a rejection of Nazi racial hierarchies and the xenophobic excesses of the First World War, with the important exception of the United States' treatment of persons of Japanese descent. Reportage documenting the liberation of Nazi concentration camps, disseminated in photo-magazines like *Life* and in eyewitness accounts such as those broadcast on the BBC, shocked international audiences and confirmed the importance of civil liberties before a broad public. When the *New York Times* asked a group of American middle-school students in 1946 whether press freedoms could help to avert future wars, one student concluded, 'Hitler would have been stopped in his tracks with one free paper'.[12]

Press and speech freedoms would be institutionalised in a range of international initiatives from 1945 onwards, notably in the creation of the United Nations in 1945 and the proclamation of the Universal Declaration of Human Rights (UDHR) three years later. Article 19 of the UDHR presented a sweeping guarantee of expressive liberties: 'Everyone has the right to freedom of opinion and expression; this right includes freedom to hold opinions without interference and to seek, receive and impart information and ideas through any media and regardless of frontiers'. While histories of human rights in the 1940s have highlighted the work of UN Human Rights Commission chair Eleanor Roosevelt and French jurist René Cassin, they have also demonstrated the contributions of figures from outside the United States and western Europe. Prominent actors on the UDHR drafting committee included Republican China's P. C. Chang and the Lebanese Christian Charles Malik. The Filipino diplomat Carlos Romulo, meanwhile, helped to push 'freedom of information' onto the agenda of international institutions, where states would debate its scope and applications in the years ahead.[13]

The symbolism of the post-war human-rights moment aside, its practical significance has been the subject of lively historiographical debate. Investigating great-power politics at the United Nations, Samuel Moyn and Mark Mazower have argued that the post-war international institutions in reality had little immediate impact on respect for human rights, including press and speech freedoms. The world's two superpowers, the United States and the Soviet Union, refused to cede sovereignty to international institutions, while the European colonial powers sought to exclude their empires from UN oversight. The UDHR was, by design, a statement of principle rather than a legally binding agreement, and the United Nations lacked the power to enforce its lofty provisions.[14] Efforts to craft a binding freedom-of-information convention would falter in the late 1940s and early 1950s, stalemated by the emerging Cold War and by widespread concern that such an agreement would abet cultural imperialism. The UN Conference on Freedom of Information opened in Geneva in March of 1948, shortly after the Soviet Union began jamming Voice of America radio broadcasts. Four years later, the United Nations would disband its Sub-commission on Freedom of Information, having made little progress on convention proposals.[15]

Positive freedoms and media development in the 1950s and 1960s

In addition to diplomatic snarls, debates over media and human rights during the early Cold War also reflected dissension over the substance of media freedoms. Did these freedoms signify the absence of governmental interference in the media, the 'negative liberties' favoured by liberal anticommunist intellectuals like Isaiah Berlin? Or could states encourage human rights through their media policies? American policymakers in the late 1940s and early 1950s tended towards the former view; and much contemporary Anglophone scholarship takes this approach. But others imagined a different political economy of rights. In Latin America, many of the foremost champions of international human rights in the 1940s wedded civil liberties to social citizenship.[16] Among the United States' closest allies in Europe, too, there was widespread consensus that post-war reconstruction demanded active governmental management of the economy.[17] Social-democratic and regulatory approaches intersected with media during the newsprint shortages that recurred in western Europe from 1945 through the early 1950s. In Britain, the average newspaper in 1950 was six to eight pages long, versus twenty before the war. One French legal expert who had been involved in post-war newsprint negotiations, capturing the mood of many in austerity-wracked Europe, wrote that government intervention was essential to surmounting 'economic obstacles' to freedom of information: 'Liberty is a hollow word if we do not give the means of its exercise to those in whom we purport to recognize it'.[18]

During the 'Development Decade' of the 1960s – so named by President Kennedy and the United Nations – a loose consensus would emerge regarding the positive role that states might play in enhancing media rights. UN Educational, Scientific and Cultural Organization (UNESCO) functionary Tor Gjesdal reported to the UN Human Rights Commission in 1962, 'No less than 70 per cent of the world's population lack information media. They are without a "window on the world" and are thus denied effective enjoyment of one of the basic human rights – the right to know'. UNESCO proposed new development standards for global media capacity: ten daily newspapers, five radio receivers and two cinema seats per one hundred people in every country.[19] Although the particulars of media-development projects varied widely, these sentiments appealed to diverse constituencies, including media industries in the United States, eager to expand their foreign markets; European powers desirous of maintaining influence in the decolonising world; and new states seeking aid.

Human rights and the cultural-imperialism debates

The 1970s and 1980s would focus increasing attention upon persistently uneven media flows between the global North and the global South. The failure of the Development Decade to live up to the expectations it had raised would fuel frustration as well as a search for new paradigms in the fields of media and communication studies. Critical communication scholars such as

Herbert Schiller would argue that information liberalism was cover for western – particularly American – cultural imperialism elsewhere in the world. This scholarship dovetailed with the concerns of a coalescing Third World bloc, which rallied to the cause of 'cultural sovereignty'. UNESCO's controversial International Commission for the Study of Communication Problems, also known as the MacBride Commission (after its Irish chair, Seán MacBride), would attempt to broker a compromise through a new 'right to communicate', intended to encompass media 'access and participation' as well as more traditional civil liberties.[20] But such a compromise would prove unacceptable to the United States and Britain, which withdrew from the organization in the mid-1980s.

Mediating human rights in the 1970s and beyond

Shifting the focus away from international institutions and towards non-governmental activism, recent scholarship has emphasized the 1970s as a 'breakthrough' moment in human-rights history. Contrasting the elite diplomacy of the 1940s to 1970s activism, Samuel Moyn writes that it was in the latter period, not the former, that liberal human rights became a genuinely 'delocalised' and 'grassroots' cause. This could happen only after UN-based advocacy, as well as the alternative ideologies of Marxism and Third Worldism, had proven disappointing in practice.[21] New non-governmental organizations (NGOs) such as Amnesty International, established in 1961, and Human Rights Watch, founded in 1978, would play an important role in publicising the human-rights violations of states around the globe.

While Moyn's periodisation has provoked debate, there is broad consensus that the increasing public-sphere prominence of human rights in the 1970s was bound up with evolving media coverage. Kenneth Cmiel has noted the dramatic increase of information about human rights which became available around this time – an 'explosion' of new books and periodicals, in the words of one university librarian trying to stay abreast of the field. This information did not remain cloistered in the ivory tower, moreover. NGOs and policymakers would begin to mobilize human-rights rhetoric – and research – to put pressure on authoritarian governments ranging from Shah Pahlavi's Iran to the Soviet Union to Latin American military dictatorships. After two-plus decades in the United States during which conservative Republicans had associated human rights with international commitments that compromised American power, by the late 1970s even Ronald Reagan was invoking human rights, albeit in the service of his own hard-line anti-communism and antistatism.[22]

Form also mattered in the popularisation of human-rights causes in the 1970s and beyond. While Amnesty International's early activism involved grassroots letter-writing campaigns on behalf of political prisoners, the organization would soon begin to market its work through everything from magazine advertisements to pens and T-shirts bearing its logo.[23] Likewise, televised events like the 'Live Aid' concerts of the mid-1980s would promote human-rights and humanitarian causes in a stylish new format, bringing them into people's homes around the world.[24] Such media innovations have helped to make human rights user-friendly. The American NGO Freedom House's easy-to-digest surveys of political and civil liberties around the world, which rank each nation as either 'Not Free,' 'Partly Free,' or 'Free', have been published annually since the early 1970s. Today the rankings are instantly available through interactive online maps.[25]

Contemporary questions

The question of how effective media are in promoting human-rights causes remains a contentious one. The American intellectual Susan Sontag famously wrote in a 1973 essay that the potential of atrocity photographs to mobilize popular conscience diminishes with prolonged exposure to them.[26] Other scholars of visual culture have more recently presented qualified defences of the ethical and civic potentialities of documentary photography and visual artefacts.[27] Less controversial is the notion that historically contingent media forms shape popular epistemologies. Kenneth Cmiel has usefully conceptualised human rights as one of the 'lingua francas' of our contemporary era of rapid transnational media flows, which can stimulate bursts of public sympathy for people in distant places and societies. But Cmiel also notes that rights talk provides only 'thin' knowledge of these places and societies, and can quickly fade from the headlines.[28]

For many recent commentators, the discourse of human rights signifies a welcome retreat from the political radicalism and grandiose modernisation schemes that plagued the 20th century – a refreshingly minimalist 'utopia', as Samuel Moyn has written. For others, contemporary liberal applications of human rights to media, such as the internet freedoms championed by Hillary Clinton's State Department around the Arab Spring, seem to reproduce the contradictions of an earlier, imperial, humanitarianism.[29] Even in the historic heartlands of empire, deep disagreements persist over the proper relationship between economic freedoms and public-interest media regulations. Recent Euro–American spats over whether internet users should enjoy a 'right to be forgotten' have exposed rifts between the Silicon Valley, which loathes the concept, and the European Union, which has embraced it.[30] If nothing else, these disagreements and divergences indicate the ongoing relevance of scholarship on the relationship between media and human rights.

Notes

1 David Copeland, *The Idea of a Free Press: The Enlightenment and its Unruly Legacy* (Evanston, IL: Northwestern University Press, 2006).
2 Stephen J.A. Ward, *The Invention of Journalism Ethics: the Path to Objectivity and Beyond* (Montreal and Kingston: McGill-Queen's University Press, 2004), 166.
3 Paul Starr, *The Creation of the Media: Political Origins of Modern Communications* (New York: Basic Books, 2004).
4 Mark Hampton, *Visions of the Press in Britain, 1850–1950* (Urbana: University of Illinois Press, 2004); Hampton, "The Fourth Estate Ideal in Journalism History," in Stuart Allan, ed., *The Routledge Companion to News and Journalism* (London and New York: Routledge, 2009), 3-12.
5 Lynn Hunt, *Inventing Human Rights: A History* (New York: W. W. Norton & Company), 20, 33.
6 Michael Barnett, *Empire of Humanity: A History of Humanitarianism* (Ithaca: Cornell University Press, 2013), 57-8.
7 Rodger Streitmatter, *Mightier than the Sword: How the News Media Have Shaped American History*, 4th ed. (Boulder: Westview Press, 2016), 16-29.
8 Patrick Joyce, *Democratic Subjects: The Self and the Social in Nineteenth Century England* (Cambridge: Cambridge University Press, 1994), 204-13; Anthony S. Wohl, "'Dizzi-Ben-Dizzi': Disraeli as Alien," *Journal of British Studies* 34 (Jul., 1995), pp. 375-411.
9 Adam Hochschild, *King Leopold's Ghost: A Story of Greed, Terror, and Heroism in Colonial Africa* (New York: Houghton Mifflin, 1999). On photography in the Congo, see Sharon Sliwinski, *Human Rights in Camera* (Chicago: University of Chicago Press, 2011), chap. 3.
10 On Lippmann and Lasswell, see Brett Gary, *The Nervous Liberals: Propaganda Anxieties from World War I to the Cold War* (New York: Columbia University Press, 1999), chap. 1 and 2.
11 Keith David Watenpaugh, 'The League of Nations' Rescue of Armenian Genocide Survivors and the Making of Modern Humanitarianism, 1920-1927', *American Historical Review* 115/5 (Dec., 2010), pp. 1315–39.
12 'Free Press Held World Peace Key', *New York Times*, 24 Feb. 1946. On popular attention to human rights in the 1940s more generally, see Paul Gordon Lauren, *The Evolution of International Human Rights: Visions Seen*, 3rd ed. (Philadelphia: University of Pennsylvania Press, 2011), chap. 5 and 6.
13 Mary Ann Glendon, *A World Made New: Eleanor Roosevelt and the Universal Declaration of Human Rights* (New York: Random House, 2001); Glenn Mitoma, *Human Rights and the Negotiation of American Power*

(Philadelphia: University of Pennsylvania Press, 2013), pp. 74–91; Kenneth Cmiel, 'Human Rights, Freedom of Information, and the Origins of Third-World Solidarity', in *Truth Claims: Representation and Human Rights*, ed. Mark Philip Bradley and Patrice Petro (New Brunswick, NJ: Rutgers University Press, 2002), pp. 109–11.

14 Samuel Moyn, *The Last Utopia: Human Rights in History* (Cambridge, MA: Harvard University Press, 2010), see esp. chap. 2; Mark Mazower, 'The Strange Triumph of Human Rights, 1933-1950', *The Historical Journal* 47(2) (June 2004), pp. 379–98.

15 Kenneth Cmiel, 'Human Rights', 115; Mitoma, *Human Rights*, pp. 91–100.

16 Greg Grandin, 'Human Rights and Empire's Embrace: A Latin American Counterpoint', in *Human Rights and Revolutions*, 2nd ed., ed. Jeffrey Wasserstrom, Greg Grandin, Lynn Hunt, and Marilyn B. Young (Lanham, MD: Rowman & Littlefield, 2007), pp. 191–212.

17 Tony Judt, *Postwar: A History of Europe since 1945* (New York: Penguin, 2005), pp. 67–77; Daniel Rodgers, *Atlantic Crossings: Social Politics in a Progressive Age* (Cambridge, Mass.: Belknap Press of Harvard University Press, 1998), pp. 485–508.

18 *World Communications: Press, Radio, Film* (Paris: UNESCO, 1950), p. 129; Fernand Terrou, '*Aspects législatifs et réglementaires de l'intervention de l'Etat dans le domaine de l'Information*', *La Revue administrative* 6(33) (May–June, 1953), p. 264.

19 Tor Gjesdal, 'Statement by Tor Gjesdal, Director of the Department of Mass Communication, UNESCO, to the 18th Session of the United Nations Commission on Human Rights, 15 March – 14 April, 1962', [spring 1962], William Benton Papers, Special Collections Research Center, University of Chicago Library, Box 393, Folder 11.

20 International Commission for the Study of Communication Problems, *Many Voices, One World: Towards a More Just and Efficient World Information and Communication Order* (New York: Unipub, 1980), pp. 172–4.

21 Samuel Moyn, 'The 1970s as a Turning Point in Human Rights History,' in *The Breakthrough: Human Rights in the 1970s,* ed. Jan Eckel and Samuel Moyn (Philadelphia: University of Pennsylvania Press, 2014), p. 6; and Moyn, *Last Utopia*, see esp. pp. 120-2.

22 Kenneth Cmiel, 'The Emergence of Human Rights Politics in the United States', *Journal of American History* 86/3 (Dec., 1999), pp. 1231–50; and Carl J. Bon Tempo, 'Human Rights and the US Republican Party in the Late 1970s', in *The Breakthrough*, pp. 146–65.

23 Cmiel, 'Emergence', pp. 1245–8.

24 Stefan-Ludwig Hoffmann, 'Genealogies of Human Rights', in *Human Rights in the Twentieth Century*, ed. Stefan-Ludwig Hoffmann (Cambridge: Cambridge University Press, 2010), p. 20.

25 Carl J. Bon Tempo, 'From the Center-right: Freedom House and Human Rights in the 1970s and 1980s', in *The Human Rights Revolution: An International History*, ed. Akira Iriye, Petra Goedde and William I. Hitchcock (New York: Oxford University Press, 2012), p. 226.

26 Susan Sontag, 'Photography', *New York Review of Books*, 18 Oct. 1973. This essay was revised and reprinted as 'On Photography' in Sontag's eponymous 1977 essay collection.

27 Sliwinski, *Human Rights in Camera*; Ariella Azoulay, *The Civil Contract of Photography* (New York: Zone Books, 2011). Sontag would modify her argument in her late work *Regarding the Pain of Others* (New York: Picador, 2003), see esp. pp. 104–13.

28 Cmiel, 'Emergence', pp. 1248–50.

29 Robin Blackburn, 'Reclaiming Human Rights', *New Left Review* 69 (May–June, 2011), p. 136. On Clinton and internet rights, see Mark Landler and Brian Knowlton, 'U.S. Policy to Address Internet Freedom', *New York Times*, 14 Feb. 2011, p. A10.

30 *New York Times* Editorial Board, 'Ordering Google to Forget', *New York Times*, 13 May 2014, p. A26; *Spiegel* staff, 'Europe: 1, Google: 0: EU Court Ruling a Victory for Privacy', trans. Daryl Lindsay and Jane Paulick, *Spiegel Online*, 20 May 2014, available at: http://www.spiegel.de/international/business/court-imposes-right-to-be-forgotten-on-google-search-results-a-970419.html [accessed 23 May, 2014].

Select Bibliography

Barnett, M. (2013). *Empire of Humanity: A History of Humanitarianism*. Ithaca, NY: Cornell University Press.

Blackburn, R. (2013). *The American Crucible: Slavery, Emancipation and Human Rights*. London: Verso.

Cmiel, K. (2002). 'Human Rights, Freedom of Information, and the Origins of Third-World Solidarity'. In: M. P. Bradley and P. Petro eds., *Truth Claims: Representation and Human Rights*. New Brunswick, NJ: Rutgers University Press, pp. 107–30.

Cmiel, K. (1999). 'The Emergence of Human Rights Politics in the United States.' *Journal of American History*, 86(3), pp. 1231–50.

Copeland, D. A. (2006). *The Idea of a Free Press: The Enlightenment and its Unruly Legacy*. Evanston, IL: Northwestern University Press.

Eckel, J. and Moyn, S., eds (2014). *The Breakthrough: Human Rights in the 1970s*. Philadelphia: University of Pennsylvania Press.

Glendon, M. A. (2001). *A World Made New: Eleanor Roosevelt and the Universal Declaration of Human Rights*. New York: Random House.

Hampton, M. (2004). *Visions of the Press in Britain, 1850–1950*. Urbana: University of Illinois Press.

Harris, B. (1996). *Politics and the Rise of the Press: Britain and France, 1620–1800*. London: Routledge.

Hunt, L. (2008). *Inventing Human Rights: A History*. New York: W. W. Norton.

International Commission for the Study of Communication Problems (1980). *Many Voices, One World: Towards a More Just and Efficient World Information and Communication Order*. New York: Unipub.

Lauren, Paul Gordon (2011). *The Evolution of International Human Rights: Visions Seen*, 3rd ed. Philadelphia: University of Pennsylvania Press.

Mazower, M. (Jun., 2004). 'The Strange Triumph of Human Rights, 1933-1950', *The Historical Journal*, 47(2), pp. 379–98.

Mitoma, G. (2013). *Human Rights and the Negotiation of American Power*. Philadelphia: University of Pennsylvania Press.

Moyn, S. (2010). *The Last Utopia: Human Rights in History*. Cambridge, MA: Belknap Press of Harvard University Press.

Sliwinski, S. (2011). *Human Rights in Camera*. Chicago: University of Chicago Press.

Sontag, S. (18 Oct. 1973). 'Photography'. *New York Review of Books*.

Sontag, S. (2003). *Regarding the Pain of Others*. New York: Picador.

Starr, P. (2005). *The Creation of the Media: Political Origins of Modern Communications*. New York: Basic Books.

Watenpaugh, K. David (2010). 'The League of Nations' Rescue of Armenian Genocide Survivors and the Making of Modern Humanitarianism, 1920-1927'. *American Historical Review*, 115(5), pp. 1315–39.

4

MEDIA FREEDOM OF EXPRESSION AT THE STRASBOURG COURT

Current predictability of the standard of protection offered

Helen Fenwick

Introduction

It is frequently said that the Strasbourg Court under Article 10 of the European Convention on Human Rights provides a high degree of protection for media expression (Fenwick and Phillipson 2006). The Court has repeatedly asserted that freedom of expression 'constitutes one of the essential foundations of a democratic society',[1] and that it 'is applicable not only to "information" or "ideas" that are favourably received or regarded as inoffensive or as a matter of indifference, but also to those that "offend, shock or disturb"'.[2]

As this chapter will argue, it is a marked feature of the Strasbourg media freedom jurisprudence that clearly political speech, which may be seen as directly engaging the self-government rationale, receives a much more robust degree of protection than other types of expression (Barendt 1987). The basic thesis is that citizens cannot participate fully in a democracy unless they have a reasonable understanding of political issues; therefore, open debate on such matters is necessary to ensure the proper working of a democracy.

By contrast, in cases involving non-political speech in the media, largely supported by the values of autonomy, truth-seeking and self-development rather than self-government, it has generally been the case that an exactly converse pattern emerges: applicants have tended to be unsuccessful[3] and a deferential approach to the judgements of the national authorities as to the expression's ability to shock or disturb is apparent. The chapter will consider selected cases to question whether the Court's current approach can be said to be too readily dismissive of speech deemed non-political, and whether the medium within which the expression appears has any bearing on its determinations.

When the Court speaks of the importance of protecting freedom of expression it is usually referring to media freedom of expression; the expression of non-media bodies, or individuals, tends not to receive the same level of protection. That is particularly apparent in respect of public protest (Fenwick and Phillipson 2000). Particular stress has been laid upon 'the pre-eminent role of the press in a State governed by the rule of law' which, 'in its vital role of "public watchdog"' has a duty 'to impart information and ideas on matters of public interest' which the public 'has a right to receive'.[4] It cannot necessarily be assumed that political expression in other mediums, including broadcasting, would inevitably receive the same level of protection.[5]

The chapter will consider the *current* predictability of the level of protection offered by the Court to media expression, asking whether it is the case that the Court has *consistently* shown a high regard for media freedom of expression, especially political expression, and, conversely, whether it is still fair to say that it quite readily dismisses free expression claims where they have little contiguity with public interest value.

The structure and application of Article 10 ECHR, European consensus analysis and the margin of appreciation doctrine

Article 10 provides a strong safeguard for freedom of expression in relation to competing interests, since it takes the primary right as its starting point. The *content* of speech will very rarely exclude it from the protection of Article 10: the Court has consistently held that a broad scope should be accorded to the first para of the Article.[6] An interference with protected speech under Article 10(1) can be justified under Article 10(2), but Article 10(1) specifically provides that the Article 'shall not prevent States from requiring the licensing of broadcasting, television or cinema enterprises', implying on its face a limitation of the primary right that is not subject to the test of para 2. However, that sentence has been found to mean that decisions of the regulatory bodies who normally grant licences and oversee broadcasting, covered by the last sentence of para 1, must be considered within para 2.[7] The preservation of a state monopoly on broadcasting must also be considered within para 2.[8]

Under Article 10(2), an interference with the guarantee of freedom of expression under Art 10 can be justified if it is prescribed by law, has a legitimate aim (one or more of the enumerated aims) and is necessary in a democratic society, meaning that interferences with the primary right should be both necessary and proportionate to the legitimate aim pursued. But interferences with expression have not all been subject to the same intensity of scrutiny at Strasbourg, due mainly to the hierarchy of expression recognised under Article 10, political expression being, as indicated, viewed as of the highest value (Harris et al. 2009a). Strasbourg views the scope for interference with political expression as very limited. Artistic/entertainment-based expression appears to have a lower place in the Article 10(1) hierarchy, partly because it may relate to varying standards of morality in the member states, and therefore if there is a lack of a European consensus on the matter the state may be accorded a broader margin of appreciation (Dzehtsiarou 2015) in respect of interferences with such expression. But even in respect of such expression, the discussion that follows indicates that decisions defending restrictions on the freedom of expression of adults are rare, *except* in respect of hard-core pornography, or where a risk to children is also present, or in the context of offending religious sensibilities, or where a clash with Article 8, providing a right to respect for private life, occurs.

In considering the demands of proportionality the Court will apply a varying level of scrutiny, based on the hierarchy of expression, in respect of the sanction applied to the expression, in terms of its impact and duration. Prior restraints on expression, such as injunctions, clearly have a strong impact in curbing it since they are intended to prevent any publication of the expression at all, meaning that it may never reach its intended audience. Criminal sanctions obviously also have a particularly strong impact, and may well have a chilling effect on expression that is as pernicious in free speech terms as prior restraints.

Sunday Times v United Kingdom[9] provides a useful illustration of the operation of the tests under Article 10(2) in the traditional context of press free expression. The case concerned such expression on a significant matter of public concern (the Thalidomide litigation) that the UK courts had found could create a risk of prejudice to court proceedings; the injunction preventing its publication had been upheld domestically. The European Court of Human Rights found that the injunction clearly infringed freedom of speech under Article 10(1); the question was whether one of the exceptions within Article 10(2) could be invoked. The imposition of the injunction satisfied the 'prescribed by law' test as based on a sufficiently clear common law offence; but it did not satisfy the 'necessary in a democratic society' test, partly due to the significance of the expression and also because the court proceedings were unlikely to be affected since they were dormant at the time. Thus, the relevant exception under Article 10(2) could not apply: Article 10 had therefore been breached. The decision provides a pertinent example of the response of the Court when confronted with expression falling within the watchdog role of the press and of a political nature – in the sense of relating clearly to the public interest. Furthermore, such expression had been interfered with by way of a prior restraint – an injunction. Thus the scene was set for finding a breach. However, the presence of one or more of those factors does not necessarily mean that a breach will be found, as further discussion will reveal.

The *Sunday Times* case concerned a typical interference by the state with an established medium. It can be contrasted with instances in which the interference arises at the instigation of a non-state actor, as will be discussed further on, and also with instances of state blocking of websites, where those claiming that an interference has occurred are not the proprietors of the websites in question – an issue more likely to arise in the internet context. That situation arose in *Cengiz and others v Turkey*:[10] the Turkish Government blocked all access to the video-sharing website YouTube in 2008 on the basis of a law that prohibited 'insulting the memory of Ataturk'; YouTube contained around ten videos viewed as insulting to Ataturk by the domestic court which had issued the blocking order. The ban remained in effect for two years. The applicants were Law Professors who relied on Youtube as part of their academic work; the Court found that they had standing to bring the claim on the basis that there was no other media platform equivalent to YouTube, so they therefore had a reasonable claim to have been affected in the exercise of their freedom of expression rights. The blocking of YouTube was not directly targeted at the applicants, as was the injunction in *Sunday Times*; however, the ban interfered with the Professors' right to receive and impart information and ideas under Article 10(1). The interference could not be justified under Article 10(2) because, again in contrast to *Sunday Times,* the ban was not 'prescribed by law' since the law in question under which it was authorised allowed only for the banning of specific publications, not for the blocking of an entire website. Had the ban had a basis in a broader domestic law, allowing for such blanket blocking, it is probable that it would have failed the 'necessary in a domestic society' test on the basis that the impugned expression would have fallen into the category of 'political expression' inviting strict scrutiny of the necessity and proportionality of the ban. Further, since it would be hard to find a European consensus as to censorship of publications 'insulting' deceased prominent state figures, a narrow margin of appreciation only would have been conceded.

Protecting political expression in the media

The 'political' media expression cases of *Sunday Times v UK*,[11] *Jersild v Denmark*,[12] *Lingens v Austria*,[13] *Thorgeirson v Iceland,*[14] all resulted in findings that Article 10 had been violated and all were marked by an intensive review of the restriction in question in which the margin of appreciation was narrowed almost to vanishing point. But while the meaning assigned to the term 'political expression' has been given a fairly broad scope at Strasbourg, it may be argued that any 'political' dimension of apparently purely entertainment-based or creative expression, has at times failed to receive recognition, as discussed further on in the chapter.[15] Further, where it can be argued instrumentally that protecting the expression in question would not advance the ultimate goals at stake in valuing political expression, expression that is self-evidently political in nature may receive a reduced protection. That was the position taken by the Court in *Animal Defenders v UK*.[16]

The Court found that the ban on political advertising in broadcasting in the UK was not incompatible with Article 10, deciding to depart from its judgement on the matter in *Vgt v Switzerland*.[17] On its face this was a surprising decision. The ban not only curbed political expression but constituted a form of prior restraint. It would have been expected therefore that a narrow margin of appreciation only would have been conceded to the UK, so strict scrutiny of the proportionality of the ban with the aims pursued would have been undertaken under Article 10(2). The Court found, however, that there was no European consensus on how to regulate paid political advertising in broadcasting. In general, under the ECHR where no such consensus can be discerned, the margin of appreciation conceded to the state tends to remain quite wide. The Court sought to balance the applicant NGO's right to impart information and ideas of general interest which the public was entitled to receive against the authorities' desire to protect the democratic debate and process from distortion by powerful financial groups using an especially influential medium: broadcasting. The possibility that powerful interest groups could unduly influence the democratic process, possibly drowning out the voices of less well-funded groups, was viewed as significant.

The Court took account of the *quality* of the legislative process that had led to the enactment of the provisions governing the ban. There had been extensive pre-legislative scrutiny of the provisions of the Act in question, and they had been enacted with cross-party support. Also judicial bodies had accorded legitimacy to the ban: its proportionality in Article 10(2) terms had been considered by the House of Lords in depth.[18] The relevant Convention case-law had received extensive analysis in finding that the ban satisfied the demands of proportionality. Further, Animal Defenders had had other outlets open to it to put forward its message since the ban only concerned broadcasting. The Court therefore came to the conclusion that the ban satisfied the demands of proportionality under Article 10(2).

Five of the dissenting judges objected to the decision of the majority on the ground that what is deemed necessary to protect political expression in a democratic society should be based on a minimum and uniform ECHR standard: 'We are particularly struck by the fact that when one compares the outcome in this case with the outcome in the case of *VgT Verein gegen Tierfabriken v. Switzerland*[19] the almost inescapable conclusion must be that an essentially identical "general prohibition" on "political advertising" – sections 321(2) and (3) of the 2003 Act in this case and sections 18 and 15 of the Federal Radio and Television Act and the Radio and Television Ordinance respectively in *VgT* – is not necessary in Swiss democratic society, but is proportionate and *a fortiori* necessary in the democratic society of the UK. We find it extremely difficult to understand this double standard within the context of a Convention whose minimum standards should be equally applicable throughout all the States parties to it'.

This decision may be said to demonstrate an acceptance by the Strasbourg Court of its role as subsidiary to that of the domestic legislature and courts, even in the context of media political expression. It is part of a recent trend at Strasbourg in which the jurisprudence gives greater weight than formerly to findings of the domestic courts and legislature *if* the Convention rights have been considered fully by the domestic bodies. So long as the domestic bodies fully rehearse the Convention arguments the Court is currently showing some reluctance to depart from their findings. The points made in the dissenting judgments in *Animal Defenders v UK,* as well as arguments of media free speech principle, render this decision questionable.

Protecting non-political expression in the media

Artistic or entertainment-based expression of no public interest value receives less protection under Article 10 and it is arguable that, for example, material grossly and gratuitously offensive on racial grounds[20] or to religious sensibilities[21] or depictions of genitals in pornographic magazines intended merely for entertainment[22] may fall outside its scope, or be found to be extremely lightly protected. However, 'hard core' pornography has been found by the Commission to fall within Art 10(1).[23] The argument from self-development – that the freedom to engage in the free expression and reception of ideas and opinions in various media is essential to human development—has received some recognition at Strasbourg (Harris et al. 2009b). The argument from autonomy – that individuals should be free to choose as to the media expression they wish to encounter – would also be applicable.

Given the breadth of para 2, it is unnecessary to seek to draw lines between artistic erotica and forms of pornography aimed at entertainment alone, even assuming that such line-drawing has any validity (Kearns 2000). The jurisprudence under Article 10 in this context, as in others, concentrates on the para 2 tests. Interferences with explicit expression may be justified if they have the legitimate aim of providing for the protection of morals or – in certain circumstances – the 'rights of others'. The use of laws on obscenity, indecency or blasphemy against explicit expression or regulation of the media with a view to upholding 'standards of taste and decency' are matters that have been addressed at Strasbourg, relying on Article 10.

The line of authority stemming from the *Handyside* case[24] suggests that although explicit expression, including some pornographic expression, is protected within Article 10(1), interference with it can be justified quite readily in certain circumstances. Once a piece of work has been accorded the label 'artistic' or entertainment-based, rather than political – and possibly when it appears in a medium not traditionally associated with the delivery of political expression, such as in a book – such ready acceptances of interference are apparent. It is clear that the scope of the domestic margin of appreciation is not the same in respect of all the aims listed in Article 10(2). The protection of morals would appear to be viewed as requiring a wide margin owing to its subjective nature, and the lack of consensus in Europe as to the standards of taste and decency to be maintained in the media. The uncertainty of the notion of the protection of morals appears in the lack of a clearly discernible common European standard. Thus expression that might shock on grounds of decency stands in contrast with the greater protection given to expression that might threaten 'the authority of the judiciary', which is seen as a more objective notion,[25] and one which reflects a consensus in Europe.

In the *Handyside* case, the European Court of Human Rights had to consider material deemed by the domestic courts to be 'obscene'. A book called The *Little Red Schoolbook*, which contained chapters on masturbation, sexual intercourse and abortion was prosecuted under the Obscene Publications Act 1959 on the basis that it appeared to encourage early sexual intercourse. The Court determined that the book fell within Article 10(1). In a famous passage, strongly favouring freedom of artistic or creative expression (the expression of information or ideas), it found that even offensive ideas fall within Article 10 due to the demands of that 'pluralism, tolerance and broadmindedness without which there is no democratic society.'[26]

However, the interference could be justified under para 2 under the protection of morals provision, which the Court considered in order to determine whether the interference with the expression was necessary in a democratic society. The Court found that the requirements of morals vary from time to time and from place to place and that the domestic authorities were therefore best placed to judge what was needed. They must 'make the initial assessment of the reality of the pressing social need implied by the notion of necessity in this context'.[27]

The judgment thus accepted that domestic authorities would be allowed a wide margin of appreciation in attempting to secure the freedoms guaranteed under the Convention in this area, although this was not to be taken as implying that an unlimited discretion was granted: the power of appreciation 'goes hand in hand with a European supervision' which concerns the legislation in question – the Obscene Publications Act – and the decision applying it. The Court placed particular weight on the fact that the book was aimed at children and might encourage them 'to indulge in precocious activities harmful for them or even to commit certain criminal offences'.[28] Thus, it was found that the English judges had been entitled to find that the book would have a 'pernicious effect on the morals' of the children who would read it. In finding that the tests under para 2 were satisfied, it was said that the fact that the book was circulating freely in the rest of Europe was not determinative of the issues, owing to the application of the margin of appreciation doctrine. Possibly that stance would not be taken now, since use of European consensus analysis (which includes granting only a narrow margin of appreciation to a state which is out of line in terms of its law and practice with the rest) is now in a more developed state, and has a greater impact on the Court's analysis.

A similar stance as to the margin of appreciation to be conceded was taken in *Müller v Switzerland*[29] in respect of a conviction arising from the exhibition of explicit paintings: the fact that the paintings had been exhibited in other parts of Switzerland and abroad did not mean that their suppression was not found to amount to a pressing social need under Article 10(2). The Court took into account the fact that the paintings were exhibited to the public at large, without a warning as to their content, and that a young girl had seen them. The strong sanction applied, which included barring exhibition of the paintings for a number of years, did not lead to a finding of disproportionality.

These two decisions give a strong indication as to the stance taken by the Court in respect of Article 10, para 2, but may be viewed as turning on their special facts, particularly the fact that children might have been affected. The thinking behind the *Handyside* decision can find some parallels from the US[30] and Canada.[31] In the US, however, there has been a greater concentration on the question whether restrictions aimed at children might impinge also on the freedom of expression of adults and on the extent to which this should be tolerated,[32] a matter which was in issue in *Handyside*, although not afforded weight by the Court.

It is notable that the Court in *Handyside* based its analysis of the justification for the protection of media freedom of expression on the arguments from democracy and self-fulfilment rather than on those from truth or moral autonomy. Those justifications, as instrumental arguments, are open to attack in the way that the argument from moral autonomy is not (Barendt 1987). This stance of the Court is especially relevant in the context of explicit expression since that argument may provide the sole justification. (It is not suggested that that was the case in *Handyside* itself; on the contrary, on the basis of the content of the book, three of the four justifications could have applied.) The Court's stance may have some bearing on the cautious nature of its jurisprudence in this area, although unlike the Supreme Court of Canada,[33] it has not explicitly addressed this issue.

These decisions at Strasbourg do not determine the question of the consumption of explicit material solely or mainly by a willing adult audience – a matter that is especially pertinent in relation to films and videos, bearing their age classifications in mind. That question was considered in *Hoare v UK*,[34] which concerned the possession of 'hard core' pornographic videos. The applicant had been convicted of possessing obscene material under s 2 of the Obscene Publications Act. The commission found quite readily that the restriction on his freedom of expression had the legitimate aim of protecting morals and was not disproportionate to that aim. But the decision was largely based on the risk that children might view the videos since once they had left the applicant's possession he would not have been able to control their eventual audience. The commission may have been influenced by the nature of the material: it had no artistic or political value and therefore the justifications underlying freedom of expression, referred to previously, were not present, apart from the justification based on moral autonomy.

That decision is broadly in harmony with that of the Commission in *Scherer v Switzerland*;[35] it was found that the conviction of the proprietor of a sex shop for showing obscene and explicit videos had breached Article 10, since access was restricted to adults and no one was likely to confront them unwittingly. *Scherer* demonstrates that Strasbourg (or at least, the Commission) is prepared to defend adult autonomy in relation to the consumption of explicit material, so long as control is retained over the ultimate consumer of the material. The difference between *Hoare* and *Scherer* related to the question of the restrictions on access to the material; in *Hoare* the penalty imposed was found to be proportionate to the aim pursued since it was viewed as capable of protecting the 'rights of others' – the rights appeared to be those of minors to be protected from harmful material; in *Scherer* such rights could not be protected by the imposition of the penalty since they were not threatened by the showing of the videos.[36] Thus Strasbourg is clearly content to restrict media expression aimed at adults in order to protect children.

Strasbourg has also shown itself to be prepared to restrict media freedom of expression to protect religious sensibilities; in *Otto-Preminger Institut v Austria*,[37] the Court considered the question of restrictions on freedom of expression in respect of a film where the expression, satirising Christianity, was aimed at a willing adult audience. A warning had been given and therefore viewers knew what to expect. Nevertheless, owing to the shock caused to particular religious sensibilities in the local region, it was found, in a much criticised decision (Pannick 1995), that the interference could be justified despite the fact that the measure had the effect of preventing the showing of the film across the whole country. A similarly restrictive decision was taken in *Gibson v UK*[38] in respect of a sculpture in an art gallery which had ear-rings made out of freeze-dried foetuses: its purpose appeared to be to make a point about trivialisation of human life. The sculptor was convicted of outraging public decency, and applied to the European Commission alleging a breach of Article 10, but the application was found inadmissible. Both *Otto-Preminger* and *Gibson* concerned expression that could be deemed 'political' as having public interest value, but in both the categorisation of the expression instead as 'artistic', partly due to the medium within which it was presented, appeared to lead to its designation as of lesser value.

Both decisions can be contrasted with the findings in *Vereinigung Bildender Kunstler v Austria* (VBK).[39] The case originated in an application against Austria by an association of artists, VBK, which claimed that the Austrian courts' decisions forbidding it to continue exhibiting a painting had violated its right to freedom of expression under Article 10. The painting showed a collage of various public figures, such as Mother Teresa and Mr Meischberger in graphic sexual positions. The Court found that the interference was 'prescribed by law' under Article 10(2) since the impugned courts' decisions were based on s78 Copyright Act. The Court also found that the interference pursued a legitimate aim, 'the protection of the rights of others'[40] on the basis that the painting debased Mr Meischberger's public standing. In relation to the necessity of the interference, the Court noted that the painting did not address details of Mr Meischberger's private life, but rather related to his public standing as a politician, and in that capacity he was required to display a wider tolerance in respect of criticism.[41]

In respect of proportionality demands, the Court noted that the Austrian courts' injunction was not limited either in time or in space; it therefore left the applicant association with no possibility of exhibiting the painting irrespective in the future. So the injunction was found to be disproportionate to the aim it pursued and therefore not necessary in a democratic society under Article 10(2); thus, a violation of Article 10 was found. The decision in *VGT* may be contrasted with those in *Otto-Preminger* and *Gibson* on the basis that an artistic work was found to have a political dimension in the latter case but not in the two former ones. On that basis strict scrutiny of the proportionality of the sanction imposed was undertaken. But had the political elements been less overt a violation might not have been found in *VGT*.

This line of cases, concerning the balance to be struck between protecting satirical and explicit expression and protecting the 'rights of others' or religious feeling, may be contrasted with a number of the decisions that have sought to balance media expression with little or no public interest value against the interest, under Article 8, in protecting the private life of celebrities. A movement towards protecting media expression, *despite* its lack of support from the arguments for democracy, or from truth or self-development, is apparent.

Von Hannover v Germany[42] made it clear that Article 8 rights are applicable in the private sphere and there is a positive obligation on the state to provide a remedy in national law for privacy-invasion by private media bodies. The case represented the culmination of a long legal fight by Princess Caroline of Monaco in the German courts to stop pictures of herself and her children, obtained by paparazzi without consent, appearing in various newspapers and magazines across Europe. The pictures were of the princess engaged in various everyday acts: shopping, horse-riding, at a beach club or restaurant. The German courts had afforded her a privacy remedy but only in relation to the more intrusive photographs she had complained of. The Strasbourg Court found, unanimously, that the failure of the German courts to provide her with a remedy in relation to a number of the unconsented-to paparazzi pictures amounted to a breach of Article 8 on the basis of securing effective respect for her private or family life. While her Article 8 rights had to be balanced against the press's Article 10 rights, the nature of the expression in question was so trivial and so lacking in public interest value, that Article 8 was found to prevail.

However, the approach taken to speech/privacy balancing in *Von Hannover v Germany (no. 2)*[43] differed significantly from that taken in the first *Von Hannover* case. The Court found, in a manner reminiscent of its approach in *Animal Defenders*, that where the balancing exercise has been undertaken by the national authorities in conformity with the criteria laid down in the Court's case-law, the Court would require strong reasons to substitute its view for that of the domestic court. It then considered a number of criteria relating to the balancing test, including the nature of the public interest involved. The Court did not criticised the approach of the German Court which found that the subject in question – the illness affecting Prince Rainier III – qualified as an event of contemporary society on which the magazines were entitled to report. It further found that the accompanying photo – which had a slight bearing on that subject – was inoffensive.[44] However, the same could have been said of the photos in the first *Von Hannover* case which nevertheless were found to have virtually no speech value.[45] The Strasbourg Court concluded that the German Court had remained within the state's margin of appreciation in carrying out the balancing act, and it did not therefore determine that it should depart from the national court's approach.

The case of *Axel Springer v Germany*[46] led to a similar outcome in which, however, the Court did depart from the stance taken in the domestic courts as to the balancing act. The case concerned publications, which were then injuncted on privacy grounds, relating to the arrest and conviction of a well-known television actor for possession of drugs. The newspaper claimed a violation of its right to freedom of expression and the Grand Chamber considered a range of factors in relation to the balancing act between Arts 10 and 8.[47] It considered in particular the contribution made by the article to a debate of general interest; the actor's prior conduct in relation to the media; the circumstances and method of obtaining the information; how well known the actor was; the content and consequences of the publications. In terms of proportionality it considered the severity of the interference. It found that there was a degree of public interest in the information, that the actor was well known and had actively sought previous publicity. The publication of the article, it was found, had not had serious consequences for the actor in terms of invasion of privacy, and while the injunction did not represent a severe sanction, it might have had a chilling effect on the press. Thus the Grand Chamber found a violation of Article 10 since the grounds advanced by the Government were not deemed to be sufficient to establish that the interference with Article 10 was 'necessary in a democratic society' to protect the actor's right to respect for his private life. Again, this decision took into account factors, such as that the actor had previously sought publicity, which were very doubtfully linked to the claimed speech value of the publications.

This trend of the Strasbourg Court towards a position in which it favours very flimsy or virtually non-existent free expression arguments when balancing Articles 8 and 10 in privacy cases was confirmed in the third *Von Hannover* case.[48] In *Von Hannover v Germany (no. 3)*[49] a German magazine had published an article about a trend among celebrities of renting out their holiday homes and it described the von Hannover family villa. The article was accompanied by a photograph of Princess Caroline and her husband on holiday, taken without consent or knowledge. The Strasbourg Court found that the German courts had given due consideration to the criteria for the balancing exercise that were set out in *Von Hannover v Germany (No. 2)* and *Axel Springer AG v Germany*. So, taking account of the margin of appreciation enjoyed by the national courts in undertaking such a balancing exercise, it was found that Germany had not failed to comply with its positive obligations under Article 8. In considering the public interest value of the photograph – its contribution to a debate of public interest – the Court appeared to accept that although there was no link between the photo and article, and the photo itself made no contribution to any potential debate about celebrities renting out holiday homes, the photo made some sort of contribution to a general interest debate, a conclusion that is very hard to understand.[50]

This third *Von Hannover* case demonstrates a clear departure from the first one, which clearly found that celebrity gossip makes no contribution to the role of the press in a democracy and therefore in such instances the free expression claim will usually be overcome by the privacy one. This third *Von Hannover* case has gone even further down the path of accepting spurious public interest arguments than the second one did, since in the second one there was a weak connection between the objected-to photo and the accompanying article. In this instance even that connection was not required. It is argued that free expression has not been advantaged by this decision since the classic free expression justifications would not have supported the publication of the photo. These recent decisions at Strasbourg, in particular *Von Hannover no. 3*, are failing to probe the true strength of the speech claim and are no longer seeking to identify with any clarity some form of contribution to public debate. As Phillipson has argued, 'what Strasbourg has done, by accepting…a broad and undefined notion of the public interest, is to rob that notion of any coherent boundaries it might once have had' (Phillipson 2016).

Conclusions

This chapter has identified a diminution in the current predictability of the standard of protection offered by the Strasbourg Court to media expression. Outside the context of press reporting it is not possible to say with full confidence, as it was previously, that the political content of expression attracting bans or sanctions in the member states will almost inevitably lead the Court to find a violation. Conversely, it is now not possible to find that the *lack* of public interest value of expression will mean that other interests – in particular that of respecting private life – will readily prevail over 'empty' free speech claims of the press. Two rising trends in the Strasbourg jurisprudence, now affecting its stance as to media free expression, have been identified as responsible. First, and of most concern, the Court is showing a preparedness to rely fairly heavily on established methods of creating self-restraint, via the margin of appreciation doctrine, increasingly closely linked to European consensus-based analysis, as was found in *Animal Defenders*. Second, the Court is paying closer attention to the recognition of Article 10 in the domestic processes, and is showing an unwillingness to depart from the conclusions reached in the member state so long as the ECHR arguments have been rehearsed, even though the conclusion may be said to fail to reflect fundamental free speech values, as in the two later *Von Hannover* cases. In an age of fear and uncertainty – in which the threat to free expression may often come from non-state actors, and journalists are murdered for printing cartoons – the need for certainty in the Court's media expression jurisprudence, and the maintenance of uniform European standards, is especially pressing.

Notes

1 *Observer and Guardian v UK* A 216 (1991) [59].
2 See e.g. *Thorgeirson v Iceland* (1992) 14 EHRR 843 [63].
3 See e.g. *Otto-Preminger Institut v Austria* (1994) 19 EHRR 3; *Delfi AS v Estonia* App No. 64569/09, judgment of 16.6.2015 concerning comments amounting to hate speech on an online news portal.
4 *Castells v Spain* A 236 (1992) [43].
5 See *Animal Defenders v UK* [2013] ECHR 362, App No. 48876/08, discussed further on, pp. 00, but compare with *Jersild v Denmark* (1994) 19 EHRR 1.
6 See e.g. *Sokolowski v Poland* App. No. 75955/01), judgment of 29.3.2005.
7 See *Groppera Radio AG v Switzerland* (1990) 12 EHRR 321, at [61].
8 See *Informationsverein Lentia v Austria* (1993) 17 EHRR 93.
9 (1980) 2 EHRR 245, 275–81.
10 Judgment of 1.12. 2015, App Nos 48226/10 and 14027/11.
11 (1980) 2 EHRR 245.
12 (1994) 19 EHRR 1.
13 (1986) 8 EHRR 407.
14 (1992) 14 EHRR 843.
15 See *Handyside v UK* (1976) 1 EHRR 737 but cf *VGT v Austria* App No. 24699/94, ECHR 2001-VI (discussed further on).
16 Grand Chamber Judgment, [2013] ECHR 362, App No 48876/08. See also reliance on consensus in *Stoll v Switzerland* App No 69698/01, judgment of 10.12.2007.
17 App No. 24699/94, ECHR 2001-VI.
18 *R (On The Application of Animal Defenders International) v Secretary of State For Culture, Media and Sport* [2008] UKHL 15.
19 App No. 24699/94, ECHR 2001-VI.
20 In *Jersild* (note 5) it was accepted that the speech of the racist group in the broadcast in question would not itself have been viewed as protected speech.
21 *Otto-Preminger Institut v Austria* (1994) 19 EHRR 34.
22 In *Groppera Radio AG v Switzerland* (1990) 12 EHRR 321, it was thought that mere entertainment might not fall within Art 10(1).
23 *Hoare v UK* [1997] EHRLR 678.
24 Eur Ct HR, A 24; (1976) 1 EHRR 737.
25 See *Sunday Times v UK* (1979) 2 EHRR 245.
26 Ibid, para 49.
27 Ibid, para 48.
28 Ibid, para 52.
29 (1991) 13 EHRR 212.
30 *Ginsberg v New York* 390 US 629 (1968).

31 *Irwin Toy Ltd v AG (Quebec)* [1989] 1 SCR 927 (concerning a broad limitation on broadcast advertising aimed at children).
32 *Reno v American Civil Liberties Union* (1997) 521 US 844.
33 See *R v Butler* [1992] 1 SCR 452.
34 [1997] EHRLR 678.
35 A 287 (1993) Com Rep (the case was discontinued in the Court owing to the death of the applicant).
36 In *Hoare* the commission, having found that the material fell within Art 10(1), went on to find under Art 10(2): 'the relationship of proportionality between the interference with the applicant's right to freedom of expression and the aim pursued is the question of whether, given that the applicant only distributed his video cassettes to people who expressed a clear interest, it can be said that the penalty imposed was capable of protecting the "rights of others"… Where no adult is confronted unintentionally or against his will with filmed matter, there must be particularly compelling reasons to justify an interference". But here, in contrast to *Scherer,* it was possible that minors would gain access to the film'.
37 (1994) 19 EHRR 34. See also *Wingrove v UK* (1996) 24 EHRR 1; *Gay News v UK* (1982) 5 EHRR 123.
38 *Gibson v UK*, Appl No. 17634.
39 (2008) 47 EHRR 5.
40 Ibid, at [29].
41 At [37]. The Court referred to *Lingens v Austria* (1986) 8 EHRR 407 at [42].
42 (2005) 40 EHRR 1.
43 (2012) 55 EHRR 15 (Grand Chamber).
44 At [123].
45 At [65].
46 (2012) 55 EHRR 6.
47 Ibid [89–95].
48 See also *Lillo-Stenberg v Norway*, Appl no 13258/09, judgment of 16 January, 2014 in which the ECtHR found that the publication of photographs concerning a wedding between a popular musician and actress came within the idea of 'general interest,' since a wedding 'cannot itself relate exclusively to details of a person's private life…' (para 37). On that basis, and with regard to the 'margin of appreciation' accorded to Norway, it was found that the publication did not unjustifiably interfere with the applicants' Art 8 right [44–45].
49 App No 8772/10, judgment of 19.9.2013.
50 *Von Hannover v Germany* ECHR 264 (2013), press release 19 September, 2013, p. 3.

References

Barendt, E. *Freedom of Speech*, 1st ed. (1987), 2nd ed. (2005), chap. 1.
Dzehtsiarou, K. (2015). European Consensus and the Legitimacy of the ECtHR, esp. chap. 2.
Fenwick, H. and Phillipson, G. (2006). *Media Freedom under the Human Rights Act*, pp. 50–72.
Fenwick, H. and Phillipson, G. (2000). 'Public Protest, the Human Rights Act and Judicial Responses to Political Expression.' *Winter Public Law*, pp. 625–48.
Harris, D. J., O'Boyle, M., Bates, E. and Buckley, C. (2009a). *Harris, O'Boyle and Warbrick Law of the European Convention on Human Rights*, 3rd ed., pp. 629–39.
Harris, D. J., et al. (2009b). *Harris, O'Boyle and Warbrick Law of the European Convention on Human Rights*, 3rd ed., pp. 632–35.
Kearns, P. (2000). 'Obscene and blasphemous libel: misunderstanding art', Crim LR 652.
Pannick, D. (1995). 'Religious feelings and the European Court', PL 7.
Phillipson G. (2016). 'Press freedom, the public interest and privacy'. In Andrew Kenyon (ed) *Comparative Defamation and Privacy Law*, p. 154.

5

COMMUNICATION FREEDOMS VERSUS COMMUNICATION RIGHTS

Discursive and normative struggles within civil society and beyond

Bart Cammaerts

In this chapter, I aim to retrace the normative implications of historical and contemporary debates and struggles between discourses and activists aiming to protect press freedom and those advocating for the need of communication rights and media regulation. I will argue that this conflict can be related to distinct normative positions concerning the role of media and communication in a democratic society, and competing views as to the balance of power in society between market forces and the state.

Press freedom is very much part of a longstanding liberal model concerned with the tyranny of the state, while a communication rights agenda pertains more to a social responsibility and public sphere paradigm which emphasises the need of state intervention. While one advocates the need to protect us from state intervention, the other precisely requires the state to intervene in order to guarantee certain rights. It was almost inevitable that these two perspectives would clash at some point, especially as the rights agenda was highjacked by many authoritarian regimes to justify limits on press freedom.

I will address this tension in the context of three key-moments of contention, 1) the conflicts relating to UNESCO's MacBride Report (1980); 2) the conflicts in view of the final declaration of ITU's World Summit on the Information Society (WSIS) which was held in Geneva (2003) and Tunis (2005); and 3) the Leveson inquiry into the ethics of the UK press held in 2011–12. In each of these cases advocates of press freedom clashed with proponents of communication rights.

Before addressing these cases, I will first present a brief theoretical framework, based on Berlin's distinction between negative and positive liberties, which will subsequently serve to contextualised the discursive and normative conflicts between communication freedoms and rights. By relating this conflict to these two competing forms of liberties, I aim to demonstrate how intra-civil society struggles are also instrumental in the ideological war of position between those resisting the regulation of media ownership and those advocating for the imposition of democratic protections against the commercialisation and commodification of the public space.

Negative and positive liberties

In his famous essay entitled 'Two Concepts of Liberty', Berlin (1958) deals with a set of inherent tensions, between: freedom and equality, a coercive and an emancipatory state, personal autonomy and collective endeavours. It concerns here, in other words, competing and intrinsically incompatible political ideas concerning freedom and rights.

The classic – and according to Berlin the preferred – way of conceptualising liberty, is in negative terms; being free from coercion, reaching your full potential without the interference by external others. To be free is, in other words, to be a fully independent agent with total control over your own destiny. With reference to Mill's (1859) position, Berlin (1969 [1958], 126–7 – emphasis in original) writes that '[t]he defense of liberty consists in the *negative* goal of warding off interference'. It is negative because it pleads for the absence of something – that is, interference or coercion. From the perspective of negative freedom, state power should thus be limited to an absolute minimum; rather individuals need to be (legally) protected from state power. Berlin is, however, also critical of this classic position as it all too easily assumes that all coercion is necessarily evil and all non-interference is inherently good, which is not always the case.

The second, competing, conceptualization of freedom starts from a radically different premise, namely a sensitivity towards the conditions which determine the nature of our freedoms and a concern with collective rather than individualistic goals and values. Positive freedom implicates the common good and the development of a collective will through which the individual is supposedly able to achieve 'true' or 'genuine' self-determination. As Berlin (1969 [1958], 132 – emphasis in original) explains:

> The real self may be conceived as something wider than the individual [...], as a social *whole* of which the individual is an element or an aspect: a tribe, a race, a Church, a State, the great society of the living and the dead and the yet unborn. This entity is then identified as being the *true* self which, by imposing its collective, or *organic* single will upon its recalcitrant *members*, achieves its own, and therefore their, *higher* freedom.

Positive freedoms thus justify emancipatory interventions (by the state or a collective) to create the conditions for freedom and self-mastery through the provision of resources to citizens to fulfil their full potential and self-determination, such as free education, health care, welfare or through guaranteeing equal opportunities for all.

As is already apparent in the quote above, Berlin was highly sceptical of positive freedoms especially due to the potential of abuse of state power in the name of a higher goal, using the Jacobin and Bolshevik revolutions as a case in point. As a result of this danger, he and many others with him, promote positive freedoms over and above negative ones.

It is, in my view, the perceived incommensurability between negative and positive freedoms that lies at the heart of the conflict between advocates of the protection of press freedom, which relates to negative freedom and those that advocate communication rights, which inevitably relies more on positive freedoms to establish and subsequently enforce rights. In what follows three cases where this tension came to a head will be addressed in more detail, first UNESCO's MacBride Report, second the UN's WSIS and lastly the Leveson Inquiry into media ethics in the UK.

UNESCO's MacBride Report (1980)

In 1977, Amadu Mohtar M'Bow, UNESCO's director general at the time, tasked an *International Commission for the Study of Communication* to write a report on the emerging problems of new communication technologies and the impact of these on the already existing asymmetries between core, semi-periphery and periphery, to refer to Wallerstein's world system model, which was published a few years earlier (Wallerstein 1974). While the appointment of the Commission was very much a means to appease the ideological confrontations and conflicts concerning information and communication between Western, Communist and non-aligned countries, the report it produced ended up exasperating them. The cold war was in full swing and information provision and communication infrastructures became unavoidably a focal point of contention.

The so-called MacBride report, named after the much respected chair of the Commission, Seán MacBride, an Irish journalist, human rights activist and politician, was in many ways an astonishing international document and statement; clear-cut and critical in its analysis and diagnosis, progressive and daring in its prognosis and proposed solutions. In the report, the authors took a critical stance against the devastating impact of marketisation and they emphasized the social importance of communication. Communication was furthermore positioned as an unalienable human right. The idea of a right to communicate was originally proposed by Jean d'Arcy in an essay published in 1969 and the Commission appropriated it to extend communication freedoms beyond press freedom (MacBride 2004 [1980], 265). As one of the co-authors of the report put it later, 'the freedom of press (and freedom of information) was enriched with the right to communicate, the right to accept and spread information and to be informed' (Osolnik 2005, 8).

The Commission unequivocally sided with citizen interests and promoted above all democratic values. Exclusive and intrusive state control as well as oligopolistic corporate control of the media were considered equally problematic. The ever-increasing concentration of ownership and the emergence of powerful oligopolies in the media market were strongly condemned. Instead, communication was approached as a genuine two-way process rather than a one-way communication flow from top to bottom or from North to South. The many asymmetries between North and South were also highlighted as troublesome and in urgent need of redress. At the same time, it was also argued – in a nuanced way – that with (press) freedom comes responsibility:

> Freedom without responsibility invites distortion and other abuses. But in the absence of freedom there can be no exercise of responsibility. The concept of freedom with responsibility necessarily includes a concern for professional ethics, demanding an equitable approach to events, situations or processes with due attention to their diverse aspects.
>
> *(MacBride 2004 [1980], 261–2)*

The Commission also proposed a set of recommendations which would lead to a New World Information and Communication Order (NWICO), a sort of third way *avant-la-lettre*, positioned in-between unbridled liberalism and monopolistic state ownership (Osolnik 2005, 10).

At a general conference in Belgrade in October 1980 UNESCO agreed on a resolution spelling out the principles of NWICO, including the elimination of 'imbalances and inequalities' and of 'the negative effects of certain monopolies, public or private, and excessive concentrations' (UNESCO 1980, 71). It goes without saying that the aftermath of this meeting, during which NWICO was approved, was marred by serious conflicts and had long-lasting repercussions. Probably the most spectacular of these was the withdrawal of the US and the UK (as well as Singapore) from UNESCO. However, less known are the fierce debates concerning the right to communicate and NWICO within civil society, mainly focusing on the tension between a negative freedom of the press and a communication rights agenda requiring positive freedoms to guarantee and protect these rights.

The World Press Freedom Committee[1] (WPFC), an international lobby group of editors and media owners specifically set-up to contest NWICO, was most vocal in opposing it. Bullen (1981, 9) wrote a highly sceptical piece on UNESCO's Belgrade meeting in which she fundamentally contested the good intentions of NWICO:

> [T]he first principle is "elimination of imbalances and inequalities" in communication. There are lots of ways to take such words, whatever the merits of the case. One person's "inequality" may be another's "editorial freedom." Another principle suggested in the resolution is that the "freedom of journalists" is "inseparable from responsibility." But there are very different ideas of what "responsible" journalism is. In some countries, it's "responsible" to follow a story wherever it leads. In others, it's "responsible" to drop a story if it leads in the wrong direction.

Throughout Bullen's report of the Belgrade meeting, a sense of deep-seated distrust can be observed. While the MacBride Report was said to contain 'some good ideas, such as opposition to censorship and free access to news sources by journalists', overall it was considered to be a 'batch of mischievous proposals' (ibid) providing the intellectual justification for Communist and authoritarian regimes to impose limits on press freedom and on the activities of journalists; it was seen to promote the abuse of positive freedom to curtail negative freedom.

It is within this context that in May 1981, about 60 delegates to the *Voices of Freedom Conference of Independent News Media*, representing many regional and international journalism organisations, agreed on a strong statement to uphold an absolute negative press freedom, free from any form of state intervention. In their so-called 'Declaration of Talloires' they pledged 'to expand the free flow of information worldwide'. They furthermore called upon 'UNESCO and other intergovernmental bodies to abandon attempts to regulate news content and formulate rules for the press'. A strong rejection of all forms of positive freedom was also adopted:

> We believe that the state exists for the individual and has a duty to uphold individual rights. We believe that the ultimate definition of a free press lies not in the actions of governments or international bodies, but rather in the professionalism, vigour and courage of individual journalists.
>
> *(Declaration of Talloires 1981)*

What is frightfully absent from these anti-NWICO discourses is a mentioning of potential issues regarding media ownership, concentration of ownership, commodification and the impact this has on the production of media content and on editorial freedom. The privileging of negative freedom over and above positive freedom in the context of information provision and communication implies an imaginary which considers 'free' and 'freedom' to be unavoidably and necessarily market-led, which is in itself never problematised or considered potentially detrimental for democracy. This subsequently fed into a broader imaginary advocating the privatization and marketization of media and telecommunication, which became the new mantras of the 1990s. This neoliberal logic reduces the provision of information and communication to a mere commodity rather than a public service or a societal democratic good.

ITU's World Summit on the Information Society (2003–05)

Fast forward to early 2000s. When it became clear that the asymmetrical introduction of the internet was re-enforcing old divides as well as producing new ones, the UN decided to act and called for a World Summit on the Information Society (WSIS) in order to address 'the whole range of relevant issues related to the information society' (UN 2001, 1). Not UNESCO, but rather the ITU, was mandated by the General Assembly to organise and run the WSIS. This was a significant and telling choice. Raboy (2003, 110) observed that '[w]ithin the UNESCO logic, media are cultural institutions, part of the process of human development. Within the ITU logic, media are technical systems for information delivery'.

This choice did not mean that the cultural perspective was absent from the WSIS, on the contrary, but these tensions did inevitably lead to a clash between different visions or what could be called 'social imaginaries' of the internet (Mansell 2012) and above all about what the role of the state should be within the information society.

In terms of process, an all-together different strategy was chosen compared to what UNESCO did in the 1980s. There was no appointed commission of wise grey-haired 'men', carefully gathering evidence and writing up an eloquent report, which would then provide the basis for debate and discussion. Instead, in true multi-stakeholder fashion, UN Resolution 56/183 encouraged 'intergovernmental organisations, including international and regional institutions, non-governmental organisations, civil society and the private sector to *contribute to*, and *actively participate in* the intergovernmental preparatory process of the Summit and the Summit itself'. (UN 2001a, 2 – emphasis added).

The UN/ITU WSIS process and the invitation of civil society to actively participate in the preparatory process was perceived by some as a golden opportunity to revive the demand for the establishment and protection of a set of communication rights (Calabrese 2004). By publishing the *People's Communication Charter* (PCC) some years earlier, Hamelink (1998) had already prepared the ground for a return of a communication rights discourse into civil society debates and the communication policy realm.

In view of the upcoming WSIS, the Communication Rights in the Information Society (CRIS) campaign was officially launched in November 2001 at the World Social Forum in Porto Alegre (Brazil) and the stated aim was to 'help build an information society based on principles of transparency, diversity, participation and social and economic justice, and inspired by equitable gender, cultural and regional perspectives'. It explicitly referred back to the MacBride-report by adopting the right to communicate as 'a means to enhance human rights and to strengthen the social, economic and regional perspectives', thereby invoking positive freedoms (CRIS Mission Statement 2001). This attempt to introduce a progressive and democratic agenda into the WSIS preparatory process was fiercely resisted, by market forces, obviously, but also by some State actors and by some civil society actors.

The World Press Freedom Committee (WPFC) voiced its continued opposition to this – according to them – cheeky attempt to revive the MacBride legacy. In a rather blunt and strong-worded piece, the European Representative of the WPFC launched a personal attack on Hamelink and wrote:

> No new rights are needed. Those who have advocated the "Right to Communicate" define it in terms that would legitimize censorship and other limits on the unrestricted practice of journalism. These advocates depict this "Right to Communicate" as a collective right that supersedes individual human rights and harks back to directly to the same proposals they made under the banner of the "New World Information and Communication Order".
>
> *(Koven 2003a, np)*

In another piece, the same representative described the CRIS campaign as 'radical' and its demands as 'extreme' (Koven 2003b). The tainted baggage of the 1980s right to communicate debate was remobilised against the communication rights agenda proposed by the CRIS campaign in the framework of the WSIS – 'The bad new ideas are the bad old ideas. In some cases, they even are being pushed by the same people', Bullen (2003, 11) wrote. Besides the WPFC, the freedom of expression NGO Article XIX also reacted strongly against all attempts by civil society actors to articulate a set of communication rights for the information society. Unlike the WPFC, Article XIX did, however, acknowledge the value of communication rights, but it considered 'that there is the potential within the framework of existing rights to accommodate the legitimate claims made in the name of the right to communicate' (Mendel 2003).

Just as was the case with NWICO in the 1980s, advocates of press freedom agreed on a declaration, this time arguing for a regulation-free internet, but also explicitly condemning all attempts to revive a communication rights agenda.

> A number of proposals for regulation and controls now being made were made and rejected during past debate over now-discredited proposals for a "new world information and communication order." There are clearly those at work who seek to revive and assert for their own purposes such restrictive proposals in the new guise of countering alleged threats and dangers posed by new communication technologies. These proposals must again be successfully resisted, just as they were earlier.
>
> *(Statement of Vienna 2002: point 9)*

Despite all the efforts of communication rights activists to deny this, communication rights were positioned by the proponents of press freedom as a mere code word for censorship and the impositions of restrictions on the negative freedom of expression.

Yet again we can observe here a clash here between those fighting for a voluntaristic agenda through positive freedoms and those who approach freedom in a negative sense, that is, the need to protect us all from state intervention, regardless of what that intervention aims to achieve. In other words, in both cases we see that a broader political struggle is being played out which crystalizes around communication and different conceptions of freedom and state intervention.

The UK's Leveson Inquiry (2011–12)

The two previous cases were situated at an international level of governance, whereas the case presented in this section relates to a national context. It could be argued that the tensions between positive and negative freedom become more concrete and real in a national context, precisely because nation states have more leeway to actually implement binding (media and communication) regulation that is enforceable. At the national level the realm of the discursive can potentially have real and actual policy implications for the media organisations that operate there.

After it emerged that large parts of the British media had been using private detectives on a large scale to hack into mobile phones of celebrities, political elites, the royal family as well as ordinary citizens, including a murdered girl (Milly Dowler), the issue of media ethics, the lack of accountability of the media and media concentration propelled itself firmly onto the political agenda in the UK. In order to address these issues the then Prime Minister David Cameron, appointed Lord Justice Leveson to lead an inquiry into two parts. The first part, which concluded in 2012, was to investigate

> the culture, practices and ethics of the press, including contacts between the press and politicians and the press and the police; it is to consider the extent to which the

current regulatory regime has failed and whether there has been a failure to act upon any previous warnings about media misconduct.

(Press Release, 14 Sept. 2011)

The second part of the Inquiry, which is supposed to address the 'extent of unlawful and improper conduct' by several news organisations, including Rupert Murdoch's News International, still has to take place (criminal investigations are ongoing).

Essentially, the Leveson Inquiry amounted to a 'damning indictment' of the UK's news industry, as pointed out by Chris Blackburn, the editor of the Independent at the time (quoted in O'Carroll 2012). Furthermore, the nature and extent of the unethical behaviour displayed by British journalists and editors also called into question the self-regulatory regime that was supposed to counter and prevent such behaviour in the first place. Overall, the Press Complaints Council (PCC) was seen to be weak, ineffective and in urgent need of reform. The broader question, however, was whether self-regulation was sufficient or whether there is a case for statutory regulation of the press, inevitably invoking positive freedoms. Leveson himself considered this question to be at the heart of his inquiry. When opening the hearings (on 14 November 2011), he explicitly referred to the importance of the watch dog role of the media, but he also asked the contentious question 'who guards the guardians?'.

Unsurprisingly, the most important recommendation of Leveson was a reform of the self-regulatory PCC, making it more independent from the media owners, but also giving it more teeth. In order to do so, Leveson controversially recommended that 'there should be legislation to underpin the independent self-regulatory system and facilitate its recognition in legal processes' (The Leveson Inquiry 2012, 17). While Leveson pointed out that this could be done without needing to resort to a statutory regulation of the press, many journalists and commentators did read it in those terms (e.g. Hislop 2012).

Besides the phone hacking scandal and ethical transgressions by journalists, Leveson was also tasked to investigate the high level of media concentration and lack of media pluralism in the UK (three companies control some 70% of newspaper circulation[2]). However, unlike the very detailed and well-argued recommendations regarding a new framework for an independent press regulator, the recommendations relating to media plurality were rather vague. Despite this vagueness, he did conclude that a new method to measure media plurality was needed (The Leveson Inquiry 2012, 30). The report also concluded that the threshold for concern in terms of the concentration of ownership should be lower in the media industry than is the case in other industries given the specific nature of media power in a democracy, but it refrained from recommending what this threshold should be.

Just as in the two other cases, we could observe a lot of activity within civil society to either support Leveson's recommendations or contest them vigorously. Regarding the former, an organisation called Hacked Off[3] campaigned for an accountable press and made the implementation of Leveson's recommendations as its *raison d'être* (Cathcart 2013). Hacked off received a lot of flak from right wing commentators and press freedom advocates for being an enemy of press freedom (Hislop 2012). Besides this, because high profile celebrities keen on privacy protection were officially backing the campaign (e.g. Hugh Grant, Steve Coogan, J. K. Rowling, John Cleese, etc.), many critics framed Hacked Off as a toy in the hand of the powerful elites in their attempts to stop journalists reporting on them negatively.

The Media Reform Coalition is another organisation that was set up in the wake of the Leveson Inquiry. It brings together civil society groups, academics and media campaigners and is committed to support media pluralism, defend ethical journalism and protect investigative and local journalism. This group was also virulently attacked by right wing commentators for being run by 'left wing academics' and being 'interventionist' (Gillian 2013). The right-wing blogger Guido Fawkes called the 'Reclaim the Media' event, organized by the Media Reform Coalition, 'sinister' (Fawkes 2014).

Besides journalists and right wing bloggers, several competing civil society organisations also rallied against Leveson and those who support his recommendations. The Freespeech Network, comprised of media owners, editors, publishers and advertisers and supported amongst others by the WPFC, was set up in reaction against the Leveson Inquiry's recommendations and was very vocal in its derision of Leveson, denoting his recommendations as 'illiberal' and stating that '[T]he fallout from the Leveson Inquiry and report has left the British press facing the most substantial threat to its freedom in the modern era' (Anthony, et al., 2015: 16). Especially the establishment of a new self-regulatory independent body through a cross-party Royal Charter, not dissimilar to how the BBC was established, was a point of contention. Article XIX refutes the claim that this body is self-regulatory and argued that it falls 'short of international standards to protect freedom of expression' (Article XIX 2013).

Yet again in this case we see a similar expression of the long-standing conflicts emerging between those advocating for the negative freedom of the press and those fighting for positive freedoms to regulate media markets for example to promote ethical behaviour amongst journalists or enforce media plurality.

Conclusion

As I have argued in this chapter, the main reason for the lack of a viable middle ground between press freedom advocates and freedom of information activists lies in the incommensurability of negative and positive forms of freedom. Each attempt to posit positive freedoms in terms of media and communication is countered by accusations of infringement to the negative freedom of expression/the press. Incidentally, the discursive equation of freedom of speech with freedom of the press is telling in this regard. O'Neill argued some years ago to decouple both given the high degree of media power. The media, she said, 'while deeply preoccupied with others' untrustworthiness–have escaped demands for accountability'. Furthermore, 'freedom of the press does not also require a licence to deceive' (O'Neill 2002).

At the same time, we can also observe a subtle and understated intertwining between the arguments of negative press freedom with a neoliberal ideology and discourse which at a meta level precisely justifies and hegemonises the superiority of negative freedoms over and above positive freedoms (Cammaerts 2015). This then in turns justifies a withdrawal of the state and feeds arguments for very minimal and preferably no intervention at all. The result of all this is a normative gridlock, which makes it impossible to argue for a voluntaristic media policy agenda aimed at guaranteeing communication as a human right and the promotion of a pluralistic democratic mediated public space. From this neoliberal perspective, freedom is pitted against regulation as fundamentally incompatible.

Positioning pubic interventions into the media and communication 'industry' as antithetical to freedom and refusing any kind of regulation to protect the communication rights of citizens, suits a number of political and economic actors particularly well, hence the very active involvement of media proprietors in these debates. Questions relating to the quality and ethics of the content produced by the capitalist 'free' media or important issues regarding the concentration of media ownership within but also across the different sectors of the media and communication industry are too easily swept aside by strongly worded arguments expressing negative freedoms when it comes to media and communication.

Overcoming this gridlock is not straightforward as press freedom and communication rights are both part of a human rights agenda and we also need to acknowledge the tensions between them. What might help, however, is articulating communication freedoms and communication rights as a productive dialectic between both negative and positive freedoms and their corresponding rights. Positive freedoms thus become essential to guarantee and underpin negative freedoms, especially if we acknowledge that a truly free press should not only protect us from abuses by the state, but crucially also from abuses by market forces abiding by commercial interests and leading to serious unethical and anti-democratic behaviour by media elites. Seen from this perspective, public and democratic interventions in the media in order to ensure that media power is made accountable, is dispersed and fosters substantial increases in the quality of news provision to citizens become legitimate. As even Berlin (1969 [1958], 124) pointed out:

> [N]o man's activity is so completely private as never to obstruct the lives of others in any way. 'Freedom for the pike is death for the minnows'; the liberty of some must depend on the restraint of others.

Notes

1   In September 2009 The WPFC ceased to exist and it subsequently became part of the US-based NGO Freedom House.
2   News Corporation (Rupert Murdoch), Daily Mail and General Trust (Viscount Rothermere) and Trinity Mirror Group (based on figures of 2013, see Media Reform Coalition 2014).
3   Hacked off established itself as an independent organisation in August of 2012, see http://mediastand-ardstrust.org/projects/hacked-off/.

References

Anthony, H., Harris, M., Nathan, S. and Reidy, P. (2015). *Leveson's Illiberal Legacy*. London: The Freespeech Network. Available at: http://freespeechnetwork.org.uk/downloads/FREEDOM_OF_PRESS_2.4.pdf. [Accessed 01/03/2017]

Article XIX (2013). *UK: Proposals to Regulate the Press*. Press Release, 9/04. Available at: https://www.article19.org/resources.php/resource/3689/en/uk:-proposals-to-regulate-the-press. [Accessed 01/03/2017]

Berlin, I. (1969 [1958]). 'Two Concepts of Liberty'. In: I. Berlin, *Four Essays on Liberty*, Oxford: Oxford University Press, pp. 118–79.

Bullen, D. (1981). 'Belgrade Report: UNESCO and the Media'. *Nieman Reports*, 35(1), pp. 8–11.

Bullen, D. (2003). 'Everything Old Is New Again', In: *Press Freedom on the Internet Working Papers*, 26–28 June. New York: WPFC, pp. 1–15.

Cammaerts, B. (2015). 'Neoliberalism and the Post-Hegemonic War of Position: The Dialectic Between Invisibility and Visibilities', *European Journal of Communication*, 30(5), pp. 522–38.

Calabrese, A. (2004). 'The Promise of Civil Society: A Global Movement for Communication Rights'. *Continuum: Journal of Media and Cultural Studies*, 18(3), pp. 317–29.

Cathcart, B. (2013). 'Hacked-off: What did we do? And Did we Win?', 25/03. Available at: http://hacking-inquiry.org/comment/hacked-off-what-did-we-do-and-did-we-win/. [Accessed 01/03/2017]

d'Arcy, J. (1969). 'Direct Broadcast Satellites and the Right to Communicate'. *EBU Review*, 118, pp. 14–18.

Declaration of Talloires (1981). *A Constructive Approach To a Global Information Order*. Talloires, France, 15–17 May.

Fawkes, G. (2014). 'Hacked Off Seek EU Diktat to Force Through New Press Laws', 29/04. Available at: http://order-order.com/2014/04/29/hacked-off-seek-eu-diktat-to-force-through-new-press-laws-watson-backs-brussels-directive-on-media-ownership/. [Accessed 01/03/2017]

Gillian, A. (2013). 'EU Pours Millions Into Groups Seeking State Control of Press', 14/04. *The Telegraph*. Available at: http://www.telegraph.co.uk/news/uknews/leveson-inquiry/9992229/EU-pours-millions-into-groups-seeking-state-control-of-press.html. [Accessed 01/03/2017]

Hamelink, C. (1998). 'The People's Communication Charter'. *Development in Practice*, 8(1), pp. 68–74.

Hislop, I. (2012). 'Why Should I Answer to David Cameron? Leveson Said Much That Was Sensible - and Much That Wasn't'. *The Independent*, 30/11. Available at: http://www.independent.co.uk/voices/comment/why-should-i-answer-to-david-cameron-leveson-said-much-that-was-sensible-and-much-that-wasnt-8372315.html. [Accessed 01/03/2017]

ITU (2003). *Geneva Declaration of Principles, First Phase of the WSIS*, 12 December, Geneva. Available at: http://www.itu.int/net/wsis/docs/geneva/official/dop.html. [Accessed 01/03/2017]

ITU (2005). *Tunis Agenda for the Information Society*. 18 November, Tunis. Available at: http://www.itu.int/net/wsis/docs2/tunis/off/6rev1.html. [Accessed 01/03/2017]

Koven, R. (2003a). *Statement for the Internet Press Freedom Conference*, 26–28 June, New York.

Koven, R. (2003b). 'New Opening for Press Controllers'. In: *Freedom of the Press 2003*, New York: Freedom House. Available at: https://freedomhouse.org/report/freedom-press-2003/new-opening-press-controllers. [Accessed 01/03/2017]

MacBride, S., Ed. (2004 [1980]). *Many Voices, One World – Towards a New, More Just, and More Efficient World Information and Communication Order*, Report of the International Commission for the Study of Communication Problems, first published by UNESCO (Paris) and reprinted by Rowman & Littlefield Publishers (Lanham, MD).

Mansell, R. (2012). *Imagining the Internet: Communication, Innovation, and Governance*. Oxford: Oxford University Press.

Media Reform Coalition (2014). *The Elephant in the Room: A Survey of Media Ownership and Plurality in the United Kingdom*. London: Media Reform Coalition. Available at: http://www.mediareform.org.uk/wp-content/uploads/2014/04/ElephantintheroomFinalfinal.pdf. [Accessed 01/03/2017]

Mendel, T. (2003). *Article 19 Critiques Right To Communicate Draft*, press release, 4 February. Available at: http://www.iris.sgdg.org/actions/smsi/hr-wsis/list/2003/msg00039.html. [Accessed 01/03/2017]

Mill, J. S. (2003 [1859]). *On Liberty*. New Haven, CT: Yale University Press.

O'Carroll, L. (2012). 'Leveson "Loading a Gun" Against Papers, Warns Independent's Editor'. *The Guardian*, 29/08. Available at: http://www.theguardian.com/media/2012/aug/29/leveson-letter-press-chris-blackhurst?INTCMP=SRCH. [Accessed 01/03/2017]

O'Neill, O. (2002). *Licence to Deceive. Reith Lectures 2002: A Question of Trust*. Available at: http://www.bbc.co.uk/radio4/reith2002/lecture5.shtml. [Accessed 01/03/2017]

Osolnik, B. (2005). 'The MacBride Report – 25 Years Later'. *Javnost/The Public*, 12(3), pp. 5–11.

Raboy, M. (2003). 'Media and Democratization in the Information Society'. In: S. Ó'Siochrú and B. Girard, eds., *Communicating in the Information Society*. Geneva: United Nations Research Institute for Social Development, pp. 103–21.

Statement of Vienna (2002). *Press Freedom on the Internet*, 21 November, Vienna.

The Leveson Inquiry (2012). 'An Inquiry into the Culture, Practices and Ethics of the Press – Executive Summary'. London: The Stationery Office.

UN (2001a). *World Summit on the Information Society, Resolution 56/183*, adopted by the General Assembly, 21 December. UN: New York. Available at: http://www.itu.int/wsis/docs/background/resolutions/56_183_unga_2002.pdf. [Accessed 01/03/2017]

UNESCO (1980). Records of the General Conference, Twenty-first Session, Belgrade, 23 September to 28 October. Available at: http://unesdoc.unesco.org/images/0011/001140/114029e.pdf. [Accessed 01/03/2017]

Wallerstein, I. (1974). *The Modern World-System: Capitalist Agriculture and the Origins of the European World-Economy in the Sixteenth Century*. New York and London: Academic Press.

6

FREEDOM OF INFORMATION AND THE MEDIA

Ben Worthy

Freedom of Information (FOI) laws represent one of the major policy innovations of the late twentieth century, having spread across the world since the 1990s. The media are a powerful constituency of users, lobbyists and defenders of these new access laws. Although few journalists actually use FOI laws, their requests have a disproportionate impact and the media are also powerful innovators and defenders. The press are often singled out by politicians as 'abusers' of these new openness rights. FOI now fits within a rapidly changing information ecosystem and a shifting and hybrid media environment.

FOI, human rights and the media around the world

FOI, and the idea of transparency it embeds, are supported by left and right, and the idea of openness permeate everyday life as an important value, norm and expectation (Schudson 2015). FOI laws entrench a public right to request information within a set timeline, subject to a set of restrictions or exemptions, frequently with an independent appeal mechanism for complaints. Laws can differ from regime to regime in terms of their legal force and the nature of their appeals system, with some using the courts and others independent commissioners.

Although relatively new, there is growing legal argument that internationally access to information now represents a fundamental human right, an idea upheld by a series of international bodies from the Council of Europe to the Inter-American Court of Human Rights to the UN Rights Committee, with the European Court of Human Rights linking article 8 and later article 10 of the ECHR to a right to access information (McDonagh 2013; Birkinshaw 2006). The right to information is often seen as an instrumental value stemming from freedom of expression though it has also been connected to privacy, social and economic rights and ideas around a fair trial (McDonagh 2013). There is also debate about whether it is also an intrinsic right in and of itself (Birkinshaw 2006; Mathiesen 2008). McDonagh (2013) argues that the 'growing recognition' of access to information will eventually make 'the case for the establishment of a stand alone [human] right to information difficult to resist' (151).

At the level of individual laws, the interaction between human and access rights varies. In some laws a right to access information is constitutionally entrenched along with other rights, while elsewhere they are not. As of 2003 around 36 countries had constitutionally entrenched rights (Peled & Rabin 2010). The India RTI law is now recognised as enshrining a constitutional

60

right whereas there is ongoing debate in the US as to whether the framers intended the US constitution to supply an implicit right to access government information (Peled & Rabin 2010; Wald 1984; Schudson 2015). Comparatively younger democracies may be more inclined to entrench laws and view them as 'essential for exercising human rights while limiting government power' (Peled & Rabin 2010, 373). A number of laws in former authoritarian regimes, such as Mexico or Chile, include a special override whereby information relating to human rights or violations must be processed in a far shorter time frame.

The spread of FOI laws, now across more than 100 countries in various legal, regulatory or voluntary forms, appears related to the strength of the media environment (Relly 2012). Accessing information is a modern offshoot of an 'age old struggle' over freedom of opinion and the press and grew out of it, championed originally by US journalists after world war two (Ackerman & Ballesteros 2006, 90; Fenster 2015). Since then journalists have been at the forefront of promoting openness with, for example, the UN Rights Committee ruling based on an appeal from a journalist being refused access to the Canadian Parliament (McDonagh 2013).

Using FOI

Although they constitute a small group, journalists have a large, disproportionate influence given their potential to disseminate access results so widely (see Cain et al. 2003). Journalists use laws but also act as innovators prepared to push cases through the appeal system, experiment with the law and push the boundaries of access. The media more generally are cheerleaders for FOI as a principle and help block any attempts to amend legislation, portraying any 'dismantling' as an attack on democracy and entrenched 'rights' (Fenster 2012). However, studies in multiple different countries have found different patterns in the media use of FOI laws shaped by the culture, the longevity of FOI regime and the general approach towards political communications.

Table 6.1 shows the variation in use. Journalists find time pressures do not fit neatly with access laws and habits and a basic lack of awareness may also condition non-use in many regimes (Cuillier 2011). Sweden's openness law, for example, has long served as a powerful source of news, while the 'dysfunctional' system in Australia blocked and discouraged use (Lidberg 2006). A US Congressional study in 2016 claimed US journalists had given up on FOI use at Federal level, plagued by delay and attempts to block release (Committee on Oversight 2016).

The two cases of India and Ireland help show the differences. In India the powerful Right to Information Act of 2005 has been largely neglected by the media, who advocate it but rarely

Table 6.1 Estimated Breakdown of Requester Groups for Selected Countries [media in bold] (%) (Michener and Worthy 2015)

Type of requester	United Kingdom (central)	United Kingdom (local)	Canada	Australia	European Union[1]
Public	39	37	31	25	23
Business	8	22	31	9	8
Organizations	12	11	41	–	–
Media	**8**	**33**	**21**	**7**	**3**
Academics	13	1–2	6	3	32
Members of parliaments	1	–	–	8	–

[1]Note the data is from different time periods from each FOI regime. The EU law refers to the Access to Documents legislation (No. 1049/2001).

make requests (Murthy et al. 2010; Relly & Schwalbe 2013). This is in spite of the Indian media's long record of anti-corruption crusades and, against downward global trends, growing news-paper readership (Relly & Schwalbe 2013). India also has the only TV programme dedicated exclusively to RTI (Raag/CES 2014). One 2013 study pointed to a series of obstacles

> Some journalists lack knowledge about freedom of information legislation... reporters rely on established channels [and] often work on tight deadlines and do not take the time to plan and implement a public records approach.
>
> *(Relly & Schwalbe 2013, 295)*

The India media does, however, regularly report the RTI activities of campaigners and watch-dogs (Relly & Schwalbe 2013).

In Ireland FOI was introduced in 1997 born from a slow burn scandal exposed by a TV investigation (McDonagh 2015). The law arrived just as the media was turning away from coverage of the troubles and had begun to pursue a role in exposing wrongdoing (Ryan 2015, 102). Since 1997 Irish journalists have used the law in a 'hit and miss' fashion, but succeeded in opening up information on prisons, church and state relations and health scandals (Ryan 2015). By 1999 journalists accounted for around 15 per cent of all requests. Although at the local level 'few seek to upset the status quo', there have been notable scandals with one FOI case leading to the imprisonment of a local councillor (Ryan 2015, 103).

Media use in Ireland has been framed by 'perceptions of [journalists'] intentions rather than their motivations' (Ryan 2015, 106). In 2003 the government introduced a series of changes, ostensibly over concerns at costs and sensitivity of the peace process (High Level Review 2003). A new upfront application fee of 10 Euro led to a 75 per cent drop in overall requests. The fees also led to a sharp drop in media use, with journalists only making up 6.5% of all requests after 2003 (OIC 2008; OIC 2004). The 'regression' in use was combined with growing delays and a 'creeping problem of interpretation' – a case Ryan, suggests of the government seeking to 'delay, deny [and] defeat' FOI (2015, 117). Nevertheless, innovations such as Gavin Sheridan's FOI news site *thestory.ie* and high-profile FOI requests continued to push the law forward. In 2014 a new FOI Act was introduced with the application fees dropped and a wider scope, including partial coverage of the police (McDonagh 2015). Though it is unclear what effect the new FOI law has had, in 2014 FOIs by journalists made up 12 per cent of all requests (OIC 2015).

Freedom of information and the media in the UK: Use, innovation and change

The media are key to the operation of the UK FOI Act 2000, which came into force in 2005. Journalists are a core user group, with a disproportionate influence as their stories, or reporting of FOI requests made by others, gain wide publicity. As we have seen elsewhere, the media use, innovate and protect FOI in the UK.

Using FOI

For journalists in the UK FOI offers potential access to information held by central and local government as well as parliament, parish councils, hospitals, the police and even institutions such as the Monarchy. The scope of the Act continues to evolve in a piecemeal way and it now extends to new bodies such as academy schools. Accidental extension has also meant that, for example, since 2015 the Act now covers the strategic rail authority, Network Rail (Burgess 2015).

In the first ten years of the Act, requests by the media have opened up information on a whole range of issues from the war in Iraq, surgeons' mortality rates to communications between the heir to the throne and government (Burgess 2015). The BBC now has a set of dedicated FOI pages online and the Society of Editors described the law as an 'essential journalistic tool' (Riddell 2013, 23). The biggest expose came in May 2009 when a series of FOI requests by journalists helped reveal abuse by several MPs of their expenses, disclosure that led to resignations, an overhaul of the Parliamentary expenses system, and, for a few MPs, imprisonment (Worthy 2014). Media requests have also played a key role in resignations from the Scottish Parliament and Northern Irish Assembly (Hazell et al. 2010, 225–26; 209–12). Another high-profile story by journalist Chris Ames pieced together the development of the Weapons of Mass destruction dossier through painstaking requests for drafts, emails and correspondence, proving that the policy was not, as politicians claimed, developed solely by intelligence reports (Hazell et al. 2010).

FOI is not only useful as a direct tool of information access. Journalists frequently pick up, publicise and pursue the results of requests made by others. As Table 6.2 shows, information from requests by MPs, Trade Unions or NGOs are all used for stories. Campaigns such as the Taxpayers' Alliance Local Council Rich list generated national and local stories across the UK.

Underneath the high-profile use, common repeat requests ask about car parks, staff payments or local policing and crime (Burgess 2015). At central and local level the national press used FOI stories to focus on the wasting of public money, unethical behaviour or poor performance, from controversial issues such as surveillance legislation to salaries, costs of away days or payment to celebrities for switching on Christmas lights (Worthy et al. 2011 23–4). Not all requests pursue public bodies. Popular FOI requests for local council restaurant inspection reports have led to the local press publishing lists and league tables of good and poor eateries.

Despite the claims of politicians, the media are not the primary user of FOI. According to a UK study in 2010, the media constituted 8 per cent of all requests to central government, fewer than 1 in 10 (Hazell et al. 2010). For other institutions the amounts appear more variable. Estimated media requests to local government went from 10 per cent in 2005 to 33 per cent by 2009 (Constitution Unit, 2010). Two local authorities sampled in 2011 identified media requests as constituting 27 per cent and 28 per cent of their total numbers respectively (MOJ 2011). Higher Education institutions in 2005 identified 22 per cent as journalists while in 2011 snapshots of the Northern Irish Executive counted 9.5 per cent of requests from the media while two hospitals sampled put the figure at 34 per cent (MOJ 2011). It is unclear if these requests are from a small group of heavy users or different journalists.

Certain newspapers, such as the Belfast Telegraph, the Guardian and the Telegraph are assiduous users of FOI and the BBC has experimented with a five minute FOI section in its Radio 5 news. Other likely users are experienced investigative reporters, such as the UK's Bureau of Investigative Journalism, as well as a small group of local and national journalists with the time and knowledge to use the law, such as the BBC's Martin Rosenbaum or Kent Messenger's Paul Francis. Outside of this are the rather harder to define groups, who sit in the grey area between citizen, activists and journalists. Matt Burgesses' FOI Directory provides details of FOI addresses, stories and advice while David Higgerson's FOI Friday blog provides regular examples of media use of the law.

As most requests, around four in every five, go to local government a former Scottish information commissioner spoke of how 'the real worth of freedom of information [is] to be found in the pages of the local rather than the national newspaper' (Dunion 2011, 458). Use by the local press varies greatly as some local authorities have had heavy use but others virtually none (see Worthy et al. 2011). Levels of use can depend on pre-existing relationships between local

Table 6.2 Selected newspaper headlines using FOI 17–22 December 2015

- Daily Echo, 'MP calls for end to "extortionate" hospital parking fees', 22 Dec. 2015
- South Wales Echo, '200 Remploy staff still out of work after factory closures', 22 Dec. 2015
- Mail on Sunday, 'A&E whitewash', 20 Dec. 2015.
- Somerset County Gazette, 'Number of rapes and sexual assaults reported to police in Somerset rises... but convictions remain low', 20 Dec. 2015.
- The Sunday Times, 'Public officials paid millions for union work; Scots taxpayers foot bill despite cuts', 20 Dec. 2015.
- Birminghammail.co.uk, 'More than £11 MILLION owed to Birmingham City Council in rent', Dec. 19, 2015.
- The Evening Standard (London), 'TFL "hypocrites" spend millions on taxi journeys', 18 Dec. 2015, Friday.
- Independent.co.uk, '110 private schools, including Prince Charles' former one, ordered by Government to 'improve standards or be closed', Dec. 18, 2015.
- Stoke, 'The Sentinel City counts the cost of freedom', Dec. 19, 2015.
- South Wales Echo, 'Council spends £480k on cuts consultancy', Dec. 18, 2015.
- Western Gazette, 'Council is accused of 'cloak of secrecy'', Dec. 17, 2015.

Source: Lexis search 17–22 December 2015.

journalists and councils as well as media resources across a dwindling local press. Those with poor relations experienced strong FOI campaigns against particular policies or even individuals.

Table 6.2 demonstrates the wide reach of FOI requests, opening up issues relating to the police, local and central government and the NHS. However, despite the potential FOI holds for journalists, there is a 'patchiness in use' (Riddell 2013, 23; Hayes 2009). Few journalists have the time and patience to use it, as the law often proves slow in relation to journalistic deadlines and is plagued by delay (Burgess 2015). At national level only a small group of journalists use FOI regularly as it can be time consuming: obtaining the MPs' expenses took from January 2004 until June 2009 (Keslo 2009).

There is also a question over what kind of information can be obtained. The BBC's Martin Rosenbaum pointed out FOI is 'inconsistent' as it works well as a means for gathering, at a 'very crude level ... facts and figures', but public bodies are 'very resistant' to releasing 'detailed minutes or information' (in Riddell 2013, 23). It is less a tool for a 'scoop' than a 'learning cycle of innovation' as the media develop approaches and themes and work and innovate with them (Burgess 2015). Common methods involve 'round robin' requests sent to a series of bodies to build a nationwide picture or 'fishing' for information that may or may not exist (Hayes 2009). Other methods including asking for schedules or correspondence on an issue, meeting minutes or 'meta-requests' about a request. Requests can also be used, if refused, for 'secrecy' or 'denial' stories or to apply pressure that may lead to disclose by other means, such as a leak (Burgess 2015). Journalists often use it alongside other tools – the MPs' expenses were partly initiated by an FOI but was eventually disclosed in full by a paid for leak (Worthy 2014). Thought they are relatively few in number journalists form part of a small group described by as 'intermediaries' or a 'vanguard' that are pushing the boundaries of FOI (Dunion 2011).

Innovators

As well as a vanguard, the media are also innovators with the law, using the appeal system and courts to push for change. Journalists have moved the boundaries where the law was unclear, from MPs' expenses to newly founded free schools (Burgess 2015). In one long running

Table 6.3 Selected media headlines on the UK FOI Commission 2015–2016

- Daily Mail, 'Freedom of Information Act MUST be protected, says Daily Mail editor', 10 Dec. 2015.
- The Daily Telegraph, 'It's our right to know', 9 Dec. 2015.
- The Sun, 'Britain has sinister cover-up fetish... we must fight it' 14 Feb. 2016.
- Daily Mail, 'The Great Public Backlash Over Bid To Curb Freedom Of Information Law', 11 Dec. 2015.
- The Sun FOI, 'Class Act', 21 Jan. 2016.
- The Daily Telegraph, 'It's our right to know what government is up to', 17 Dec. 2015.
- Belfast Telegraph, 'We must fight watering down of Freedom of Information Act', 10 July 2015.
- Birmingham Post, 'A tax on journalism; New campaign to keep vital Freedom of Information Act free for all', 29 Oct. 2015.
- The Times, 'Greater secrecy "will put Britain back in Dark Ages"', 8 Dec. 2015.
- Daily Mail, 'How Whitehall spends £289million of YOUR cash on propaganda and marketing... but just £5.6 million of freedom law it now claims is "too expensive"', 14 Nov. 2015.
- Oxford Mail 'FOI: We have a right to know how all public money is spent', 16 Nov. 2015.
- Northern Echo 'We need to shine a light our masters', 16 Feb. 2016.
- Guardian 'Government's FoI review threatens to damage democracy, says PA', 9 Nov. 2015.
- Daily Mail, 'Scandals That Would Never Have Been Exposed', 13 Nov. 2015.
- Guardian 'Freedom of Information Act: 103 stories that prove Chris Grayling wrong', 30 Oct. 2015.
- Daily Mail, 'How right to know law has saved taxpayers cash: public sector waste revealed by threatened Freedom of Information Act', 7 Dec. 2015.

Source: Lexis Search July 2015–March 2016.

campaign, a Financial Times journalist sought to prove that a government Minister was using private email to evade FOI, leading to an ICO ruling that private emails are covered by FOI for public business (Burgess 2015). A request by a Guardian journalist to see pre-2010 correspondence between the Prince of Wales and government departments was eventually upheld by the Supreme Court after a six-year court battle (*R (Evans) v Attorney General, [2015] UKSC* 21). This led to a 'landmark' legal ruling that reduced the government's veto power under the Act and raised fundamental questions about Executive-Judiciary relations (Elliott 2015). Outside of the Act, two journalists' pursuance of a politician led to the UK Supreme Court ruling on the existence on separate common law rights to access information (*Kennedy v the Charity Commission*, [2014] UKSC 20). FOI also feeds into new innovations such as the 'Help Me Investigate' website and a series of 'hybrid' political observatories that are now part of the media monitoring of government (Bradshaw 2013; Schudson 2015).

Defender

In the UK there have been repeated attempts to restrict the Act, with a weakening reform floated roughly every 18 months. This has included an attempt to introduce upfront application fees in 2006, to remove Parliament from the scope of FOI via a Private Members' Bill in 2007–08, to exclude Cabinet papers and discussion of deterring 'industrial users' between 2012 and 2013. All failed amid strong opposition in the media that also served to galvanise powerful opposition within Parliament. Only one change, with considerable less publicity, was successfully made in 2010 when the Monarch and heir to the throne were removed from the scope of the Act.

In 2015, following the ruling in *R v Evans*, an independent commission was created by the Cameron government with a remit looking to strengthen the veto power and protections around decision making and examine the potential 'burden'. The inquiry illustrated the depth of division between supporters of FOI in the media and opponents in government.

The commission generated unified criticism across more than 300 articles in 147 different national, regional and local papers, as Table 6.2 shows. The media opposition went far beyond the 'traditional' FOI supporting Guardian, involving right wing Conservative papers such as the Daily Telegraph and, most effectively, the Daily Mail, alongside a range of regional and local newspapers (House of Commons Library 2016). The Press Association ran a 'Hands Off FOI campaign', attracting 43,0000 signatures on a petition via Change.org. A personal submission to the commission from the Head of Associated Press argued that 'curtailing FoI will inevitably contribute to even greater voter cynicism about an elitist political class protecting its own interests, rather than the public's' and was 'entirely antipathetic to the mood of the times, in which voters expect more, not less transparency in the way they are governed' (*Daily Mail*, 1 Dec. 2015: *Daily Mail*, 10 Dec. 2015).

In March 2016 the commission, rather to the media's surprise, concluded that 'the Act is generally working well … it has enhanced openness and transparency [and] there is no evidence that the Act needs to be radically altered, or that the right of access to information needs to be restricted' (Independent Commission on Freedom of Information 2016, 3).

FOI and media: Abuse, resistance and trust?

Transparency remains a 'contested political issue that masquerades as an administrative tool' (Fenster 2012, 449). FOI is shaped as much by perceptions as the reality of use. One study describes an iceberg effect, whereby views are shaped by the small percentage that cause controversy and headlines (White 2007). Media use and reporting causes accusations from politicians of abuse, resistance and claims that that FOI has actually reduced public trust.

For politicians, FOI can generate concern or even hostility. In a hostile media environment like the UK, the media is often singled out for blame by government, while journalists complain of evasion and resistance from government. Tony Blair, in his memoirs, put forward the case for media as abusers:

> The truth is that the FOI Act isn't used, for the most part, by 'the people'. It's used by journalists. For political leaders, it's like saying to someone who is hitting you over the head with a stick, 'Hey, try this instead', and handing them a mallet.
>
> *(2011, 516–17)*

Tony Blair later argued that FOI 'results in a battle between the government and media' and 'tilted the scales on various contentious issues towards the media' (Justice Committee 2012a). His Chief of Staff Jonathan Powell repeated the erroneous claim that the media made most requests, saying 'unfortunately the number of requests lodged by the public was dwarfed by those from journalists, and their aim was not illumination but harassment' (2010, 197). Both have also claimed FOI leads to a diminution of paper trails, though there is little clear evidence for this effect (Worthy & Hazell 2016: Justice 2012).

For media sensitive public bodies, requests by the media are likely to be perceived as a hostile act. As Snell (2002) points out any FOI regime is 'unpredictable in terms of requestor, type of request, timing and outcome' and 'government information management techniques are apt to be portrayed as excessive secrecy or cover-ups' (188). Moreover, how senior politicians and officials meet transparency may have a powerful influence on their views. Most officials or politicians high up in an organisation only see a very small percentage of requests, copied in to the 1 or 2 per cent of particularly troublesome requests, sensitive cases or, worst of all, the ones involving them: a very selective, and very negative, view of what is being asked. Two different sources detail Tony Blair's unhappiness at the releasing of an FOI relating to who had visited the Prime Ministerial residence (Rawnsley 2010; Powell 2010).

A study by the MOJ (2011) concluded that:

> FOI requests from media may not be geared towards the public interest and accountability, but to sourcing news stories of little relevance to accountability of public authorities. This concern has been reflected in ... concern at a large number of requests from journalists who were 'fishing' for a story (57).

The narrative of media abuse has continued. In 2015, Leader of the House of Commons Chris Grayling claimed FOI 'is, on occasion, misused by those who use it as, effectively, a research tool to generate stories for the media, and that is not acceptable' (House of Commons Library 2016). The claim was echoed at local government level by the Local Government Association, in a submission to the Independent Commission on FOI, who spoke of how some councils complained of 'requests from journalists and researchers for a specific research or media purpose, often provided as a round robin request to fish for news stories' and argued that 'requestors are effectively using the FOI route as a short cut to undertaking proper research'.

FOI does undoubtedly raises uncomfortable headlines and exposes by its nature. As the Justice Select Committee (2012) pointed out, such friction is inevitable in an environment such as the UK:

> Evidence of irregularities, deficiencies and errors is always likely to prove more newsworthy than evidence that everything is being done by the book and the public authority is operating well. Greater release of data is invariably going to lead to greater exposure ... which may sometimes be unfair or partial.

The Committee concluded that 'while regrettable [it] is a price well worth paying for the benefits greater openness brings to our democracy' (18).

Whether media use of FOI leads to a 'battle' is unclear. Snell, drawing on Roberts, elaborated a series of degrees of response from public bodies ranging from co-operation, to neglect to outright adversarialism (2006). In Canada Roberts (2005) identified a series of sophisticated strategies developed by government agencies to minimise the fallout from sensitive or controversial requests through delay and developing 'lines to take'. In the UK such game playing is rare but can occur with delay, or simultaneous publication designed to deprive journalists of a scoop (Hazell et al. 2010; Hayes 2009). In the UK the ANL claimed some public bodies engaged in redaction, misrepresenting spending and 'hiding' detail in footnotes (2015).

A further claim is that media's highlighting of negative stories undermines trust: Blair spoke of how greater openness 'sullied' politicians' reputations (2011, 127) In a 'low trust, high blame' environment like the UK, FOI may become a 'gotcha tool' for shock exposure rather than a serious tool of democratic scrutiny (Fung and Weil 2010; O'Neill 2006). The FOI Act came amid decades of declining political trust, evidenced by continued falls in perceptions of government competence and politicians' truth telling (Whiteley et al. 2013; IPSOS Mori 2015). A series of tracker surveys between 2005 and 2010 by the MOJ found that 'respondents tend to disagree that public authorities are open and trustworthy' since FOI was introduced and public trust has continued to decline in the ten years of the law's operation (2010; Curtice 2010; Whiteley et al. 2015). However, trust is a complex bundle of perceptions, heuristics and causality and proving any cause and effect is problematic (Whiteley et al. 2013). The Justice Committee concluded FOI had 'no generalisable impact' on trust (2012, 17–18). Even the seemingly clear case of a decline in trust triggered by the MPs' expenses scandal shows nuance, as the disclosure of Parliamentary corruption came as a confirmation of the poor view the public have of their representatives, rather than a revelation (Hansard Society 2010; Fox 2012).

Whatever the evidence, to some critics, especially senior politicians, FOI has now become a negative symbol, symptomatic of a system in which there is too much of the 'wrong kind' of democracy and too little of the 'right', with the media as the central culprit (Flinders 2015, 10). While openness 'offers access to voices that would not otherwise be heard' and 'encourages exposure of political failures and wrongdoing'. However, and here the media are made responsible, it also 'promotes grandstanding, needless disputation ... perhaps worst of all, it creates ... a pervasive sense of contentiousness, mistrust, and even outright viciousness' (Heclo 1999, 65). David Cameron put it rather more colourfully when he spoke of FOI as part of a series of impediments on modern government:

> What I call the buggeration factor, of consulting and consultations and health and safety and judicial review and FOI [the Freedom of Information Act] … Just generally, if you want to do something, build a road, start a new college, launch a programme to encourage people to build more houses – it takes a bloody long time.
>
> *(The Times, 28 Mar. 2015)*

The future ecology of transparency

FOI now sits in both a changing transparency and media landscape. FOI is part of an ever-evolving 'ecology of transparency' composed of 'countervailing mechanisms of control' and a 'network of other structural checks' (Kreimer 2008, 1016; Schudson 2015). Fenster (2016) maps theses differing 'laws, institutions, and technologies' that include 'legal rights and administrative obligations that FOI and related laws have created' as well as 'open data [and] open source platforms' all the way to 'vigilante leaking of massive caches of government documents ... most famously by WikiLeaks and Edward Snowden' (276) Some of these new tools, such as Open Data, broadly follow the path and pattern of FOI while others are more dynamic and less controlled (Birchall 2014, 84). Schudson argues that an alternative way of viewing FOI is as part of a series of instruments of 'democratic distrust' or a safety net for scepticism, going back to Bentham's system of distrust (2015, 237).

This ecology can clash and interact in unexpected ways, as seen in early 2016 when David Cameron's promises of greater transparency of company ownership and tax were undercut by the Panama papers mega-leak. This not only exposed Cameron's own inherited offshore wealth but led to the publication of his and other leading politicians' tax returns and greater promises of private sector openness.

In the UK FOI now exists alongside a whole series of legislation, regulations and experiments (Burgess 2015). These include Environmental Information Regulations, Subject Access via the Data Protection Act as well as a host of 'targeted' sector specific transparency instruments granting access to medical records all way to local government accounts. Since 2010, UK governments have championed a series of Open Data initiatives and technological innovations that offer a growing series of datasets, apps and innovations allowing access to reusable data.

FOI is a central part of this new 'hybrid' system. Schudson (2015) points out how there is an ever growing network of 'political observatories' within this ecosystem, from citizen bloggers to NGOs and independent auditors, using FOI and other means to gather information and challenge. FOI now forms part of an armoury for a powerful group of potential 'veto wielders' who are exercising 'counter-democratic control' (Schudson 2015). The fruits of this new system can be seen in the emergence of collaborative news sites such as Muck Rock in the US, which brings together journalists, researchers, activists, and regular citizens to 'analyze, and share government documents, making politics more transparent and democracies more informed'. Similarly, in

Ireland the new site Right To Know is a combined 'media outlet and a transparency organisation', a 'self-sustaining organisation' intended to 'act as a watchdog, an advocate, an investigator, a trainer, and a partner to other NGOs and the media' while the EU Wobbing site brings together journalists who use access laws across Europe to share tips, experiences and disclosures.

Outside of this ecology, FOI now also exists in a very different media environment where broadcast era distinctions between the journalist, activist and passive audience no longer apply (Vaccari et al. 2015). The new 'political information cycle' that is gradually supplementing the mainstream media offers new participants avenues into influencing politics (Chadwick 2013). In the new 'hyper-accelerated news cycles', filled with 'complex and rapidly evolving events', there are 'greater opportunities for active and strategic intervention … framing, and reframing by a wide array of actors – from elite journalists and campaign staff to committed activists, celebrities, and, of course, lay members of the wider public' (Vaccari et al. 1042). The new 'information abundance' and array of tools means that citizens can 'pursue democratic surveillance on their own terms by seeking out untold stories and unreported data' (Blumler & Coleman 2015, 120–21). FOI may well suit a new 'postmaterial political culture' of 'citizen initiated campaigning', movement-like party structures and increasingly fluid and individualised media and political interaction (see Chadwick and Stromer-Galley 2016).

References

Ackerman, J. M. and Sandoval-Ballesteros, I. E. (2006). 'The Global Explosion of Freedom of Information Laws'. *The Administrative Law Review*, 58(1), pp. 85–130.

Birchall, C. (2014). 'Radical Transparency?' *Cultural Studies Critical Methodologies*, 14(1), pp. 77–88.

Birkinshaw, P. (2006). 'Freedom of Information and Openness: Fundamental Human Rights?'. *Administrative Law Review*, 1, pp. 177–218.

Birmingham Post (2015). 'A Tax on Journalism; New Campaign to Keep Vital Freedom of Information Act Free For All'. *The Birmingham Post*, p. 5.

Blair, T. (2011). *A Journey*. London: Hutchinson.

Blumler, J. G. and Coleman S. (2015). 'Democracy and the Media—Revisited', *The Public*, 22(2), pp. 111–28.

Bradshaw, P. (2013). 'The Transparency Opportunity: Holding Power to Account – or Making Power Accountable?'. In: N. Bowles, J.T. Hamilton, and D. Levy, eds., (2013) *Transparency in Politics and the Media: Accountability and Open Government*, Oxford: I.B. Tauris, pp. 147–61.

Burgess, M. (2015). *Freedom of Information: A Practical Guide for UK Journalists*. London: Routledge.

Cain, B., Fabbrini, S., and Egan, P. (2003) 'Towards More Open Democracies: The Expansion of FOI Laws', in B. E. Cain, R. J. Dalton, and S.E. Scarrow (eds) *Democracy Transformed? Expanding Political Opportunities in Advanced Industrial Democracies*. Oxford: Oxford University Press, pp. 115–39.

Chadwick, A. and Stromer-Galley, J. (2016, in press). 'Digital Media, Power, and Democracy in Parties and Election Campaigns: Party Decline or Party Renewal?' *International Journal of Press/Politics*, 21(3).

Committee on Oversight and Government Reform (US House of Representatives) (2016). *FOIA Is Broken: A Report*. Washington: Congress.

Cuillier, D. (2010). 'Honey vs. Vinegar: Testing Compliance-gaining Theories in the Context of Freedom of Information Laws'. *Communication Law and Policy*, 15(3), pp. 203–29.

Cuillier, D. (2011). 'Pressed for Time: U.S. Journalists' Use of Public Records During Economic Crisis'. Presented at the Global Conference on Transparency Research, Newark, NJ.

Curtice, J. (2010). 'Rebuilding the Bonds of Trust and Confidence? Labour's Constitutional Reform Programme'. *The Political Quarterly*, 81, pp. S65–S77.

Daily Mail (2015). 'The Great Public Backlash Over Bid to Curb Freedom of Information Law'. *The Daily Mail*, p. 16.

Daily Mail. (2015). 'Freedom of Information Act MUST be protected, says Daily Mail editor'. *The Daily Mail*. Available at: http://www.dailymail.co.uk/news/article-3353682/Freedom-Act-protected-says-Daily-Mail-editor.html

Daily Mail (2015). 'How Right to Know Law has Saved Taxpayers Cash: Public Sector Waste Revealed by Threatened Freedom of Information Act'. *The Daily Mail*. Available. at: http://www.dailymail.co.uk/news/article-3348775/How-freedom-law-saved-taxpayers-cash.htm

Daily Mail (2015). 'How Whitehall spends £289million of YOUR Cash on Propaganda and Marketing.. But Just £5.6 Million of Freedom Law it Now Claims is 'Too Expensive'', and 'Scandals That Would Never Have Been Exposed'. *The Daily Mail.*

Daily Mail (2015). 'Minister for Hypocrisy: Chris Grayling Said Reporters 'Misused' Freedom Law But Crowed As Stories Shamed Labour'. *The Daily Mail.* Available at: http://www.dailymail.co.uk/news/article-3296119/Outrage-Cabinet-minister-says-wrong-use-Freedom-Information-laws-news-stories.html.Daily

Darch, C. and Underwood, P. (2010). *Freedom of Information in the Developing World: Demand, Compliance and Democratic Behaviours.* Oxford: Chandos.

Dunion, K. (2011). *Freedom of Information in Scotland in Practice.* Dundee: Dundee University Press.

Elliott, M. (2015). *A Tangled Constitutional Web: The Black-Spider Memos and the British Constitution's Relational Architecture.* University of Cambridge Faculty of Law Research Paper No. 34/2015. Available at SSRN: http://ssrn.com/abstract=2621451

Felle, T. and Adshead, M. L. (2009). *Democracy and the Right to Know: 10 Years of Freedom of Information in Ireland.* University of Limerick Politics and Public Administration Working Paper, (4).

Fenster, M. (2015). 'Transparency in Search of a Theory'. *European Journal of Social Theory*, 18(2), pp. 150–67.

Fenster, M. (2012). 'The Transparency Fix: Advocating Legal Rights and Their Alternatives in the Pursuit of a Visible State'. *University of Pittsburgh Law Review*, 73(3). Available at: SSRN:http://ssrn.com/abstract=1918154

Flinders, M. (2015). 'The General Rejection? Political Disengagement, Disaffected Democrats and "Doing Politics" Differently'. *Parliamentary Affairs*, 68(suppl 1), pp. 241–54.

Fox, R. (2012). 'Disgruntled, Disillusioned and Disengaged: Public Attitudes to Politics in Britain' Today'. *Parliamentary Affairs*, 65(4): 877–87.

Fung, A. (2013). 'Infotopia: Unleashing the Power of Democratic Transparency'. *Politics and Society*, 41: pp. 183–212.

Fung, A., and Weil, D. (2010). 'Open Government, Open Society'. In T. Lathrop and L. Ruma, eds., *Collaboration, Transparency, and Participation in Practice.* New York: O'Reilly Media, pp. 105–14.

Guardian (2015). 'Government's FoI Review Threatens to Damage Democracy, says PA'. *The Guardian.* Available at: https://www.theguardian.com/media/2015/nov/09/government-foi-review-pa-freedom-of-information-act

Guardian (2015). 'Freedom of Information Act: 103 Stories that Prove Chris Grayling Wrong'. *The Guardian.* Available at: https://www.theguardian.com/media/2015/oct/30/freedom-of-information-act-chris-grayling-misuse-foi

Guardian (2015). 'Freedom of Information Act Misused by Media to Create Stories, says Grayling'. *The Guardian.* Available at: https://www.theguardian.com/media/2015/oct/29/freedom-of-information-journalists-chris-grayling-foi

Hansard Society (2010). *Audit of Political Engagement 7: The 2010 Report with a focus on MPs and Parliament.* London: Hansard Society.

Hayes, J. (2009). A Shock to the System: Journalism, Government and the Freedom of Information Act 2000. Available at: https://reutersinstitute.politics.ox.ac.uk/fileadmin/documents/Publications/Hayes_A_Shock_to_the_System.pdf [Accessed 12 Nov. 2014].

Hazell, R., Bourke, G. and Worthy, B. (2012). 'Open House? Freedom of Information and its Impact on the UK Parliament'. *Public Administration*, 90(4), pp. 901–21.

Hazell, R., Worthy, B. and Glover, M. (2010). *The Impact of the Freedom of Information Act on Central Government in the UK.* Palgrave: London.

Hazell, R. and Worthy B. (2010). 'Assessing the Performance of FOI in Different Countries'. *Government Information Quarterly*, 27(4), pp. 352–59.

Heclo, H. (1999). 'Hyperdemocracy'. *The Wilson Quarterly* (1976-), 23(1), pp. 62–71.

High Level Review (2003). *Report of the High Level Review Group on the FOI Act.* Dublin: Department of the Taoiseach. Available at: http://www.taoiseach.gov.ie/eng/Publications/Publications_Archive/Publications_for_2003/hlrgReportOnFOI.pdf [Accessed 12 Oct. 2015].

House of Commons Library (2016). *Freedom of Information: Changing the Law?* Commons Briefing paper SN07400 London: TSO.

ICO (2015). *Working Effectively: Lessons From 10 Years of the Freedom of Information Act.* Available at: https://ico.org.uk/about-the-ico/news-and-events/news-and-blogs/2015/10/working-effectively-lessons-from-10-years-of-the-freedom-of-information-act/ [Accessed 1 Nov. 2015].

Independent Commission on Freedom of Information (2016). *Independent Commission on Freedom of Information Report.* London: TSO.

IPSOS/Mori (2015). *Politicians Trusted Less Than Estate Agents, Bankers and Journalists.* Available at: https://www.ipsos-mori.com/researchpublications/researcharchive/3504/Politicians-trusted-less-than-estate-agents-bankers-and-journalists.aspx [Accessed 1 Nov. 2015].

Justice Committee (House of Commons) (2012). *Post-legislative Scrutiny of the Freedom of Information Act 2000; Volumes 1 and 2* [HC 96-i]. London: TSO.

Justice Committee (2012a). Letter from Rt Hon Tony Blair to Rt Hon Sir Alan Beith MP, Chair, Justice Committee, re: *Post-legislative Scrutiny of the Freedom of Information Act 2000*, dated July 2012. Available at: http://www.publications.parliament.uk/pa/cm201213/cmselect/cmjust/96/tb01.htm [Accessed 1 Nov. 2015].

Kelso, A. (2009). 'Parliament on its knees: MPs' expenses and the crisis of transparency at Westminster'. *The Political Quarterly*, 80(3), 329–38.

Kreimer, S. F. (2008). 'The Freedom of Information Act and the Ecology of Transparency'. *University of Pennsylvania Journal of Constitutional Law*, 10(5), pp. 1011–79.

Lidberg, J. (2006). '*Keeping the Bastards Honest': the Promise and Practice of Freedom of Information Legislation.* PhD. Murdoch University.

McDonagh, M. (2015). *Freedom of Information Law in Ireland*, 3rd ed., Dublin: Thomson Round Hall.

McDonagh, M. (2013). 'The Right to Information in International Human Rights Law'. *Human Rights Law Review*, 13(1), pp. 25–55.

Mail (2015). 'He Would, Wouldn't He? Sir Cover Up Attacks Law'. *The Daily Mail.* Available at: http://www.dailymail.co.uk/news/article-3248428/He-wouldn-t-Sir-Cover-attacks-Freedom-Information-laws-saying-make-harder-ministers-formulate-policy.html

Mathiesen, K. (2008). *Access to Information as a Human Right.* Available at SSRN: http://ssrn.com/abstract=1264666

Michener, G. and Worthy, B. (2015). 'The Information-Gathering Matrix A Framework for Conceptualizing the Use of Freedom of Information Laws'. *Administration & Society*, 0095399715590825 [Early View].

Ministry of Justice [MOJ] (2011). Memorandum to the Justice Select Committee. London: TSO.

MOJ (2010). Information rights tracker survey: key wave 14 results. Available at: https://www.gov.uk/government/uploads/system/uploads/attachment_data/file/217865/foi-tracker-survey-wave-14.pdf [Accessed 1 Nov. 2015].

Murthy, C. S. H. N., Ramakrishna, C. and Melkote, S. R. (2010). 'Trends in First Page Priorities of Indian Print Media Reporting: A Content Analysis of Four English Language Newspapers'. *Journal of Media and Communication Studies*, 2(2), pp. 39–53.

National Centre for Social Research (2015). *British Social Attitudes Data.* Available at: http://www.bsa-data.natcen.ac.uk/

Office of the Information Commissioner (2015). *Annual Report 2014.* Dublin: OIC.

Office of the Information Commissioner (2008). *Freedom of Information: The First Decade.* Dublin: OIC.

OIC (2004). Review of the Operation of the Freedom of Information (Amendment) Act 2003. Available at: http://www.oic.gov.ie/en/Publications/Special-Reports/Investigations-Compliance/Review-of-the-Operation-of-FOI2003/Up-front-Fees.html [Accessed 2 Nov. 2014].

O'Neill, O. (2006). 'Transparency and the Ethics of Communication'. In: C. Hood and D. Heald, eds., *Transparency: The Key to Better Governance?* Oxford: Oxford University Press, pp. 75–91.

Oxford Mail. (2015). 'FOI: We Have a Right to Know How All Public Money Is Spent', *Oxford Mail* 16 Nov 2015.

Pasquier, M., and Villeneuve, J. (2007). 'Organizational Barriers to Transparency a Typology and Analysis of Organizational Behaviour Tending to Prevent or Restrict Access to Information.' *International Review of Administrative Sciences*, 73(1), pp. 147–62.

Peled, R. and Rabin, Y. (2010). 'The Constitutional Right to Information'. *Columbia Human Rights Law Review*, (42)2, pp. 357–401.

Powell, J. (2010). *The New Machiavelli: How to Wield Power in the Modern World.* London: Random House.

R (Evans) v Attorney General, [2015] UKSC 21 https://www.supremecourt.uk/cases/docs/uksc-2014-0137-press-summary.pdf [Accessed 1 Nov. 2015].

Rawnsley, A. (2010). *The End of the Party.* London: Penguin UK.

Relly, J. E. (2012). 'Freedom of Information Laws and Global Diffusion: Testing Rogers's Model'. *Journalism & Mass Communication Quarterly*, 89(3), pp. 431–57.

Relly, J. E., & Schwalbe, C. B. (2013). Watchdog journalism: India's three largest English-language newspapers and the Right to Information Act. *Asian Journal of Communication*, 23(3), 284–301.

Riddell, P. (2013). 'Impact of Transparency on Accountability'. In: Bowles, N., Hamilton, J. T. and Levy, D., eds., *Transparency in Politics and the Media: Accountability and Open Government*. London: IB Tauris, pp. 19–31.

Right to Information Assessment and Analysis Group and Centre for Equity Studies (Raag/CES) (2014). *Peoples' Monitoring of the RTI Regime in India 2011–13*. New Delhi: NCPRI.

Ryan, C. (2015). 'Freedom of Information and the Media: A Case of Delay, Deny, Defeat?' In: M. Adshead and T. Felle, eds., *Ireland and the Freedom of Information Act*. Manchester: MUP, pp. 102–22.

Schudson, M. (2015). *The Rise of the Right to Know: Politics and the Culture of Transparency, 1945-1975*. Harvard: Harvard University Press.

Schudson, M. (2010). 'Political Observatories, Databases & News in the Emerging Ecology of Public Information'. *Daedalus*, 139(2), pp. 100–109.

Snell, R. (2002) 'FoI and the Delivery of Diminishing Returns, or How Spin-Doctors and Journalists have Mistreated a Volatile Reform'. *The Drawing Board: An Australian Review of Public Affairs*, 3 (2): 187–207.

Snell, R. (2006). 'Freedom of Information Practices'. *Agenda*, 13(4), pp. 291–307.

Snell, R., (2001). 'Administrative Compliance – Evaluating the Effectiveness of Freedom of Information'. Available at: http://papers.ssrn.com/abstract=2540700 [Accessed 30 Jun. 2015].

Sun. (2015) 'Britain Has Sinister Cover-up Fetish .. We Must Fight It'. *The Sun*, p. 14.

Sun FOI. (2015) 'Class Act'. The Sun, p. 8.

Times (2015). 'Greater Secrecy 'Will Put Britain Back in Dark Ages'. *The Times*, p. 2.

Times (2015). '24 Hours With David Cameron'. The Times. Available at: http://www.thetimes.co.uk/tto/magazine/article4391549.ece

Vaccari, C., Chadwick, A. and O'Loughlin, B. (2015). 'Dual Screening the Political: Media Events, Social Media, and Citizen' Engagement'. *Journal of Communication*, 65, pp. 1041–61.

Wald, P. M. (1984) 'Freedom of Information Act: A Short Case Study in the Perils and Paybacks of Legislating Democratic Values'. *The Emory Law Journal*, 33: 649–79.

White, N. (2007). *Free and Frank: Making the Official Information Act Work Better*. Wellington: Institute of Policy Studies.

Whiteley, P., Clarke, H. D., Sanders, D. and Stewart, M. (2015). 'Why Do Voters Lose Trust in Governments? Public Perceptions of Government Honesty and Trustworthiness in Britain 2000–2013'. *The British Journal of Politics & International Relations*. doi:10.1111/1467-856X.12073

Worthy, B., Hazell, R., Amos, J. and Bourke, G. (2011). 'Town Hall Transparency? The Impact of FOI on Local Government in England'. Constitution Unit: London.

Worthy, B. and Hazell, R. (2016). 'Disruptive, Dynamic and Democratic? Ten Years of Freedom of Information in the UK'. *Parliamentary Affairs*. doi:10.1093/pa/gsv069

Worthy, B. (2015). 'The Impact of Open Data in the UK: Complex, Unpredictable and Political', *Public Administration*, 93(3), pp. 788–805.

Worthy, B. (2014). 'Freedom of Information and the MPs' Expenses Scandal'. In: J. Hudson, ed., *At the Public's Expense? The Political Consequences of the 2009 British MPs' Expenses Scandal*. London: OUP, pp. 27–43.

Worthy, B. (2013). '"Some Are More Open Than Others": Comparing the Impact of the Freedom of Information Act 2000 on Local and Central Government in the UK'. *Journal of Comparative Policy Analysis: Research and Practice*, 15(5), pp. 395–414.

Worthy, B. (2010). 'More Open But No More Trusted? The Impact of FOI on British Central Government'. *Governance*, 23(4), pp. 561–82.

7

FREEDOM OF EXPRESSION AND THE CHILLING EFFECT

Judith Townend[1]

Introduction to the chilling effect

The notion of speech, or expression, being 'chilled' is a pervasive and popular one. It metaphorically suggests a negative deterrence of communication: that a person or organisation is made physically colder by inhibiting the exercise of their right to free expression.

The chilling effect is not an esoteric legal metaphor: journalists and campaign groups cite it frequently. It can, but does not have to mean, an outright obstruction of human rights relating to speech. 'Chilling' does not necessarily mean to make ice cold; the metaphorical suggestion of temperature suggests a scale of deterrence from cool to freezing. The chilling effect is used to describe overt censorship such as a government banning publication of a book, as well as subtler controls such as ambiguous legislation and high legal costs that provoke uncertainty and fear among writers and journalists.

The judiciary has played an important role in the popularisation of this highly flexible metaphor. Since the mid-1950s judges – first in the United States but now all over the world – have used it to explain decisions relating to individuals' and organisations' right to freedom of expression. Despite its global prevalence, there has been very little interrogation of what it actually means and the rare attempts to systematically document the chilling effect of statutes and judicial decisions on freedom of expression are stymied by a lack of reliable and available data.

With a focus on the chilling effect's origins in the US and the jurisdiction of England and Wales, this chapter first traces the historical roots of the 'chilling effect' concept in relation to human rights, and in particular, laws of defamation and privacy, and the areas of freedom of information and state surveillance. It then considers the difference between its judicial and social use within and between these distinct areas of law. Second, it turns to the question of measurement, examining attempts to systematically document the chill. Third, it considers the impact of the chilling effect metaphor on communication law and policymaking and argues that in order to better protect fundamental human rights, there is a need for clearer articulation by lawmakers of desired boundaries for legitimate speech.

Historical development of the chilling effect

First Amendment origins

The first documented appearance[2] of the 'chill' metaphor to describe the future deterrence of free activity and speech is in a First Amendment case which recognised that demanding a loyalty oath from state employees in Oklahoma had 'an unmistakable tendency to chill … free play of the spirit' and made 'for caution and timidity in their associations by potential teachers' (US 1952, 195). Ten years later, the 'chilling effect' concept made its debut; the court identified a 'deterrent and "chilling" effect on the free exercise of constitutionally enshrined rights of free speech' when NAACP membership records for alleged 'Communists' were demanded by a legislative investigating committee in Florida (US 1963, 557).

The chilling effect may have originated in an even earlier undocumented example, but its precise origin is perhaps less relevant than the growing prevalence and import of the metaphor in the 20th and 21st centuries. Writing 15 years after the first judicial utterance of the chilling effect, Schauer found that the concept of the chilling effect had 'grown from an emotive argument into a major substantive component of first amendment adjudication' and that its use 'accounts for some very significant advances in free speech theory, and, in fact, the chilling effect doctrine underlies the resolution of many cases in which it is neither expressed nor clearly implied' (1978, 685). The metaphor regularly appears in a variety of legal contexts, connected by the theme of freedom of expression, but quite different in nature from those early cases concerning freedom of political expression and association.

Defamation

The 'chilling effect' concept is perhaps best known in the context of defamation law and in particular, in the permanent form of defamation known as libel. This is partly because the chilling effect has been taken on as the war cry of individuals and organisations calling for the relaxation of onerous libel laws and the reform of high libel costs, and was a motif of the high-profile libel reform campaign of 2009–13[3] that led to the introduction of the Defamation Act 2013 in England and Wales.[4] The metaphor was also appropriated by the British government when it asserted that the new Act would 'reverse' the chill on freedom of expression (Ministry of Justice 2013); a claim which is difficult to assess, as will be further discussed (see 'Measurement').

For many media lawyers, it is *New York Times v Sullivan* (US 1964) that most closely resonates with the chilling effect, which held that a state cannot award a public official damages for defamatory falsehood relating to his official conduct unless he or she proves 'actual malice', that is, that the defendant made a statement with knowledge that it was false or with reckless disregard of whether it was false or not. This landmark ruling has been widely perceived to reduce the chilling effect of defamation actions against US media organisations, but this came 'at a price', in Schauer's view (1978, 708). It was, he argues, an imperfect solution; it requires that 'we must prohibit the imposition of sanctions in instances where ideally they would be permitted' (1978, 685). Some commentators refer to this as another kind of chilling effect, where potential claimants may be deterred from pursuing a claim in defamation owing to legal uncertainty or relaxed provisions (see, for example, Kenyon 2013, 228; Page 2015, 1).

It was several decades after the ruling in *New York Times v Sullivan* that the chilling effect concept really took hold in the English courts, although related issues had been considered. In *Derbyshire County Council v Times Newspapers* (UKHL 1993), which considered whether a local authority could maintain a claim for defamation damages, the House of Lords drew on *New York*

Times v Sullivan to explain that while the decision was related to the US constitutional right to freedom of speech, 'the public interest considerations which underlaid them are no less valid in this country'. 'What has been described as 'the chilling effect' induced by the threat of civil actions for libel is very important', observed Lord Keith (UKHL 1993, 8).

The 'chilling effect' was again directly discussed in *Reynolds v Times Newspapers Ltd* (UKHL 1999) although, as Cheer has pointed out (2008, 66), the dicta 'reveal a House of Lords which is wary of the press and somewhat sceptical of a chilling effect'. Lord Nicholls acknowledged that unpredictability and uncertainty, coupled with the high costs of defending an action, affects a journalist's decision and may '"chill" the publication of true statements of fact as well as those which are untrue'. The chill should not, however, be exaggerated and could vary between different types of publications. '[W]ith the enunciation of some guidelines by the court, any practical problems should be manageable' (UKHL 1999).

Ambiguity remained central to the chilling effect concept in Eady J's ruling in *Jameel v The Wall Street Journal Europe* (EWHC 2004), which found 'there is no more "chilling effect" upon freedom of communication … than uncertainty as to the lawfulness of one's actions' (para. 17). His point was underlined, perhaps, by the House of Lords' decision in the *Wall Street Journal's* favour, overturning the Court of Appeal's and Eady J's earlier decision that the publication did not have recourse to the qualified privilege defence established in *Reynolds* as the requirements of responsible journalism had not been satisfied; the Lords held that they had been (UKHL 2006). Indeed, the lawfulness of one's actions is not easily predictable!

The subjectivities of the chilling effect were clearly demonstrated in the House of Lords ruling: Lord Bingham found 'the weight placed by the newspaper on the chilling effect' of the existing rule was in his opinion 'exaggerated' (UKHL 2006, para. 21). Baroness Hale, on the other hand, was more sympathetic to the newspapers' position, describing a 'disproportionately chilling effect upon freedom of speech' (para. 154).

Though receiving mixed reception, the chilling effect is an increasingly common consideration in English defamation cases, since its first appearance in the late 20th century. While the doctrine may hold more sway in cases based in the US than in England and Wales, it has arguably affected influential judicial decisions in defamation cases, as well as broader policy; namely, the introduction of the Defamation Act 2013. It has also been a central consideration in a number of privacy cases.

Privacy

The courts' extension of the chilling effect concept to privacy law has been fairly seamless and widely adopted by the courts and the media. In *Mosley v News Group Newspapers Ltd* (EWHC 2008), in which the claimant Max Mosley successfully sued the *News of the World* newspaper for breach of privacy, exemplary damages were refused; in Eady J's view, such damages would have provided a form of relief in a new area of law that was unnecessary, nor legally prescribed. For that reason, 'the "chilling effect" would be obvious"' (para. 173).

Chilling effect claims have tended to focus on costs even when making a broader point about threats to freedom of expression. For example, when various freedom speech groups intervening in *Mosley v United Kingdom* (ECtHR 2011, para. 103) were concerned that any requirement to notify the subject of a story ahead of publication would give rise to a chilling effect, the focus was on the high cost of (even successfully) defending injunction proceedings arising from compulsory notification.

This case also highlighted several other facets of the 'chilling effect' principle. Beyond costs, the court considered the effectiveness of a pre-notification obligation and a possible exception for newspapers if they could show that the public interest was at stake. In this context, a narrowly defined understanding of public interest is identified as a potential chilling effect (para. 126). Additionally, the judgment reinforces another element of the chilling effect doctrine: that it anticipates the implications of future behaviour outside the case under consideration. Mosley's bid for a legally binding pre-notification requirement is examined beyond the facts of his case, considering the 'chilling effect to which a pre-notification requirement risks giving rise' (para. 132).

Whereas discussion of chilling effects in defamation have tended to concentrate on the damage to journalists' ability to hold political and financial power to account, it is not generally so in privacy, where many claims against the media have concerned the private lives of celebrities and sportspeople. In a speech in 2009, Sir David Eady observed that few privacy cases are contested with a public interest defence.

Freedom of information

In the past few years, a chilling effect has been described in a very different context relating to communication: in relation to freedom of information (FOI) laws that enable public access to information. In this context, it would be a stretch to describe the chilling effect as a developed doctrine as such, but the concept has played an influential role in shaping discussions on the development of FOI.

It is not the public or press which has been described as chilled in this context but ministers and civil servants. It has been claimed that freedom of information laws can cause public servants to avoid frank and candid discussion during policy deliberations and to keep inadequate records (see Bannister 2015, 342). It remains a contentious claim that has been treated somewhat sceptically, however. Lord McNally told the UK's Independent Freedom of Information Commission that he had not witnessed ministers choosing to exchange views privately rather than commit them to writing although he had heard 'mandarins' speak of this phenomenon (Gov.uk 2016, 36).

In the FOI context, the chilling effect argument has received markedly different treatment between tribunals and other bodies considering disclosure of the same information. A First-Tier Tribunal which considered a likely 'discouragement of candour, imagination and innovation' (FTT 2014, para. 60) resulting from disclosure of information on the implementation of universal work credit, found there was 'no evidence to support the claim' (2014, para. 62). In contrast, the Upper Tribunal subsequently found that expecting such evidence was an 'unrealistic and unattainable standard for the Department [of Work and Pensions] to meet' and that such effects might be 'subtle' and without paper trail. (UT 2015, para. 18).[5]

More generally, a parliamentary committee examining the issue was 'not able to conclude, with any certainty, that a chilling effect has resulted from the FOI Act' (House of Commons 2012, 75). The former Information Commissioner Christopher Graham has suggested that 'if mandarins keep talking about a chilling effect, theirs is a self-fulfilling prophecy' (ICO 2015).

Surveillance

How does knowledge that you are being watched affect your behaviour? This is the question at the heart of the discussion on the chilling effect of surveillance powers – whether used by the state or a private entity such as Google or Facebook, for example. Survey research indicates that knowledge of monitoring programmes causes writers and journalists to self-censor what they search for (PEN American Center 2013), although the relationship between surveillance and individuals' behaviour may be more nuanced than a 'blanket silencing' (see Stoycheff 2016).

The chilling effect is alluded to in surveillance-related case law, but not extensively or explicitly. In the *Digital Rights Ireland* case, Advocate General Cruz Villalón's non-binding opinion identified a 'vague feeling of surveillance' which may affect rights to freedom of expression. But, he noted, the court did not have 'sufficient material' to give a ruling in that regard, and that the '[chilling] effect would be merely a collateral consequence of interference with the right to privacy …' (CJEU 2013, para. 52).

In this context, the claimed effect is perhaps even more pernicious than the defamation or privacy chills previously described, as it affects not only what an individual might write but also what they might read.

Distinctions in use

Observed chilling effects are not limited to the communication areas described previously; they have also been claimed in other areas of media law: as a result of the use of copyright, data protection, contempt of court and various criminal sanctions for speech.[6] Within these various communication contexts the chilling effect takes different forms. To date, scholars have tended to define these in binary terms.

Benign and invidious chills

Schauer defines the 'benign' deterrence as 'an effect caused by the intentional regulation of speech or other activity properly subject to governmental control' (1978, 690). This is comparable to what a previous UK Information Commissioner saw as the 'beneficially chilling effect' of penalties to deter illegal data protection breaches (Graham, cited in Leveson 2012, para. 2.8, 1089). Cheer's study of defamation in New Zealand also emphasises the distinction that some chilling effects are permissible and desirable (2008, 62), suggesting that 'in order to protect reputation, defamation must chill some speech' (63). These interpretations suggest that a chilling effect can be understood as benign and desirable, where a restriction is usefully and appropriately applied.

In contrast, Schauer describes what he sees as an undesirable chill: an 'invidious' deterrence: 'this can occur not only when activity shielded by the first amendment is implicated, but also when any behaviour safeguarded by the [US] Constitution is unduly discouraged' (1978, 690). The danger of 'invidious' deterrence, argues Schauer, lies in the fact 'deterred by the fear of punishment, some individuals refrain from saying or publishing something that which they lawfully could, and indeed, should'. As well as the harm that arises from the non-exercise of a constitutional right, this could cause 'general societal loss' (693).

Direct and indirect chills

Barendt et al. provide a two-part classification, which allows for both 'direct' and 'structural' illegitimate deterrence, or 'chilling effects'. The direct chill takes place when material is specifically changed as a result of legal considerations, of which the 'if in doubt, take it out' philosophy 'exemplified by most magazine editors and publishers' is part and described as 'conscious inhibition' or 'self-censorship' (Barendt et al. 1997, 191). Significantly, they identify that this is not necessarily 'uniform': 'different media experience [it] with notably different force'.

The second category, the 'structural' and indirect chilling effect refers to a 'deeper, subtler way in which libel inhibits media publication'. This prevents the very creation of media content, with avoidance of 'taboo' organizations and individuals: 'certain subjects are treated as off-limits,

Table 7.1 Types of chills

Type of chill	Direct	Indirect
Benign	Where a specific threat of legal action deters illegitimate speech	Where a broad concern about legal action deters illegitimate speech
Invidious	Where a specific threat of legal action deters legitimate speech	Where a broad concern about legal action deters legitimate speech

Table 7.2 Harm to freedom of expression caused by different types of 'chilling effect'

Less harmful	More harmful
Benign/Indirect → Benign/Direct → Invidious/Indirect → Invidious/Direct	

minefields into which it is too difficult to stray. Nothing is edited to lessen libel risk because nothing is written in the first place' (192).

Additionally, there is a secondary form within this 'structural' deterrence, a tendency towards a more polemical and opaque style, favouring comment over 'clear' and 'hard-edged' investigative journalism, which the authors suggest could be a result of the journalists' interpretation of the fair comment defence, perceived as more lenient than the defence of justification in defamation cases[7] (193). They emphasise, however, that the idea that style has been moulded by the law of defamation is 'untestable', a commonly identified problem for researchers in this area.

The two sets of characteristics described by Schauer and Barendt et al. can manifest themselves as shown in Table 7.1.

At worst (for their freedom of speech), a publisher might encounter an invidious and direct chill; at best (for their freedom of speech), a benign and indirect chill. This scale is depicted in Table 7.2.

Chills arising from speech protection

Finally, there is evidence of alternative chills, which can be understood as side effects of attempts to reduce the chill on speech. In the context of defamation and privacy, some commentators have worried about the potential chilling effect on claimants and the inclination of individuals to enter public life. It has even been suggested that law-enforcing authorities are themselves chilled. L. J. Leveson, for example, suggested that a 'special enforcement regime' in the Data Protection Act 1998, giving the press special exemptions from legislative provisions, had a 'chilling effect on reasonable law enforcement and, equally, had a high risk of impacting unfairly on individuals' (Leveson 2012, para. 2.55, 1081).

Measurement

Though chilling effects are widely cited and claimed to be systematic and reliable, evidence is difficult to locate within and outside case law. The overall methodological challenge is that one is seeking to prove a negative – or a counterfactual assertion – and looking for evidence that could be seen to reflect badly on those 'chilled' or 'chilling' (see Knight 2015). In the context of FOI, it would require asking civil servants to admit they had been deliberately obfuscating information which could be seen as unprofessional conduct (Worthy 2017). My own empirical research on the relationship between defamation, privacy law and journalism, suggests that while journalists and lawyers were often willing to discuss the chilling effect in general, they can be reluctant – or are unable – to give specific examples from their own experience (Townend 2015).

Kendrick suggests that problem with the application of the chilling effect concept is that 'both the detection of a problem and the imposition of a remedy involve intractable empirical difficulties' and unambiguously suggests that the US Supreme Court 'has founded the chilling effect on nothing more than unpersuasive empirical guesswork' (2013, 1633). Worthy points out two obstacles to documenting the chill in the FOI context: first, locating hard evidence rather than anecdotes; and second, isolating FOI as the causal factor rather than departmental or ministerial leaks, or a tendency for informal meetings enabled by new technology. In his view, it is impossible to say if there is or is not an effect (Worthy, 2017).

Nonetheless, efforts have been made, particularly in the context of defamation and copyright. In the US, a Harvard-born project called the Chilling Effects Clearinghouse, now known as Lumen, has documented defamation and copyright threats in the form of cease-and-desist letters. One reason for changing its name in 2016 was that it could lead people to think that it only included 'notices that have in fact had a "chilling effect" on conduct or speech', which was too 'limiting' for its role as a 'neutral third party' collecting and monitoring notices (Lumen 2015). This points to a critical issue for any researcher documenting chills: to determine whether a threat could be described as a chill, one has to consider first whether a threat has deterred, or is likely to deter, speech; and second, whether such deterrence is necessarily undesirable. Given the variety of judicial interpretation on the desirability of speech, let alone everyday interpretation, this is not easy.

Kenyon argues that there are better ways than theoretical conjecture to assess the potential for defamation reform (2001, 546) and there have been a number of attempts to go beyond the case law and document the chill of defamation law in comparative studies using content analysis (Dent & Kenyon 2004) interviews and surveys (Kenyon & Marjoribanks 2008; Weaver et al. 2004; Cheer 2008; Townend 2014, 2015) but all indicate some of the methodological difficulties.

Kenyon's observation that the area deserves greater attention from researchers and their funders still stands over a decade later, certainly in the UK context. Researchers need not confine themselves to self-reporting surveys and interviews to gather data: observational techniques that record users' actual online behaviour could prove a fruitful if challenging methodology for monitoring deterring effects. Additionally, we might learn from the judicial consideration of the chilling effect in different communication and information law settings.

Seeking clarity

One of the few scholars to dig beneath the metaphor, Haig Bosmajian, warns that while tropes such as the chilling effect 'can help us comprehend what may have been incomprehensible', there is a danger that they can lead us to 'mislead, conceal, create misunderstandings, and come to rely on clichéd thinking' (1992, 205). Though the chilling effect and other communication metaphors have been used to develop doctrines and principles in law there is insufficient examination of their function and implication on judicial decisions (Bosmajian 1992, 7).

Academic empirical studies, public statements in speeches and the media and case law all indicate that chilling effect definitions in different communication contexts are indeed as 'slippery' and 'amorphous' as US Justice Harlan warned in the metaphor's younger days (US 1967). This does not, however, mean that the phenomena described by the chilling effect metaphor are necessarily imagined or non-existent. Even those scholars engaged in critical analysis of the concept, are reluctant to suggest the chilling effect is not 'real' or should play no role in the development of law relating to freedom of expression.

The concept should not, however, be used without interrogation, especially when it is deployed as legal doctrine. This requires relevant parties, lawyers and judges to be specific about what they are describing. Are they talking about benign or invidious effects, that is, where speech is deterred legitimately or illegitimately under current law? Are they referring to direct or indirect effects, that is, where speech is directly deterred as the result of a specific threat, or indirectly because there is a more general concern? Does speech risk being deterred because of a clear legal provision, or because of uncertainty in the law and the legal process? Is the issue the substantive law, or procedural factors such as cost? On what evidence have they drawn their conclusion, and why? This is especially important if the determination of a chilling effect forms part of the central reasoning in a case, or if a specific legal reform is being sought.

A clearer understanding of chilling effect claims would lead to a more appropriate application. Certainly, this would be helpful as a point of reference in lawmaking: for judges, parliamentarians and policymakers. But it would not reflect the way the metaphor is used in society and understood by individuals interacting with communication law, that is journalists, charity and NGO professionals and ordinary members of the public wishing to express themselves online and access information. A further problem is that boundaries between legitimate/desirable and illegitimate/undesirable speech are keenly contested, both within and outside courts. Even if one formed a definition based on, let's say, the public interest, it is clear that interpretations of the public interest can vary dramatically (see e.g. Morrison & Svennevig 2002).

However, the chilling effect is defined in relation to the exercise of human rights, some deterrence of expression is inevitable owing to the uncertainty of law and the fact that individuals are risk averse (see Schauer, 731), although lawmakers should seek to minimise this uncertainty in the clear design of foreseeable and accessible legislation and through comprehensible case law. Given that some sort of deterrence will always exist, the chilling effect doctrine applied by the courts allows judges to favour the protection of speech rights even in the absence of specific evidence predicting the future behaviour of individuals (see Schauer, 731–2).

Conclusion

In lieu of positing a firm definition for the social concept or legal doctrine, I propose that greater clarity in research, law and policymaking might be achieved through specificity about what is claimed when a chilling effect is asserted, and ideally, evidence of its existence (or its non-existence, if the opposite is claimed). This will help the formulation of better laws and legal processes relating to human rights and communication: reforming law where it is seen to have an overly and detrimentally restrictive effect on freedom of speech and simplifying court processes to reduce its burdens of mental stress, money and time.

Notes

1   With thanks to Judith Bannister, Eric Barendt, Natali Helberger, Nora Ni Loideain, Lorna Woods and Ben Worthy for their suggestions and feedback, which will also inform my future work. All errors and omissions remain my own.
2   This is the first instance of its use reported by Schauer (1978) and Bosmajian (1992). There may be earlier undiscovered judicial uses.
3   The campaign has not formally ended: although it considers the passage of the 2013 Act a marker of success in England and Wales and it is less active since that time, it continues to publicise the situation in Northern Ireland, where the Act has not been extended, and in Scotland, where it only partially applies.

4　See, for example, Glanville 2009; Glanville and Heawood 2009.

5　When the case was later re-heard in the First-Tier Tribunal, the court was not convinced that risk of disclosure would create pressure to cause a change in civil servants' behaviour (FTT 2016, para. 63).

6　In England and Wales this would include, for example, offences under the Communications Act, 2003, section 127 or the Malicious Communications Act, 1988, section 1. There are also criminal offences associated with data protection, contempt of court and copyright. In other countries, defamation and breach of privacy may be treated as criminal offences.

7　The authors emphasise that it would be inaccurate for a journalist to act on the belief that presenting allegations of fact as statements of opinion will provide an automatic protection from libel action (Barendt et al. 1997, 193). These defences are now known as truth and honest opinion.

References

Bannister, J. (2015). 'Accountability or Participation? Disentangling the Rationales for FOI Access to Deliberative Material'. *Revue Internationale des Gouvernements Ouverts*. Paris: IMODEV, pp. 327–44.

Barendt, E., Lustgarten, L., Norrie, K. and Stephenson, H. (1997). *Libel and the Media: the Chilling Effect*. Oxford: Clarendon Press.

Bosmajian, H. A. (1992). *Metaphor and Reason in Judicial Opinions*. Carbondale: Southern Illinois University Press.

Cheer, U. J. (2008). *Reality and Myth: The New Zealand Media and the Chilling Effect of Defamation Law*. PhD. Christchurch, New Zealand: University of Canterbury.

CJEU, 2013. Opinion of A. G. Cruz Villalón in *Digital Rights Ireland* [2013] Case C-293/12 (European Court of Justice, 13 December). Available at: http://curia.europa.eu/juris/document/document_print.jsf?do clang=EN&text=&pageIndex=0&part=1&mode=lst&docid=145562&occ=first&dir=&cid=218559

Dent, C. and Kenyon, A. T. (2004). 'Defamation Law's Chilling Effect: A Comparative Content Analysis of Australian and US Newspapers'. *Media & Arts Law Review*, 9(89), pp. 1–39.

Eady, D. (2009). *Sir David Eady's Speech on Privacy*. Available at: http://www.publications.parliament.uk/pa/cm200809/cmselect/cmcumeds/memo/press/uc7502.htm [Accessed 18 May, 2014].

ECtHR, (2007). *Hachette Filipacchi Associés v. France* [2007] App no. 71111/01 (ECtHR (First section), 14 June).

ECtHR. (2011). *Mosley v United Kingdom* [2011] App no. 48009/08 (ECtHR (Fourth Section), 10 May).

EWHC. (2008). *Mosley v News Group Newspapers Ltd* [2008] EWHC 1777 (QB).

EWHC. (2004). *Abdul Latif Jameel Company Ltd. v The Wall Street Journal Europe Sprl* [2004] EWHC 37 (QB).

FTT. (2014). *John Slater v ICO and DWP* [2014] Case No. EA/2013/0145 (First Tier Tribunal (Information Rights)).

FTT. (2016). *John Slater v ICO and DWP* [2016] Case No. EA/2013/0145 (First Tier Tribunal (Information Rights)).

Glanville, J. (2009). 'Slightly Chilled'. *Index on Censorship*, 38(2), pp. 3–5.

Glanville, J. and Heawood, J. (2009). *Free Speech Is Not for Sale*. London: Index on Censorship/English PEN, pp. 1–29.

Gov.uk, (2016). *Independent Commission on Freedom of Information Oral Evidence*, session transcript, 20 January, 2016. Available at: https://www.gov.uk/government/uploads/system/uploads/attachment_data/file/504067/Independent_Commission_on_Freedom_of_Information_Oral_Evidence_Session-_20_January_2016_transcript.pdf [Accessed 6 May, 2016].

House of Commons (2012). *House of Commons Justice Committee - Post-legislative scrutiny of the Freedom of Information Act 2000*. HC 96-I.

ICO (2015). *Working Effectively: Lessons from 10 Years of the Freedom of Information Act*. Available at: https://ico.org.uk/about-the-ico/news-and-events/news-and-blogs/2015/10/working-effectively-lessons-from-10-years-of-the-freedom-of-information-act/ [Accessed 6 May, 2016].

Kendrick, L. (2013). 'Speech, Intent, and the Chilling Effect'. *William and Mary Law Review*, 54(5), p. 1633.

Kenyon, A. T. (2001). 'Defamation and Critique: Political Speech and New York Times v. Sullivan in Australia and England'. *Melb. UL Rev.*, 25, p. 522.

Kenyon, A. T. (2013). *Defamation: Comparative Law and Practice*. London: UCL.

Kenyon, A. T. and Marjoribanks, T. (2008). 'Chilled Journalism?: Defamation and Public Speech in US and Australian Law and Journalism'. *New Zealand Sociology*, 23(2), pp. 18–33.

Knight, C. (2015). *Is it Getting Chilly in Here?* 11KBW Panopticon Blog. Available at: http://panopticon-blog.com/2015/10/07/is-it-getting-chilly-in-here/ [Accessed 6 May, 2016].

Leveson, B. (2012). *An Inquiry into the Culture, Practices and Ethics of the Press: Volume III*. London: The Stationery Office.

Lumen (2015). *Chilling Effects Announces New Name, International Partnerships*. Lumen Database. Available at: https://lumendatabase.org/blog_entries/763 [Accessed 6 May, 2016].

Ministry of Justice (2013). Defamation Laws Take Effect. Available at: https://www.gov.uk/government/news/defamation-laws-take-effect [Accessed 5 May, 2016].

Morrison, D. E. and Svennevig, M. (2002). *The Public Interest, the Media and Privacy*. BBC. Available at: http://downloads.bbc.co.uk/guidelines/editorialguidelines/research/privacy.pdf

Page, A. (2015). Section 1 of the Defamation Act 2013. Available at: http://www.5rb.com/wp-content/uploads/2015/02/Section-1-Defamation-Act-2013-APQC-2.pdf [Accessed 6 May, 2016].

PEN American Center (2013). *Chilling Effects: NSA Surveillance Drives US Writers to Self-Censor*. New York. Available at: http://www.pen.org/sites/default/files/Chilling%20Effects_PEN%20American.pdf [Accessed 6 May, 2016].

Schauer, F. (1978). 'Fear, Risk and the First Amendment: Unraveling the Chilling Effect'. Boston University Law Review, 58(5), pp. 685–732.

Stoycheff, E. (2016). 'Under Surveillance Examining Facebook's Spiral of Silence Effects in the Wake of NSA Internet Monitoring'. *Journalism & Mass Communication Quarterly*, 93(2), 296–311.

Townend, J. (2014). 'Online Chilling Effects in England and Wales'. *Internet Policy Review*. Available at: http://dx.doi.org/10.14763/2014.2.252 [Accessed 6 May, 2016].

Townend, J. (2015). *Defamation, Privacy & the Chill: A Socio-legal Study of the Relationship Between Media Law and Journalistic Practice in England and Wales, 2008-13*. PhD. City University London.

UKHL (1993). *Derbyshire CC v Times Newspapers Ltd* [1993] UKHL 18 (House of Lords).

UKHL (1999). *Reynolds v Times Newspapers Ltd and Others* [1999] UKHL 45 (House of Lords).

UKHL (2006). *Jameel & Ors v Wall Street Journal Europe Sprl* [2006] UKHL 44 (House of Lords).

US (1952). *Wieman v Updegraff* [1952] 344 US 183 (US Supreme Court).

US (1963). *Gibson v Florida Legislative Investigation Committee* [1963] 372 US 539 (US Supreme Court).

US (1964). *New York Times Co. v. Sullivan* (No. 39) [1964] 376 US 254 (US Supreme Court).

US (1967). *Zwickler v Koota* [1967] 389 US 241 (US Supreme Court).

UT, (2015). *Department for Work and Pensions v Information Commissioner & Ors* [2015] UKUT 535 (AAC).

Weaver, R. L., Kenyon, A. T., Partlett, D. F. and Walker, C. P. (2004). 'Defamation Law and Free Speech: Reynolds v. Times Newspapers and the English Media'. *Vanderbilt Journal of Transnational Law*, 37, p. 1255.

Worthy, B. (2017). *The Politics of Freedom of Information: How and Why Governments Pass Laws That Threaten Their Power*. Manchester: MUP.

8

HUMAN RIGHTS
AND PRESS LAW

Julian Petley

Introduction

In this chapter I wish to examine the impact which the European Convention on Human Rights has had on laws which have a significant bearing on media, and especially press, content. My aim is to show how the Convention, and, in the UK the Human Rights Act 1998, have helped to protect responsible journalism whilst at the same time restraining intrusion and privacy invasion by sections of the press. In the course of this process, laws – and national courts' interpretations of those laws – which have proved particularly burdensome for serious journalism have been successfully challenged, and legislatures have been made forcefully aware of the fact that any new laws which they pass must be compatible with the Convention, not least its requirement that freedom of expression be protected.

Of all the human rights enshrined in the European Convention on Human Rights, the most important to the media is surely Article 10. This states that 'everyone has the right to freedom of opinion and expression. This right shall include freedom to hold opinions and to receive and impart information and ideas without interference by public authority and regardless of frontiers'.

However, it is extremely important to note that this right is qualified by Article 10(2). This lays down that

> [t]he exercise of these freedoms, since it carries with it duties and responsibilities, may be subject to such formalities, conditions, restrictions or penalties as are prescribed by law and are necessary in a democratic society, in the interests of national security, territorial integrity or public safety, for the prevention of disorder or crime, for the protection of health or morals, for the protection of the reputation or the rights of others, for preventing the disclosure of information received in confidence, or for maintaining the authority and impartiality of the judiciary.

This means that, under certain circumstances, the right to freedom of expression may be trumped by laws covering, for example, defamation, official secrecy, the operation of the justice system, obscenity, and so on. But the operative words here are 'under certain circumstances'. As the European Court of Human Rights pointed out in a case arising from the British government's attempts to ban newspapers from publishing details of Peter Wright's memoir

Spycatcher, the exceptions contained in 10(2) 'must be narrowly interpreted and the necessity for any restrictions must be convincingly established'.[1]

And as Geoffrey Robertson and Andrew Nicol explain:

> Once the court is satisfied that there has been an infringement [of Article 10], the burden shifts to the Government or to the party seeking to justify the breach to prove that the infringing law is a clearly defined restriction which legitimately serves an Article 10(2) value and its application is necessary – not expedient – to serve a pressing social need in a democratic society, and is a reasonably proportionate response to that need.
>
> *(2008, 80)*

A balancing act

The relationship between Article 10 and articles protecting other rights is also crucial. In this respect it is extremely important to understand that there are very few absolute rights in the ECHR – these are the right to life (Article 2), the right not to be subjected to torture or to inhuman or degrading treatment or punishment (Article 3), the right not to be held in slavery or servitude (Article 4), and the right not to be held guilty of any criminal offence on account of any act which did not constitute a criminal offence at the time it was committed (Article 7). All other rights are subject to balancing exercises by the courts. In cases involving the media, the press in particular, it is frequently Articles 8 and 10 which find themselves being balanced against each other. Article 8 lays down that

> [e]veryone has the right to respect for his private and family life, his home and his correspondence. There shall be no interference by a public authority with the exercise of this right except such as is in accordance with the law and is necessary in a democratic society in the interests of national security, public safety or the economic wellbeing of the country, for the prevention of disorder or crime, for the protection of health or morals, or for the protection of the rights and freedoms of others.

As Lord Steyn argues in *Re S (FC) (a Child) (Appellant)*, 2004, which involves an attempt to prevent newspapers publishing information which might lead to the identification of a child whose mother was accused of murdering her other child, when it comes to balancing Articles 8 and 10, 'neither article has *as such* precedence over the other', and so 'an intense focus on the comparative importance of the specific rights being claimed in the individual case is necessary'. The justifications for interfering with or restricting each right must be taken into account, and a proportionality test must be applied to each[2]. Similarly in the case in which Max Mosley successfully sued the *News of the World* in 2008 for publishing details of a party in which he had been involved, Mr Justice Eady described this 'intense focus' on the individual facts of the specific case as

> a 'new methodology' which is obviously incompatible with making broad generalisations of the kind which the media often resorted to in the past, such as, for example, 'Public figures must expect to have less privacy' or 'People in positions of responsibility must be seen as "role models" and set us all an example of how to live upstanding lives'. Sometimes factors of this kind may have a legitimate role to play when the 'ultimate balancing exercise' comes to be carried out, but generalisations can never be determinative. In every case 'it all depends' (i.e. upon what is revealed by the intense focus on the individual circumstances).[3]

We shall return in greater detail to the matter of privacy later, but the important points to grasp here are the manner in which non-absolute (that is, qualified and restricted) rights have to be weighed up against each other in particular cases, and the necessity in such circumstances of bringing to bear an 'intense focus' on the facts of each particular case.

'Free speech does not mean free speech'

Blackstone's Statutes on Media Law (2013) lists 58 statutes which in one way or another have a significant bearing on media content, and it is extremely important to understand that, notwithstanding windy rhetorical invocations of England as the 'home of free speech' and misleading descriptions of the Human Rights Act as representing 'rights brought home', the right to free expression enshrined in Article 10 had never had a home in Britain until the passing of the Act in 1998 and its coming into force in 2000. But, even then, it's important to understand that 'the Act does not, as such, incorporate the rights into UK law ... it gives rights particular effects in particular contexts: the two most important are as interpretative aids where statutes apply and as a duty binding upon public authorities' (Fenwick & Phillipson 2006, 124). Contrary to much popular mythology, Magna Carta has absolutely nothing to say about freedom of expression, and the continued absence of any constitutional or statutory provision protecting such freedom meant that, until 1998, the right to such freedom was largely residual – in other words, that which was not expressly forbidden by law was permitted to be published. As the Law Lords put it in 1936: 'Free speech does not mean free speech: it means speech hedged in by all the laws against defamation, blasphemy, sedition and so forth. It means freedom governed by law' (quoted in Robertson & Nicol 2008, 2). Or as Lord Goff of Chieveley stated in one of the many cases occasioned by *Spycatcher*:

> We may pride ourselves on the fact that freedom of speech has existed in this country perhaps as long as, if not longer than, it has existed in any other country in the world. The only difference is that, whereas article 10 of the Convention, in accordance with its avowed purpose, proceeds to state a fundamental right and then to qualify it, we in this country (where everybody is free to do anything, subject only to the provisions of the law) proceed rather upon an assumption of freedom of speech, and turn to our law to discover the established exceptions to it.[4]

However, the problem with such an approach is that the exceptions, as represented by both statute and common law, are nothing if not numerous. Furthermore, some of the exceptions, however 'established' in statute or common law, have turned out to be incompatible with Article 10, which is why, in the 1980s and 1990s, before the English legal system had come to take full account of the Convention and the jurisprudence occasioned by it, the UK found itself so often before the European Court.

The authority of the judiciary

The first case in which the UK was found guilty of a breach of Article 10 by the European Court, *The Sunday Times v UK* (1979), actually resulted in a change to one of the laws which have a distinct bearing on what the media can and cannot report, namely the law of contempt. The British government had stopped *The Sunday Times* publishing an article about the marketing of thalidomide in case it prejudiced court cases involving claims for civil damages by victims of the drug, although these had long been stalled in the courts. They did so on the grounds that publication would undermine the authority of the judiciary as well as the legal rights of the drug's manufacturer, and the Lords upheld the ban. According to the Court,

> Since the proposed article was couched in moderate terms and did not present just one side of the evidence, its publication would not have had adverse consequences for the 'authority of the judiciary' … In view of all the circumstances, the interference did not correspond to a social need sufficiently pressing to outweigh the public interest in freedom of expression; the reasons for the restraint were not therefore sufficient under Article 10 (2); it was not proportionate to the legitimate aim pursued; and it was not necessary in a democratic society for maintaining the authority of the judiciary.[5]

As a result of this ruling, the government was obliged to change the law via the Contempt of Court Act 1981, which decreed that stories could not be injuncted simply because they might prejudice future litigation.

The 1981 Act also strengthened the protection afforded to journalists' sources by stating that

> [n]o court may require a person to disclose, nor is any person guilty of contempt of court for refusing to disclose, the source of information contained in a publication for which he is responsible unless it is established to the satisfaction of the court that it is necessary in the interests of justice or national security or for the prevention of disorder or crime.

However, this did not stop the courts from repeatedly insisting that Bill Goodwin, a trainee journalist working for *The Engineer*, must disclose the identity of a source who, in 1989, leaked to him confidential information which showed that the financial position of a private company, Tetra, was far less strong than it publicly claimed. He refused to do so and was threatened with prison, eventually being fined for contempt, the courts repeatedly agreeing with Tetra, albeit on the basis of very little evidence, that the source must be an employee motivated by a desire to damage the company, who would leak again unless unmasked. It was thus in the 'interests of justice' that the source be revealed so that they could face disciplinary action. Thus, and by no means for the first or last time, a company's property rights trumped a journalist's attempt to expose a matter which was in the public interest. Goodwin then took his case to the European Court, whose ruling in 1996 stated:

> Having regard to the importance of the protection of journalistic sources for press freedom in a democratic society and the potentially chilling effect an order of source disclosure has on the exercise of that freedom, such a measure cannot be compatible with Article 10 of the Convention unless it is justified by an overriding requirement in the public interest.

In this case, the Court found that such a requirement was absent, and declared that

> [t]he applicant and the Commission were of the opinion that Article 10 of the Convention required that any compulsion imposed on a journalist to reveal his source had to be limited to exceptional circumstances where vital public or individual interests were at stake. This test was not satisfied in the present case.

It thus concluded:

> In sum, there was not, in the Court's view, a reasonable relationship of proportionality between the legitimate aim pursued by the disclosure order and the means deployed to achieve that aim. The restriction which the disclosure order entailed on the applicant journalist's exercise of his freedom of expression cannot therefore be regarded as having been necessary in a democratic society, within the meaning of paragraph 2 of Article 10, for the protection of Tetra's rights under English law.[6]

On this occasion, however, the law remained unreformed, in spite of numerous complaints that the phrase 'the interests of justice', which had originally been inserted into the Act in order to protect defendants in criminal cases, could mean almost anything that a litigant wanted. Perhaps unsurprisingly, then, the Goodwin scenario was repeated in 2001 when the English courts insisted that the *Financial Times* and other newspapers hand over documents to the Belgian brewing giant Interbrew SA in order to identify the source of leaks about its plans to take over another brewing company. The papers refused and took their case to the European Court, which, unsurprisingly, ruled that Interbrew's interests in eliminating 'the threat of damage through future dissemination of confidential information and in obtaining damages for past breaches of confidence were, even if considered cumulatively, insufficient to outweigh the public interest in the protection of journalists' sources'[7].

Defamation

Laws concerning defamation are also of considerable concern to the media, and here the European Court has made significant interventions in order to protect responsible journalism. A key case concerned the Austrian journalist Peter Lingens who, in 1975, was convicted of criminal libel for accusing the Chancellor, Bruno Kreisky, of protecting and helping former SS officers for political reasons. The Court overturned his conviction on the grounds that

> [w]hilst the press must not overstep the bounds set, inter alia, for the 'protection of the reputation of others', it is nevertheless incumbent on it to impart information and ideas on political issues just as on those in other areas of public interest. Not only does the press have the task of imparting such information and ideas: the public also has a right to receive them ... Freedom of the press furthermore affords the public one of the best means of discovering and forming an opinion of the ideas and attitudes of political leaders. More generally, freedom of political debate is at the very core of the concept of a democratic society which prevails throughout the Convention. The limits of acceptable criticism are accordingly wider as regards a politician as such than as regards a private individual. Unlike the latter, the former inevitably and knowingly lays himself open to close scrutiny of his every word and deed by both journalists and the public at large, and he must consequently display a greater degree of tolerance. No doubt Article 10(2) enables the reputation of others – that is to say, of all individuals – to be protected, and this protection extends to politicians too, even when they are not acting in their private capacity; but in such cases the requirements of such protection have to be weighed in relation to the interests of open discussion of political issues.[8]

Another important case in this respect concerned a Spanish opposition politician, Miguel Castells, who, in 1979, was convicted of 'insulting the government' by publishing an article in which he accused it in detail of supporting right-wing death squads in the Basque region. In 1992 the Court ruled that

> [t]he limits of permissible criticism are wider with regard to the Government than in relation to a private citizen or even a politician. In a democratic system the actions or omissions of the Government must be subject to the close scrutiny not only of the legislative and judicial authorities but also of the press and public opinion. Furthermore, the dominant position which the Government occupies makes it necessary for it to display restraint in resorting to criminal proceedings, particularly where other means are available for replying to the unjustified attacks and criticisms of its adversaries or the media.[9]

Judgements such as these came to have a significant impact on English defamation law, the interpretation of which has, historically, heavily favoured the reputation of the plaintiff over the right of the accused to express themselves. But as Eric Barendt et al. point out, by the end of the 1990s it had come to be recognised that the common law had to be developed and applied consistently with Article 10 of the Convention; in particular, 'there was legitimate concern about the "chilling effect" that the existing law was having on public interest speech – especially as a result of the high evidentiary burdens that the common law imposed on media defendants in proving the truth of the allegations that they publish' (2014, 423).

The crucial case which signalled a shift in how the law of defamation was developing under the influence of the Convention, and particularly the cases mentioned previously, was *Reynolds v Times Newspapers* (1999), in which the former Premier of the Republic of Ireland, Albert Reynolds, sued *The Sunday Times* for alleging that he had lied to the lower house, and principal chamber, of the Irish legislature. When the paper successfully appealed the case to the House of Lords in 1999, Lord Steyn spoke of the 'new landscape' of the Human Rights Act, arguing that

> [t]he starting point is now the right of freedom of expression, a right based on a constitutional or higher legal order foundation. Exceptions to freedom of expression must be justified as being necessary in a democracy. In other words, freedom of expression is the rule and regulation of speech is the exception requiring justification. The existence and width of any exception can only be justified if it is underpinned by a pressing social need. These are fundamental principles governing the balance to be struck between freedom of expression and defamation.

What the judgement itself essentially did was to develop the doctrine of 'qualified privilege', so that balanced, responsible journalism about matters of serious public concern could be 'privileged' from libel actions, even if subsequently the allegations turned out to be untrue. Thus Lord Nicholls laid out ten factors that should be taken into account when deciding whether a piece of journalism should be considered worthy of being protected by qualified privilege:

1. The seriousness of the allegation. The more serious the charge, the more the public is misinformed and the individual harmed, if the allegation is not true.
2. The nature of the information, and the extent to which the subject-matter is a matter of public concern.
3. The source of the information. Some informants have no direct knowledge of the events. Some have their own axes to grind, or are being paid for their stories.
4. The steps taken to verify the information.

5. The status of the information. The allegation may have already been the subject of an investigation which commands respect.
6. The urgency of the matter. News is often a perishable commodity.
7. Whether comment was sought from the plaintiff. He may have information others do not possess or have not disclosed. An approach to the plaintiff will not always be necessary.
8. Whether the article contained the gist of the plaintiff's side of the story.
9. The tone of the article. A newspaper can raise queries or call for an investigation. It need not adopt allegations as statements of fact.
10. The circumstances of the publication, including the timing.[10]

As things turned out, the Reynolds defence failed to work well in practice from the media's point of view. All too often the journalism in question was judged by the courts not to be responsible (sometimes with good reason), judges tended to regard the aforementioned factors as a checklist all of whose boxes had to be ticked, the journalistic item was not judged as a whole, and the defence 'was usually rejected by trial judges brought up to believe that a "privilege" could only be claimed when there was a moral or legal *duty* to publish – and news stories, however newsworthy, rarely had this morally imperative quality' (Robertson & Nicol 2008, 98). It was thus left to the House of Lords, in the case of *Jameel v Wall Street Journal Europe* (2006), again taking the Convention into full consideration, to recast the Reynolds defence as a thoroughgoing public interest defence. Briefly, the Lords argued that although the Reynolds factors may be used to give guidance to the court's analysis, they should not be used as a checklist; the piece of journalism before the court must be read as a whole; the defamatory material must make a real contribution to the public interest element of the story and must have been believed to be true at the time of publication; and due weight must be given to the editorial judgements of the journalists concerned in determining whether they took steps to investigate and publish the article in a fair and responsible manner.[11]

These cases, allied with growing judicial and journalistic dissatisfaction with the existing legislation on defamation, eventually led to the Defamation Act 2013, which, in line with the ECHR and the HRA, attempted to strike a fair balance between the right to freedom of expression and the right to the protection of reputation. Thus the Act includes a requirement that a claimant must show that a publication which they wish to sue has caused or is likely to cause serious harm to their reputation, and it also incorporates the Reynolds principles (thereby abolishing the Reynolds defence in common law) in that the defendant is permitted to mount the defence that 'the statement complained of was, or formed part of, a statement on a matter of public interest; and the defendant reasonably believed that publishing the statement complained of was in the public interest'. The Act also adds that

> [i]n determining whether it was reasonable for the defendant to believe that publishing the statement complained of was in the public interest, the court must make such allowance for editorial judgement as it considers appropriate. For the avoidance of doubt, the defence under this section may be relied upon irrespective of whether the statement complained of is a statement of fact or a statement of opinion.

Privacy, confidentiality and intrusion

Thus far I have examined the way in which the Convention, both before and after the passing of the Human Rights Act, has helped to protect responsible journalism from laws which had all too often stifled it. This has happened because the Court has overturned the judgements of national courts which are incompatible with Article 10, and the resulting jurisprudence has encouraged those courts to act in ways which are compatible with it. Lawmakers have also been encouraged to do likewise. It might therefore be expected that media organisations would strongly welcome the protections provided by the Convention. In most European countries this has indeed been the case, but, uniquely in Britain, significant sections of the press have led what can only be called a virulent and vicious crusade against both the Convention and the Act (Mead 2015). As I have explained in some detail elsewhere (Petley 2006), this is partly because both were seen as emanations of the hated 'Brussels' by newspapers absolutely fanatically opposed to the EU; that the ECHR is actually the creation of the Council of Europe, that Britain was a founder member, and that it is based in Strasbourg have long been matters of utter indifference to such publications. But the other reason was that newspapers, and especially those whose speciality is delving into people's private lives in pursuit of salacious stories, espied in Article 8 the threat of a privacy law which might interfere with this highly lucrative business. Privacy is actually the subject of another chapter in this book, so what I want to do here is simply to explain how the ECHR actually works to protect serious journalism in cases involving balancing Articles 8 and 10, whilst at the same time discourages unwanted and unwarranted intrusion into people's private lives.

As is well known, English common law has long resisted any single overarching claim for 'invasion of privacy', although, greatly aided by the Convention, the courts have developed the common law in a number of relevant areas, most notably that concerning confidentiality (particularly in the protracted battles between Michael Douglas, Catherine Zeta-Jones and *OK!* magazine, on the one hand, and *Hello!* on the other), in order to protect what would now be called privacy rights. At the same time, in spite of numerous invitations to protect privacy by members of both Houses, judges, Sir David Calcutt's *Review of Press Self-Regulation* (1993), and the Culture, Media and Sport select committee report *Privacy and Media Intrusion* (2003), successive governments have refused point blank to introduce an actual privacy law. The evidence of press/government relations exposed by the Leveson Inquiry, not to mention the events following it, would strongly suggest that they were simply too terrified of press retaliation, and too concerned to keep newspapers onside, even to contemplate such legislation. It has thus been left to the courts to do so – and consequently to face tirades of populist, anti-juridical abuse from the press for having the temerity to do so.

A particularly important series of cases involved Naomi Campbell and Mirror Group Newspapers. These arose as a result of the super-model, who had denied using illegal drugs, suing the *Daily Mirror* in 2001 after it had published a story about her addiction, including a photograph of her leaving a Narcotics Anonymous meeting. She argued that although the paper was entitled to correct the false image she had presented, it had breached her confidence by referring to her attending NA and by publishing the photograph. In the final judgement, in 2004, the majority of the Lords of Appeal argued that her attendance at the Narcotics Anonymous clinic was analogous to other forms of medical treatment whose privacy the law should be particularly ready to protect, and that Campbell's right to privacy in this matter outweighed the newspaper's right to report her visit to NA. Laying out very clearly what the common law now understands by breach of confidence, Lord Nicholls pointed out that it no longer entailed 'improper use of information disclosed by one person to another in confidence', or involved an 'initial confidential relationship'. Rather, 'now the law imposes a "duty of confidence" whenever a person receives information he knows or ought to know is fairly and reasonably to be regarded as confidential'. However, in his view, 'information about an individual's private life would not, in ordinary usage, be called "confidential". The more natural description today is that such information is private. The essence of the tort is better encapsulated now as misuse of private information'.

'A debate of general interest'

Equally important in the context of this chapter's central concern with legal protections for responsible journalism, was Baroness Hale's intervention. Noting that the information revealed by the *Mirror* was indeed both private and confidential, she pointed out that its publication thus required specific justification under Article 10, and went on to examine the nature of the freedom of expression which was being asserted by the paper. Thus she argued:

> There are undoubtedly different types of speech, just as there are different types of private information, some of which are more deserving of protection in a democratic society than others. Top of the list is political speech. The free exchange of information and ideas on matters relevant to the organisation of the economic, social and political life of the country is crucial to any democracy. Without this, it can scarcely be called a democracy at all. This includes revealing information about public figures, especially those in elective office, which would otherwise be private but is relevant to their participation in public life. Intellectual and educational speech and expression are also important in a democracy, not least because they enable the development of individuals' potential to play a full part in society and in our democratic life. Artistic speech and expression is important for similar reasons, in fostering both individual originality and creativity and the free-thinking and dynamic society we so much value. No doubt there are other kinds of speech and expression for which similar claims can be made. But it is difficult to make such claims on behalf of the publication with which we are concerned here. The political and social life of the community, and the intellectual, artistic or personal development of individuals, are not obviously assisted by pouring over the intimate details of a fashion model's private life.[12]

This was a crucial and much cited aspect of the judgement, and a very similar and equally influential approach was taken by the European Court in the case of *Princess Caroline von Hannover v Germany* (2004). This concerned pictures taken of the princess and her family in various public places. The Princess had tried to block their publication on the grounds that that they infringed her right to protection of her personality rights guaranteed by sections 2(1) and 1(1) of the Basic Law and her right to protection of her private life and to the control of the use of her image guaranteed by sections 22 et seq. of the Copyright (Arts Domain) Act. However, the German courts had refused her request, on the grounds that she was a public figure and had to tolerate her picture being published when she appeared in public, even on private business. She thus appealed to Strasbourg, which upheld her case. The court argued that

> [a] fundamental distinction needs to be made between reporting facts – even controversial ones – capable of contributing to a debate in a democratic society relating to politicians in the exercise of their functions, for example, and reporting details of the private life of an individual who, moreover, as in this case, does not exercise official functions. While in the former case the press exercises its vital role of 'watchdog' in a democracy by contributing to imparting information and ideas on matters of public interest … it does not do so in the latter case. Similarly, although the public has a right to be informed, which is an essential right in a democratic society that, in certain special circumstances, can even extend to aspects of the private life of public figures, particularly where politicians are concerned … this is not the case here. The situation here does not come within the sphere of any political or public debate because the

published photos and accompanying commentaries relate exclusively to details of the applicant's private life.

It concluded that

[t]he decisive factor in balancing the protection of private life against freedom of expression should lie in the contribution that the published photos and articles make to a debate of general interest. It is clear in the instant case that they made no such contribution, since the applicant exercises no official function and the photos and articles related exclusively to details of her private life.

'Up for a three-way'

The extent to which such thinking has now become firmly ingrained within the legal process is particularly clearly illustrated by the case of *PJS v Newsgroup* (2016). This concerns two well-known individuals in the entertainment business, PJS and YMA, who are married to each other and have young children. Between 2009 and 2011 PJS had occasional sexual encounters with AB, and in 2011 PJS asked AB if his partner, CD, was 'up for a three-way', which indeed he was. In 2016 AB and CD approached the *Sun on Sunday* and told the editor of their liaison with PJS. The paper's lawyers then contacted PJS's representatives and informed them of their possession of the story. The celebrity stated that publication would be an invasion of privacy and applied for an injunction on the grounds that it would breach his Article 8 rights to privacy and confidentiality. The case then began its journey through the courts, and the reasons that the Supreme Court gave for upholding the injunction clearly demonstrate the extent to which the English courts are now prepared to protect privacy and confidentiality. Thus Lord Mance argued that

[c]riticism of conduct cannot be a pretext for invasion of privacy by disclosure of alleged sexual infidelity which is of no real public interest in a legal sense. It is beside the point that the appellant and his partner are in other contexts subjects of public and media attention – factors without which the issue would hardly arise or come to court. It remains beside the point, however much their private sexual conduct might interest the public and help sell newspapers or copy.

He also stated that any public interest in publishing the story was so limited that it should be 'effectively disregarded in any balancing exercise' and added that

[i]t may be that the mere reporting of sexual encounters of someone like the appellant, however well known to the public, with a view to criticising them does not even fall within the concept of freedom of expression under Article 10 at all. For present purposes, any public interest in publishing such criticism [of the appellant's sexual encounters] must, in the absence of any other, legally recognised, public interest, be effectively disregarded in any balancing exercise and is incapable by itself of outweighing such Article 8 privacy rights as the appellant enjoys.

The Supreme Court was also thoroughly unpersuaded by the *Sun on Sunday*'s argument that it should be allowed to publish the identities of those involved in the case because these had already been revealed on the Internet, in social media, and in certain publications in Scotland

and abroad. In Lord Mance's view, which distinctly echoes that of Mr Justice Eady in the Mosley case mentioned earlier, this

> did not give due weight to the qualitative difference in intrusiveness and distress likely to be involved in what is now proposed by way of unrestricted publication by the English media in hard copy as well as on their own internet sites. There is little doubt that there would be a media storm. It would involve not merely disclosure of names and generalised description of the nature of the sexual activities involved, but the most intimate details. This would be likely to add greatly and on a potentially enduring basis to the intrusiveness and distress felt by the appellant, his partner and, by way of increased media attention now and/or in the future, their children.

As distinct from the law of confidence, the law of privacy both protects the confidentiality of private information and protects against intrusion into private lives. In this respect, Lord Mance quoted Mr Justice Eady in *CTB v News Group Newspapers* (2011) to the effect that 'it is important always to remember that the modern law of privacy is not concerned solely with information or "secrets": it is also concerned importantly with intrusion [... That] also largely explains why it is the case that the truth or falsity of the allegations in question can often be irrelevant'.[13]

In the High Court on Friday 4 November, Mr Justice Warby announced that PJS and News Group Newspapers had agreed a final order in the action for breach of confidence and misuse of private information. The proceedings were 'stayed' on the basis that NGN pay a 'specified sum' in full and final settlement of PJS's claim for damages and costs. NGN also agreed to give undertakings not to use, disclose or publish certain information and to remove and not republish certain existing articles. The undertakings also extended to not publishing any information which identified or was liable to identify PJS as a party to the action, including identifying his partner or three other individuals.

Conclusion

This is an extremely important judgement in that it renders insignificant the fact that information which the press wishes to publish in England is widely available elsewhere, with the consequence that a degree of confidentiality has already been lost. From a claimant's point of view, this decision underlines the considerable advantages of misuse of private information, as compared to breach of confidence, as a cause of action for seeking to restrain the publication of information. It thus demonstrates, once again, the importance of the Convention and the Human Rights Act in developing the common law in the areas of both confidentiality and privacy. That it has been met with howls of execration from a press which clearly longs to be able to compete on a level playing field with Internet gossip, thus debasing its journalistic standards yet further, is entirely predictable. But its all-out attacks on the judiciary, and its determination to push at the very outer limits of the laws of the land in its reporting of this and other similar stories, does give a particular urgency to the point made during the Supreme Court hearing by Desmond Browne, QC for PJS: 'The court needs to consider whether we are living in a country under the rule of law or under the rule of the press'.[14] It is also a sobering thought that press hostility to both the Convention and the Human Rights Act – on the grounds that they threaten to introduce privacy legislation 'by the back door', as newspapers habitually, and entirely inaccurately, put it – has undoubtedly been one of the key reasons why so many papers, all of the main privacy invaders among them, have campaigned so vociferously for over two decades for the UK to withdraw from the Convention and to abolish the Human Rights Act. Whether they will be as successful in this campaign as in that which contributed to Britain withdrawing from the EU remains to be seen.

Notes

1 http://www.worldlii.org/eu/cases/ECHR/1991/50.html
2 http://www.5rb.com/wp-content/uploads/2013/10/Re-S-HL-28-Sept-2004.pdf
3 http://www.bailii.org/ew/cases/EWHC/QB/2008/1777.html
4 http://www.bailii.org/uk/cases/UKHL/1988/6.html
5 http://www.hrcr.org/safrica/limitations/sunday_times_uk.html
6 http://www.5rb.com/wp-content/uploads/2013/10/Goodwin-v-United-Kingdom-ECHR-27-Mar-1996.pdf
7 https://www.theguardian.com/media/2009/dec/15/court-rules-interbrew-leaked-documents
8 http://www.bailii.org/eu/cases/ECHR/1986/7.html
9 https://www.article19.org/resources.php/resource/2308/en/castells-v.-spain
10 http://www.bailii.org/cgi-bin/markup.cgi?doc=/uk/cases/UKHL/1999/45.html
11 file://acfs4/pfsf/pfstjjp/My%20Documents/Human%20Rights/Case%20Jameel%20v.%20Wall%20Street%20Journal%20%202006.html
12 http://www.bailii.org/uk/cases/UKHL/2004/22.html
13 https://www.supremecourt.uk/cases/docs/uksc-2016-0080-judgment.pdf
14 https://www.theguardian.com/media/2016/apr/21/lifting-of-celebrity-threesome-injunction-would-be-devastating

References

Barendt, E., Bosland, J., Crauford-Smith, R. and Hitchens, L. (2014). *Media Law: Text, Cases and Materials*. Harlow: Pearson Education.
Caddell, R. and Johnson, H. (2013). *Blackstone's Statutes on Media Law*, 4th ed. Oxford: Oxford University Press.
Fenwick, H. and Phillipson, G. (2006). *Media Freedom under the Human Rights Act*. Oxford: Oxford University Press.
Mead, D. (2015). '"You Couldn't Make It Up"; Some Narratives of the Media's Coverage of Human Rights'. In: K. S. Ziegler, E. Wicks and L. Hodson, eds, *The UK and Human Rights: A Strained Relationship?* Oxford: Hart Publishing, pp. 453–72.
Petley, J. (2006). 'Podsnappery; or Why British Newspapers Support Fagging', *The International Journal of Communications Ethics*, 3(2/3), pp. 42–50.
Robertson, G. and Nicol, A. (2008). *Media Law*, 5th edn. London: Penguin.

9

HUMAN RIGHTS AND THE DIGITAL

Kari Karppinen

Introduction

Terms such as 'digital rights' and 'internet rights' now have a prominent place in political and academic debates around the world. While not so long ago it was possible to argue that the perspective of human rights had only received marginal attention in debates on the global information society (Drake & Jørgensen 2006, 5), it now seems that individual rights constitute a central normative framework for approaching policy issues related to new digital technologies and the Internet.

The calls for the protection of digital rights have resulted in a number of reports, projects and political declarations. The United Nations World Summit on Information Society (WSIS) process (2003–05) is often seen as the first global attempt to assert the status of human rights principles in the development and global governance of the information society. While views on its results in promoting human rights were mixed, in recent years the rhetoric of digital rights has gained even more prominence as several governments and international organizations have produced their own declarations on rights and freedoms in the digital age.[1] Digital rights have also become a prominent cause for political activism and civil society organizations both nationally and globally (e.g. APC 2006; IRPC 2015; Padovani & Calabrese 2014).

Declarations alone do not mean that human rights are realized in practice or that current communication and information policies would actually be guided by human rights consideration any more than before. The prominence of rights may also reflect the perception that human rights are increasingly threatened in the digital era, as continuing concerns over new architectures of control and revelations of widespread surveillance practices online imply.

Few would deny that the political and regulatory choices related to digital technologies have profound impacts on freedom of expression, access to information, privacy and a range of other human rights related to development, culture and social equality among other areas (for different perspectives, see e.g. Akrivopoulou & Garipidis 2012; Jørgensen 2006; Klang & Murray 2005). There are a range of concrete policy and legal issues that currently raise human rights concerns related to issues, such as net neutrality, copyright and piracy, surveillance and privacy, data protection and content filtering. Aside from specific legal issues, human rights principles also bear upon broader concerns about the future development and governance of digital media, such as equal access to the Internet or the 'structural power' of dominant Internet platforms and corporations who increasingly control data flows (e.g. Horten 2016).

As a widely recognized and institutionalized normative framework, human rights clearly offer a useful normative basis for these debates. Yet current debates on digital rights do not constitute a unified approach to concrete policy problems. It can be argued that the digital transformation has only exacerbated disagreements about the meaning and interpretation of relevant rights, the means by which they can be realized, and how they should be balanced with other concerns, such as security or economic efficiency. The convergence of digital media across borders and industry sectors has challenged existing normative and regulatory frameworks in communication policy and introduced new issues, tensions and arenas of political contestation. Does the new digital environment then create a need for new human rights, and what kinds of institutions are needed to uphold and enforce these rights in the non-territorial, regulation-averse and rapidly changing digital environment?

Instead of focusing on individual regulatory issues or legal frameworks, this chapter takes a broader view of digital rights as emerging normative principles for the governance of digital communication environment. In this sense, the framework of digital rights is open to multiple narratives that reflect different political visions and interests. The chapter begins by first broadly outlining different perspectives from which the interface between human rights and new digital technologies can be approached. After that, the chapter reviews the evolution of digital rights discourses from the early emphasis on negative rights and the uncontrollable nature of digital technologies towards a broader agenda of digital rights and threats. Finally, the chapter highlights the variety of approaches to digital rights in academic research and in current digital rights activism. As the main thread, the chapter emphasizes that debates on digital rights do not consti-tute a fixed set of demands that can be ever fully settled or realized. Instead, the debates are can be seen as part of an ongoing process of negotiating and contesting the ethical frameworks and principles for the regulation of new digital technologies.

Human rights and the digital transformation: Four perspectives

The interface between human rights and the new digital technologies can be approached from diverse angles and at different levels, including philosophical debates, concrete legal and policy analyses, studies of social movements and activism, and a range of more specific themes related, for instance, to development, gender, child protection or cultural minorities' rights. Furthermore, rights can refer to existing formal, legally binding norms, but especially in non-legal discourses they are also used more broadly to refer to normative principles or ethical ideals, against which real-world developments are assessed (Mathiesen 2014). For the purposes of grasping the differ-ent of levels of debate, I highlight here four different perspectives in the digital rights debates.

The first, and perhaps dominant perspective, from which all new media technolo-gies have been discussed, concerns how digital technologies extend and challenge existing communication-related rights and freedoms, particularly freedom of expression. In both aca-demic debates and popular commentary, much has been written on how digital technologies boost freedom of communication and democracy by opening up new opportunities for self-expression and political participation for new voices (e.g. Benkler 2006; Castells 2009). Yet many critical scholars remind us how the same digital tools can also be used for censorship and surveillance, and new forms of communicative inequalities and concentrations of power (e.g. Curran, Freedman & Fenton 2013; McChesney 2013). Besides the vast attention given to the contentions between digital optimists and pessimists and their perspectives on the realisation of communicative rights and freedoms, new digital technologies have at least revitalised and re-politicised legal, political and philosophical debates on the meaning and interpretation of free speech and its regulatory implications.

The prominent debates on freedom of expression and privacy protection, however, cover only part of the broader international human rights agenda (see Drake & Jørgensen 2006, 5). Second, digital technologies have also been seen as an infrastructure for the realization and promotion of human rights more generally. As a 2011 United Nations Human Rights Council report notes, because of 'the transformative nature of the digital technologies' the access to these technologies and the ability to utilize them effectively should be seen as a 'an indispensable tool for globalising a range of human rights' (UNHRC 2011). Besides their obvious impact on freedom of expression, this perspective sees digital tools more broadly as tools that enable the promotion of broader human rights related goals, such as economic development, political participation, combating inequality and societal progress in general. The perspective of digital technologies' facilitative role has also raised the question of whether access to the Internet or other digital tools, should be seen as a human right in itself, which would create a positive obligation for states to ensure connectivity (De Hert & Kloza 2012). As Mathiesen (2014) argues, Internet access can be seen as a 'derived human right' that stems from more primary human rights, whose realization increasingly depends on access to the use digital technologies.

Thirdly, beyond the debate on Internet access as a human right, new technologies have generated demands of other, more specific new human rights. A good example is the right to data protection, including the ownership and fair use of personal data. Now protected in the EU Charter of Fundamental Rights, for instance, the right to data protection can be seen as a new right that branches off from established interpretations of privacy as an established human right. Another controversial example is 'the right to be forgotten', which allows individuals to ask for outdated or irrelevant information about them to be removed from search results. As with all other new human rights, it can be argued that the proliferation of new rights might lead to the inflation and fragmentation of the human rights framework (De Hert & Kloza 2012). However, the framework of human rights is historically not unchanging or locked, and as the current wave of Internet rights declarations indicate, new rights emerge in response to new contexts and challenges.

Finally, the interface between human rights and the digital environment can also be approached from the perspective of the regulatory regimes or institutions needed to uphold and enforce rights. Beyond their impact on public communication, the digital convergence and the globalization of information flows have influenced the capacity of states to implement policies designed to fulfil citizens' communication rights (e.g. Flew, Iosifides & Steemers 2016; Lunt & Livingstone 2012). The global and distributed nature of digital media networks thus raises questions of 'who has the authority and the ability to govern, and in response to what goals' (Mansell 2012, 171), and whether there a need for new global institutions or regulatory frameworks to enforce policies based on human rights principles (e.g. Mueller 2010; Brown & Marsden 2013). In the context of Internet governance, in particular, the new forms of global politics and transnational institutions are often discussed with terms such as 'multi-stakeholderism' or 'network governance', which seem to imply that the locus of regulation has fundamentally shifted from states, and treaties between states, towards non-state actors and different types of soft governance.

While these perspectives are by no means exhaustive, they illustrate the range of human rights issues that digital technologies raise. Beyond these different levels of analysis, I will now turn to discuss the question of against whom, or what threats, digital rights are typically claimed.

Negative and positive rights in the digital environment

The distinction between *negative* rights, which protect individuals from unjustified government interference, and *positive* rights, which oblige states to guarantee individuals some basic goods, provides one way to examine the underlying ideals of the digital rights debate.

Historically, the debates on free expression and human rights in the new digital environment have been dominated by a negative rights perspective. Both academic and early activist debates largely focused on opposing governments' attempts to impose laws and restrictions on free speech and privacy on the Internet, rather than focusing on the broader international human rights agenda and its issues, such as the rights to development, gender equality, non-discrimination or the right to take part in cultural life (see Drake & Jorgensen 2006, 5–6). As Ithiel de Sola Pool (1983, 10) argued in the early academic debates on new communication technologies, the question was 'whether the electronic resources for communications can be as free of public regulation in the future as the platform and printing press have been in the past', or 'whether that great achievement will become lost in the confusion about new technologies'.

A decade later, *A Declaration of the Independence of Cyberspace* by John Perry Barlow (1996) reflected the same ideas even more dramatically:

> Governments of the Industrial World, you weary giants of flesh and steel, I come from Cyberspace, the new home of Mind. On behalf of the future, I ask you of the past to leave us alone. You are not welcome among us. You have no sovereignty where we gather.
>
> We have no elected government, nor are we likely to have one, so I address you with no greater authority than that with which liberty itself always speaks. I declare the global social space we are building to be naturally independent of the tyrannies you seek to impose on us. You have no moral right to rule us nor do you possess any methods of enforcement we have true reason to fear.

This often heard libertarian utopia conceived new digital technologies as independent of the terrestrial political, economic and legal systems, and as a naturally egalitarian and uncontrollable space for the exchange of information and free communication (Kreiss 2015). The idea that governments should not interfere in the development of digital technologies because it inevitably stifles innovation, creativity and individual rights is still familiar in current policy debates (Mansell 2012; Kreiss 2015). On the other hand, the idea that digital media are somehow naturally beyond terrestrial politics and its methods of enforcement has lost much of its conviction in the last two decades. Few would now deny that new digital technologies are intimately entangled in economic power relations and governmental and regulatory structures. While this is certainly the case in authoritarian societies like China, the Snowden leaks and other revelations of mass-surveillance have increasingly revealed how states, often in cooperation with powerful corporations, aim to exert control also in western liberal democracies (e.g. Horten 2016; Lyon 2015).

The UNESCO report on the new ecology of freedom of expression concludes: 'The control of information on the Internet and Web is certainly feasible, and technological advances do not therefore guarantee greater freedom of speech' (Dutton et al. 2011, 40). Similarly the UN Human Rights Council (2011) has noted: 'States are increasingly censoring information online, namely through: arbitrary blocking or filtering of content; criminalisation of legitimate expression; imposition of intermediary liability; disconnecting users from Internet access, including on the basis of intellectual property rights law; cyberattacks; and inadequate protection of the right to privacy and data protection'. As another sign of increasing prominence of these concerns, the UNHRC appointed in 2015 a first special rapporteur on the right to privacy in the digital age.

Despite recurring predictions of the diminishing role of states in communication policy, national policies remain key factors that influence the development and use of digital media (Goldsmith & Wu 2006; Flew et al. 2016). On the one hand, this points to the continued relevance of a negative rights perspective, and the basic function of human rights to vertically shield individuals against abuses of power by states. On the other hand, the exclusive focus on government censorship ignores how commercial and other types of power relations can also constrain digital rights and freedoms.

As Horten (2016) among others describes, a small number of large companies have 'structural power' to shape access to information in the digital realm. A select few search engines and content platforms, and their algorithms determine what we can do, with abilities to track user behaviour, control personal data, and give preference to or even block specific contents. These new algorithmic architectures of control, or 'regulation by code' (Lessig 1999), now raise a broad range of human rights concerns over freedom of expression, privacy and other potential forms of discrimination and manipulation. As a consequence, the assumption that free expression and other human rights exist if there is no government intervention is a very narrow way to approach the interface between human rights and digital media (see Kenyon 2014).

In contrast to the early rhetoric that emphasized freedom from the state, in current policy debates around copyright and access to knowledge, net neutrality and data protection, for instance, the choice is usually not between regulation and no regulation at all. In contrast to the imaginary of an uncontrollable virtual space, digital media are regulated all the time, although not always in a democratically accountable way, and they are intimately related to 'terrestrial' economic and political power structures (e.g. Braman 2009; Goldsmith & Wu 2006). Instead of a choice between freedom and non-freedom, digital policies are about conflicts between different interests and aims, and different modes of regulation promoting different values.

From a positive rights perspective, regulation is not seen only as an obstacle to the realization of human rights. Instead, it can be argued that the realization of human rights, broadly understood, creates obligations for policymakers to promote equality of access, limit the concentration of power in the hands of few, place restrictions on commercial forms of surveillance and censorship, and to create other means to protect vulnerable and weak online.

The perspective of positive rights thus presents a more complex discourse of digital rights as a counterbalance to the new inequalities and forms of control and domination in the digital environment. Instead of a dichotomy between individual rights and government control, human-rights-based policies are increasingly seen as an alternative to industrial control and a more closed, market-led, ecosystems. In both academic and activist digital rights discourses, such non-state threats to digital rights include the commodification of communication, the creation of new oligopolies, and other forces that may create or exacerbate social and cultural inequalities (Curran, Freedman & Fenton 2013; Fuchs 2013; Horten 2016; McChesney 2013).

In terms of freedom of expression, the positive rights approach thus emphasizes the structural preconditions for citizens' equal and effective use of public speech. Furthermore, the second and third generation human rights, such as the right to development or the right to participation in cultural life, relate even more clearly to equal conditions and opportunities to take advantage of digital tools (Jørgensen 2013). Instead of non-intervention, they raise the questions of the regulatory and institutional arrangements needed to actually protect and fulfil these rights (Mathiesen 2014).

In terms of this wider understanding of human rights, non-interference and the legal protection of individuals' negative rights are not sufficient to maintain realization of human rights. Instead, as Mansell (2012) argues, the anti-regulatory imaginary inherited from the early debates on Internet freedom has actually favoured established power structures and enabled the continuing concentration of power in the digital media.

Paradigms and politics of digital rights

Despite claims of how new technologies intrinsically either expand or threaten human rights, these dangers and opportunities do not emerge independently of politics and regulation.

As McChesney (2013, 99) notes, the entire realm of digital communications largely resulted from state intervention and government-subsidized research, and even the lack of intervention in its development is a political decision. The different narratives associated with digital rights thus involve different political assumptions with complex implications for regulation and policy.

Much has been written on how new digital technologies and uses have disrupted existing frameworks and paradigms of media and communication policy. In the converged digital environment, distinct normative and regulatory traditions associated with previously separate media (print, broadcasting, telecommunications) have clashed, and as Duff (2012, 6) argues, the information society has inherited 'a baggage of discordant normative traditions' – and a need for a new and rigorous normative debate on values and principles that public policies should be based on. Van Cuilenburg and McQuail (2003) speak of an emerging 'new communications policy paradigm', which is to reflect entirely 'new political ideas and social values'. Similarly, Mansell (2012, 4) argues that the dominant imaginaries of the Internet as an uncontrollable or market-driven space, controlled by corporations and software engineers, has led to paralysis of regulatory imaginaries and a need for new imaginaries to 'guide the evolution of the communication system along a pathway that is more consistent with aspirations for the good society'.

While human rights clearly provide a normative basis for these debates, the perspective of rights itself can be associated with several different normative frameworks. Jørgensen (2013) argues that debates on human rights challenges in the context of the Internet and information society involve different framings which highlight different human rights aspects: The infrastructure dimension focuses on the Internet as a global resource that enables communication; the public sphere perspective highlights the Internet as a public space for democratic participation; the media dimension draws attention to the Internet as a new media platform, and to its differences with conventional media; and finally the cultural dimension focuses on the social norms and practices of the Internet.

In the academic literature, several scholars have approached the new digital policy problems from the normative perspective of the public sphere and democratic participation (Dahlberg 2011; Lunt & Livingstone 2012). Others have approached the same problems from a distributive justice perspective, emphasising the importance of equal access and the fair distribution of information resources (Duff 2012; Schejter & Tirosh 2015). Yet another perspective, especially pertinent in the debates on digital technologies and development (e.g. Kleine 2014), is provided by the 'capabilities' approach to human rights, and its focus on the real communicative opportunities that people enjoy and the structural preconditions that they entail. All of these approaches employ the framework of human rights, yet they frame the normative questions differently and focus on different aspects of freedom, equality and rights in the digital era.

Besides academic debates, a growing range of social movements and digital activism groups have framed their aims and activities in the language of human rights. These movements do not share a fixed conception of digital rights but cover various positions and ideologies.

The spectrum of these movements includes established human rights organizations, such as Amnesty International or Human Rights Watch; more specifically digital rights and information-policy-oriented organizations like the Electronic Frontier Foundation or the Internet Rights and Principles Coalition; and even new political parties like the Pirate Parties in different countries. Much of the digital-rights groups' work still reflects the ideals of the early cyberliberties movements, which largely mobilized against rights violations by governments around the world (Drake & Jorgensen 2006; Dahlberg 2011). On the other hand, newer digital rights movements, such as the Pirate Parties born in Northern Europe, have adopted a different type of thinking, which combines cyberlibertarian ideals with 'cultural environmentalism' and the notion of 'commons' to defend Internet culture against both corporate and state colonization (Burkart 2014).

Yet other strands of communication rights activism focus more on the democratic and participatory aims associated with digital technology. The Communication Rights in the Information Society (CRIS) Campaign, for example, which mobilized a range of civil society organizations around the WSIS process in the early 2000s, defended a broader conception of 'communication rights', which included not only negative freedoms but also positive rights of individuals to access and effectively deploy information and knowledge to promote democratic participation and the diversity of cultures and identities online (Alegre & Ó Siochru 2005; Mueller et al. 2007).

Various groups and movements with less organisational unity and more free-form activities and causes, such as Wikileaks, Anonymous and even individual hacktivists, have emerged to defend human rights and freedom of information against various forms of restrictions in the digital world (Beyer 2014; Brevini et al. 2013). Many of these have been seen as disruptive forces, which bring attention to a range of injustices and political issues, without necessarily following any specific political program or manifesto. While all of these groups claim to promote human rights, there is also criticism of their activities. Sorell (2015, 7), for example, criticises the means and forms of Wikileaks and Anonymous for their lack of transparency, arbitrary selection of causes and their lack of concern for the rights of their 'targets', which can make their activities even 'subversive of central tenets of human rights'.

Rather than a specific framework or a paradigm, digital rights can thus be understood as a broad umbrella framing for a host of normative ideals. Beyond their status as existing legal obligations, rights can be articulated with a variety of framings and associations employed by different actors for different purposes. From this perspective, one crucial challenge for research on human rights and in the digital context is to clarify the concrete policy and practical implications of these different alternative visions.

Conclusions

Instead of focusing on human rights as an institutionalized legal framework, this chapter has focused more on debates on digital rights as expressions of different political and ideological visions and interests. The emphasis on the contested nature of rights does not mean to understate the importance of human rights as an established, legally defined and internationally recognized framework that can be invoked to challenge state and commercial surveillance, digital censorship and various other forms of discrimination and rights violations. As a counterforce to other interests that drive the development of digital policies, such as state security, surveillance and corporate influence, upholding human rights principles as existing legal norms is clearly a central task for policymakers and researchers.

Beyond this task, however, human rights also have another role in providing a long-term normative vision for the information and communication policies that are taking shape. In this broader meaning, the current academic and political debates on digital rights and their meaning are about negotiating and contesting the values and principles that guide future policies. This is no different from older media, where questions about the meaning and realization of communication rights, and whether policymakers should refrain from intervention or actively promote citizens' rights to diverse information, are continually contested. In the digital context, the number of policy issues and their complexity has only increased, which means that the debates on 'digital rights' and their implications for regulation are not likely to be settled any time soon.

Note

1 At the international level, these include reports by the United Nations Human Rights Council, UNESCO, and even OECD and G8, as well as regional declarations, such as the African Declaration on Internet Rights and Freedoms and several European Union and the Council of Europe documents. At the national level much attention was given to the Brazilian Civil Rights Framework for the Internet (2014), and its provisions on net neutrality, privacy and freedom of expression online. Following the NSA spying scandal and Edward Snowden's leaks, similar documents have been prepared by countless other national and international bodies.

References

Akrivopoulou, C. and Garipidis, N., eds. (2012). *Human Rights and Risks in the Digital Era: Globalization and the Effects of Information Technologies*. Hershey, PA: IGI Global.

Alegre, A. and Ó Siochrú, S. (2005). 'Communication Rights'. In: A. Ambrosi, V. Peugeot and D. Pimienta, eds., *Word Matters. Multicultural Perspectives on Information Societies*. Caen: C&F Éditions, pp. 49–72.

APC, Association of Progressive Communication (2006). 'APC Internet Rights Charter'. Available at: https://www.apc.org/en/node/5677/ [Accessed 10 Apr. 2016]

Barlow, P. (1996). *A Declaration of the Independence of Cyberspace*. Available at: http://www.eff.org/cyberspace-independence[21 Apr. 2016]

Benkler, Y. (2006). *How Social Production Transforms Markets and Freedom*. New Haven and London: Yale University Press.

Beyer, J. L. (2014). 'The Emergence of a Freedom of Information Movement: Anonymous, WikiLeaks, the Pirate Party, and Iceland'. *Journal of Computer-Mediated Communication* 19(2), pp. 141–54.

Braman, S. (2009). *Change of State*. Cambridge, MA: MIT Press.

Brevini, B., Hintz, A. and McCurdy, P. (2013). *Beyond Wikileaks: Implications for the Future of Communications, Journalism and Society*. Basingstoke, UK: Palgrave.

Brown, I. and Marsden, C. (2012). *Regulating Code. Good Governance and Better Regulation in the Information Age*. Cambridge, MA: MIT Press.

Burkart, P. (2014). *Pirate Politics. The Information Policy Contests*. Cambridge, MA: MIT Press.

Castells, M. (2009). *Communication Power*. Oxford: Oxford University Press.

Curran, J, Fenton, N. and Freedman, D. (2013). *Misunderstanding the Internet*. London & New York: Routledge.

Dahlberg, L. (2011). 'Re-constructing Digital Democracy: An Outline of Four "Positions"'. *New Media & Society*, 13(6), pp. 855–72.

De Hert, P. and Kloza, D. (2012). 'Internet (access) as a New Fundamental Right. Inflating the Current Rights Framework?'. *European Journal of Law and Technology* 3(3). Available at: http://ejlt.org/article/view/123/268 [21 Apr. 2016]

Drake, W. J. and Jørgensen, R. F. (2006). 'Introduction'. In: R. F. Jørgensen, ed., *Human Rights in the Global Information Society*. Cambridge, MA: MIT Press, pp. 1–49.

Duff, A. (2012). *A Normative Theory of the Information Society*. New York: Routledge.

Dutton W. H., Dopatka, A., Law, G. and Nash, V. (2011). 'Freedom of Connection, Freedom of Expression: the Changing Legal and Regulatory Ecology Shaping the Internet'. *Division for Freedom of Expression, Democracy and Peace*. Paris: UNESCO.

Flew, T., Iosifides, P. and Steemers, J. eds. (2016). *Global Media and National Policies. The Return of the State*. Basingstoke, UK: Palgrave.

Fuchs, C. (2013). *Social Media: A Critical Introduction*. London, UK: Sage.

Goldsmith, J. and Wu, T. (2006). *Who Controls the Internet? Illusions of a Borderless World*. Oxford and New York: Oxford University Press.

Horten, M. (2016). *The Closing of the Net*. Cambridge: Polity Press.

IRPC, Internet Rights and Principles Coalition (2015). *The Charter of Human Rights and Principles for the Internet*. Available at: http://internetrightsandprinciples.org/site/charter/ [21 Apr. 2016]

Jørgensen, R. F., ed. (2006). *Human Rights in the Global Information Society*. Cambridge, MA: MIT Press.

Jørgensen, R. F. (2013). *Framing the Net. Human Rights and the Internet*. Cheltenham, UK: Edgar Elgar.

Kenyon, A. (2014). 'Assuming Free Speech'. *The Modern Law Review*, 77(3), pp. 379–408.

Klang, M. and Murray, A., eds. (2005). *Human Rights in the Digital Age*. London: Glasshouse Press.

Kleine, D. (2014). *Technologies of Choice? ICTs, Development, and the Capabilities Approach*. Cambridge: MIT Press.

Kreiss, D. (2015). 'A Vision of and for the Networked World. John Perry Barlow's A Declaration of Independence of Cyberspace at Twenty'. In: J. Bennett and N. Strange, eds., *Media Independence: Working with Freedom or Working for Free?* New York: Routledge, pp. 117–36.

Lessig, L. (1999). *Code: And Other Laws of Cyberspace*. New York: Basic Books.

Lunt, P. and S. Livingstone (2012). *Media Regulation: Governance and the Interests of Citizens and Consumers*. London: Sage.

Lyon, D. (2015). *Surveillance after Snowden*. Cambridge: Polity Press.

Mansell, R. (2012). *Imagining the Internet. Communication, Innovation, and Governance*. Oxford: Oxford University Press.

Mathiesen, K. (2014). 'Human Rights for the Digital Age'. *Journal of Mass Media Ethics*, 29(1), pp. 2–18.

McChesney, R. (2013). *Digital Disconnect: How Capitalism Is Turning the Internet Against Democracy*. New York: The New Press.

Mueller, M. L. (2010). *Networks and States. The Global Politics of Internet Governance*. Cambridge, MA: MIT Press.

Mueller, M. L, Kuerbis, B. and Pagé, C. M. (2007). 'Democratizing Global Communication. Global Civil Society and the Campaign for Communication Rights in the Information Society'. *International Journal of Communication*, 1, pp. 267–96.

Padovani, C. and Calabrese A., eds. (2014). *Communication Rights and Social Justice: Historical Accounts of Transnational Mobilizations*. Basingstoke, UK: Palgrave Macmillan.

Schejter, A. and Tirosh, N. (2015). '"Seek the Meek, Seek the Just": Social Media and Social Justice'. *Telecommunications Policy*, 39, pp. 796–803.

Sola Pool, I. (1983). *Technologies of Freedom*. Harvard, MA: Harvard University Press.

Sorell, T. (2015). 'Human Rights and Hacktivism. The Cases of Wikileaks and Anonymous'. *Journal of Human Rights Practice*, 7(3), pp. 391–410.

van Cuilenburg, J. and McQuail, D. (2003). 'Media Policy Paradigm Shifts: Towards a New Communications Policy Paradigm'. *European Journal of Communication* 18(2), pp. 181–207.

United Nations Human Rights Council (2011). 'Report of the Special Rapporteur on the Promotion and Protection of the Right to Freedom of Opinion and Expression'. Frank La Rue. Available at: http://www2.ohchr.org/english/bodies/hrcouncil/docs/17session/A.HRC.17.27_en.pdf [21 Apr. 2016]

10

CHILDREN'S RIGHTS IN THE DIGITAL AGE

Sonia Livingstone

In the couple of decades since Internet use has become commonplace in everyday life, especially in the global North, a growing body of research has examined the meanings, practices and consequences of people's engagement with an ever-new array of digital media. Within this context of social, technological and regulatory change, the position of children has been sometimes prominent – with them being celebrated as creative pioneers of the digital age or worried about for their vulnerability. But mostly they are rendered invisible, the discursive blurring of 'the population' with 'adults' obscuring the specific conditions, concerns and rights of children in the digital age. The age-blind nature of most academic and policy discourses on media and human rights parallels their neglect of gender, ethnicity, disability, religion or region yet it generates little sense of injustice or effort towards redress.

Children constitute an estimated one-third of the world's population, and, significantly, one-third of the world's Internet users (Livingstone, Carr & Byrne 2015).[1] In the global North, long the locus of debates over the Internet and rights, four in five people are online but only around one in five people are under 18, making for many more adults than children online. But the global North constitutes only around one-sixth of the world's population, and we have reached a crucial tipping point: Two-thirds of the world's nearly 3 billion Internet users live in the global South, where at least one third of the population is under 18, and that's where the next billion Internet users live too. Moreover, as society increasingly embeds digital networks and services into its fundamental infrastructure, the rights of non-users in a digital age also matter.

To understand how children's rights in particular are being reconfigured in and through digital networks and services, we must address a series of problems and paradoxes. This chapter examines these in order to evaluate current research, policy and practice in relation to children's rights in the digital age. I argue that to understand children's rights in the digital age, it is time to adopt a more global focus, and to understand the rights of Internet users globally it is time to include a child-centred focus.

Definitional challenges – child, rights, digital

In this chapter I will use the following definitions, while recognising their complexities:

1. By 'child', I follow the United Nations (UN) Convention on the Rights of the Child (CRC) in defining 'a "child" as a person below the age of 18, unless the laws of a particular country set the legal age for adulthood younger' (UN 1989; see also Holzscheiter 2010). This upper limit can be contentious in countries where the legal age for marriage or sexual consent is much lower than 18, or when society (often via parents) seeks to protect teenagers from certain forms of sexual, identity or political expression. While the lower age limit (birth) is not generally controversial, as the age of first Internet use drops, the challenge grows of supporting the rights of those too young to exercise informed and digitally literate decision making in an (online) ecology largely designed for adults.

2. By 'rights', my focus is on fundamental human rights as these apply to everybody. I take the UN CRC as my framework, since (a) it spells out that human rights (e.g. to freedom of expression, assembly and privacy) also apply to children, a point commonly overlooked; (b) it calls for specific child-focused mechanisms to ensure that these rights are respected and not infringed (over and above those human rights instruments designed primarily for adults who can, for instance, bear full responsibility for their actions or seek independent redress); and (c) it includes rights that apply especially or only to children (such as the right to development, play and a caring upbringing). Note that the CRC is addressed primarily to states, notwithstanding that these already struggle to underpin rights in relation to the transnationally networked and heavily commercial Internet.

3. In focusing on 'the digital,' the point is not to endorse a technologically determinist account of social change; after all, digital media have been invented, designed, produced, marketed and appropriated by people (Lievrouw and Livingstone 2006). Nor is it to claim that society is radically transformed by the digital, bearing no relation to previous periods. Nor even that the digital constitutes the most important change in today's society. Rather, what matters here is the recognition that society is becoming dependent on interactive, networked, remixable and ubiquitous media, as once-optional technologies used by the privileged few become part of the taken-for-granted infrastructure for all levels of society, from the domestic to the global (Star and Bowker 2006).

With these definitions in mind, this chapter asks: Is the digital ecology reconfiguring children's rights and if so, how, and with what implications?

Scoping children's rights in the digital age

A good place to begin is with children's views, since recognition of children's voices on matters that affect them is central to the CRC. A recent multinational consultation with children showed that they are now convinced of an indelible and positive connection between their rights and the Internet (Third et al. 2014). Their reasoning can be summarised in four points:

1. The Internet and mobile technologies are becoming a key means by which children exercise their rights to information, education and participation.

2. Consequently, access to the Internet and mobile technologies must also be a basic right, a view endorsed by the UN in 2011 (UN General Assembly 2011).

3. Since access is insufficient without media or digital literacy, that too is now fundamental to exercising rights in a digital age.

4. Children expect their voices to be heard in formal and informal processes of deliberation wherever their rights in a digital age are at stake, including in relation to Internet governance (Nordic Youth Forum 2012).

For researchers, this opens up a fascinating new agenda that demands new theory, methods and findings (see Cortesi and Gasser 2014; Livingstone and Bulger 2014; van der Hof, van den Berg & Schermer 2014). But for stakeholders concerned with children's rights and/or Internet provision and governance, this sets out a problematic agenda new to both sides. Notwithstanding that both the World Wide Web and the UN CRC celebrated their quarter centuries in 2014, many of the key organisations involved (e.g. Council of Europe, UN Committee on the Rights of the Child, Internet Governance Forum) are only now taking steps to address children's rights in the digital age.

The task ahead is challenging. From a child rights point of view, despite considerable optimism over what the Internet could offer children, there are concerns that children use online services not targeted toward them, or where site or service providers are unaware of or negligent of their status as minors. Children's data are collected and often sold without informed consent and irrespective of child protection issues or child-friendly mechanisms for redress (Montgomery & Chester 2015). Insofar as children's informational and educational needs are increasingly provided online, stakeholders (states, welfare services, educators, parents) find themselves relying on commercial services providers that deny specific obligations to children, while children may find that vital services are inaccessible to them for reasons of cost or child protection filters (CRIN 2014). Absorbing most attention are sexual risks including exploitation and abuse, themselves longstanding problems offline but now increasingly mediated and possibly amplified by the affordances (anonymity, convenience, connectivity, etc.) of the Internet (Palmer 2015).

These challenges concern matters of principle and practice, and I will focus on four – the problem of ensuring rights online as well as offline, of prioritising among potentially clashing rights, of distinguishing opportunities from risks and of identifying 'the best interests of the child'.

The problem of ensuring rights online as well as offline

Although it is readily proclaimed that rights offline are equally rights online (see e.g. NETmundial 2014), this is difficult in practice to conceptualise or implement. Consider that though human rights frameworks are age-generic, the CRC ensures they apply to children, but while it may be argued that Internet provision and governance also operates in an age-generic way, there is no equivalent of the CRC to ensure it works for children (which, as the Committee on the Rights of the Child recently observed [2014], it does not). Several notable problems exist. One is the problem of age verification: There is, at present, no satisfactory way of knowing who is a child or an adult online (nor, for an Internet content or service provider, is there a reliable way of matching a child to a parent able to give consent on their behalf). Some providers (e.g. Disney) have tried expensive mechanisms, while more (e.g. Facebook) have tried cheaper, but ineffective mechanisms, and most do not try at all (see Montgomery & Chester 2015).

This takes us to the second problem. Children's rights have traditionally been guaranteed by public bodies – think not only of education, health and welfare systems, but also of the town planners who arrange traffic and zoning rules partly to empower and protect children. But the implementation of online rights benefits from few such powerful mediators in 'cyberspace'. Instead, this relies either on formal legislation (often seen to be too heavy-handed or dated given the pace of technological innovation) or on the social responsibility or self-regulation of those powerful corporations whose commercial services increasingly underpin children's communication, play, learning – and even their exploitation and abuse – in ways that are historically unprecedented. In consequence, it is proving difficult to treat children according to 'their best interests' (as the CRC requires, and as some guidelines seek to ensure; see Rutgers 2014).

The third problem is that, since the Internet is a fundamentally global network, the responsibilities of the state for child rights are increasingly mediated by a system that escapes national jurisdiction, again, to a historically unprecedented degree. Indeed, arguing that the Internet is too fast-changing, too international and too complex, states are now outsourcing their responsibilities for child rights (and rights more generally) to a fragile mix of good practice guidelines, haphazard self-regulation, sporadic efforts towards corporate social responsibility and multinational, multi-stakeholder fora (van der Hof et al. 2014).

The problem of prioritising among potentially clashing rights

The articles of the CRC are commonly classified in terms of the '3 P's':

1. Rights to protection concern the wide array of threats to children's dignity, survival and development. In the digital age, policy makers should attend to research showing the extent of sexual grooming and sexual exploitation of children online, the creation and distribution of child abuse images, the availability of (diverse, extreme) pornography, and new threats to privacy, identity and reputation posed by personal data exploitation, misuse, tracking by companies, and hostility, hate, bullying and self-harm-related content and conduct from other people online.
2. Rights to provision concern the resources necessary for children's survival and their development to their full potential. In the digital age, consider the development and provision of online formal and informal learning resources and curricula, on children's use of the wealth of accessible and specialised information along with education to support the digital literacies to use them well and more casual opportunities for creativity, exploration and entertainment as well as some distinctive provision of content that represents (minority) children's culture and heritage.
3. Rights to participation enable children to engage with processes that affect their development and enable them to play an active part in society. In the digital age, policy makers can draw on research on the use of children's peer-to-peer connections for sharing, networking and collaboration, including the development of user-friendly fora for child/youth voice and expression and child-led initiatives for local and global change.

Stakeholders often turn to research to figure out how to maximise children's online opportunities for provision and participation while minimising the risks that merit protection. And as indicated previously, both research and policy are developing the underpinning to support these three categories of child rights. But as yet, no robust way has been found to deal with the not-infrequent clash of competing rights – most often between rights to protection and participation.

As the work of the EU Kids Online network has shown, online risks and opportunities are positively correlated (Livingstone, Haddon & Görzig 2012). This means that efforts to keep children safe online tend to restrict their freedoms, while efforts to promote their freedoms – to explore the Web, to make new friends, to get involved in wider networks – bring more risks. In a simple sense, this is obvious: The more we act in the world the more we have good and bad experiences, and using the Internet is no different. Indeed, we can sum up a lot of the available research in the idea of the more, the more: The more children go online, the more they do there, the more they gain digital skills, the more online opportunities they enjoy – and the more risk of harm they encounter too.

It is thus the case that the more effort is put into maximising the opportunities of children's Internet use, the harder it is also to minimise the risks and vice versa, thereby putting policy for protection at odds with policy for provision and participation. The 2016 draft General Data Protection Directive from the European Commission provided recent illustration of this problem, when it became public that setting the age for verifiable parental consent at 16 directly prioritised child protection (against data exploitation) at the cost of child participation (on social networks etc. from the age of 13). It seems this occurred without recourse to evidence, impact assessment or a process of consultation with children or relevant child rights organisations.

The problem of distinguishing opportunities over risks

Adding to the difficulty of prioritising among potentially clashing rights is the challenge even of distinguishing them. Consider the arguments over 'sexting', where some teenagers have been criminalised for what they and others would consider legitimate sexual expression, as part of an equally vital effort to protect children from being groomed and exploited (Salter, Crofts & Lee 2013).

Online activities can be particularly ambiguous in terms of whether they turn out to be opportunities or risk. Adults do not always see eye to eye with children about what counts as a risk or an opportunity online, and they have little tradition to guide them. Meanwhile, children – often interested in transgressive or 'risky opportunities' – are particularly likely to pursue these online, especially insofar as risk-averse societies restrict their offline freedoms. Further, children's online activities depend in part on the design of the interface, and the Internet is primarily designed to facilitate usage irrespective of beneficial or harmful outcomes; social networks facilitate new contacts whether helpmates or paedophiles; search engines suggest new sites whether constructive or pernicious; and so on.

It can even be argued that some degree of risk is itself beneficial, building resilience in children. Here it is pertinent that most research is about risk but not about harm – for instance, studies tend to measure exposure to pornography rather than any actual or long-term harm that may result from such exposure (Livingstone 2013). Indeed, while we know that some risk results in some harm for some children, we do not yet know enough about when and for whom this happens, nor about when some exposure to risk can have positive results. Moreover, just as some exposure to risk may build resilience, it is also possible that some exposure to opportunity can have negative results. Consider the problems of the 'one laptop per child' initiative, along with the many others that provide children with mobile devices or Western information resources with little grasp of how these may undermine or disrupt local hierarchies or traditions (Kleine, Hollow, and Poveda 2014; World Bank 2016). Without considerable care in managing the contexts surrounding even well-intentioned interventions, benefits can prove elusive.

The problem of identifying 'the best interests of the child' online

The CRC asserts that children's voices should be heard 'in all matters that concern them' and that this should be implemented 'according to the evolving capacity of the child' and 'in the best interests of the child'. But just what is in the best interests of the child, and what is their capacity to influence decisions that affect them? These are questions on which research as well as policy is divided and contested. So often the decision is conservative, risk-averse, tending to favour protection over participation. Hence in the global North at least, restrictive approaches to children's Internet use in homes and schools are dominant (O'Neill et al. 2013). To be sure, in public fora, there are interesting experiments inviting even relatively young children to participate and express their views meaningfully. But research also shows that in practice, it is often only the already advantaged who gain such opportunities, and that opportunities for expression and voice are often ineffective and unheard (Lansdown 2014).

The question of participation, especially on a global scale, also points to a more general problem with child rights frameworks. Child rights, like all statements of fundamental rights, are couched in a universal language. This brings considerable rhetorical and normative/legal advantages for policy and practice within and across countries. But children's lives are profoundly shaped by particular, cultural contexts and their meaning is grounded locally. The application of a universal framework in particular contexts can, at the extreme, make rights into wrongs – this representing another paradox – with outsiders trumpeting foreign values as they trample on local meanings and misinterpret or disrupt established community practices, at least in their unintended if not intended consequences (Hanson 2014). The assumption of a universalising framework comes under especial fire when it embodies Western values yet is applied (or imposed) in the global South. Advocating for children's right to express their sexual identity online, or facilitating children's voice and agency when this clashes with familial or community traditions, can pose especially acute problems if local contexts are not well understood or local agencies and institutions are not carefully engaged in mutual dialogue (Kleine, Hollow & Poveda 2014).[2]

Let me refer to Isaiah Berlin's (1958) classic distinction between positive and negative freedoms to focus the problem. Children's protection rights represent a case of negative freedom – for example, that children should be free from sexual or violent abuse. Negative freedoms are usually less controversial than positive ones, because they seek to remove harms according to a minimalist approach to rights. But children's provision (and, in fact, participation rights) represents claims for positive freedom. And these can be controversial because they tend to assert a maximalist vision – often implicitly normative, Western, capitalist – of what the good life could or should be. So, the right to education (or play or identity or culture) is easily asserted, but who are we to assert that children should live not only without fear of harm but according to a late-modern vision of participatory democracy or a Western capitalist vision of learning for the information economy?

Thinking ahead

Over a decade ago, the 2003 phase of the World Summit on the Information Society (WSIS 2003) process culminated in the adoption of the Geneva Declaration of Principles and Plan of Action, in which the position of children was expressly recognised:

> We are committed to realizing our common vision of the Information Society for ourselves and for future generations. We recognize that young people are the future workforce and leading creators and earliest adopters of ICTs [information and tele-communications technologies]. They must therefore be empowered as learners, developers, contributors, entrepreneurs and decision-makers. We must focus especially on young people who have not yet been able to benefit fully from the opportunities provided by ICTs. We are also committed to ensuring that the development of ICT applications and operation of services respects the rights of children as well as their protection and well-being.

But since then, although children's Internet use has been widely celebrated, worried about and planned for, it would be hard to claim that much progress has been made in relation to children's rights in the digital age. In this chapter I have identified several problems that contribute to and help account for this unsatisfactory state of affairs.

Some readers will protest that these problems matter little since children are first and foremost the responsibility of their parents who surely act to enable and protect their rights, online as well as offline. In many cases, this is fair and indeed, asserted by the CRC (Articles 3 and 18). But here arise yet more problems. Many parents lack the awareness, competence, will, time and resources or the understanding, to protect and empower their children online. And the less parents are themselves digitally literate, the more they tend to restrict rather than empower their children online. Then, especially in the global South, where most Internet users now live, it cannot be safely assumed that children have the benefit of parents or adequate schooling (Livingstone & Byrne 2015). Last, among the children whose rights are most infringed, parents can be as much part of the problem as the solution (Finkelhor et al. 2015). So paradoxically, parents can be good representatives for happy well-resourced children but they can be poor representatives for the children who most need representation. For all these reasons, the CRC calls on states and the expert welfare and legal bodies they appoint to act on their behalf to provide special assistance and protection to the child when parents do not or cannot fulfil their responsibilities.

In responding to this call, it matters that child rights and adult rights online have become discursively entangled so that each seems to threaten to undermine the other. Notably, some institutional and regulatory efforts to protect children from sexual or violent offences online have – deliberately or inadvertently – been used by censorious or surveillant governments to curtail or infringe (adult) rights to freedom of expression (La Rue 2014). So, given justified concern about adult expression and privacy rights online, children have been discursively positioned as a hindrance to adult rights online, with advocates for (adult) Internet rights and freedoms often reluctant to acknowledge children's rights to either protection or participation (Livingstone 2011). It is thus unsurprising yet disappointing that in the burgeoning array of Internet bills of rights being proposed nationally and internationally, children's rights figure little if at all, especially in terms other than protection from illegal abuse (for a review, see Weber 2015).

In short, it appears that when rights clash, policy makers, academics and the public appear tacitly to agree that child protection should trump child participation and that adult freedom of expression should trump both. Consequently, although providing for children online and encouraging their participation might seem straightforwardly positive goals, in practice it remains more straightforward to argue for addressing children's (negative) rights to protection than to support their positive rights online. This situation is not helped by the fact that, it appears, few policy makers can convincingly elaborate just what would constitute great opportunities and provision for children online. Possibly, as argued in relation to positive and negative freedoms, they sense that to articulate a positive vision would somehow overstep the mark into maximalist prescriptions that impose 'our' values on 'others'? But while a minimalist approach may be politically circumspect, any resulting vacuum in the digital imaginary (Mansell 2012) will be filled by a market rather than by those acting primarily in children's best interests.

Emerging now on the horizon, as researchers and policy makers begin to think about the coming agenda in terms of the Internet of Things, smart homes and schools, and big data (Foucault Welles 2016), as further conceptual challenges. Most notably, it is timely to consider whether the design, regulation and use of digital technologies is beginning to reconfigure the very nature of child rights. Some digital media scholars are rethinking the core phenomena (abuse, privacy, identity, expression, education) of human rights frameworks in the digital age (see e.g. Cohen 2014). From new concepts to new 'digital rights' (as in 'the right to be forgotten';

Schillings 2015), to asking whether human rights legislation itself needs to be revised, opens up a hazardous path where, according to the law of unintended consequences, the losses may exceed the gains. It may be better to argue, more conservatively, that while the phenomena are always changing, the concepts embedded in legal frameworks are sufficiently abstract as to encompass these changes. This is to say, for instance, what is at stake is not so much new rights (to, say, digital identity or e-learning or protection from online abuse) but, rather, the (long-established) rights to identity or education or freedom from abuse, albeit now differently instantiated and regulated in a digital age. Whether or not I am right in this view, addressing the coming agenda will, I have argued, require a truly global process of dialogue and deliberation, and this dialogue must include children's voices and experiences too.

Notes

1   According to UNICEF (2014), nearly one-third (30%) of the world's population is aged under 18: this figure is lower in the global North and higher in the least developed countries. According to the International Telecommunications Union (ITU, 2015), over one-third (43%) of the world's population is online. In Livingstone et al. (2015), noting first that no reliable statistics exist on the proportion of Internet users aged under 18, we analysed such ITU data as exists to infer that children worldwide go online in a similar proportion to adults (albeit less at the younger and more at the older end of the age span 0–17). On this basis we estimate that one in three children are now online, and that one in three Internet users is a child.
2   The same may be said for research, insofar as it is tempting to sit in the global North designing research for the global South. Instead, we need a partnership approach for cross-national research, marrying rigorous research methods with dialogue to understand and respond to local circumstances and, as a result, a welcome widening of the evidence base (Livingstone and Bulger 2014).

References

Berlin, I. (1958). *Two Concepts of Liberty: An Inaugural Lecture Delivered Before the University of Oxford on 31 October 1958*. Oxford: Clarendon Press.
Cohen, J. E. (2014). *Configuring the Networked Self: Law, Code and the Play of Everyday Practice*. New Haven, CT: Yale University Press.
Committee on the Rights of the Child (2014). *Report of the 2014 Day of General Discussion on 'Digital Media and Children's Rights'*. Office of the United Nations High Commissioner for Human Rights. Available at: www.ohchr.org/Documents/HRBodies/CRC/Discussions/2014/DGD_report.pdf
Cortesi, S. and Gasser U. eds. (2014). *Digitally Connected: Global Perspectives on Youth and Digital Media*. Cambridge, MA: Berkman Centre for Internet and Society, Harvard University. Available at: http://papers.ssrn.com/sol3/papers.cfm?abstract_id=2585686
CRIN (Child Rights International Network) (2014). *Access Denied: Protect Rights—Unblock Children's Access to Information*. Available at: www.crin.org/sites/default/files/access_to_information_final_layout.pdf
Finkelhor, D., Turner, H. A., Shattuck, A. and Hamby, S. L. (2015). 'Prevalence of Childhood Exposure to Violence, Crime, and Abuse'. *JAMA Pediatrics*, 169, p. 746.
Foucault Welles, B. (2016). 'Computational CAM: Studying Children and Media in the Age of Big Data'. *Journal of Children and Media*, 10, pp. 72–80.
Hanson, K. (2014). '"Killed by Charity" – Towards Interdisciplinary Children's Rights Studies.' *Childhood*, 21(4), pp. 441–446.
Holzscheiter, H. (2010). *Children's Rights in International Politics: The Transformative Power of Discourse*. Basingstoke: Palgrave Macmillan.
ITU (International Telecommunications Union) (2015). *Measuring the Information Society Report*. Geneva, Switzerland: ITU. Available at: http://www.itu.int/en/ITU-D/Statistics/Documents/publications/misr2015/MISR2015-w5.pdf
Kleine, D., Hollow, D. and Poveda, S. (2014). *Children, ICT and Development: Capturing the Potential, Meeting the Challenges*. Florence: UNICEF Office of Research-Innocenti. Available at: http://www.unicef-irc.org/publications/715

Lansdown, G. (2014). '25 Years of UNCRC: Lessons Learned in Children's Participation'. *Canadian Journal of Children's Rights*, 1, pp. 172–190.

La Rue, F. (2014). *Report of the Special Rapporteur on the Promotion and Protection of the Right to Freedom of Opinion and Expression*, A/69/335. New York: United Nations General Assembly. Available at: http://www2.ohchr.org/english/bodies/hrcouncil/docs/17session/A.HRC.17.27_en.pdf

Lievrouw, L. and Livingstone, S. eds. (2006). *Handbook of New Media: Social Shaping and Social Consequences*. London: Sage.

Livingstone, S. (2011). 'Regulating the Internet in the Interests of Children: Emerging European and International Approaches'. In: R. Mansell and M. Raboy, eds., *The Handbook on Global Media and Communication Policy*. Oxford: Blackwell, pp. 505–524. Available at: http://eprints.lse.ac.uk/44962/

Livingstone, S. (2013). 'Online Risk, Harm and Vulnerability: Reflections on the Evidence Base for Child Internet Safety Policy'. *ZER: Journal of Communication Studies*, 18, pp. 13–28. Available at: http://www.ehu.eus/zer/hemeroteca/pdfs/zer35-01-livingstone.pdf

Livingstone, S. and Bulger, M. (2014). 'A Global Research Agenda for Children's Rights in the Digital Age'. *Journal of Children and Media*. doi:10.1080/17482798.2014.961496

Livingstone, S. and Byrne J. (2015). 'Challenges of Parental Responsibility in a Global Perspective'. In: U. Gasser, ed., *Digitally Connected: Global Perspectives on Youth and Digital Media*. Cambridge, MA: Berkman Center for Internet and Society, Harvard University, pp. 26–29.

Livingstone, S., Carr, J. and Byrne, J. (2015). 'One in Three: The Task for Global Internet Governance in Addressing Children's Rights'. *Global Commission on Internet Governance: Paper Series*. London: Centre for International Governance Innovation and Chatham House. Available at: https://www.cigionline.org/sites/default/files/no22_2.pdf

Livingstone, S., Haddon, L. and Görzig, E. eds. (2012). *Children, Risk and Safety Online: Research and Policy Challenges in Comparative Perspective*. Bristol: Policy Press.

Mansell, R. (2012). *Imagining the Internet: Communication, Innovation, and Governance*. Oxford: Oxford University Press.

Montgomery, K. C. and Chester, J. (2015). 'Data Protection for Youth in the Digital Age: Developing a Rights-based Global Framework'. *European Data Law Protection Review*, 1(4), pp. 277–291. Available at: http://edpl.lexxion.eu/article/EDPL/2015/4/6

NETmundial (2014). *NETmundial Multistakeholder Statement*. Available at: http://netmundial.br/netmundial-multistakeholder-statement/

Nordic Youth Forum (2012). *Youth Have Their Say on Internet Governance*. Gothenburg: Nordicom. http://www.nordicom.gu.se/en/publikationer/youth-have-their-say-Internet-governance

O'Neill, B., Staksrud, E. and McLaughlin, S. eds. (2013). *Children and Internet Safety in Europe: Policy Debates and Challenges*. Gothenburg, Sweden: Nordicom.

Palmer, T. (2015). *Digital Dangers: The Impact of Technology on the Sexual Abuse and Exploitation of Children and Young People*. Barkingside: Barnardo's. Available at: http://www.barnardos.org.uk/onlineshop/pdf/digital_dangers_report.pdf

Rutgers, C., ed. (2014). *Guidelines for Industry on Child Online Protection*. Geneva, Switzerland: International Telecommunications Union. Available at: www.itu.int/en/cop/Documents/bD_Broch_INDUSTRY_0909.pdf

Salter, M., Crofts, T. and Lee. M. (2013). 'Beyond Criminalisation and Responsibilisation: "Sexting," Gender and Young People'. *Current Issues in Criminal Justice*, 24, pp. 301–316.

Schillings (2015). *iRights – The Legal Framework*. London: Schillings. http://5rightsframework.com/resources.html

Star, L. and Bowker, G. (2006). 'How to Infrastructure'. In: L. Lievrouw and S. Livingstone, eds., *The Handbook of New Media* (Updated Student Edition). London: Sage, pp. 230–254.

Third, A., Bellerose, D., Dawkins, U., Keltie, E. and Pihl. K. (2014). *Children's Rights in the Digital Age: A Download from Children Around the World*. Melbourne: Young and Well Cooperative Research Centre. Available at: http://www.unicef.org/publications/index_76268.html

UNICEF (2014). *Every Child Counts*. New York: United Nations Children's Fund. Available at: www.unicef.org/sowc2014/numbers/

UN (United Nations) (1989). *Convention on the Rights of the Child*. Available at: www.ohchr.org/EN/ProfessionalInterest/Pages/CRC.aspx.

UN General Assembly (2011). *Report of the Special Rapporteur on the Promotion and Protection of the Right to Freedom of Opinion and Expression, Frank La Rue*. Human Rights Council, A/HRC/17/27. Available at: www2.ohchr.org/english/bodies/hrcouncil/docs/17session/A.HRC.17.27_en.pdf van der Hof, S., van den Berg, B. and Schermer, B. eds. (2014). *Minding Minors Wandering the Web: Regulating Online Child Safety*. Berlin: Springer.

Weber, R. H. (2015). 'Principles for Governing the Internet: A Comparative Analysis'. *UNESCO Series on Internet Freedom*. Paris: UNESCO. Available at: http://unesdoc.unesco.org/images/0023/002344/234435e.pdf

World Bank (2016). *World Development Report 2016: Digital Dividends*. Washington, DC: World Bank. Available at: http://www.worldbank.org/en/publication/wdr2016

WSIS (World Summit on the Information Society) (2003). *Declaration of Principles. Building the Information Society: A Global Challenge in the New Millennium*. Available at: www.itu.int/net/wsis/docs/geneva/official/dop.html

11

MEDIA AND INFORMATION LITERACY (MIL)

Taking the digital social turn for online freedoms and education 3.0

Divina Frau-Meigs

The expression 'Media Literacy' conjures up a complex set of notions: a socioeconomic right, a political project and a pedagogical practice with a specific set of competences. In terms of political project, it oscillates between protection of young people and consumers from the propaganda and the harmful content conveyed by media and participation as a means of maximising the benefits of freedom of expression and information. In terms of pedagogical practice, it promotes a set of competences that foster citizenship and creativity about the production and consumption of media as a result of critical thinking (Hobbs and Jensen, 2009; Potter, 2013). In terms of socioeconomic right, it posits that exposure to media literacy generates personal empowerment and social and cultural engagement, buttressed by the main human right that legitimates media: freedom of expression (Frau-Meigs, 2008). As a result, media literacy is the locus of several competing frameworks, with recurring key notions whose weight varies according to national configurations. They construct an epistemology that posits media exposure, consumption and production in relation to engagement and empowerment (Figure 11.1).

Media literacy is grounded mostly in the multidisciplinary fields of education and information and communication sciences. It is presented as a transversal domain rather than a fully established discipline. As a result, it occupies an ancillary position within the two scientific fields that provide an umbrella for it. This subordinate status can be partly explained because of its project-based and problem-solving pedagogies, often carried by a mix of activists and professionals, in empirical settings, working from the bottom up, without necessarily calling on theoretical constructs and academic methodologies.

Over time, Media literacy has moved from the critical analysis of mass media in the early 1950s to the reflexive practices of social media in the digital era (Hoechsmann and Poyntz, 2012). As a result, the term 'information' has been added by researchers and adopted by UNESCO, to produce 'media and information literacy' (MIL) that integrates the multiple meanings of information in the digital era. MIL emerged at UNESCO as a follow-up of the *Kit for Media Education* (2007) and the ensuing collaborative elaboration of the *Paris Agenda for Media Education* (2008). The Fez Declaration on Media and Information Literacy of 2011 completed the transformation. The purpose was to provide an alternative and a complement to ICT-based pedagogies as

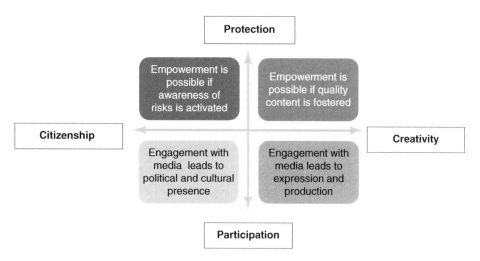

Figure 11.1 MIL epistemology

they penetrated the world of education, together with the rise of the Internet and social media. The 2014 Paris Declaration *MIL in the Digital Era* explicitly states the need for critical thinking, competencies and values over operational skills for the real empowerment of citizens.[1]

The fundamental nature of the challenge deals with the transformation of MIL and human rights by the digital, social and smart turn. This moment took place in 2005–06 with the arrival of Web 2.0 platforms such as Facebook, Twitter and YouTube, together with the rise of big data and learning analytics. They increased sociability and participation in the social turn, and they amplified creativity and distributed intelligence in the smart turn. This augmentation is a burning issue as the Internet extends its Web and three billion users are already engaged in online activities. Among these users, about a third are children and young people (Livingstone et al., 2016), which adds the onus of considering their rights as they are spending considerable time online. This implies to develop a critical perspective on the assumptions embedded in the deployment of human rights and education, by teachers as well as by policy makers.

The question of MIL and human rights in the digital age has yet to receive sustained scholarly attention, especially as all issues related to education and MIL in particular tend to deal with it as a matter of subsidiarity, devolved to states and communities despite the transborder nature of digital tools. So the analysis of the reciprocal relations between MIL and human rights needs to build on the latest theoretical approaches in the field. New constructs in social cognition, with notions such as identity, privacy, attribution, distributed intelligence as well as notions coming from information and communication sciences like data, networks, social media and Internet governance can help understand the complexity of the digital transition. The delicate balance in human rights and education alike between abstract norms that imply duties and responsibilities on the one hand and operational uses and practices that imply participation and civic agency on the other hand also needs to be considered. In this radically new context, what are the constructs and the new competences required to produce human-rights-savvy media users and producers?

Integrating the impact of Internet on human rights: Towards a new rights-based approach

Human rights and the Internet are relatively recent, both being born after the trauma of the Second World War. The Universal Declaration of Human Rights (UDHR) was adopted by the

United Nations General Assembly in 1948, followed in 1959 by the Declaration of the Rights of the Child (which became a UN Convention in 1989).[2] The Advanced Research Projects Agency Network (ARPAnet), the first multiple-site computer network, was effectively created in 1969 and the World Wide Web, the Internet's best-known application, in 1989. Their trajectory is increasingly meshed with new literacies, such as media education that started emerging in the public policy programmes in the 1980s (Kellner and Share, 2005; Lee, 2010). It was reasserted, in Europe especially, by the Audiovisual Media Services Directive of 2010 that required states to introduce it in their national policies (Frau-Meigs, Velez, Flores, 2017).

Internet governance principles as part of human rights and MIL

The momentum has grown more and more since the World Summit on Information Society (WSIS) in 2003–05. The WSIS Geneva Declaration of 2003 reaffirmed 'the universality, indivisibility, interdependence, and interrelation of all human rights and fundamental freedoms, including the right to development', in the information society. In 2012, following on the Arab Springs – where the social and smart turn went political – the United Nations General Assembly adopted its first resolution on the Human Rights on the Internet. The resolution asserts that 'the Internet can be an important tool for development and for exercising human rights'.[3]

The interdependence of rights and the Internet was thus established as mutually reinforcing. Issues related to how the Internet is governed are taking centre stage as the pure players are reaching a phase of institutionalization: no longer pioneering, they are playing a critical role in economic and social affairs that affect offline matters as much as online freedoms. Consequently and accordingly, the principles governing the Internet have matured, crystallising into a rough consensus with 'NETmundial' that has helped to establish a consolidated list of international processes and principles.[4] The main Internet governance (IG) processes are considered to be: multi-stakeholder, open, transparent, accountable, inclusive and equitable, distributed, collaborative and enabling of meaningful participation. The core principles currently posited are: universality, openness, interoperability, security, neutrality and diversity (Frau-Meigs & Hibbard 2016).

IG recognizes the role of the Internet in promoting human rights, while at the same time showing that it is also used to violate such rights, with additional concerns about the infringement and enhancement of children's rights. This in turn affects the complex set of MIL core notions, especially protection and participation. On the protection side, new risks deal with children's human rights such as online grooming, cyberporn, cyber-harassment, and increasingly youth radicalisation via social networks. But adults are not spared, as they can be affected by hacking, phishing and trolling, with chilling effects on empowerment because of privacy encroachments. On the participation side, increased hate speech, gender stereotyping, big data profiling and tracing lead to concerns of poor engagement and risks of exclusion because of freedom of expression encroachments. Altogether, on the content level, new forms of propaganda, censorship, biased representations and stereotypes have appeared, while on the industry production level, digital convergence and pure player consolidation have impacted on diversity, pluralism and quality.

Progressive interpretations of these issues by member states, international and regional organisations, and by national and regional courts can enable human rights to evolve in cyberspace in a seamless manner, regardless of frontiers or media formats. For example, access to Internet is increasingly considered as an integral part of the right to freedom of expression. So is the right to information, mostly concerned with access to materials held by public bodies and, increasingly, certain private bodies. The growing attention for such a right comes from a variety of reasons: rising political participation, increased anti-corruption measures, growing advocacy groups from within civil society (Callamard, 2008). It is also vindicated by investigative journalists' pressure for increased access to transborder news and data, as evidenced by the three major data-mining-related scandals that combine 'leaks' and 'gates': WikiLeaks (2010), Snowden (2013) and Panama Papers (2016). They bring back the heyday of watchdog journalism, forgotten since the Watergate and the Pentagon Papers.

Embracing what data do to media

Understanding the interpenetration of media and data is crucial to fathom the current debates on online freedoms (Article 19 of the Universal Declaration of Human Rights, UDHR). Media have become participatory with the social turn but they also have become smart with the impact of data aggregation and curation. They are impacted by data analytics, defined as the measurement of and reporting about online data from users of social media; their purpose is to optimise the understanding of complex events via data aggregation on smart networks. So knowledge is gained not just by fact-checking the traditional way, in a linear causation way, but also by data-curating that reveals unexpected non-linear relations and patterns.

Online freedoms vs. mass surveillance

This evolution gives a new spin to 'information' with statistical means of representation that are computer-generated and data-visualised. Media reporting has been impacted, with data journalism becoming increasingly part of news feeds. The Snowden revelations have shown how data analytics can enhance political mass surveillance while Amazon recommendations and Facebook scandals regularly reveal monitoring for unauthorised commercial purposes that can put citizens at risk. 'Data' has gained enormous cultural currency as pure player platforms especially the GAFAMs (Google Apple Facebook Amazon Microsoft) profile people's habits and behaviours, but also as Internet users can have access to their own data, building their reputation systems according to their followers, as they become publishers online, in direct competition with heritage media. The features of data in all media tell stories and have purpose but they tend to elide the stakes and the finalities from the public discourse, which is a concern especially as data are more and more often influential in decision shaping and making.

This data currency is going to increase considerably with the arrival of the Internet of Things (IoT), where captors and sensors embedded in all kinds of devices will lead citizens to send data about themselves automatically. There is a risk to freedom of expression due to this networked freedom of emission. Characteristically, most maps of IoT have erased media and education from their prospective services while featuring prominently safety and cybersecurity (Figure 11.2 IoT Mindap).[5]

Beyond naturalising media and education as part of the DNA of the IoT, such maps reveal the pure players' intent to suppress all intermediaries between users and their mindsets. A lot of consumer knowledge will be required to avoid the 'filter bubble' denounced by Eli Pariser (2011), who worries about how the Internet can narrow people's worldview and enclose them in platforms that will only conform to their data profiles, behaviours and tastes, based on their navigation traces.

Currently this ever-increasing variety of statistics, together with cross-correlation of big data and IoT convergence, is not regulated. And yet their uses and the conditions of their availability (anonymous or public, for sale or not for sale, etc.) should be clearly specified, in the best interests of citizens at large. The governance of the Internet implies to think about who is going to manage and own such data and for what uses, within and beyond media and education as the protection of such data is important for democracy and for the preservation of the public value of the Internet (Frau-Meigs & Hibbard, 2016).[6]

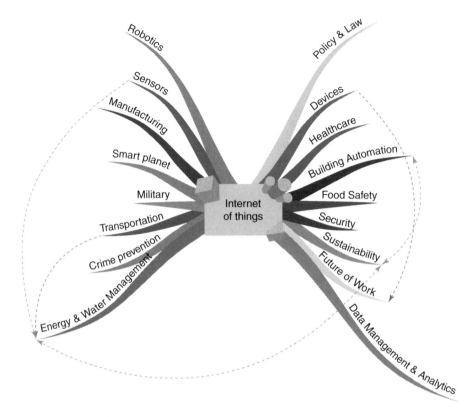

Figure 11.2 IoT Mindmap
Source: press.teleinteractive.sourcenet

How to prevent misuse should be an important part of IG in education, with new rules for preventing mass surveillance while respecting online freedoms. This may encourage the rise of citizen initiatives around 'self' data (rather than big data), already perceivable in tools such as Quantified Self, Customer Commons, PDS (personal datastores) or Smart Disclosure. Such initiatives need to be presented as a viable alternative so that people do not fall prey to the fatality of data but regain control over their data destiny. Individuals can be empowered if they are given control over their data, with notions such as data portability, allowing them to take their data with them when they decide to leave a specific service. To counterbalance the Internet of Things, IG needs to nurture and expand the Internet of Citizens.[7]

Privacy vs. security

Data also affect the current debates on privacy (article 12 of UDHR) as most of the pure players who try to disqualify it as a right are distorting it. Vint Cerf, Internet pioneer now working for Google, expressed the strategy clearly in 2013: 'Privacy may actually be an anomaly'.[8] The new moral injunction seems to be 'publicness' so as to expand the data mining options of pure players (Brin, 1998; Rosen, 2000; Casilli et al., 2014). Publicness is increasingly presented as a new norm if not a new right. In 2010, Mark Zuckerberg, Facebook founder, stated as obvious that 'Public is the new social norm'.[9] And everybody has to conform, especially young people who are malleable and can be groomed early. They are the targets of pure players tech companies that are trying to drive the age limit of access to social media down to 8 (instead of 13). This pressure has led parental associations in the USA to push for extended protection to 16 via the Do Not Track Act of 2015 that amends the Children's Online Privacy Protection Act (COPPA) of 1998. The Act effectively defines 'a "minor" as an individual over the age of 12 and under the age of 16'.[10] In a similar move, the emergence of the right 'to be forgotten,' is important for children's right to privacy as it enables the removal of their online traces, under specific circumstances.

Most often however, privacy is pitched against security (article 3 of UDHR). Striking the right balance between privacy and security is a traditional concern of democracies. In the past, over-protection of privacy has been construed as having chilling effects on freedom of expression as it allows governments to erect barriers to information flows. But with big data, over-protection of security may have chilling effects on both privacy and online freedoms. The risk of misusing security can lead to political polarisation, even extremism, and to silencing minorities (Frau-Meigs, 2010, 2013).

Data produce a displacement in privacy, as suggested by Daniel Solove (2008). He identifies four areas of activities when data present a 'risk of harm to privacy' (Solove, 2008, 104): data collection (surveillance), data processing (aggregation, identification, insecurity), data dissemination (disclosure, breach of confidentiality, exposure, blackmail, distortion, appropriation) and data invasions (intrusion, decisional interference). These breaches due to exposure are related to reputation and are potentially harmful because they can affect self-development and freedom, when people lose control over the capacity to create their own life and benefit from social regard that is so key to interaction with peers as evinced in social networks and Web 2.0 activities. Being able to create intimate and safe territories of the self is essential to the well-being of a person and to the maintenance of a healthy public sphere.

Shifts in privacy also impact identity as online presence. The emerging phenomenon of 'reputation systems' associates identity with daily actions, giving others greater opportunities to bear judgment on those actions. Such systems could lead to harmful mistakes, difficult to correct, 'if the systems are operated entirely by private parties and their ratings formulas are closely held trade secrets' (Zittrain 2008, 221). Zittrain proposes to empower users to contribute to their own security models, which accounts for current claims in the transparency of algorithms. Unmonitored data mining by third parties can have chilling effects on free speech and social participation, in the absence of public accountability. Gate-keeping the gatekeepers implies the addition of privacy to MIL, so that all citizens are empowered to protect themselves from third parties and can hold governments accountable, which could account for the increase of interest for whistle blowers and their protection.

The impact of data implies the revisiting of the pre-digital competing MIL epistemology frameworks which may yield very diverse options in terms of the advancement of human rights in the digital era (see Figure 11.3).

A rights-based approach to MIL is necessary; one that incorporates key Internet governance principles to deal with online freedoms and privacy as they are impacted by data. Such a development is necessary to have a people-centred approach to new media, as advocated by civil society groups in WSIS, the Internet Corporation for Assigned Names and Numbers (ICANN), Internet Governance Forum (IGF) and so on. This approach also guarantees a child-sensitive approach in terms of protection and participation.

Augmenting MIL with IG competences for the 21st century

Considering these outcomes, the content of the MIL curriculum needs to be upgraded, to include Internet Governance issues as part of the emerging human rights of the post-WSIS era

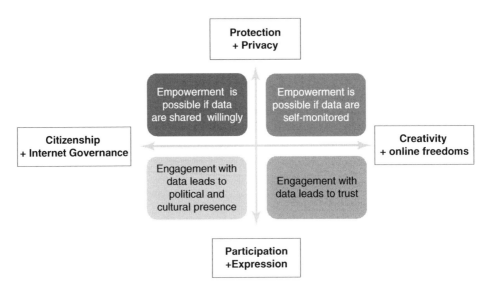

Figure 11.3 MIL epistemology augmented by data

that also coincides with new UN Sustainable Goals for development. Also at play is the digital transition from education 2.0, where information and communication technologies are seen as support tools, to education 3.0 where MIL augmented with IG are the new basics. MIL is necessary to bring changes in values and attitudes, to redress structural imbalances and to empower users, especially young people (Frau-Meigs & Hibbard, 2016).

MIL as transliteracy

This vision is not only supported by the social and smart turn but also by the paradigm shift around the notion of 'information'. It incorporates three cultures that augment MIL to the power of 3: 'news' (media and communication), 'documents' (library and information sciences) and 'data' (code and informatics). This paradigmatic change is fostered by the digital convergence of three major fields: computation sciences (computer literacy), communication sciences (media literacy) and information/library sciences (information literacy). The terms to describe this MIL[3] compete among researchers. Some use 'digital literacy' (Buckingham 2008), others 'compétences médiatiques' (De Smedt and Fastrez, 2012), or 'information literacy' (Serres 2012) or even 'multiliteracies' (Provenzo et al., 2011).

Beyond the conceptual inflation, what remains is the empowerment afforded by the Internet as a ubiquitous medium, supported by smart platforms and social networks, within and outside the school environment. This radically modifies the learning skills needed to participate in this environment. The revisited epistemology and the knowledge categories that are intrinsic to MIL[3] and which make it recognisable and distinguishable from other forms of literacies, all point to the emergence of MIL[3] as 'transliteracy':

1. [T]he ability to embrace the multimedia layout that encompasses skills for reading, writing and counting with all the available tools (from paper to image, from book to wiki);

2. [T]he capacity to navigate through multiple domains that includes the ability to search, to evaluate and to modify information according to its relevant contexts of use (as code, news and document).

(Frau-Meigs, 2015)

Transliteracy revisits MIL to embrace the multimodal layout of the Internet with a repertoire of e-strategies such as searching, remixing, pooling, networking and gaming (Jenkins et al. 2009). It also points to a meta set of e-strategies for dealing with the convergence of the three information cultures: editorial strategies (being able to comment, publish online), organisational strategies (being able to search and navigate) and operational strategies (being able to code and play).[11] (See Figure 11.4)

MIL as transliteracy takes advantage of online participation and social networking for the co-construction of knowledge, not just on a textual basis but also on a multimodal basis (sound, image, text). It treats coding as a literacy practice to deal with the interpenetration of media and data, not as a set of e-skills per se, but as part of computational thinking based on the three information cultures.

The seven Cs for a human-rights-based approach to MIL

Beyond the learning skills and e-strategies integral to transliteracy, there are overall competences that relate to a human-rights-based approach to MIL. These can be summed up as the seven Cs: comprehension, criticism, creativity, citizenship, consumption, cross-cultural communication and conflict resolution (Frau-Meigs 2012). The first three Cs are mostly applicable within schools, the four other Cs tend to be more easily applied in various contexts, to foster a culture

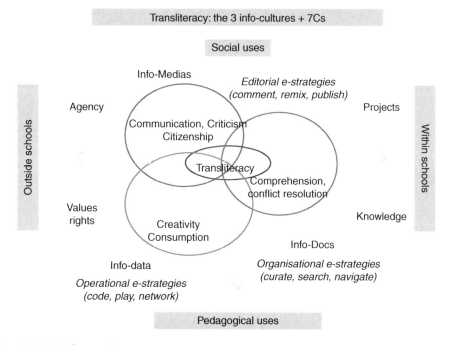

Figure 11.4 MIL[3] as transliteracy

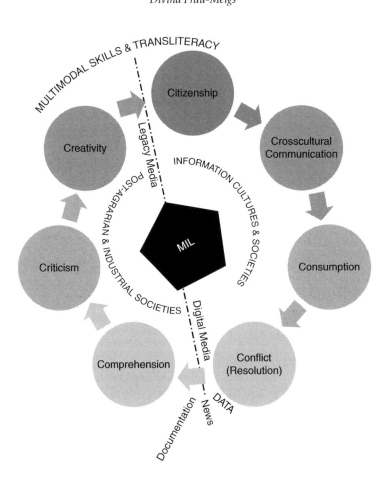

Figure 11.5   MIL[3] and 7Cs

of peace, social justice and cultural diversity (See Figure 11.5). They reflect the need to integrate computing and big data with media and the need for critical and creative skills to move towards transformative literacies based not only on skills but also on values and ethics. They go beyond current policies for IT or e-skills that are mainly operational and dilute human rights by reducing them to a "safer internet" version of responsible behaviour. They point to the need for shared values that make sense for children and educators alike. They are holistic, recombining complex problem solving with technical, social and soft skills in order to lead to self-management and 'learning to become' or 'savoir devenir' (Frau-Meigs, 2015).[12]

MIL can play a crucial role in the protection and promotion of human rights online, to build sustainable information and knowledge societies. It provides a counter-point to the growing discourse on security and surveillance that has been invading Internet governance debates since Snowden's case and others like it, with an acceleration happening around the terrorist attacks during the Syrian conflict, where the social networks tended to be blamed for the radicalization of young people.

The seven Cs can be developed for educational purposes and a critical thinking of media as they go digital, to help in the understanding and management of the paradigm shifts in MIL epistemology, without the hurdles that abstract principles create in young people's minds. They can help strike the delicate balance in human rights between principles and ethics, between conceptual norms with attendant responsibilities on the one hand and operational uses with attendant agencies on the other hand. They point to everyday ethics, with project-based learning and problem-solving pedagogies. Projects such as ECFOLI for instance can train children to solve conflicts via the media production of stories based on their common shared heritage.[13]

Maybe more than ever, MIL implies to revisit the perspective on 'critical' thinking as expressed by John Dewey (1910) to help young people gain some sense of agency. Critical thinking applied to media is not only about understanding and evaluating information as news, docs and data, but also about the credibility of evidence, the capacity to detect hidden agendas and the ability to solve ethical dilemmas. More than ever, young people need to be able to identify distortion, misinformation and propaganda to fight the bias, stereotypes and prejudices conveyed via the media … and resolvable via the media.

Many initiatives point to the sensible practices where MIL provides benefits for critical thinking. The Massive Open Online course DIY MIL for instance elaborates on issues of freedom of expression to help participants create their own resources and coursework to fight bias and rumours, as well as to help detect radicalisation.[14] Data visualisation can be mastered by bringing journalists and young people together to work with public data, as in the Dataviz initiative.[15] Editing online with Wikipedia can be done by training young people with Wikipedians to produce their own articles, as in the CLEMI project 'wikiconcours'.[16]

Such initiatives show how radically MIL can change access to digitally-mediated knowledge and should be a frontier field for education and research. Placing MIL in the curriculum means recognising the importance of issues that are crucial for active citizenship and creativity, such as privacy protection, freedom of expression and (self)data management. There is also an urgency to recognize it as a discipline on its own that can then be mainstreamed into the others, to reshuffle heritage disciplines with creative humanities. MIL needs to be a stand-alone matter, in a trans-border world where the Internet is a global resource. Bringing together the principles of Internet governance with educational principles (competences, ethics, etc.) transforms MIL into an educational field in itself, that has the potential to help schools make the transition to the 21st century. Disciplinary lines of differentiation need to be reshuffled to embrace MIL as a frontier field for research so that these highly political and legal constructs that increasingly join the human and the digital are fully mastered.

Notes

1 Paris Declaration on "Media and information Literacy in the Digital Era", 2014, drafted under the direction of Divina Frau-Meigs by ANR TRANSLIT and COST 'Transforming Audiences/Transforming Societies' for UNESCO (Divina Frau-Meigs, Christine Trueltzsch-Wijnen, Igor Kanizaj, María del Mar Grandío Pérez, Nora Schleicher, Brian O'Neill, Julian McDougall, Kirsten Drotner, Pieramarco Aroldi, Pascale Thumerelle and Christian Gautellier). Available at: http://www.unesco.org/new/fileadmin/MULTIMEDIA/HQ/CI/CI/pdf/In_Focus/paris_mil_declaration_final.pdf

2 The UN Convention on Rights of the Child concurs with two MIL notions, asserting rights to protection (threats to children's dignity, survival and development) and rights to participation (empowerment and engagement with processes that affect their development).

3 UN Human Rights Council, Twentieth Session (June 29, 2012), *The Promotion, Protection and Enjoyment of Human Rights on the Internet*, A/HRC/20/L.13. Office of the High Commissioner for Human Rights. Available at: http://ap.ohchr.org

4 The NETmundial process is a consolidation of prior events and discussions (WSIS, IGF, ICANN…) http://netmundial.br/wp-content/uploads/2014/04/NETmundial-Multistakeholder-Document.pdf

5 Many other examples can be found online, see also IoT map, available at http://mapcbinsights.com. (Accessed on 13 May, 2016).

6 See Council of Europe Recommendation on measures to promote the public service value of the Internet, https://wcd.coe.int/ViewDoc.jsp ?id=1207291

7 http://www.coe.int/en/web/portal/-/recommendation-on-the-internet-of-citizens

8 http://techcrunch.com/2013/11/20/googles-cerf-says-privacy-may-be-an-anomaly-historically-hes-right/

9 http://mashable.com/2010/01/10/facebook-founder-on-privacy/#fpmyMqMDuqqj

10 See the Do Not Track Bill, https://www.congress.gov/bill/114th-congress/house-bill/2734

11 See the work of the research group TRANSLIT, funded by the French National Research Agency (ANR), conducted by Divina Frau-Meigs: http://www.translit.fr

12 The UNESCO chair *Savoir devenir à l'ère du développement numérique durable: maîtriser les cultures de l'information* was created by Divina Frau-Meigs in order to analyse MIL[3] and transliteracy as a 5th pillar of knowledge besides the four pillars delineated by the Delors report *Learning: The Treasure Within* (UNESCO 1996): learning to be, learning to learn, learning to do, learning to live together. The chair *Savoir devenir* points at learning to become and to project oneself as a 5th pillar, empowered by MIL and supported by a digital ecosystem. www.divina-frau-meigs.fr

13 ECFOLI is an Erasmus + funded project, involving five countries (Cyprus, France, Morocco, Palestine and Portugal). https://www.ecfoli.eu

14 MOOC DIY MIL is part of the ECO MOOC project funded by the EU. https://www.ecolearning.eu

15 https://frequence-ecoles.org/2014/05/20/43-posters-de-dataviz-exposes-a-la-region-ra/

16 https://fr.wikipedia.org/wiki/Wikipédia:Wikiconcours

References

Brin, D. (1998). 'The Transparent Society'. *Will Technology Force Us to Choose Between Privacy and Freedom?* New York: Perseus.

Buckingham, D. (2008). 'Defining Digital Literacy. What Do Young People Need to Know About Digital Media?' C. Lankshear and M. Knobel, eds. *Digital Literacies: Concepts, Policies, and Practices*. Oxford: Peter Lang, pp. 73–91.

Callamard, A. (2008). 'Towards a Third Generation of Activism for the Right to Freedom of Information'. *Freedom of Expression, Access to Information and Empowerment of People*. Paris: UNESCO, pp. 46–7.

Casilli, A., Tubaro, P. and Sarabi Y. (2014). *Against the Hypothesis of the End of Privacy*. New York: Springer.

De Smedt, T. et Fastrez, P. (dir.). (2012). 'Les compétences médiatiques des gens ordinaires'. *Recherches en communication*, 34(7), pp. 140–7.

Dewey, J. (1910). *How We Think*. Lexington, MA: D.C. Heath & Co.

Frau-Meigs, D. (2008). 'Media Literacy and Human Rights: Education for Sustainable Societies'. *Croatian Journal of Communication and Psychology*, 5(3), pp. 145–57.

Frau-Meigs, D. (2015). 'Augmented Media and Information Literacy (MIL): How Can MIL Harness the Affordances of Digital Information Cultures?' S. Kotilainen and R. Kupiainen, eds., *Media Education Futures*. Goteborg: Clearinghouse, pp. 13–26.

Frau-Meigs, D. (2010). 'From Secrecy 1.0 to Privacy 2.0: Who Controls What?' *Revue Française d'Etudes Américaines*, 123(2), pp. 79–95.

Frau-Meigs, D. ed. (2013). 'Internet Governance/La gouvernance d'internet'. *Revue Française d'Etudes Américaines*, 134(1), pp. 1–128.

Frau-Meigs, D. and Hibbard, L. (2016). 'Education 3.0 and Internet Governance: A New Global Alliance for Children and Young People's Sustainable Digital Development'. *Global Commission on Internet Governance*, Series no. 27. London: Chatham House.

Frau-Meigs D., Velez, I. and Flores Michel J., eds. (2017). *MIL Public Policies in Europe: A Cross-Country Comparison*. London: Routledge.

Frau-Meigs, D. (2012). 'Transliteracy as the new research horizon for media and information literacy'. *Media Studies*, Special issue on *Critical insights in European media literacy research and policy* 2 (Dec. 2012): 5–25.

Frau-Meigs, D. and Torrent, J., eds. (2009). *Mapping Media Education Policies in the World: Visions, Programmes and Challenges*. New York: UN-Alliance of Civilizations.

Hobbs, R. and Jensen, A. (2009). 'The Past, Present, and Future of Media Literacy Education'. *Journal of Media Literacy Education*, 1(1), pp. 1–11.

Hoechsmann, M., and Poyntz, S. R. (2012). *Media Literacies: a Critical Introduction*. Malden, MA: Wiley-Blackwell.

Jenkins, H. with Purushotma, R., Weigel, M., Clinton, K. and Robison, A. J. (2009). *Confronting the Challenges of Participatory Culture: Media Education for the 21st Century*. Cambridge: MIT and The John D. and Catherine T. MacArthur Foundation.

Jones, R. H., Hafner, C. A. (2012). *Understanding Digital Literacies: A Practical Introduction*. New York: Routledge.

Kellner, D. and Share, J. (2005). 'Toward Critical Media Literacy: Core Concepts, Debates, Organizations and Policy'. *Discourse: Studies in the Cultural Politics of Education*, 26(3), pp. 369–86.

Lee, A. Y. L. (2010). 'Media Education: Definitions, Approaches and Development Around the Globe'. *New Horizons in Education*, 58(3), pp. 1–13.

Livingstone, S. (2004). 'Media Literacy and the Challenge of New Information and Communication Technologies'. *Communication Review*, 1(7), pp. 3–14.

Livingstone, S., Papaioannou, T., del Mar Grandío Pérez, M., & Wijnen, C. W., eds. (2012). 'Critical Insights in European Media Literacy Research and Policy', Special issue, *Media Studies* 3(6), pp. 2–12.

Livingstone, S., Carr, J. and Byrne, J. (2016). 'One in Three: The Task for Global Internet Governance in Addressing Children's Rights'. *Global Commission on Internet Governance Series*. London: Chatham House, pp. 1–37.

McGonagle, T. (2011). *Media Literacy: No Longer the Shrinking Violet of European Audiovisual Media Regulation?* (IRIS Plus No. 2011-3). Strasbourg: European Audiovisual Observatory.

Pariser, E. (2011). *The Filter Bubble: What the Internet Is Hiding from You*. New York: Penguin.

Potter, W. J. (2013). 'Review of Literature on Media Literacy'. *Sociology Compass*, 7, pp. 417–35.

Provenzo, E. F., Goodwin, A., Lipsky, M. and Sharpe, S., eds. (2011). *Multiliteracies: Beyond Text and the Written Word*. Charlotte, NC: Information Age Pup.

Rosen, J. (2000). *The Unwanted Gaze. The Destruction of Privacy in America*. New York: Vintage.

Serres, A. (2012). *Dans le labyrinthe. Évaluer l'information sur internet*. Caen: C&F éditions.

Silverstone, R. (2004). 'Regulation, Media Literacy and Media Civics'. *Media, Culture & Society*, 26(3), pp. 440–49.

Solove, D. G. (2008). *Understanding Privacy*. Cambridge, MA: Harvard University Press.

UNESCO (2007). *Media Education. A Kit for Teachers, Students, Parents and Professionals*. Frau-Meigs, D., ed. Paris: UNESCO Publishing. Available at: http://unesdoc.unesco.org/images/0014/001492/149278e.pdf

UNESCO (1996). *Learning: The Treasure Within*. Report to UNESCO of the International Commission on Education for the Twenty-first Century. Paris: UNESCO Publishing.

UNESCO (2007). Paris Agenda for Media Education. *L'éducation aux médias. Avancées, obstacles, orientations nouvelles depuis Grunwald: vers un changement d'échelle?* [CD-Rom] Frau-Meigs, D., Souyri, C., Bévort, E. et Jacquinot, G., eds. Paris: Commission nationale française pour l'Unesco, 2007. (English and French). Available at: http://www.nordicom.gu.se/sv/clearinghouse/paris-agenda-12-recommendations-media-education

von Feilitzen, C., and Carlsson, U., eds. (2004). *Promote or Protect? Perspectives on Media Literacy and Media Regulations*. Göteborg: UNESCO International Clearinghouse on Children, Youth and Media, NORDICOM.

Zittrain, J. (2008). *The Future of the Internet and How to Stop It*. London: Allen Lane.

12

THEORISING DIGITAL MEDIA CULTURES
The politics of watching and being watched

Gavin J.D. Smith

Introduction

> Someone has my dental records. Someone has my financial records. Someone knows
> just about everything about me. You have no privacy. Get over it.
>
> *(Scott McNealy, former CEO of Sun Microsystems[1])*

McNealy's opening remarks are a telling indictment of how transformations in the organisation of social life have significantly compromised, if not annihilated, liberal principles such as the right to privacy. In particular, the extensive creation, gathering and analysis of digital information for social, commercial and governmental ends has become a customary characteristic of most of the world's polities. For instance, recent estimates by IT giant IBM suggest that 'every day, we create 2.5 quintillion bytes of data – so much that 90% of the data in the world today [have] been created in the last two years alone'.[2] While traditional media and state practices have, since their inception, encroached on personal life through either public reportage or registration of private details (see Woo 2006), the rapid proliferation of networked digital devices (NDD hereafter) – and flows of media – into the social fabric have dramatically increased the *connectivity* and *visibility* of their users in terms of their whereabouts, preferences, habits and relationships. But these sensor-enabled mediums, such as the personal computer, the smartphone or the Fitbit tracker, perform two discrete, if intertwined, functions. They permit the user to access, consume and interact with content created by other individuals and institutions, but in doing so, they also produce and circulate additional data that act as 'virtual testimonies' of the user's physical location and behavioural practices (Smith 2016a). That is, today's media systems operate as informational conduits: they both *represent* and *distribute* data. They double up as platforms and as sources of knowledge, both for the bearer of the device and for those audiences implicitly referred to in the opening epigraph who, by virtue of their social location within digital networks, are privy to the data trails the former leaves in her/his wake. As Gus Hunt, the CIA's Chief Technology Officer, recently put it: 'The agency would also like to be able to save and analyse all of the digital breadcrumbs people don't even know they are creating. You're already a walking sensor platform'.[3]

The advent of portable NDD, globally distributed technical infrastructures which facilitate data dissemination and the related 'Internet of Things' has facilitated a revolution in terms of how individuals conduct and experience their personal and public affairs. At any particular moment, around 2.5 billion people around the world are connected to one another in a virtual sense through the webbed medium of the Internet,[4] with young people in developed regions spending approximately nine hours each day participating in forms of online activity.[5] As a result, progressively more aspects of social life are being intermediated by NDD, from sexual practices and ideologies to expressions of self-identity and police brutality. Conveying details of physiologies, thoughts, moods, whereabouts, behaviours and social networks in real time, such data have the capacity to transcend spatial and temporal confines, situate individuals in global exchange systems and facilitate processes of 'action' and 'government' *at a distance* (Latour 1987, 219; Miller & Rose 1990, 9). This has meant that spatially and socially separated individuals have the means to form virtual identities, communities and campaigns around mutual interests and issues, just as distanciated marketers and authorities can exploit the details derived from widespread practices of online browsing, consumption and communication to garner insights on user preferences and to red flag or gold star them in accordance with their attributed persona. Witnessing the mediation of *glocal* events (events that are simultaneously local and global) as represented in flows of digital content, and the resultant effect of time-space compression, has become a naturalised experience in the digital era, and it has inspired a 'cosmopolitan consciousness' (Beck 2006) while making individuals acutely susceptive to data-sharing repertoires and the challenges of living in an info-saturated world (Smith 2016b). The online ecology is a vast data mine that facilitates unbridled experiences of connectivity, sociality, exhibitionism, learning and surveillance. For this reason, it is a social terrain mired in complex politics and power dynamics.

This chapter explores some key issues arising from the use and experience of media in the digital era. It entails conceptualising media as being simultaneously a *relation of visibility*, a *type of commodity* and a *mode of power*. We ponder whether a privacy framework is an adequate (or desirable) legal and moral device for regulating and protecting the vast flows of personal information qua media being routinely leaked or expelled into the surrounding 'digital enclosure', as people participate in social life via digital mediums (Andrejevic 2009). I wish to demonstrate how democratic practice is paradoxically *served* and *undermined* by the quasi-free flow of information to and from nodal points in what is an 'endless' and 'lively' network (Lupton 2016, 2). Such data make individuals aware of abuses of power, alternative ideas and spatially remote – if virtually proximate – events. They help educate, entertain and connect them and, as conduits for the transference of personal experience and outlooks, they provide a means for the expression of political sentiment. But data are equally used to track, profile, manipulate and persecute those whom they represent, and when configured by algorithmic codes, they can deterministically anticipate the future trajectories and life-chances, of their referents in ways that are far from apparent and poorly regulated (Gandy 2006). In other words, the fact that data mediate and are mediated by socio-cultural relations entails that they are used relativistically to serve desirable and undesirable ends: outcomes which are very much dependent on the intentions, interests and placement of the actors they represent and audiences they stimulate. This fact, of course, makes it necessarily difficult to place the heterogeneity of contemporary media practices in a clearly defined and normative rights-based framework.

Media in the digital era: The watched and watching world

The rapid diffusion of NDD into the social world has profoundly transformed the nature and means of communication and everything that goes with it, from the mechanics of work and consumption to the dynamics of politics and criminality. Almost every social activity imaginable is supplemented, and prefixed, with a cyber equivalent. It is overwhelmingly the case that individuals now receive and transmit information about all manner of social events and experiences, and participate in social life via Internet-enabled mediums and infrastructures. These processes and practices have radically de-stabilised traditional notions of media, especially with respect to how knowledge about various issues is created, disseminated and encountered. Where in the pre-digital age the means of communication was predominantly in the hands of a small power elite who exercised significant control over how and what people thought within a bounded geographical territory, today's media environment is both interactive and pluralised in character. It comprises a multitude of biographical and speculative perspectives from users who were previously disconnected socially and spatially.

In today's media-rich ecology, it is now appropriate to talk about individuals as being 'prosumers' of information (Ritzer & Jurgenson 2010). People are said to engage in practices of 'value co-creation' (Prahalad & Ramaswamy 2004) that reflect (a) the aspirations of companies to put unwaged consumers to work in the services of global capital, and (b) the personal desires of individuals to court attention and share mediated experiences. Onlookers might include intimate familiars, but just as easily, unknown strangers in the case of mobile software applications, or 'apps', like Periscope: a platform that lets users anonymously watch in real time the staged (often graphic) broadcasts of complete strangers.[6] In the context of media, prosumption is irrevocably changing repertoires of story telling and meaning making, enabling users to be active generators of their own narratives while also consuming and contributing to the content of other providers be they of a professional or an amateur status. This is exemplified in the increasing appearance of 'comments' sections at the end of online articles which enable readers to assume the role of debate commentators (Poster 1995) and to post either supportive or critical responses.

These developments, specifically the open-ended properties of digital media, have been framed as heralding new opportunities for democratic practice, in which previously passive audiences have become reconstituted as active contributors of content (see Poster 1995; Negroponte 1996; Kellner 1997). Because this content is personalised and authentic in tone, it is thought to possess more resonance in terms of its capacity to galvanise the audiences it contacts. From this perspective, media and connectedness facilitate relations of empowerment and mobilisation, spelling the rise of the 'citizen journalist', the 'wiki blogger' and 'enlightened publics', who can take to the digital airwaves to document the embodied ills caused by – and thereby challenge the dominance of – prevailing social conditions. The transition from a mediacorp-run media environment (a narrow and thin informational sphere) that was unidirectional, reductionist and dogmatic in composition to one that is more omnidirectional and collaborative (and thus broad and thick) in scope, has been construed as a move that destabilises hegemonic systems of knowledge and propaganda that operate in ways that merely represent and serve the interests of ruling groups.

The pluralisation in platforms of communication is praised for its capacity to feature the voices and experiences of the hitherto marginalised, to foster grass-roots activism and community, and to initiate new modes of accountability.[7] The Arab Spring uprisings in 2011, the George Holliday videotape depicting Rodney King being unlawfully assaulted by LA police in 1991, and the release by WikiLeaks in 2010 of the 'Collateral Murder' video each epitomise the populist promise assumed of this 'splintered' media environment, where the control of ideas and information – specifically, the framing of events – is no longer the exclusive preserve of a powerful minority, but is instead a contested field mutually constructed by the sense-making practices of a throng of NDD-equipped 'citizen sensors'. Moreover, because of the networked character of these devices and platforms, media – in the form of tweets, blogs, images and posts – can be made and shared instantaneously with third-party audiences who become connected in situational and emotional ways by virtue of their being not just privy to the shared media referent, but able to cumulatively adapt and extend the meaning of it. In this time-space compressing process, the sense of context or boundedness is increasingly collapsed, meaning that technologies of media function as both conduits and continuums between an actual embodied or experiential event, and its subsequent unfettered representation in cyberspace (Smith 2016a).

The virality and intrinsically leaky nature of digitally harvested media has both engineered – and been an offshoot of – a broader *culture of scopophilia* (see Lyon 2006), where via NDD and media use contemporary individuals occupy the role of watchers (as networked audiences) and the watched (as networked performers). A key facet of this culture, what Thomas Mathiesen (1997) called the synoptical 'viewer society', is the coupling of mediated voyeurism with that of mediated exhibitionism. Technological means and cultural desire has created a circumstance where the many now see and gaze – both cynically and adoringly – upon *the few* (especially with regards reality television shows and soap operas), but also, in an Internet and data-driven era, *the many* (via digital apps and social media platforms). Equally, the many reveal their bodies, thoughts and actions to the mediated gaze of the few, but also of the many. The existence of these mediums and media, for Mathiesen, invert Michel Foucault's seminal characterisation of modernity's panoptic ethos and structures. Rather than a disciplinary authority gazing hierarchically upon the bodies and behaviours of the mad, the sick, the worker and the criminal in order to inspect them and formulate diagnoses, or as part of an asymmetrical diagram of power, technological advancements have increasingly placed these privileges and capabilities in the hands of the many: that is to say, in the hands of the non-expert performer and audience.

It is not just designated experts who now systematically monitor and problematise the physical and mental functions of bodies. Formerly closed systems of knowledge are being unfurled via the digitalisation of information (read availability and porousness) and related acts of citizen science, just as previously backstage intimacies are being increasingly transferred to front-stage regions for public viewing. A brief browse on popular video sharing site, YouTube, for example, registers approximately 302,000 childbirth videos, 51,600 abortion procedure videos, 540,000 autopsy videos and 115,000 videos of people in different stages of dying. Many of these films contain highly graphic and personal content and feature the mediated bodily exposure of people in contrasting states of vulnerability. The flood of NDD into the weave of social relations, and their connectedness to technological infrastructures, has resulted in a decentralisation of the means of observation and a consequent upsurge in practices of watching and experiences of being watched. Of course, this process has contributed to enriched public understandings of all manner of embodied conditions and historical taboos while simultaneously desensitising the subjectivities of people to *practices of exposure* and *spectacles of suffering* (Smith 2015). A key upshot is that subjects are structurally and socially conditioned to see, and to share, more (Smith 2016b). A further implication has been the gradual eclipsing of boundaries between private and public life, radically disrupting traditional distinctions made between the clean and the unclean, purity and pollution, sacred and profane (Douglas 1991). The existence of digital media, and their capacity to transcend if not obliterate a sense of context, makes it steadily more difficult to distinguish the belonging of things. As Nicholas Negroponte, the founder and Chairman Emeritus of Massachusetts Institute of Technology's Media Lab, recently asserted: 'The digital world creates convergence, overlap and blur in previously separate, distinct and crisply defined areas. Simple definitions, such as being inside or outside something, being part of or not part of something else, being for or against just about anything ... all of these are suddenly subject to reinterpretation'.[8]

As a result of the affordances NDD provide, users develop intricate attachments to these mediums, often imbuing them with a quasi-vitalism. They are often the last thing handled at night and the first thing touched the following morning. I'm sure many readers will attest to reading emails or social media updates on their smartphones before they even regard their partners, children or pets. Indeed, more of us are sleeping with gadgets attached to our bodies or positioned under our pillows.[9] As digital devices get progressively embedded in sociocultural relations as facilitators of sociality, convenience and entertainment, so their symbolic status has metamorphosed. They are no longer inanimate objects, but rather *sentient companions* that increasingly orient our attention and behaviours. In thinking of them in these terms, I mean that we – to apply Donna Haraway's (2008, 3) phrase – progressively 'become with' the technologies carried in our bags or implanted on our bodies, we co-evolve and mutate together in complex sociotechnical entanglements. As Deborah Lupton (2016, 2) notes, 'The devices that we carry with us literally are our companions: in the case of smartphones regularly touched, fiddled with and looked at throughout the day'. In this process, individual device carriers are rendered into what I have previously called, 'technovisuals' (Smith 2016a, 110), their bodily actions being continuously converted into discrete traces of data that come, as bodily proxies, to represent and visualise them in different ways. As Stalder (2002, 120) explains:

> Our physical bodies are being shadowed by an increasingly comprehensive 'data body'. However, this shadow body does more than follow us. It does also precede us. Before we arrive somewhere, we have already been measured and classified. Thus, upon arrival, we're treated according to whatever criteria have been connected to the profile that represents us.

How individuals consciously/unconsciously perceive and manage their data proxies – those details 'leaking' from their bodies as they interact with NDD and other sensor-laden structures – and profile the data signatures of visualised others, are issues still to be empirically understood. Evidently, this coded and liminal persona, as a key signifier of selfhood in today's data-driven economies, is increasingly a source of knowledge/power interplays between dataveillance systems and data sharing subjects. As compressed flows of history and biography, these entities circulate in the intersectional spaces and margins between bodies. The significance of data proxies entails that technovisuals need develop and exercise a 'data consciousness' that is orientated to the avoidance of data-based victimisation on the one hand and the accumulation of desired returns for projecting an effective datafied self on the other. As Irma van der Ploeg (2012, 177) states, 'who you are, how you are, and how you are going to be treated in various situations, is increasingly known to various agents and agencies through information deriving from your own body; information that is processed elsewhere, through the networks, databases, and algorithms of the information society'. As they intersect with the risk and value driven codes of the dataveillant analysts, these virtual figures 'have implications for our lives in a rapidly growing array of contexts, from the international travel we are allowed to undertake to the insurance premiums, job offers, discounts or credit we are offered' (Lupton 2016, 3). Tellingly, when former US President Barack Obama was recently invited to give advice to a young person aspiring to be president, he said: 'I want everybody here to be careful about what you post on Facebook, because in the YouTube age, whatever you do, it will be pulled up again later somewhere in your life'.

Thus, the permeation of NDD into the mechanics of modern social relations and the resultant effects on consciousness they imprint as media making and sharing apparatuses, has contributed to our embrace of a hybrid audience/performer identity. We presume media in ways which satisfy existential urges and, of course, organisational imperatives *to see* as voyeurs and *be seen* as exhibitionists. As a consequence, the digital mediums that come to be a focal point of our attention take on new symbolic significance, assuming a prominent position in our daily repertoires while paradoxically disappearing from awareness. Not unsurprisingly, a number of critical data scholars are concerned about this naturalisation and the relations of passivity, exploitation and subjugation it initiates.

Media as visibility, commodity and power

Beyond affording services and pleasures to users, NDD double up as *visibility*-producing dispositifs of surveillance: exposing the bodies of people to the gaze of the few and the many. The digital traces they recursively expel into the surrounding 'technosphere' make device users transparent to unknown third party observers, be they state officials, insurance actuaries and marketers, qua the flows of media they voluntarily and involuntarily distribute. But as I have also suggested, the effect of this visibility is to (a) normalise subjective experiences of watching and being watched, and (b) desensitise people to the value and significance of their data.

In today's data-driven knowledge economies, personal information is a valuable commodity. It makes 'data barons' – those owning and managing the technical infrastructures – such as Mark Zuckerberg not only extraordinarily wealthy but also immeasurably powerful. As Joris Toonders recently wrote in *WIRED* magazine: 'Data in the 21st Century is Like Oil in the 18th Century: an Immensely, Untapped Valuable Asset'.[10] Yet, as Mark Andrejevic notes, notwithstanding the primacy that is placed by state agencies and corporate firms in data scraping and mining – in establishing correlations in the data for prediction and optimisation: 'we [the general public] have very little access to the forms of information collection and circulation that are taking place "behind the scenes"'(2009, 57). In this way, data afford those who retain it exceptional powers to construct, define and manipulate reality, to even engineer what we see, think, and feel:

> Every click, every like, every comment and every connection is used to build up a rich profile of each user ... Facebook already uses artificial intelligence to personalise your newsfeed, identify you in photos and translate your posts ...The ultimate aim is to develop algorithms that can understand the nuances of people's physical interactions.
>
> *(Olivia Solon[11])*

The consequence of datum flows being routinely syphoned off from the actions of oblivious technovisuals to vast data silos for profiling 'is that 'they' know more than ever about 'us', while we still know very little about them, including who they are and what they know about us' (Stalder 2002, 121). This asymmetrical situation raises three primary issues, each of which will be touched on briefly.

Processing opacity

It is overwhelmingly the case that most data sharers have extremely limited awareness of *when* and *why* data are collected from them, *where* they end up and *how* they get used. And yet the virtual portrait of them assembled from the aggregation of disparate data traces has the means to exercise determinative powers over their life chances and trajectories, either enabling or constraining particular behaviours or mobilities on the basis of how it is actuarially positioned and arranged. Because there is a patent asymmetry in the relation between the watcher and the watched, in terms of their respective positions as unknown and known, unaccountable and accountable, uninformed and informed, impotent and potent, the data sharer is symbolically placed in a situation of vulnerability. The system programmer/data profiler, by contrast, remains unseen and thereby immune from the adverse effects of her/his codifications (or 'its' in the case of an algorithm). There is, for instance, little to no recourse for understanding, let alone objecting to, the probabilistic assumptions and rules that are applied as a means to assign a risk/ value rating to social factors like ethnicity, age, income, sexuality and postcode. Moreover, there is grave concern that software protocols – which make automated judgements and discriminate on the basis of abstract machine-learned logics – operate with limited oversight, treating individuals in markedly different ways as a consequence of their assumed (or appointed) positioning in a wider social field.

Privacy annihilation

The fact that, by choice and design, most aspects of a person's life are now routinely monitored has presented an almighty challenge to historical civil liberties like the right to be let alone. Policies and practices in a digitally saturated world seem to undercut the possibility of a private or anonymous existence. In an age of 'porous bodies' and 'leaky devices' (Smith 2016a), and in a culture where repertoires of sharing and visibility are expected in organisational and community contexts, limited opportunities exist for the autonomous management of impressions. The truth is, even though we might cling to the romantic aspiration of maintaining 'personal space' or a 'private life', in an ecology of mass surveillance and information exchange, this notion is entirely quixotic. Even super rich celebrities, those with exceptional power and resources, find themselves living under a microscope of intensive digital scrutiny, even if this attention is intentionally courted). As Stalder (2002, 122) contends: 'From an individual's point of view, making dozens of complex decisions each day about which data collection to consent to and which to refuse, i.e. to actively exercise informational self-determination, is clearly impractical'. This has produced a situation where, for Haggerty and Ericson (2000, 619), it is no longer possible to live off the grid:

> The coalescence of [data-traces] into the surveillant assemblage marks the progressive 'disappearance of disappearance' – a process whereby it is increasingly difficult for individuals to maintain their anonymity, or to escape the monitoring of social institutions.

I have previously written about the 'embodied exhaustion' that stems from a life of near constant visibility, where the instigators and sources of the gaze remain predominantly indistinct and the exposed subject attempts to manage the digital impressions their bodies and actions generate so as to avoid undesired treatment (Smith 2016a).

Dispossession and disempowerment

Notwithstanding the fact that technovisuals experience pleasures from their use of NDD, it is they who perform *the work* of data sharing in contexts where the texts created are the exclusive property of those administering the technical infrastructures. Mark Andrejevic (2009, 47, 57) introduces the notion of the 'digital enclosure' to describe how the corporate owners of these mediums/platforms strategically convert user content into surplus value: 'This feedback becomes the property of private companies that can store, aggregate, sort and, in many cases, sell the information in the form of a database or cybernetic commodity to others'. He illustrates the ways in which technovisuals become 'feedback devices' for marketing agencies that exploit 'their free [value-generating] participation ... as a form of productive labour [that is] captured by capital' (ibid, 59). Echoing this observation, venture capitalist Om Malik has pointed out with respect to the underlying logics of social networking firms: 'If you're not paying, you're the product'.[12] In this way, the colonisation of the Internet of things by state and market forces can produce relations of digital estrangement and alienation, for example, when we are dispossessed and lose control of the data we create, when it is later used to disadvantage/harm us (especially via racial profiling (Monahan and Palmer 2009)) or when it is sold for a profit that is never remunerated to the data sharer. Andrejevic (ibid, 60–1) accentuates the fact that 'much of the celebratory hype over the way in which the internet creates a new generation of audience-producers blurs the important line between *access* to the means of online content production and *ownership or control* over these resources'. We thus become the experimental 'lab rats' of behavioural economists, who analyse our daily habits and apply psychological heuristics to develop customised advertisements for manipulating desire and orchestrating consumption.

Whither media rights?

I have suggested that digital media, as forms of *visibility* (as a means of making relations legible), *commodity* (as a means of generating capital) and *power* (as a means of exerting influence), pose some important opportunities/risks for rights discourses and practices that require further empirical analysis. The spread of NDD enables new modes of political representation and mobilisation to organically emerge that hold diverse power brokers to account, but in the course of seeking convenience and connectivity technovisuals have traded their anonymity and privacy. The picture is complex, and in constant motion, but it is clear that innovative *post-privacy* frameworks and methodological designs are urgently needed to trace the flows of power, labour and inequality being leveraged in the digital era, as media are created, disseminated, captured and exhibited in the course of everyday social practices and as they simultaneously refigure both public and organisational means of knowing.

There is a call by some to replace 'terms of contract' user agreements with prescriptive 'Rule of Law' precepts that stipulate how data is processed. As Nicolas Suzor has argued: 'Finding a way to interpret and apply the values of the Rule of Law to the corporations that provide our new public spheres – the social media platforms, the content hosts, the search engines, and those that provide the infrastructure – is what needs to change to make sense of the growing concerns about the way that Facebook and others exercise their power'.[13] This kind of call reinforces Andrejevic's (2009, 48) critique that: 'For both legal and regulatory purposes, the notion of privacy, narrowly construed, is insufficient for the task of thinking about the pressing issues surrounding information collection and use ... personal privacy is something that individuals surrender in exchange for access to resources – and they do so under structured power relations that render the notion of free or autonomous consent at best problematic'. For instance, even though individuals repeatedly report in attitudinal surveys that 'privacy' is important to them, they freely trade personal details for discounted products, as in the case of store loyalty cards, just as they register concerns about declining privacy protections in one context while sharing personal intimacies, such as foetal scans, in another. The individualistic notion of privacy has just too many inconsistencies and contradictions that weaken its stake as an antidote to the injurious social effects of mass data-driven surveillance.

Stalder (2002, 123) argues that a more 'offensive' liability approach is needed that demands 'accountability of those whose power is enhanced by the new connections'. This proposal requires Internet Service Providers (ISPs), media platforms, data controllers and governments to be (a) more transparent with regards their data profiling and configuring techniques, and (b) subject to greater oversight by better resourced data commissioners and ombudsman. It also requires citizens to be better educated in digital literacy skills and ethics (that go beyond mere advice on how to avoid being a victim of identity theft), in knowing and exercising their rights and responsibilities with respect to data sharing repertoires, but also in developing a more informed understanding of data politics and ontologies. This is especially the case for the younger generations who have grown (and are growing) up entirely familiar with – and dependent on – digital interfaces as sites of quasi-public space, and who do not necessarily remember or appreciate historical instances from the recent past where data have been used in politicised ways to intimidate and persecute.[14]

Future research is required to identify more robust regulatory tools that can curb the worst excesses of the data sharing economy, especially the marked asymmetries this arrangement consolidates. Post-privacy frameworks that are going to be appropriate for protecting and delivering rights in the digital age must start from a research-driven and user-led evidence base. Thus, there needs to be a sharper focus on how media is coded both by those creating it and those reviewing it. This entails conducting more interdisciplinary research on how technovisuals construe their data, what and why they share online, how they perceive the audience to whom they are posturing and performing, how much they know about dataveillance and cybercrime, and what kinds of meanings they assign to their data presence and that of others. Although this strand must consider the situated social experiences and practices of data sharers, it equally demands that research investigates the operations of those behavioural trackers, be they human or otherwise, who profile and process the digital media that is scraped from diverse sources. Focusing on the axis of assumptions, meanings, targets and logics that mediate their decisions, and what ends their actions serve, will provide clues as to the optimal way of ensuring that regulatory bodies can identify the cultural and experiential structures which tend to perpetuate processes of data-based discrimination and marginalisation, specifically on the grounds of factors like race, ethnicity and poverty.

Notes

1 http://www.sfgate.com/business/ontherecord/article/On-the-Record-Scott-McNealy-2557428.php [Accessed 11 May, 2016].
2 http://www-01.ibm.com/software/data/bigdata/what-is-big-data.html, [Accessed 18 May, 2016].
3 http://www.huffingtonpost.com.au/2013/03/20/cia-gus-hunt-bigdata_n_2917842.html, [Accessed 18 May, 2016].
4 http://www.thecultureist.com/2013/05/09/how-many-people-use-the-internet-more-than-2-billion-infographic/, [Accessed 11 May, 2016].
5 http://edition.cnn.com/2015/11/03/health/teens-tweens-media-screen-use-report/, [Accessed 11 May, 2016].
6 https://www.periscope.tv/, [Accessed 25 May, 2016].
7 http://www.huffingtonpost.com/pierre-omidyar/social-media-enemy-of-the_b_4867421.html, [Accessed 23 May, 2016].
8 http://www.wired.co.uk/article/negroponte-20, [Accessed 27 May, 2016].
9 https://www.theguardian.com/technology/2016/apr/25/how-to-sleep-better-with-technology, [Accessed 25 May, 2016].
10 http://www.wired.com/insights/2014/07/data-new-oil-digital-economy/, [Accessed 10/2/2016].
11 https://www.theguardian.com/technology/2016/apr/23/facebook-global-takeover-f8-conference-messenger-chatbots, [Accessed 27 May, 2016].
12 https://www.theguardian.com/technology/2016/apr/23/facebook-global-takeover-f8-conference-messenger-chatbots, [Accessed 24 May, 2016].
13 https://medium.com/dmrc-at-large/governing-the-internet-the-rule-of-law-in-decentralized-regulation-c9af23d28f6b#.wlhry1i0d, [Accessed 26 May, 2016].
14 http://www.britannica.com/topic/Stasi, [Accessed 28 May, 2016].

References

Andrejevic, M. (2009). 'Privacy, Exploitation, and the Digital Enclosure'. *Amsterdam Law Forum*, 1(4), pp. 47–62.
Beck, U. (2006). *The Cosmopolitan Vision*. Cambridge: Polity Press.

Douglas, M. (1991). *Purity and Danger: An Analysis of the Concepts of Pollution and Taboo*. London: Routledge.

Gandy, O. H. (2006). 'Data Mining, Surveillance, and Discrimination in the Post-9/11 Environment'. In: K. D. Haggerty and R.V. Ericson, eds., *The New Politics of Surveillance and Visibility*. Toronto: University of Toronto Press.

Haggerty, K. D. and Ericson, R.V. (2000). 'The Surveillant Assemblage'. *British Journal of Sociology*, 51(4), pp. 605–622.

Haraway, D. J. (2008). *When Species Meet*. Minneapolis, MN: University of Minnesota Press.

Kellner, D. (1997). 'Intellectuals, the New Public Spheres, and Techno-politics'. *New Political Science*, 41(2), pp. 169–188.

Latour, B. (1987). *Science in Action*. Cambridge, MA: Harvard University Press.

Lupton, D. (2016). 'Digital Companion Species and Eating Data: Implications for Theorising Digital Data–Human Assemblages'. *Big Data & Society*, 3(1), pp. 1–5.

Lyon, D. (2006). '9/11, Synopticon, and Scopophilia: Watching and Being Watched'. In: K.D. Haggerty and R.V. Ericson, eds., *The New Politics of Surveillance and Visibility*. Toronto: University of Toronto Press.

Mathiesen, T. (1997). 'The Viewer Society: Michel Foucault's "Panopticon" Revisited'. *Theoretical Criminology*, 1(2), pp. 215–234.

Miller, P. and N. Rose. (1990). 'Governing Economic Life'. *Economy and Society*, 19(1), pp. 1–31.

Monahan, T. and N. A. Palmer. (2009). 'The Emerging Politics of DHS Fusion Centers'. *Security Dialogue*, 40(6), pp. 617–636.

Negroponte, N. P. (1996). *Being Digital*. New York: Vintage Books.

Poster, M. (1995). *Cyberdemocracy: Internet and the Public Sphere*. Available at: http://www.humanities.uci.edu/mposter/writings/democ.html

Prahalad, C. K. and V. Ramaswamy. (2004). 'Co-Creation Experiences: The Next Practice in Value Creation'. *Journal of Interactive Marketing*, 18(3), pp. 5–14.

Ritzer, G. and N. Jurgenson. (2010). 'Production, Consumption, Prosumption: the Nature of Capitalism in the Age of the Digital "Prosumer"'. *Journal of Consumer Culture*, 10(1), pp. 13–36.

Smith, G. J. D. (2015). *Opening the Black Box: The Work of Watching*, London: Routledge.

Smith, G. J. D. (2016a). 'Surveillance, Data and Embodiment: On the Work of Being Watched'. *Body & Society*, 22(2), pp. 108–139.

Smith, G. J. D. (2016b). 'Companion Surveillance and Surveillant Subjectivities: On the Seduction of Seeing and Being Seen'. *Media Fields Journal: Critical Explorations in Media and Space* 11. Available at http://mediafieldsjournal.squarespace.com/companion-surveillance/

Stalder, F. (2002). Opinion. 'Privacy Is Not the Antidote to Surveillance'. *Surveillance & Society* 1(1), pp. 120–124.

van der Ploeg, I. (2012). 'The Body as Data in the Age of Information'. In: K. Ball, K.D. Haggerty and D. Lyon, eds., *Routledge Handbook of Surveillance Studies*. London: Routledge.

Woo, J. (2006). 'The Right Not to be Identified: Privacy and Anonymity in the Interactive Media Environment'. *New Media & Society*, 8(6), pp. 949–967.

13

ALL HUMAN RIGHTS ARE LOCAL

The resiliency of social change

Jan Servaes

Our world has apparently, once again, entered a deep and fundamental crisis in ecological, economic, social, cultural and spiritual ways. Nobel Prize Winner Amartya Sen observes that 'there is a compelling need in the contemporary world to ask questions not only about the economics and politics of globalization, but also about the values, ethics and sense of belonging that shape our conception of the global world' (Sen 2006, 185). Over the course of history it becomes apparent that we are positioned between the material and the non-material, and between our individuality and the 'others'. 'Throughout the ages and from all sides man (s/he) is called upon to retain the equilibrium within that force field. Time and again, the message is that developments can only continue if a certain middle way is found between fundamental opposites within that social value pattern' (Van Egmond 2013, 133). While worldviews and social values were in the past mainly looked upon as bipolar and limited to national contexts, now they have become increasingly global and multidimensional. Unfortunately, we are again experiencing a loss of equilibrium, resulting in more extreme and fundamentalist value patterns.

Let's start with a brief assessment of freedoms and rights in an historical perspective to summarise the three generations of human rights. Though each generation adds new perspectives and complexity, they all remain very much grounded in Western individualism. As similar waves can be identified in the history of communication for social change theory and praxis, this chapter argues that we need to start analysing human rights from a real-world and localised perspective. As Phil Bloomer argues – 'human rights often lend a vital inspirational role (endorsing the rightness of the struggle); a powerful and universal language (understood nationally and globally and bringing diverse interests together); and a compelling rationale for fair treatment in the face of injustice' (Bloomer 2014, 120) – human rights remain a vital and effective tool for social change. Especially because human rights, besides being a legal category, 'must be understood as a social construction that has been developed and demonstrated in many different ways throughout human history' (Alvarez Icaza 2014).

Three generations

The concepts 'freedom of information', 'free flow of information', 'freedom of expression' or 'freedom of the press' have often been associated with the core of Western thinking, as they emphasise the individualism and liberty ingrained in it. This emphasis can be seen quite prominently in the content of international legal instruments, which uphold the individual as the fundamental unit of value, concludes Michael Elliott (2007, 359–60): 'Human rights instruments are directed overwhelmingly towards the protection of individuals themselves (i.e. everyone/all persons) and categorical groups of individuals (e.g. women, children, the disabled), rather than truly collective or corporate entities (e.g. peoples) ... Given the history and entrenchment of Western cultural assumptions in world society, it is difficult to imagine another entity usurping the ontological primacy of the individual'.

These rights, the so-called civil or freedom rights, can be said to be the first generation of human rights. A second generation of human rights was inspired by socialist revolutions at the turn of the twentieth century, and emphasize the economic and sociocultural rights of people. The right to work, education, shelter and the right to participate in cultural life, belong to this second generation of human rights. These first and second generations of human rights were reformulated as binding international law in two conventions that were adopted in 1966 and came into effect in 1976: the International Covenant on Economic, Social and Cultural Rights, and the International Covenant on Civil and Political Rights.

The third generation of human rights – the so-called solidarity or collective rights – emerged through anti-colonialist revolutions emphasizing national self-determination and non-discrimination. Solidarity rights pertain primarily to certain collective concerns, such as peace, development, ecological balance, culture and communication. These third generation of human rights has seen a greater emphasis on groups but, once again, this tends to manifest itself more in terms of entitlements for sets of individuals rather than for corporate entities themselves (Boli & Elliott 2008).

At the same time, human rights continue to be diffused around the world, with increasing activism by various non-governmental and civil society organizations. Therefore, the content of human rights ideology has become more diverse, but not endlessly so. Despite the 'glocalising' tendencies of world culture, human rights have not been 'localized'. In other words, while some degree of regional differentiation has occurred (in terms of African, European or Islamic Declarations), we have not seen separate human rights documents at many national levels; nor have we seen them for prominent ethnic groups at the subnational levels. Indeed, 'the articulation of human rights continues to be a largely universal endeavour because, for the most part, we continue to believe that we are all part of the same 'human family' – a family of equal and sovereign individuals' (Elliott 2007, 360).

In the domain of the freedom of expression and the freedom of press, one can observe a double evolution since the 1950s. Whereas originally the active right of the so-called sender-communicator to supply information without externally imposed restrictions was emphasized; nowadays the passive as well as active right of the receiver to be informed and to inform gets more attention. Gradually the principle of the right to communicate, which contains both the passive and active right of the receiver became popular. The principle first appeared in 1969 in an article of Jean D'Arcy, the then director of the UN information bureau in New York. D'Arcy (1969, 14) wrote that 'the time will come when the Universal Declaration of Human Rights will have to encompass a more extensive right than man's right to inform, first laid down 21 years ago in Article 19. This is the right of man to communicate'. This principle made its entrance in the UNESCO discourse only after five years, in 1974. Both individual and social rights and duties were included in this right to communicate.

About the same time, another shift took place in the discussions on communication rights and responsibilities; that is, from the so-called maintenance duty of the government towards the media, to an emphasis on the government's duty to take care of and to create the conditions and infrastructure in which the freedom of communication can be realized and stimulated as a fundamental social right. These rights embody the duty of the state and all social organizations to place people's collective interests before national and individual interests. There is also the related recognition that individual rights under international law are linked with the notion that individuals have duties and obligations (Hamelink 2004). For more details, see Servaes (1996), Servaes (1998) and Servaes et al. (2009).

Four pressing questions

An interesting philosophical essay by Richard Thompson Ford (2011), 'Universal Rights down to earth', published in the Amnesty International Global Ethics series edited by Kwame Anthony Appiah, one of our current global philosophers, starts from the assumption that 'Modern human rights are a unique fusion of universal morality, political activism and legal formalism: an approach to social justice that codifies moral intuitions and seeks to enforce them through a combination of political lobbying, public relations campaigning and litigation' (Thompson Ford 2011, 5). Thompson Ford argues that, in certain regions, human rights ideals clash with the limits of institutional capabilities or civic culture; while, elsewhere, rights enforcement leads to further human rights violations. Four pressing questions form the backbone of his review:

- Are rights universal?
- Can abstract rights guide concrete reforms?
- How do rights affect political consciousness?
- Can too many rights make a wrong?

This leads to the conclusion that 'thinking of rights as tools, rather than as abstract moral imperatives, would encourage us to consider alternative approaches to humanitarianism' (Thompson Ford 2011, 121).

Indeed, while the United States proudly self-identifies as the major purveyor of peace, democracy and human rights across the world, one could ask whether this perception of self matches up to the actual policies and history of military actions throughout recent decades? Are the United States' seemingly constant wars (Guatemala, Vietnam, El Salvador, East Timor, Afghanistan, Iraq to name a few) befitting to achieving peace, establishing democracy and guaranteeing human rights? Perhaps most oppressive yet is the US policy in the Middle East, where the US provides Israel with more than $3 billion per year in military assistance – which is roughly one-fifth of America's entire foreign aid budget and more aid than they give to the entire continent of Africa. We see how American policy is determined by the corporate sector, tightly linked to the state, which makes decisions in their own self-interest – in stark opposition to the rhetoric of democracy and human rights (Kaplowitz 2003; Mitchell & Schoeffel 2002; Zinn 2005).

In addition, we know of the different perceptions on humanity, culture and individual and collective rights in Western, Asian and African contexts. Already in the eighties (see, e.g. Servaes 1989) we argued in favour of a triple and dialectically integrated framework for the study of the so-called normative media theories: at a philosophical, a political-economic and a cultural-anthropological level. Others (see, for instance, Christians et al 2009; Lee 2015; Gunaratne 2005; Thissu 2015; Wang 2011) have developed similar arguments. The increasing multiplicity and convergence of ICTs, the Internet and social networks, the deregulation of media markets and the cultural globalization/localisation of media products and services have forced a reassessment in both theory and praxis. Nestor Garcia Canclini (2012), in an overview of communication and human rights in Latin America (Vega Montiel 2012), further argues that the differences between cultures and the way in which they understand human rights are also complicated by the differences between knowledge disciplines, from philosophy and theology to the social sciences. He therefore advocates the need for an interdisciplinary approach to cultural and communication rights.

'Botched abstractions and foggy history' (Sen 2006, 57)

With such a position we are a long way from the noble calls for a global universal ethics. Only about twenty years ago, the report to UNESCO of the World Commission on Culture and Development, chaired by Javier Pérez de Cuéllar (1996, 36–7), noticed 'There is evolving in our time a global civic culture, a culture which contains further elements to be incorporated in a new global ethics. The idea of human rights, the principle of democratic legitimacy, public accountability and the emerging ethos of evidence and proof are the prime candidates for consideration ... Today, the idea of human rights, though still challenged by recalcitrant governments, is a firmly entrenched standard of political conduct and will have to be a cornerstone of any global ethics'. The Commission on Culture and Development suggested that the following principal ideas should form the core of a new global ethics: (a) human rights and responsibilities; (b) democracy and the elements of civil society; (c) the protection of minorities; (d) commitment to peaceful conflict-resolution and fair negotiation; and (e) equity within and between generations. The report started from the above third generation of human rights. It argued that development divorced from its human or cultural context is growth without a soul. This means that culture cannot ultimately be reduced to a subsidiary position as a mere promoter of economic growth. It went on arguing that 'governments cannot determine a people's culture: indeed, they are partly determined by it' (De Cuéllar 1996, 15).

The report observed that many elements of a global ethics were absent from global governance. Therefore, the Commission defined several areas of policy and action for governments, international organizations, private voluntary associations, profit-seeking firms, trade unions, families and individuals, culminating in an international agenda and the principles of cultural respect. The purpose was to mobilize the energies of people everywhere in recognition of new cultural challenges. The Agenda was intended to be selective and illustrative, not comprehensive.

The basic principle should be 'the fostering of respect for all cultures whose values are tolerant of others. Respect goes beyond tolerance and implies a positive attitude to other people and a rejoicing in their culture. Social peace is necessary for human development: in turn it requires that differences between cultures be regarded not as something alien and unacceptable or hateful, but as experiments in ways of living together that contain valuable lessons and information for all' (De Cuéllar 1996, 25).

Cultural freedom differs from other forms of freedom in a number of ways. First, most freedoms refer to the individual. Cultural freedom, in contrast, is a collective freedom. It is the condition for individual freedom to flourish. Second, cultural freedom, properly interpreted, is a guarantee of freedom as a whole. It protects not only the collectivity but also the rights of every individual within it. Third, cultural freedom, by protecting alternative ways of living, encourages creativity, experimentation and diversity, the very essentials of human development. Finally, freedom is central to culture, and in particular the freedom to decide what we have reason to value, and what lives we have reason to seek. 'One of the most basic needs is to be left free to define our own basic needs' (De Cuéllar 1995, 26).

Applying this principle of Cultural Respect universally has proven to be difficult, if not impossible; not only in theory but even more so in the reality of our increasingly fundamentalist world. This has, as Amartya Sen observes in his critique of Huntington's *Clash of Civilizations*, 'possibly terrible consequences of classifying people in terms of singular affiliations woven around exclusively religious identities' (Sen 2006, 76). Joining Mahatma Gandhi, Sen argues that 'there are many identities other than religious ethnicity that are also relevant for a person's self-understanding and for the relations between citizens of diverse backgrounds within the country' (Sen 2006, 168). Putting the discussion in the British context he contends: 'What has to be particularly avoided … is the confusion between multiculturalism with cultural liberty, on the one side, and plural monoculturalism with faith-based separatism on the other. A nation can hardly be seen as a collection of sequestered segments, with citizens being assigned fixed places in predetermined segments. Nor can Britain be seen, explicitly or by implication, as an imagined national federation of religious ethnicities' (Sen 2006, 165). In other words, 'the point is not for everyone to hold the same worldview. The issue rather is whether there would be a common denominator, a common ground between people with differing worldviews' (Van Egmond 2013, 21–2).

So, returning to Thompson Ford's argument – 'To best serve humanity, universal human rights must come down to earth' (Thomson Ford 2011, 123) – we better go 'local'.

Communication for development and social change (CDSC)

The study of communication for development and social change has gone through similar paradigmatic changes.

In general, social change (or development) can be described as a significant change of structured social action or of the culture in a given society, community or context. Such a broad definition could be further specified on the basis of a number of 'dimensions' of social change: space (micro, meso, macro), time (short, medium, long-term), speed (slow, incremental, evolutionary versus fast, fundamental, revolutionary), direction (forward or backward), content (sociocultural, psychological, sociological, organizational, anthropological, economic and so forth) and impact (peaceful versus violent) (Servaes 2011). In Servaes (1999) we distinguished between three general development paradigms (modernisation, dependency and multiplicity), which were narrowed down to two communication paradigms: diffusion versus participatory communication. From the modernization and growth theory to the dependency approach and the multiplicity or participatory model, these latter traditions of discourse are characterised by a turn towards local communities as targets for research and debate, on the one hand, and the search for an understanding of the complex relationships between globalization and localization, on the other hand. While income, productivity and gross domestic product (GDP) are still essential aspects of human development, they are not the sum total of human existence. Previously held traditional modernization and dependency perspectives have become more difficult to support because of the growing interdependency of regions, nations and communities in our globalised world. Just as this has important implications for the way we think about social change and development, so too does it present opportunities for how we think about the role and place of communication and human rights in development and social change processes (Servaes 2015).

The right to communication as a fundamental human right clearly indicates that another communication model necessitates participatory democratisation and thus a redistribution of power on all levels. The point of departure is not an elitist position, but development from the grass-roots level. Even the renowned MacBride Report suggested that the right to communicate 'promises to advance the democratization of communication on all levels – international, national, local, individual' (MacBride 1980, 171).

Fundamental here is the other vision of the role of the authorities in processes of social change. Unlike the confidence in and respect for the role of the state, which is characteristic of the modernization and dependency paradigms, the third multiplicity paradigm has a rather reserved attitude towards the authorities and their power. Policies therefore had to be built on more selective participation strategies of dissociation and association, with less predictable, potentially positive and/or negative consequences.

Over the years, the problems have become more complex and wicked, especially when we add 'sustainability' and 'resiliency' to the discussion on social change (Servaes 2013). Different perspectives – based on both 'Western' and 'Eastern' philosophical starting points – have resulted in a more holistic and integrated vision of sustainable development or social change. Nowadays, four dimensions are generally recognized as the 'pillars' of sustainable development: economic, environmental, social and cultural. At the same time, a unifying theme is that there is no universal development model. Development is an integral, multidimensional and dialectic process that differs from society to society, community to community, context to context. In other words, each society and community must attempt to delineate its own strategy to sustainable development starting with the resources and 'capitals' available (not only physical, financial and environmental but also human, social, institutional etc.) and considering needs and views of the people concerned. In addition, resilience – defined as 'the capacity of individuals, communities and systems to survive, adapt and grow in the face of stress and shocks, and even transform when conditions require it. Building resilience is about making people, communities and systems better prepared to withstand catastrophic events – both natural and manmade – and able to bounce back more quickly and emerge stronger from these shocks and stresses' (Rockefeller Foundation 2013) – refers to three dimensions: the ability to resist, cope and bounce back in the face of disturbance; the capacity to adapt to change and uncertainty; and the capacity for transformation (Brown 2016, 10–11).

In other words, sustainable development or social change implies a participatory, multi-stakeholder approach to policymakingper Oxford and for consistency and implementation, mobilizing public and private resources for development and making use of the knowledge, skills and energy of all social groups concerned with the future of the planet and its people.

Communication and/for change

Over the years we have studied different CSSC approaches that remain being used and applied. Some of these are more traditional, hierarchical and linear, some more participatory and interactive. Most contain elements of both. From an epistemological and ontological perspective, that doesn't always make sense; but in practice that seems to be a given. Generally speaking we identified two approaches: One aims to produce a common understanding among all the participants in a development initiative by implementing a policy or a development project; that is, the top-down model. The other emphasizes engaging the grassroots in making decisions that enhance their own lives, or the bottom-up model. Despite the diversity of approaches, there is a consensus in the early 21st century on the need for grassroots participation in bringing about change at both social and individual levels.

The connection between human rights and communication for development and social change should be obvious. A bottom-up perspective on development or social change argues in favour of empowerment; the ability of people to influence the wider system and take control of their lives. Therefore, this perspective argues that a communication rights based approach needs to be explicitly built into development plans and social change projects to ensure that a mutual sharing/learning process is facilitated. Such communicative sharing is deemed the best guarantee for creating successful transformations.

In other words, the new starting point is examining the processes of 'bottom-up' change, focusing on self-development of local communities. The basic assumption is that there are no countries or communities that function completely autonomously nor completely self-sufficient;

nor are there any nations whose development is exclusively determined by external factors. Every society is dependent on the other in one way or another, both in form and in degree.

Consequently, we further subdivided communication strategies for development and social change at five levels:

1. Behaviour change communication (BCC) (mainly interpersonal communication),
2. Mass communication (MC) (community media, mass media and ICTs),
3. Advocacy communication (AC) (interpersonal and/or mass communication),
4. Participatory communication (PC) (interpersonal communication, community media and social media) and
5. Communication for structural and sustainable social change (CSSC) (interpersonal communication, participatory communication, online media and mass communication).

Interpersonal communication and mass communication form the bulk of what is being studied in the mainstream discipline of communication science. Behaviour change communication is mainly concerned with short-term individual changes in attitudes and behaviour. It can be further subdivided in perspectives that explain individual behaviour, interpersonal behaviour and community or societal behaviour.

Looking at desired or expected outcomes, one could think of four broad headings:

1. approaches that attempt to change attitudes (through information dissemination, awareness building, public relations …)
2. behavioural change approaches (focusing on changes of individual behaviour, interpersonal behaviour and/or community and societal behaviour)
3. advocacy approaches (primarily targeted at policy makers and decision makers at all levels and sectors of society)
4. communication for structural and sustainable change approaches (which could be either top-down, horizontal or bottom-up)

The first three approaches, though useful by themselves, are in isolation not capable of creating sustainable change. Only participatory communication (PC) and communication for structural and sustainable social change (CSSC) are more concerned about long-term sustained change at different levels of society.

That's why we have argued that sustainable social change can only be achieved in combination with and incorporating aspects of the wider environment that influences (and constrains) structural and sustainable change. These aspects include: structural and conjunctural factors (e.g. history, migration, conflicts); policy and legislation; service provision; education systems; institutional and organizational factors (e.g. bureaucracy, corruption); cultural factors (e.g. religion, norms and values); sociodemographic factors (e.g. ethnicity, class); sociopolitical factors; socioeconomic factors; and the physical environment.

Sen's capabilities and freedom framework

With Richard Heeks (2016) we believe that an integration of rights based approaches to social change, linking the 'universally shared values' of 'localized' rights with the subjectivity of Sen's capabilities and freedom framework, might be a 'means of addressing the new forces that impinge on capabilities and functionings as a result of global informationalism; as a struggle between foundational models of organizing and identity' (Heeks 2016, 51).

Sen (1992) argues that humans are different in the environment they live, in physical characteristics, in communities they belong to, and in opportunities available to them. Serious problems and conflicts are often the result of people's identities being narrowed down to only one (religious, ethnic, physical, …) aspect of their being. For instance a disabled person functions differently in society than an able-bodied person will, even if they receive the same income. Therefore, Sen prefers to define the quality of life on the basis of capabilities rather than on functionings. He proposed to stop measuring factors that were only indirectly related to well-being by focusing on functionings or 'the various things a person may value doing or being'. (Sen 2001, 75).

Functioning may range from achieving basic health wellness, participating in a community, attaining educational qualifications or whatever an individual values or hopes to achieve. Capability, on the other hand, refers to the ability to achieve functioning (well-being), it is the freedom and rights of an individual to achieve well being. Expanded to social inequalities, the capabilities approach addresses the issues of social justice, basic rights as a set of fundamental entitlements for all citizens, and opportunities available for citizen to function in society. As we have argued elsewhere, the absence of all these exacerbate social inequalities (Servaes & Oyedemi 2016a).

A person's well-being could than be evaluated by analysing the various functionings achieved in that person's life. It is however important to note the difference between well-being and agency, as highlighted by Marien et al. (2016), because not all functionings are achieved by a single person only (Robeyns 2005). However, a focus on mere functionings would be similar to utilitarian approaches only. Individuals may still choose to disregard these life goals because they favour other goals, or are unable to change resources in functionings due to a lack of particular resources, which are indirectly related to a good. To escape the shortcomings of utilitarian approaches and account for individual heterogeneity, Sen introduces capability sets that constitute all feasible functionings available to a person (Sen 2001, 75), including freedom of choice. It is up to the individual to decide not to convert a possible functioning into an achieved functioning. Robeyns (2005, 99) deepened and diversified the definition of conversion factors by identifying three groups: (1) personal conversion factors (e.g. metabolism, physical condition, sex, reading skills, intelligence) influence how a person can convert the characteristics of a commodity into a functioning; (2) social conversion factors (e.g. public policies, social norms, discriminating practices, gender roles, societal hierarchies, power relations); and (3) environmental conversion factors (e.g. climate, geographical location).

Sen sees freedom as the ultimate goal of development. Freedom can be either instrumental or intrinsic. Instrumental freedoms are basic freedoms required to develop and enable other types of freedom that in turn can again be instrumental or intrinsic. The ultimate goal of Sen's framework for development is intrinsic freedom, or in other words, to have a complete capability set. However, as pointed out by Nussbaum (2003), Sen refrains from defining intrinsic capabilities because they depend on individual and cultural preferences. Therefore, Nussbaum criticizes Sen's lack of fundamental freedoms 'that are to some extent independent of the preferences that people happen to have, preferences shaped, often, by unjust background conditions' (Nussbaum 2003, 48).

Ilse Marien, Rob Heyman, Koen Salemink and Leo Van Audenhove (2016) then raise the issue of ICTs as entitlements. They pose that translating Sen's approach to digital inequalities implies that ICTs can only be entitlements if they are not merely considered as functionings, but also conversion factors for other functionings. However, reflections on ICTs as entitlements should also be reframed more critically, they argue. If a society has to rely on a technology it does not control, such as the Internet or social media, should we strive to make it an entitlement? Especially if this technology in itself is not yet finished or stabilised see (also Klein 2013).

Hence, they warn: 'Defining unfinished ICTs as entitlements is a dangerous game where one risks to drive capitalist expansion while at the same time increasing digital(ised) conversion factors for fundamental freedoms. It means that entitlements are used to primarily drive economic considerations and only secondly fundamental freedoms. Also, non-users, whether by choice or not, beg the question if ICTs should ever be taken as the overall normative stance within society. These non-users may have valid arguments to resist progress and these are nullified if digital by default is set as the overall norm or better said as an unwanted entitlement. One might argue that many self-excluded users rely on proxy users, but they are particular and spontaneous. It is impossible to depend on the benevolence of proxy users in a universal human rights perspective. An ICTs-as-entitlements approach should make claims about the right to proxy technologies or proxy-conversion factors. In other words, an entitlement approach has to question the digital by default instead of vindicating this default' (Marien et al. 2016, 181). An argument which is being echoed in the Latin American context by Jesus Martin Barbero (2012, 166): 'We come to the point of asking what are appropriate cultural rights and communication policies in a time of economic concentration and polarization of what here we will call unequaled differences. We know that diversity exists not only because different sectors of society choose to develop in different ways but also because they had unequal chances to access goods. In conclusion, there are ethnic, linguistic, gender and age differences that are not necessarily conditioned by inequity and there are other differences caused by inequity'.

A promising and much-needed trend?

According to Bloomer (2014), Blackeley (2013), Harris (2010), Nelson & Dorsey (2003), Mander & Tauli-Corpuz (2006), Mitlin et al (2007), Polet (2007), Postigo (2012), Rootes (2008), Wronka (2008) and others, the interaction between human rights and development/social change is growing rapidly, and on several institutional fronts. A more explicit and detailed rights based approach to development/social change, advocacy by human rights, development NGOs, civil society and indigenous peoples and increased attention to cultural, economic and social concerns (based on the second and third generation of human rights) have become a fundamental challenge to a market – 'no end to growth' – view of development which is still dominating the modernization approach of most governments and businesses.

The local bottom-up initiatives are asserting their commitment to (human-) rights-based strategies and mandates, and are now struggling with the implications of those commitments for project and program planning in diverse political and social settings and in diverse organizational structures. They have also begun to explore the underexploited links between development, environment and the protection of civil and political rights in a more systematic and strategic way. Another aspect of the nexus is the emergence of movements to assert and gain leverage from internationally recognized economic and social rights. 'Driven largely by the work of networks of smaller NGOs, and outside the sphere of the major international human rights NGOs, the economic and social rights (ESC) movement aims to mobilize international affirmations of universal rights to a range of social and economic goods—education, health care, water, food, even the right to "development"—to encourage concrete changes in policy and practice by states, corporations and international organizations' (Nelson & Dorsey 2003, 2022).

However, the reality on the ground, the rising inequality and broader social injustice in our societies (ICIJ 2016, Oxfam 2016, Servaes & Oyedemi 2016b) tells us that redistribution of wealth and power, and the right to equal and fair livelihood, health, education etc. needs to go beyond well-intended speeches and declarations. It needs to lead to social change. In other words, the great challenge is making human rights a reality for everyone.

All these dimensions and movements, and the theoretical advances mentioned in this chapter, are essential to understanding the present dynamic interaction of human rights and development/social change. The nexus of human rights and social change is complex and multidimensional, but it also allows for hope and optimism.

References

Alvarez Icaza, E. (2014). 'Human Rights as an Effective Way to Produce Social Change'. *Conectas Human Rights*, 11(20), June. Available at: http://www.conectas.org/en/actions/sur-journal/issue/20/1007257-human-rights-as-an-effective-way-to-produce-social-change [Accessed 15 May, 2016].

Blakeley, R. (2013). 'Human Rights, State Wrongs, and Social Change: the Theory and Practice of Emancipation'. *Review of International Studies*, 39(3), pp. 599–619, doi:10.1017/S0260210512000186

Bloomer, P. (2014). 'Are Human Rights an Effective Tool for Social Change?: A Perspective on Human Rights and Business'. *SUR - International Journal On Human Rights*, 11(20), Jun./Dec 2014. Available at: http://ssrn.com/abstract=2552790 [Accessed 1 April, 2016].

Boli, J. and Elliott, M. (2008). 'Facade Diversity. The Individualization of Cultural Difference'. *International Sociology*, 23(4), pp. 540–60.

Brown, K. (2016). *Resilience, Development and Global Change*. London: Routledge.

Canclini, N. G. (2012). 'Communication and Human Rights'. In: Vega Montiel, A., ed., *Communication and Human Rights*. Mexico: Universidad Nacional Autonoma de Mexico (UNAM), pp. 18–28.

Christians, C. G., Theodore L. G., McQuail, D., Nordenstreng, K. and White, R. A. (2009). *Normative Theories of the Media. Journalism in democratic societies*. Champaign IL: University of Illinois Press.

D'Arcy, J. (1969). 'Direct Broadcast Satellites and the Right to Communicate'. *EBU-Review*. 118, p. 118.

De Cuellar, J. P., ed. (1996). *Our Creative Diversity: Report of the World Commission on Culture and Development*. Paris: United Nations Educational, Scientific, and Cultural Organization.

Elliott, M. (2007). 'Human Rights and the Triumph of the Individual in World Culture'. *Cultural Sociology*, 1(3), pp. 343–63.

Gunaratne, S. (2005). *The Dao of the Press. A Humanocentric Theory*. Cresskill, NJ: Hampton Press.

Hamelink, C. (2004). *Human Rights for Communicators*. Cresskill, NJ: Hampton Press.

Harris, P. (2010). *World Ethics and Climate Change. From International to Global Justice*. Edinburgh: Edinburgh University Press.

Heeks, R. (2016). 'Seeking a New Link between ICTs and Human Development'. *Information Technologies & International Development*, 12(1), pp. 51–4.

ICIJ (2016). The Panama Papers. Washington DC: The International Consortium of Investigative Journalists. Available at: https://panamapapers.icij.org/ [Accessed 1 April, 2016].

Kaplowitz, D. (2003). *In Whose Interest?* [Online]. Available at: http://thoughtmaybe.com/in-whose-interest/ [Accessed 1 April, 2016].

Kleine, D. (2013). *Technologies of Choice? ICTs, Development, and the Capabilities Approach*. Cambridge MA: MIT press.

Lee, Chin-Chuan, ed. (2015). *Internationalizing 'International Communication'*. Ann Arbor MI: University of Michigan Press.

MacBride, S., ed. (1980). *Many Voices, One World: Communication and Society, Today and Tomorrow*. Paris: UNESCO.

Mander, J. and V. Tauli-Corpuz, eds. (2006). *Paradigm Wars. Indigenous Peoples' Resistance to Globalization*. San Francisco: Sierra Club Books.

Marien, I., Heyman, R., Salemink, K. and Van Audenhove, L. (2016). 'Digital by Default. Consequences, Casualties and Coping Strategies'. In: J. Servaes & T. Oyedemi, eds., *Social Inequalities, Media and Communication: Theory and Roots*. Lanham, MD: Lexington Books, Rowman and Littefield.

Martin - Barbero, J. (2012). 'Strategic Challenges: Information Society and Human Rights'. In: A. Vega Montiel, ed., *Communication and Human Rights*. Mexico: Universidad Nacional Autonoma De Mexico (UNAM).

Mitchell, P. and Schoeffel, J., eds. (2002). *Understanding Power. The Indispensable Chomsky*. New York: The New Press.

Mitlin, D., Hickey, S. and Bebbington, A. (2007). 'Reclaiming Development? NGOs and the Challenge of Alternatives'. *World Development*, 35(10), pp. 1699–1720.

Nelson, P. and Dorsey, E. (2003). 'At the Nexus of Human Rights and Development: New Methods and Strategies of Global NGOs'. *World Development*, 31(12), pp. 2013–26.

Nussbaum, M. (2003). 'Capabilities as Fundamental Entitlements: Sen and Social Justice'. *Feminist Economics*, 9(2–3), pp. 33–59.

Oxfam (2016). *An Economy for the 1%. How Privilege and Power in the Economy Drive Extreme Inequality and How This Can be Stopped*. Available at: https://www.oxfam.org/sites/www.oxfam.org/files/file_attachments/bp210-economy-one-percent-tax-havens-180116-en_0.pdf [Accessed 15 May, 2016].

Polet, F., ed. (2007). *The State of Resistance. Popular Struggles in the Global South*. London: Zed Books.

Postigo, H. (2012). *The Digital Rights Movement. The Role of Technology in Subverting Digital Copyright*. Cambridge, MA: The MIT Press.

Robeyns, I. (2005). 'The Capability Approach: A Theoretical Survey'. *Journal of Human Development*, 6(1), pp. 93–117.

Rockefeller Foundation (2013). *100 Resilient Cities*. Available at: http://www.100resilientcities.org/#/-_/ [Accessed 29 Mar. 2016].

Rootes, C., ed. (2008). *Acting Locally. Local Environmental Mobilizations and Campaigns*. London: Routledge.

Sen, A. (1992). *Inequality reexamined*. Cambridge MA: Harvard University Press.

Sen, A. (1993). 'Capability and Well-being'. In: M. Nussbaum and A. Sen, eds., *The Quality of Life*. Oxford: Clarendon Press, pp. 30–53.

Sen, A. (2001). *Development as Freedom*. Oxford/New York: Oxford University Press.

Sen, A. (2004). 'Cultural Liberty and Human Development'. In: S. Fukuda-Parr, ed., *Human Development Report: Cultural Liberty in Today's Diverse World*. New York: United Nations Development Programme.

Sen, A. (2006). *Identity and Violence. The Illusion of Destiny*. New York: Norton.

Servaes, J. (1989). 'Beyond the Four Theories of the Press', *Communicatio Socialis Yearbook, Journal of Christian Communication in the Third World. Vol.* 8, pp. 35–46.

Servaes, J. (1996). *Mensenrechten en conflictbeheersing (Human Rights and Conflict Resolution)*. Leuven: Acco.

Servaes, J. (1998). 'Human Rights, Participatory Communication and Cultural Freedom in a Global Perspective'. *Journal of International Communication*, 5(1–2), pp. 122–33.

Servaes, J. (1999). *Communication for Development. One World, Multiple Cultures*. Cresskill NJ: Hampton Press.

Servaes J., Malikhao P. and Pinprayong T. (2009). 'Communication Rights are Human Rights. A Case Study of Thailand's Media', In: A. Dakroury, M. Eid and Y. Kamalipour, eds., *The Right to Communicate: Historical Hopes, Global Debates, and Future Premises*. Dubuque, IA: Kendall Hunt Publishers, pp. 227–54.

Servaes, J. (2011). 'Social Change', Oxford Bibliographies Online. Oxford University Press. Available at: http://www.oxfordbibliographiesonline.com/display/id/obo-9780199756841-0063 [Accessed 1 April, 2016].

Servaes, J., ed. (2013). *Sustainability, Participation and Culture in Communication. Theory and Praxis*. Bristol-Chicago: Intellect-University of Chicago Press.

Servaes, J. (2015). 'Studying the Global from within the Local'. *Communication Research and Practice*, 1(3), pp. 242–50.

Servaes, J. and Oyedemi, T., eds. (2016a). *Social Inequalities, Media, and Communication: Theory and Roots*. Lanham, MD: Lexington Books, Rowman and Littefield.

Servaes, J. and Oyedemi, T., eds. (2016b). *The Praxis of Social Inequality in Media: A Global Perspective*, Vol. 2, Lanham, MD: Lexington Books, Rowman and Littefield.

Thissu, D. (2015). *International Communication. Continuity and Change*. New York: Bloomsbury Academic.

Thompson Ford, R. (2011). *Universal Rights Down to Earth*. New York: Norton.

Van Egmond, K. (2013). *Sustainable Civilization*. New York: Palgrave Macmillan.

Vega Montiel, A., ed. (2012). *Communication and Human Rights*. Mexico: Universidad Nacional Autonoma de Mexico (UNAM).

Wang, G., ed. (2011). *De-Westernizing Communication Research. Altering Questions and Changing Frameworks*. New York: Routledge.

Wronka, J. (2008). *Human Rights and Social Justice*. Los Angeles: Sage.

Zinn, H. (2005). *A People's History of the United States. 1492-Present*. New York: HarperPerennial.

PART II

Media performance and human rights

Political processes

14

POLITICAL DETERMINANTS OF MEDIA FREEDOM

Sebastian Stier

Introduction

As stated in the United Nations Universal Declaration of Human Rights, press freedom is a universal right.[1] However, states blatantly violate these obligations. The rights of journalists are infringed by restrictive regulations, manipulations of the media market, informal pressures and outright coercion. The degree of freedom in the reporting of print and broadcast media thus crucially depends on political context.

The present literature review outlines how political systems shape media freedom differentiating two mechanisms. Political scientists mostly explained variations in media freedom with political institutions such as parliaments, party competition, checks and balances and the rule of law. These factors shape media policy and also condition a government's coercive capacity towards the media. The literature in political economy explored how governments shape the economic environment in which news media operate. The chapter reviews relevant studies and identifies favourable and adverse political conditions for the media. The article outlines future research avenues and discusses the effects of increasing Internet use on media freedom. There are indications that the spread of the Internet yet again reconfigures state–media relations.

Conceptualizing and measuring media freedom

What is the role of the political system in determining media freedom? For a long time, comparative politics regarded the protection of civil liberties and political persecution as static phenomena inherently tied to certain political systems (Davenport 2007). Correspondingly, the press was considered as being free in democratic and unfree in authoritarian or totalitarian regimes (Friedrich & Brzezinski 1965; Siebert et al. 1963). According to Dahl, media freedom is even one of the preconditions of 'large-scale democracy' (Dahl 2005). But applying such a rigid criterion to the analysis of the press hides many shades of grey found in the real world and ignores the more subtle variations in media freedom between but especially within regime groups. Just compare, for instance, the media in Berlusconi's Italy with Scandinavian media systems, or the brutal suppression of opposing voices by the military government in Egypt with Tunisia's relatively liberal media environment. Recent developments in Hungary and Turkey show that nominally democratic regimes[2] are not immune to government interference with the media.

Normative liberal perspectives conceptualise the press as a Fourth Estate that keeps the government in check, sets the political agenda, distributes political information and presents diverse political viewpoints to the public (Bennett 2010; Gurevitch & Blumler 1990; Norris 2006). However, governments interfere with news production in a multitude of ways, which impedes the press from fulfilling these functions. All over the world, media organizations are censored and journalists are politically persecuted, killed or jailed. More subtly, tight libel laws and restricted access to sources makes investigative news reporting difficult. In many countries, the interests of the government and the owners of large media corporations overlap to a large degree, which narrows the editorial freedoms granted to journalists. The magnitude of government interference critically depends on the political context in which governments and news media operate (Bennett 2010).

Academics from several disciplines have studied how political systems shape the media.[3] A significant share of this discussion has been devoted to the operationalisation of media freedom (McQuail 2005). Here, I follow the definition of Freedom House in which media freedom is regarded as the 'degree to which each country permits the free flow of news and information' (Freedom House 2015), which depends on (1) the extent of political interference, e.g. through intimidation, censorship or political persecution (political environment); (2) constitutional and regulatory means (legal environment); and (3) independence of editorial decisions from commercial or private interests (economic environment). Although the link between the political system and the economic environment is less apparent, the rulemaking authority of the political system ultimately shapes economic activity in general and the media market in particular (see Part 1 of this volume on media regulation). Accordingly, the economic environment has consistently been regarded as an important parameter in normative theories of the press (Bennett 2010; Gurevitch & Blumler 1990; Herman & Chomsky 1988). The discussed operationalization is prevalent in the literature on the political determinants of press freedom, as authors have overwhelmingly relied on the *Freedom of the Press* index (Freedom House 2015). Freedom House annually assesses the degree of media freedom in 199 countries.[4]

Figure 14.1 displays the temporal distribution of media systems as categorised by Freedom House. The most obvious pattern in the data is clearly related to changes in the geopolitical environment: After the end of the Cold War, media systems around the world underwent dramatic changes. Most post-communist and Sub-Saharan media systems have become more liberal and in general, global democratization tendencies throughout the 1990s improved the situation of the media significantly so that the number of free media systems increased until 2003. Afterwards, however, we observe a reversion of the trend, as the number of partly free media systems has risen dramatically. These contexts, in which the major obstacles for the media are rarely blatant censorship or political persecution, but rather indirect government interference, make up the majority of media systems in 2014 (35%). Strikingly, the percentage of free media systems is currently the lowest since 1988 (32%). These temporal patterns will be revisited in the following literature review. The downward trend can be related to changes in the political environment and to technological developments.

Political mechanisms

The following section lays out several mechanisms of how characteristics of political systems affect media freedom. It starts out by discussing the relevance of 'formal-democratic' institutions like parliaments and multiparty systems which have spread significantly since the end of the Cold War (Gandhi 2008; Magaloni & Kricheli 2010).

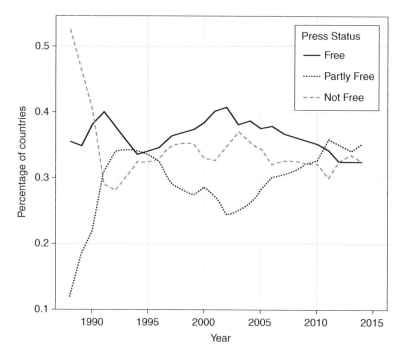

Figure 14.1 Press freedom status 1988–2014 (Freedom House, 2015)

On the one hand, democratic institutions enhance the protection of human rights (Davenport 2007). Facing political competition and participation by citizens, governments have to consider electoral consequences when applying repressive policies. In addition to that, institutional checks and balances limit the coercive capacity of governments. Accordingly, the presence of parliaments and opposition parties increases media freedom, even in non-democratic contexts (Gandhi 2008). Gandhi illustrates how the political opposition in Jordan's parliament impacted the long-lasting political negotiations on media laws during the 1990s. Improvements in the relative power of the parliament and opposition parties lead to more liberal media policies (Gandhi 2008, 108–9). In line with this argument, the level of democratization, as measured by the Polity index, is correlated positively with media freedom (Egorov et al. 2009; Norris 2006). The media liberalisation accompanying worldwide democratization tendencies during the 1990s corroborate these institutionalist arguments (Figure 14.1).

On the other hand, the number of partly free media systems has increased since 2003. This development coincides with the rise of 'electoral' or 'competitive authoritarian regimes' (Levitsky & Way 2010; Schedler 2002). These regimes hold elections but the electoral 'playing field' (Levitsky & Way 2010) is manipulated in favour of incumbent governments. One of the main tools of dominant political elites to bias the playing field is interference with the news media. Guriev and Treisman (2015) even regard 'information based dictatorships' as the main manifestation of autocracy in the 21st century. Authoritarian governments rarely repress their citizens, because this would signal their unpopularity and failed policies to the public. Yet, restrictive media policies and other propagandistic means are used strategically in order to portray the incumbent government as beneficial to the people while presenting the opposition as incompetent. According to this literature, the media is not blatantly persecuted, but trapped in a tightly defined role within such semi-pluralist political systems.

Comparative politics has devoted increasing attention to the study of authoritarian regime subtypes. Stier (2015) shows that electoral autocracies, despite the previously described deficiencies, still have the highest media freedom. At the other end of the non-democratic spectrum are communist regimes, a category that includes contemporary China, Cuba, North Korea and Vietnam, notorious violators of human rights. The totalitarian ideology not only aims to transform politics, but society as a whole. In order to control the flow of information and spread a coherent ideology, the communist party maintains a communications monopoly, i.e. many mass media platforms are nationalised and independent outlets tightly controlled (Friedrich & Brzezinski 1965; Voltmer 2008, 29). Monarchies and military regimes have also had surprisingly high levels of media freedom until 2010, the last year in Stier's statistical analysis. However, these results should be regarded as preliminary, especially in light of the media suppression by the recently instated military governments in Egypt and Thailand and the deteriorating situation of the media in Middle Eastern monarchies as a consequence of the Arab Spring (Lynch 2015).

Further studies investigated how institutional configurations of formal-democratic political systems are related to media freedom. Bairett (2015) demonstrates that in Central and Eastern Europe, the situation of the media is precarious in presidential regimes, during periods of enhanced executive power and when governments have considerable legislative competencies. Prime examples for this are the judicial media harassment and violence against journalists in Putin's Russia or recent legislative media reforms in Poland and Hungary. Kellam and Stein (2016) report similar results showing that the institutional and political strength of presidents as well as leftist ideologies are the major impediments to media freedom in South America. In contrast, institutional and judicial checks and balances serve as protections for the media.

Another group of studies investigated how endogenous or exogenous political conditions that vary in the short term influence state-media relationships. One important variable in authoritarian contexts is bureaucratic performance. By permitting certain levels of independent watchdog journalism, a regime can improve political control over bureaucratic agents and enhance economic and political performance. Such a fine-grained media policy 'reduces corruption while still maintaining citizens' uncertainty about the true level of discontent' (Lorentzen 2014, 405). In the model of Lorentzen (2014), the degree of media freedom is adjusted by the central government depending on the level of social tensions. When the political situation is unstable and thus the circulation of true information potentially more damaging, media policies become more restrictive. Building on similar assumptions, Egorov et al. (2009) introduce an additional source of variation in their model and empirical panel analyses: natural resources. When oil prices and oil reserves are high, governments in resource rich states can extract and distribute rents freely and rely less on bureaucratic performance. However, this calculation changes with declining resource revenues. When the quality of governance and with it economic growth becomes the primary pillar of state performance, the political dangers of independent media reporting can become a risk worth taking for governments.

In weak democratic contexts, media policies are also subject to short-term political considerations of governments. In Africa, periods of political instability like public protests, coups or constitutional reform efforts by the government are accompanied by harassment of the media (VonDoepp & Young 2013). Kellam and Stein (2016) unveil the same mechanism in South America with regard to strikes, demonstrations and economic crises. In a follow-up study, VonDoepp and Young (2015) concentrate on factors constraining government interference with the media. Media freedom is higher in democratic and hybrid regimes in Africa when the rule of law is strong and the media is embedded in civil society. In further correlations, the authors show that more active media consumption correlates with less media harassment. This indicates that attentive audiences limit the role of the state. Finally, several studies have identified a negative impact of violent conflicts and weak state institutions on media freedom (Stier 2015; VonDoepp & Young 2013; Waisbord 2002). In politically unstable contexts, violence against journalists is not only perpetrated by governments but also by other conflict parties.

While there is agreement on the positive effects a powerful judicial branch has on media freedom, the literature is ambiguous regarding the role of formal-democratic institutions. It has been argued that elections, parliaments and opposition parties serve as checks and balances protecting the media. However, democratically elected governments use their power to influence news coverage in illegitimate ways and formal-democratic institutions are also strategic tools of ruling authoritarian elites to maintain their grip on power. The mere presence of elections and opposition parties does therefore not guarantee media freedom. In many contexts, interference with news coverage is even one of the primary instruments of electoral manipulation (Levitsky & Way 2010). Diverging academic assessments of the relationship between institutional pluralism and media freedom are also a matter of perspective. If the status of the media under semi-authoritarian rule and in weak democratic contexts is assessed according to normative ideals of the press, the situation certainly looks dire. But such volatile environments are still preferable to the hostile media policies of closed autocracies.

The literature review and the negative trend displayed in Figure 14.1 have made apparent that the media is under severe pressure in large parts of the world. We are observing 'new hybrid forms of political communication [...] that blend liberal ideals of a free press with the trajectories of the past, indigenous values and the constraints and experiences of transition' (Voltmer 2008, 23). Further research needs to be conducted on the precise mechanisms shaping state-press relations in non-Western contexts. How are discursive boundaries defined? What is the role of the media in non-democratic electoral processes? How credible and persuasive are the news to audiences in partly free media systems?

Economic mechanisms

A substantial body of literature, especially from political economy, concentrates on the economic environment of the media. Authors investigate the sources of media bias, which can be defined as 'distortions that originate on the supply side of the media market' (Gentzkow & Shapiro 2008, 134). I review studies that explicitly relate the economic context to political processes and the intentions of governments.

The central finding of this literature is that private ownership of the media reduces media bias (Besley & Prat 2006; Djankov et al. 2003; Gentzkow & Shapiro 2008; Petrova 2011). Djankov et al. (2003) compiled a dataset of media ownership and identify positive correlations between private media ownership and diverse outcome variables, including press freedom. They conclude that governments interfere with state owned media outlets in order to hold onto power and impede government oversight. The formal model of Besley and Prat (2006) concurs with this finding but demonstrates the importance of competition in news markets, since ownership concentration facilitates media capture by political interests. When ownership is heterogeneous, government capture of parts of the media increases the commercial incentives of competitors to report non-biased information (Gentzkow & Shapiro 2008). Petrova (2011) adds that only after advertising revenues had reached a certain threshold, US newspapers emancipated themselves from partisan political interests. Gehlbach & Sonin (2014) develop a model that indicates greater media bias in autocracies and small media markets where advertising revenues from governments are an important source of income for media corporations. Media bias decreases with growing advertising markets, but not linearly, as governments, especially non-democratic ones, may target advertising revenues and nationalise the media.

In contrast to this literature that presents an 'argument for economic liberalization before political liberalization' (Petrova 2011, 806) in democratization processes, there is a long tradition in media studies addressing the deficiencies of media commercialization (Herman & Chomsky 1988; McChesney 2008). Private media ownership is often concentrated in the hands of a small number of media barons or families (Djankov et al. 2003) who have their own political interests which are often aligned to the government. While it has long been thought that economic liberalization of the media would enhance the democratization of political regimes (Lerner 1958), it has been shown empirically that media commercialization can preserve the political status quo depending, in accordance with the previous chapter, critically on political context (Akser & Baybars-Hawks 2012; Stockmann 2013; Stockmann & Gallagher 2011). Stockmann (2013) demonstrates that the introduction of market principles has not improved media freedom in China, but contributed to the legitimacy of the communist one-party state. In South America, intensified media competition fits well with the personalisation of presidential politics and the entertainment orientation of audiences, while the political diversity of media coverage has remained notoriously underdeveloped (Voltmer 2008; Waisbord 2002, 2010). The continued importance of government advertising also preserves the influence of the state (Waisbord 2010).

Taken together, the literature indicates that private ownership constitutes an enabling condition for media freedom. However, the relationship between economic liberalization and media freedom is not a linear one. Critical research on the political economy of the mass media shows that market mechanisms can severely constrain journalistic work. In addition to that, the state still considerably shapes the media market, as demonstrated by the political path dependencies in China and South America. Further research should thus concentrate on the entanglement of political and economic interests. Since the economic literature prefers formal models over empirical analysis, we still lack robust evidence at the organizational and individual level of how economic mechanisms influence journalism, in particular outside established democracies.

Old and new media

The emergence of the Internet and the growing use of digital technologies by citizens have not only fundamentally transformed journalism (see Allan in this volume) and news consumption (see McPherson in this volume), but have induced structural shifts in the communication environment at the macro level, as institutionalized power relations and the roles of state actors are reconfigured in the new realms of communication (Castells 2007). These transformations also affect the role of traditional media. Recent developments point towards an inverse relationship between Internet diffusion and media freedom. Yet, in accordance with the preceding discussions, the causal mechanisms behind these processes vary in different political regimes.

There are indications that authoritarian regimes restrict the coverage of traditional media in order to compensate for the availability of additional sources of information on the Internet. As more and diverse information opportunities arise for citizens, governments seem to have ramped up their efforts to control the mass media. Stier (2015) included Internet diffusion as a control variable in his panel analysis of media freedom and indeed identified a negative relationship. Newland and Lorentzen (2015) ran multiple panel regressions to investigate the relationship between Internet diffusion and media freedom in more depth. They mostly get insignificant results, except for authoritarian party regimes which have reduced media freedom in parallel with the growing Internet use by their citizens. This is consistent with the model of Lorentzen (2014) in which one-party states in particular use their central control of the mass media to adjust information controls. In the Middle East, where the mobilizing potential of social media became apparent during the Arab Spring, the mass media also suffers from a tightening grip of state authorities (Lynch 2015).

The Internet also seems to have negative repercussions for media freedom in democracies, although the effect is more indirect (McChesney 2008). It is not only or mainly the political use of the medium by citizens that unsettles governments but also considerations related to national security and geopolitics. The use of the Web by criminals and terrorists serves as a justification to expand national regulation, jurisdiction, prosecution and surveillance on the Internet (see Briant in this volume). These measures also target the use of the Web for whistleblowing by the likes of Wikileaks and Edward Snowden. In the aftermath of the uncovering of NSA spying, journalists were harassed by government agencies. The Guardian, for instance, had to destroy hard drives with leaked data from Edward Snowden in order to avoid legal action by the British government. The partner of investigative journalist Glenn Greenwald was kept in custody for nine hours based on dubious legal justifications. US writers have severely self-censored due to the knowledge of mass surveillance and journalistic work has been exacerbated in general, since the integrity of communication with and the trustfulness of sources have deteriorated sharply (PEN America 2013).

There is also an economic dimension at play: The Internet has suppressed the advertising revenues of mass media organizations (Zentner 2012). As circulation and viewership of traditional media declined, publishers had to cut newsroom staff and resources. Especially the newspaper industry has been hard-hit by several bankruptcies and an increasing concentration of the newspaper market. In 2013 for instance, Jeff Bezos, ironically the founder of Internet company Amazon, bought The Washington Post in a package with other assets. In addition to these aggravated economic circumstances, the media has to adjust to the accelerated information environment of social media in which breaking news get rewarded with more clicks than well-researched and fact-checked articles. In the digital age, it is challenging for the media to fulfill the functions normative theories of the press ascribe to it. McChesney comments: 'generating effective policies for the establishment of viable news media is a central dilemma [sic!] our times. It has always been an issue, but with the twin blades of neoliberalism and the Internet it is approaching crisis stage' (McChesney 2008, 20).

Conclusion

Press freedom is an endangered human right in all parts of the world. Political science and economics revealed several mechanisms of how the political context impacts news reporting. It is apparent that the presence of democratic institutions is a necessary but not a sufficient condition for the emergence and preservation of a free media system. Authoritarian as well as democratic governments use political and economic instruments to pressurise, regulate, harass or persecute the media in order to undermine government oversight by the public, prevent the spread of alternative political viewpoints and impede reporting on human rights violations. Empirical press freedom data records the lowest number of free media systems since the early 1990s, while the highest share of contemporary media systems belongs to the partly free category, where the role of the press as a Fourth Estate is precarious.

This chapter has mostly concentrated on the institutionalized mass media. Yet, theoretical models and empirical research on state-media relationships need to increasingly incorporate varying media logics. In (semi-)authoritarian regimes like Russia or Venezuela and weak democratic contexts like Hungary or Turkey we can observe targeted policies constraining certain aspects of journalistic work coupled with more diffuse information controls on the Internet. State actors impose regulation on contents and internet service providers, block websites and censor contents. Guriev and Treisman (2015) regard such 'information based dictatorships' as the current model of choice for dominant elites to sustain their rule by less repressive means. As Internet diffusion in autocracies grows, political interventions in the digital realm should become more widespread. Latent chilling effects online and offline also affect journalism and political expression in democratic countries. It is of utmost academic and political importance that researchers look beyond the surface and reveal the increasingly obscure violations of media freedom which not only limit the role of the media as a public watchdog but in consequence endanger human rights in general.

Notes

1 The terms 'media' and 'press' are used interchangeably and refer to the traditional non-digital media newspapers, TV and radio. Internet freedom is an entirely different subject, which should be investigated by taking the more technical Internet governance into account.
2 According to standard regime datasets used in comparative politics.
3 The literature review excludes the lively debate on the role of the media in democratization processes (Lerner 1958; Norris 2006; Voltmer 2008) and also studies using media freedom as an independent variable, for example as an impeding factor of corruption (e.g. Brunetti & Weder 2003). The literature on media systems in established democracies (e.g. Hallin & Mancini 2004) is also not featured in this global assessment of media freedom, since these studies mostly focus on the Western world.
4 See for an evaluation of the methodology: Becker et al. (2007). The level of agreement between the Freedom House measurement and alternative indicators of press freedom is high (Becker et al. 2007; Stier 2015).

References

Akser, M. and Baybars-Hawks, B. (2012). 'Media and Democracy in Turkey: Toward a Model of Neoliberal Media Autocracy'. *Middle East Journal of Culture and Communication*, 5(3), pp. 302–21.

Bairett, R. L. (2015). 'Executive Power and Media Freedom in Central and Eastern Europe'. *Comparative Political Studies*, 48(10), pp. 1260–92.

Becker, L. B., Vlad, T. and Nusser, N. (2007). 'An Evaluation of Press Freedom Indicators'. *International Communication Gazette*, 69(1), pp. 5–28.

Bennett, W. L. (2010). 'The Press, Power and Public Accountability'. In: S. Allan, ed., *The Routledge Companion to News and Journalism*, Oxford: Routledge, pp. 105–15.

Besley, T. and Prat, A. (2006). 'Handcuffs for the Grabbing Hand? Media Capture and Government Accountability'. *American Economic Review*, 96(3), pp. 720–36.

Brunetti, A. and Weder, B. (2003). 'A Free Press Is Bad News for Corruption'. *Journal of Public Economics*, 87(7–8), pp. 1801–24.

Castells, M. (2007). 'Communication, Power and Counter-power in the Network Society'. *International Journal of Communication*, 1(1), pp. 238–66.

Dahl, R. A. (2005). 'What Political Institutions Does Large-scale Democracy Require?'. *Political Science Quarterly*, 120(2), pp. 187–97.

Davenport, C. (2007). 'State Repression and Political Order'. *Annual Review of Political Science*, 10, pp. 1–23.

Djankov, S., McLiesh, C., Nenova, T. and Shleifer, A. (2003). 'Who Owns the Media?'. *The Journal of Law and Economics*, 46(2), pp. 341–82.

Egorov, G., Guriev, S. and Sonin, K. (2009). 'Why Resource-poor Dictators Allow Freer Media: A Theory and Evidence from Panel Data', *American Political Science Review*, 103(4), pp. 645–68.

Freedom House (2015). *Freedom of the Press 2015: Harsh Laws and Violence Drive Global Decline*. Available online at: https://freedomhouse.org/report/freedom-press/freedom-press-2015 [Accessed 1 March, 2017].

Friedrich, C. J. and Brzezinski, Z. (1965). *Totalitarian Dictatorship and Autocracy*, 2nd ed, Cambridge, MA: Harvard University Press.

Gandhi, J. (2008). *Political Institutions Under Dictatorship*. New York, NY: Cambridge University Press.

Gehlbach, S. and Sonin, K. (2014). 'Government Control of the Media'. *Journal of Public Economics*, 118, pp. 163–71.

Gentzkow, M. and Shapiro, J. M. (2008). 'Competition and Truth in the Market for News'. *Journal of Economic Perspectives*, 22(2), pp. 133–54.

Gurevitch, M. and Blumler, J. G. (1990). 'Political Communication Systems and Democratic Values'. In: J. Lichtenberg, ed., *Democracy and the Mass Media*, New York, NY: Cambridge University Press, pp. 269–89.

Guriev, S. and Treisman, D. (2015). *How Modern Dictators Survive: An Informational Theory of the New Authoritarianism*, NBER Working Paper (No. 21136).

Hallin, D. C. and Mancini, P. (2004). *Comparing Media Systems: Three Models of Media and Politics*. New York, NY, UK   : Cambridge University Press.

Herman, E. S. and Chomsky, N. (1988). *Manufacturing Consent: The Political Economy of the Mass Media*. London: Random House.

Kellam, M. and Stein, E. A. (2016). 'Silencing Critics: Why and How Presidents Restrict Media Freedom in Democracies'. *Comparative Political Studies*, 49(1), pp. 36–77.

Lerner, D. (1958). *The Passing of Traditional Society: Modernizing the Middle East*, Glencoe, IL: Macmillan Pub Co.

Levitsky, S. and Way, L. (2010). *Competitive authoritarianism: Hybrid regimes after the Cold War*. New York: Cambridge University Press.

Lorentzen, P. (2014). 'China's Strategic Censorship'. *American Journal of Political Science*, 58(2), pp. 402–14.

Lynch, M. (2015). 'The Rise and Fall of the New Arab Public Sphere'. *Current History*, December 2015, pp. 331–36.

Magaloni, B. and Kricheli, R. (2010). 'Political Order and One-party Rule'. *Annual Review of Political Science*, 13(1), pp. 123–43.

McChesney, R. W. (2008). *The Political Economy of Media: Enduring Issues, Emerging Dilemmas*. New York: Monthly Review Press.

McQuail, D. (2005). *McQuail's Mass Communication Theory*. 5th ed. London and Thousand Oaks: Sage Publications.

Newland, S. A. and Lorentzen, P. (2015). 'Countering Liberation Technology: Internet Access and Media Freedom in Autocracies'. Available at: http://peterlorentzen.com/research_files/Newland_Lorentzen_Media.pdf [Accessed 1 March, 2017].

Norris, P. (2006). 'The Role of the Free Press in Promoting Democratization, Good Governance and Human Development'. In: Global Forum for Media Development, ed., *Media Matters*, Brussels, pp. 66–75.

PEN America (2013). *Chilling Effects: NSA Surveillance Drives U.S Writers to Self-censor*. Available at: https://www.pen.org/sites/default/files/Chilling%20Effects_PEN%20American.pdf [Accessed 1 March, 2017].

Petrova, M. (2011). 'Newspapers and Parties: How Advertising Revenues Created an Independent Press', *American Political Science Review*, 105(4), pp. 790–808.

Schedler, A. (2002). 'The Menu of Manipulation'. *Journal of Democracy*, 13(2), pp. 36–50.

Siebert, F. S., Peterson, T. and Schramm, W. (1963). *Four Theories of the Press: The Authoritarian, Libertarian, Social Responsibility, and Soviet Communist Concepts of What the Press Should Be and Do*. Urbana: University of Illinois Press.

Stier, S. (2015). 'Democracy, Autocracy, and the News: The Impact of Regime Type on Media Freedom'. *Democratization*, 22(7), pp. 1273–95.

Stockmann, D. (2013). *Media Commercialization and Authoritarian Rule in China*, New York, NY: Cambridge University Press.

Stockmann, D. and Gallagher, M. E. (2011). 'Remote Control: How the Media Sustain Authoritarian Rule in China'. *Comparative Political Studies*, 44(4), pp. 436–67.

Voltmer, K. (2008). 'Comparing Media Systems in New Democracies: East Meets South Meets West'. *Central European Journal of Communication*, 1(1), pp. 23–40.

VonDoepp, P. and Young, D. J. (2013). 'Assaults on the Fourth Estate: Explaining Media Harassment in Africa'. *The Journal of Politics*, 75(1), pp. 36–51.

VonDoepp, P. and Young, D. J. (2015). 'Holding the State at Bay: Understanding Media Freedoms in Africa'. *Democratization*, doi:10.1080/13510347.2015.1044524

Waisbord, S. (2002). 'Antipress Violence and the Crisis of the State'. *The Harvard International Journal of Press/Politics* 7(3), pp. 90–109.

Waisbord, S. (2010). 'Latin America'. In P. Norris, ed., *Public Sentinel: News Media and Governance Reform*. Washington, DC: World Bank, pp. 305–28.

Zentner, A. (2012). 'Internet Adoption and Advertising Expenditures on Traditional Media: An Empirical Analysis Using a Panel of Countries'. *Journal of Economics & Management Strategy*, 21(4), pp. 913–26.

15

BEYOND THE BINARY OF UNIVERSALISM AND RELATIVISM

Iran, media and the discourse of human rights

Mehdi Semati

Introduction

Advocating human rights is a perilous activity. Human rights activists who live in authoritarian states pay the heaviest price for their writings and for their political and legalistic activities. For academics who live in the West and write about human rights in their native country such writing poses a different kind of challenge. On the one hand, if one writes unapologetically in defence of human rights and universal normative principles, one runs the risk of being viewed an accomplice to the forces of empire, ignoring the specificity of the local and betraying the natives. On the other, if one cautions against universal claims and advocates for an approach that attends to the agency of the local population in the face of political constraints, one runs the risk of being called an apologist for the authoritarian regimes.

Writing about human rights and communication media presents its own set of challenges as the discourses of human rights, with their universal normative foundations, run the risk of being abused by imposing a top-down model that not only ignores the local cultural practices and legal frameworks, but also promotes an ineffectual approach. In this chapter I address media and the discourse of human rights as they relate to the Islamic Republic of Iran. I argue that advocating human and communication rights in a global framework built on universal normative principles without considering the local legal, cultural, political and technological contexts is trafficking in abstractions at best, and, at worst, an abuse of human rights principles and a silencing of native voices that are articulating such principles locally. In a framework that rejects the binary of 'universalism' and 'cultural relativism', I highlight the local discourses that attempt to rearticulate or reclaim normative principles as compatible with local traditions (e.g. reformist figures claiming normative principles underpinning the Universal Declaration of Human Rights as compatible with Islamic traditions). Moreover, I show how these principles are fought for or lived out in specific cultural practices. The approach I suggest allows us to advocate for human rights while attentive to the contexts in which media institutions and practices emerge as products of a state's social and media policies. Additionally, it allows us to account for the ways in which local individual and collective agency deploys communication media to assert itself, and to challenge the state.

In doing so I address communication technologies and media with respect to issues of press freedom, media access, political communication, performing citizenship and political structures in the Islamic Republic of Iran. Iran is a significant and interesting case for addressing human rights issues because it is at once, and paradoxically, one of the most vilified countries in the Western imagination and one of the brightest spots in an otherwise troubled Middle East. Iran is often characterized as a theocracy and an authoritarian state, ruled by religious fanatics. Yet, Iranian social space, unlike its formal political space, remains relatively open. Iranian cultural and communication space is fairly dynamic and conducive to empowering individual and collective agency in spite of the state's wish to deny this agency. These realities of the Islamic Republic of Iran suggest we cannot approach the discourse of human rights without acknowledging the ambiguities, contradictions and complexities that characterise each context, complexities that make it impossible to impose a ready-made approach that only demands implementation without understanding local transformations and dynamics.

In the first part of this chapter I review some of the theoretical difficulties that haunt the human rights discourses. In the second part, I present the case of the Islamic Republic of Iran in two sections: First, I discuss these theoretical ambiguities in the case of Iran in terms of the debate that pits 'universalists' against 'cultural relativists'; second, I present the state of media and communication space in Iran in order to reflect on those issues that animate the human rights discourse. I would argue that although we should not stop demanding respect for human and communication rights, placing emphasis solely on the state's attempt at censorship and intimidation is misleading. This is so because such emphasis tends to abstract the individual and collective agency in the face of such attempts. This agency is exercised through different means and in the performance of citizenship outside the arena of formal politics. If in the title of this chapter I use Iran instead of the Islamic Republic of Iran it is because in much of the discourse of human rights and Iran, Iranians and their practices of defiance are often erased when the state becomes the only focus in human rights discussions. Moreover, in such discussions the state's own communication and media policies in facilitating the infrastructure that individuals use to exercise their agency are ignored.

The theoretical foundations of human rights discourse

The main initial difficulty with international human rights law is that it does not account for the theoretical foundation upon which it is based (Donnelly, 2006). It asserts that human beings are free and entitled to equal dignity and rights (Article 1, Universal Delectation), and that such rights are founded on the 'inherent dignity of the human person' (Covenants, Preamble). As Donnelly (2006) argues, while the social contract tradition merely assumes such rights exist, the moral theory tradition in Western thought doesn't address it at all. This difficulty reveals itself in the proliferation of the literature on a debate between the proponents of 'universalism' of rights and their opponents who argue for 'cultural relativism', as the local applicability of normative universal principles becomes a vexing issue. In addressing this binary, Donnelly (2007) writes in defence of 'functional, international legal, and overlapping consensus universality' because 'anthropological and ontological universality' are not defensible empirically and philosophically (281). The push to 'negotiate culture and human rights' has produced notions such as 'tempered universalism' and 'chastened universalism' (See Bell, Nathan, & Peleg, 2000).

In 'rethinking human rights', Chandler's (2002) contribution raises significant 'questions which challenge the radical claims of the proponents of human rights approaches and suggest that rather than challenging political and economic inequalities in the international system, the human rights framework is facilitating new hierarchies of control and regulation' (2). Chandler goes on to argue that the discourses of human rights have been deployed to recast the international order in its unipolar rendition, where we have, in Kosovo, our 'first international military intervention against a sovereign state for purely human rights purposes' (4). Furthermore, human rights discourse, especially women's rights, has been deployed to frame the so-called war on terror by the United States and Great Britain (5).[1] The abuse of insinuations of human rights became 'scandalous' when it was announced that Saudi Arabia, arguably one of the worst violators of human rights in the world, was chosen as 'Chair of a key UN Human Rights Council panel, with the power to select top officials who shape international human rights standards and report on violations worldwide'.[2]

Another difficulty with the discourse of human rights is that of neatly separating the civil and political rights from economic, social and cultural rights, which presents a problem in advancing arguments in favour of communication and media rights as human rights. This is a difficulty because the relationship between human rights and communication rights revolves around issues grounded in civil and political rights. As many international treaties treat freedom of expression and unfettered access to information as elements of human rights, they tend to ground them in civil and political domains. The right to freedom of opinion and expression is, in fact, enshrined in the articles 19 and 20 of the International Covenants on Civil and Political Rights.[3]

However, it is the concern with the specificity of the cultural[4] and the preoccupation with 'media systems' that interest communication and media scholars in discussing rights. Studying communication space or 'media system' of other countries in a global framework involving normative principles is difficult to conduct without addressing the legal framework and the political context in which media institutions and practices exist. It might be useful to remember that one of the most well-known academic books in communication that tried to explain media systems failed to deliver on some of its most basic premises simply because it ignored local legal traditions and the way they give rise to specific conceptualizations of rights. *Four Theories of the Press* (Siebert, Peterson, & Schramm, 1956), one of the most influential and enduring books on the subject in international communication, which tried to offer normative principles in a global framework, never mentions the Universal Declaration of Human Rights.[5] In the next part, I relate the preceding discussion to the discourse of human rights in the Islamic Republic of Iran in terms of the debate between universalism and cultural relativism.

Human rights and the case of the Islamic Republic of Iran

In this part of the chapter, in the first section I discuss the theoretical difficulties of human rights discourse in the case of Iran. In the second section, I present the state of media and communication space in Iran to reflect on those issues that animate the human rights discourse.

Between universalism and relativism, the Iranian case

The debates about human rights in the Islamic Republic have not been immune from the larger discursive formations of international human rights regime. As far back as 2001, for example, a book was published that warned us of the evils of 'cultural relativism' in the discourse of human rights on Iran. Afshari's (2001) book, *Human Rights in Iran: The Abuse of Cultural Relativism*, deploys a no-nonsense approach that seeks to expose the 'curse of the religious state' (54). The subtitle of the book makes the author's commitments clear. He briskly does away with 'the mirage of cultural authenticity' in a space of thirteen pages. Advocating 'universalism', the rest of the book is devoted to listing how the Islamic Republic has violated various rights of its people. Such an approach does not really tell us much beyond a list of offenses committed by 'the religious state' against hapless and helpless 'victims'. Not only does it ignore the complexity of the character of 'the state', it is oblivious to any local articulations of the universal principles it seeks to advocate. Moreover, its binary opposition of universalism and relativism renders both culture and rights as static and ahistorical.

Others have advocated a more nuanced approach. Arzoo Osanloo's *The Politics of Women's Rights in Iran* (2009), for example, focuses on how local cultural, legal and social conditions determine urban middle class women's conceptualization of rights. Her research on Tehran Family Court proceedings, female Qur'anic meetings and other formal and informal settings shows the 'renewed emphasis on a language of rights marks an ideological shift in the meaning of rights – one that emerges through the confluence of Islamic principles and republicanism' (4). Osanloo attempts to demonstrate that rights and 'rights talk' belong inside culture, since they 'are themselves cultural practices emerging from a specific Euro-American historical and political trajectory' (1). She rejects the false opposition of universalism and relativism because it 'conflates rights, the object of our study, with the challenge posed by how to study rights in non-Western societies' (2).

To quarrel with Osanloo about the what is or isn't 'Islamic' is to miss the point of studying local articulations of rights or practices that are informed by the logic of normative principles of rights. The universalists tend to ignore even the mere existence of debates inside Iran about the compatibility of normative principles of human rights and local religious views, which are far from static, as a notion such as 'dynamic jurisprudence' suggests. Prominent theologians and religious thinkers have contributed to a debate that challenges the hardliners' religious interpretations of rights.[6] A clear sign that these local articulations have made an impact in Iran is that even the hardliners have been forced to justify their actions by invoking Islamic foundations for social justice, even only if to shift from the Universal Declaration of Human Rights to a local re-articulation. As Ghamari-Tabrizi (2000) points out, this 'shift in the point of reference is an important one, for it points to one of the main dilemmas of human rights in the era of globalization: namely, on what grounds should civil and human rights be defined, justified, and defended'? (38). In order to develop a politics of human rights in Iran as an alternative to the universalist-relativist binary, he suggests we should: 'demystify the idea of human rights by historicising and politicising it'; take into account the internal debates on human rights in specific cultural contexts; 'scrutinize human rights based on its praxis, that is, to bring together its textual references and justifications with its actual practices and the ways in which it is understood by its practitioners' (38).

The emphasis on practices is a guard against collapsing local articulations, legal and sociocultural contexts into abstractions. It is noteworthy that Afshari (2001), who vehemently opposes 'cultural relativism', had argued (1994) earlier that 'the success or failure of Muslims to internalise a secular outlook and values should be determined by *what they actually do*' (emphasis added, 239). Although I have no interest in debating what 'internalising secular outlook' means, I want to take him up on examining 'what they actually do' in order to avoid generalities and abstractions. If the authoritarian elements of the state in the Islamic Republic attempt to curtail the freedom of speech and access to information by Iranians, shouldn't we try to find out 'what they actually do'?

In the following section, I address communication space in Iran as it relates to the normative components and concerns of human rights discourses. In order to do that I offer interrelated discussions that are central to the topic of human rights discourse and communication media: the legal framework of Iranian communication media, while keeping in mind the media and communication policies of the state; Iranian communication space, a space that is a result of both communication and media policies and specific characteristics of Iranian sociopolitical and cultural contexts; aspects of performing citizenship outside formal politics in Iran that addresses 'what they actually do'.

Communication space in Iran in context and the human rights discourse

The Islamic Republic of Iran's constitution as a legal framework addresses freedom of the press and freedom of expression. Article 24 of the constitution states that, 'Publications and the press have freedom of expression', adding 'except when it is detrimental to the fundamental principles of Islam or the right of the public'. Likewise, with respect to broadcasting, article 175 of the constitution states, 'The freedom of expression and dissemination of thoughts in the Radio and Television of the Islamic Republic of Iran must be guaranteed', but must be 'in keeping with the Islamic criteria and the best interests of the country'. Article 2 of the constitution makes an explicit commitment to 'cultural independence', while article 3 states that in order to achieve the objectives of article 2, the government has a duty to create 'favorable environment for the growth of moral virtues based on faith and piety and the struggle against all forms of vice and corruption'.[7] It is not difficult to see how such a legal framework has been inadequate to safeguard freedom of the press and freedom of expression. The tension between a commitment to free expression and 'Islamic criteria', written into the very constitution that founded the Islamic Republic, was a harbinger of the many contradictions that characterize many aspects of life and politics in contemporary Iran. The ultimate goal of the legal framework for the operation of media in the Islamic Republic appears to be the propagation of 'Islamic culture', and the production of Islamic subjects who freely abide by the Islamic principles prescribed by the state.

The 1979 Iranian revolution ushered in an 'Islamic Republic', a governing system that combines elements of theocracy, republicanism and direct democracy. The electorates elect the president (who has the power to appoints the cabinet), the parliament and the Assembly of Experts, made up of clerics who oversee the appointment of the 'Supreme Leader'. However, the Supreme Leader, who occupies the pinnacle of power in the Iranian political system, is unelected. He appoints the head of the national broadcasting system, the head of judiciary and half of the members of the Council of Guardians from among the members of the Assembly of Experts (the other half is elected by the parliament). The Council of Guardians is a powerful body that interprets the constitution and the adherence of bills in parliament to Islamic laws and to the constitution. Moreover, it has veto power over the list of candidates for different offices (president, parliament, Assembly of Experts and local councils). Although we should not forget that Iran has produced an indigenous democracy debate and a nascent democracy movement that predate the Islamic Republic going back to the constitutional revolution of 1906 (Gheissari & Nasr, 2005; Semati 2007), the afore-mentioned contradictory tendencies characterize not only Iranian political system, but also its communication and media policies.

The Islamic Republic of Iran Broadcasting (IRIB) is a mammoth organization owned and operated by the state. It is a sprawling organization with terrestrial and satellite operations engaged in internal and external radio and television production and broadcasting. It has its own publishing arm and film production company, among other holdings. Although the constitution makes explicit reference to freedom of expression in broadcasting, IRIB's commitment to its ideological agenda of 'Islamisation' of culture as a policy goal has meant a firm grip on broadcasting. The charter of the IRIB (clause 9) characterises IRIB as a 'public university' with the 'main objective of propagating Islamic culture'. In articulating broadcasting as a 'public university', and in keeping with the title of the Ministry of Culture and Islamic *Guidance*, the instrumentalisation of media and culture in the production of Islamic subjects is fairly explicit. IRIB reflects the views of the office of the Supreme Leader, and some of the most hardline elements of the 'factional' politics of Iran.

Although IRIB produces some of the most popular entertainment and sports programming, it currently faces a crisis of legitimacy for two sets of reasons. First, it is a failing business venture for the state (it is not unusual to read about the wasteful spending on it in major newspapers in Iran). Second, it has very little credibility when it comes to news, public affairs and matters of national interests. It is viewed as the mouthpiece of the faction close to the Supreme Leader. In contrast to broadcasting, the print press is not government owned, and has been a relatively rambunctious press. The press has been partisan, in the sense that different factions have their own newspapers voicing oppositional views functioning as the de facto political parties. The press relies on subsidies by the state for both papers (the rise of price for paper has made it too expensive to run a profitable newspaper) and for advertising revenue (as many of state owned companies, organizations and ministries are the major purchasers of ad space in the print press).

Apart from the attempt to pressure newspapers through subsidies and ad buys, the state engages in newspaper closures and intimidation of journalists and imprisoning some to make examples out of them. These acts of intimidation are based on perceived transgressions of the infamous 'red lines' in Iranian political discourse. However, the attempt at censorship of the print press does not go unchallenged. Reform-minded journalists find ways to challenge the state and its hardline institutions using different strategies. For example, if they perceive a specific foreign policy position of a conservative president is a red line, they will find other policy positions to criticize and undermine his credibility (e.g. harsh criticism of his environmental policy becomes a substitute for undermining him on foreign policy position). They might, to offer another example, soften the lead and write a neutral headline, and bury the criticism deep inside the reporting. To take another example, if they can't criticize leaders for sanctions against Iran, they write about the calamitous economics conditions as a result of the sanctions. In short, resourceful and resilient journalists do not simply roll over because the state orders them to do so.

IRIB might be the official organ of the state, but its discourse does not go unchallenged. It competes with hundreds of foreign-language and Persian-language satellite channels beamed into Iran from outside. These satellite channels include foreign-language entertainment and news channels (e.g. BBC, CNN International).[8] More troubling for the state, these channels include Persian-language entertainment, and public affairs programming, some of which belong to the various 'opposition groups' based abroad. Satellite dishes and receivers are illegal to own, but the state is either unwilling or incapable of enforcing the ban, although it has occasionally raided apartment buildings to confiscate dishes or receivers. The hard line elements of the state even use technology to scramble the signal for (especially Persian-language) satellite signals, even as warnings about the health hazard to the publics of transmitting scrambling signals have been debated in the press. These efforts have been futile in preventing Iranians from consuming satellite channels. According to Ali Janati, the Ministry of Culture, 71 per cent residents in Tehran watch satellite television. As a 'reformist' Minister in a reformist President's cabinet, he is opposed to placing such restrictions, and even cites examples of other failed efforts in the past to ban communication technologies (e.g. VCRs and video clubs).[9]

Challenging the state's discourses and ideology is even more significant when the challenge is issued by ordinary individuals in everyday life through the most mundane and ubiquitous everyday technological means. Cell phones capable of sending texts or SMS (short-message-service) have long presented a challenge for the state, and have contributed significantly to a widening of the gap between the official culture as espoused by the state (Islamic culture) and a popular culture, which is more in tune with global popular (youth) secular culture. According to the Chair of the Centre for Communication Technologies and Digital Media in the Ministry of Culture, there are 40 million smart phone in use in Iran today.[10] In a country with a total population of 82 million[11], where 60 per cent of the population is under the age of 30, this is a significant development. The circulation of jokes, photoshopped images, poems, songs, bloopers and different textual forms that challenge and undermine the official discourse of the state on various topics has been ongoing since the arrival of mobile telephony in Iran. Here the individual expression of preferences, opinion and voices is the performance of a politicized cultural citizenship, a citizenship that increasingly takes a textual form.[12] To the extent that formal politics is constrained, culture becomes a space for struggle over competing articulations of what it means to be Iranian, what it means to be a Muslim or live in an 'Islamic' republic (Semati 2008). Yes, free expression is constrained in the 'public sphere' of the Islamic Republic of Iran, but its communication space is far more difficult to govern than individual acts of intimidation and censorship seem to suggest to outside observes.

A contrarian view expressed by a serving Minister of Culture, under a president who shares his cabinet member's view on communication and media policy, complicates a simple notion of 'the state', as it points to a divided political authority. It highlights a power struggle between different forces within the governing structure in the Islamic Republic. It is a struggle that intensified with the election of the enormously popular reformist president Mohammad Khatami (1997–2005) with his discourses of 'civil society' and 'dialog among civilisations'. The first two years of Khatami's presidency, sometimes dubbed 'Tehran Spring', saw unprecedented optimism and measures of freedom, which prompted hardliners in the judiciary and other centres of power to push back by closing newspapers. This kind of action often lead the same team to start another newspaper by a different name in a cat and mouse game with the conservatives. Such political dynamics became even more intensified with the arrival of the Internet in Iran.

Iran was one of the first countries in the Middle East to go online. Qom, a city located about 100 miles southwest of Tehran, is where main theological seminaries and the centre of religious learning and scholarship are located. In a short order, the Internet and many IT resources were used in 'digitising' religious research centres, seminaries, voluminous religious texts and in establishing portals for information on religious matters. Almost all of the grand Ayatollahs (a source of emulation) have a substantial web presence. Iran has had one of the most vibrant blog scenes, making Persian at one point the third most common language of blogging in the world. The topics for these bloggers varied considerably and included literature, arts, cooking and a host of other subjects. However, the most significant aspect of blogging was in the sociopolitical registers where a diverse range of views were expressed both in support of the state and, more significantly, in challenging the conservative elements of the ruling structure (Sreberny & Khiabany, 2010).

As social media arrived in Iran, Facebooks pages, Instagram and Twitter accounts began to replace blogs. Reform-minded journalists, artists, intellectuals and other citizens have joined various social media. A recent report, quoting Morteza Mousavian, the Chair of the Centre for Communication Technologies and Digital Media in the Ministry of Culture, claims that while 53 per cent of Iranians are active users of social media, that number among people between 18 to 29 years of age is 72 per cent. The same report claims that the penetration rate for the Internet in Iran is at 80 per cent. Although this number for penetration rate seems to be an exaggeration,[13] in a country with a young population where 73 per cent live in urban areas with easy access to the Internet, it becomes clear why the hardliner elements of the state are unsettled.

Among the measures that the hardline elements of the state have taken to roll back the affordances of the Internet were the intimidation and jailing of bloggers who did not hide their identities. These measures have been widely and rightly condemned as gross violations of human rights of Iranians. Other measures have included filtering websites to block access by users. Filtering of websites is an inconvenience for users. However, anti-filtering software is widely and readily available. The filtering of social media is selective: while Facebook and Twitter are filtered, Instagram is not. Mobile-based social media platforms tend not to be filtered (e.g. WhatsApp, oovoo, Viber, imo). The latest mobile-based platform (which is also available as a desktop application) is Telegram. The controversy surrounding this app is a telling case of Internet policy, which reflects the larger internal media policy debates within the state. These debates are symptomatic of the power struggle among different centres of power and the political structure of the Islamic Republic of Iran.

Telegram is a cloud-based instant messaging service that enables users to send and receive texts, videos, audio files, photos, stickers and files to each other or to groups. Much to the chagrin of authoritarians, this app has joined others that provide end-to-end encryption, allowing 'secret chats'. Since its introduction in 2013, Telegram has garnered 28 million users in Iran, according to a recent University of Tehran study.[14] Its user-friendly design has made it a widely used app not only among Iranians inside Iran, but also among Iranian diaspora and expats to stay in touch with family members and friends throughout the world. Telegram makes a smartphone a powerful communication tool in the hands of citizen who find entry points to politics in their quotidian social interactions. More important, its capability to form 'channels', which are basically one-to-many broadcasting channels, has allowed individuals with followers (like a former President Khatami who is barred from appearing on the official media in the country) to have their own broadcasting channel, bypassing the state-controlled media altogether. The proliferation of 'channels' in the hundreds of thousands has rattled many of the conservative elements of the state.

A policy debate has erupted in Iran about why Telegram should or should not be filtered (it currently is not filtered). President Rouhani is engaged in the same type of struggle that Khatami was engaged in with the conservative voices during his administration. This struggle is not merely a struggle over media policy. It is more; it is a struggle over two competing visions of what the Islamic Republic should be. And the headlines reflect that: the headline that reads, 'Rouhani battles judiciary over Internet censorship', indicates that old battles are being fought between the new administration and the old conservative guard in the judiciary.[15] And much the same way Khatami relied on the independent reformist print press to convey his reformist message against a broadcasting system controlled by the conservative voices, Rouhani needs the social media to bypass the conservative-controlled IRIB to garner support for his agenda against the hardline elements of the state. So far Rouhani has been successful in pushing back against attempts to create a stronger censorship regime, especially regarding Telegram.[16]

The question is why the state has allowed this communication space to emerge in the first place. I do not have the space to discuss social policies that have lead a young population to be inclined to reject propaganda by the state, or to seek access to alternative sources of information online, or to pursue global youth culture (e.g. post-revolution social policy of offering 'mass-education'). I only point out two sets of reasons as to why the state has allowed this communication space and its infrastructure to materialise. The first is the ideological needs of the state: various media are developed to project the state's ideological outlook both internally and externally. The other set of reasons has to do with the commercial logic of communication media or economic imperatives. Although the state has paid lip service to following the constitution's mandate on privatising industries, the telecommunication industry is at best 'semi-private', where major stakeholders are connected to the state. In this context, media policies (fuelled by commercial imperatives), social policies (e.g. education for the masses, strong female social presence and participation in the workforce) and other factors such as demographics (a largely young, educated and urban population) have articulated to create a citizenry that resists propaganda, has access to means of expression and engages politics in terms of cultural citizenship, and has turned elections (as imperfect as they are) unpredictable, often in the direction of moderation and reform.

It should be emphasized that the conservative forces are not conceding defeat, and will not in the foreseeable future. The authoritarian elements of the state would like to continue to monopolise all means of control, be they symbolic expressive or material. One sign that they are busy trying to put the genie of the communication technology back in the bottle is their efforts to create a National Information Network, which is a form of Intranet (an internal network cut off from the larger Internet)[17]. The efforts have largely been shrouded in secrecy and ambiguity, and seems destined to fail for technical and commercial reasons. The epic struggle between the reformists and the conservatives continues.

The global implications for the advocacy of human and communication rights should be clear by now. The binary of 'universalist' and 'relativist' is not helpful in finding an approach to address human rights in various local settings. To the extent that human rights discourse is a product of a specific history, local conceptions of universal normative principles are a product of specific histories. As Ghamari-Tabrizi (2000) argues, 'any successful human rights policy needs to shift its emphasis from the predicament *of implementation* and *accommodation,* to the politics of *articulation* of rights and the dynamics of *generation* of change, respectively' (35). In addressing communication and media rights in specific contexts, a more useful approach takes into account those factors that lead to empowering local individual and collective agency, one that reflexively rearticulates communication and human rights discourse at the local level.

Conclusion

Principles of human rights are worth fighting for, and I believe we should condemn those states that engage in gross violations of them. At the same time, we should be wary of abuses of human rights discourse. More important, advocating human and communication rights in a global framework involving normative principles should also require us to study local legal, cultural, political and technological traditions. Such an approach allows us to advocate for human rights and be aware of the contexts in which media institutions and practices exist and how they may enable local individual and collective agency to assert itself. Such an approach should also make us aware of the local attempts in rearticulating or reclaiming normative principles as compatible with local traditions. Human rights abuses in the Islamic Republic are not defensible. In fact, they are beneath the dignity of a cosmopolitan people who has a proud and rich history that has contributed to the foundations upon which such normative principles are based.

Notes

1 See Stabile & Kumar (2005), and Semati & Brookey (2014).
2 See the report by UN Watch, a non-governmental human rights organization based in Geneva, here: http://www.unwatch.org/again-saudis-elected-chair-of-un-human-rights-council-panel/
3 https://treaties.un.org/doc/publication/unts/volume%20999/volume-999-i-14668-english.pdf. For more on ICT and human rights see Jørgensen (2006).
4 For a discussion of Cultural Studies and human rights, see Erni (2010) and Coombe (2010). For a discussion of cultural citizenship as it relates to rights, see Miller (2007).
5 For an insightful discussion of the reasons for popularity of this book as the politics of its production and reception see Nerone (2004).
6 A comprehensive review of this literature is beyond the scope of this paper. For examples of this literature, see Mir-Hosseini (2002), Ghamari-Tabrizi (2000), Soroush (2000), Kadivar (2008).
7 For a translation of the text of the constitution of the Islamic Republic (accessed May 15, 2016) see http://irandataportal.syr.edu/wp-content/uploads/constitution-english-1368.pdf
8 For more on satellite television in Iran, see Alikhah (2008).
9 For a report on Ali Janati's remarks, see http://www.bbc.co.uk/persian/iran/2013/12/131217_l39_satellite_ban_jannati
10 See http://www.mehrnews.com/news/3721091/۵۳-درصد-مردم-عضو-شبکه‌های-اجتماعی-علاقه‌ای-ایرانیان-به جستجوی-خبر

166

11 For statistics on the population of Iran, see https://www.cia.gov/library/publications/the-world-factbook/geos/ir.html

12 I draw from the literature on cultural citizenship (see Jones 2010), and would argue that in places like Iran culture is even more politicized because formal politics is constrained.

13 That Internet penetration rate in Iran is reported by Internet World Stats to be at 68.5% (see http://www.internetworldstats.com/me/ir.htm). Mousavian's comments are reported here: http://www.mehrnews.com/news/3721091/۵۳-درصد-مردم-وضع-کشـبک-هـا-تجامتجی-علـاقـی-اهونیاری-هب-جتـسـوی-خ-بر

14 See the report here: http://www.mehrnews.com/news/3768129/۲۸-میلیون-نفر-عـضو-گلـتـارم-هسـتند

15 See http://www.al-monitor.com/pulse/originals/2014/05/iran-rouhani-battled-judiciary-internet-censorship.html

16 International Campaign for Human Rights in Iran has addressed social media censorship in Iran. See https://www.iranhumanrights.org/2016/06/social-media-servers-transfer-to-ran/

17 See the report by BBC on the proposed "national Internet" here: http://www.bbc.com/news/world-middle-east-22281336

References

Afshari, R. (1994). 'An Essay on Islamic Cultural Relativism in the Discourse of Human Rights'. *Human Rights Quarterly*, 16, pp. 235–76.

Afshari, R. (2001). *Human Rights in Iran: The Abuse of Cultural Relativism*. Philadelphia: University of Pennsylvania Press.

Alikhah, F. (2008). 'The Politics of Satellite Television in Iran'. In: M. Semati, ed., *Media, Culture and Society in Iran: Living with Globalization and the Islamic State*. London: Routledge, pp. 94–110.

Bell, L., Nathan, A. and Peleg, I. eds. (2000). *Negotiating Culture and Human Rights*. New York: Columbia University Press.

Chandler, D., ed. (2002). *Rethinking Human Rights: Critical Approaches to International Politics*. New York: Palgrave Macmillan.

Coombe, R. J. (2010). 'Honing a Critical Cultural Study of Human Rights'. *Communication and Critical/Cultural Studies*, 7(3), pp. 230–46.

Donnelly, J. (2006). 'Human Rights'. In: J. Dryzek, B. Honig, and A. Phillips, eds., *The Oxford Handbook of Political Theory*. New York: Oxford University Press, pp. 601–20.

Donnelly, J. (2007). 'The Relative Universality of Human Rights'. *Human Rights Quarterly*, 29(2), pp. 281–306.

Erni, J. N., (2010). 'Reframing Cultural Studies: Human Rights as a Site of Legal-cultural Struggles'. *Communication and Critical/Cultural Studies*, 7(3), pp. 221–29.

Ghamari-Tabrizi, B. (2000). 'Globalization, Islam, and Human Rights: The Case of Iran'. *Political and Legal Anthropology Review*, 23(1), pp. 33–48.

Gheissari, A., and Nasr, V. (2009). *Democracy in Iran: History and the Quest for Liberty*. New York: Oxford University Press.

Jones, J. (2010). *Entertaining Politics: Satiric Television and Political Engagement*. Lanham, MD: Rowman & Littlefield.

Jørgensen, R. F., ed. (2006). *Human Rights in the Global Information Society*. Cambridge, MA: MIT Press.

Kadivar, M. (2008). 'Human Rights and Intellectual Islam'. In K. Vogt, L. Larsen, C. Moe, eds., *New Directions in Islamic Thought: Exploring Reform and Muslim Tradition*. New York: i.b. Tauris, pp. 47–73.

Miller, T. (2007). *Cultural Citizenship: Cosmopolitanism, Consumerism, and Television in a Neoliberal Age*. Philadelphia: Temple University Press.

Mir-Hosseini, Z. (2002). 'The Conservative and Reformist Conflict Over Women's Rights in Iran'. *International Journal of Politics, Culture and Society*, 16(1), pp. 37–53.

Nerone, J. (2004). '*Four Theories of the Press* in Hindsight: Reflections on a Popular Model'. In: M. Semati, ed., *New Frontiers in International Communication Theory*. Lanham, MD: Rowman & Littlefield, pp. 21–32.

Osanloo, A. (2009). *The Politics of Women's Rights in Iran*. Princeton, NJ: Princeton University Press.

Semati, M. (2007). 'Media, the State, and the Pro-democracy Movement in Iran'. In I. A. Blankson and D. Murphy, eds., *Globalization and Media Transformation in New and Emerging Democracies*. Albany, NY: SUNY Press, pp. 143–60.

Semati, M. (2008). 'Living with Globalization and the Islamic State: An Introduction to Media, Culture, and Society in Iran'. In M. Semati, ed., *Media, Culture, and Society in Iran: Living with Globalization and the Islamic State*. London: Routledge, pp. 1–13.

Semati, M., and Brookey, R. (2014). 'Not for Neda: Digital Media, (Citizen) Journalism, and the Invention of a Post-feminist Martyr'. *Communication, Culture & Critique*, 7(2), pp. 137–53.

Siebert, F. S., Peterson, T, and Schramm, W. (1956). *Four Theories of the Press: The Authoritarian, Libertarian, Social Responsibility and Soviet Communist Concepts of What the Press Should Be and Do*. Urbana: University of Illinois Press.

Soroush, A. (2000). *Reason, Freedom, and Democracy in Islam: Essential Writing of Abdolkarim Soroush* (translated and edited by M. Sadri and A. Sadri). New York: Oxford University Press.

Sreberny, A., and Khiabany, G. (2010). *Blogistan: The Internet and Politics in Iran*. New York: i.b. Tauris.

Stabil, C. and Kumar, D. (2005). Unveiling Imperialism: Media, Gender and the War on Afghanistan. *Media, Culture, & Society*, 27(5), pp. 765–82.

16

RIGHTS, MEDIA AND MASS-SURVEILLANCE IN A DIGITAL AGE

Emma L. Briant

This chapter discusses important challenges posed for media, journalism and public debate by recent massive domestic and global surveillance of US National Security Agency (NSA), and Britain's Government Communications Headquarters (GCHQ).[1] It focuses on contemporary developments concerning these countries with a stated intention of protecting our liberties, security and rights during global conflict; mass-surveillance that transformed our media environment, journalism and relations with the state, raising important implications for human rights.

Surveillance, rights and the media

Surveillance Studies traditionally suffered from problems of access, with official restrictions[2] punctuated by the revelations of the occasional persecuted whistle-blower. Gatekeeper policing plus targeting of academics (Keen 1999) and journalists with surveillance has meant research often focused on historical accounts, or was dominated by 'official' accounts. Gilliom points to political and conceptual failings in debate over surveillance and privacy which overlooked experiences, and resistance by, 'the watched' (2001). While 'Surveillance is a central – and, now, necessary – feature of today's advanced societies' David Lyon observed as recently as 2002, 'exactly how it developed, how it works, and what its consequences are is as yet unclear' (Lyon 2002, 4). The field developed rapidly after 9/11 as new surveillance technologies, and online leaking and encryption opportunities for whistle-blowers, researchers and journalists, flourished.

Security measures are legitimated in so far as they protect our human rights, including free speech or privacy. Surveillance debates emphasise a so-called security vs liberty problematic, where, in seeking to protect certain rights, security places other rights under pressure (Hocking 2004).[3] Privacy secures our autonomy and is argued to be especially necessary for journalists, who must be confident they are not spied upon to investigate and confront power in their 'fourth estate' role. Article 10 of the European Convention on Human Rights (ECHR) gives journalists the right to protect their sources from being revealed, and a state cannot obtain this information unless there is an overriding public interest requiring disclosure and no alternative (See: Article 19, May 1998). The unequal power relations implied by surveillance run counter to democracy, but, as we seek human rights protections, real-world challenges present uncomfortable realities to navigate and negotiate (Haggerty and Samatas 2010). Privacy rights often come under tension (Garfinkel 2001; Rosen 2004; Taylor 2002; Whittacker 1999) yet security arguments are claimed to be overstated and extreme measures frequently normalised during crisis (Hocking 2004, 89, 237; McGrath 2004).

Surveillance is a product of modernity (Bauman 1988; Lyon 2003); bureaucratic systems that are ambivalent in function. While not inherently malicious, efforts towards our protection may conversely increase our control. Academic understandings of surveillance transitioned away from the 'panopticon' metaphor (Foucault 1977) through increasing awareness of how 'watched' see the watchers, where 'synoptic' self-control operates (Matthieson 1997). Today's scholarship illuminates a networked, dynamic and flexible assemblage[4] (Haggerty and Ericson 2000) where surveillance occurs within a world of 'flows' and movements of people and information (Castells 1996, 376f.; Bauman & Lyon 2013). 'The watched' also *watch* and 'hierarchies of observation' allow some scrutiny of power (Haggerty and Ericson 2000). Surveillance can 'empower journalism and the civil sphere to monitor unfolding conflicts and human rights abuses' (Cottle et al. 2016, 167); or protect human rights, bringing prosecutions, supporting pre-emptive actions and advocacy (Stanyer & Davidson 2011). Yet, as transparency becomes increasingly inescapable,[5] a 'phenetic fix' also emerges – a trend to capture 'personal data triggered by human bodies and to use these abstractions to place people in new social classes of income, attributes, habits, preferences, or offences, in order to influence, manage, or control them' (Lyon 2002, 3). Central to understanding surveillance and contemporary media systems are relations between state and corporate power (Hintz 2014; Lyon 2001; Parenti; 2003; Zuboff, 5 Mar. 2016). And Mattelart stresses how examining the 'dark side of democracy' in historical and global context, reveals 'new ways of seeing the inextricable ties that have gradually developed between states of emergency and exception, surveillance and security, crises and the means of social control, with special emphasis on the means for influencing opinion' (2010, 2). Matthieson (1997) and Lyon (in Ericson and Haggerty 2006, 35–54) point to the media's crucial synoptic role which puts public awareness, understanding and response at the heart of how surveillance functions. The assertion those who have 'nothing to hide ... have nothing to fear' appears increasingly shallow (Lyon 2003, 1) as research now seeks to establish, just what we *do* have to fear; the implications of 'social sorting' (Lyon 2002) for human rights, accountability and legitimate security practises in a digital age.

Contemporary surveillance

Governments worldwide utilise surveillance, and many present a far more hostile environment for journalism than Britain and US. However, thousands of classified documents leaked in 2013–14 by Edward Snowden, revealed extensive reach of these countries' surveillance capabilities and corporate collaborations, setting them apart from similar democracies – in *scale* and *form* of surveillance, as well as the *ease* of domestic spying. Digital technologies provide 'unprecedented capacity to interfere with the rights to freedom of opinion and expression' (David Kaye, UN Special Rapporteur quoted in Clarke et al. 2015, 6). Both countries substantially expanded their security and intelligence agencies, the NSA seeking to 'own the net': dominate our global computing and communication systems (Gallagher & Greenwald 2014). They collaborated extensively with GCHQ across programmes like ECHELON, PRISM and TEMPORA; The Patriot Act (2001) allowing collection of US citizens' communications, which may violate the Fourth Amendment of the Constitution[6]. Domestic spying and reciprocal spying powerfully challenged popular notions of privacy, media freedom and relations between citizens and state.

Yet these revelations follow a long history of reciprocal spying (Johnson 2004, 165) and domestic surveillance activities on citizens deemed communist, anti-colonial or somehow radical justified with reference to security in both the UK and US.[7] Anglo-American intelligence-sharing grew through two world wars, secured the British post-war residual world power status (Aldrich 2002; Reynolds 2000; Smith 1995) and remains today, with Britain as a crucial hub, transiting 10–25 per cent of global Internet traffic (Clarke et al. 2015, 10). British intelligence has traditionally been less transparent, and in surveillance, this was revealed to be a US 'selling point'. Britain's dependence on the US, leads it to fear weakening US perceptions of partnership 'leading to loss of access, and/or reduction in investment ... to the UK' (Hopkins & Borger 2013). Many kinds of data are obtained through covert or overt channels or purchased;[8] but this chapter will focus on media and communications.[9]

Bulk interception involves large-scale interception of citizens' communications; enabling data (broken down pre-transmission) to be reconstituted and understood. GCHQ use this and tap undersea cables for 'target discovery' – analysing patterns and characteristics to identify a specific threat or collect general information on networks and individuals (Clarke, et al. 2015, 18). Where both sender and recipient are domestic it is subject to 'more rigorous safeguards' (Clarke, et al. 2015, 18).

Surveillance by public bodies (under the UK Regulation of Investigatory Powers Act (RIPA) (2000)) distinguishes between *communications data*[10] ('metadata') and communications' *content*. US metadata surveillance falls under S215 of The Patriot Act (2001) and the Foreign Intelligence Surveillance Act (FISA) (1978), amended in 2008 to cover US persons abroad and demand mass Internet and metadata from private companies (Hopkins and Ackerman, 2013). For some, the size of metadata depersonalises it, removing the question of privacy; thought 'non-intrusive' as no human examines the content (Introna and Wood 2004). Security services stress their need to manage large datasets effectively. YouGov found 52 per cent of British people believe security services need more access to their communications, 63 per cent said they trust the intelligence agencies to behave responsibly with information obtained (January 2015, 6). However, given the specialist, technical nature of these activities, it is unclear how much knowledge those polled would have of existing capabilities and their use. Often the public cannot fully comprehend the scale of mass-surveillance as technologies, capacities and threats develop at a bewildering rate. The assertion that interception of communication content (covered by PRISM) is more intrusive than metadata, becomes less meaningful as powerful mathematical tools allow substantial profiles on individuals to be built without accessing *content,* by *aggregating* expansive data we produce including browsing history and shopping habits.

The Independent Reviewer of Terrorism Legislation, argues 'Cyber espionage allows information to be stolen remotely, cheaply and on an industrial scale at relatively little risk' to a hostile state (Anderson 2015, 44). And, justifying surveillance, the UK Home Secretary claimed metadata is used in 95 per cent of serious organised crime cases (Clarke et al. 2015, 23–4). Whether these capabilities have been effective in preventing terrorist attacks is contested (Walsh and Miller 2016, 353). One former US Delta Force Commander observed technical overreliance: collecting 'things that sound sexy but do nothing for us' (Stein 2015).

As correlations are identified, new algorithms are created and applied to particular cases until 'certain kinds of behaviour can be predicted' (Clarke et. al. 2015, 16). Dencik et al. warn unpredictability might then be interpreted as 'risk' and 'become conducive to an environment of "overintervention" by the policy' (2015, 53), particularly if contractors are capable of more intrusive monitoring. Bauman and Lyon warn 'surveillance streamlines the process of doing things at a distance, of separating a person from the consequences of an action' (2013, 7). Police often have superficial understandings of how the algorithms they employ (often produced originally for other purposes) work. These then 'inform policing strategies and pre-emptive tactics' which is 'a significant issue regarding the lack of accountability' (Dencik et al. 2015, 51). Stored data may prejudice an individual's unknowable future.[11] Algorithmic prediction exists alongside pre-emption in wide-reaching counterterrorism strategies. The Home Office 'Prevent' strategies in the community, are criticised for extending surveillance to students, schoolchildren and toddlers (e.g. Mendick & Verkaik, 2015).

Data can be held for long periods and be difficult to access (Norris and L'Hoiry 2015). The European Court of Justice in Digital Rights stated the EU Data Retention Directive entailed 'interference with the fundamental rights of practically the entire European population' (quoted in Don't Spy on Us 2014, 6). GCHQ director Robert Hannigan argued fighting ISIS online is a 'huge' challenge requiring 'greater co-operation from technology companies' (2014). Online threats are, to most, an intangible threatening unknown, yet public trust in responses has been shaken. In the UK, in three years 82 journalists had their metadata obtained by police, and crucially Article 10 (freedom of speech) was not considered (Turvill 2015). As governments surveil citizens, journalists and NGOs, some argue this threatens the liberties they claim to protect.

In 2015, the US Congress passed legislative changes clarifying US surveillance powers, an NSA phone-spying programme was ruled illegal (Stempel 2015). The USA Freedom Act 2015 imposed some limits on the bulk collection of metadata on US citizens but capabilities remain extensive. Battles continue, as corporations test their power relative to government in the courts (as in the recent Apple-FBI case). The European Court of Human Rights ruled this kind of mass surveillance is illegal, as it fails 'to include 'sufficiently precise, effective and comprehensive' measures that would limit surveillance to only people it suspected of crimes' (McCarthy 2016).

Oversight often lags behind technological change and after small improvements, criticism of US surveillance oversight remains; none of 1457 NSA requests in 2015 were rejected or even modified by the foreign intelligence surveillance court (Reuters 2016). The UN criticised US failure to ensure 'effective remedies in cases of abuse.' (McLaughlin 2015). Similarly, British police were found to request metadata every two minutes, obtaining access in 96 per cent of cases[12] (Clarke, et al. 2015, 44). Gavin Millar QC argues the new draft Investigatory Powers Bill[13] replacing RIPA keeps extensive bulk surveillance and won't guarantee journalists' right to protect sources. The Court of Human Rights says a judge should decide whether a source may be obtained by the state, and 'have the benefit of evidence and argument from the journalist as well'. This Bill proposes *police* decide and only need 'reasonable grounds' rather than 'overriding public interest' (as Article 10). A judge will review the police's argument but the journalist will remain unawares so 'the case for protecting press freedom will not be articulated' (Millar 2015). New legislation often seeks to solidify and legitimate powers.

Activist groups'[14] efforts and international pressure have produced resolutions to force states to respect privacy rights, including the Inter-Parliamentary Union resolution 'Democracy in the digital era and the threat to privacy and individual freedoms'. But Icelandic MP and early Wikileaks activist Birgitta Jónsdóttir argued, 'Europe really thinks that they are so developed that they don't even have to take the resolutions that they adopt. It seems like they think that we are participating in making resolutions for the developing world' (Interview: 6 May 2016).

Creeping capitalism?

While data storage and collection by government raises more concern than private corporations due to their legal and coercive powers, but we should *not* underestimate the potential for politically and commercially motivated private corporations to wield data in a way that influences democratic political systems. Shoshana Zuboff argues a 'wholly new species of capitalism' has evolved in which 'profits derive from the unilateral surveillance and modification of human behaviour' using surveillance capabilities that are 'the envy of every state security agency' (2016). Hintz shows corporations' key role in 'policing' online activity, regulation and setting policy (2014). Everyday devices increasingly store an interconnected bewildering universe[15] of data on users' behaviour.[16] Facebook track web browsing of anyone visiting the page, without their consent and has breached European law (Gibbs 2015). Facebook users 'like' or comment 'nearly three billion times a day' (Clarke, et al. 2015, 16) and 'emoticon' engagements collect (and profit from) increasingly nuanced reaction data. Terms and Conditions and privacy tools[17] raise issues of consent and may give a false sense of control (Fiddler 2015). Algorithms and 'reactions' allow Facebook to select news feed content that will best provoke emotions in a user, making them more receptive to promoted messages or advertisements (Oremus 2016). Overtly political, Facebook has removed activist pages including 'Anarchist Memes' a page 'dedicated to anti-capitalist, anti-racist and feminist rights' (Hintz 2014, 362).

The public value their ability to control their online representation.[18] The Internet has clear democratic potential and can facilitate governance (Williamson 2010). However, as Birgitta Jónsdóttir points out, some areas are more e-appropriate than others: "UK parliament are really super-keen on e-governance … the main problem is that you want to be able to vote anonymously – it's a very sacred right … and you can't do that in online voting. There is always going to someone who has access to how you voted … it's very easy to hack in and manipulate it. So how are those that are pushing for e-governance – where are the going to draw the line on there being no guarantees for your privacy?' (Interview: 6 May 2016). Facebook encourage users to declare their votes, using a popular tool purposefully used for mass-manipulations of a political nature (Griffin 2016). The potential for combining data on personality, consumer patterns, emotions and relationships to bear on an election or referendum looms darkly.

Curtailing inquiry, dominating debate

Concerning numbers of journalists, politicians and Human Rights Organisations have been targeted by mass-surveillance. What is concerning is what is within the law. In 2015 the UK's Investigatory Powers Tribunal ruled that GCHQ intercepting emails of Human Rights Organisations was legal (Correra 2015). GCHQ has placed investigative journalists on an information security 'threat' list alongside terrorists and obtained emails from 'the BBC, Reuters, the Guardian, the New York Times, Le Monde, the Sun, NBC and the Washington Post' – among 70,000 emails obtained through bulk interception 'in the space of less than 10 minutes on one day in November 2008'. They were 'shared on the agency's intranet as part of a test exercise' and included 'correspondence between reporters and editors discussing stories' (Ball 2015). A spokesman stressed the legal framework GCHQ operates within: a framework of little worth if it allows journalists to become targets. One document stated 'journalists and reporters representing all types of news media represent a potential threat to security', attempting to get information to which 'they are not entitled'. This should be reported 'immediately' leaving little tolerance for investigative journalism (Ball 2015). Over 100 editors appealed to the UK Prime Minister stressing the implications of excessive intrusion: 'whistleblowers will not come forward to journalists in future if law enforcement agencies have the power to view journalists' phone records at will' (Press Gazette 2015).

Commissioners providing oversight also 'have not publicly found a warrant to be disproportionate, have refused to provide adequate statistics and are under-resourced' (Don't Spy on Us 2014, 27). An independent surveillance review concluded arrangements were inadequate despite compliance due to an inadequate legal framework. For public confidence, surveillance activities must be 'demonstrably lawful, necessary and proportionate' (Clarke et al. 2015, xi–xii).

To counter perceived public mistrust, intelligence services increased efforts to communicate with domestic and international publics. Increased transparency is welcome, increasing propaganda is not. This information is highly selective and engagement with the media seeks to justify existing and extensions of activities, rather than facilitating debate. CIA efforts to collaborate or recruit media professionals risks their being perceived as propagandists, threatening journalists' safe reporting of human rights in hostile countries. Johnson criticises journalists' often uncritical acceptance of this relationship: 'Every time this type of behaviour is normalised, or shrugged off, or made sexy, real journalists and real filmmakers overseas are put further at risk' (2016). Governments *must* communicate benefits and costs of surveillance measures, allowing space for public debate (Walsh and Miller 2016). Other avenues for transparency are shrinking; Britain's intelligence agencies are already exempt from the embattled Freedom of Information Act, and in 2004 the US eroded established rules leaving 'CIA's ability to deny FOIA requests at will' without legal challenge (Meissner 2016, 361).

Surveillance capabilities must be understood within wider propaganda and security strategies. 'Prevent' includes covert propaganda production, shaped around 'keywords and paid-for Google and Facebook adverts to target people whose browsing history suggests they are Muslims'. Using 'promotion and diversion techniques', an external partner 'promotes ... messages to browsers who are searching for terms such as Isis, Khalifa and "What does the Qur'an say about jihad?"' (Cobain et al, 2016). Propagandists stress their 'cultural awareness' (Briant 2015, 87–8), in psychological profiling and audience analysis shaping 'narratives' to impose attitude or behavioural change. Rather than engaging with communities, such activities alienate them by seeking to more effectively dominate.

Emerging research indicates impacts on dissent and free speech; Stoycheff found 'the government's online surveillance programs may threaten the disclosure of minority views and contribute to the reinforcement of majority opinion' (2016, 12). Some more vulnerable members of society feel unable to voice opinions online, damaging their ability to deliberate and suppressing democratic engagement.[19] Stoycheff concludes the 'spiral of silence' effect of alienation (individuals monitoring and adjusting expression according to their perceptions of whether theirs is a majority or minority opinion) may be further accentuated when this includes the possibility of alienation from *government* (2016, 12). Similar findings regarding political activists prompt concern over whether they 'are able to adapt as the state adapts and ... keep open a space for radical protest within the overall political ecosystem' (Ramsay et al. 2016).

Despite whistle-blowers' efforts challenges remain in researching surveillance. As media technologies and mass-surveillance remain in continual flux, research is needed exploring how surveillance relates to coercion and persuasion. Pressure must be placed on policymakers to implement resolutions and constant vigilance is necessary protect human rights. Researching impacts on activism, free speech and journalistic debate could facilitate adaptation and resilience, securing space for the future exercise of democracy in an evolving media environment.

Notes

1 And other 'Five Eyes' governments: Australia, Canada, New Zealand.
2 Including the '30 year rule' and Official Secrets Act in the UK.
3 See Walsh and Miller (2016) attempting to delineate a practical, ethical framework to balance privacy and security.
4 The idea of an assemblage understands surveillance as different flowing phenomena and processes working together.
5 In the UK ONS data indicates 54% of adults participated in social networking in 2014 (Clarke et al. 2015: 6) and Pew data shows of US adults 65% use social networking (Perrin, 8 Oct. 2015).

6 Against unreasonable searches and seizures. This is contested, see Walsh and Miller, 2016: 353.
7 The UK spied on Trade Union activists during the Miners' strike, members of the The Campaign for Nuclear Disarmament are two famous examples, but in the 70's and 80's the BBC was also allowing 'MI5 to investigate the backgrounds and political affiliations of thousands of its employees' (Hastings, 2 July, 2006). In US Weiner, 2008, p. 223) gives an account of this. Other examples include MHCHAOS, COINTELPRO.
8 The Intelligence Services Act (1994) and Security Service Act (1989) allow access to bulk personal datasets including those on citizens' health and tax records (Clarke, et al., 2015: 19–20).
9 Surveillance of digital communications takes place at different layers in our communication infrastructure, the device layer (hardware such as computers, smartphones etc); the network layer (transmission of data in 'packets' via routers and across networks using IP addresses to identify a device, facilitated by communication and internet service providers such as Virgin Media or BT); and a physical layer (major lines, switching centres and nodes of the telecommunications services including fibre-optic cables underneath our oceans) (Clarke, et al. 2015: 8–10). Massing Facebook posts, internet browsing history and calls is then possible. Beneath what we usually access (the world wide web, or 'surface web'), there is a less accessible but extensive 'deep web' comprised of email and company and governments intranets and 'dark web' which can be accessed using software like The Onion Router (Tor).
10 Including traffic data, service-use information and subscriber information held by a communication service provider.
11 In the UK The Data Retention and Investigatory Powers Act (2014) set a metadata-retention period of 12 months, enabling use by government under warrant. Don't Spy on Us argue this was 'plainly contrary to existing rights under the European Charter of Fundamental Rights and the ECHR and it was pushed through without sufficient time to enable the public to discuss and debate its proposals' (September 2014: 6).
12 Although Interception of Communications Commissioner's Office (IOCCO) stated police statistical requirements were flawed and have since changed.
13 The Bill passed by 281 votes to 15 during its second reading in the House of Commons on 15th March 2016.
14 Including Privacy International, Reform Government Surveillance (an alliance of global internet companies), Don't Spy on Us, Big Brother Watch, Open Rights Group and Global Commission on Internet Governance.
15 According to Clarke, et al. 'some estimates suggest that 90 per cent of all data in the world has been generated over the last two years' and Google now 'processes more than 24 petabytes of data' per day (2015: 16).
16 Wearable technologies and the 'internet of things' make this extraordinarily expansive.
17 Londoners in one experiment unwittingly surrendered their first born child for wifi access (Fox-Brewster, 29 Sept. 2014).
18 In a US survey by Microsoft 45% of respondents said they have little or no control over the information companies gather such as their browsing data (23 Jan. 2013). And Big Brother Watch found 79% of British people are concerned about online privacy, younger generations more so (Mar. 2015: 2).
19 Interestingly, those most susceptible to the 'silencing' effect were those who supported surveillance and felt they had 'nothing to hide'; the small minority of those sampled who had strong views about surveillance being unjustified were less likely to let it influence their expression online (Stoycheff, 2016: 12).

References

Aldrich, R. (2002). *The Hidden Hand: Britain, America and Cold War Secret Intelligence*. London: John Murray.
Anderson, D. (2015). *A Question of Trust: Report of the Investigatory Powers Review*. Available at: https://terrorismlegislationreviewer.independent.gov.uk/wp-content/uploads/2015/06/IPR-Report-Print-Version.pdf [Accessed 14 May, 2016].
Article 19. (May 1998). *Briefing Paper on Protection of Journalists' Sources*. Available at: https://www.article19.org/data/files/pdfs/publications/right-to-protect-sources.pdf [Accessed 14 May, 2016].
Ball, J. (19 Jan 2015). 'GCHQ Captured Emails of Journalists from Top International Media'. *The Guardian*: http://www.theguardian.com/uk-news/2015/jan/19/gchq-intercepted-emails-journalists-ny-times-bbc-guardian-le-monde-reuters-nbc-washington-post [Accessed 14 May, 2016].
Bauman, Z. (1988). 'Sociology after the Holocaust'. *The British Journal of Sociology*, 39(4), pp. 469–497.
Bauman, Z. and Lyon, D. (2013). *Liquid Surveillance*. London: Polity.

Big Brother Watch (2015). *UK Public Research – Online Privacy*. Available at: https://www.bigbrotherwatch. org.uk/wp-content/uploads/2015/03/Big-Brother-Watch-Polling-Results.pdf [Accessed 14 May, 2016].

Briant, E. L. (2015). *Propaganda and Counter-terrorism: Strategies for Global Change*. Manchester: Manchester University Press.

Castells, M. (1996). *The Rise of the Network Society*. Oxford: Wiley Blackwell.

Clarke, M., Brooke, H., Cowley, L., Evans, J., Fox, M., Grieve, J., Hall, W., Hennessy, P., Ormand, D., O'Neill, O., Rooker, J., Scarlett, J. and Walden, I. (2015). *A Democratic License to Operate: Report of the Independent Surveillance Review*. London: Royal United Services Institute. Available at: https://rusi.org/ publication/whitehall-reports/democratic-licence-operate-report-independent-surveillance-review [Accessed 14 May, 2016].

Cobain, I., Ross, A., Evans, R. and Mahmood, M. (2016). 'Revealed: UK's covert propaganda bid to stop Muslims joining Isis'. *The Guardian*. Available at: https://www.theguardian.com/uk-news/2016/ may/02/uk-government-covert-propaganda-stop-muslims-joining-isis.

Cottle, S., Sambrook, R. and Mosdell, N. (2016). *Reporting Dangerously: Journalist Killings, Intimidation and Security*. London: Palgrave.

Correra, G. (2015). 'GCHQ 'Broke Rules' When Spying on NGOs'. *BBC News* (22 June). Available at: http://www.bbc.com/news/technology-33225194 [Accessed 14 May, 2016].

Dencik, L., Hintz, A., Carey, Z. and Pandya, H. (2015). *'Managing Threats': Uses of Social Media for Policing Domestic Extremism and Disorder in the UK*. Cardiff: Cardiff School of Journalism.

Don't Spy on Us. (2014). Don't Spy on Us: Reforming Surveillance in the UK. Available at: https://www. openrightsgroup.org/assets/files/pdfs/reports/DSOU_Reforming_surveillance_old.pdf [Accessed 14 May, 2016].

Ericson, R. and Haggerty, K., eds., (2006). *The New Politics of Surveillance and Visibility*. Toronto: University of Toronto Press.

Fiddler, S. (2015). 'Facebook Policies Taken to Task in Report for Data-Privacy Issues'. *Wall Street Journal* (23 Febr.). Available at: www.wsj.com/articles/facebook-policies-taken-to-task-in-report-for-data-privacy-issues-1424725902 [Accessed 14 May, 2016].

Foucault, M. (1977). *Discipline & Punish: The Birth of the Prison*. New York: Vintage Books.

Fox-Brewster, T. (2016). 'Londoners Give Up Eldest Children in Public Wi-Fi Security Horror Show'. *The Guardian* (29 Sept.). Available at: https://www.theguardian.com/technology/2014/sep/29/londoners-wi-fi-security-herod-clause [Accessed 14 May, 2016].

Gallagher, R. and Greenwald, G. (2014). 'How the NSA plans to infect "millions" of computers with malware'. *The Intercept* (12 Mar.). Available at: https://theintercept.com/2014/03/12/nsa-plans-infect-millions-computers-malware/ [Accessed 14 May, 2016].

Garfinkel, S. (2001). *Database Nation: The Death of Privacy in the 21st Century*. Cambridge, MA: O'Reilly.

Gilliom, J. (2001). *Overseers of the Poor: Surveillance, Resistance and the Limits of Privacy*. Chicago: University of Chicago Press.

Gibbs, S. (2015). 'Facebook "tracks all visitors, breaching EU law"'. *The Guardian*. Available at: https://www. theguardian.com/technology/2015/mar/31/facebook-tracks-all-visitors-breaching-eu-law-report.

Greenberg, A. (April 2016). 'How Reporters Pulled Off the Panama Papers, the Biggest Leak in Whistleblower History'. *Wired*. Available at: http://www.wired.com/2016/04/reporters-pulled-off-panama-papers-biggest-leak-whistleblower-history/ [Accessed 14 May, 2016].

Griffin, A. (2016). 'UK Elections 2016: How Facebook Is Manipulating You to Vote'. *The Independent* (5 May). Available at: www.independent.co.uk/life-style/gadgets-and-tech/news/uk-elections-2016-how-facebook-is-manipulating-you-to-vote-a7015196.html [Accessed 14 May, 2016]

Haggerty, K. and Ericson, R. (2000). 'The Surveillant Assemblage'. *British Journal of Sociology*. 51(4), pp. 605–622.

Haggerty, K. and Samatas, M. (2010). *Surveillance and Democracy*. New York: Routledge-Cavendish.

Hannigan, R. (2014). Opinion: The Web is a Terrorist's Command-and-control Network of Choice. *Financial Times* (3 Nov.). Available at: www.ft.com/cms/s/2/c89b6c58-6342-11e4-8a63-00144feabdc0. html [Accessed 14 May, 2016].

Hastings, C. (2006). 'Revealed: How the BBC Used MI5 to Vet Thousands of Staff'. *The Telegraph* (2 July). Available at: http://www.telegraph.co.uk/news/uknews/1522875/Revealed-how-the-BBC-used-MI5-to-vet-thousands-of-staff.html [Accessed 14 May, 2016].

Hintz, A. (2014). 'Outsourcing Surveillance—Privatising Policy: Communications Regulation by Commercial Intermediaries'. *Birkbeck Law Review*. 2(2), pp. 349–368.

Hocking, J. (2004). Terror Laws: ASIO, Counter-Terrorism and the Threat to Democracy. Sydney: UNSW Press.

Hopkins, N. and Ackerman, S. (2013). 'Flexible Laws and Weak Oversight Give GCHQ Room for Manoeuvre'. *The Guardian*, August 2. Available at: http://www.theguardian.com/uknews/2013/aug/02/gchq-laws-oversight-nsa.

Hopkins, N. and Borger, J. (2013). 'Exclusive: NSA Pays £100m in Secret Funding for GCHQ'. *The Guardian*, August 1. Available at: http://www.theguardian.com/uk-news/2013/aug/01/nsapaid-gchq-spying-edward-snowden.

Introna, L. and Wood, D. (2004). 'Picturing Algorithmic Surveillance: The Politics of Facial Recognition Systems'. *Surveillance and Society*. 2(2/3), pp. 177–198.

Johnson, C. (2004). *The Sorrows of Empire: Militarism, Secrecy, and the End of the Republic.* London: Verso.

Johnson, A. (2016). 'CIA's Work With Filmmakers Puts All Media Workers at Risk'. *FAIR* (8 Apr.). Available at: http://fair.org/home/cias-work-with-filmmakers-puts-all-media-workers-at-risk/ [Accessed 14 May, 2016].

Keen, M. F. (1999). *Stalking the Sociological Imagination: J. Edgar Hoover's FBI Surveillance of American Sociology.* London: Greenwood Press.

Lyon, D. (2001). *Surveillance Society: Monitoring Everyday Life: Issues in Society*. Maidenhead: Open University Press.

Lyon, D. (2002). Editorial. 'Surveillance Studies: Understanding Visibility, Mobility and the Phenetic Fix'. *Surveillance and Society*, 1(1), pp. 1–7.

Lyon, D. ed. (2002). *Surveillance as Social Sorting: Privacy, Risk, and Digital Discrimination.* London and New York: Routledge.

Lyon, D. (2003). *Surveillance after September 11.* London: Polity.

Mathieson, T. (1997). 'The Viewer Society: Michel Foucault's "Panopticon" revisited'. *Theoretical Criminology*, 1(2), pp. 215–34.

Mattelart, A. (2010). *The Globalization of Surveillance.* London: Polity.

May, A. (2015). 'Report of the Interception of Communications Commissioner'; *IOCCO.* Available at: http://www.iocco-uk.info/docs/IOCCO%20Report%20March%202015%20(Web).pdf [Accessed 14 May, 2016].

McCarthy, K. (2016). 'European Human Rights Court Rules Mass Surveillance Illegal'. *The Register* (20 Jan.). Available at: www.theregister.co.uk/2016/01/20/human_rights_court_rules_mass_surveillance_illegal/ [Accessed 11 Jan. 2016].

McGrath, John. (2004). *Loving Big Brother: Surveillance Culture and Performance Space.* London: Routledge.

McLaughlin, J. (2015). 'UN Gives US Flunking Grades on Privacy and Surveillance Rights'. *The Intercept* (28 July). Accessed at: https://theintercept.com/2015/07/28/un-review-u-s-flunking-privacy-national-security-surveillance-rights/ [Accessed 14 May, 2016].

Meissner, J. (2016). 'Eliminating the No Number, No List Response: Keeping the CIA within the Scope of the Law Amidst America's Global War on Terror'. *Nevada Law Journal*, 16(1), pp. 345–72.

Mendick, Robert. and Verkaik, Robert. (2015). '"Anti-terror Plan to Spy on Toddlers" Is Heavy-handed'. *The Telegraph* (4 Jan.). Available at: www.telegraph.co.uk/news/uknews/terrorism-in-the-uk/11323558/Anti-terror-plan-to-spy-on-toddlers-is-heavy-handed.html [Accessed 14 May 2016].

Microsoft. (2013). 'Survey Shows People Need More Help Controlling Personal Info Online'. [Online]. Available at: https://news.microsoft.com/2013/01/23/survey-shows-people-need-more-help-controlling-personal-info-online/ [Accessed 14 May, 2016].

Millar, Gavin. (2015). 'This Surveillance Bill Threatens Investigative Journalism'. *The Guardian* (6 Nov.). Available at: http://www.theguardian.cm/commentisfree/2015/nov/06/surveillance-bill-threatens-investigative-journalism [Accessed 14 May, 2016].

Norris, C. and L'Hoiry, X. (2015). *IRISS: The Unaccountable State of Surveillance.* University of Sheffield. Unpublished.

Oremus, W. (2016). 'Facebook's Five New Reaction Buttons: Data, Data, Data, Data, and Data'. *Slate* (24 Feb.). Available at: www.slate.com/blogs/future_tense/2016/02/24/facebook_s_5_new_reactions_buttons_are_all_about_data_data_data.html [Accessed 14 May, 2016].

Parenti, C. (2003). *The Soft Cage: Surveillance in America from Slave Passes to the War on Terror.* New York: Basic Books.

Perrin, A. (2015). 'Social Media Usage: 2005-2015'. *Pew Research Data* (8 Oct.). Available at: http://www.pewinternet.org/2015/10/08/social-networking-usage-2005-2015/ [Accessed 14 May, 2016].

Press Gazette. (2015). 'Every UK National Newspaper Editor Urges Prime Minister to Stop RIPA Spying on Journalists'. Available at: http://www.pressgazette.co.uk/every-national-newspaper-editor-dacre-rusbridger-signs-save-our-sources-protest-letter [Accessed 14 May, 2016].

Ramsay, G.; Ramsay, A. and Marsden, S. (2016). 'Report: Impacts of surveillance on Contemporary British Activism'. *Open Democracy* (24 May). Available at: https://www.opendemocracy.net/uk/gilbert-ramsay/report-impacts-of-surveillance-on-contemporary-british-activism [Accessed 11 June, 2016].

Reuters. (2016). 'US Foreign Intelligence Court Did Not Deny Any Surveillance Requests Last Year'. *The Guardian* (30 Apr.). Available at: http://www.theguardian.com/law/2016/apr/30/fisa-court-foreign-intelligence-surveillance-fbi-nsa-applications [Accessed 14 May, 2016].

Reynolds, D. (2000). *Rich Relations: The American Occupation of Britain, 1942–1945.* London: Phoenix Press.

Rosen, J. (2004). *The Naked Crowd: Reclaiming Security and Freedom in an Anxious Age.* New York: Random House.

Senker, K. (2012). *Privacy and Surveillance.* New York: Rosen Publishing.

Smith, B. (1995). 'The Road to the Anglo-American Intelligence Partnership'. *American Intelligence Journal.* 16(2/3), pp. 59–62.

Stanyer, J. and Davidson, S. (2011). 'The Global Human Rights Regime and the Internet: Non-democratic States and the Hyper-visibility of Evidence of Oppression'. Cottle, S. and Lester, L. eds. *Transnational Protests and the Media.* New York: Peter Lang Publishing.

Stein, J. (2015). US Spies May be Back in Action Against ISIS. *Newsweek* (1 Dec.). Available at: http://europe.newsweek.com/us-spies-back-action-against-isis-400146 [Accessed 14 May, 2016].

Stempel, J. (2015). 'NSA's Phone Spying Program Ruled Illegal by Appeals Court'. *Reuters* (7 May). Available at: www.reuters.com/article/us-usa-security-nsa-idUSKBN0NS1IN20150507 [Accessed 14 May, 2016].

Stoycheff, E. (2016). 'Under Surveillance: Examining Facebook's Spiral of Silence Effects in the Wake of NSA Internet Monitoring'. *Journalism & Mass Communication Quarterly*, 93(2) pp. 296–311.

Taylor, N. (2002). 'State Surveillance and the Right to Privacy'. *Surveillance and Society*, 1(1), pp. 66–78.

Turvill, W. (2015). 'Interception Commissioner: 82 journalists' phone records grabbed by police in three years, judicial oversight needed'. *Press Gazette.* Available at: http://www.pressgazette.co.uk/interception-commissioner-82-journalists-phone-records-targeted-police-three-years-forces-should/.

Walsh, P. and Miller, S. (2016). 'Rethinking "Five Eyes" Security Intelligence Collection Policies and Practice Post Snowden'. *Intelligence and National Security*, 31(3), pp. 345–68.

Weiner, T. (2008). *Legacy of Ashes: History of the CIA.* London: Penguin.

Whitaker, R. (1999). *The End of Privacy: How Total Surveillance Is Becoming a Reality.* New York: The New Press.

Williamson, A. (2010). *Digital Citizens and Democratic Participation.* London: Hansard Society.

Yougov/Sunday Times. (2015). Survey Results. Accessed at: https://d25d2506sfb94s.cloudfront.net/cumulus_uploads/document/wt26kxdn72/YG-Archive-Pol-Sunday-Times-results-160115.pdf [Accessed 14 May, 2016].

Zuboff, S. (2016). 'The Secrets of Surveillance Capitalism'. *Frankfurter Allgemeine Zeitung* (5 Mar.). Accessed at: http://www.faz.net/aktuell/feuilleton/debatten/the-digital-debate/shoshana-zuboff-secrets-of-surveillance-capitalism-14103616.html [Accessed 14 May, 2016].

17

CIVIL SOCIETY AND POLITICAL-INTELLIGENCE ELITES

From manipulation to public accountability

Vian Bakir

Intelligence agencies are used by political elites to further the national interest and protect national security. Despite the existence of international human rights treaties, sometimes, human rights get in the way, and are sacrificed. Nation-states can be upfront about sacrificing certain human rights via the process of 'derogation' from human rights treaties, but this requires a specific set of circumstances. For instance, it is only in times of public emergency threatening the life of nation, that nations can adjust their obligations under human rights treaties. Furthermore, derogation is only temporary and only allowed for certain types of human right (such as the right to privacy). Other human rights are non-derogable: They cannot be compromised or reduced, at least in theory, because they are considered as too important – for instance the right to be free from torture and other inhumane or degrading treatment or punishment (Rule of Law in Armed Conflict Project n.d.) and the right not to be disappeared (United Nations 2006). However, nation-states may still wish to sacrifice such human rights if they perceive their nation to be sufficiently threatened. In such circumstances, the human rights sacrifices occur in secret, raising challenges for civil society in holding political-intelligence elites to account. It is this relationship between civil society and political-intelligence elite accountability that this chapter centrally addresses, paying particular attention to the secretive torture-intelligence policies of the George W. Bush administration (Jan. 2001–Jan. 2009).

Following the events of '9/11' and developed in the context of the War on Terror, the Bush administration developed highly secretive torture-intelligence policies (the Detention and Interrogation Program), and tasked the Central Intelligence Agency (CIA) with carrying them out. Because intelligence agencies normally operate in secret, the ability of civil society to hold political-intelligence elites publicly to account for any such human rights contraventions is limited. Compounding this difficulty, most research examining relationships between civil society and intelligence agencies confirms political-intelligence elite manipulation of civil society rather than civil society's ability to publicly hold intelligence agencies to account. Yet, civil society can play an important role in exposing secretive, human-rights-compromising policies. This may happen, via the press, through unauthorised leaks and investigative journalism; and via non-governmental organisations (NGOs), through original and critical research, campaigns and

179

protests. Such civil society activity can move issues forward to challenge political-intelligence elite claims and to hold them publicly accountable.

This chapter will critically examine the challenges faced by the press and NGOs (as key civil society actors) in holding political-intelligence elites to account on secretive policies that abuse non-derogable human rights. It does so first, through a multidisciplinary literature review (drawing from journalism, media, history and international relations) on relationships of influence between civil society and intelligence agencies. Second, it refers to a paradigmatic contemporary case study of civil society's attempts and challenges in holding political-intelligence elites to account, namely the Bush-era torture-intelligence policy during its most secretive phase (Autumn 2001 – Spring 2004). While ultimately, a network of international civil society actors challenged the torture-intelligence policy so robustly that the policy was ended as Barack Obama became US president (in 2009), during its most secretive phase, civil society efforts to expose the policy were greatly stymied by political-intelligence elite manipulation (Bakir 2013). This case study, then, examines key successful strategies used by political-intelligence elites to keep the policy secret from civil society. Reflecting on this, and key themes identified by the literature review this chapter concludes with directions for future research into the public accountability of political-intelligence elites in the area of human rights.

The field of intelligence, influence and civil society

There is very little research examining the relationships of influence between intelligence agencies and civil society. The little that exists largely examines the media, especially the press and film (Dover and Goodman 2009, Jenkins 2012, Bakir 2015), with a lesser focus on NGOs (Caparini 2004, Caparini et al. 2006, Aldrich 2009). Most of the research focuses on intelligence agencies' strategies, techniques and successes in manipulating different nodes (media and NGOs) within civil society, while very little addresses the question of whether it is possible for civil society to publicly hold political-intelligence elites to account (although see Caparini et al. 2006, Robarge 2009, Hillebrand 2012, Van Puyvelde 2013, Johnson 2014, Lashmar 2015). Prominent themes are delineated in the following sections.

Intelligence agencies' strategies and techniques of manipulating civil society

Much attention within this field is focused on intelligence agencies' strategies and techniques of manipulating the media, with comparatively little written on manipulating NGOs. The three main strategies of influence directed at the media are secrecy, censorship and propaganda. The strategy of secrecy has been desired since the inception of both the intelligence agencies and the mass-market press (Shpiro 2001), and continues today. For instance, Hess (2009) describes the German intelligence agency, BND's, efforts during the Cold War and up to the 2000s to protect its sources, methods and organisation from press coverage. The strategy of censorship is achieved through three main techniques. These comprise the use, or threatened use, of legal force (Sweeney and Washburn 2014); blacklisting, harassing and threatening non-compliant media and journalists (Spaulding 2009); and self-censorship by media employees persuaded by government arguments on national security (Eldridge 2000).

The strategy of propaganda is achieved through many techniques. These include developing propaganda-oriented policy and organizational machinery and institutions (Cull 2010); creating propaganda films (Willmetts 2015); exporting merchandise and products of popular culture and high culture to influence foreign publics (Gienow-Hecht 2003); using opinion-leaders to propagate propaganda (Pullin 2011); and using disinformation and psychological warfare techniques (Chanan 2009). While targeted at a wide range of media including film, radio, novels and the press, an array of techniques are focused specifically on the press. Propaganda techniques aimed at the foreign press include creating or financially supporting foreign news and radio services that can then be exploited when needed (de Vries 2012), and providing propagandistic content for the foreign press, newsreels and radio to persuade foreign publics (Chang 2014). The provision of propaganda to the domestic press to persuade domestic audiences is often viewed as the most ethically problematic given that the press in liberal democracies are regarded as a vehicle of ensuring political – and intelligence – accountability. Such propaganda techniques include selective authorized leaks, declassification and misdirection (Hastedt 2005); cultivating or directly employing sympathetic journalists (Magen 2014); and using the press as a cover for agents overseas (Hess 2009).

While less is written on intelligence agencies' strategies and techniques of manipulating NGOs, the small amount of research in this area reveals an anti-communist impetus during the Cold War (Mariager 2013), and following the Cold War, a desire to promote democracy (Anable 2006). The most commonly researched technique of influence by intelligence agencies regarding NGOs is the setting up of 'state-private networks' and the launch and financing of covertly run front organizations, these techniques documented during the Cold War (Aldrich 2003) and beyond (Barker 2008). For instance, Barker (2008) examines the role of the congressionally funded NGO, the National Endowment for Democracy, as a means of legally channelling funding from larger agencies, like the United States Agency for International Development (USAID) and the CIA, to promote, via independent media institutions, 'low-intensity', public-relations-friendly democracy in Iraq and Afghanistan post-9/11. Other techniques used by intelligence agencies to influence NGOs, but limited to the Cold War period, are propaganda campaigns against groups, as in the case of press coverage of a pro-Soviet Danish peace group in 1986, the coverage claiming that an upcoming international nonpartisan peace conference, the World Peace Congress, was a communist propaganda event (Mariager 2013).

Civil society's practices in engaging with intelligence agencies

A number of civil society's practices in engaging with intelligence, and with intelligence agencies, agents and sources, have been documented. These practices range from those that collaborate with intelligence agencies, to those that oppose them.

Collaborative journalistic practices include acting as intelligence informants (Alwood 2007); spreading intelligence-sourced propaganda (Holland 2009); uncritical use of intelligence sources (Lashmar 2013); uncritical tone of coverage of intelligence issues (de Vries 2012); and failure to report on intelligence failures (Gup 2004). NGOs also engage in collaborative practices with intelligence agencies. Motivations for NGOs' cooperation with intelligence agencies during the Second World War and the Cold War included patriotism, anti-colonialism (Dow 2011) and the desire to promote peace in the nuclear age (Laville 2003).

Oppositional journalistic practices include exposing secret or little-known policies (Chung 2014); attempting to maintain editorial independence and freedom of speech (Sweeney and Washburn 2014); highlighting intelligence failures and demanding reform (de Vries 2012); questioning political administration's presentation and interpretation of intelligence (Bean 2013); uncovering intelligence agents' identity (Bar-Joseph 2008); and resorting to opinion when facts are unforthcoming or unclear (Matei 2014). All of these practices can be used to hold political-intelligence elites publicly to account, although some have far more sway than others (the latter two run the greatest risk of being seen as commercial ploys to win audience attention rather than upholding any fourth estate ideals).

Motivations for NGOs adopting a more critical role towards intelligence agencies revolve around their efforts to improve the accountability of intelligence agencies. For instance, Van Puyvelde (2013) describes the role of interest groups in the US since the 1950s to the present day in helping to hold intelligence agencies to account. Deibert (2003) describes how, in the Internet age, NGOs and hackers have merged to become hacktivists, their aims being to engage in activism ranging from protests against state policies to surveillance of state activities and treaties, and surveillance of state intelligence agencies. A wide variety of oppositional practices used by NGOs seeking greater intelligence accountability are documented. Focusing on the project on government secrecy at the Federation of American Scientists, the Project on Government Oversight and the American Civil Liberties Union, Van Puyvelde (2013) observes that techniques include obtaining and circulating information to potential intelligence overseers; supporting whistleblowers; targeting and mobilizing the US people, providing them with opportunities for civic engagement and communication with institutions; using litigation and relying on the judgment of the courts; lobbying; and testifying before congressional committees. Another NGO technique of influence involves generating and sharing a pool of knowledge and analysis. Sometimes this is focused on the secret side of the government (Van Puyvelde 2013); sometimes on broader state activities and policies; and sometimes on the secret side of activism such as using encryption tools to secure private or sensitive exchanges, and to allow street activists to engage in 'real-time' strategic organization of protest (Deibert 2003).

To summarise, the literature shows that key organs of civil society, namely the media (especially the press) and NGOs have long been targets of influence by political-intelligence elites, but do have resistive capacity, which sometimes succeeds in holding political-intelligence elites publicly accountable. However, this is far from an easy task. The difficulties faced by civil society in this area are illustrated below by examining the relationship between intelligence agencies and civil society in the most secretive phase of the Bush administration's torture-intelligence policy (2001–4), where the non-derogable right to be free from torture and other inhumane or degrading treatment or punishment was secretly taken apart.

The Bush administration's torture-intelligence policy

On 11 September 2001, within the first year of George W. Bush's US presidency, Sunni Islamic fundamentalists, al-Qaeda, conducted a spectacular terrorist attack on American soil – '9/11'. Four hijacked airplanes were spectacularly transformed into Weapons of Mass Destruction (WMD), attacking America's economic headquarters (The World Trade Center) and military headquarters (the Pentagon), simultaneously, killing nearly 3,000 people. After 9/11, for the Bush administration, the perception of the risk of terrorism changed, along with what it was prepared to do to mitigate that risk. Frequently invoked by US officials was the idea that 9/11 ushered in a new threat – a new risk – which required a new way of thinking (The 9/11 Commission Report 2004, 10).

Between the end of the Second World War and pre-9/11, warfare was more to do with the mutually assured destruction of nuclear weaponry, guerilla warfare and civil war. In contrast, for the Bush administration, 9/11 ushered in the jihadist-terrorist model of warfare, where terrorists were unafraid of embracing death to achieve their aims. The ability of terrorists to blend into the civilian population decreased their vulnerability to signal intelligence (from radio messages, radio signals and radar) and imagery intelligence (long-range photography to gain images). Consequently, human intelligence (information gained from human sources, including interrogation) was seen as essential. The Bush administration believed that what it terms 'enhanced interrogation techniques' (EITs) (and what others term torture) along with what became known as 'extraordinary rendition' (enforced disappearances to secret prisons where torture occurred) were necessary to extract intelligence from al-Qaeda terrorist suspects. It put the CIA at the forefront of implementing this secret torture-intelligence policy (Bakir 2013). The need for secrecy stemmed from the fact that the US historically has been a leading proponent of the ban on torture. It participated in the 1929 conference that produced the first Geneva Convention governing the humane treatment of prisoners; and in the 1949 re-writing of humanitarian law for the Geneva Conventions. In 1994 the US ratified the UN Torture Convention [1984]. Secrecy, then, would avoid protracted and embarrassing debates in Congress and the media, on the US's human rights obligations regarding the right to be free from torture and other inhuman or degrading treatment or punishment.

The secret policy only started to surface publicly in spring 2004 through leaked user-generated content – photographs of torture of security detainees by US Military Police (MP) at abu Ghraib prison in Iraq, the photos taken by an in-crowd of MP torturers and other MP onlookers. With the help of a global network of journalists, NGOs, citizens, lawyers and political investigations, the secret policy was gradually exposed after US media, *CBS* and *The New Yorker*, published some of the leaked photos in 2004, and in 2005 *The Washington Post* reported the existence of a global network of secret prisons where detainees subject to extraordinary rendition had been sent for further torture. As the secret policy was exposed, the Bush administration deflected attention by presenting perpetrators caught on camera (a small number of MPs at abu Ghraib) as isolated examples of 'bad apples' who were abusing policy rather than enacting a secret torture-intelligence policy (Bakir 2013). The Bush administration also took care to distinguish the torture depicted in the abu Ghraib photos from what it termed EITs used in places like Guantanamo Bay prison on captured al-Qaeda suspects, claiming that EITs were legal and necessary in preventing a future terrorist attack. Despite the Bush administration's generation of numerous secret legal memoranda from the Department of Justice's (DoJ) Office of Legal Counsel to argue for the legality of the torture-intelligence policy, the legal argument over whether EITs constitute torture has long been settled (they do), with US President Obama reiterating this on taking office in 2009. The argument over EIT's effectiveness was left hanging for several more years as the secrecy of the intelligence community about their techniques and impact allowed EIT proponents to continue to claim their effectiveness without providing evidence. However, declassification in December 2014 of the US Senate Intelligence *Committee Study of the Central Intelligence Agency's Detention and Interrogation Program* (US Senate Intelligence Committee Report 2012) for the first time publicly evidenced the ineffectiveness of the torture-intelligence programme, including EITs.

A key question is how the torture-intelligence policy remained secret from its initiation soon after 9/11 until the abu Ghraib leaks in Spring 2004. Over this period of 2.5 years why was civil society failing to do its job of holding political-intelligence elites to account?

Problematic relationships with civil society

Between 9/11 and the publication of the abu Ghraib photographs in Spring 2004, occasional news stories emerged pointing to US torture and extraordinary renditions of al-Qaeda suspects. However, they were countered by Bush administration media manipulation, which: tested American attitudes to the idea of torture; normalized the practice of extraordinary renditions; publicly portrayed interrogations as harsh but legal; attempted to discredit accounts from former detainees in the War on Terror; and denied NGOs' requests for release of records under the US's Freedom of Information Act (FOIA). Each of these efforts at controlling wider civil society is examined below.

In terms of the Bush administration testing American attitudes to the idea of torture, very soon after 9/11, news stories appeared in American mainstream press suggesting that torture might be used in the War on Terror, and presenting this as potentially a good idea. For instance, on 21 October 2001, the *Washington Post* reported impatience expressed by a senior official from the Federal Bureau of Investigation (FBI) over the interrogation of four suspected terrorists arrested after 9/11, because none were talking, with the official stating: 'We are known for humanitarian treatment But it could get to that spot where we could go to pressure where we won't have a choice, and we are probably getting there.' Reflecting anything from ideological capture of journalists through to infiltration by intelligence agencies, such trial balloons from the FBI drew support for torture by media commentators across the political spectrum. For instance, as McCoy (2006, 111) records, on 5 November 2001, *Newsweek*'s columnist Jonathan Alter wrote: 'In this autumn of anger, even a liberal can find his thoughts turning to … torture' adding 'some torture clearly works' and advocating the transfer of suspects to 'our less squeamish allies.' Indeed, as noted by Bernie Hamilton in his address to the Annual General Meeting of Doctors for Human Rights on 24 November 2001, the idea of torture in interrogations: 'is only talk that has appeared in a number of US newspapers. But that is the way changes happen. You run an idea up the flagpole and see if anyone salutes' (Doctors for Human Rights n.d.).

Alongside the apparent testing by the Bush administration of US public attitudes towards torture following 9/11, occasional reports of extraordinary rendition surfaced in the international press – but these were quickly made to appear 'normal' rather than a highly unusual (and illegal) activity. For instance, on 26 October 2001, Pakistan's *The News International* ran a story headlined 'Mystery man handed over to US troops in Karachi'. According to an unnamed source at Karachi airport:

> Pakistani authorities handed over a 'suspected foreigner' to the US authorities in a mysterious way.' The man was taken away in a 'Falcon aircraft owned by the US air force'. 'The entire operation was so mysterious that all persons involved in the operation, including US troops, were wearing masks … A masked US trooper was also making a video film of the entire operation.

This story – a witnessing of an extraordinary rendition – was picked up by the *Los Angeles Times* two days later, on 28 October 2001, but heavily citing a military intelligence source that normalized the then unusual event: 'This is not unusual. Over the last six months, many people have been deported if they had false documents or suspect links with terrorist organizations in African and Middle Eastern countries'. The Bush administration also offered a range of pragmatic explanations for extraordinary rendition. Such inoculations appeared to work. For instance, the *Washington Post* on 11 March 2002 reported on the rendition from Indonesia to Egypt of Muhammad Sa'ad Iqbal Madni (suspected of being an al-Qaeda operative). This story was attributed to unnamed 'Western diplomats and intelligence sources.' Although noting that rendition to places like Egypt and Jordan 'whose intelligence services have close ties to the CIA' meant that detainees could be 'subjected to interrogation tactics - including torture and threats to families - that are illegal in the United States,' this story also noted that:

> diplomats said it is preferable to render a suspect secretly because it prevents lengthy court battles and minimizes publicity that could tip off the detainee's associates. Rendering suspects to a third country, particularly Muslim nations such as Egypt or Jordan, also helps to defuse domestic political concerns in predominantly Muslim nations such as Indonesia, the diplomats said.

Having probed American public opinion on detainee torture, across 2002 the Bush administration prepared the American public to accept the idea that EITs did not constitute torture, and that, combined with renditions, were vital for intelligence gains to minimise the risk of another 9/11 happening. For instance, several years into the War on Terror, *CNN*, on 3 March 2003, reported that CIA had captured Khalid Shaikh Mohammed (KSM) (billed as the mastermind behind 9/11). While KSM was subjected to the harshest of EITs (for instance, subjected to simulated drowning ('water-boarding') at least 183 times (US Senate Intelligence Committee Report 2012), in *CNN*'s news report the issue of torture is not raised. Instead, the headline is: '"Appropriate pressure" being put on al Qaeda leader'. This is followed by the lede: '"All appropriate pressure" is being put on Khalid Shaikh Mohammed, the man believed to be the key planner of the terrorist attacks of September 11, 2001, to reveal plots for any future operations, a senior US intelligence official said Sunday'.

Where examples of torture became known through accounts from former detainees, the Bush administration (together with some of its allies in the 54 other countries suspected of complicity in this policy) attempted to discredit the former detainees. A prominent example is the case of Canadian and Syrian citizen, Maher Arar. Arar was erroneously subject to extraordinary rendition to Syria in 2001, torture in Syrian jails, and then smeared as a terrorist by unnamed Canadian officials on his return. The smears came from Canadian reporters reporting unnamed government officials who were leaking false information about Arar (Commission of Inquiry into the Actions of Canadian Officials in Relation to Maher Arar 2006). This was designed to pre-emptively discredit his claims, and was intensified as, on 4 November 2003, Arar, spoke publicly for the first time about his ten-month-long extraordinary rendition to Syria, and his torture there (Bakir 2013).

Given such examples of political-intelligence elite manipulation of journalism, or of journalistic complicity with political-intelligence elites, it is perhaps unsurprising that in the first few years in the War on Terror, it was not journalists who publicly pointed to a torture-intelligence policy. Rather, this task was largely taken up NGOs. Given the early media accounts of threats of torture and of extraordinary rendition, a network of NGOs joined forces to further direct public attention to these practices. For instance, noting that: 'The level of secrecy surrounding 9/11 detainees has made fact finding and analysis difficult' (Amnesty International 2002, 4), in an effort to gain information about the identity and location of detainees, Amnesty International and several other human rights organizations made a joint formal request to the US DoJ on 29 October 2001 for the release of records under the FOIA. However, several weeks earlier, on 12 October 2001, the Bush administration had issued new guidelines for responding to FOIA requests. These guidelines reversed the previous Clinton administration's policy that agencies should release information unless harm would result from disclosure. Now, heads of federal agencies were directed to identify reasons to deny access to information by invoking one of the FOIA's exemptions, even if no harm would result from disclosure (US House of Representatives Committee on the Judiciary 2009). When the government failed to respond to NGOs' formal request for records, the NGOs filed a joint civil action in December 2001 against the DoJ and FBI, alleging violations of the FOIA. In a counter-attack, on 19 March 2004, Andrew Card, then White House Chief of Staff, issued a memorandum advising executive departments and agencies to use FOIA exemptions to withhold 'sensitive but non-classified' information; and to re-classify certain types of unclassified or previously declassified information (US House of Representatives Committee on the Judiciary 2009, 252).

Directions for future research

The multidisciplinary literature review points to the various ways in which civil society has been manipulated by political-intelligence elites. This potential is confirmed by the previously discussed contemporary case study on the torture-intelligence policy while in its most secretive phase. The case study shows that where the US political-intelligence elite views a policy as central to national security, but where that policy also contravenes non-derogable human rights, resources are deployed to divert attention from the policy to keep it secret. To divert attention, the US domestic mainstream press is activated as a conduit for political-intelligence elite sourced propaganda. Such propaganda aims to: test and shape domestic public attitudes towards the acceptability of policies that contravene human rights; damage the credibility of human rights whistle-blowers (such as Arar); and deflect attention from inadvertent exposures (such as through eye-witness accounts of extraordinary rendition) of secret policies involving intelligence agencies.

Arising from this analysis, three important areas of research are needed. Given that the US domestic press is meant to be exempt from state propaganda activities, it would be useful, first, to establish the broad patterns of mainstream press attention to problematic policies that involve intelligence agencies and the contravention of human rights. This is not an easy task given the secretive and propagandistic nature of political-intelligence elite-supplied material. As such, close attention should be paid to news stories' stated sources, and the evidentiary basis of any publicised intelligence claims made, bearing in mind that intelligence reports, being based on uncertain knowledge with the evidentiary base largely kept secret from the public, are particularly vulnerable to political manipulation.

Second, it is important to inquire into how the mainstream press can be encouraged and enabled to ask more critical questions of their nation's political-intelligence elites, especially when human rights are being contravened. Of course, this is a line of inquiry not just applicable to intelligence and human rights, but to all issues. Scholars of journalism decry the poor state of critical and investigative journalism more generally, noting that journalists are increasingly time-constrained, and resource-poor, as declining paying audiences generate job redundancies and pressures on remaining journalists to produce copy for multiple news forms (Jackson & Moloney 2015). These factors mitigate against in-depth, time-consuming, investigative or critical journalism, increasing the press' susceptibility to manipulation. Added to these problems, however, involving political-intelligence elites and breaches of non-derogable human rights is that: (a) to save face, manipulation is highly likely (no liberal democracy, least of all one which has historically projected itself as at the forefront of human rights, would want to be seen leading the world into norm regress on the torture ban); and (b) given that intelligence agencies are involved, issues of national security are at stake, which means that emotive claims stoking fear about threats, such as terrorism, are likely, making critical journalistic coverage susceptible to charges of anti-patriotism.

Third, more action-oriented research is needed into how human rights NGOs can make their own critical research into this area better heard through societies' various organs of public accountability such as the press. Journalism studies suggests that NGOs will struggle here, as the press generally indexes the range of debate made by elites, adopting critical positions only if part of the political elite publicly do so, but otherwise failing to criticise (Bennett 1990; Bennett, Lawrence & Livingston 2007). Hence, if a policy is secret, and not the subject of elite debate, NGOs will struggle to get their position heard. This becomes even harder if also faced with manipulative political-intelligence elite activity. Yet, with NGOs forming a crucial node of holding political-intelligence elites to account, as mainstream press succumb to strategies of secrecy and propaganda, NGOs surely deserve much more attention, and help, from the academic community.

References

Aldrich, R. J. (2003). 'Putting Culture into the Cold War: the Cultural Relations Department (CRD) and British Covert Information Warfare'. *Intelligence and National Security*, 18(2), pp. 109–33.

Aldrich, R. J. (2009). 'Global Intelligence Co-operation Versus Accountability: New Facets to an Old Problem'. *Intelligence and National Security*, 24(1), pp. 26–56.

Alwood, E. (2007). 'Watching the Watchdogs: FBI Spying on Journalists in the 1940s. *Journalism & Mass Communication Quarterly*, 84(1), pp. 137–50.

Amnesty International (2002). *USA: Amnesty International's Concerns Regarding Post-September 11 Detentions in the USA.* Available at: https://www.amnesty.org/en/documents/amr51/044/2002/en/ [Accessed 1 March, 2017].

Anable, D. (2006). 'The Role of Georgia's Media - and Western Aid - in the Rose Revolution'. *The Harvard International Journal of Press/Politics*, 11(3), pp. 7–43.

Bakir, V. (2015). 'News, Agenda Building, and Intelligence Agencies: A Systematic Review of the Field from the Discipline of Journalism, Media, and Communications'. *The International Journal of Press/Politics*, 20(2): 131–44.

Bakir, V. (2013). *Torture, Intelligence and Sousveillance in the War on Terror: Agenda–building Struggles.* London & New York: Routledge.

Bar-Joseph, U. (2008). The Intelligence Chief Who Went Fishing in the Cold: How Maj. Gen. (res.) Eli Zeira Exposed the Identity of Israel's Best Source Ever'. *Intelligence and National Security*, 23(2), pp. 226–48.

Barker, M. J. (2008). 'Democracy or Polyarchy? US-funded Media Developments in Afghanistan and Iraq post 9/11'. *Media, Culture & Society*, 30(1), pp. 109–30.

Bean, H. (2013). 'Rhetorical and Critical/Cultural Intelligence Studies'. *Intelligence and National Security*, 28(4), pp. 495–519.

Bennett, W. L, Lawrence, R. G. and Livingston S. (2007). *When the Press Fails: Political Power and the News Media from Iraq to Katrina.* Chicago: University of Chicago Press.

Bennett, W. L. (1990). 'Toward a Theory of Press-state Relations in the United States'. *Journal of Communication*, 40(2), pp. 103–27.

Caparini, M. (2004). 'Media and the Security Sector: Oversight and Accountability'. In M. Caparini, ed., *Media in Security and Governance: The Role of the News Media in Security Accountability and Oversight*, Baden-Baden: Nomos, pp. 15–49.

Caparini, M., Fluri, P. and Molnar, F. eds. (2006). *Civil Society and the Security Sector: Concepts and Practices in New Democracies.* Geneva Centre for the Democratic Control of Armed Forces.

Chanan, M. (2009). 'Reporting from El Salvador: A Case Study in Participant Observation'. *Journal of Intelligence History*, 9(1–2), pp. 53–73.

Chang, K. (2014). 'Muted Reception: U.S. Propaganda and the Construction of Mexican Popular Opinion During the Second World War'. *Diplomatic History*, 38(3), pp. 569–98.

Chung, P. (2014). The "Pictures in our Heads": Journalists, Human Rights, and U.S.–South Korean Relations, 1970–1976'. *Diplomatic History*, 38(5), pp. 1136–55.

Commission of Inquiry into the Actions of Canadian Officials in Relation to Maher Arar (2006). *Report of the Events Relating to Maher Arar, Factual Background,* Vol. I, II and Analysis and Recommendations, Addendum.

Cull, N. J. (2010). 'Speeding the Strange Death of American Public Diplomacy: the George H. W. Bush Administration and the US Information Agency'. *Diplomatic History*, 34(1), pp. 47–69.

de Vries, T. (2012). The 1967 Central Intelligence Agency Scandal: Catalyst in a Transforming Relationship Between State and People'. *Journal of American History*, 98(4), pp. 1075–92.

Deibert, R. J. (2003). 'Deep Probe: the Evolution of Network Intelligence'. *Intelligence and National Security*, 18(4), pp. 175–93.

Doctors for Human Rights (n,d.). *The Attack on Human Rights: Time Line of Events.* Available at: http://phall.members.gn.apc.org/timeline.05-01-10.doc

Dow, P. E. (2011). 'Romance in a Marriage of Convenience: The Missionary Factor in Early Cold War U.S.-Ethiopian Relations, 1941–1960'. *Diplomatic History*, 35(5): 859–95. doi:10.1111/j.1467-7709.2011.00988.x.

Dover, R. and Goodman, M. S. (Eds.) (2009). *Spinning Intelligence: Why Intelligence needs the Media, Why the Media needs Intelligence.* London: C. Hurst and Co.

Eldridge, D. N. (2000). '"Dear Owen": The CIA, Luigi Luraschi and Hollywood, 1953'. *Historical Journal of Film, Radio and Television*, 20(2), pp. 149–96.

Gienow-Hecht, J. (2003). '"How Good Are We?" Culture and the Cold War'. *Intelligence and National Security*, 18(2), pp. 269–82.

Gup, T. (2004). 'Covering the CIA in Times of Crisis: Obstacles and Strategies'. *The Harvard International Journal of Press/Politics*, 9(3), pp. 28–39.

Hastedt, G. (2005). 'Public Intelligence: Leaks as Policy Instruments–the Case of the Iraq War'. *Intelligence and National Security*, 20(3), pp. 419–39.

Hess, S. (2009). 'German Intelligence Organizations and the Media'. *Journal of Intelligence History*, 9 (1–2), pp. 75–87.

Hillebrand, C. (2012). 'The Role of News Media in Intelligence Oversight'. *Intelligence and National Security*, 27(5), pp. 689–706.

Holland, M. (2009). 'I. F. Stone: Encounters with Soviet Intelligence'. *Journal of Cold War Studies*, 11(3), pp. 144–205.

Jackson, D. and Moloney, K. (2015). 'Inside Churnalism: PR, Journalism and Power Relationships in Flux'. *Journalism Studies*, 1–18, doi:10.1080/1461670X.2015.1017597

Jenkins, T. (2012). *The CIA in Hollywood: How the Agency Shapes Film and Television*. Austin: University of Texas Press.

Johnson, L. K. (2014). 'Intelligence Shocks, Media Coverage, and Congressional Accountability, 1947–2012'. *Journal of Intelligence History*, 13(1), pp. 1–21.

Lashmar, P. (2013). 'Urinal or Conduit? Institutional Information Flow Between the UK Intelligence Services and the News Media'. *Journalism*, 14(8), pp. 1–17.

Lashmar, P. (2015). 'Spies and Journalists: Towards an Ethical Framework?'. *Ethical Space: The International Journal of Communication Ethics*, 12(3/4), pp. 4–14.

Laville, H. (2003). 'The Memorial Day Statement: Women's Organizations in the "Peace Offensive"'. *Intelligence and National Security*, 18(2), pp. 192–210.

Magen, C. (2014). 'Mossad Directors and the Media: a Historical Perspective'. *Journal of Intelligence History*, 13(2), pp. 144–60.

Mariager, R. (2013). 'Surveillance of Peace Movements in Denmark During the Cold War'. *Journal of Intelligence History*, 12(1), pp. 60–75.

Matei, F. C. (2014). 'The Media's Role in Intelligence Democratization'. *International Journal of Intelligence and CounterIntelligence*, 27(1), pp. 73–108.

McCoy, A. W. (2006). *A Question of Torture: CIA Interrogation, from the Cold War to the War on Terror*. New York: Metropolitan Books.

Pullin, E. D. (2011). 'Money Does Not Make Any Difference to the Opinions That We Hold': India, the CIA, and the Congress for Cultural Freedom, 1951–58'. *Intelligence and National Security*, 26(2–3), pp. 377–98.

Robarge, D. (2009). 'CIA in the Spotlight: The Central Intelligence Agency and Public Accountability'. *Journal of Intelligence History*, 9(1–2), pp. 105–26.

Rule of Law in Armed Conflict Project (n.d). *Derogation From Human Rights Treaties in Situations of Emergency*. http://www.geneva-academy.ch/RULAC/derogation_from_human_rights_treaties_in_situations_of_emergency.php

Shpiro, S. (2001). 'Intelligence, Media, and Terrorism: Imperial Germany and the Middle East'. *Journal of Intelligence History*, 1(1), pp. 21–35.

Spaulding, S. (2009). Off the Blacklist, but Still a Target'. *Journalism Studies*, 10(6), pp. 789–804.

Sweeney, M. S. and Washburn, P. S. (2014). '"Aint Justice Wonderful." The Chicago Tribune's Battle of Midway Story and the Government's Attempt at an Espionage Act Indictment in 1942'. *Journalism & Communication Monographs*, 16(1), pp. 7–97.

The 9/11 Commission Report (2004). *The National Commission on Terrorist Attacks Upon the United States*. Available at: https://www.9-11commission.gov/ [Accessed 1 March, 2017].

United Nations (2006). *International Convention for the Protection of All Persons from Enforced Disappearance*. Available at: https://treaties.un.org/Pages/ViewDetails.aspx?src=IND&mtdsg_no=IV-16&chapter=4&lang=en

US House of Representatives Committee on the Judiciary (2009). *Reining in the Imperial Presidency: Lessons and Recommendations Relating to the Presidency of George W. Bush. House Committee on the Judiciary Majority Staff Report to Chairman John Conyers, Jr.* (Released 13 Jan. 2009). http://www.house.gov/delahunt/imperialpresidency.pdf

US Senate Intelligence Committee Report (2012). *Executive Summary: Committee Study of the Central Intelligence Agency's Detention and Interrogation Program* (Released Dec. 2014). Available at: http://www.washingtonpost.com/wp-srv/special/national/cia-interrogation-report/document/

Van Puyvelde, D. (2013). 'Intelligence Accountability and the Role of Public Interest Groups in the United States'. *Intelligence and National Security*, 28(2), pp. 139–58.

Willmetts, S. (2015). 'The CIA and the Invention of Tradition'. *Journal of Intelligence History*, 14(2), pp. 112–28.

18

FOREIGN POLICY, MEDIA AND HUMAN RIGHTS

Ekaterina Balabanova

The increased salience of human rights in media coverage since the 1990s is a recognition of media becoming 'more receptive to human rights issues today than at any time in the modern history of the media' seeing them as more newsworthy than ever before (ICHRP 2002, 32, 16; Ramos et al. 2007; Cole 2010; Caliendo et al. 1999; Ovsiovitch 1993). However, despite this increased frequency and salience, there has been no shortage of criticisms of the way media cover human rights issues. During the Cold-War period the information available through the media was seen as sporadic (Berry & McChesney 1988), 'incomplete, thus skewing the public's perception of human rights around the world' (Ovsiovitch 1993, 685) and biased (Herman & Chomsky 1988). In the post-Cold-War era the media has been accused of a 'serious lack of knowledge', 'inadequate understanding', even 'ignorance' of what human rights are; how they are created, promoted and enforced; what governments' responsibilities in relation to them are (ICHRP 2002, Internews 2012). This has negative repercussions for the quality of reporting, leads to human rights often wrongly being regarded as only relevant to the reporting of conflict and a focus on civil and political rights rather than abuses of social and economic rights (Internews 2012, ICHRP 2002, Ramos et al. 2007).

Why does this matter? Ideas about human rights now appear to play an important role in setting, communicating and critiquing political agendas on foreign policy. From the 'humanitarian interventions' of the 1990s to the ethnic and religious conflicts of the 2010s the language of choice for all sides is overwhelmingly one of human rights, and these are increasingly struggles that are mediatized in different ways. It is now almost impossible to discuss violent conflicts between and within states or between state and non-state actors without including a role for the media. The media has become one of the key battlegrounds for contemporary political actors on all sides of 'war', with some arguing it can even constitute an independent actor creating pressure for action (Gilboa et al. 2016, 1).

Yet there is very little agreement on the role of the media and its contribution to any impact of human rights in foreign policymaking. Competing claims raise a series of questions about the complex interplay between a developing system of international norms, the transformation of the media environment and technology and international relations. Has the embedding of human rights norms in the international system combined with a new capacity for media to reach nearly all parts of the globe challenged traditional statecraft based on realpolitik? Has the rise of global media platforms and social media influenced the agenda for foreign policy – forcing governments to deal with the horrors of human rights abuses around the world? Has there been a shift in power dynamics where whistleblowers and Internet-based information exchange has disrupted the capacity for states to control and dominate the public sphere? Has a radically reconstituted media environment altered the relationship between human rights and foreign policy? Or perhaps these influences and the role of the media have been exaggerated and overplayed – a brief post-Cold-War period that has, or will soon, pass? Did the advent of the 'war on terror' signal a shift back to normal service, where media coverage served state interests and human rights concerns were secondary in foreign policy formulation? Were the televised so-called humanitarian wars of the 1990s little more than a carefully curated mirage?

This chapter does not pretend to answer all these questions, but it does aim to make sense of many of these competing claims by locating them both in historical perspective and within the broader traditions of thought about international relations. It identifies how different perspectives at different points in time have informed the research agenda and led to arguments over the nature of the media-human-rights relationship in the context of foreign policies.

It proceeds in three main sections: The first uses an historical lens to explore the developing media-human-rights relationship in foreign policy. The next section explores in a more technical sense how these competing claims have been tested through research that has aimed to detect and assess the influence of the media. The third and final sections address more specifically the claims about system change resulting from the radical developments in the media environment in the 21st century, and what these may mean for the media-human-rights relationship. It is argued that the expansion of existing scholarship should move beyond the usual liberal-realist axis and test more thoroughly and systematically the claims made by those assigning revolutionary effects to the transformation of media in the 21st century.

Human rights and foreign policy

In order to understand the role of the media it is worth briefly pausing to consider how human rights are thought to have played a role in foreign policymaking. Can a straight line be drawn between contemporary discussions of human rights norms in 21st century foreign policy and the 1948 Universal Declaration on Human Rights (UDHR), or even further back – to the bold declarations about the 'rights of man' during the French or American revolutions? There has certainly been change over time – the relevance of human rights norms to foreign policymaking has not been widely accepted across liberal democracies –foreign policy and diplomacy have traditionally been considered 'high politics', insulated from moral concerns, accountability and transparency. A good example of this is provided by the Cold-War period. Occurring in parallel to the codification of the international regime designed to 'reaffirm faith in fundamental human rights' (UN Charter 1945) policymakers had no hesitation in placing human rights ideas secondary to the realist logic of superpower rivalry where interests trumped ethics.

This should not be mistaken for a complete absence of ethical thinking, however, because each 'side' would argue they were suspending normal moral limits of behaviour in the international sphere in order to overcome the enemy and protect their own particular system of human rights. Thus rhetorical references to rights and appeal to notions of justice fill the history of foreign policy – as endless iterations in a long tradition of *ius bellum iustum* – just war theory. Appealing to human rights norms creates the requisite 'moral responsibility' for sovereign states to act as they see fit 'to stop the terrible atrocities' (Wheeler 2000, 266) wherever these occur across the globe. But the contemporary international human rights system is more than this – it constitutes a set of shared norms codified through public declarations and instruments such as the UDHR. They represent something close to a common moral language (Beitz 2009, 1) and the UDHR and the norms it set out to propagate have received widespread global public acceptance (Powers 2016). They have become part of the public debate and this has become reflected in the media, in various ways (Caliendo et al. 1999; Cole 2010; Ovsiovitch 1993; ICHRP 2002; Ramos et al. 2007).

It is possible, however, to detect a shift in the prominence of human rights in foreign policy debates from the 1970s onwards. This was the point at which there was a revival in interest towards human rights from a foreign policy perspective and there was a definite public relations resonance. It was the presidency of Jimmy Carter that turned human rights into 'an American rallying cry and a global sensation' (Keys 2014, 2) making him the first leader of a major country to elevate the international promotion of human rights to a central role in foreign policy. Perhaps less known but equally notable were the efforts of a number of smaller countries, such as Norway and the Netherlands, who also emphasised human rights in their foreign policies since the mid-1970s. In 1973, for example, the Netherlands officially stressed the 'close relationship between peace, a just distribution of wealth, international legal order and respect for human rights' (quoted in Donnelly 2013, 129).

It would be wrong, then, to suggest that the language of human rights in public debates over foreign policy was specific to the period between the end of the Cold War and the start of the war on terror (Bahador 2011). However, it was the 1990s when the Western governments use of human rights discourses became really prominent in the context of the so-called humanitarian wars. This continued into the 2000s through the pro- and anti-Iraq war rhetoric incorporating human rights language. The interventions that took place in the 1990s in response to the humanitarian crises in Africa and Southeastern Europe often advanced ethical and moral arguments as key justifications (Chandler 2006, Hehir 2010a). In rhetorical terms the association between foreign policy and human rights perhaps reached a peak when NATO intervened to defend the human rights and the individual-level security of Kosovo Albanians (Solana 1999).

This was the era of a new set of 'doctrines' that fused human rights with foreign policy objectives. First was the so called 'Clinton Doctrine', committing American power not only to defend vital national interests in a specific region, but to protect human rights wherever and whenever they are violated (Daalder 1999). Then there was the Doctrine of the 'International Community' proclaimed by the then British Prime Minister Tony Blair, who put forward the idea that 'we cannot turn our backs on conflicts and the violation of human rights within other countries if we want still to be secure' (Blair 1999). This statement came in the context of an already declared commitment to an 'ethical dimension' in foreign policy made by the then British Foreign Minister Robin Cook (in 1997). But perhaps the most significant commitment to human rights to come out of the 1990s was the so called 'Responsibility to Protect' (R2P). As with humanitarian intervention more generally, R2P (proposed in 2001 and adopted in 2005) has divided opinions – while some have defended it arguing that it has 'moved from being a controversial and indeterminate concept seldom utilised by international society to a norm utilized almost habitually' (Bellamy 2015), others have claimed that it lacked substance and was merely 'sound and fury signifying nothing', a 'slogan employed for differing purposes shorn of any real meaning or utility' (Hehir 2010b, 218, 219, 235).

Events in the early 21st century made it blindingly clear that Fukuyama's (1992) narrative of a progressive series of victories for liberal democratic principles, including human rights norms, leading to the 'end of history', was premature at best. The story has since proven to be much more multidirectional – dynamic, uneven and with liberal democratic principles spreading, but just as easily being 'rolled back' (Zakaria 1997). Human rights remained at the centre of the emotively and ideologically charged Bush era with its more aggressive US foreign policy haunted by the spectre of international terrorism. Despite the damage the post-9/11 period did to the credibility of ethical foreign policy the language of human rights continued to be invoked by policymakers; for example, in Libya in 2011 where intervention was presented as 'necessary, legal and right' (Cameron, cited in *The Economist* 2011). It was Syria's long civil war that provoked a wave of debates questioning the international community's 'responsibility to protect' (ICISS 2001) and the ways to 'help revitalise the world's desire and ability to protect human rights' (Gottlieb 2013).

Interestingly, the Obama administration is seen by some as having done little to push forward the human rights agenda instead allowing the language and the very idea of human rights in foreign policy to fade (Keys 2014). The gap was filled somewhat by Britain and France in relation to Libya – they championed the human rights language constructing the intervention as a 'mélange of concepts: protection of civilians and the responsibility to protect' (Adler-Nissen & Pouliot 2014, 899). The human rights narrative, however, was also used by countries such as Russia defending its actions in Crimea in 2014. The Russian Foreign Minister Lavrov was cited saying that 'this is a question of defending our citizens and compatriots, and ensuring human rights' (cited in *Telegraph* 2014). While this defence of the intervention was disputed by Ukraine, the US and the European Union, it provides a clear example of the ubiquity of the rhetoric of human rights.

Underlying this brief survey one can detect vague assumptions about 'progress' towards democratic principles based on international norms: where foreign policymaking has moved away from decisions made 'behind gilded doors' towards a model where it is at least beginning to be informed by human rights. In this story the media appears to have played some sort of role, but it is not very clear how patterns of influence and power operate, how they might have changed and what this means for human rights. Laying bare these assumptions raises a host of questions about how foreign policy happens, about cause and effect – relating to the connections between developing human rights regimes on the one hand, and the changing media environment on the other.

What role for the media?

How has the media played a role in this story of human rights and foreign policy? It was in the end of the 20th and beginning of the 21st centuries that the role of the media became central to theories about how 'soft power' could change international relations (Nye 2004). A potential influence for the media and human rights made a perfect fit with a renewed interest in the role of ideas and 'ideas-infused institutions' in the crafting of foreign policy (Drezner 2000). It was also during this period that the theory of a 'CNN effect' was proposed – where media coverage of humanitarian crises could push governments to intervene (Robinson 1999). Since then there have been new debates around new media technologies and information sharing techniques and how they might disrupt and re-order the international system.

The media and the struggle for human rights has become central to many of the defining conflicts of the 21st century; for example, the wars involving al-Qaeda and 'Islamic State', and in Eastern Europe, with the conflict between Ukraine and Russia. Contested ideas about human rights are of course central to these conflicts, with a mixture of familiar and less familiar causal arguments in relation to the media. In a throwback to the Cold War the Russian media stand accused of propagating stories of horrific human rights abuses as part of a strategy to invoke memories of Nazi atrocities and support for a 'patriotic war' (Horbyk 2015). By contrast there are claims that something entirely different is happening in the Middle East and in parts of Africa and Asia. Much as Kaldor (2003) argued that 'new wars' had replaced old ones, control of the war narrative via the tried and tested methods of propaganda via mass media has become increasingly displaced by the availability of new technologies that have spawned new modes of control (Bauman et al 2014) and resistance (Postill 2014).

The realist-liberal axis

Many of the aforementioned ideas challenge what could be described as realist assumptions about the role of media in time of conflict: to communicate the war narrative on behalf of the protagonists as effectively as possible; a propaganda tool for the state to extend influence; a means of maintaining societal support for war aims. In this context the abuse or betrayal of human rights by the enemy might of course be secondary to actual causes of war, but can often become central to its justification. The status of human rights and their institutionalisation as common moral language from the late 20th century, and the development of new media technologies together provide the ideal material and instruments with which to weave a narrative to discredit your opponent and claim the moral high ground. For the sceptics, this is merely the natural marriage of justificatory language and communication techniques that have always been used to support military adventures: something that can be traced right back to the crusades up to the present-day R2P (Bosignore 2011).

Against the backdrop of such realist analyses, the idea of a 'CNN effect' suggests something quite counter-intuitive. This is the notion that the same embedding of human rights values in the international system and the same technological advances in communications technologies have fundamentally shifted the nexus between the media, human rights and foreign policy. If such a CNN effect were to exist, the advent of 24/7 'real-time' global news has changed something, because of something else: a consensus over common values of humanity – human rights – and the fact that they should be protected beyond national borders. The central claim is that this could lead to occasions where, instead of a conduit for selling decisions already made, media coverage of humanitarian crises could actually influence foreign policy (Robinson 2002).

The CNN effect presents the relationship between human rights and the media as central, but in an apparently radical new way: as a combination that challenges, and acts independently of, the state. Examples that are commonly cited in discussions about the CNN effect include the actions of the US in Iraq during the 1991 uprising by the Kurdish minority, the US-led intervention in Somalia in 1992–3, the NATO intervention in Bosnia in 1994–5 and in Kosovo in 1999. Research into the role of the media in prompting these military actions provides evidence that is 'mixed, contradictory and confusing' (Gilboa 2005, 34). One of the many difficulties with the tracing of media influence in foreign policymaking is complexity. There are so many different types of conflict and different types of media and these have changed over time – alongside the impacts of technological advances and the forces of globalisation (on both conflict and the media). Then there is the challenge of considering *when* media has influence when there are multiple different stages which conflicts tend to go through; for example, before, during and then following a military intervention. A valiant attempt to capture this is Gilboa et al (2016) 'multilevel hybridity' approach, complete with five 'streams' of interaction and six 'levels' of media. Another issue relates to the breadth of foreign relations. There is a great tendency to focus on military intervention when a great deal of the business of foreign policy concerns non-military means. For example, Payaslian (1996) and Van Belle et al. (2000) found that media coverage of human rights issues did have a systematic effect on US foreign economic and military aid during the Reagan and Bush administrations.

But are the propositions of the proponents and detractors of the CNN effect truly radical? In IR-theory terminology they could easily be located within the context of the broader realist-idealist (liberal) axis. As EH Carr (1946) argues in his seminal text on international relations in the interwar years idealists will always point to the possibility of more rational, reasonable and peaceful foreign policies based on universal norms, while realists will emphasise the continuing threat of war due to the importance of national interests and states' hunger for power.

As at the beginning of the 20th century, the notion that foreign policymaking in the 21st century is shaped by universal norms faces widespread criticism from 'realists' who doubt the power of human rights and the moral certainty explicit in humanitarian interventions. In the US (but also the NATO-dominated West more generally) this critique is closely associated with the public intellectual Noam Chomsky. Following his analysis of the intervention in Kosovo (1999), Chomsky's stinging critique of the language and 'practice' of human rights in foreign policy has come to represent the 'counterorthodoxy of the anti-globalization left' (Isaac 2002, 506). From this perspective, those who see the media as performing anything beyond the usual role of a conduit for government propaganda are idealists or 'utopians'.

It is certainly true that since the end of the 1990s the chorus of 'realist' voices, dismissing the idea of the birth of a new era of human rights and the role of media as midwife, has become ever-louder. They have been quick to point out that the language of human rights with regards to the post-Cold-War interventions might better be understood as a cover for the pursuit of Western interests. As Hehir (2010a, 172) noted, '[r]hetorical support for human rights […] is one thing; implementing measures to constrain the capacity of states in this regard is quite another'. The 'too little and too late' (Weiss 2010, 88) response of the international community to the genocide in Rwanda in 1994, the US's retreat from Somalia in 1993, the reaction to the ethnic cleansing in Bosnia became all examples of massive human rights violations that took place while the world stood by and watched. They raised doubts about the will to halt suffering and act in the name of human rights that appeared to be selective, driven by considerations of national interest, 'morally hypocritical, a rhetorical instrument that rationalises the projection of force by the powerful' (Wheeler & Morris 2007, 448). Likewise, the increasingly elusive evidence of a CNN effect was all but abandoned by media scholars (Gilboa 2005).

This could be seen as a victory for the realists with their mirror image of the CNN effect. Instead it is the media holding back the prospect of maintaining or furthering human rights standards in foreign policy. Illegal wars abroad and the encroachment of civil liberties at home are not scrutinised and the media turns from hero to villain. The example of the UK is a case in point, with its government's abandonment of terminology suggesting foreign policy should have an 'ethical dimension' only a few years after it was first proclaimed. The reversal was put down to the toxic influence of the media. Coverage of foreign policy purposefully simplified the role of ethics to create a 'conduit for criticism' (Gaskarth 2013, 192). Specifically, this was the way in which the British media reinterpreted Cook's declaration of an 'ethical dimension' as an 'ethical foreign policy', setting up a false dichotomy where foreign policy was either ethical or unethical and leading to a focus on short-term failures at the expense of the complex challenges in promoting human rights in the foreign policy arena (Williams 2002, 56–7).

The strongest argument in this realist/sceptical perspective on the role of the media in furthering human rights concerns relates to the response to the terrorist attacks of 9/11. Although Operation Iraqi Freedom was supposed to be about 'tearing down the apparatus of terror' (White House 2003), and 'lessening the suffering of the Iraqi people' (Howard [cited in Hehir 2010a: 225] 2003) by getting rid of Saddam Hussein as 'an act of humanity' (Hinsliff 2003), critics have argued strongly that humanitarian justifications were abused and the 2003 invasion of Iraq undermined the very idea of humanitarian intervention (Bellamy 2004, Hehir 2010a).

The media, revolution and resistance in the international system

In his famous lectures on the history of international thought, Martin Wight distinguished between three different streams: realism, rationalism and revolutionism (Wight 1991). While this typology has been described by its critics as simplistic, naïve and Eurocentric (Dunne 1993) it has proven rather resilient over time. This is because it is useful in distinguishing how the presumption that the world exists in a Hobbesian state of war competes with rational ideas about the possibility of an international system based upon shared rules and norms. It also points out that both are fundamentally opposed by ideas about transnationalism and international solidarity that threaten to overturn the order of states.

While the debate over humanitarian intervention and the role of the media in foreign policy sits between realist and rationalist streams, there are a host of new claims for a revolutionary role for the media in the context of shifts in international relations and communications technologies in the 21st century. Examples include the role of social media, for example, in the Arab Spring, and the impact of mass release of data by Wikileaks and Edward Snowden. Some have argued that the novelty of these developments have been overblown and are more of a continuation than a paradigm shift (Morozov 2011). But if instead they truly, as some argue, challenge 'dominant articulations of power' (Brevini, et al. 2013, 4) then it is still to be determined what they mean for the central questions of this chapter concerning media, human rights and foreign policy.

It is possible, however, to begin to understand the extent to which states have disregarded certain human rights to extend their international reach and allow their security and intelligence services to make use of mass (cyber) surveillance (Bauman et al. 2014). It is also becoming evident how this is complicated by the rise of new modes of resistance that themselves turn on similar technologies; for example, new protest movements, hacktivists and 'freedom technologists' (Postill 2014), or via anti-Western ideologies that have adopted guerrilla tactics such as the so-called media jihad (Galloway 2016).

In one sense there is nothing completely new. The actions of Wikileaks and Snowden in the 21st century can be understood as a repetition of previous leaks throughout history embarrassing great powers; for example, the Pentagon papers (released by Daniel Ellsberg through the *New York Times* in 1971) or publication of the Sykes-Picot agreement (exposed in the Russian and British press in 1917). Yet these latest protagonists claim they are doing something different (Abrams 2010). They believe that the contemporary information environment can act to weaken authoritarian forms of governance. This is no less than the radical instrumentalisation of media to further an 'ethic of transparency' with consequences for the foreign policies of both illiberal and liberal states (Assange 2006).

Conclusions

If human rights now figure more prominently in the process of foreign policymaking, what does this mean in terms of broader questions about the causal interactions between media and conflict? It is difficult to argue against the proposition that there is something novel and fundamentally different about the contemporary media environment. The way that we communicate has been transformed through technological advances and multiplication of forms, channels and types. But how does this matter and what does it really change? History is littered with declarations about the consequences of new media technologies for the progression of human relations, but also scepticism about the truthfulness of such claims. There is something that appeals to the cosmopolitan imaginary about the media transforming the world into 'no more than a village' (McLuhan 1964, 5). It prompts some to think about all sorts of potential ways in which we can begin to feel a greater sense of responsibility to act and stop distant human suffering (Silverstone 2007), how we can begin to feel like a global civil society (Kaldor 2003), and where journalists can leverage the 'cosmopolitanising potential of reporting' (Chouliaraki & Blaagaard 2013, 150). In short, the media somehow promises the possibility of solidarity between peoples and nations: a humanitarian future. Yet despite the recognition of this potential, the results for many seem rather disappointing – the cosmopolitan promise has been transformed into a deficit (Balabanova 2014, 50–1). Instead of transnational solidarity media coverage of human rights tragedies from across the world seems to be delivering 'compassion fatigue' (Moeller 1999).

References

Abrams, F. (2010). 'Why WikiLeaks is unlike the Pentagon Papers'. *The Wall Street Journal*, 29 December.

Adler-Nissen, R. and Pouliot, V. (2014). 'Power in Practice: Negotiating the International Intervention in Libya', *European Journal of International Relations*, 20(4), pp. 889–911.

Assange, J. (2006). 'State and Terrorist Conspiracies' and 'Conspiracy as Governance'. Originally published on *IQ.org*. Available at: http://cryptome.org/0002/ja-conspiracies.pdf

Bahador, B. (2011). 'Did the Global War on Terror End the CNN Effect?', *Media, War & Conflict*, 4(1), pp. 37–54.

Balabanova, E. (2014). *The Media and Human Rights: The Cosmopolitan Promise*. London: Routledge.

Bauman, Z., Bigo, D., Esteves, P., Guild, E., Jabri, V., Lyon, D. and Walker R. B. J. (2014). 'After Snowden: Rethinking the Impact of Surveillance', *International Political Sociology*, 8(2), pp. 121–44.

Beitz, C. (2009). *The Idea of Human Rights*. Oxford: Oxford University Press.

Bellamy, A. (2015). 'The Responsibility to Protect Turns Ten', *Ethics & International Affairs*, 29(2), pp. 161–85.

Berry, V. and McChesney, A. (1988). 'Human rights and foreign policy-making'. In *Human Rights in Canadian Foreign Policy*, T. O. Matthews & C. Pratt (Eds.) Kingston: McGill-Queen's University Press.

Blair, T. (1999). *Doctrine of the International Community*. Speech to the Economic Club of Chicago, 22 April.

Brevini, B., Hintz, A. and McCurdy, P. (Eds.). (2013). *Beyond WikiLeaks: Implications for the Future of Communications, Journalism and Society*. Basingstoke: Palgrave Macmillan.

Bosignore, E. (2011). 'From "White Man's Burden" to "Right to Protect"', *Military Technolology* 35(1), pp. 14–17.

Caliendo, S. M., M. P. Gibney and A. Payne. (1999). '"All the news that's fit to print?" *New York Times* coverage of human rights violations'. *Harvard International Journal of Press/Politics*, 4: 48–69.

Carr, E.H. 1946. *The Twenty Years' Crisis, 1919–1939*. 2/e. London: Macmillan & Co, Ltd

Chandler, D. (2006). *From Kosovo to Kabul and Beyond: Human Rights and International Intervention*. London: Pluto Press.

Chomsky, N. (1999). *The New Military Humanism: Lessons from Kosovo*. Monroe, ME: Common Courage Press.

Chouliaraki, L. and Blaagaard, B. (2013). 'Introduction'. *Journalism Studies*, 14(2): 150–5.

Cole, W. M. (2010). 'No news is good news: Human rights coverage in the American print media, 1980-2000'. *Journal of Human Rights,* 9(3): 303–25.

Daalder, I. (1999). 'And now, a Clinton Doctrine?' *Haagsche Courant*, 10 July.

Donnelly, J. (2013). *International Human Rights: Dilemmas in World Politics*. 4/e. Boulder, CO: Westview Press.

Drezner, D. (2000). 'Ideas, Bureaucratic Politics, and the Crafting of Foreign Policy', *American Journal of Political Science*, 44, pp. 733–49.

Dunne, T. (1993). 'Mythology or Methodology? Traditions in International Theory', *Review of International Studiesi*, xix(3), pp. 305–18.

Fukuyama, F. (1992). *End of History and the Last Man*. New York: Avon.

Galloway, C. (August 2016). 'Media Jihad: What PR Can Learn in Islamic State's Public Relations Masterclass', *Public Relations Review*, 42(4), pp. 582–590.

Gaskarth, J. (2013). 'Interpreting Ethical Foreign Policy: Traditions and Dilemmas for Policymakers', *British Journal of Politics & International Relations*, 15(2), pp. 192–209.

Gilboa, E. (2005). 'The CNN Effect: The Search for a Communication Theory of International Relations', *Political Communication*, 22(1), pp. 27–44.

Gilboa, E., Jumbert, M. G., Miklian, J. and Robinson, P. (2016). 'Moving media and conflict studies beyond the CNN effect'. *Review of International Studies,* 42(4): 654–72.

Gottlieb, S. (2013). 'Syria and the Demise of the Responsibility to Protect', *The National Interest*, 5 November.

Hehir, A. (2010a). *Humanitarian Intervention: An Introduction*. Basingstoke: Palgrave Macmillan.

Hehir, A. (2010b). 'The Responsibility to Protect: 'Sound and Fury Signifying Nothing?', *International Relations*, 24(2), pp. 218–39.

Herman, E. and N. Chomsky. (1988). *Manufacturing Consent: The Political Economy of the Mass Media*. London: Vintage.

Hinsliff, G. (2003). 'Blair stakes his political future on beating Iraq'. *Observer*, 16 February

Horbyk, R. 2015. 'Little Patriotic War: Nationalist Narratives in the Russian Media Coverage of the Ukraine-Russia Crisis', *Asian Politics and Policy*, 7(3), pp. 505–11.

International Commission on Intervention and State Sovereignty (ICISS). 2001. *The Responsibility to Protect*. Ottawa: International Development Research Centre.

International Council on Human Rights Policy (ICHRP). (2002). *Journalism, Media and the Challenge of Human Rights Reporting*. Geneva: ICHRP.

Internews. (2012). *Speak Up, Speak Out: A Toolkit for Reporting on Human Rights Issues*. Washington: Internews.

Isaac, J. (2002). 'Hannah Arendt on Human Rights and the Limits of Exposure, or Why Noam Chomsky is Wrong About the Meaning of Kosovo', *Social Research: An International Quarterly Volume*, 69(2), pp. 505–37.

Kaldor, M. (1999). *New and Old Wars: Organised Violence in a Global Era* (1st ed.). London: Polity Press.

Keys, B. (2014). *Reclaiming American Virtue. The Human Rights Revolution of the 1970s*. Cambridge, MA: Harvard University Press.

McLuhan, M. (1964). *Understanding Media*. New York: Mentor.

Moeller, S. (1999). *Compassion Fatigue: How the Media Sell Disease, Famine, War and Death*. New York: Routledge.

Morozov, E. (2011). The *Net Delusion: The Dark Side of Internet Freedom*. New York: Public Affairs.

Nye, J. (2004). 'Soft Power and American Foreign Policy', *Political Science Quarterly*, 119(2), pp. 255–70.

Ovsiovitch, J. S. (1993). 'News Coverage of Human Rights', *Political Research Quarterly*, 46, pp. 671–89.

Payaslian, S. (1996). *US Foreign Economic and Military Aid: The Reagan and Bush Administrations*. New York: University Press of America.

Postill, J. (2014). 'Freedom Technologists and the New Protest Movements: A Theory of Protest Formulas', *Convergence: The International Journal of Research into New Media Technologies*, 20(4), pp. 402–18.

Powers, M. (2016). 'Opening the News Gates? Humanitarian and Human Rights NGOs in the US Media, 1990-2010', *Media, Culture and Society*, 38(3), pp. 315–31.

Ramos, H., J. Ron and O. N. T. Thoms. (2007). 'Shaping the Northern media's human rights coverage, 1986-2000'. *Journal of Peace Research*, 44(4): 385–406.

Robinson, P. (2002). *The Myth of the CNN Effect*. London: Routledge.

Silverstone, R. (2007). *Media and Morality: On the Rise of the Mediapolis*. Cambridge: Polity Press.

Solana, J. (1999). 'NATO's Success in Kosovo', *Foreign Affairs*, 78(6), pp. 114–20.

Telegraph (2014). 'Ukraine Crisis: "We Had to Defend our Citizens", says Russia'. *Telegraph*, 3 March.

The Economist (2011). 'David Cameron's War'. *The Economist*, 27 August. Available at: http://www.economist.com/node/21526887

Van Belle, D. A. and Hook, S. W. (2000). 'Greasing the Squeaky Wheel: News Media Coverage and US Foreign Aid', *International Interactions*, 26(3), pp. 321–46.

Weiss, T. G. (2010). *Humanitarian Intervention*. Cambridge: Polity Press.

Wheeler, N. J. (2000). *Saving Strangers: Humanitarian Intervention in International Society*. Oxford: Oxford University Press.

Wheeler, N. and Morris, J. (2007). 'Justifying the Iraq War as a Humanitarian Intervention: The Cure is Worse than the Disease'. In: R. Thakur and W. P S. Sidhu, eds., *The Iraq Crisis and World Order: Structural, Institutional and Normative Challenges*. New York: United Nations University Press.

White House. (2003). 'President Says Saddam Hussein Must Leave Iraq Within 48 Hours: Remarks by the President in Address to the Nation', 17 March. Available at: https://georgewbush-whitehouse.archives.gov/news/releases/2003/03/20030317-7.html

Williams, P. (2002). 'The Rise and Fall of the "Ethical Dimension": Presentation and Practice in New Labour's Foreign Policy', *Cambridge Review of International Affairs*, 15(1), pp. 53–63.

Wight, M. (1991). *International Theory: The Three Traditions*, G. Wight and B. Porter, eds. Leicester and London: Leicester University Press.

Zakaria, F. (1997). 'The Rise of Illiberal Democracy', *Foreign Affairs* (November/December).

19

PUBLIC DIPLOMACY, MEDIA AND HUMAN RIGHTS

Amelia H. Arsenault

Public diplomacy (PD) commonly refers to efforts by nation states to engage, inform and influence foreign publics in service of foreign policy goals. Particularly since 9/11, states and multilateral organizations at all ends of the geopolitical spectrum have taken a greater interest in PD activities, which range from exchange programs, to international broadcasting, to social media outreach. The relationship between public diplomacy, the media and human rights is complex and multifaceted. This is because old and new media systems are a critical conduit for PD *about* human rights issues and the subject of PD campaigns advocating particular normative conceptions of the human right to receive and impart information. Moreover, 'promoting human rights' has become a catchall rationale as well as a tagline embedded in a range of disparate PD activities. To fully explore these dimensions, this chapter unfolds in three separate but interconnected sections. First, it explores the theory and practice surrounding PD and human rights. Second, it examines how the media activities of advocacy organizations have complicated human rights PD. Finally, it examines the evolution of PD surrounding freedom of expression and communicative rights.

Public diplomacy and human rights in theory and practice

In an effort to solicit foreign public support for short and long term foreign policy goals, nation states utilise a bevy of PD activities that range from state-initiated or funded person-to-person exchange programs, to public events and summits, to press conferences and speeches, to the establishment of media organizations designed to promote particular world views (i.e. international broadcasting). When it comes to human rights, PD objectives vary from broad (and often vague) agenda items like 'promoting human rights' to lobbying for foreign domestic support of or opposition to the passage of particular pieces of legislation (e.g. the 2013 Nigerian Same Sex Marriage Prohibition act) or the humane treatment of a specific person or population. Encouraging the humane treatment of Eastern European human rights dissidents like Vaclav Havel and Lach Walesa, for example, was a cornerstone of Cold-War–Era Radio Free Europe/Radio Liberty broadcasts. Moreover, 'human rights' is a trope that is commonly tacked on to even the most tangential PD effort, often by states considered to be violators of human rights norms. Human rights PD thus also includes activities that challenge the universality of human rights norms as well as initiatives that that use human rights as a frame to improve the palatability of other foreign policy objectives or a nation's brand. The English language Twitter feed of the Russian Foreign Ministry (@MFA_Russia), for example, frequently features tweets framing Russia as an advocate for human rights and debunking allegations of domestic human rights abuses. Middle Eastern nations, particularly Iran, have also used PD efforts to advocate for a model of human rights that respects cultural diversity and framed Western promotion of universal human rights as, 'growing attempts to create a new form of colonialism and uniculturalism (Non Aligned Movement 2007, Annex 4)'.

The practitioners involved in human rights PD are equally variegated. Human rights, for example, is a key feature of United States Code § 2732 Public Diplomacy Responsibilities of the Department of State (DOS): 'The Secretary shall continue to articulate the importance of freedom, democracy, and human rights as fundamental principles underlying United States foreign policy goals'. Human rights promotion is ostensibly headquartered in the Bureau of Democracy, Human Rights and Labor, Office of Policy Planning and Public Diplomacy, which utilises PD tools to promote respect for human rights and strengthen democratic institutions and civil society. Its public communication projects include Humanrights.gov: a portal launched in 2014, which catalogues human rights issues by topic and country and profiles annual reports such as the *Country Reports on Human Rights Practices* and *The Advancing Freedom and Democracy Report*.[1] It also hosts 'State of Rights', a series of live stream episodes in which viewers are asked to participate using the #stateofrights hashtag. Human rights, however, is also a part of the mission statement of other PD arms of the DOS (e.g. the Bureau of International Information Programs and the Office of Public Affairs, Planning and Coordination) as well as media platforms supervised by the Broadcasting Board of Governors (BBG) (e.g. Voice of America and Radio Free Asia). Similarly, Australia maintains a staff of three to four PD officers within the human rights section of the Department of Foreign Affairs and Trade (DFAT), but all PD programs are guided by directions to 'highlight Australia's core values that underpin our commitment to democracy, rule of law, human rights and freedom of speech (DFAT 2014, 4)'.

Mapping out the terrain of human rights PD is further complicated by the ambivalence of many government bureaucrats towards 'public diplomacy', a term often equated with strategic influence or dismissed as a kinder, gentler term for propaganda (Brown 2008). Few government officials refer to themselves as PD practitioners or work specifically in PD departments or bureaus. President Barack Obama, for example, almost exclusively uses the term 'engagement' or 'strategic communication (Gregory 2011, 353)'. Indeed, while academics and pundits commonly equate international broadcasting efforts like Voice of America (VOA) and the BBC World Service with PD, organizational employees often bristle at any implication that their work reflects strategic communication and is influenced by state interests. Similarly, those working in the development sector (particularly in media for development) resist any suggestion that foreign aid projects can or should be linked to nation branding or strategic influence (see for example, Kumar 2006, GAO 2005, 8). The Office of the United Nations High Commissioner for Human Rights (OHCHR), in another example, makes little to no reference of PD. The majority of UN public communication is headquartered in the Strategic Communication Division of the UN DPI (Department of Public Information). PD scholars would argue, however, that a DPI and OHCHR activities like Human Rights Day – which commemorates the day the UN General Assembly signed the Universal Declaration of Human Rights (December 10) – reflects a PD exercise because it is accompanied each year by events (including its own hashtag, #humanrightstoday) designed to raise public awareness about UN activities related to human rights.

Academic inquiry into the relationship between PD and human rights is similarly hard to quantify. The majority of PD literature is largely atheoretical, concerned with evaluating the effectiveness of larger campaigns rather than exploring or testing particular explanatory models or theories (Entman 2008). In so far as there is a theoretical approach to the study of PD, scholars often focus on the extent to which PD, particularly mediated diplomacy, solidifies or undermines existing power relationships in the international system (see for example Nye 2004 and Miskimmon et al. 2014). Human rights PD literature typically centres on the United States (as does most PD literature in general). The majority of this literature focuses on how American human rights abuses, (e.g. the treatment of Abu Ghraib and Guantanamo Bay prisoners) have derailed larger US PD efforts related to the War on Terror or provided diplomatic cover for countries like China and Russia accused of human rights violation (e.g. Melissen 2005; Van Ham 2005; Foot 2008). The most robust literature on human rights PD involves the efforts of middle powers (e.g. Canada and Norway), whom researchers posit are better positioned than major powers, because 'public human rights initiatives from the big powers run the risk of being misunderstood and counter-attacked as neo-imperialistic acts of interference (Egeland 1988, 176–7; Batora 2005, 8)'.

Public diplomacy, strategic communication, global engagement or propaganda – depending upon your preferred moniker – is an ever increasing part of international diplomacy. More often than not, these activities evoke human rights as a signifier of values rather than as a concrete agenda. Changes in the global media system, however, have expanded the number of players involved in the global conversation on human rights, prompting two significant and mutually constitutive trends in contemporary PD. These will be discussed in the two subsequent sections, (1) in response to the proactive old and new media strategies of human rights advocacy organizations, states are either more vigorously defending their human rights records or initiating PD campaigns capitalising on the activities of human rights advocates that cohere to broader foreign policy goals, and (2) PD practitioners are paying exponentially more attention to the right to communicate as a fundamental human right.

Human rights 2.0

Every new advancement in communication technologies—from parchment, to the telegraph, to social media – has propelled changes in the conduct of diplomacy, particularly public diplomacy (Archetti 2012; Davison 1974; Nikles 2003). While civil society has long utilized different media to advocate for social change, the rapid evolution of mobile and social media has opened up new avenues for championing particular causes or policies. Traditional media organizations are no longer gatekeepers between diplomacy and publics. State officials frequently bypass the press, communicating directly with foreign governments through or supplemented by social media exchanges designed to influence foreign publics, or what is popularly referred to as 'public diplomacy 2.0 (Arsenault 2008)'. Particularly in recent years, human rights NGOs and activist groups have leveraged these same changes in the media system, with significant implications for PD.

Civil society organizations increasingly create and distribute media and communications regarding human rights (as well as other issues) independent of traditional private and state media flows, creating PD problems for states accused of committing human rights abuses and encouraging other states to conduct PD campaigns capitalizing on the lobbying activities of these organizations. (Powers 2014). Social media technologies, which blend interpersonal and public communication, provide a host of new human rights advocacy tools. Where advocacy used to be bifurcated between raising public awareness through the media and direct government lobbying via activities like letter writing campaigns, new media technologies are converging and expanding these activities. As Scoble and Weiserberg (1974) documented, during the

60s and 70s, Amnesty International (AI) lobbied offending governments through member letter writing campaigns, creating a two-step flow of advocacy – from AI to publics and from publics to governments. Today, these campaigns take place in the public eye in the form of online petitions, where signatories can simultaneously send messages to government officials, notify their friends and colleagues of their activities and raise the profile of the action to hopefully (but not always) solicit media attention. This is just the tip of the iceberg. Human rights NGOs were some of the first to leverage the communicative power of the Web and some of the first movers in utilising and building crowdsourcing technologies like Ushahidi and the Hub (defunct as of 2010) to document human rights violations in a public forum. As technologies have become easier to use, human rights groups have moved to leverage amateur videos for witnessing and documentation purposes (Thijm 2010). WITNESS, for example, posted videos documenting human rights atrocities on its website as early as 1998, seven years before the birth of YouTube. Today, NGOs increasingly bypass traditional media organizations by producing their own advocacy brand of news. Audiences can now subscribe to YouTube channels maintained by organizations like Human Rights Watch (HRW) and Article 19. AI, for example, maintains Amnestymedia.org its own 'multimedia newsroom' featuring 'products including visual content and expert comment about human rights issues around the world' that can be shared by journalists and other activists free of charge.

There is, of course, a robust debate between those who believe that new media empowers activists (e.g. Shirky 2008; Kimport & Earl 2011) and those that believe that social media activism is largely symbolic and often ineffective (e.g. Hindman 2008). A detailed study of 257 transnational NGOS by Thrall et al. (2014) found that, 'the ability to conduct traditional information politics on a global scale is restricted to organizations with annual budgets in the hundreds of millions, groups like AI, HRW, Doctors Without Borders, and Save the Children (p. 10)'. Bob (2011) also points out that, while these elite INGOs are disproportionately powerful gatekeepers, they are also critical tools used by local human rights organizations to insert issues into the global political agenda and pressure states into accepting new norms (4). Although some NGOs are more empowered than others, collectively human rights NGOS are prompting states to engage in both defensive (i.e. defending their human rights record) and offensive (i.e. capitalizing on NGO activities that coincide with foreign policy priorities) PD activities.

In *Activists beyond Borders*, Margaret E. Keck and Kathryn Sikkink (1998) outline how transnational advocacy networks (TANs) create a 'boomerang effect' by lobbying foreign governments to place pressure on the target government. While they do not mention 'public diplomacy' per se, their detailed case studies of the ways in which TANs pressured the Argentinian and Mexican governments to enact human rights reforms was in many ways prescient of future trends. Risse and Sikkink (1999) maintain that 'moral consciousness-raising by the international human rights community often involves a process of shaming … shaming then implies a process of persuasion, since it convinces leaders that their behaviour is inconsistent with the identity to which they aspire (15)'. It is outside the scope of this chapter to comment on the extent to which this shaming leads to considered human rights policy changes. It can, however, point to numerous examples of states using PD to respond to or mitigate these TAN shaming efforts. As previously mentioned, the Russian MFA aggrandises Russia's human rights performance, both in social media (@MFA_Russia) and in the popular press. *Russia Beyond the Headlines* is an international multimedia project launched by *Rossiyskaya Gazeta* (the official government newspaper) in 2007. Its website, rbth.com, is only part of the effort. RBTH frequently purchases multi-page supplements (e.g. Russia Now and Russia in India) in marquis global media outlets such as the *New York Times, The Washington Post, the Daily Telegraph* (UK) and *the Times of India* (see Golan & Viatchaninova 2013). These advertorials commonly feature editorials and 'news stories' responding to critical evaluations of Russia's human rights record, such as those found in HRW's annual *World Report* and Reporters Without Borders *World Press Freedom Rankings*. China has also made advocating a division of human rights into two distinct types – political and civil rights and social and economic rights – central to its 'Chinese charm offensive' (i.e. expanded PD activities) over the last two decades, particularly in Africa and South East Asia (Kurlantzick 2007; Tang & Li 2011). The Chinese position is that social and economic rights (i.e. not living in poverty) are paramount in developing countries such as China and thus a rationale for why China does not follow universal (Western) human rights norms (Tang & Li 2011, 101). Many credit the further expansion of Chinese soft power activities to international TAN campaigns in the lead up to the 2008 Beijing Olympics. According to Chen (2011), one of the four government representative talking points was that 'hosting the Olympics would inevitably improve China's human rights outlook' because it would encourage the country's entrance into the global community.

Conversely, states design offensive PD campaigns that leverage the new media activism of civil society organizations that complement their foreign policy priorities. The US DOS, for example, manages the Global Equality Fund for civil society organizations working to protect and advance LGBT rights globally. Each award is accompanied by major publicity drives designed to highlight government-NGO partnerships. In 2014, two Nobel Peace Prize laureates, Adolfo Pérez Esquivel and Mairead Maguire, joined by 100 scholars, wrote an open letter questioning whether collaboration between HRW and the US DOS had reached such a level that it corrupted the organization's mission and advocacy activities (Esquivel et. al 2014). In another example, in 2015, the Dutch Government formed a strategic partnership with PAX surrounding 'lobby and advocacy'. As Hicks (2011) argues, increasingly media savvy NGOs play a critical role in human rights diplomacy. Domestic human rights organizations provide diplomatic cover for foreign governments to lobby publically for domestic changes and avoid being labelled as 'foreign interventionists'; and TANs and INGOS help to instigate more expansive government PD surrounding human rights, particularly because human rights diplomacy has historically been characterized by secret or 'closed-door diplomacy'. (Hicks 2011, 218, 221)

International non-governmental networks such as the Open Rights Group, the Index on Censorship, Article 19, and the Internet Freedom Coalition have also been instrumental in highlighting the importance of Internet technologies for freedom of expression and the right to connect as a human right, enlisting media businesses and other activist organizations to sign on to such global projects as the 2012 Declaration of Internet Freedom. The DOS, for example, has capitalised on these activities by providing major funds for Internet activists through its well advertised Digital Defenders Partnership as has the EU through its No Disconnect Strategy. While PD officials frequently use old and new media to advocate for particular conceptions of human rights, as will be discussed in more detail in the next section, particularly over the last decade PD about freedom to receive and impart information as a fundamental human right has taken centre stage.

The right to communicate

Diplomacy regarding communicative rights first emerged in the 19th century in negotiations surrounding the formation of the International Telecommunications Union (1865) and the Universal Postal Union (1874), the second and third oldest multilateral organizations in the world, respectively. As electronic telegraph wires proliferated, so too did discussion and debate about ownership and access to these all-important means of communication. Early diplomatic debates inculcated two of the central tensions in contemporary PD surrounding the right to communicate: (1) state interests in maintaining informational as well as geographic sovereignty versus the right to receive and impart information across borders, and (2) the desire of states to maximise economic gains from the infrastructure of communication versus concerns regarding the content that flows through communication systems. For nation states and scholars of international communication alike, the critical and perhaps distinct feature of new and old media is that communication resources play a dual role. They are both the subjects of power struggle and the conduits through which increasingly almost all power struggles are exacted (see also Castells 2009). Thus states of varying sizes, power configurations and polities have taken a keen interest in—and put forward corresponding narratives about—how and why media should be and are constructed, distributed, consumed, produced and—importantly for this chapter – how communicative rights should be interpreted.

As a consequence, PD about the right to communicate is generally bifurcated—divided between discussions that present communication resources as necessary tools for economic development and opportunity and those that frame the right to communicate and access information as human rights necessary for democratization and good governance. Economic rights, for instance, took centre stage during telecommunications regulation negotiations leading to the establishment of the World Trade Organization in 1995. While the Soviet Union and the US focused on questions of communicative rights and the free flow of information during bilateral negotiations regarding the Vienna Agreement (1989) of the Helsinki Accords, which included clauses addressing the use of satellites, the privacy of mail and telecommunications, as well as the right of Soviet citizens to outside information sources. While interrelated, these two groups of activities are often compartmentalised in different bureaus and initiatives. Development and economic agencies (e.g. the Swedish International Development Cooperation Agency and the Office of International Communications and Information Policy in the US DOS) manage media and Internet infrastructure development and legal reform programs while ministries of foreign affairs typically focus on public communication efforts designed to promote appreciation for communicative rights as outlined by the respective country's foreign and domestic policy priorities. Both factions, however, are involved in programs designed to raise foreign domestic appreciation for government initiatives and policies related to media and communications norms.

The overlap between outreach efforts designed to promote appreciation for normative conceptions of communicative rights and economically focused media infrastructure and law and policy programs has only intensified in the last decade with the rise of the Internet and social media. Particularly since the thwarted 2009 Green Revolution in Iran, nicknamed the 'Twitter Revolution', Internet freedom has become a central tenet of the Western diplomatic agenda. In 2010, then Secretary of State, Hillary Clinton moved the Internet freedom agenda into the global spotlight when she presented her 'Remarks on Internet Freedom' at the Newseum in Washington, DC. In this speech, Clinton made the case that 'Internet freedom' should be added to the essential four freedoms (i.e. freedom of speech and worship and freedom from want and fear) outlined by Franklin Delano Roosevelt in his 1941 State of the Union Address in which he urged a break with US policies of non-intervention in the Second World War.

The series of Arab Spring protests that began in December 2010 added fuel to the Internet freedom fire, kicking off a wave of similar rhetoric by organizations in the global north. In May 2011, the Obama administration announced its 'International Strategy for Cyberspace', reflecting America's 'core commitments to fundamental freedoms, privacy, and the free flow of information (Office of the President 2011, 5)'. In December 2011, the European Commission outlined a 'no disconnect strategy', premised on developing circumvention tools, educating activists, monitoring censorship and building cooperative networks of stakeholders interested in increasing access to information. Global multilateral efforts also began to emerge in 2011, such as the twenty-nine-member-state Freedom Online Coalition. Not limited to the West, Internet freedom has been championed in regional stakeholder meetings like the Asia Pacific Regional Internet Governance Forum, the Central Africa Internet Governance Forum, the East Africa Internet Governance Forum, the West Africa Internet Governance Forum, the European Dialogue on Internet Governance, and the Latin America and Caribbean Internet Governance Forum (Kalathil 2010).

PD practitioners have begun to take a more visible role in supporting these efforts through bi- and multilateral public statements as well as specific programs designed to raise public awareness. In 2014, Russian President, Vladimir Putin bemused the human rights community when he labelled the 'right to information [as] one of the most important and inalienable human rights' at the launch of Russia Today's (Russia's state-owned international broadcasting organization) Spanish language channel in Argentina (Kremlin.ru 2014). Major Internet freedom projects either maintained or supported by organizations traditionally considered to be agents of public diplomacy include: the Internet Anti-Censorship Division of the Broadcasting Board of Governors; the Swedish Ministry of Foreign Affairs Annual Swedish Internet Forum; and the #Diplohack initiative of the Dutch and Norwegian Embassies to the United Kingdom. These programs range from those that advocate for free global communication flows and freedom of expression to those that call for the ability of states to assert information sovereignty that protects the economic and cultural rights of their domestic publics. Radio Free Asia, a US international broadcast organization founded in 1951, for example, has branched out into the Internet freedom agenda through its Open Technology Fund. OTF projects include the Weibo Detector, a publically accessible tool that documents specific topics and voices censored on China's most popular social media platform and an anonymous mobile human rights reporting tool for Burmese human rights abuse victims and witnesses.

The DOS Bureau of Public Diplomacy and Public Affairs is perhaps the most visible public diplomacy actor promoting, 'long-standing values of openness and human rights in a networked world (Office of International Communications and Information Policy 2016)'. Two policy priorities have been central to these efforts: (1.) promoting the idea that the Internet is a public space where people should have the freedom 'to assemble and associate' regardless of geography or state and (2) championing the idea of a *single* Internet, while resisting any attempts by states like Iran, Russia and China to create sectioned off national Internets (Clinton 2011). The UNHRC echoes this conception of the Internet as a globally accessible space; in a resolution signed by 47 member states in 2012 (including China and Russia) it *'affirm[ed]* that the same rights that people have offline must also be protected online'. This is perhaps one of the central differentiators of current PD efforts surrounding the right to communicate. While freedom of expression as a universal norm has been espoused for centuries (see for example, Milton 1643), what separates contemporary activities is this conception of a digital and global space – which in turn has implications for sovereignty.

Not surprisingly, calls for greater information sovereignty have paralleled the rise of the Internet freedom agenda. At the December 2015 second annual World Internet Conference organized by the Cyberspace Administration of China, for example, Chinese President Xi Jinping called on other governments to respect 'network sovereignty" as well as efforts by states (e.g. Russia, China and Iran) to control the digital content accessible by its citizens (McDonald 2015). At a press conference preceding the event, Lu Wei, Deputy Head of the Publicity Department of the Communist Party of China explained that information sovereignty was a critical part of Internet freedom, because, 'freedom without order doesn't exist (AFP 2015)'. The US and other Western nations have often been accused of using the Internet freedom agenda as a disingenuous and strategic foreign policy tool because they aggressively promote reforms in pariah states like Iran and Syria while remaining silent on allied countries like Saudi Arabia and espouse the primacy of free information flows while downplaying their disproportionate share of the profits from media globalization. Criticisms of inconsistencies in the US approach to Internet freedom only expanded in the wake of the 2013 revelations of mass global NSA surveillance of the Internet. In a high profile speech at the UN General Assembly, Brazilian President Dilma Rousseff, for example condemned US surveillance activities and called for a UN-led Internet governance system free of US control. The Snowden leaks also provided more fuel to the fire of Russian and Chinese calls for greater media and Internet sovereignty from the global Internet, or what in an international press conference Putin labelled as a 'CIA project (MacAskill 2014)'.

Conclusion

As mobile and Internet proliferation increases, it is likely that these PD efforts to frame and advocate for particular visions of the Internet, connectivity and the right to communicate will only proliferate, so too will both proactive and reactive public diplomacy campaigns designed to advocate for or defend particular conceptions or treatments of human rights. As this chapter has demonstrated, the challenges of unpacking the relationship between the media, public diplomacy and human rights are many. Public diplomacy is both an object of academic study (i.e. how states attempt to leverage foreign public opinion and improve relationships with foreign publics in order to promote short and long term foreign policy goals) and an area of practice conducted by both individuals who label themselves as 'public diplomacy officers' and leaders and other government actors who want to raise the profile of their particular position or project on a foreign domestic or world stage but eschew the PD label. There are no easy dividing lines or definitions. Human rights is sometimes a tagline tacked on to tangential public diplomacy activities and at other times the direct objective of particular PD initiatives. Further complicating this relationship is the fact that media and communication systems are both the conduits for public diplomacy and the object of debates and initiatives about human rights. Moreover, human rights activists can at times be partners and at other times adversaries to these public diplomacy activities. It is likely that over time, this relationship will only grow more complicated.

Note

1   The reach of Human Rights.gov is relatively minor, with most of the links coming from the United States and Western Europe, but its content is designed for a global audience (ACPD 2015: 143; Alexa.com 2016).

References

AFP (9 Dec. 2015). 'China Internet Czar Defends Web Censorship Policies'. *Agency France Press*. Available at: http://www.dawn.com/news/1225249 [Accessed 19 May, 2016].

Archetti, C. (2012). 'The Impact of New Media on Diplomatic Practice: An Evolutionary Model of Change'. *The Hague Journal of Diplomacy*, 7(2), pp. 181–206.

Arsenault, A. (2009). 'Public Diplomacy 2.0'. In Philip M Seib, ed. *Toward a New Public Diplomacy: Redirecting U.S. Foreign Policy*. Boston: Palgrave, pp. 135–53.

Batora, J. (2005). 'Public Diplomacy in Small and Medium-Sized States: Norway and Canada. Discussion Papers in Diplomacy'. *Netherlands Institute of International Relations Clingendael*. Available at: http://www.clingendael.nl/publications/2005/20050300_cli_paper_dip_issue97.pdf

Bob, C. ed. (2011). *The International Struggle for New Human Rights*. Philadelphia: University of Pennsylvania Press.

Brown, J. (2008). 'Public Diplomacy and Propaganda: Their Differences'. *American Diplomacy*. Available at: http://www.unc.edu/depts/diplomat/item/2008/0709/comm/brown_pudiplprop.html [Accessed 5 March, 2017].

Bureau of Public Affairs (2011). 'International Cyber Diplomacy: Promoting Openness, Security and Prosperity in a Networked World'. Fact Sheet. U.S. Department of State. Available at: https://obamawhitehouse.archives.gov/sites/default/files/rss_viewer/international_strategy_for_cyberspace.pdf [Accessed 5 March, 2017].

Castells, M. (2009). *Communication Power*. New York: Oxford University Press.

Chen, Ni (2011). 'The Evolving Chinese Government Spokesperson System '. In: J. Wang, ed., *Soft Power in China: Public Diplomacy Through Communication*. New York: Palgrave Macmillan, 73–93.

Clinton, H. R. (2010). *Remarks on Internet Freedom*. Available at: https://tavaana.org/sites/default/files/Remarks%20on%20Internet%20Freedom_0.pdf [Accessed 5 March, 2017].

Clinton, H. R. (2011). *Internet Rights and Wrongs: Choices & Challenges in a Networked World*. Available at: https://www.eff.org/document/secretary-clintons-internet-rights-and-wrongs-choices-and-challenges-networked-world-speech [Accessed 5 March, 2017].

Davison, W. Phillips (1974). 'News Media and International Negotiation'. *Public Opinion Quarterly*, 38(2), pp. 174–191.

Department of Foreign Affairs and Trade (2014). *Public Diplomacy Strategy 2014-2016*. Canberra: Australian Government. Available at: http://dfat.gov.au/people-to-people/public-diplomacy/Documents/public-diplomacy-strategy-2014-16.pdf [Accessed 5 March, 2017].

Egeland, J. (1988). *Impotent Superpower--Potent Small State: Potentials and Limitations of Human Rights Objectives in the Foreign Policies of the United States and Norway*. Oslo: Norwegian University Press.

Entman, R. M. (2008). 'Theorizing Mediated Public Diplomacy: The U.S. Case'. *The International Journal of Press/Politics*, 13, 87–102. doi:10.1177/1940161208314657.

Esquival, A. P, Maguire, M. et al. (2014). 'Letter to Human Rights Watch Urges Independence from US Government'. *Human Rights Investigations*. Available at: https://humanrightsinvestigations.org/2014/05/17/human-rights-watch-independence-us-government/

Foot, R. (2008). 'Exceptionalism Again: The Bush Administration, the "Global War on Terror" and Human Rights'. *Law and History Review*, 26(3), pp. 707–25.

GAO (2005). *U.S. Public Diplomacy Interagency Coordination Efforts Hampered by the Lack of a National Communication Strategy. GAO-05-323*. Washington, D.C.: Government Accountability Office.

Golan, G. J. and Viatchaninova, E. (2013). 'Government Social Responsibility in Public Diplomacy: Russia's Strategic Use of Advertorials'. *Public Relations Review*, 39(4), pp. 403–05.

Gregory, B. (2011). 'American Public Diplomacy: Enduring Characteristics, Elusive Transformation'. *The Hague Journal of Diplomacy*, 6(3–4), pp. 351–72.

Hicks, P. (2011). 'Human Rights Diplomacy: The NGO Role'. In: M. O'Flaherty, Z. Kedzia, A. Müller and G. Ulrich, eds., *Human Rights Diplomacy: Contemporary Perspectives*. Leiden: Martinus Nijhoff Publishers, 217–22.

Hindman, M. (2008). 'What Is the Online Public Sphere Good For?'. In: J. Turow and L. Tsui, eds., *The Hyperlinked Society: Questioning Connections in the Digital Age*. Michigan: Digital Culture Books, pp. 268–88.

Kalathil, S. (2010). *Internet Freedom: A Background Paper*. Prepared for the Aspen Institute International Digital Economy Accords (IDEA) Project. Aspen: Aspen Institute.

Keck, M. E. and Sikiink, K. (1998). *Activists Beyond Borders: Advocacy Networks in International Politics*. Ithaca, NY: Cornell University Press.

Kremlin.ru, (2014). 'Today TV Channel Starts Broadcasting in Argentina'. *President of Russia*, October 9. Available at: http://en.kremlin.ru/events/president/news/46762 [Accessed 18 May, 2016].

Kimport, K. and Earl, J. (2011). *Digitally Enabled Social Change: Activism in the Internet Age*. Boston: MIT Press.

Kumar, K. (2006). *Promoting Independent Media: Strategies for Democracy Assistance*. Boulder, CO: Lynne Rienner Publishers.

Kurlantzick, J. (2007). *Charm Offensive: How China's Soft Power Is Transforming the World*. New Haven: Yale University Press.

MacAskill, E. (2014). 'Putin Calls Internet a "CIA Project" Renewing Fears of Web Breakup'. *The Guardian*. Available at: http://www.theguardian.com/world/2014/apr/24/vladimir-putin-web-breakup-internet-cia [Accessed 5 March, 2017].

McDonald, J. (2015). 'China Calls for Global "Governance System" For Internet'. *The Huffington Post*. Available at: http://www.huffingtonpost.ca/2015/12/16/china-internet-regulation_n_8822434.html [Accessed 6 Jan. 2016].

Melissen, J. (2005). *The New Public Diplomacy: Soft Power in International Relations*. New York: Palgrave Macmillan.

Milton, J. (1643). *Areopagitica. A Speech of Mr. John Milton for the Liberty of Unlicenc'd Printing to the Parliament of England*. Available on: https://www.dartmouth.edu/~milton/reading_room/areopagitica/text.shtml [Accessed 5 March, 2017].

Miskimmon, A., O'Loughlin, B. and Roselle, L. (2014). *Strategic Narratives: Communication Power and the New World Order*. New York: Routledge.

Nikles, D. P. (2003). *Under the Wire: How the Telegraph Changed Diplomacy*. Boston: Harvard University Press.

Non-Aligned Movement (2007). *Information on the Non-Aligned Movement Ministerial Meeting on Human Rights and Cultural Diversity*. Tehran, Islamic Republic Of Iran, 3–4 September 3–4. Distributed in the provisional agenda of the 179th session of the Executive Board UNESCO. 179 EX/48. Available at: http://unesdoc.unesco.org/images/0015/001581/158163e.pdf [Accessed 5 March, 2017].

Nye, J. S. (2004). *Soft Power: The Means to Success in World Politics*. New York: Public Affairs.

Office of the President (May 2011). *International Strategy for Cyberspace: Prosperity, Security, and Openness in a Networked World*.

Office of International Communications and Information Policy (2016). *Internet Freedom*. US Department of State. Available at http://www.state.gov/e/eb/cip/netfreedom/index.htm

Powers, M. (2014). 'The Structural Organization of NGO Publicity Work: Explaining Divergent Publicity Strategies at Humanitarian and Human Rights Organizations'. *International Journal of Communication*, 8, p. 18.

Risse, T. and Sikkink, K. (1999). 'The Socialization of Human Rights Norms into Domestic Practices Introduction'. In: Ropp, S. C. and Sikkink, K. eds., *The Power of Human Rights: International Norms and Domestic Change*. Cambridge: Cambridge University Press, pp. 1–38.

Shirky, C. (2008). *Here Comes Everybody: The Power of Organizing Without Organizations*. New York: Penguin Press.

Scoble, H. M. and Wiseberg, L. S. (1974). 'Human Rights and Amnesty International'. *The ANNALS of the American Academy of Political and Social Science*, 413(1), pp. 11–26.

Tang, L. and Li, H. (2011). 'Chinese Corporate Diplomacy: Huawei's CSR Discourse in Africa'. In: Wang, J. ed., *Soft Power in China*. Palgrave Macmillan Series in Global Public Diplomacy. Palgrave Macmillan, pp. 95–115.

Thijm, Y. A. (2010). 'Update on The Hub and WITNESS' New Online Strategy'. *Witness.org*, August. Available at: http://blog.witness.org/2010/08/update-on-the-hub-and-witness-new-online-strategy/ [Accessed 5 March, 2017].

Thrall, A. T., Stecula, D. and Sweet, D. (2014). 'May We Have Your Attention Please? Human-Rights NGOs and the Problem of Global Communication'. *The International Journal of Press/Politics*, doi: 1940161213519132

United Nations (2012). *Resolution L13, the Promotion, Protection and Enjoyment of Human Rights on the Internet*. Human Rights Council. Twentieth Session. Agenda item 3.

Van Ham, P. (2003). 'War, Lies, and Videotape: Public Diplomacy and the USA's War on Terrorism'. *Security Dialogue*, 34(4): 427–44.

PART III

Media performance and human rights

News and journalism

20

GLOBAL MEDIA ETHICS, HUMAN RIGHTS AND FLOURISHING

Stephen J. A. Ward

This chapter argues that human rights should play a major role in the construction of a global media ethics, an ethics that transcends parochial journalism norms and practices. It envisages a global media ethics with human rights expressing many of its core principles.

The chapter is not a chapter in the philosophy of human rights.[1] It is chapter in the philosophy of journalism ethics. It does not chart the history and diversity of theories of human rights, and associated philosophical debates such as which list of human rights is correct. Rather, the focus is on developing an appropriate conception of human rights for an ethics of global news media, a conception that I call contractual naturalism. The chapter explores how this conception of human rights shapes the principles and aims of global media ethics.[2]

Section 1, 'Journalism ethics', argues that the ethics of pre-digital journalism, which historically has been parochial, needs to be reconstructed as a digital, global ethics. In explaining why journalism ethic should 'go global', the section examines how parochial journalism ethics has prioritised nation-based political rights yet has struggled to deal adequately with human rights. Section 2, 'Human rights and global ethics', puts forward a contractual conception of human rights based on the idea of ethics as a matter of human invention, proposal and social agreement. It then shows how such a conception can be used to construct a global ethics that takes human flourishing as its ultimate aim. Section 3, 'Application to journalism', explains how human rights are central to global media ethics.

Journalism ethics: From parochial to global

Journalism ethics

Journalism ethics is the study and application of the norms and aims that should guide the social practice of journalism, in its many technological and cultural forms. Journalism ethics is the responsible use of the freedom to publish. Since journalism has significant impact on persons and societies, journalists cannot escape responsibilities and the expectation of their publics to follow a code of ethics. Journalism principles include impartiality, serving the public, editorial independence, truth-seeking, accuracy, minimising harm and verification. Under these principles fall a large number of specific norms and protocols for dealing with recurring situations, such as the use of deceptive techniques to obtain information.

Among media cultures globally, the aims and principles of responsible practice overlap and vary. Some principles are shared, such as truth-seeking, and others are not, such as objectivity. Some cultures value an aggressive watchdog journalism to expose official wrongdoing; other cultures stress the role of media in maintaining social solidarity.

The history of Western journalism can be divided into two parts: a pre-digital, non-global journalism from the 17th century onwards, whose modern form is professional mainstream journalism; and a digital, global journalism, from the late 20th century to today, which includes professional and non-professional.

The history of journalism ethics exhibits a similar division, between a pre-digital, non-global ethics for professional, mainstream journalism, and an emerging, digital, global ethics for a news media that is professional and non-professional. There have been four previous revolutions in journalism ethics – the invention of a journalism ethics in the 17th century, the ethics of the Enlightenment 'public' press of the 18th century, the liberal theory of the press in the 19th century and the professional ethic of journalism in the previous century.[3] Currently, we are in the middle of a fifth revolution due to the emergence of digital global media. This media revolution has undermined the pre-digital ethical framework, and created new forms of journalism, and new practitioners. Accepted principles such as objectivity are questioned, and journalists debate who is a journalist and what constitutes journalism. The result is that journalism ethics lacks a moral framework for the new digital and global journalism.

Parochial journalism ethics

The rise of digital, global journalism has made evident a crucial presumption of journalism ethics, which I call the 'parochial thesis': that the primary duty of a journalist is to support and promote the interests of a group of which the journalist is a member – typically the public of a nation, or the members of a religious or ethnic group.

Journalism parochialism is an expression of ethical localism: the claim that parochial values and principles dealing with what is near and dear – family, ethnic group, nation – should have more ethical weight than global values and principles, where the parochial and the global conflict. Localism tends towards moral relativism, arguing that ethical norms exist and have validity mainly (or only) in specific cultures and countries (see Ward 2015c). Ethical globalism asserts the opposite: Global values have priority over parochial values, where they conflict. Global values include a concern for all of humanity, the moral equality of all humans and strong support for foreigners in need.

In this chapter I deal with the dominant form of ethical localism in journalism: moral nationalism, the duty of journalists to nation. On this view, the primary allegiance of journalists is to their co-patriots. This loyalty to co-nationals trumps talk of serving citizens in other countries. Journalists are citizens of a nation, first; and journalists, second. When media practitioners consider their actions, they should emphasize the impact on the local and national, not the global. The prevalence of ethical localism means that many codes of ethics say little about the duties of journalists towards foreigners, humanity or human rights.[4]

Journalism ethics, it seems, stops at the border.

Across the revolutions in media ethics, the common presumption has been that any press philosophy or code of ethics is a parochial, group-defined philosophy or code. When American codes of journalism ethics call on journalists to serve the public, they mean American journalists serving the American public. Similarly, Canadian, Indian and Russian journalists have their own nation-based codes and duties. *Not* that such a presumption was explicitly stated in many codes of ethics. The parochial thesis has seemed obvious and correct, perhaps too obvious to state in an era of non-global journalism and in a world divided into nation states.

Despite its apparent correctness, the parochial thesis created, and continues to create, conceptual and practical tensions in journalism ethics. At times, the tensions have undermined other journalistic principles and have challenged the consistency of journalism ethics as a whole. Conceptually, for example, it is difficult to explain how journalists could be objective and impartial in reporting *yet* favour their nation when reporting on issues affecting their nation, such as global trade patterns. Practically, principles of truth-telling and independence have been comprised during war. Often, the parochial thesis – in the form of patriotic calls from government and citizens – insists that journalists uncritically support their nation at war, distribute propaganda for the war machine and demonise other nations and races.

Journalism and rights

How has Western journalism ethics treated rights? In general, political and civil rights (and liberties) *within* a nation have been of the greatest interest and concern, in two senses: the liberties of the press and the liberties of the public. It is argued that the press require freedom to publish to support the liberties and rights of the public. Press philosophy in the 1700s, for example, argued that journalism fell under a social contract whereby journalists served the Enlightenment public by carrying out essential information functions in return for constitutional guarantees of freedom of the press. In the mid- to late-1800s, journalists adopted a liberal democratic view which portrays them as protectors of the political and civil rights of free and equal citizens against the power of government. Journalists do so through the provision of news and by acting as a watchdog on official wrongdoing. In the 20th century, the press expanded its notion of rights to include issues of equality within its national boundaries, such as a woman's right to vote and the right of American blacks to attend non-segregated schools.

To be sure, journalists and their codes affirmed more than rights. They also claimed to support many social and individual goods for their co-patriots, from economic development to entertainment. However, for journalism ethics, the original and fundamental concern was that of an independent journalism, as a political institution, fulfilling its rights 'mission' in society.

Why go global?

The emergence of global news media raises serious questions about the adequacy of a journalism ethics developed for a non-global media. However, it is also true that few people would deny that journalists should have some parochial values. They may argue that journalists, who live and work in their polity, should promote the national interest. Such parochial values are not to be dismissed lightly. Parochial values, from love of family to love of one's country, have ethical weight. Yet, we cannot rest with the sanguine conclusion that parochialism in journalism is normal and to be accepted, and sufficient for journalism ethics. There are reasons for 'going global' in media ethics. Ideally, we want a global ethics that recognizes but limits the influence of parochial values on journalism, especially where global issues are in focus. The difficult ethical problem is how to properly weigh and balance parochial and global values, when both sets of values demand different responses from us.

The first, and most general, reason to go global is that we live in a different world than when media codes were first created over a century ago. We live in a world where "reality" is defined and mediated by a ubiquitous and powerful global media. News media are global in content because they report on global issues or events, whether the issue is immigration, climate change, world trade policies or international security. News media are global in reach because they have the technology to gather information from around the world with incredible speed, and to use this information to create stories for a global public. News media are global in impact because the production of stories has impact across borders, sparking riots in distant lands or prompting global responses to natural disasters.

The argument for global journalism ethics can be summarized in one short sentence: Global power entails global responsibilities. It is therefore appropriate – some would say urgent – to ask about the ethics of global media, and to what extent it differs from the previous ethics of a non-global media rooted in individual nations and regions of the world. The need for a global ethics is due not only to technological innovation and new ownership patterns; it is due to changes in the world that journalism inhabits. Of primary importance is the fact that our media-connected world brings together a plurality of different religions, traditions, ethnic groups, values and organizations with varying political agendas, social ideals and conceptions of the good. Media content deemed offensive by certain groups can spark not just domestic unrest but global tension. In such a climate, the role of media, and its ethics, must be re-examined.

A globally minded media is of great value because a biased and parochial media can wreak havoc in a tightly linked global world. North American readers may fail to understand the causes of violence in the Middle East or of drought in Africa if they are not reported properly. Jingoistic reports can portray the inhabitants of other regions of the world as a threat. Reports may incite ethnic groups to attack each other. In times of insecurity, a narrow-minded, patriotic news media can amplify the views of leaders who stampede populations into war or the removal of civil rights for minorities. We need a cosmopolitan media that reports issues in a way that reflects this global plurality of views and helps groups understand each other better. We also need globally responsible media to help citizens understand the daunting global problems of poverty, environmental degradation and political instability.

A second reason, directly relevant to this chapter, is that a parochial journalism ethics cannot be entrusted with the vital role of supporting human rights around the world. An ethical localism that prioritises parochial interests, in journalism and without, cannot be the strong voice (or global moral conscience) needed to protect and advance human rights. History teaches us that parochialism is an unsteady guide for ethics, especially for international issues. One only has to review the history of the two world wars of the last century, and the horrific Holocaust, to question the moral competency of parochialism in global affairs.

Moreover, it seems today that, at almost every turn, some form of parochialism threatens to weaken our resolve to deal effectively with global issues, such as immigration, climate change or human rights. Global interests face counterbalancing parochial interests which range from a xenophobic nationalism and distrust of strangers to a milder but still powerful belief that nations need strong self-interested reasons to act on any global issue.

Moral parochialism can erode the will to work from global principles. People justify their inaction by citing slogans such as 'charity begins at home', or they soft-peddle crucial assistance to foreigners as a laudable but optional form of benevolence. Or, hard-nosed realists warn us that, in a dog-eat-dog world of competing nations, globalism is a soft-headed luxury we cannot afford. For a recent example of distorted media coverage due to strong parochial feelings, consider the coverage in Europe and the United States of the 2015-2016 refugee crises, as thousands fleeing war in Syria and elsewhere sought to reach parts of Europe. In many countries, such as Italy and Greece, journalists and news publications became megaphones for populists and right-wing groups with their inaccurate facts, xenophobic fears and proposals that violated existing human rights treaties.[5]

Parochialism in society and in the media seems always in need of being corrected, limited and counterbalanced by global ethical principles.

Human rights and global ethics

A conception of human rights

Having described why journalism ethics should become a global ethic, we are ready to address the question that motivates this chapter: What is the place of human rights in global media ethics? The short answer is: Human rights should be among the core values of a cosmopolitan, global ethics.

What conception of human rights is appropriate for global media ethics? Boylan (2014) divides human rights theories according to how they justify human rights claims. He notes three kinds: (1) Theories that justify human rights legally and contractually, for example, there are laws that endorse human rights. (2) Theories that justify human rights as promoting the basic interests and welfare of people. (3) Theories that justify human rights as providing the freedom and autonomy that people need to become self-directed agents, and to develop their capacities.

I put forward a view that I call contractualism naturalism.[6] My theory cuts across all three of Boylan's categories. I define a right as an ethical claim that certain freedoms and forms of activity are so important to human welfare and social cooperation that it would be wrong for anyone, or society, to deny such activity. Society has a duty to respect, support and protect such rights. Human rights are the most fundamental of all our rights. They are whatever is necessary for the flourishing of human beings. Flourishing can be defined, following Nussbaum (2011, 33–4), as what is necessary to develop human's natural 'central capacities'. Nussbaum provides a list of 10 central capacities, from being able to live a life of normal length and being able to have good health to the right of affiliating with others and being able to participate in decisions that affect one's interests. These rights to exercise the freedoms that develop capacity and agency are the rights of every person anywhere in the world, irrespective of citizenship, residence, race, ethnicity, class, caste or community. These are rights a person has by being human.

To this view I add a contractual rider: Any candidate for a human right must be able to be recognized and ratified by a fair and rational process of deliberation. The contractual test is: Might these proposed human rights be agreed to by rational and reasonable persons seeking moral principles to guide their social interaction?

For contractual naturalism, an ethical norm or assertion is not a factual description of an external, independent moral property or moral fact, as most ethical realists believe (Shafer-Landau 2005, 1–3). It is a pragmatic proposal for a rule that says how, morally speaking, we should regulate conduct and practice. Parties to the discussion should adopt what Sen has called an attitude of 'open impartiality' (Sen 2009, 358–9), which is an interactive process of critical scrutiny, open to arguments from others and their perspectives and interests. The ground of ethics is nothing more, and nothing less, than what reasonable people, reviewing their experience and listening to others, believe should be the rule.

Human rights are typically universal statements – rights that apply to all people, such as the right not to be subjected to torture or the right of free expression. I regard human rights as 'contractual universals' (Ward 2010, 175–6). The human right is put forward as an epistemologically and ethical reasonable candidate for a basic principle in our ethical belief system. To say that x is a universal human right is a covert way of proposing that x should be recognized as a basic ethical principle.

Human rights and global ethics

How does this conception of human rights become part of global ethics and global media ethics? The linkage is not one of entailment or necessity. It is possible to agree that human rights are basic rules of conduct without adopting a global ethics.

The linkage is this: The principles of the human rights approach should be a major part the content of global ethics. Human rights are among the basic values of global ethics. At the same time, human rights claims express the meaning and inspiration behind global ethics. When we claim, as a human right, the right to not be imprisoned without just cause, we express deep moral emotions that motivate people to embrace global ethics.

In particular, the human rights approach provides important principles for a theory of right (or justice). A moral theory has two main components: (1) A theory of the right: principles of right and duty which define proper conduct among humans, or what Scanlon (1998) calls what we owe each other. This is deontological ethics, and stems largely from Kant. And (2) a theory of the good: principles that state and prioritise the many valued things that contribute to a good life: pleasures, friendship, love, adequate wealth and so on. Utilitarianism and consequentialism are ethical theories of the good. Human rights are content for a theory of the right.

Also, human rights are compatible with cosmopolitan ethics, a form of ethics that is used to support arguments for global ethics. Cosmopolitanism is an ethical theory with ancient roots.[7] The basic moral principle is that all humans have equal value and dignity as members of humanity. This rules out social arrangements that discriminate on the basis of caste, gender, race or nationality. Our concern for others is not parochial but universal. We have duties to foreigners, not only charity. The ideas of cosmopolitanism – moral equality and duties to strangers – should be part of any theory or practice of human rights.

Human rights and flourishing

I contend that human rights theory, and any theory of the right, is based on some general conception of the human good as a whole, such as a conception of human welfare, happiness or flourishing. We draw a portrait of a good life, over time, as an integrated composite of goods, and we make this portrait the ultimate aim of action and ethics.

Contractual naturalism grounds its justification of rights on a theory of flourishing. On this view, goods and rights combine to promote the most fundamental of all moral goods: human flourishing. Flourishing means the exercise of one's intellectual, emotional and other capacities to a high degree in a supportive social context. Ideally, flourishing is the fullest expression of human development under favourable conditions. In reality, humans flourish in varying degrees. Few people flourish fully. Life often goes badly; many live in desperate conditions where flourishing is a remote ideal. Nevertheless, the ideal of flourishing is important for evaluating social and political systems.

We can define 'human rights' in terms of human flourishing. Following Nussbaum, we think of flourishing as the development of our central capacities. Then, we define human rights as the claim that the development of such capacities is a fundamental right. Questions of human rights revolve around the right (and the freedom) to develop these core capacities, and how to provide the material and social conditions that allow such development to occur.

Therefore, I propose that a global ethics should be based on the supremely general principle of promoting human flourishing. It is the ultimate moral aim. Any ethics, including any media ethics, should be guided by a cosmopolitan desire to create, maintain or advance the flourishing of all humans. Through this idea we express our love of humanity.

We can further explicate the idea of ethical flourishing as the capacity to enjoy four levels of goods: individual, social, political and ethical goods.[8] To achieve the goods of each level is to achieve a corresponding form of human dignity: individual, social, political and ethical dignity.

By individual goods, I mean the goods that come from the development of each individual's capacities. This level includes the physical goods that allow physical dignity. All persons need food, shelter and security to live a normal length of life in health. This level also contains the rational and moral goods that allow physical capacity to flower into distinct human traits. The social goods arise when we use our rational and moral capacities to participate in society. Among the social goods are the freedom to enter into and benefit from economic association, the goods of love and friendship; the need for mutual recognition and respect. In this manner, we achieve social dignity. By 'political goods', I mean the goods that accrue to us as citizens living in a just political association. The latter, in my view, is a participatory, dialogic democracy. These goods include the basic liberties, such as freedom of speech, combined with the opportunity and resources to exercise these freedoms. Citizens are able to participate in political life, to hold office and to influence decisions. A citizen who enjoys these goods has political dignity, through self-government.

By 'ethical goods', I mean the goods that come from living among persons and institutions of ethical character. We can rely on them to act ethically. To flourish, we need to live among people who are disposed to be what Rawls (1993, 48) calls morally 'reasonable'. Such people pursue their goods, morally, that is, within the boundaries of justice and fairness.

The aim of global ethics is affirming humanity by aiming at ethical flourishing, understood as the promotion of our core capacities on four levels. The aim is global. It is not the promotion of flourishing only in Canada or China. The goal is flourishing across all borders. The individual, social, political and ethical dignity that we seek for citizens in our society, we seek for humanity at large.

Application to journalism

What does all of this mean for global journalism ethics?

It means journalism should support human flourishing, as freedom of agency and as capacity building, on all four levels. This makes the moral aim of journalism global, not parochial. In accepting flourishing as aim, journalists subscribe to the priority of moral globalism and to cosmopolitan values. We ground journalism ethics on a *global thesis*: that the primary duty of a journalist is to support and promote the flourishing of the global public, or humanity at large. Journalists are citizens of the world (or members of humanity) first, and members of a nation (or group) second.

If journalists were to adopt these moral notions, it would begin a chain of reinterpretations of primary concepts, revisions of codes of ethics and new practices.

The first change would be in the self-consciousness of responsible journalists. They would see themselves as citizens of the world, as agents of a global public sphere. The goal of their collective actions is a well-informed, diverse and tolerant global 'info-sphere' that challenges the distortions of tyrants, the abuse of human rights and the manipulation of information by special interests. The second change would involve the idea of journalism's social contract. In a global public sphere, if global journalism has a social contract, it is not with a particular public or society; instead, it seems to be something much more diffuse – a multi-society contract. The cosmopolitan journalist is a transnational public communicator who seeks the trust and credence of a global audience.

Also, principles would be reinterpreted. The ideal of objectivity in news coverage takes on an international sense. Traditionally, news objectivity asks journalists to avoid bias towards groups within one's own country. Global objectivity would discourage allowing bias towards one's country as a whole to distort reports on international issues. The norms of accuracy and balance become enlarged to include reports with international sources and cross-cultural perspectives. Global journalism ethics also affects the principle of minimizing harm. It asks journalists to be more conscious of how they frame major stories, how they set the international news agenda, and how they can spark violence in tense societies.

Global journalism ethics would require journalists to act so that principles of human rights and social justice take precedence over personal interests and national interests, when they conflict. When my country embarks on an unjust war against another country, I, as a journalist (or citizen), should say so. If I am a Canadian journalist and I learn that Canada is engaged in trading practices that condemn citizens of an African country to continuing, abject poverty, I should not hesitate to report the injustice.

A globally minded media would alter how journalists approach covering international events such as a conference on climate change. With regard to the climate conference, parochial journalists would tend to ask: What is in it for our country? A global attitude would require that journalists take on the wider perspective of the global public good. What is the global problem concerning climate change and how should all countries cooperative to reach a fair and effective agreement? Globally minded journalists from the West would report the legitimate complaints that developing nations have against the environmental policy of their own country.

A global journalism ethics rethinks the role of patriotism. In a global world, patriotism should play a decreasing role in ethical reasoning about media issues. At best, nation-based forms of patriotism remain ethically permissible if they do not conflict with the demands of a global ethical flourishing. Global journalism ethics requires that journalists commit themselves only to a moderate patriotism, subjecting the easily inflamed emotion of love of country to rational and ethical restraint.

Therefore, in sum, a global ethics limits parochial attachments in journalism by drawing a ring of broader ethical principles around them. When there is no conflict with human rights or other global principles, journalists can report in ways that support local and national communities. They can practice their craft parochially.

Conclusion

This chapter has argued for three things: (1) The need for a global media ethics; a parochial ethics is inadequate for today's journalism, and it provides inadequate support for human rights; (2) A contractual naturalism that understands human rights as proposals to govern global interaction. Human rights are basic principles of global ethics and they promote human flourishing. (3) To create a global media ethics, and to advance human rights, journalists should adopt the notions of moral globalism, cosmopolitan values and global human flourishing.

If these concepts were embraced, journalism ethics, once parochial, would have new global aims and principles, and its practices would support human rights. At the same time, appeals to human rights would express, powerfully, the content of global media ethics. Human rights and global media ethics would provide mutual support to each other.

Notes

1   On the philosophy of human rights and human rights practice, see Hayden (2001); Boersema (2011); and Goodale and Merry (2007).
2   In this chapter I will use, alternately, "journalism ethics" and "media ethics" for stylistic variation. I treat both terms as equivalent in meaning, as referring to the practice of journalism.
3   For the history of journalism ethics, see Ward (2015b).
4   However, for an example of a global code of media ethics, see Ward (2015a), the Appendix.
5   On media coverage of the refuge crisis, see a study by the Ethical Journalism Network at http://ethicaljournalismnetwork.org/en/contents/moving-stories-international-review-of-how-media-cover-migration

6   Contractualism (see Darwall, 2003; Sayre-McCord, 2000) views morality as based on an agreement among members of a culture or society. Naturalism explains morality by appeal to natural processes and capacities, without appeal to deities or non-natural forces.

7   Cosmopolitanism begins in ancient Greece and Rome with Dionysus the Cynic, Cicero, and the Stoics. Enlightenment cosmopolitan thinkers include Voltaire, Bentham, and, most importantly, Kant. Modern cosmopolitans include Beitz (2009), Nussbaum (1997), Wiredu (1996), and Singer (1995).

8   For extended treatment of the human good and flourishing, see Ward (2010), chapters 3 and 5.

References

Beitz, C. (2009). *The Idea of Human Rights*. Oxford: Oxford University Press.

Boersema, D. (2011). *Philosophy of Human Rights.* Boulder, CO: Westview Press.

Boylan, M. (2014). *Natural Human Rights: A Theory.* Cambridge, UK: Cambridge University Press.

Darwall., S. ed. (2003). *Contractarianism/Contractualism*. Malden, MA: Blackwell.

Goodale, M. and Merry, S. E. (2007). *The Practice of Human Rights.* Cambridge, MA: Cambridge University Press.

Hayden, P. ed. (2001). *The Philosophy of Human Rights*. St. Paul, MN: Paragon House.

Nussbaum, M. C. (2011). *Creating Capabilities*. Cambridge, MA: Belknap Press.

Nussbaum, M. C. (1997). *Cultivating Humanity: A Classical Defence of Reform in Liberal Education.* Cambridge, MA: Harvard University Press.

Rawls, J. (1993). *Political Liberalism*. New York: Columbia University Press.

Sayre-McCord, G. (2000). 'Contractarianism'. In: Hugh LaFollette, ed., *The Blackwell Guide to Ethical Theory*. Malden, MA: Blackwell Publishing, pp. 247–67.

Scanlon, T. (1998). *What We Owe to Each Other*. Cambridge: Harvard University Press.

Sen, A. (2009). *The Idea of Justice*. Cambridge, MA: Belknap Press.

Singer, P. (1995). *How Are We to Live? Ethics in an Age of Self-Interest.* New York, NY: Prometheus Books.

Ward, S. J. A. (2010). *Global Journalism Ethics*. Montreal: McGill-Queen's University Press.

Ward, S. J. A. (2015a). *Radical Media Ethics: A Global Approach*. Malden, MA: Wiley.

Ward, S. J. A. (2015b). *The Invention of Journalism Ethics.* 2nd edition. Montreal: McGill-Queen's University Press.

Ward, S. J. A. (2015c). 'The Moral Priority of Globalism in a Digital World'. In: Herman Wasserman and Shakuntala Rao, eds., *Media Ethics and Justice in the Age of Globalization*. Houndmills, UK: Palgrave/McMillan, pp. 23–42.

Wiredu, K. (1996). *Cultural Universals and Particulars: An Africa Perspective*. Bloomington, IN: Indiana University Press.

21

INVESTIGATIVE JOURNALISM AND HUMAN RIGHTS

Michael Bromley

Investigative journalism has played a prominent role in the recognition, protection and promotion of human rights (Lublinski, Spurk et al. 2015, 8). This has derived from its status as an idealised form of journalism (Bromley 2005, 319–20). Investigative journalists have been described as the 'special forces' of journalism (Hunter & Hanson 2011, 9), and widely presented, if not always viewed, as heroic figures (Bromley 2008, 184). Thus, investigative journalism has epitomised the normative functions of journalism in asserting the rights of journalism itself to assure free flows of communication as enshrined in a number of international and national conventions and legal frameworks of human rights (most notably, Article 19 of the Universal Declaration of Human Rights) (Johnston 2015; White 2011), while undertaking a 'watchdog' oversight of human rights (and specifically their violation) (Chambers 2000, 112ff) as well as 'triggering change' (Lublinski, Spurk et al. 2015) in its role as an actor independent of government and its institutions. Investigative journalism has been posited as the most effective operationalisation of the journalistic mission to hold all forms of power to account by robustly promulgating a combative right to bring information into the public domain; challenging the *status quo*, and sponsoring freedom of expression through the exposure of 'matters that are concealed – either deliberately by someone in a position of power, or accidentally, behind a chaotic mass of facts and circumstances that obscure understanding' (Hunter & Hanson 2011, 8). In this way, investigative journalism extends the boundaries of mundane journalism, going 'beyond conventional reporting' to enforce social accountability (Peruzzotti & Smulovitz 2002, 214; Waisbord 2002, 377). This has suggested that 'journalists, at least as much as governments, have a vested interest in the defence and promotion of high standards of human rights' (White 2011). As the former British newspaper editor, Harold Evans, put it, investigative journalism seeks to stop 'evil practices' (Spark 1999, 8) albeit that neither what constitutes 'evil', nor investigative journalism's response to it in all cases, are necessarily universally agreed (Waisbord 1996, 357).

Key to understanding investigative journalism's role in relation to human rights is its function as the custodian of public conscience (Ettema & Glasser 1998), patrolling 'the boundaries of ... civic consciousness' and locating transgressions (Protess et al. 1991, 5). A distinction between reporting and investigative journalism was expressed by Hodgson (2010), a former member of the London *Sunday Times* newspaper Insight investigative team: reporting is focussed on the manifest and episodic, whereas investigative journalism involves 'seeking out the larger, less obvious truth' of the systemic. Tulloch (2011, 320) differentiated between the 'simple-minded narrative' of ordinary reporting and the 'imaginary understanding' required of investigative journalism; as well as between the information needs of citizens (suggesting a circumscribed geo-political interest) and those of humans (implying universality). A further distinction has been drawn between 'responsible journalism in the public interest [... and] infringing privacy through intrusive photographs or "kiss and tell" revelations' (Whittle and Cooper 2009, 95). However, 'coverage of human rights issues is often difficult to fit into the breaking news format' of contemporary local, national and global 24/7 news channels and websites (Kaplan et al. 2002, 46), leading to human rights being 'reported more than covered' (Gregory 2006, 197), and their import submerged in 'the daily inundations of news broadcasts showcasing violence, militancy and condemnations of rights violations framed in lifeless legalese' (Avni 2006, 212). The emergence of citizen journalists has acted as something of a corrective to this tendency, providing alternative, direct and often personal accounts of human rights and their violations (Allan, Sonwalkar & Carter 2007). Finally, there has been both a withdrawal of mainstream Western journalists from what are termed 'hostile environments' (a factor which itself has prompted the intervention of citizen journalists (Ciobanu 2015)) and a shift in the sponsorship of those who still travel to such destinations from the media to NGOs and others (Cooper 2011, 30; Powers 2016; Sullivan 2013, 17).

A contrast may be drawn, therefore, between journalists who report the evidence, claims and campaigns of external actors, such as human rights organisations and victims of abuse (sometimes sponsored by those organisations), or NGOs and charities reporting directly (Turvill 2015b), which then amplifies those data, claims and campaigns, thereby raising public awareness, and journalists who pursue their own investigations into human rights (Peruzzotti & Smulovitz 2002, 221–5). In this second role in particular, investigative journalists are autonomous agents in a system of vertical social management (Peruzzotti & Smulovitz 2006, 11–15).

Insofar as investigative journalism addresses lapses in proclaimed public morality, it contributes to eradicating, correcting, redefining or even disregarding – but always making public – violations (Aucoin 2007, 7–8). Investigative journalism proceeds from regarding declarations, codes and bills of human rights as representing an agreed moral position; that deviations from this affront the settlement, and are likely to be effected in conditions of attempted or realised concealment. Investigative journalists hold that it is their duty to expose digressions to public scrutiny, and where necessary to penetrate any obfuscation shielding 'the truth' from open view. This has led investigative journalists to be proactive in their approach to freedom of information; to adopt specific ways of reporting, and to utilise a common range of methods. Enumerating the distinctive practices of investigative journalists, the executive editor of the Global Investigative Journalism Network argued, 'There is a moral compass to investigative journalism, and that's why the field attracts men and women who want to right wrongs, stick up for the dispossessed and forgotten, and stop abuses of power' (Kaplan 2015).

Thus, it can be said that investigative journalism acts as a private regulator of public actions, including the operation of human rights, but without a legally sanctioned mandate, relying on its ability to acquire information and then disseminate it; the trust it builds in society, and its capacity to undertake this work. In this way, it acts like interest, pressure and social action groups perhaps more than mainstream journalism (Scott 2002, 62, 66–8). According to the UK's Centre for Investigative Journalism, this regulatory attention is brought to bear in 'the public interest' on 'the principles of social justice, human rights, whistleblowing and the protection of the environment'.[1] That has led to investigative journalism claiming 'rights' specific to its own condition. While not always precisely expressed, these appeared to include the 'rights' not to be stymied in investigations by vested interests; to protect sources, particularly whistle-blowers; to undertake undercover reporting, and to make clandestine recordings (Bebawi 2016, n.p.; Fratkin, Hwang and O'Brien 2011; Basson et al. 2010; Investigative Reporters and Editors, nd; Public Interest Journalism Foundation, 2014). Underpinning these claims is the operation of the rule of law. When David Miranda, the partner of the investigative journalist Glenn Greenwald, who was responsible for the disclosure in 2013 of networks of global state surveillance, was arrested in the UK under anti-terrorism legislation, it was claimed that this constituted intimidation designed to restrain investigative journalism (although the UK's high court found that the arrest was justified on the grounds of 'national security'). Similarly, the editor-in-chief of WikiLeaks, the online publisher of secret documents, and the founders of the German news site *Netzpolitik* have been pursued by the authorities, not for practising investigative journalism, but for espionage, theft, treason and conspiracy (Nyst 2015; Pilger 2015). Investigative journalism may expose wrongdoing (Coronel 2010, 113) but it is unlikely that it can do so without provoking use of the criminal law 'as a tool for disposing of those who use their right of free speech to embarrass or inconvenience the authorities' (cf. Robertson 1999, 104).

As the formalisation and adoption of human rights, including the right to know, have been extended (driven in part by investigative journalism) (Blanton 2002) so, somewhat paradoxically, has the criminal law been used increasingly to curtail investigative journalism (Peters 2003, 45; Shaw 2012, 31). Whereas the European Court of Human Rights has reasserted the right of 'press freedom [... especially] in circumstances in which state activities and decisions escape democratic or judicial scrutiny on account of their confidential or secret nature' (cited Voorhoof and Cannie 2010, 415), for example, in the United Kingdom, the Human Rights Act 1998 which incorporated the European Convention on Human Rights (ECHR) into domestic law, effectively introduced a right to privacy (contained in Article 8 of the ECHR which has its equivalence in the Fourth Amendment of the US Constitution) somewhat at odds with the right to free expression (Article 10 – Europe's version of the First Amendment) which had been previously paramount in the UK. Moreover, under Article 8 journalists could be compelled to reveal their sources (Welch 2011). In 2015 the Bureau of Investigative Journalism claimed that the Regulation of the Investigatory Powers Act 2000, which permitted the authorities to intercept journalists' communications, breached journalists' own rights to privacy and contravened the right to free expression (Turvill 2015a). The investigations editor of *The Sun* newspaper claimed that the Bribery Act 2010, which provides no public interest defence, led to journalists declining offers of information from whistle-blowers if they asked for financial remuneration (Ponsford 2012). Investigative journalists relying on public office holders for information have been charged with conspiracy to commit misconduct in public office, a common law offence carrying a maximum sentence of life imprisonment (Haria and Turvill 2015). Investigative journalists have been threatened with arrest under the Protection from Harassment Act 1997 if they continued to pursue individuals (Ponsford 2014). Yet, as Tumber and Waisbord (2004, 1145) noted, although the scope for investigative journalism may have narrowed in parts of the global West, it has gained new impetus elsewhere as democratisation has promoted a concern with human rights (Coronel 2012, 19).

This burgeoning of the application of investigative journalism to the oversight of human rights has been supported by international efforts to effect democratisation. Between 2007 and 2015 the United Nations Democracy Fund (2016) financed organisations with more than $US2.5m to deliver projects connecting the promotion and defence of human rights and journalism in Africa, the Middle East, central and southern Asia and Latin America. While not always explicitly identifying investigative journalism, the projects implied the use of investigative techniques and approaches. In 2015 the European Union and the Norwegian government funded a project 'Creating a culture of investigative journalism for furthering democratic reform –

linking human rights organisations, government officials and the media to promote change' in Kyrgyzstan (Kabar 2015). In 2004 the Norwegian Agency for Development Cooperation sponsored the establishment of a Master's programme in journalism at Addis Ababa University in Ethiopia with an emphasis on investigation (Skjerdal 2009, 26). At the same time, there has been an escalation in the threats to journalists, and particularly those doing investigative work, resulting in murder, kidnapping, imprisonment and physical assaults: of more than 1,000 media personnel killed between 1992 and 2014, 18 per cent were reporting on human rights (Daly 2014; Shaw 2012, 30). In conditions where not only freedom of expression was not guaranteed, but state censorship and control operated, providing an alternative, more critical version of events through investigative journalism was particularly difficult (Kaplan et al. 2002, 64). In Malaysia, journalists' failure to 'ask [...] probing questions and investigate' contributed to a situation in which human rights were disregarded (Anuar 2012). Conversely, a study of the coverage of human trafficking in the US newspapers the *New York Times* and *Washington Post* found that articles initiated by investigative journalists were more likely to publicise views which differed from official policy, including raising human rights as an issue (Gulati 2011, 375). Thus, investigative journalism plays a crucial role in 'providing information that facilitates political competition and accountability' which in turn lead to greater respect for human rights (Whitten-Woodring 2009, 596). Additionally, investigative journalism assists in creating conditions in which people demand their rights through reference to them and exposure of their violation (Kaplan et al. 2002, 76; Wang 2016, 31).

Nevertheless, investigative journalism has its limits. Whitten-Woodring (2009, 616) argued that its effectiveness was predetermined by the degree of contextual democratisation. More environments deemed to be hostile, unstable, insecure and contested and a decline in corporate and statal media investment in investigative journalism, have given rise to anxieties about the nature and functioning of the practice (Downie 2012; House of Lords 2012). In turn, this has put an onus on journalists themselves to 'take charge of their profession' (Shaw 2012, 35). Proposing a reorientation of journalism more effectively to bring issues of human rights into the public domain, Shaw (2012, 37–8, 40) appeared to draw in part on the approaches and techniques of orthodox investigation journalism, including going beyond 'just reporting the facts of the news'; producing 'in-depth analysis'; practising journalism which was 'diagnostic', and exploring 'people behind the story and the story behind the people'. With others (for example, Galusca 2012) he suggested that investigative journalism adopt a broader approach to human rights beyond the exotic, extremes of conflict and the transitorily 'newsworthy' to focus on the often more mundane manifestations of 'indirect forms of cultural and structural violence' (Shaw 2012, 11). While the so-called Arab Spring brought to the world's attention the power of the Facebook generation to call authoritarianism to account, less noticed was the investigative journalism in the region exposing the mistreatment of domestic workers in Bahrain; child abuse in Jordan; neglect in Syrian nursing homes; pesticide poisoning in Palestine, and cancer risks from depleted uranium weapons in Iraq (Feldstein 2012).

Investigative journalists located outside the global west have focused on human rights issues arising out of the daily experiences of land grabs; environmental degradation; dangerous working conditions; the treatment of indigenous peoples; strike breaking; miscarriages of justice; criminal impunity; child abductions; medical misconduct; excessive profiteering; poverty; sexploitation; disenfranchisement; discrimination; extremism; police brutality, and migration (African Network of Centers for Investigative Reporting nd; Coronel 2016; JARING 2015; Philippine Center for Investigative Journalism 2016; Scoop 2015; Svensson 2014, 160). In several places, organisations have been established specifically to defend the rights of investigative journalists rather than investigating wider human rights (Foundation 19/29 nd; P-24 nd).[2] Globally, the practice of investigative journalism addressing human rights issues has spread beyond media organisations and individual journalists to include not-for-profits, NGOs, academic units, associations, foundations, bureaux, centres and training institutions in more than 60 countries (Clark 2015). By 2016 there were 18 university-based investigative journalism centres in the US and two in the UK.

Where Western media have maintained consistency over many years in pursuing investigative journalism, they have also been able to address the more day-to-day social reality of abuses of human rights. As a former executive editor of *The Washington Post* and co-founder of the Investigative Reporters and Editors group observed

> Their journalism went deeper, explaining while revealing, sometimes illuminating solutions while exposing problems. Investigative reporting in the pages of *The [Washington] Post* has helped reduce police shootings in the District; reform the treatment of helpless wards of the government, change practices of the United Way, the Nature Conservancy and the Smithsonian; expose corruption in Congress; and improve the rehabilitation and living conditions of severely disabled veterans at Walter Reed Army Medical Center.
>
> *(Downie 2012)*

In the UK, too, over at least 40 years investigative journalists, such as the late Paul Foot, the BBC television series *Rough Justice* and *Panorama*, Central Broadcasting's TV strand *The Cook Report,* Granada Television's *World in Action* and the *Guardian, Observer* and *Sunday Times* newspapers, among others, exposed where human rights had been denied almost routinely through miscarriages of justice; the operation of protection rackets; loan sharking; child pornography; the hidden health dangers of asbestos; abuses by UK companies overseas; police malfeasance; hospital failures; cruelty towards and neglect of the elderly, and the persecution of minorities (de Burgh 2008a; de Burgh 2008b, 343; de Burgh 2008c, 55, 64–6; de Burgh 2008d, 76–7; Greenslade 2008, 335–7).[3] In many ways, these investigations of human rights violations culminated in the investigative journalist Nick Davies' exposure in *The Guardian* of British journalists' own denial of human rights in the so-called newspaper phone hacking scandal (Davies 2014; for a full archive, see http://www.nickdavies.net/).

Investigative journalism and human rights were interconnected from the seventeenth and eighteenth centuries as the modernising state grappled with maintaining control over growing populations with an enhanced sense of 'civil rights' in resistance to the arbitrariness of absolute power, providing an opportunity for an 'entrepreneurship in information' both to supply social data and to 'speak the truth to power' (de Burgh 2008e, 34; Feldstein 2006, 3–4).[4] During the long 19th century many practitioners combined social inquiry, social activism and social realist literary activities with journalism which investigated human rights in rapidly industrialising economies – poverty; prostitution; alcohol abuse; poor housing; debilitating working conditions; crime; failures in education; colonialism, and, in the US, slavery and the status of indigenous peoples – paralleling state inspections, commissions and committees (Frankel 2006, 1–19). They included Friedrich Engels; Harriett Beecher Stowe; Charles Dickens; Nellie Bly; Émile Zola; Frederick Law Olmstead; Anton Chekhov; William Cobbett; William Lloyd Garrison; W. T. Stead; Jacob Riis; Henry Mayhew; Ida B. Wells; Henry Melville, and Fyodor Dostoevsky (Aucoin 2007, 25–32; Carson 2013, 11; Donovan and Rubery 2012; Feldstein 2009, 789–92; Schiffrin 2014b).

This configuration of a demand for social information at times of profound change, a concern with human rights and a greater capacity to supply evidence through improved communications, it has been suggested, provides a model for the waxing of investigative journalism and its focus on the condition of human rights – emerging again in the US during the Progressive era at the beginning of the 20th century, and the period of civil rights agitation in the 1960s (Feldstein 2006, 9–10); as well as in Australia (indigenous and women's rights) (Minchin 2001) and the UK (women's and gay rights) (de Burgh 2008c, 54–6). Interestingly, this coincidence of circumstances appeared to be replicated once more as economic reforms exposed human rights issues in China in the 1990s (Tong 2011, 34–5). If this analysis holds good, then it could explain why, at a time of globalisation, democratisation and digitisation, with their disruptive impact on social relations, some believe that the early 21st century has become a new global 'golden age' for journalists investigating human rights (Schiffrin 2014a).

Notes

1   http://www.tcij.org/about-cij
2   Foundation 19/29 (Foundation for the Support of Investigative Journalism) was declared by the Russian Ministry of Justice in 2015 to be a 'foreign agent' in an attempt to curtail its activities (Human Rights Watch 2016).
3   A declaration of interest: with my then colleague Deric Henderson at the *Belfast Telegraph*, and Gavin Esler (1980), of the BBC, I was one of the first journalists to investigate the miscarriage of justice of what became known as the Guildford Four and Maguire Seven cases.
4   The phrase is attributed to the US civil rights leader Bayard Rustin (1942) (Long 2012, 2).

References

African Network of Centers for Investigative Reporting (nd). 'Fatal Extraction: the Human Cost of Australia's Mining Empire in Africa'. Available at: https://fatalextraction.investigativecenters.org/ [Accessed 24 Apr. 2016].

Allan, S., Sonwalkar, P. and Carter, C. (2007). 'Bearing Witness: Citizen Journalism and Human Rights'. *Globalisation, Societies and Education*, 5(3), pp. 373–89.

Anuar, M. K. (2012). 'Reporting the Environment: Human Rights, Development and Journalism in Malaysia'. *Asia Pacific Media Educator*, 22(2), pp. 253–62.

Aucoin, J. L. (2007). *The Evolution of American Investigative Journalism*. Columbia, MO: University of Missouri Press.

Avni, R. (2006). 'Mobilizing Hope: Beyond the Shame-based Model in the Israeli-Palestine Conflict'. *American Anthropologis*, 108(1), pp. 205–14.

Basson, A., Dennen, T., Djokotoe, E., Gayala, S.-F., Groenink, E., Hanlon, J., Mulama, J., Mwamba, E., Rukuni, C., Schutze, E., Serino, T.K. and wa Simbeye, F. (2010). *Investigative Journalism Manual*. Available at: http://www.investigative-journalism-africa.info/ [Accessed 17 Apr. 2016].

Bewabi, S. (2016). *Investigative Journalism in the Arab World: Issues and Challenges*, London: Palgrave Macmillan.

Blanton, T. (2002). 'The World's Right to Know'. *Foreign Policy*, 131, pp. 50–8.

Bromley, M. (2005). 'Subterfuge as Public Service: Investigative Journalism as Idealized Journalism', pp. 313–27. In: S. Allan, ed., *Journalism: Critical Issues*, Maidenhead, UK: Open University Press.

Bromley, M. (2008). 'Investigative Journalism and Scholarship'. In: H. de Burgh ed., *Investigative Journalism*, 2nd ed. London: Routledge, pp. 174–88.

Carson, A. (2013). 'The History of Investigative Journalism in Australia'. In: S. J. Tanner and N. Richardson, eds., *Journalism Research and Investigation in a Digital World*. South Melbourne, VIC: Oxford University Press, pp. 10–20.

Chambers, D. (2001). 'Globalising Media Agendas: the Production of Journalism'. In: H. de Burgh, ed., *Investigative Journalism: Context and Practice*. London: Routledge, pp. 108–25.

Ciobanu, M. (15 Oct. 2015). 'Citizen Journalists in Syria "start writing history"'. *Journalism.co.uk*. Available at: https://www.journalism.co.uk/news/writing-history-training-citizen-journalists-in-syria-/s2/a574666/ [Accessed 25 Apr. 2016].

Clark, A. (2015). 'How an Investigative Journalist Helped Prove a City Was Being Poisoned with its Own Water'. *Columbia Journalism Review* (3 Nov.). Available at: http://www.cjr.org/united_states_project/flint_water_lead_curt_guyette_aclu_michigan.php: [Accessed 6 May, 2016].

Cooper, G. (2011). *From Their Own Correspondent? New Media and the Changes in Disaster Coverage: Lessons to be Learnt.* Oxford: Reuters Institute for the Study of Journalism.

Coronel, S. S. (2012). *Digging Deeper: A Guide for Investigative Journalists in the Balkans.* 2nd ed. Sarajevo: Balkan Investigative Reporting Network.

Coronel, S. S. (2010). 'Corruption and the watchdog role of the news media'. In P. Norris, ed., *Public Sentinel: News Media & Goverance Reform.* Washington, DC: World Bank, 111–36.

Coronel, S. S. (2016). 'Against the Odds, Investigative Journalism Persists in the Middle East'. *Global Investigative Journalism Network* (13 Apr.). Available at: http://gijn.org/2016/04/13/against-the-odds-investigative-journalism-persists-in-middle-east/ [Accessed 24 April 2016].

Daly, E. (2014). 'Why We Need Journalism', *Human Rights Watch* (2 May). Available at: https://www.hrw.org/news/2014/05/02/why-we-need-journalism [Accessed 22 Apr. 2016].

Davies, N. (2014). *Hack Attack: How the Truth Caught up with Rupert Murdoch.* London: Chatto & Windus.

de Burgh, H. (2008a). 'Exposing Miscarriages of Justice: An Example from BBC's *Rough Justice*'. In H. de Burgh, ed., *Investigative Journalism* 2nd ed. London: Routledge, pp. 289–99.

de Burgh, H. (2008b). 'Pillaging the Environmentalists: *The Cook Report*'. In: H. de Burgh, ed., *Investigative Journalism* 2nd ed. London: Routledge, pp. 340–57.

de Burgh, H. (2008c). 'Forty Years: A Tradition of Investigative Journalism'. In: H. de Burgh, ed., *Investigative Journalism* 2nd ed. London: Routledge, pp. 54–69.

de Burgh, H. (2008d). 'The Blair Years: Mediocracy and Investigative Journalism'. In: H. de Burgh, ed., *Investigative Journalism,* 2nd ed. London: Routledge, pp. 70–95.

de Burgh, H. (2008e). 'The Emergence of Investigative Journalism'. In: H. de Burgh, ed., *Investigative Journalism,* 2nd ed. London: Routledge, pp. 32–53.

Donovan, S. and Rubery, M., eds., (2012). *Secret Commissions: An Anthology of Victorian Investigative Journalism.* Peterborough, ONT: Broadview Press.

Downie, L. (2012). 'Forty Years after Watergate, Investigative Journalism is at Risk'. *The Washington Post* (7 June). Available at: https://www.washingtonpost.com/opinions/forty-years-after-watergate-investigative-journalism-is-at-risk/2012/06/07/gJQArTzlLV_story.html [Accessed 24 Apr. 2016].

Esler, G. (1980). 'Giuseppe Conlon and the Bomb Factory'. *Spotlight,* BBC Television (26 February). Available at: http://www.bbc.co.uk/programmes/p00hp9gv [Accessed 25 Apr. 2016].

Ettema, J. S. and Glasser, T. L. (1998). *Custodians of Conscience: Investigative Journalism and Public Virtue.* New York: Columbia University Press.

Feldstein, M. (2006). 'A Muckraking Model: Investigative Reporting Cycles in American History'. *Press/Politics,* 11(2), pp. 1–16.

Feldstein, M. (2009). 'Investigative Journalism'. In: C. H. Sterling, ed., *Encyclopedia of Journalism.* Thousand Oaks, CA: Sage, pp.788–94.

Feldstein, M. (2012). 'Muckraking Goes Global', *American Journalism Review* (April/May). Available at: http://ajrarchive.org/Article.asp?id=5294 [Accessed 24 Apr. 2016].

Foundation 19/29 (nd). Available at: http://en.foundation19-29.com/ [Accessed 24 Apr. 2016].

Frankel, O. (2006). *States of Inquiry: Social Investigations and Print Culture in Nineteenth-Century Britain and the United States.* Baltimore, MY: Johns Hopkins University Press.

Fratkin, J., Hwang, J. and O'Brien, S. (2011) '*Crude*'. *Followthethings.com.* Available at: http://www.followthethings.com/crude.shtml [Accessed 15 Apr. 2016].

Galusca, R. (2012). 'Slave Hunters, Brothel Busters, and Feminist Interventions: Investigative Journalists as Anti-sex-trafficking Humanitarians'. *Feminist Formations,* 24(2), pp. 1–24.

Gregory, S. (2006). 'Transnational Storytelling: Human Rights, WITNESS, and Video Advocacy', *American Anthropology,* 108(1), pp. 195–204.

Greenslade, R. (2008). 'Subterfuge, Set-ups, Stings and Stunts: How Red-tops Go About Their Investigations'. In H. de Burgh, ed., *Investigative Journalism* 2nd ed. London: Routledge, pp. 319–39.

Gulati, G. J. (2011). 'News Frames and Story Triggers in the Media's Coverage of Human Trafficking'. *Human Rights Review,* 12, pp. 363–79.

Haria, R. and Turvill, W. (2015). 'Jailed for More Than 20 Years: the Sources Convicted of Selling Stories to Journalists', *Press Gazette* (28 July). Available at: http://www.pressgazette.co.uk/jailed-more-20-years-sources-convicted-selling-stories-journalists [Accessed 22 April 2016].

Hodgson, G. (2010). 'Obituary For Murray Sayle'. *Guardian* (21 September). At http://www.theguardian.com/media/2010/sep/21/murray-sayle-obituary [Accessed 16 Dec. 2015].

House of Lords (2012). 'The Future of Investigative Journalism'. *Communications Committee – Third Report.* Available at: http://www.publications.parliament.uk/pa/ld201012/ldselect/ldcomuni/256/25602.htm: [Accessed 24 Apr. 2016].

Human Rights Watch (2016). 'Russia: Government Against Rights Groups' (16 April). Available at: https://www.hrw.org/russia-government-against-rights-groups-battle-chronicle [Accessed 6 May, 2016].

Hunter, M. L. and Hason, N. (2011). 'What Is Investigative Journalism?'. In: M. L. Hunter, ed., *Story-Based Inquiry: A Manual for Investigative Journalists*, Paris: UNESCO, pp. 7–10.

Investigative Reporters and Editors (nd). Available at: https://www.ire.org/about/ [Accessed 15 Apr. 2016].

JARING (Indonesian Network for Investigative Journalism) (2015). At http://www.jaring.id/ [Accessed 24 Apr. 2016].

Johnston, D. C. (2015). 'The World Needs Investigative Journalism', *Human Rights Freedoms* (13 October). Available at: http://hrf.report/the-world-needs-investigative-journalism/ [Accessed 26 Oct. 2015].

Kabar (2015). 'IWPR Conducted Training on Analytical Radio Journalism for Reporters in Kyrgyzstan' (2 March). Available at: http://kabar.kg/eng/society/full/12345 [Accessed 21 Apr. 2016].

Kaplan, D. E. (2015). '8 Lessons on Investigative Journalism from *Spotlight*'. Global Investigative Journalism Network (7 December). Available at: http://gijn.org/2015/12/07/8-lessons-on-investigative-journalism-from-spotlight/ [Accessed 17 Dec. 2015].

Kaplan, R., Mohamedu, M.-M. O, Cook, M., Gutman, R., Karikari, K., Mathoz, J.-P. White, A., Khatib, N., Macari, M., Molivic, Y., Sindauigaya, A., Freih, L. and Moeller, S. D. (2002). *Journalism, Media and the Challenge of Human Rights Reporting*. Versoix, Switzerland: International Council on Human Rights Policy.

Long, M. G. ed. (2012). *I Must Resist: Bayard Rustin's Life in Letters*. San Francisco, CA: City Lights.

Lublinksi, J., Spurk, C. et al. (2015). 'Triggering Change – How Investigative Journalists in Sub-Saharan Africa Contribute to Solving Problems in Society', *Journalism*, doi:1464884915597159

Minchin, L. (2001). 'Digging the Dirt: Investigative Journalism in Australia from the 1950s to 2000'. *Four Corners*, ABC Television. Available at: http://www.abc.net.au/4corners/4c40/essays/minchin.htm [Accessed 6 May, 2016].

Nyst, C. (2015). 'Investigative Journalism is Vital for Democracy as State Surveillance Increases', *The Guardian* (5 August). Available at: http://www.theguardian.com/commentisfree/2015/aug/05/investigative-journalism-surveillance-democracy-germany-netzpolitik [Accessed 24 Apr. 2016].

P-24 (Platform for Independent Journalism, Turkey) (nd). At http://platform24.org/en/about-us [Accessed 24 Apr. 2016].

Peruzzotti, E. and Smulovitz, C. (2002). 'Held to Account: Experiences of Social Accountability in Latin America'. *Journal of Human Development*, 3(2), pp. 209–30.

Peruzzotti, E. and Smulovitz, C. (2006). *Enforcing the Rule of Law: Social Accountability in the New Latin American Democracies*. Pittsburgh, PA: Pittsburgh University Press.

Peters, B. (2003). 'The Media's Role: Covering or Covering Up Corruption?'. In *Global Corruption Report: Access to Information*. Berlin: Transparency International, pp. 44–56.

Philippine Center for Investigative Journalism (2016). Available at: http://pcij.org/ [Accessed 24 Apr. 2016].

Pilger, J. (2015). 'Julian Assange: the Untold Story of an Epic Struggle for Justice'. *New Matilda* (31 July). Available at: https://newmatilda.com/2015/07/31/julian-assange-untold-story-epic-struggle-justice/ [Accessed 24 Apr. 2016].

Ponsford, D. (2012). '*Sun* Investigations Chief: Bribery Act as Forced Us to Turn Away Whistle-blowers'. *Press Gazette* (13 November). Available at: http://www.pressgazette.co.uk/sun-investigations-chief-bribery-act-has-forced-us-turn-away-genuine-whistle-blowers [Accessed 22 Apr. 2016].

Ponsford, D. (2014). 'Journalist Investigating £100m Investment Fraud Given "Absurd" Harassment Warning by Met Police', *Press Gazette* (25 April). Available at http://www.pressgazette.co.uk/journalist-investigating-%C2%A3100m-investment-fraud-given-absurd-harassment-warning-met-police [Accessed 22 Apr. 2016].

Powers, M. (2016). 'The New Boots on the Ground: NGOs in the Changing Landscape of International News', *Journalism*, 17(40), pp. 401–16.

Project V. (2016). 'First Amendment Right Upheld in New Hampshire Secret Recording Case' (25 March). Available at: http://projectveritas.com/posts/news/first-amendment-rights-upheld-new-hampshire-secret-recording-case/ [Accessed 15 Apr. 2016].

Protess, D., Lomax Cook, F. Gordon, M. and Ettema, J. (1991). *The Journalism of Outrage: Investigative Reporting and Agenda Building in America*, New York: Guilford.

Public Interest Journalism Foundation (2014). Available at: http://www.pijf.com.au/dont-miss-new-news-in-melbourne-in-october/ [Accessed 15 Apr. 2016].

Robertson, G. (1999). *The Justice Game*. London: Vintage.

Schiffrin, A. (2014a). 'Why We're Living in the Golden Age of Investigative Journalism', *Salon* (31 August). Available at: http://www.salon.com/2014/08/31/why_were_living_in_the_golden_age_of_investigative_journalism/ [Accessed 24 Apr. 2016].

Schiffrin, A. (2014b). 'Introduction'. In: A. Schiffrin, ed., *Global Muckraking: 100 Years of Investigative Journalism from around the World*. New York: The New Press, pp. 1–14.

Scoop (Eastern Europe) (2015). 'Dangerous Smoke from a Giant'. Available at: http://i-scoop.org/scoop/ [Accessed 24 Apr. 2016].

Scott, C. (2002). 'Private Regulation of the Public Sector: A Neglected Facet of Contemporary Governance', *Journal of Law and Society*, 29(1), pp. 56–76.

Shaw, I. S. (2012). *Human Rights Journalism: Advances in Reporting Distant Humanitarian Inverventions*. Basingstoke, UK: Palgrave Macmillan.

Skjerdal, T. S. (2009). 'Between Journalism "Universals" and Cultural Particulars: Challenges Facing the Development of a Journalism Programme in an East African Context', *Journal of African Media Studies*, 1(1), pp. 23–34.

Spark, D. (1999). *Investigative Reporting: A Study in Technique*, Oxford: Focal Press.

Sullivan, D. (2013). *Investigative Reporting in Emerging Democracies: Models, Challenges, and Lessons Learned* Washington. DC: Center for International Media Assistance.

Svensson, M. (2014). 'Reporting on Law and Injustices: Investigative Journalism and the Legal System'. In M. Svensson, E. Sætler and Z. Zhang, eds. *Chinese Investigative Journalists' Dreams: Autonomy, Agency, and Voice*. Lanham, MD: Lexington, pp. 157–77.

Tong, J. (2011). *Investigative Journalism in China: Journalism, Power, Society*. London: A&C Black.

Tulloch, J. (2011). 'Confronting Evil: Literature and Investigative Journalism'. In: J. Mair and R. L. Keeble, eds., *Investigative Journalism: Dead or Alive?* Bury St Edmunds, UK: Abramis, pp. 318–33.

Tumber, H. and Waisbord, S. (2004). 'Introduction: Political Scandals and Media Across Democracies, Volume II', *American Behavioral Scientist*, 47(9), pp. 1143–52.

Turvill, W. (2015a). 'European Court Fast-tracks Decision on Challenge to State Surveillance of Journalists', *Press Gazette* (20 January). Available at: http://www.pressgazette.co.uk/european-court-fast-tracks-decision-legality-uk-surveillance-journalists [Accessed 22 Apr. 2016].

Turvill, W. (2015b). 'Greenpeace Expands into Journalism with Launch of Investigations Team', *Press Gazette* (10 September). Available at: http://www.pressgazette.co.uk/greenpeace-expands-journalism-launch-investigations-team [Accessed 25 Apr. 2016].

United Nations Democracy Fund (2016). Project database. Available at: http://www.un.org/democracy-fund/searchform [Accessed 21 Apr. 2016].

Voorhoof, D. and Cannie, H. (2010). 'Freedom of Expression and Information in a Democratic Society: the Added but Fragile Value of the European Convention on Human Rights'. *The International Communication Gazette*, 72(4–5), pp. 407–23.

Waisbord, S. R. (1996). 'Investigative Journalism and Political Accountability in South American Democracies', *Critical Studies in Mass Communication*, 13(4), pp. 34–363.

Waisbord, S. (2002). 'The Challenges of Investigative Journalism', *University of Miami Law Review*, 5, pp. 377–95.

Wang, H. (2016). *The Transformation of Investigative Journalism in China: From Journalists to Activists*. Lanham, MD: Lexington.

Welch, J. (2011). 'Striking the Balance Between Personal Privacy and Media Freedom', *Liberty* (10 May). Available at: https://www.liberty-human-rights.org.uk/news/blog/striking-balance-between-personal-privacy-and-media-freedom [Accessed 22 Apr. 2016].

White, A. (2011). Ethical Journalism and Human Rights. Commissioner for Human Rights, Strasbourg: Council of Europe, CommDH (2011), p. 40.

Whitten-Woodring, J. (2009). 'Watchdog or Lapdog? Media Freedom, Regime Type, and Government Respect for Human Rights', *International Studies Quarterly*, 53(3), pp. 595–625.

Whittle, S. and Cooper, G. (2009). *Privacy, Probity and Public Interest*. Oxford: Reuters Institute for the Study of Journalism.

22

INTERNATIONAL REPORTING

Giovanna Dell'Orto

The free flow of information across national borders, cultures and political systems should be a crucial human right in this era of unprecedented globalization and migration, as well as a necessary prerequisite for the exposure of human rights violations perpetrated far from the major media capitals. But the human right of journalists, and of citizen journalists, to exercise their freedom of expression by doing their job unimpeded, and the impact of coverage of human rights abuses on political and public mobilization are only two of the most evident linkages between human rights and international reporting. The latter also intersect because the growing attacks on international reporting, especially for political gain, violate the much broader public's right to know, its awareness of both its surroundings and the decision-making that directly affects it. Mass communication has always been inextricably linked to international politics because of its power to project not only events but also national identities, and intentions, in ways that help set foreign policy permissibility parameters. For this very reason, international newsgathering and transmission have been increasingly targeted by groups in power, and those aspiring to be, with censorship, access prohibitions, distribution restrictions and all too often, tragically, with deadly violence – a violation of human rights that affects not just reporters but their audiences, which today are unrestricted by geography.

This chapter traces the history of the major trends in international reporting in this context, from the de facto diplomatic role of some Western correspondents and news organizations to the efforts in developing countries to combat perceived media imperialism. It focuses especially on the role of international reporting as a mediator of meanings across national boundaries, because from that perspective, transformations in journalism inevitably have major repercussions on the human rights of both its public and the public it covers. The chapter then discusses changes in international reporting over time up to the embattled present, when foreign news in general media is under sustained attack by crash-strapped publishers, a distrustful and uninterested public and rising levels of unpunished violence – the latter of which are further explored in the following chapter.

Unpacking the dimensions of international reporting

In early 2016, actor Sean Penn's write-up in *Rolling Stone* magazine of his meeting in Mexico with the world's most-wanted drug trafficker, Joaquín 'El Chapo' Guzmán, led to much handwringing about who is a journalist and what is a legitimate story in the context of both foreign news and the grievous human rights abuses that Guzmán's notoriously violent Sinaloa cartel is accused of perpetrating (Penn 2016; Simon 2016). There are many serious ethical and legal questions surrounding the mixing of movie and criminal stardom under the guise of journalism in that piece. Foremost among the ethical concerns is the submission of the article for pre-publication approval to Guzmán, since pre-publication censorship is the one unambiguous red line in US media law. At a human level, even more disturbing is the fact that the meeting – calling it an interview does a disservice to one of the most critical and challenging tools in a journalist's box – happened in one of the world's deadliest countries for reporters. But there is a deeper question that the journalistic outcry over this piece implied: Who is, and has been, actually reporting news from a particular country to publics beyond its borders, and how?

The case of reporting foreign news in the context of US journalism is particularly emblematic, and therefore the focal interest of this chapter, because of a unique combination of factors: An almost exclusively commercial media system largely based on advertising, supported by solid foundational press freedoms enshrined in the eighteenth-century First Amendment to the Constitution and repeatedly affirmed and broadened by the Supreme Court since, and operating in the country whose political, military, commercial and ideological power has dominated world affairs for the last eight decades. Furthermore, both the study of modern mass communication as well as the scholarly and popular resistance to what has often been perceived as 'cultural imperialism' have focused heavily on US media, from the *New York Times* to Mickey Mouse cartoons and movies. So has the analysis of the directionality of impact between foreign news and foreign policymaking (often triangulated through public opinion), particularly when centred on the anticipated effects of 'new media', from the CNN effect (and the humanitarian interventions in Rwanda or Bosnia) to the supposed Twitter revolutions (and Washington's response to turmoil in Iran or Syria).

In the United States, news media have long struggled between the constitutionally protected duty to inform a democratic public and the imperative to stay commercially viable, so sensationalism and fluff pieces, even in the deadly serious context of foreign news, are nothing new. Penn's endeavour is not dramatically different from those by the 'occasional correspondents' that filled early-Republic newspapers with tales from abroad, or even from today's breathless accounts of major TV personalities parachuting into the world's disaster du jour, and most literature on foreign correspondence in particular focused on the most colourful characters and their exploits (cfr. Hamilton 2009). Two anecdotes from arguably the dawn and the peak of US presence on the international scene vividly illustrate how US journalism has often been perceived overseas as a quasi-actor in diplomacy: Before the 1898 Spanish-American war that catapulted Washington into a world power, the *New York Times* published verbatim addresses to the American public by both Cuban rebels and Spanish leaders, the latter lamenting how the US Congress was too easily swayed by public opinion; and in December 1991, Soviet leader Mikhail Gorbachev signed his resignation with a pen borrowed from the president of CNN, which was inside the Kremlin for the very end of the Cold War (Dell'Orto 2013, 2).

Perhaps the most widely examined aspect of international reporting has been its purported effect on political and social institutions, either from the perspective of policymaking and intervention, usually from Western powers in less developed countries, or more generally globalization, usually from the perspective of the periphery coping with influences from the West. The concern is critical to an analysis of media and human rights. On the one hand, independent news media (particularly still and video photography) with a global reach are one of the crucial factors in revealing, and mobilizing Western public support against, human rights abuses perpetrated by Western and non-Western actors (cfr. Shaw 1999). On the other hand, the free expression of indigenous cultures is a human right that can be threatened by the blind adoption of homogenous values spread by massive media conglomerates and originating in the global North/West.

The inquiry into global news flows, rooted in post-war efforts and modernization theories, dominated early attempts to understand the impact of communication on the international order and continues to shape the scholarly field (e.g. Chang 1998; de Beer & Merrill 2004; Löffelholz & Weaver 2008; Thussu 2006), often alerting to major economic and political power disparities among countries at both the generating and receiving end of news. Studies of how covered/receiving countries, usually in the global South, have been affected by international flows of information and communication have found a gamut of impacts, from aids to development and democratization to radicalization to the fragmenting or even the reinforcing of cultural identity (e.g. eds. Blankson & Murphy 2007; Cottle 2009; Norris & Inglehart 2009; Tehranian 1999).

On the issue of the nexus between news and policy, findings from a wealth of studies fail to point to a single conclusion as to direct influence, let alone its direction (from policymaking elites to the media or viceversa; Miller 2007). While some scholars have pointed to sourcing practices, hegemony and national identity as the causes for the media to follow their governments' policy lines, especially during war time (e.g. Bennett 1990; Hallin 1987; Herman 1993; Luther 2001), others argue that media can drive foreign policy under certain circumstances, instigating often ill-advised ventures overseas ranging from the Spanish-American War to Black Hawk Down (e.g. Aday 2010; Gilboa, 2002; eds Nikolaev & Hakanen 2006; Robinson 2002; Seib 1997; Strobel 1997).

Since the introduction of 24-hour cable news, and particularly with the digital revolution, the dramatic transformation in communication technologies that can connect almost anyone around the world instantaneously and at virtually no reputational or resource cost has driven other studies to conclude that the means of spreading information themselves have an effect on world politics, either at the policy or the structural levels (e.g. Deibert 1997; Hanson 2008; Serfaty 1991) – again with obvious implications for human rights, especially the ability to alert the global community to abuses via social media and user-generated content.

International reporting as mediator across national boundaries

My historical research (Dell'Orto 2008; Dell'Orto 2013), informed by a constructivist perspective that sees the creation of countries' images as central to the power relations among them, has proposed and tested a different, arguably even deeper impact of foreign news on foreign policymaking and international relations than revealed in many studies aiming to prove directionality of influence. Briefly, the more restricted the news discourse, the less nuanced the public understanding and policy debate, with ultimately devastating consequences for action and its implications. This is of critical importance given that humanising other countries, instead of reducing them to caricaturised players in established narratives (be they Communism or Islamism or, for that matter, climate change), is necessary for human rights to become part of the discourse, as Balabanova (2015) shows they increasingly have. From Beijing to Mostar, victims of gross human rights abuses long have taken their plight to international reporters to ensure a global audience would hear about it, and although their ultimate success in provoking resolution has been debated (e.g. Bloch-Elkon 2007), the compassionate reporting certainly increased visibility and likely constructed the moral desirability of intervention.

Twenty case studies of American news coverage of major international events from the European revolutions of 1848 to the terror attacks in Mumbai in 2008 (Dell'Orto 2013) suggest a striking correlation between oversimplified narratives and disastrous foreign policy decisions, and conversely between nuanced, grounded coverage and realistic leadership – a frightening finding given the current crisis in the profession of foreign correspondence, as discussed later in this chapter. Since the news media serve as one of the essential loci for the formation of public opinion and the definition of policy parameters regarding international affairs (and the United States' role in them), the real consequences of reporting and narrative failures are dire, regardless whether they are dictated by a lack of resources on the ground or by the growing strength of domestic and foreign spin.

Surely no reader could be enlightened, and no substantive political debate sustained, by coverage that offered statements such as that even if Mexican voters in 2000 dethroned the party that had ruled for 70 years the country would still 'be Mexico', or that South Africa in 1994 risked becoming an 'African' country if the apartheid regime was defeated, or that the key to the Israeli-Palestinian conflict is atavistic hatred – no further explanation, leaving those shorthand, off-hand references to speak to readers' most basic stereotypes. On the contrary, the most multifaceted and informative correspondence paralleled the (relatively) bloodless implosion of the Soviet Union, a surprising end for both an oppressive, bankrupt regime and a bipolar world. Instead of facile references to Communism and nuclear weapons, the robust press corps in Moscow discussed rising threats such as ethnic tensions, economic crisis and the unclear prospects of leadership.

That far rarer, more challenging investigation into what actually happens overseas, on its own terms albeit with US implications, is the kind of reporting that correspondents undertook from Spain and China in the 1930s as the powers that would become the Axis turned on civilians with unprecedented viciousness – and that permanently shook American isolationism. Or that led some correspondents in Afghanistan during the Soviet invasion to delve into the rise of Islamist power and question whether Washington's prolific aid to the mujahedeen was not 'merely substituting one sort of trouble for another' (cited in Dell'Orto 2013, 109), a perspective sorely missing from domestic US media and political discourse.

International reporting practices: Changes and continuities

Clearly, the content of international reporting has been shaped by the evolution of its practices, at the core of which for over a century has been the painstaking, often hazardous effort by increasingly objective professionals who sought to bring news of the world home to the US public and, in so doing, helped build the box within which public opinion and policymaking were formed. While the last decades have witnessed a drastic change in information and communication technologies, and a subsequent revolution in the distribution of news, core professional practices in foreign correspondence have remained relatively unaltered (Dell'Orto 2015). Already in the 1850s, a New York editor warned not to entrust foreign news solely to 'a single electrician at a seaport town' (Dell'Orto 2013, 39). He meant the operator of the day's new technological marvel, the telegraph, but the logic applies just as well to today: A smartphone and an opinion do not make a foreign correspondent. A senior UN official in Sudan in the early 2000s was quoted as wondering whether technological improvements would 'prevent a future Darfur' or barely provide more elegant, faster accounts of the international community's failure to do so (Mody 2010, xi).

A techno-utopian delusion that in the era of social media and citizen journalism 'being there' is no longer necessary to tell the world's stories is gaining ground in some academic circles, conveniently supported by the entirely realistic observation that the financial crisis plaguing most Western media makes a new golden age of foreign correspondence extremely unlikely, at least in quantity. But it is directly contradicted by the findings of an oral history of foreign correspondence practices from the Second World War to today – eight decades of US dominance on global affairs – based on 61 interviews conducted with reporters who worked for The Associated Press for a cumulative 1,710 years and covered all continents, each producing thousands of stories (Dell'Orto 2015).

New technologies have indeed revolutionised news distribution practices – correspondents can push further and farther (although they must also produce faster) now that they no longer have to worry about finding a pay phone to dictate their story or entrusting news cables and photos to random trustworthy-looking strangers at an airport willing to serve as 'pigeons'. (Up until the end of the twentieth century and the widespread use of satellite phones and Internet communications, correspondents covering countries ranging from Bangladesh to Biafra to Bolivia that had either damaged infrastructure or regimes censoring cabled and phoned information often had no option but to find 'somebody at the airport who seemed nice', give the willing strangers film, stories and a contact at an AP bureau in whatever friendlier country they were flying to, and hope they would relay the package.)

But for all the dramatic transformations in communications, the story behind the stories shows strong continuities in the methods, and motives, of foreign correspondents. To see through the spin and stereotypes, to sniff out the big trends without falling for grand and simplistic storylines and to narrate engagingly for readers halfway across the world (or steps across the border) – simply put, to produce stories both truthful and impactful – foreign correspondents have first and foremost needed to be on the ground, not only to cover breaking news but also to analyse long-term issues. Whether in mid-1940s Italy or late-1970s China or early-1990s South Africa or today's Afghanistan, correspondents, often in partnership with local journalists, have needed the time and resources (languages included) to be in a country long enough to learn its essence and quirks and to find and develop sources among those holding court in princely palaces and squatting underneath highway bridges.

With full immersion, and the undaunted commitment to being on the scene not only when news breaks but before and after, they have had to develop the necessary skills to understand what the crucial stories are, and to tell them in a way that engages faraway audiences through a sense of shared humanity and common concerns, while also staying true to the always nuanced realities on the ground. Neither apologists nor advocates or diplomats, correspondents have had to master getting the multiple sides of each story, no matter how unpalatable. Having dug and probed and gotten popes, presidents, terrorists and street children to share what they knew and felt on the record for worldwide publication, correspondents have often consequently had to bear the responsibility of doing their best to prevent deadly harm from befalling those who dared speak to journalists (or Americans or Westerners or women or people of other races ...).

No matter how much 'vox pop' – the journalistic shorthand for *vox populi*, the voice of the people obtained through interviews with ordinary individuals – might be pushed online by the millions with social media accounts, real journalists do not simply troll Facebook for a quote. Rather, they have run tremendous risks to give a chance to have their voices heard to those whose faces are literally never seen, for example by traveling deep into Taliban-controlled territory to interview female survivors of a US soldier who had gone on a rampage and killed 16 Afghan civilians (Gannon 2013).

Current challenges to international reporting

The costs of this kind of international reporting, however, are increasingly high, both in financial and security terms, at a time when the public seems to devalue it among a deluge of information.

As the example of Penn's article on Guzmán illustrates, entertainers from Hollywood to late-night comedy shows are ever more participating in public debates, and many younger Americans especially are learning about weighty social and political matters from comedians rather than politicians and anchors as the distinctions are increasingly seen as blurred (Williams & Delli Carpini 2011; Mazzoleni & Sfardini 2009). Theoretically, the more voices contribute to conversations on grave public matters the better the chances that something useful will emerge from the cacophony, since a relevant nugget about the narco violence that has devastated Mexico can indeed be gleaned from an Oscar-winner's 11,000-word narrative (that's more than 10 times the length of the average news article) or, for that matter, from the published text messages between Guzmán and Mexican actress Kate del Castillo, who acted as liaison and appeared to have been the drug lord's real bait to agree to the meeting and publication.

In practice, however, those bits of 'news' today are thrown into an undifferentiated digital mix, where the serious eyewitness reporting and investigative pieces that can advance public understanding and buttress realistic foreign policymaking have been plummeting for decades now. Most legacy media have slashed foreign coverage as they struggle to stay in business while their advertising revenue vanishes into the online world. For the sizable majority of Millennials who now get their political news from Facebook and Twitter instead of TV or newspapers, information about, say, Mexico comes from an entirely mixed-source feed, where their friend's selfie in Cancún snaps into place above the celebrity profile that pushes down into screen-oblivion a 150-word straight-news account about the latest victims of human rights violations. It is not clear whether Millennials pay more attention to, and trust more, the selfie or the news – but there are fewer and fewer professionals providing less and less of the latter in the digital age, which is especially dangerous since the online media environment is highly imitative. The instantaneous ability to monitor online both the competition and the public's interest in media outputs has led many news producers to focus on matching and updating content instead of breaking news or developing investigative pieces, so that despite the apparent plethora of digital information, 'what most consumers get is more of the same' (Boczkowski 2010, 6).

International coverage on network TV is down by more than half since the end of the Cold War, and two thirds of newspapers give foreign news decreasing space, in addition to all but a handful of them shutting down overseas bureaus and reducing the ranks of foreign correspondents by about a third, according to the Pew Research Center (2014), Jurkowitz (2014) and other researchers. The few areas of growth are in 'digital native' organizations like Vice News and Buzzfeed. Already Millennials are significantly more likely to have heard of Buzzfeed than of *The Economist* (Mitchell et al. 2015), which – based on a quick, recent perusal of top stories on their respective homepages – means America's young voters and future leaders are more likely to read about '21 Dogs Named Bob' than about 'A bomb blast kills 10 in Istanbul'.

In 1900, *New York Tribune* editors published a summary of the ongoing Boxer Rebellion in Beijing and added the following, rather snarky note to their readers: '[The events] are here briefly reviewed for the benefit of those readers of The Tribune who did not pay that attention to them which they would have done had they appreciated the grave historical importance which now attaches to them' (cited in Dell'Orto 2013, 64). Given that public apathy and the ability of events in far-flung locales to resonate anywhere else in the world have both increased by orders of magnitude in the twenty-first century, eyewitness foreign correspondents seem to remain an endangered but necessary public good, contrary to the spreading misperception that global connectivity and social media translate into the irrelevancy of foreign correspondents and professional correspondence. But in addition to their dramatically dwindling numbers and the public's confusion as to who they are and what they do, the growing deadliness of practicing journalism in a frighteningly large part of the world has exacerbated the challenges to this kind of international reporting.

Foreign correspondents have indeed faced a near-constant level of personal danger that news audiences become aware of only through the most horrifying assassinations. The Committee to Protect Journalists has tallied 1234 journalists killed between 1992 and early April 2017, so many with impunity that self-censorship is increasingly widespread in particularly lethal areas. Thirty-eight" of those journalists were working in Mexico – "74" per cent of them covering 'crime' news." Lastly, in the next sentence, it should be "That is just ahead of Afghanistan (31 killed there), a country that has been constantly at war, between foreign occupations and/or civil conflict, since the late 1970s (Committee to Protect Journalists 2017). Throughout the world, journalists working in their own country suffer worse conditions and deadlier threats than foreign correspondents.

Even farther from the public view, but no less chilling, are the omnipresent surveillance, manipulation, denials of access and intimidation of sources by governments, militaries, criminal organizations and insurgents of all stripes. Journalists fight against these constraints on a daily basis – from the relatively banal visa struggles to interview subjects that are 'disappeared' shortly after a story is published. They push right up against 'no-go' zones, as one AP correspondent did by traveling into Ciudad Mier, just across the Texas border, after its residents had fled in what the story called 'the most dramatic example so far of the increasing ferocity of war between rival drug cartels, and the government's failure to fight back' (Stevenson 2010). Mexico was saying the crisis was over, even encouraging tourism – the correspondent, walking on streets carpeted in shell casings past a bullet-riddled army truck, wrote that 'The scenes witnessed by The Associated Press say something else'.

International reporting and human rights: Conclusions

What appears to have driven many correspondents to face these dangers has been the idealistic but ultimately irrefutable notion that if only more people could be made aware and to care, something good might happen. And sometimes it has, especially on human rights.

Less than half the length of Penn's El Chapo tale, and greeted with infinitesimally less media buzz until it won a Pulitzer Prize for public service, a 2015 Associated Press investigation into how the seafood landing on US dining tables was gotten out of Southeast Asian waters led directly to the rescuing of more than 2,000 enslaved fishermen (The Associated Press 2015). After a year-long investigation that used everything from satellite data to dangerous shoe-leather reporting, the four AP writers demonstrated that the fish 'caught by men who were savagely beaten and caged' in an Indonesian island, some for more than a decade, went into the supply chains of American food giants like Wal-Mart and Kroger. Less than two weeks after the story hit the wire, Indonesian officials evacuated more than 300 former and current slaves from the island village of Benjina, the first in many rescues, and ongoing governmental investigations, over the next months. Arriving back in his village, one Burmese fisherman held for 22 years as a slave fell to the ground when he spotted his 60-year-old mother running towards him: 'She swept him up in her arms and softly stroked his head, cradling him as he let everything go'.

As many journalists operating within the model of independent, objective newsgathering have noted repeatedly, their job as professional reporters and editors is not to be advocates – not even for human rights, no matter their sense of outrage at the many abuses they encounter. Nevertheless, today's grave threats to international and domestic journalists' ability to carry out their duties are bound to have major implications for the global public's right to be informed in accurate, impactful ways of the progress (or not) of human rights norms. And while citizen-oriented communication technologies have opened new, promising venues to augment the global flow of information, they constantly run into the harsh realities of faltering infrastructure and political censorship, even violence. One needs to look no further than the Middle

East, where authoritarian regimes have risen anew from the much-heralded, communication networks-fueled movements known as 'the Arab Spring' and where by far the most astute, successful user of social media has been the Islamic State, which seems bent on ferociously obliterating every vestige of freedom and dignity from the region.

Finally, one might ask a provocative question: By opening a window onto different realities, challenging preconceptions and most of all allowing previously muted voices a moment on the global stage, is not the very act of international reporting a form of advocating for that most essential human right, the right to have one's existence recognized by unknown others?

References

Aday, S. (2010). 'Leading the Charge: Media, Elites, and the Use of Emotion in Stimulating Rally Effects in Wartime'. *Journal of Communication*, 60(3), pp. 440–65.

Balabanova, E. (2015). *The Media and Human Rights: The Cosmopolitan Promise*. London: Routledge.

Bennett, W. L. (1990). 'Toward a Theory of Press-State Relations in the United States'. *Journal of Communication*, 40(2), pp. 103–25.

Blankson, I. A. & Murphy P. D., eds. (2007). *Negotiating Democracy: Media Transformations in Emerging Democracies*. Albany: State University of New York Press.

Bloch-Elkon, Y. (2007). 'Studying the Media, Public Opinion, and Foreign Policy in International Crises: The United States and the Bosnian Crisis, 1992–1995'. *The Harvard International Journal of Press/Politics*, 12(4), pp. 20–51.

Boczkowski, P. J. (2010). *News at Work: Imitation in an Age of Information Abundance*. Chicago: University of Chicago Press.

Chang, T. K. (1998). 'All Countries not Created Equal to be News'. *Communication Research*, 25(5), pp. 528–63.

Committee to Protect Journalists (2017). Available from https://www.cpj.org/killed/

Cottle, S. (2009). 'Journalism and Globalization'. In: K. Wahl-Jorgensen and T. Hanitzsch, eds., *The Handbook of Journalism Studies*. New York: Routledge, pp. 341–56.

de Beer, A. S. and Merrill, J. C. (2004). *Global Journalism: Topical Issues and Media Systems*. Boston: Pearson.

Deibert, R. J. (1997). *Parchment, Printing, and Hypermedia: Communication in World Order Transformation*. New York: Columbia University Press.

Dell'Orto, G. (2008). *The Hidden Power of the American Dream: Why Europe's Shaken Confidence in the United States Threatens the Future of U.S. Influence*. Westport, CT: Praeger Security International.

Dell'Orto, G. (2013). *American Journalism and International Relations: Foreign Correspondence From the Early Republic to the Digital Era*. Cambridge: Cambridge University Press.

Dell'Orto, G. (2015). *AP Foreign Correspondents in Action: World War II to the Present*. Cambridge: Cambridge University Press.

Gannon, K. (2013). 'Afghans Tell of US Soldier's Killing Rampage'. *The Associated Press*, 16 May.

Gilboa, E., ed. (2002). *Media and Conflict*. Ardsley, NY: Transnational Publishers.

Hallin, D. C. (1987). 'Hegemony: The American News Media from Vietnam to El Salvador, a Study of Ideological Change and its Limits'. In: D. Paletz, ed., *Political Communication Research*. Norwood, NY: Ablex, pp. 3–25.

Hamilton, J. M. (2009). *Journalism's Roving Eye: A History of American Foreign Reporting*. Baton Rouge: Louisiana State University Press.

Hanson, E. (2008). *The Information Revolution and World Politics*. Lanham: Rowman and Littlefield.

Herman, E. S. (1993). 'The Media's Role in U.S. Foreign Policy'. *Journal of International Affairs*, 47(1), pp. 23–45.

Löffelholz, M. and Weaver D., eds. (2008). *Global Journalism Research: Theories, Methods, Findings, Future*. Malden, MA: Blackwell.

Luther, C. A. (2001). *Press Images, National Identity, and Foreign Policy: A Case Study of U.S.-Japan Relations from 1955–1995*. New York: Routledge.

Mazzoleni, G. and Sfardini A. (2009). *Politica pop [Pop politics]*. Bologna: Il Mulino.

Miller, D. B. (2007). *Media Pressure on Foreign Policy: the Evolving Theoretical Framework*. New York: Palgrave Macmillan.

Mitchell, A., Gottfried, J. and Matsa K. E. (2015). *Millennials and Political News: Social Media – the Local TV for the Next Generation?* Pew Research Center, 1 June. Available from http://www.journalism.org/2015/06/01/millennials-political-news/ [Accessed 9 April, 2017].

Mody, B. (2010). *The Geopolitics of Representation in Foreign News: Explaining Darfur.* Lexington Books, Lanham.

Nikolaev A. G. and Hakanen E. A., eds. (2006). *Leading to the 2003 Iraq War: The Global Media Debate.* New York: Palgrave Macmillan.

Norris P. and Inglehart R. (2009). *Cosmopolitan Communications: Cultural Diversity in a Globalized World.* Cambridge: Cambridge University Press.

Penn, S. (2016). 'El Chapo Speaks: a Secret Visit With the Most Wanted Man in the World'. *Rolling Stone* (9 January).

Pew Research Center (2014). 'State of the News Media 2014'. Available at: http://www.journalism.org/2014/03/26/state-of-the-news-media-2014-overview/ [Accessed 5 March, 2017].

Robinson, P. (2002). *The CNN Effect: The Myth of News, Foreign Policy and Intervention.* London: Routledge.

Seib, P. (1997). *Headline Diplomacy: How News Coverage Affects Foreign Policy.* Westport CT: Praeger.

Seib, P. (2008). *The Al Jazeera Effect: How the Global Media Are Reshaping World Politics.* Washington: Potomac Books.

Serfaty, S., ed. (1991). *The Media and Foreign Policy.* New York: St. Martin's Press.

Shaw, M. (1999). 'Global Voices: Civil Society and the Media in Global Crises'. In: T. Dunne and N. J. Wheeler, eds., *Human Rights in Global Politics.* Cambridge University Press, Cambridge, pp. 214–32.

Simon, J. (2016). 'Who Says Sean Penn isn't a Real Journalist?' *Columbia Journalism Review* (12 January).

Stevenson, M. (2010). 'Refugees: No Return to Town Hit by Mexico Drug War'. *The Associated Press*, 22 November.

Strobel, W. P. (1997). *Late-breaking Foreign Policy: The News Media's Influence on Peace Operations.* Washington DC: United States Institute of Peace Press.

Tehranian, M. (1999). *Global Communication and World Politics: Domination, Development, and Discourse.* Boulder CO: Lynne Rienner.

The Associated Press (2015). 'Seafood From Slaves'. Available at: http://www.ap.org/explore/seafood-from-slaves/ [Accessed 5 March, 2017].

Thussu, D. K. (2006). *International Communication: Continuity and Change.* New York: Oxford University Press.

Williams, B. A. and Delli Carpini M. X. (2011). *After Broadcast News: Media Regimes, Democracy, and the New Information Environment.* Cambridge: Cambridge University Press.

23

GLOBAL VIOLENCE AGAINST JOURNALISTS

The power of impunity and emerging initiatives to evoke social change

Jeannine E. Relly and Celeste González de Bustamante

This chapter focuses on anti-press violence, legal institutions, the role of historical and cultural context with impunity and research focused on the concept of social change. The literature on anti-press violence is explored as is the critical relationship of anti-press violence with factors such as political development, economic constraints and cultural traditions. These complicating factors include anti-press violence related to stateless regions lacking rule of law and other issues deterring press protection. The chapter provides a chronology of declarations, resolutions, decisions and other instruments addressing the issue of violence against journalists. We then review frameworks that may be utilized as a foundation for anti-press violence and social change theorising and research.

Beheadings. Torture. Unthinkable assaults and crimes. Attacks on journalists have tripled in the new millennium compared with the last decade of the 20th century, as the number of journalists threatened, beaten, kidnapp`ed and killed have climbed (Freedom House 2013). In only about 10 years, more than 700 journalists were killed in nations around the world with 90 percent of the cases going without punishment of the perpetrators (UNESCO 2015a, 1). As Heyns and Srinivasan (2013, 305) concluded, 'If journalists are deliberately targeted, or if those who attack them go unpunished, the media cannot be free'.

In contrast to even 20 years ago, lightweight technologies and the speed in which information is transmitted have contributed to journalists facing an increasing number of 'threats, attempted or actual assaults, abductions, disappearances, and even death' for their reports; and citizens are reached in locales never thought possible before with the continuing growth of a global digital ecosystem, increasing the risk (Heyns & Srinivasan 2013, 305; Tumber 2006, 440).

For years, journalists have been targeted because of their 'occupational duty to investigate controversial matters' and their professional role in covering regional conflicts or wars filing news reports that may run counter to propaganda battles of adversaries (Kirby & Jackson 1986, 2). In recent times, as well, many journalists have been targeted because of their work exposing corruption or other improprieties (Levin 2013, 216).

Frontline correspondents continue to face challenging times. However, the lines among opposition groups in conflict zones have become ever more murky with journalists finding themselves 'on the receiving end of missiles from 'their' side, and are targeted by some for kidnap (or worse) because of their appearance or because they point their cameras at an inappropriate object' (Tumber 2006, 440). Further complicating these issues is the blurring of reporting on war and terror with the growing number of global attacks (Tumber 2002, 251). However, it has become clear that foreign correspondents are at less risk of being killed than local journalists working within their own countries (UNESCO 2015b).

Beyond the dangerous global and domestic landscape in which journalists report, grey areas exist in the latest conflicts and war zones, where the 'methods' of combat often are asymmetric and there are numerous opposition groups fighting one another on the ground in ideological propaganda battlefields; and there is an increasing demand for reports on conflicts (Lisosky & Henrichsen 2009, 130). The issue of not bringing perpetrators of anti-press violence to justice – impunity – has driven many from the profession into exile. One of the most serious consequences of institutionalized impunity leads to the 'chilling effect' of self-censorship, or total silence (Article 19 et al. 2008, 20).

This chapter examines the narrow strand of literature focused on anti-press violence, the issue of impunity, and legal instruments introduced over time in an attempt to provide limited and broader protections for journalists. We also provide a synopsis of the emerging literature focused on social change research and how it has been, and could be, applied to growing global concerns about violence against journalists.

There have been initiatives in the international community with partners in states around the world to consider journalists to have 'special concern', designation or protections because of the role that they play in society (Heyns & Srinivasan 2013, 306; Lisosky & Henrichsen 2009). A host of domestic, international and intergovernmental organizations, including governments, have introduced legal instruments, laws, international proposals, mechanisms and strategies to address the inadequate legal protection of journalists facing violence in its many forms. However, we argue that there exists a delicate balance between protection and control, domestic sovereignty and lack of monitoring and accountability mechanisms, which have marred many of the attempts over the years. A new wave of initiatives are afoot with some of the old concerns, and new ones, surfacing.

Anti-press violence

Scholars and others around the world have written about worsening conditions for journalists in environments in which violence is perpetrated against news media by corrupt government officials, organized crime groups, militias, terror groups and others engaged in practices outside of the law (Chu & Lee 2014; Relly & González de Bustamante 2014; Kim & Hama-Saeed 2008; Tumber & Palmer 2004; Tumber & Webster 2006; Tumber 2011; Waisbord 2002; Waisbord 2007). Contrasted against the First World War when two journalists were killed and the Vietnam War that took 66 journalists (Lisosky & Henrichsen 2009, 130), the last quarter century was a brutal one for the profession, claiming the lives of 1,236 journalists who largely were covering war, corruption, human rights issues and politics before their deaths (Committee to Protect Journalists 2017). Those perpetrating the crimes, according to Heyns and Srinivasan (2013, 311) are political groups (30%), government officials (23%), criminal groups (13%), paramilitary groups (6%), military officials (5%), residents (2%), mobs (2%) and a large group of unknown perpetrators (19%).

Waisbord (2002, 94–6) outlined several patterns that have emerged with anti-press violence in Latin America, areas which could be utilized in studies in other regions of the world. In that region, violence towards journalists varied across countries and it rose and fell over time. Many of the conflicts that journalists find themselves in seem to fit the 'localized, unstructured, scattered violence that lacks the logic of conventional civil wars' (Waisbord 2002, 100). Relly and González de Bustamante (2014) found that violence against journalists and others along the northern Mexico border was episodic and transient with intense periods for some journalists, including losing colleagues in a sea of casualties in the city of Juárez, which had nearly 3,000 total deaths in one year as the government launched a war on organized crime. A common thread across countries and regions: impunity (UNESCO 2015a; Waisbord 2002).

In a study of 601 journalists in Arab countries, Pintak and Ginges (2009) found that government control (70%), physical violence (37%), religious groups (31%) and US threats (30%) were among the most significant challenges in the profession. Other scholars (Kim & Hama-Saeed 2008; Kim 2010; Relly, Zanger and Fahmy 2015) found that violence had a significant influence on journalists and their work. In Pakistan, Pintak and Setiyono (2011) found in a survey of near 400 journalists that physical violence was among the top four types of threats.

Other research has found journalists outside metropolitan areas were more at risk than those in large cities, and journalists seemed to be attacked for controversial work or investigations involving human rights issues, corruption, the environment or drug trafficking (Waisbord 2002, 94–6). Park (2002, 237) argued that anti-press violence and other restraints limited 'the quality of Argentina's transitional democracy'. A narrow body of literature also has examined the conditions in which journalists work during formal and informal conflicts (Relly & González de Bustamante 2014; Tumber 2006, 2011). Other work has considered lawless environments and the repercussions of lack of rule of law (Waisbord 2002, 2007).

Historical context for journalists as a special designation – legal instruments

A myriad of declarations, covenants, agreements and resolutions acknowledge that freedom of expression is a human right. During conflicts, International Humanitarian Law and International Human Rights Law operate simultaneously as protections for journalists (Levin 2013, 224). International Humanitarian Law mandates the protection of journalists, whereas the International Covenant of Civil and Political Rights codifies International Human Rights Law, offering protections of freedom of expression, which embodies the rights of the press (Levin 2013, 224).

Though early discussion of international law to protect journalists has been traced to the Civil War when the Lieber Instructions were authorized by President Lincoln (Kirby & Jackson 1986, 4), by the 1920s there were countries introducing ways to protect journalists through the enhanced Hague Conventions (1899 and 1907) leading up to the 1929 Geneva Convention (Lisosky & Henrichsen 2009) of which Article 81 notes:

> Persons who follow the armed forces without directly belonging thereto, such as correspondents, newspaper reporters, sutlers, or contractors, who fall into the hands of the enemy, and whom the latter think fit to detain, shall be entitled to be treated as prisoners of war, provided they are in possession of an authorization from the military authorities of the armed forces which they were following.
>
> *(Geneva Convention 1929)*

The global recognition for the need to protect human rights, in general, was institutionalized following the Second World War. The genocide and incomprehensible human rights violations during that war and the 'failure of an international system that was based on the principle of absolute sovereignty, which excluded the acts of governments against its own citizens from the protections of human rights' largely drove the development of global rights institutions (Grossman 2012, 366). By 1949, the Fourth Geneva Conventions protected civilians during wartime, though scholars point out that Article 2 of the conventions applied to only armed conflicts that were international, offering protections to journalists after capture, and covering journalists who were authorized to cover the conflict by the armed forces (Kirby & Jackson 1986, 6). Howard (2002, 512) suggested the 'failure to provide journalists with special status under the Geneva Conventions was a lost opportunity to provide an added level of protection to journalists'.

The next major effort to address the safety of journalists occurred after 17 journalists disappeared in Cambodia in 1970 (Howard 2002; Levin 2013). A convention, known as the Montecatini Draft, which would focus on journalists' safety, was prepared yet it was not referred to the UN to be considered (Levin 2013, 238). Similarly, the United Nations created the International Professional Committee for the Safety of Journalists, which like the Montecatini Draft, would have issued identification cards to journalists and would have maintained records that followed journalists sent out on 'dangerous missions'; there were no enforcement provisions (Levin 2013, 238). Though both draft plans proposed a special designation for journalists, neither moved forward. In Chapter III of the 1977 Geneva Convention Protocols, journalists were addressed as civilians receiving protection in armed conflict (Lisosky & Henrichsen 2009, 133). By 1989, a draft resolution titled 'Protection of Journalists' was introduced to the UN Committee on Human Rights, which noted the role of journalists in reporting on human rights violations and requested governments to 'provide journalists 'with maximum protection and support'' (Mukerjee 1995, 108). The resolution, however, did not make it out of the committee (Levin 2013).

It was years later that Mukerjee (1995, 112) concluded that from the 1970s to the 1990s 'there was little interest' in drafts for global protections for journalists, which were initiated by the United Nations, with priorities of 'security, trade, and economic growth' instead garnering more attention, and issues of other human suffering, such as 'hunger, disease, disaster, and severe political repression' making provisions for the protection of journalists appear 'trivial'. Looking back at the proposals, Howard (2002, 535) neatly summarises that the approaches included identification cards for those working in 'war-torn regions, international criminalization of violence against journalists, temporary UN Tribunals or "regional human rights tribunals"'.

A number of key issues have emerged as impediments to advancing instruments that protect journalists. Among them are geographic scarcity of human rights norms in some regions of the world, sovereignty and political-sensitivity concerns in countries, and lack of resources for law enforcement and judicial systems (Centre for Law, Justice & Journalism 2011, 27). Further, the majority of global instruments already adopted are nonbinding in nature and do not appear to be having a significant effect on their own. Current instruments also are designed largely for formalised conflicts rather than internal conflicts in countries that include firefights among cartel members, militias or warlords battling for territory. It has been argued by some countries, as well, that responsibilities of monitoring and enforcing civil and political rights obligations often are beyond the resource capacities of nations and their governing bodies (Centre for Law, Justice & Journalism 2011, 27–8).

A growing number of scholars and others have been advocating for the adoption of a new global protection status for journalists that includes monitoring and enforcement of the norms. To date, a functional definition of a journalist has been widely accepted as any 'person who is regularly or professionally engaged in the collection and dissemination of information to the public via any means of mass communication' (Heyns & Srinivasan 2013, 307). Given that the nature of conflict has changed dramatically in recent years, including weapons advancements, the growing number of threat groups, digital communication advances and the insidious nature of psych-ops in the 21st century, Levin argued that the weak reliability and vulnerability of 'protections afforded' journalists is evident (2013, 219, 215).

Table 23.1 Intergovernmental organization instruments focused on journalist protection

Organization	Instrument	Initiative	Date
United Nations General Assembly	Resolution 3058 (XXVIII)	Aims for the Protection of Journalists Engaged in Dangerous Missions in Areas of Armed Conflict.	November 2, 1973
Organization of American States	Declaration of Chapultepec	"Suggests working to eradicate acts of "murder, terrorism, kidnapping, intimidation," and the "unjust imprisonment of journalists." The Declaration also call for investigating and punishing harshly the perpetrators.	March 11, 1994
United Nations Educational, Scientific, and Cultural Organization (UNESCO)	Resolution 29	Presses for Condemnation of Violence Against Journalists.	November 12, 1997
Inter-American Commission on Human Rights	Declaration of Principles on Freedom of Expression, Principle 9	Holds it is the state's obligation to prevent threats, assaults, and killing of journalists and to investigate such cases.	October 24, 2000
African Commission on Human and People's Rights	Resolution on the adoption of the Declaration of Principles on Freedom of Expression in Africa, Principle XI	Indicates states' obligations to prevent intimidation, attacks, and murders against journalists, provide access to effective redress, investigate potential perpetrators, and follow obligations under international humanitarian law for journalists to be granted the status of non-combatants.	October 23, 2002
UNESCO	Belgrade Declaration on Media in Conflict Areas and in Countries in Transition	Aims to ensure journalists' safety and address impunity	May 3, 2004
African Commission on Human and People's Rights	Resolution on the Situation of Freedom of Expression in Africa	Notes concerns about reports and mistreatment and alleged murders of journalists and calls on member states to take measure to uphold the principles of regional and international freedom of expression and human rights instruments.	November 29, 2006
United Nations Security Council	Resolution 1738	Emphasizes the states' role to comply with international law to prosecute violations against the press and condemns intentional news media attacks in armed-conflict environments.	December 23, 2006
Parliamentary Assembly of the Council of Europe	Resolution 1535	Focuses on "threats to the lives and freedom of expression of journalists," noting states' legal obligations to investigate threats, violence, and killings of journalists.	January 25, 2007
UNESCO	Medellin Declaration Securing the Safety of Journalists and Combating Impunity	Calls to investigate crimes against news media, provide witness protection, and prosecute.	May 3, 2007

Organization	Document	Date	Description
Committee of Ministers of the Council of Europe	Declaration by the Committee of Ministers on the Protection and Promotion of Investigative Journalism	September 26, 2007	Emphasizes physical safety of journalists and sources and freedom of movement of news media. Calls on member states to protect and promote investigative journalism.
UNESCO International Programme for the Development of Communication (IPDC)	Decision on the Safety of Journalists and the Issue of Impunity	March 27, 2008	Urges member states to address violence against journalists and comply with international law to address impunity. Invites the Bureau of the Intergovernmental Council of the IPDC to prioritize support of projects that build capacity for protection and safety of journalists.
United Nations Human Rights Council	Resolution 12/16	October 12, 2009	Calls for measures to investigate threats and violence against journalists.
UNESCO International Programme for the Development of Communication Intergovernmental Council	IPDC Decision on the Safety of Journalists and the Issue of Impunity	March 24, 2010	Requests UNESCO Director General to consult with member states to ascertain the feasibility of developing a plan that would address the issue of journalist safety and impunity.
UNESCO International Programme for the Development of Communication Intergovernmental Council	IPDC Decision on the Safety of Journalists and the Issue of Impunity	March 23, 2012	Requests member states to address impunity for violence against journalists, comply with international law, and prosecute violators. Requests that UNESCO continues to provide reports every two years through voluntarily supplied information from member states that list killings of journalists and non-response.
United Nations	UN Plan of Action on the Safety of Journalists and the Issue of Impunity	April 12, 2012	Produces a plan to work toward secure environments for journalists in conflict and non-conflict contexts. The plan includes indicators for monitoring interventions conducted in states around the world.
UNESCO	The Carthage Declaration	May 3, 2012	Calls for stakeholders, member states, professional associations, industry, media outlets, and others to promote and/or advance independent investigations focused on violence and killing of journalists through criminal justice systems.
United Nations	Implementation Strategy 2013–2014	March 5, 2013	Provides a UN plan of action on the safety of journalists and the impunity issue.
United Nations General Assembly	Resolution 68/163	December 18, 2013	Addresses safety of journalists and the issue of impunity.
UNESCO International Programme for the Development of Communication Intergovernmental Council	Decision Taken by the 29th IPDC Council Session	November 21, 2014	Includes Council reaffirming previous decisions related to security of journalists and notes in two-thirds of reported cases of journalists being killed there was no information submitted to UNESCO.
United Nations Security Council	Resolution 2222	May 27, 2015	Condemns abuse against journalists in armed conflicts and calls on member states to prevent these violations and to create and continue to enforce laws that enable and protect journalists to perform their duties.

Historical and cultural context and impunity

A decade and a half ago, anti-press violence was linked in the literature to nations, or swaths of countries, that were disintegrating (Waisbord 2002, 100). More recently, as well, research has shown that historical context, rule of law and political and societal culture are closely related to violence against journalists in regions around the world (Hughes 2003; 2006; González de Bustamante 2014; Relly & González de Bustamante 2014; Kim & Hama-Saeed 2008; Kim, 2010; Tumber 2006; 2011; Waisbord 2007).

A narrow but growing body of literature has examined journalists' perceptions of rule of law and human rights for those practicing journalism in their countries (Relly & González de Bustamante, 2014; Pintak & Ginges 2008; Pintak & Setiyono 2010). When rule of law is weak, journalists cannot be ensured safety and security, much less protection (Waisbord 2002, 90). Waisbord (2007) noted that 'statelessness', a condition that has largely impacted the global south, 'facilitates anti-press violence, undermines the economic basis for news organizations, and weakens the rule of law' (115).

The literature has demonstrated a significant and inverse relationship between news media rights in a country and human rights violations (Apodaca 2007), making the context in which violence is committed against journalists critical for grounding research. Scholarly work has explored how investigative journalism in some contexts straddles 'ambiguous traditions' often 'mired in cultural contradictions and economic boundaries' of local news media (Waisbord 1996, 343), all of which exacerbate conditions for journalists working in zones of conflict or swaths of countries that appear 'stateless'.

Scholars point out that impunity has been one of the most daunting challenges related to journalists' security for 'often the suspects are drawn from the very institutions and authorities responsible for upholding and enforcing a protective regime' (Heyns & Srinivasan 2013: 311). Various dimensions of impunity have been described by the Inter-American Court for Human Rights (2002, 13) as 'total lack of investigation, prosecution, capture, trial and conviction of those responsible for violations of the rights protected … in view of the fact that the State has the obligation to use all the legal means at its disposal to combat that situation'. It is becoming common knowledge that the perpetuation of anti-press violence lays at the feet of those who permit impunity to continue, and it should be noted that 'the effect of exemption from punishment of those who commit a crime', may largely play a role in repeated violations with 'arbitrary arrests and detention, enforced disappearance, harassment and intimidation' often aimed at silencing journalists (UNESCO 2014, 87).

Over time, impunity for assaulting and killing journalists in countries around the world has been identified as one of the key issues underlying the growing incidents of crimes against journalists. More specifically, Heyns and Srinivasan (2013) write that, though lack of evidence may at times be the reason that perpetrators of crimes against journalists are not pursued, 'all indications are that impunity is intentional', for a myriad of reasons, including weak criminal justice systems that have corrupt law enforcement, prosecutors and judges, and the issue of witness influence by organized crime groups and corrupt bureaucrats and politicians (326, 312). Quite simply, impunity is a dominant factor that fosters an environment that permits violence against journalists.

Social Change

For more than a decade, major news media advocacy organizations, governments, intergovernmental organizations, such as the UN affiliates, academics and others have noted the 'importance of protecting those who gather information about war' (Lisosky & Henrichsen 2009: 131). Little theorizing or research has examined this phenomenon (González de Bustamante & Relly 2014; Tumber 2006; 2011; Waisbord 2002; 2007).

In an early call for social change research, Waisbord (2002, 92, 103) asked, 'What conditions foster antipress violence? ... What solutions can be instrumented?' A myriad of 'ideal-type' responses to the violence against journalists have been written about with a combination of approaches being advocated: civil society and global pressure, judicial strength and the absence of those in opposition to change (Grossman 2015, 743). Davies and Crawford (2013, 2157) concluded from their work 'that advocacy energies would be better spent promoting enforcement of existing laws'. Lublinski et al. (2015) found in eight of the ten cases examined in Sub-Saharan Africa that journalists were able to trigger societal change through investigative journalism and interacting with actors outside of the news media. Chan and Lee (2011) found from a survey of journalists that when attitudes and beliefs of journalists cluster, they serve as a counterforce to the power centre in a jurisdiction.

More generally, scholars have found that nongovernmental organizations and the rest of civil society can be instrumental in pressing for change in human rights culture (Heyns & Srinivasan 2013; Relly & González de Bustamante 2014; Zafarullah & Rahman 2002). Waisbord (2007, 115) noted that the news media alone 'cannot address entrenched problems of violence, security, and lawlessness', yet it can monitor government responses to violence and raise awareness of violence and impunity issues.

An independent judiciary also has been suggested as a necessary force to combat human rights abuses and violations of press freedom (Ogbondah 1991). Others have noted, as well, that 'even in highly repressive societies, courts can sometimes provide useful entry points for an active civil society when it is not available in the political realm' (Heyns & Srinivasan 2013, 327). It has been noted that with increasing attention being paid to human rights around the world, the number of human rights trials have increased; however scholars have remained 'cautious regarding the impact of the age of accountability on overcoming barriers to justice' (Payne, Lessa, & Pereira 2015, 729).

Conclusion

In the nearly 70 years since the signing of Article 19 of the UN (1948) Universal Declaration of Human Rights, which outlines the right to 'seek, receive and impart information and ideas through any media', there have been concerted initiatives by the international and supranational communities to call attention to and to reduce anti-press violence. However, despite the continued efforts, anti-press violence persists and in some cases is increasing. The global community's focus on developing monitoring and enforcement tools is a new frontier, which is worthy of future theorizing and research. Scholars should follow social change in this area and adapt and develop social change frameworks for conceptual and empirical work.

References

Apodaca, C. (2007). 'The Whole World Could be Watching: Human Rights and the Media'. *Journal of Human Rights*, 6(2), pp. 147–64.

Article 19, Committee to Protect Journalists, Foundation for Press Freedom, Inter-American Press Association, International Federation of Journalists, International Media Support, International News Safety Institute, International Press Institute, Open Society Foundation – Media Programme, Reporters Without Borders, The Rory Peck Trust, UNESCO, World Association of Community Radio Broadcasters. (2008). *Press Freedom in Mexico: The Shadow of Impunity and Violence.* Available at: https://

245

www.mediasupport.org/publication/press-freedom-in-mexico-the-shadow-of-impunity-and-vio-lence/ [Accessed 6 March, 2017].

Centre for Law, Justice and Journalism (2011). *The Initiative on Impunity and the Rule of Law: A Policy Research and Advocacy Project*. Centre for Law, Justice and Journalism, City University London, and the Centre for Freedom of the Media, University of Sheffield. Available at: http://www.city.ac.uk/__data/assets/pdf_file/0014/124304/Impunity_report_9th_FINAL-August.pdf [Accessed 6 March, 2017].

Chan, J. M. and Lee, F. L. (2011). 'The Primacy of Local Interests and Press Freedom in Hong Kong: A Survey Study of Professional Journalists'. *Journalism*, 12(1), pp. 89–105.

Chu, D., and Lee, A.Y. L. (2014). 'Media Education Initiatives by Media Organizations: The Uses of Media Literacy in Hong Kong Media'. *Journalism & Mass Communication Educator*, 69(2), pp. 127–45.

Committee to Protect Journalists. (2017). '1236 Journalists Killed Since 1992'. New York: Committee to Protect Journalists. https://cpj.org/killed/

Davies, K. and Crawford, E. (2013). 'Legal Avenues for Ending Impunity for the Death of Journalists in Conflict Zones: Current and Proposed International Agreements'. *International Journal of Communication* 7, pp. 2157–77.

Freedom House (2013). *Freedom of the Press*. New York: Freedom House.

Geneva Convention (1929). Available at: https://www.icrc.org/ihl.nsf/52d68d14de6160e0c12563da005fdb1b/eb1571b00daec90ec125641e00402aa6) [Accessed 5 March, 2017].

González de Bustamante, C. and E. Relly, J. (2014). 'Journalism in Times of Violence: Social Media Use by U.S. and Mexican Journalists Working in Northern Mexico'. *Digital Journalism*, 2(4), pp. 507–23.

Grossman, C. (2012). 'Challenges to Freedom of Expression Within the Inter-American System: A Jurisprudential Analysis'. *Human Rights Quarterly*, 34(2), pp. 361–403.

Heyns, C. and Srinivasan, S. (2013). 'Protecting the Right to Life of Journalists: The Need for a Higher Level of Engagement'. *Human Rights Quarterly*, 35(2), pp. 304–332.

Howard, D. (2002). 'Remaking the Pen Mightier than the Sword: An Evaluation of the Growing Need for the International Protection of Journalists'. *Georgia Journal of International and Comparative Law*, 30(3), pp. 505–42.

Hughes, S. (2003). 'From the Inside Out How Institutional Entrepreneurs Transformed Mexican Journalism'. *The International Journal of Press/Politics*, 8(3), pp. 87–117.

Hughes, S. (2006). *Newsrooms in Conflict: Journalism and the Democratization of Mexico*, Pittsburgh: University of Pittsburgh Press.

Inter-American Court for Human Rights (2002). Bámaca Velásquez Case, Judgment of February 22, 2002, Inter-Am. Ct. H.R., (Ser. C) No. 91. https://www1.umn.edu/humanrts/iachr/C/91-ing.html [Accessed 6 March, 2017].

Kim, H.S. and Hama-Saeed, M. (2008). 'Emerging Media in Peril: Iraqi Journalism in the Post-Saddam Hussein Era'. *Journalism Studies*, 9(4), pp. 578–94.

Kim, H. S. (2010). 'Forces of Gatekeeping and Journalists' Perceptions of Physical Danger in Post-Saddam Hussein's Iraq'. *Journalism & Mass Communication Quarterly*, 87(3–4), pp. 484–500.

Kirby, M. D., and Jackson, L. J. (1986). 'International Humanitarian Law and the Protection of Media Personnel'. *University of New South Wales Law Journal*, 9(1), pp. 1–16.

Levin, E. (2013). 'Journalists as a Protected Category: A New Status for the Media in International Humanitarian Law'. *UCLA Journal of International Law & Foreign Affairs*, 17, p. 215.

Lisosky, J. M. and Henrichsen, J. (2009). 'Don't Shoot the Messenger: Prospects for Protecting Journalists in Conflict Situations'. *Media, War & Conflict*, 2(2), pp. 129–148.

Lublinski, J., Spurk, C., Fleury, J. M., Labassi, O., Mbarga, G., Nicolas, M. L. and Rizk, T. A. (2015). 'Triggering Change–How Investigative Journalists in Sub-Saharan Africa Contribute to Solving Problems in Society'. *Journalism*, 17(8), pp. 1074–1094.

Mukherjee, A. (1995). 'The Internationalization of Journalists' Rights: An Historical Analysis'. *Journal of Internationall Law & Practice*, 4, pp. 87–113.

Ogbondah, C.W. (1991). 'The Pen is Mightier than the "Koboko": A Critical Analysis of the Amakiri Case in Nigeria'. *Political Communication*, 8(2), pp. 109–24.

Park, D. (2002). 'Media, Democracy, and Human Rights in Argentina'. *Journal of Communication Inquiry* 26(3) pp. 237–60.

Payne, L. A., Lessa, F. and Pereira, G. (2015). 'Overcoming Barriers to Justice in the Age of Human Rights Accountability', *Human Rights Quarterly*, 37(3), pp. 728–54.

Pintak, L. and Ginges, J. (2009). 'Inside the Arab Newsroom: Arab Journalists Evaluate Themselves and the Competition', *Journalism Studies*, 10(2), pp. 157–77.

Pintak, L. and Setiyono, B. (2011). 'The Mission of Indonesian Journalism: Balancing Democracy, Development, and Islamic Values'. *The International Journal of Press/Politics*, 16(2), pp. 185–209.

Relly, J. E. and de Bustamante, C. G. (2014). 'Silencing Mexico A Study of Influences on Journalists in the Northern States'. *The International Journal of Press/Politics*, 19(1), pp. 108–31.

Relly, J. E., Zanger, M. and Fahmy, S. (2015). 'News Media Landscape in a Fragile State: Professional Ethics Perceptions in a Post-Ba'athist Iraq'. *Mass Communication and Society*, 18(4), pp. 471–97.

Tumber, H. (2002). 'Reporting under Fire'. In: B. Zelizer and S. Allan, eds., *Journalism after September 11*. London: Routledge.

Tumber, H. (2006). 'The Fear of Living Dangerously: Journalists who Report on Conflict'. *International Relations*, 20(4), pp. 439–51.

Tumber, H. (2011). 'Reporting under Fire: The Physical Safety and Emotional Welfare of Journalists'. In B. Zelizer and S. Allan, eds., *Journalism after September 11*. London: Routledge, pp. 247–62.

Tumber, H. and Palmer, J. (2004). Media at War: The Iraq Crisis. Thousand Oaks: Sage Publications.

Tumber, H. and Webster, F. (2006). *Journalists Under Fire: Information War and Journalistic Practices*. London: Sage.

United Nations (1948). Universal Declaration of Human Rights. Available at: http://www.un.org/en/universal-declaration-human-rights/[Accessed 6 March, 2017].

United Nations (1929). *Geneva Convention*. Available at: http://www.un-documents.net/gc-3.htm and https://www.icrc.org/eng/resources/documents/misc/57jnws.htm [accessed on 6 March, 2017].

UNESCO (2014). 'World Trends in Freedom of Expression and Media Development'. Available at: http://www.unesco.se/wp-content/uploads/2016/01/World-Trends-in-Freedom-of-Expression-and-Media-Development-2014.pdf [Accessed 6 March, 2017].

UNESCO (2015a). 'Ending Impunity for Crimes against Journalists'. Available at: http://www.unesco.org/new/en/unesco/events/prizes-and-celebrations/celebrations/international-days/int-day-to-end-impunity/international-day-to-end-impunity-2015/ [Accessed 6 March, 2017].

UNESCO (2015b). 'International Day to End Impunity for Crimes against Journalists'. Available at: http://www.un.org/en/events/journalists/background.shtml [Accessed 6 March, 2017].

Waisbord, S. R. (1996). 'Investigative Journalism and Political Accountability in South American Democracies'. *Critical Studies in Media Communication*, 13(4), pp. 343–63.

Waisbord, S. (2002). "Antipress Violence and the Crisis of the State," *The Harvard International Journal of Press/Politics*, 7(3), pp. 90–109.

Waisbord, S. (2007). 'Democratic Journalism and 'Statelessness'. *Political Communication*, 24(2), pp. 115–29.

Zafarullah, H. M. and Rahman, M. (2002). 'Human Rights, Civil Society and Nongovernmental Organizations: The Nexus in Bangladesh'. *Human Rights Quarterly*, 24(4), pp. 1011–34.

24

CIVIC ORGANIZATIONS, HUMAN RIGHTS AND THE NEWS MEDIA

Matthew Powers

Civic organizations – groups like Amnesty International and Human Rights Watch – play a key role in the production and circulation of human rights discourses (Clark 2001; Keck & Sikkink 1998). Such groups investigate potential abuses, cultivate public support on human rights issues and petition political and economic elites to end human rights violations (Dawes 2007; Hopgood 2006). In all these efforts, the news media are an essential ally. Media coverage can bring attention to neglected issues, detail the institutional processes whereby human rights violations are adjudicated, and potentially influence the actions of political and economic leaders (Krain 2012). For all these reasons, one important aspect of human rights scholarship examines the relationship between civic organizations and the news media with whom they interact. Scholars have examined the strategies civic organizations use to attract media coverage (Ron et al 2005; Waisbord 2011), the permeability of the news media to human rights messages (Ramos et al 2007; Powers 2016a), and the effects of these interactions on civic organizations, journalism and human rights discourses more generally (Cottle & Nolan 2007; Tumber 2009).

Today, changes in media, human rights and civic organizations drive growing interest in this topic. Diminished revenues have led to budget cuts at news organizations across North America and Western Europe: Foreign news bureaus – long the source of most human rights coverage – have been especially hard hit (Sambrook 2010). During this same period, human rights discourses have multiplied: Once used primarily to describe violations of bodily integrity, human rights frames are now applied to a wide range of social issues (Moyn 2010). Finally, professionalization within the advocacy sector and the proliferation of digital technologies has led civic organizations to ramp up and diversify their content offerings (Powers 2015). Taken together, these changes raise a number of important questions. Will changes in journalism open up the news gates to civic organizations interested in making the news? What types of social problems will assume the human rights frame? How and in what ways will civic organizations integrate digital tools into their established publicity efforts?

This chapter explores these questions by reviewing the available scholarship on civic organizations and the news media. It suggests that despite new developments in journalism and advocacy, civic organizations continue to face an uphill – and uneven – battle in the struggle for publicity. In order to boost their chances of making the news, these groups adapt to – rather than challenge – established news norms, and this adaptation favours political and civil violations of human rights, while downplaying economic frames. Finally, despite the potential for digital technologies to circumvent these established patterns, it suggests that such tools are used primarily to interact with journalists and protect organizational credibility, rather than explore alternative forms of public engagement. On the whole, then, the scholarship finds that in the relationship between journalism and advocacy, the news media continue to hold the upper hand in shaping human rights news.

In what follows, I begin by briefly overviewing the key changes in media, human rights and civic organizations that drive growing interest in their interrelations. I then synthesise the key findings of the available literature. I conclude by discussing potential areas for future scholarship. Specifically, I argue that three concerns deserve to be at the forefront of future inquiries on civic organizations, human rights and the news media. First, I suggest that scholarship needs to move from describing the relationship between civic organizations and the news media and develop more parsimonious explanations for the relationship. Second, I argue that empirical analyses should diversify their foci to account for human rights organizations operating at various scales (local, regional, international). Third, I underscore the need for greater normative clarity about the various benefits and drawbacks provided by civic organizations that pursue media coverage. Greater attention to these three questions, I suggest, can diversify inquiries empirically, strengthen claims analytically and clarify the normative stakes inherent in scholarship on civic organizations, the news media and human rights.

The changing contexts of media, human rights and civic organizations

Scholarly interest in the relationship between media, human rights and civic organizations arises in the context of changes within each. Consider the news media first: Across Western Europe and North America, diminished revenues have led news organizations to reduce the resources they commit to international news coverage (Sambrook 2010). Foreign news bureaus have been especially hard hit: Since the end of the Cold War, news organizations have cut back on the number of foreign news bureaus and full time staff (Kumar 2011). In their place, freelance reporters and parachute journalists are increasingly common (Hannerz 2004; International Council on Human Rights Policy 2002). As a result of these changes, news organizations find it increasingly difficult to adequately monitor international affairs with their own correspondents.

During this same period, civic organizations have undergone changes that lead them to increase both the amount and types of information they produce. For starters, many civic organizations have become institutionalized. No longer ephemeral social movements, these groups are established as durable social organizations with budgets and sizeable staffs (Lang 2013). These organizations have also professionalised, which has led them to hire staff whose expertise lies in part in their ability to produce specific information materials (e.g. research, press releases, multimedia) (Powers 2015). Finally, these organizations are increasingly competitive, as they differentiate themselves from other civic groups in pursuit of limited funds and public attention. This leads many to manage their 'brands' so as to maximise positive impact (Orgad 2013). Together, and in conjunction with digital tools that lower costs while expanding publishing options, these changes mean that civic organizations produce a greater variety of information products today than in the past, and that they place a growing emphasis on generating publicity.

In addition to these institutional changes, the discursive meanings of human rights have multiplied. For much of the 20th century, human rights discourses mostly described violations of political or civil rights (e.g. free speech, torture, illegal detention). Indeed, it was coverage of these issues that led Amnesty International to become the first non-governmental organization to win the Nobel Prize in 1977 (Clark 2001; Hopgood 2006). Today, though, human rights are used to describe a much wider range of social issues, including but not limited to business and labour rights, and environmental degradation (Moyn 2010). This discursive change means that human rights discourses may be attached to a growing number of social causes. Whether and to what extent such changes are mirrored in news coverage of human rights issues is thus an analytically important question that can help ascertain how discourses evolve over time.

Technological developments cut across these changing contexts, and create new possibilities for civic organizations to garner media attention. Where civic organizations once relied almost exclusively on the news media for publicity, today such groups have a range of tools (e.g. websites, social media accounts) at their disposal. This has led some to suggest that civic organizations may bypass the news media and directly target relevant stakeholders (Bennett and Segerberg 2013). Relatedly, others see such tools functioning as a force multiplier by allowing advocacy groups to more easily gain a voice in the media (Chadwick 2013). The precise outcome remains uncertain but the general idea is straightforward: Digital technologies are expected to diversify publicity options for civic organizations and give them a heightened degree of informational independence.

Taken together, these changes raise a number of important questions. Most basically, they raise the possibility that civic organizations may be more likely to have their messages picked up by the news media, that those messages will describe a growing number of human rights issues, and that digital tools will strengthen the capacity of civic groups to shape public awareness of human rights concerns. Beyond that, these changes also introduce debates about their potential impacts on journalism and advocacy. Some worry that the growing prevalence of civic organizations as news providers threatens to turn the news media into a platform for advocacy and fundraising (Rothmyer 2011). Others worry that the pursuit of publicity will distract civic organizations from issues with less media appeal (Cottle and Nolan 2007; Fenton 2010). In recent years, scholars have made substantial advances in answering these questions. It is to these answers to which I now turn.

What the research says

Despite the changes that have been discussed, the available research suggests that civic organizations continue to face an uphill – and highly uneven – battle in the struggle for publicity. Moreover, this research finds that in order to increase their chances of making the news, civic groups adapt to – rather than challenge – established news norms, which favours dramatic stories about political violations while eschewing coverage of economic-related human rights concerns. Finally, despite the potential for digital technologies to circumvent these established patterns, it seems that such tools to date are used primarily to interact with journalists and protect organizational credibility, rather than explore alternative forms of public engagement. Together, this scholarship portrays the relationship between civic organizations and the news media as one where journalists hold the upper hand in defining, selecting and shaping human rights news.

The most consistent finding in the available literature is that civic organizations struggle to make the news. Professional norms lead journalists to rely on government officials to set the news agenda, and this puts civic groups at a structural disadvantage in garnering publicity (Lang 2013). The journalistic beat system further reinforces this bias towards government officials, as few news organizations have dedicated human rights beats (Waisbord 2011). As a result, when civic organizations do appear in the news, they tend to be in places or on issues where the media spotlight is already shining (Ramos et al 2007). Statistical analyses have shown that this spotlight is not strictly correlated with real world human rights conditions and is instead more closely linked to topics in which American and European government officials are most interested (Hafner-Burton and Ron, 2013).

Recent cost-cutting trends in journalism do not substantially alter this pattern. While leading human rights groups appear more in the news today than twenty years ago, they continue to appear in countries where the media spotlight is already shining (Van Leuven & Joye 2014; Powers 2016a). In any given year, nearly half of all media mentions of leading human rights groups occur in just five countries (Powers 2016a). Within news stories, human rights groups appear late in articles and typically after government officials (Van Leuven & Joye 2014). Finally, freelancers, who work on a contract basis, shift between jobs for human rights groups and news organizations, but seem to privilege their journalistic identity in both roles (Conrad 2015; Wright 2015). Together, these findings show that breaking into the news continues to be an uphill struggle for most civic groups.

In addition to being uphill, research also finds that the struggle for publicity is highly uneven. A study of the prevalence of 250 human rights organizations in more than 600 news outlets finds that 10 percent of organizations account for 90 percent of all media coverage (Thrall et al 2014). This finding extends to the relationship between smaller and larger human rights organizations. In principle, larger groups are said to 'boomerang' issues from transnational settings back to local contexts (Keck and Sikkink 1998). In practice, scholars find that large human rights organizations – like Amnesty International and Human Rights Watch – typically choose issues on the basis of organizational matches more than objective need (Bob 2006; Wright 2015). This suggests that the human rights issues discussed in the mainstream media largely reflect the agenda of a few leading human rights organizations.

A second consistent finding is that civic organizations interested in attracting the media spotlight adapt to – rather than challenge – established news norms. Such groups monitor news coverage in an effort to identify human rights angles in extant news stories (Powers 2015). They also package their press releases in formats that mimic or 'clone' news formats (Fenton 2010; Waisbord 2011). These efforts are sometimes successful in capturing media attention and influencing the actions of government officials (Krain 2012). However, the broader effect seems to be a bias on the part of civic groups towards issues that emphasize conflict, celebrities and spectacles (Chouliaraki 2013). This makes more radical forms of human rights criticism – for instance, calling attention to the economic conditions underpinning various human rights issues – difficult (Fenton 2010; Cottle and Nolan 2007). In a longitudinal content analysis, Caliendo et al (1999, 64) find that NGO reporting on inhumane living conditions is 'not the kind of human-rights story that the media would generally pick up on' for the simple fact that it does not correspond to news norms of timeliness, drama and novelty.

Digital tools provide civic organizations with a seemingly endless number of ways to pursue publicity. Research shows that most groups have extended their information offerings by boosting their Web presence. Nearly all civic organizations have websites on which they publish news (Waisbord 2011). Most have social media accounts and publish a variety of multimedia items (McPherson 2015; Powers 2015). Furthermore, there is evidence to suggest that some of the larger groups see opportunities in these new technologies to target relevant stakeholders directly. Human Rights Watch, for example, regularly sends photographers to supplement their verbal reporting with visual imagery. In doing so, they hope to attract the attention of policymakers and human rights advocates sympathetic to their issues (Powers 2015). Such tools raise important questions about the types of publicity that are most effective in achieving advocacy goals: If the relevant policy makers can be targeted directly online, why struggle to get the *New York Times* to cover your issue?

For the most part, though, extant research finds that civic organizations use digital tools primarily to attract the attention of journalists and to boost their organizations' brands. One analysis of the websites and social media accounts of 100 human rights NGOs found that most used these tools to boost their extant publicity efforts by making it easier for users to donate and for journalists to find press releases (Kingston and Stam 2012). Very few of the sites provided users with information about protests to join or actions to be taken, and social media accounts are mostly oriented to capturing the attention of journalists. Interviews with communication staffers at civic organizations corroborate and extend these survey findings. Cottle and Nolan (2007, 866) note that 'today's 24/7 news environment ... demands constant updates and information on request [by journalists]', which leads digital tools to be used first and foremost to meet the needs of the news media. Related research finds civic groups worried about negative publicity, and thus reluctant to use digital tools to cultivate alternative forms of public engagement (Powers 2014).

This thus serves as a general summary of the available literature on human rights organizations and the news media. Civic organizations still wish to garner coverage in the mainstream media, even though their relative chances of doing so remain low. Cutbacks in newsroom resources may allow civic groups to appear more frequently in the news, but journalistic norms and beat structures continue to favour the statements of government officials over advocacy groups. Civic groups seem to respond to these challenges mostly by accommodating to media norms and using digital tools to pursue mainstream media coverage. These findings reflect the current state of scholarly knowledge, and this state is of course subject to change. However, the findings also raise questions about why civic organizations favour media coverage and what, normatively, scholars ought to make of these findings. It is to these and related questions to which I now turn.

Future directions

Given what we know about the relationship between human rights, civic organizations and the news media, what are possible directions for future research? Here, I will suggest three: one which touches on the need for explanation, a second which suggests a need for expanded inquiry beyond the Western world and a third which seeks to clarify the normative implications of the research findings. While hardly exhaustive, these three directions extend and in some cases correct for blind spots in the existing scholarship. Moreover, they reflect my view of where scholarship ought – and, in some cases, is – moving.

The first suggestion is for more explanation of the relationship between civic organizations and the news media. To date, much of the scholarship has focused on documenting key dimensions of this relationship (e.g. how advocacy groups elicit media attention, when they are successful). Less attention has been given to explaining these outcomes. As a result, scholars know *that* civic organizations prioritize coverage in the mainstream media, but lack a coherent explanation as to *why* this should be the case. A small but growing literature has endeavoured to provide such explanations. In my own work, I have tried to show how donor demands, organizational cultures and political environments shape the publicity strategies of civic groups (Powers 2014). While some groups remain heavily invested in garnering coverage in broadcast media, other organizations concentrate almost exclusively on placement within elite publications like the *New York Times* and *Financial Times*. These differences are not mere preferences; rather, they reflect the incentives generated by donors, political officials and organizational dynamics. Relatedly, Shani Orgad (2013) has shown how tensions within civic organizations, especially between marketing and research departments, shape the types of publicity strategies that civic organizations pursue (see also Nolan and Mikami 2012 and Waisbord 2008). By taking civic organizations as their own institutional 'field' (Bourdieu 1994), this scholarship seeks to move beyond describing the relations between civic organizations and the news media.

Clearly, more work remains to be done within this area. Surprisingly little research, for example, explores why the news media continues to minimise the contributions of civic organizations. For the most part, research has emphasized the importance of 'indexing' norms in journalism, which favour political officials. Less explored are the relationships between journalists and NGO professionals (Tumber 2009), and the structure of news beats (Waisbord 2011). Given the widespread growth of freelancing in international news, there is a need to further examine the specific mechanisms by which human rights coverage gets produced despite ongoing reductions in editorial staff (Wright's (2015) work on freelancers is very important in this regard).

A second suggestion for future scholars has to do with expanding the lens of inquiry. To a great extent, what we know about human rights and the media is limited to coverage of Amnesty International and Human Rights Watch in leading European and American news outlets. To the extent that scholars do look beyond these organizations, there is often little integration with key debates about human rights and journalism (for important exceptions see Thrall et al. 2014 and Waisbord 2011). To be sure, this state of affairs is shaped partly by convenience and cultural proximity. Amnesty International, for example, archives its materials in ways that are relatively easy for quantitatively oriented researchers to use (see e.g. Ron et al. 2005). Moreover, for many scholars, debates about changes in the news media are informed by cutbacks in Western news organizations. Given the dominant positions of both leading NGOs and news organizations, these groups are important to study in their own right.

Yet knowing the actions of leading organizations is not the same thing as grasping the larger field in which they operate. Consider the proliferation of human rights at the local, regional and international levels over the past twenty years (Moyn 2010). Apart from knowing that most appear in the news rarely, we know relatively little about their aims and strategies. To what extent are they interested in garnering media coverage? To the degree that they are, what strategies do they use in order to pursue it? What are the relationships between different groups at varying scales? The answers to these questions are important for a fuller understanding of the relationship between civic organizations and the news media more generally.

A third issue has to do with clarifying the normative stakes implicit in research on human rights organizations and the news media. Elsewhere, I have suggested that scholarly evaluations of the relationship between civic organizations and the news media oscillate between tropes of boon and bane (Powers 2016b). To some, civic organizations take seriously the ethical precepts of factual reporting and provide news coverage from locales that otherwise receive scant coverage (Schudson 2011). By contrast, others worry that the growing presence of civic organizations augur a troubling conflation of the lines separating journalism from advocacy, with worrisome consequences befalling both parties as a result (Cottle and Nolan 2007; Fenton 2010; Rothmyer 2011). Each of these arguments contains elements of truth, as the civic sector and the news media are too diverse to be captured by any one overarching argument. What this lacks, however, is a direct engagement with the values underpinning evaluations on either side of the debate. This blind spot makes it difficult to move beyond the current debate.

Normative theories of public communication provide an important tool that can be used in these debates. Such theories specify the roles that journalists and advocates are tasked with assuming in order to satisfy their civic obligations. Such roles are not singular; instead, arguments about the role of advocacy groups and journalists are linked broader ideals of democratic governance (Benson 2008). With respect to human rights organizations, I have suggested that normative theories identify at least four distinct roles: an expert role associated with the representative liberal tradition and oriented primarily towards norms of accuracy and transparency in gathering and distributing information; an advocacy role drawn from participatory democracy and geared towards a norm of public awareness; a facilitative role rooted in discursive ethics that encourages reasoned exchanges across diverse social groups; and a critical role found in radical democratic theory that aims to expose systemic injustices (Powers 2016b).

Obviously, these four theories merely scratch the surface of potential normative frameworks for evaluating the actions of civic organizations. In suggesting them, my aim is less to say whether advocacy groups are a boon or bane for public communication; instead, I want to explore which types of public communication their efforts seem most likely to support. At this juncture, and based on my reading of the literature, it seems that civic organizations most often perform roles associated with representative liberal and democratic participatory models. They do this by emphasizing their roles as experts and awareness-raising advocates. By contrast, discursive and radical norms, which require facilitative and critical roles, seem to be less frequently achieved. How and in what ways this may change as a result of ongoing transformations in journalism and advocacy is a question for future scholarship.

Conclusion

This chapter has reviewed extant scholarship examining the relationship between civic organizations and the news media. Despite changes in journalism, advocacy and human rights discourses, this research suggests that civic organizations continue to face substantial and uneven challenges in garnering media attention. In order to attract the media spotlight, most groups develop publicity strategies that adapt to media norms and biases. As a result, human rights news tends to focus on issues that emphasize conflict, spectacle and celebrities, while downplaying economic frames for understanding human rights issues. Finally, while digital tools in principle provide civic organizations with ways to bypass the news media, most research suggests that to date such tools are utilized primarily to attract the attention of journalists and to promote and protect the organizational brands of civic organizations.

Scholars of human rights organizations and the news media are still working to put together a parsimonious explanation for this state of affairs. In this chapter, I have highlighted the need for accounts that move beyond description and towards explanation of the relationship between civic organizations and the news media. Beyond that, I have also suggested that future research can do to more expand from its usual focus on leading human rights organizations and elite news media providers and incorporate advocacy and news organizations working at various scales on human rights issues. Finally, I have suggested that while normative concerns implicitly lie at the heart of much scholarship, evaluations of scholarly findings could be made far more explicit. There is genuine excitement about the potential for advocacy groups to find a greater voice in the news as a result of changes in journalism and advocacy. At the same time, sceptics express reasonable concerns about the impacts of these developments on journalism and advocacy, respectively. Rather than decide the issue in general, I have suggested that scholarship can advance by examining the various dimensions on which advocates and journalists do – and do not – approximate the roles and responsibilities set out for them in normative theories of public communication. Such theories will not settle debates once for all; they should, however, clarify the stakes involved in such debates.

References

Bennett, W. L. and Segerberg, A. (2013). *The Logic of Connective Action*. Cambridge: Cambridge University Press.
Benson, R. (2008). 'Normative Theories of Journalism'. In: W. Donsbach, ed., *The Blackwell International Encyclopedia of Communication*. New York: Blackwell, pp. 2591–97.
Bob, C. (2006). *The Marketing of Rebellion*. Cambridge: Cambridge University Press.
Bourdieu, P. (1994). *The Field of Cultural Production*. New York: Columbia University Press.

Caliendo, S., Gibney, M. and Payne, A. (1999). 'All the News that's Fit to Print: New York Times Coverage of Human-rights Violations'. *International Journal of Press/Politics* 4(4), pp. 48–69.

Chadwick, A. (2013). *The Hybrid Media System*. New York: Oxford University Press.

Chouliaraki, L. (2013). *The Ironic Spectator*. Cambridge: Polity.

Clark, A. M. (2001). *Diplomacy of Conscience*. Princeton NJ: Princeton University Press.

Cottle, S. and Nolan, D. (2007). 'Global Humanitarianism and the Changing Media-aid Field'. *Journalism Studies* 8(6), pp. 862–78.

Conrad, D. (2015). 'The Freelancer-NGO Alliance: What a Story of Kenyan Waste Reveals About Contemporary Foreign News Production'. *Journalism Studies* 16(2), pp. 27–288.

Dawes, J. (2007). *That the World May Know*. Cambridge, MA: Harvard University Press.

Fenton, N. (2010). 'NGOs, New Media and the Mainstream News'. In: N. Fenton, ed., *New media, old news*. Sage, London, pp. 153–68.

Gore, W. (2009). 'Privacy and the PCC - adapting to changing circumstances'. *Press Complaints Commission*. Available from: http://www.pcc.org.uk/news/index.html?article=NjA3OQ== [Accessed 20 May, 2012].

Hafner-Burton, E. and Ron, J. (2013). 'The Latin Bias: Regions, the Anglo-American Media, and Human Rights'. *International Studies Quarterly* 57(3), pp. 474–91.

Hannerz, U. (2004). *Foreign News*. Chicago: University of Chicago Press.

Hopgood, S. (2006). *Keepers of the Flame*. Ithaca, NY: Cornell University Press.

International Council on Human Rights Policy (2002). *Journalism, Media and the Challenge of Human Rights Reporting*. Available from: http://www.ichrp.org/files/reports/14/106_report_en.pdf [Accessed 28 Mar. 2016].

Keck, M. and Sikkink, K. (1998). *Activists Beyond Borders*. Ithaca, NY: Cornell University Press.

Kingston, L. N. and Stam, K. R. (2012). 'Online Advocacy: Analysis of Human Rights NGO Websites.' *Journal of Human Rights Practice* 5(1), pp. 75–95.

Krain, M. (2012). 'J'accuse! Does Naming and Shaming Perpetrators Reduce the Severity of Genocides or Politicides?'. *International Studies Quarterly* 56(3), pp. 574–89.

Kumar, P. (2011). 'Shrinking Foreign Coverage'. *American Journalism Review*, December/January. Available at: http://ajrarchive.org/article.asp?id=4998. [Accessed 8 Mar. 2016].

Lang, S. (2013). *NGOs, Civil Society and the Public Sphere*. Cambridge: Cambridge University Press.

McPherson, E. (2015). 'Advocacy Organizations' Evaluations of Social Media Information for NGO Journalism'. *American Behavioral Scientist* 59(1), pp. 124–48.

Moyn, S. (2010). *The Last Utopia*. Cambridge, MA: Harvard University Press.

Nolan, D. and Mikami, A. (2012). 'The Things That We Have to Do: Ethics and Instrumentality in Humanitarian Communication'. *Global Media and Communication* 9(1), pp. 53–70.

Orgad, S. (2013). 'Visualizers of Solidarity: Organizational Politics in Humanitarian and International Development NGOs'. *Visual Communication* 12(3), pp. 295–314.

Powers, M. (2014). 'The Structural Organization of NGO Publicity: Explaining Divergent Publicity Strategies at Humanitarian and Human Rights Organizations'. *International Journal of Communication* 8(1), pp. 90–107.

Powers, M. (2015). 'The New Boots on the Ground: NGOs in the Changing Landscape of International News'. *Journalism: Theory, Practice & Criticism*. Available at: http://jou.sagepub.com/content/early/2015/01/27/1464884914568077 [Accessed 8 Mar. 2016].

Powers, M. (2016a). 'Opening the News Gates? Humanitarian and Human Rights NGOs in the American News Media, 1990-2010'. *Media, Culture & Society* 38(3), pp. 315–31.

Powers, M. (2016b). 'Beyond Boon or Bane: Using Normative Theories to Evaluate the Newsmaking Efforts of NGOs'. *Journalism Studies*. Available at: http://www.tandfonline.com/doi/abs/10.1080/1461670X.2015.1124733 [Accessed 9 Mar. 2016].

Ramos, H., Ron, J. and Thoms, O. (2007). 'Shaping the Northern Media's Human Rights Coverage, 1986-2000'. *Journal of Peace Research* 44(4), pp. 385–406.

Ron, J., Ramos, H. and Rodgers, K. (2005). 'Transnational Information Politics NGO Human Rights Reporting, 1986-2000', *International Studies Quarterly* 49(3), pp. 557–88.

Rothmyer, K. (2011). 'Hiding the Real Africa: Why NGOs Prefer Bad News'. *Columbia Journalism Review*, 17 March. Available at: http://www.cjr.org/reports/hiding_the_real_africa.php [Accessed 8 Mar. 2016].

Sambrook, R. (2010). 'Are Foreign Correspondents Redundant? The Changing Face of International News'. *Reuters Institute for the Study of Journalism*. Available at: http://reutersinstitute.politics.ox.ac.uk/publication/are-foreign-correspondents-redundant [Accessed 8 Mar. 2016].

Schudson, M. (2011). *The Sociology of News*. New York: Norton.

Thrall T., Stecula, D. and Sweet D. (2014). 'May We Have Your Attention Please? Human-rights NGOs and the Problem of Global Communication'. *International Journal of Press/Politics* 19(2), pp. 135–59.

Tumber, H. (2009). 'Journalists and War Crimes'. In: S. Allan ed., *The Routledge Companion to News and Journalism*. New York: Routledge, pp. 533–41.

Van Leuven, S. and Joye, S. (2014). 'Civil Society Organizations at the Gates? A Gatekeeping Study of Newsmaking Efforts by NGOs and Government Institutions'. *International Journal of Press/Politics* 19(2), pp. 160–85.

Waisbord, S. (2008). 'The Institutional Challenges of Participatory Communication in International Aid'. *Social Identities* 4(4), pp. 505–22.

Waisbord, S. (2011). 'Can NGOs Change the News?', *International Journal of Communication*, 5(1), pp. 142–65.

Wright, K. (2015). 'These Grey Areas: How and Why Freelance Works Blurs INGOs and News Organizations'. *Journalism Studies*. Available at: http://www.tandfonline.com/doi/abs/10.1080/14616 70X.2015.1036904 [Accessed 9 Mar. 2016].

25

RIGHTS AND RESPONSIBILITIES WHEN USING USER-GENERATED CONTENT TO REPORT CRISIS EVENTS

Glenda Cooper

On 26 December 2004 when the tsunami struck, none of Reuters' 2,300 journalists or 1,000 stringers were on the beaches. 'For the first 24 hours', Tom Glocer, the former head of Reuters pointed out: 'the best and the only photos and video came from tourists armed with telephones, digital cameras and camcorders. And if you didn't have those pictures, you weren't on the story' (Glocer 2006). By the time the Nepal earthquake happened a decade later, video of the scene was posted within minutes on YouTube. Drone footage, and live streaming by the Periscope app were used by the media and there was even a tie-up between the BBC and the chat app Viber (Reid 2015).

Use of user-generated content (UGC)[1] by mainstream media outlets has risen dramatically, particularly in crisis events and humanitarian disasters where dramatic stills and video taken by onlookers is often considered 'more newsworthy than professional content' (Hermida & Thurman 2008, 344). The result however has often been a smash-and-grab approach with insufficient consideration by journalists about how to treat the creators of this content. This chapter aims to address some of the key issues that journalists now face when considering the human rights of the people who create such content, and the responsibilities these media outlets have when distributing it more widely than the creator ever thought possible.

Of particular interest are the rights to privacy, intellectual property and freedom of expression. These are well-established rights both legally and normatively in traditional journalism, but the use of content created by ordinary people has thrown up new issues. Different countries have different legal regimes but these are universal issues. In this chapter, I will focus on UK and European examples, using as a basis the European Convention on Human Rights and in particular, Article 8 (which states that everyone has the right to respect for private and family life, home and correspondence), Article 1 Protocol 1 (which states that everyone has the right to peaceful enjoyment of possessions) and Article 10 (which provides the right to freedom of expression). But this is meant as a starting point for debate rather than a comprehensive legal summary, and any discussion should go further than specific legal regimes to encompass professional and self-regulatory norms.

Intellectual property

As the earthquake struck Haiti on 12 January 2010, Daniel Morel took photographs that would appear on front pages around the world, thanks to the decision he made a couple of hours later to post them via Twitpic.[2]

Morel had a four-year fight in the courts to successfully prove that AFP and Getty who had picked them up and distributed them to their clients had infringed his copyright by lifting his pictures from Twitter (Estrin 2013)[3]. But Morel was not an 'accidental journalist' – someone caught up in the disaster, and posting on social media because he had nowhere else to display his work. If it took Morel, an experienced former Associated Press photographer, nearly four years to resolve this, creators of UGC who upload pictures rather than sell them directly are even more vulnerable.

Key questions that journalists who use other people's video, photographs or tweets should be asking themselves are as follows:

> What is the nature of the work?
> Is it copyright protected?
> Who was the author, and who is the rightful owner?
> What might exceptions/defences to copyright protection be?
> What possible problems with reuse and linking might there be?

The nature of the work (whether it is a photograph, film clip, sound or text) is significant because different rules often apply to different forms of content. For example (as discussed more fully later) in the UK regime there is no 'fair dealing' defence for photographs.

But can a UGC work be copyright protected? Certainly, copyright is protected under Article 1 Protocol 1 of the European Convention of Human Rights (ECHR) as a property right. But content created in the aftermath of a disaster is often hurried, muddled and unedited – it is not carefully designed or created. But copyright often focuses on the *expression* of an idea rather than the idea itself, and does not concern itself with the quality or merit of a piece of work. So judgments from the European Court of Justice (ECJ) may favour creators of UGC. For example, in the case of *Painer v Standard Verlags GmbH & Ors* [ECJ, 2011], Eva-Maria Painer, who had taken a portrait of Natascha Kampusch[4], and then found it reproduced without her consent in newspapers successfully sued media companies saying she was entitled to copyright. Pertinent to UGC creators, the court ruled that because Painer had chosen how to frame the shot, the angle and the atmosphere, and then also selected which snapshot to use afterwards, even a standard portrait could be protected by copyright.

In fact, the main problem may be establishing authorship – both for creators claiming ownership or mainstream media looking for permissions in fast-moving news events. This goes further than copyright and also embraces moral rights as well (that is, rights of attribution, the right to have it published anonymously or pseudonymously and the integrity of the work).

The 2016 Brussels terror attacks saw a case in point. Anna Ahronheim, a defence correspondent with a Middle East TV channel, shared a video on Twitter of the explosions at the airport. It was retweeted nearly 27,000 times and Ahronheim was commonly credited with it – even though she had merely taken the video from a WhatsApp group. Even after the social news agency Storyful tracked down the real creator, Pinchas Kopferstein, and Ahronheim tweeted 'Just FYI, this is NOT my video. Im [sic] not in #Brussels. It was shared with me on whatsapp. I dont have a name for credit but please DONT use mine',[5] she was still commonly credited (Cobben 2016).

David Clinch, of Storyful concluded that journalists were asking the wrong questions when seeking to establish the ownership of such content:

> Instead of asking 'can we use it?' journalists need to ask: where does this video come from, where were you when this happened? Do you have any other images to show that you were there?
>
> *(quoted in Cobben 2016)*

Agencies such as Scoopt and Demotix (now both defunct) were set up to help UGC creators get credit or earn money for their work. Storyful, continues to search, verify and distribute UGC. But it has subscription agreements with newsrooms such as the BBC, *Wall Street Journal*, and ABC (the company itself was bought by News Corp) and thus its focus is more on providing verified content to the traditional media, rather than focusing on the UGC creators. In its frequently asked questions page, Storyful says it does not sell content or make a commission, it instead 'requests permission to use content … on behalf of our clients' (storyful.com/faq).

Defences

When newsworthy stories need reporting, there are however defences to copyright – principally the media's right to freedom of expression and, in the UK, what is known as 'fair dealing'. In the first case, the media often mounts a vigorous defence. To take one example, in *British Broadcasting Corporation (in the case of HM Advocate v Kimberley Mary Hainey) Petitioners* [ScotHC 2012] the BBC argued that in a high-profile case the judge should release pictures of a murdered two-year-old otherwise it was an unjustifiable interference with the media and public's right to freedom of expression under Article 10. These photographs had been shown to the jury, but were not originally given to the media because the it was argued that the copyright was owned by Kimberley Hainey, who had taken the pictures (and who was also on trial for her son's murder[6]).

Lord Woolman ordered the release of six photographs citing *Ashdown v Telegraph Group Ltd* [EWCA 2001] and *Tarsasag A Szabadsagjogokert v Hungary* [ECHR 2011] as allowing greater press freedom and making sure the 'law cannot allow arbitrary restrictions which may become a form of indirect censorship' (para 27, cited by Lord Woolman in para 37).

The media in the UK (and similar jurisdictions such as Australia, Canada and New Zealand) also have another defence for infringing copyright – what is known as 'fair dealing'. Less flexible than the US concept of fair use, fair dealing covers use of copyrighted material for research, criticism and reviews, parodies but most pertinently for news reporting. Photographs however are exempted from this.

This debate came to the fore after coverage of three nights of rioting in London in August 2011, when the BBC used pictures posted on people's Twitter feeds to illustrate the mayhem. Andy Mabbett, a blogger, took issue with a BBC report on 6 August, which used pictures labelled 'from Twitter'. Mabbett wrote to the BBC, complaining:

> You may have found them via that website but they would have been hosted elsewhere and taken by other photographers, whom you did not name and whose copyright you may have breached. You have done this with other recent news stories such as the Oslo attacks. This is not acceptable. In future, please give proper credit to photographers.
>
> *(Mabbett 2011)*

A representative of the BBC initially replied:

> Twitter is a social network platform which is available to most people who have a computer and therefore any content on it is not subject to the same copyright laws as it is already in the public domain.
>
> *(Cited in Mabbett 2011)*

However, following an outraged response from Mabbett, the then BBC News social media editor, Chris Hamilton, admitted the corporation's initial response was inaccurate. He said that the BBC always made strenuous efforts to reach copyright holders although 'in exceptional situations, i.e. a major news story, where there is a strong public interest in making a photo available to a wide audience, we may seek clearance after we've first used it' (Hamilton 2011).

Reuse, linking and consent

But is it fair to (re)publish work from Internet sites with the defence of reporting current events, if that material was not initially made widely available? It may seem self-evident that anything on an Internet site is already published, and the Court of Justice of the European Union's ruling in *Svensson v Retriever Sverige AB* [EUECJ, 2014a] was that once content has been made available to the public, it does not breach copyright to make it available by linking to it.

This may be the legal position. But it can be argued that the originator did not intend for it to be published more widely – and that journalists should bear in mind the intentions of the creator and the impact of reuse particularly when caught up in such traumatic events.

Consent as it applies to journalism practice goes beyond legal constraints and raises peculiarly difficult problems, especially in the aftermath of disasters when an eyewitness/survivor/victim's ability to fully comprehend the consequences of what they are doing may be diminished. And while obtaining consent is a basic ethical requirement for journalists, it is often implicitly rather than explicitly understood.

Muller (2013, 37), in his investigation into the 2009 Australian 'Black Saturday' bushfires, puts forward the idea of the 'four abilities' model described by Grisso and Appelbaum (1998, cited in Muller, 2013). This measures people's capacity to consent by assessing their ability: 1) to make a choice; 2) understand the meaning of what is being proposed; 3) to appreciate the implications and consequences; and, 4) when equipped with the necessary facts, to be able to arrive at a reasoned decision.

Muller (2013, 39–42) talked to the survivors of the fires and found that while most had ability 1, not everyone had abilities 2 and 3, and ability 4 was almost entirely absent. The journalist therefore has to take responsibility for recognising and respecting a survivor's autonomy.

At this point, some researchers may feel it is wrong for journalists to approach survivors; however, in an important news story such as a humanitarian crisis, it would be wrong to erase the voices of the victims and leave them silent.

Privacy

When a crime, tragedy or natural disaster occurred in the past, a journalist was faced with rites of passage: the doorstep and the death knock[7] confronting the survivors or their families face to face. The growth of social networking sites has changed all this. Any 'collect' [a family photograph from the past] in the media these days is likely to have come from Facebook. As Paul Fievez, a former night picture editor wrote:

> Within seconds of a story breaking, news and picture desks are all assigning reporters, photographers and picture researchers to log in to Facebook, Twitter, Linked-In, Friends Reunited. All of the other social networks and personal websites are Googled and scoured for pictures and information.
>
> *(Fievez 2011)*

Unlike other jurisdictions, the law of England did not specifically recognise a right to privacy until 2 October 2000 when the *Human Rights Act 1998* came into effect, so the media and the courts are still wrestling with weighing up the conflicting needs of the ECHR's Article 8 guaranteeing a right to privacy, and Article 10 which safeguards freedom of expression.

Initially Article 8 seemed to take precedence, particularly following *von Hannover v Germany* [ECHR 2004] (in which the ECHR ruled respect for the private life of Princess Caroline of Monaco had been breached by photographs of her shopping or on holiday in public places), *McKennitt v Ash* [EWHC 2005] in which a folk singer attempted to stop publication of a former employee's book about their friendship and *CC v AB* [EWHC 2006] when a prominent sportsman secured an injunction after a betrayed husband wanted to publicise the sportsman's adulterous relationship with his wife.

But subsequent cases have seen the pendulum swing back to Article 10 favouring freedom of expression, – those of *Axel Springer AG v Germany* [ECHR 2012a] and *Von Hannover v Germany no 2* [ECHR 2012b]. In the first, the European Court of Human Rights ruled that Article 10 was violated after the German newspaper *Bild* was prevented from revealing the arrest and conviction of a well-known actor for drugs possession. In the second, *Frau im Spiegel* had taken pictures of Princess Caroline on a skiing holiday while her father was very ill; she claimed this was a breach of Article 8, but the court ruled that the photographs contributed to a debate in the public interest.

These cases however were focused on public figures. What about ordinary members of the public? To take one possible scenario: if someone films the survivor of an earthquake which is then used by the BBC and viewed by millions, has privacy been breached?

Peck v UK [ECHR 2003] suggests that those who use UGC of dramatic events without seeking the permission of those they feature may lay themselves open to legal action. This case revolved around a man called Geoffrey Peck who was suffering from depression and tried to commit suicide on his local high street. But the local council had installed CCTV, and when an operator saw what was happening, s/he called summoned medical help. To show how useful CCTV could be, the council later released both photographs and short clips to local newspapers and TV.

The ECHR found that releasing these images without Peck's consent, and without masking his identity sufficiently infringed his right to privacy under Article 8.

This has however been seen as a problematic case. First it could be argued that natural disasters have a public dimension that suicides usually do not. Second, Robertson and Nicol argue that Peck '*created* a public event by his actions' (2007, 275) [their emphasis]. The reality is, though, that courts would have to consider Peck's case in weighing up any action taken by for example, an earthquake victim, clearly in distress, broadcast on the evening news.

This argument came into focus again in 2015 after the use of Jordi Mir's footage in the aftermath of the attacks on the Charlie Hebdo offices in Paris. He had filmed the attackers Cherif and Said Kouachi in the act of killing a police officer, Ahmed Merabet and uploaded the video onto Facebook, before deleting it 15 minutes later (Satter 2015). By then, however, he had lost control of the film: it had been uploaded to YouTube and widely used. Merabet's brother later said they were traumatised by the continual reuse of the footage, and attacked journalists, saying:

How dare you take that video and broadcast it? I heard his voice. I recognized him. I saw him get slaughtered and I hear him get slaughtered every day. (Alexander, 2015) Mir, who said his decision to upload had been a 'stupid reflex reaction' turned down offers of payment, while authorising some media organisations to use the film as long as they cut the moment of death; some, he said, continued to run it without permission (Satter 2015; Sargent 2015).

These discussions around privacy encompass self-regulatory and sociological considerations here too. As the privacy theorist Helen Nissenbaum points out, the fundamental problem with social media is a breakdown in what she calls 'contextual integrity' (Nissenbaum 2004, 138).

Nissenbaum explains that privacy means different things in different situations, and that it is violated when people do not respect two types of contextual norms – those of appropriateness (what information may be shared) and those of flow and distribution (with whom the information is shared). Grimmelmann (2009) calls this a 'flattening' of relationships – the erosion of the fine divisions in social relationships that there are in real life. When material is pilfered from social networking sites by the media, then this transgression of contextual norms is taken even further.

In the most extreme cases, this can result in widespread vilification and even loss of a job and social status, as in the case of Lindsey Stone. Her bad-taste photograph in which she pretended to shout and swear in front of a sign asking for silence and 'respect' at the Arlington National Cemetery, led to her being 'trolled' and then fired after it was shared widely online (Ronson 2015). Zimmer (2010), in his critique of the contextual privacy failings of the Taste, Ties and Time case[8], concludes:

> Future researchers must ... recog[nize] that just because personal information is made available in some fashion on a social network does not mean it is fair game for capture and release to all.
>
> *(Zimmer 2010, 323)*

For those who have found images and text scattered over the media in the aftermath of a traumatic situation, self-regulation in the UK at least has offered scant comfort. The former regulator, the Press Complaints Commission took the view that there should be an expectation that information posted online should not be republished 'unless they, and/or the information they have published, are newsworthy' (Gore 2009) – but that definition of 'newsworthiness' was broad. This led to the PCC's upholding newspaper's rights to publish of a civil servant's tweets about feeling hungover at work, a serving police officer's view on the death of Ian Tomlinson at the G20 protests[9] – despite the comments being behind strict privacy settings and even a spoof MySpace page written by an Oxford student who went on to kill himself.

The PCC did rule there were limits – most seriously in the Mullan case concerning survivors of the Dunblane massacre[10] – where it was made clear that it was not acceptable to trawl the net for information.

At the time of writing, the Independent Press Standards Organisation (IPSO), the PCC's 'successor', had not dealt with many cases involving social media, (personal communication, 10 November 2015), although it did uphold a complaint of breach of privacy in *A woman v Lancashire Evening Post* (2015) where pixelated (non-sexual) photographs of children taken from Facebook had been used to illustrate a story about how these pictures had been found on a file-sharing website for paedophiles.

The General Data Protection Regulation, which has just come into force may help with its 'right to be forgotten' (that is, to delete data that was previously publically available from social networking sites) and the need to have more explicit consent to process private information. This is in the aftermath of cases such as *Google v Costeja Gonzales* [EUECJ 2014b] – Mario

Costeja Gonzales had fought for home foreclosure notices from a decade earlier to be deleted. After the ruling, Google rapidly launched an online form by which members of the public could identify search links that were irrelevant, outdated, inadequate, inaccurate or without public interest. By March 2015, nearly 220,000 requests to 'be forgotten' had been made to Google, 95 per cent of them by private citizens (Tippman & Powles 2015).

While there have been concerns from academics about the way Google has taken the initiative and about lack of transparency over the delisting process (Goodman 2015), it is possible that the right to be forgotten could be used by people who find their social media content and profiles used (or abused) by mainstream media in the aftermath of traumatic events.

Defamation

Disasters are moments of crisis, and high drama. The stories that the media often tell include heroism – but also cowardice, bad behaviour and even corruption. There is also considerable potential for the producers of the content themselves to defame someone online.

A common story in the aftermath of a disaster is the amount of looting that goes on – as was the case after the Haiti earthquake, for example (Pilkington 2010). What if someone – whether through genuine belief or otherwise – tweeted, retweeted, put up a picture on Flickr or video on YouTube insinuating that a clearly identified person had been involved in looting – and it was then republished by a mainstream media site?

These problems are still being debated. In the UK, for example, tweeters should be aware that the Defamation Act 2013 covers anything on the Internet and any forms of electronic communication. They may also want to bear in mind cases of 'Twibel' (defamation via Twitter), such as *Cairns v Modi* [EWHC 2012] [11] in which a New Zealand cricketer received £75,000 for a defamatory comment about match-fixing, despite the fact the tweet had only been seen by 65 people and the website by 1,000.

Perhaps the most well-known case in the UK is Lord McAlpine's action against Sally Bercow (EWHC 2013) after her tweet 'Why is Lord McAlpine trending? *innocent face*' (in relation to false claims of sex abuse). The wife of the Speaker of the House of Commons eventually settled out of court, paying undisclosed damages after the tweet was ruled to be defamatory in a preliminary ruling.

But it is not just the tweeter who risks a suit. Websites – including media organisations – which allow derogatory tweets or online messages to be put on their sites, may also find themselves liable. In the UK, 'secondary' publishers such as Internet service providers (ISPs) can avoid liability for defamation under provisions in the E-Commerce Regulations if they are 'mere conduits' – i.e. they do not initiate the transmission of defamatory comments, select who receives the comments or select or modify information – although if alerted to such material they must act 'expeditiously' to ensure the information is deleted or access disabled.

The problem was this provided a clear disincentive for website operators to actively moderate their sites. To try to deal with this, the UK's Defamation Act 2013 gave website operators a new defence for defamation: if the ISP can 'show that it was not the operator who posted the statement on the website' then it would be for the claimant to pursue the person who actually put up the UGC. So in the Lord McAlpine case, for example, he pursued Sally Bercow and other tweeters for their defamatory comments. However, if the claimant can prove it is not possible for them to identify the person who posted the statement, s/he can give the website a notice of complaint which the operator must respond to.

In cases of serious online defamation, most website owners act rapidly – for example, Twitter quickly took down numerous tweets in the McAlpine case. The problem is in the greyer areas – is something defamatory or honest comment? – and when anonymous posters do not identify themselves. In the aftermath of a humanitarian disaster, there could be comments from whistle-blowers or ordinary members of the public questioning the aid effort or why so many people have been affected.

Finally, instead of putting defamatory comments directly on a website, people might put up hyperlinks to such material instead. In the Canadian case *Crookes v Newton* [SCC 2011] the Supreme Court ruled that merely including hyperlinks to defamatory material is not equivalent to publishing that content; instead such links should be considered similar to footnotes or references. Only when a hyperlinker presents content in a way that actually repeats the defamatory content will s/he be considered a publisher and be potentially liable.

Conclusion

In the aftermath of the 7/7 bombings, John Naughton wrote of his concern at the idea of 'cameraphone ghouls' (Naughton 2005), whose first reaction was to film the tunnels and the injured after escaping serious injury themselves. A decade on, Tony Kemp, the first medic at the scene of the Shoreham air crash in August 2015, said those who did the same there were in 'shock' and 'victims' too, while police warned against posting such graphic footage online (Merrill 2015).

Despite Naughton's disgust, user-generated content is now a firmly established part of disaster reporting in the mainstream media. The idea of reporting an earthquake, a tsunami, a flood or a cholera outbreak and not using footage filmed or tweets written by amateurs seems unthinkable for most media professionals. The result has been a laissez-faire attitude to the public's words and images, often while paying lip service to consent, privacy and taste.

While copyright has been more widely accepted in the use of images, with text it continues to be contentious and the application of copyright law to user-generated content remains sketchy. The basics of consent – even with no monetary recompense at stake – still appears to be a fraught area, with confusion over whether republishing requires additional permission.

With successive cases, privacy appears to have moved on from the argument that if putting something online means that it is fair game for the media to reproduce it to considering the implications of the ability to send an impulsive tweet or picture around the world in seconds. But the complications of other people's access to an individual's online pictures, coupled with the idea that a new artefact may be created once an image or post has been shared and commented on, that is completely devoid of context, means that much still rests on normative and deontological journalistic approaches.

At the time of writing there is little empirical data on whether 'Twibel' defamation cases are on the increase, but the potential for such defamation remains high. What may also need to be considered is the fact that caution by ISPs may result in the deletion of fair comments (such as why an aid effort took so long to get through, the role of a government minister in safety regulations, a whistle-blower's account of the housing that could not withstand an earthquake)

Finally there is one last issue to be considered. The growth of apps such as Periscope suggest that our chances of being confronted by graphic content is higher – and for families or survivors to see distressing scenes played on over and over again. So this new ability of a citizen, to establish him or herself as a co-witness, is not the same as controlling how a story is framed.

All too often, the focus is on obtaining copyright approval rather than engaging in a conversation with a (possibly) traumatised individual. Rarely, it seems, do journalists think about what it is like for an eyewitness to be repeatedly contacted on Twitter or Facebook after being caught up in a disaster. While the legal and regulatory aspects need to be considered, and intellectual property, privacy and freedom of expression as outlined by the ECHR and other conventions need to be respected, in these particularly traumatic stories, journalists should also bear in mind the situation the creator of content finds themselves in; just because they are meeting them online rather than face to face.

Notes

1 The term 'user-generated content' is highly contested, with many alternatives being suggested, including 'citizen journalism', 'citizen witnessing' and 'accidental journalism', but it is generally accepted as the least bad option. In this context I am using as a basis the OECD's definition – that it requires some kind of creative effort, publication and it is created outside normal professional routines and practices – i.e. it is produced by non-professionals, 'without expectation of profit or remuneration but the primary goals being to connect with peers, level of fame and desire to express oneself' (OECD 2007).
2 A website that allows people to post pictures on to Twitter.
3 Morel successfully sued AFP and Getty Images – see *Agence France Press v Morel* [S.D.N.Y. 2014]. He won $1.22m after a jury ruled that the organisations had willfully infringed his copyright of eight pictures.
4 The Austrian kidnap victim who was held in a cellar for eight years before escaping in 2006.
5 This second tweet was retweeted 10 times in comparison by 8 April 2016.
6 Her conviction was later quashed on appeal in 2013.
7 These shorthand terms refer to a reporter waiting outside someone's house for a comment, or trying to persuade a grieving family to talk about the deceased.
8 Researchers used Facebook to carry out a longitudinal study into undergraduates in an unidentified New England private college (Lewis et al, 2008). It was quickly identified as Harvard and thus students themselves could be identified.
9 A newspaper vendor who died in the 2009 G20 summit protests. An inquest later ruled he had been unlawfully killed.
10 Mullan, Weir, Campbell (PCC, 2009). The *Sunday Express* had trawled Facebook for comments and pictures made by the Dunblane survivors as they turned 18, and wrote a piece criticising their drinking habits.
11 Cairns was also subsequently found not guilty in a perjury case (Norquay, 2015).

References

Alexander, H. (2015). *Funeral for French Policeman Ahmed Merabet Held in Paris*. Available at: http://www.telegraph.co.uk/news/worldnews/europe/france/11338404/Funeral-for-French-policeman-Ahmed-Merabet-held-in-Paris.html [Accessed 18 April, 2016].
Cobben, I. (2016). *Mass Misattribution of Viral Brussels Video*. Available at: http://blog.wan-ifra.org/2016/03/24/mass-misattribution-of-viral-brussels-video [Accessed 8 April, 2016].
ECJ (2011). *Painer v Standard Verlags GmbH* [2011] EUECJ C-145/10. Available at: http://www.bailii.org/eu/cases/EUECJ/2011/C14510.html [Accessed 5 March, 2017].
ECHR (2003). *Peck v the United Kingdom* [2003] ECHR 44. Available at: http://www.bailii.org/eu/cases/ECHR/2003/44.html [Accessed 5 March, 2017].
ECHR (2004). *Von Hannover v Germany* [2004] EMLR 21. Available at: http://www.bailii.org/eu/cases/ECHR/2012/228.html [Accessed 5 March, 2017].
ECHR (2011). *Társaság A Szabadságjogokért v Hungary* (2011) 53 EHRR 3, [2009].
ECHR 618 Available at: http://www.bailii.org/eu/cases/ECHR/2009/618.html [Accessed 5 March, 2017].
ECHR (2012a). *Axel Springer AG v Germany* [2012] EMLR 15. Available at: http://www.bailii.org/eu/cases/ECHR/2004/294.html [Accessed 5 March, 2017].
ECHR (2012b). *Von Hannover v. Germany (no. 2)* [2012] ECHR 228. Available at: http://www.bailii.org/eu/cases/ECHR/2012/227.html [Accessed 5 March, 2017].
Estrin, J. (2013). *Haitian Photographer Wins Major US Copyright Victory*. Available at: http://lens.blogs.nytimes.com/2013/11/23/haitian-photographer-wins-major-u-s-copyright-victory/?_r=0 [Accessed 8 January, 2015].
EUECJ (2014a). *Svensson and Others v Retriever Sverige AB* [2014] 3 CMLR 4. Available at: http://www.bailii.org/eu/cases/EUECJ/2014/C46612.html [Accessed 5 March, 2017].

EUECJ (2014b). *Mario Costeja Gonzalez v Google Spain and Google* [2014] C-131/12. Available at: http://www.bailii.org/eu/cases/EUECJ/2014/C13112.html [Accessed 5 March, 2017].

EWCA (2001). *Ashdown v Telegraph Group Ltd* [2001] EWCA Civ 1142. Available at: http://www.bailii.org/ew/cases/EWCA/Civ/2001/1142.html [Accessed 5 March, 2017].

EWHC (2005). *McKennitt v Ash* [2005] EWHC 3003 (QB). Available at: http://www.bailii.org/ew/cases/EWHC/QB/2005/3003.html [Accessed 5 March, 2017].

EWHC (2006). *CC v AB* [2006] EWHC 3083 (QB). Available at: http://www.bailii.org/ew/cases/EWHC/QB/2006/3083.html [Accessed 5 March, 2017].

EWHC (2012). *Cairns v Modi* [2012] EWHC B1 (QB). Available at: http://www.bailii.org/ew/cases/EWHC/QB/2012/756.html [Accessed 5 March, 2017].

EWHC (2013). *McAlpine v Bercow* [2013] EWHC 1342 (QB). Available at: http://www.bailii.org/ew/cases/EWHC/QB/2013/1342.html [Accessed 5 March, 2017].

Fievez, P. (2011). *Borrowed Photos (2)*. Available at: http://gentlemenranters.com/page_325.html#pf220 [30 November, 2011].

Glocer, T. (2006). *We Media Speech*. Available at: http://tomglocer.com/blogs/sample_weblog/archive/2006/10/11/98.aspx [Accessed 18 April, 2016].

Goodman, E. P. (2015). *Open Letter to Google from 80 Internet Scholars*. Available at: https://medium.com/@ellgood/open-letter-to-google-from-80-internet-scholars-release-rtbf-compliance-data-cbfc6d59f-1bd#.yu1qbamid [Accessed 2 November, 2015].

Grimmelmann, J. (2009). '"Saving Facebook" NYLS Legal Studies Research Paper No. 08/09-7', *Iowa Law Review*, 94, p. 1137.

Hamilton. C. (2011). *Use of Photographs from Social Media in our Output*. Available at: http://www.bbc.co.uk/blogs/theeditors/2011/08/use_of_photographs_from_social.html [Accessed 18 April, 2016].

Hermida, A. and Thurman, N. (2008). 'A Clash Of Cultures', *Journalism Practice*, 2(3), pp. 343–56.

IPSO (2015). *A Woman v Lancashire Evening Post*. Available at: https://www.ipso.co.uk/IPSO/rulings/IPSOrulings-detail.html?id=139 [Accessed 6 January, 2016].

Lewis K., Kaufman, J., Gonzalez, M., Wimmer, A. and Christakis, N. (2008). 'Taste, ties and time: A new social network dataset using Facebook.com'. *Social Networks*. 30(4), pp. 330–42.

Mabbett, A. (2011). The BBC's Fundamental Misunderstanding of Copyright. Available at: http://pigsonthewing.org.uk/bbc-fundamental-misunderstanding-copyright/ [Accessed 20 May, 2012].

Merrill, J. (2015). 'Shoreham Airshow: Medic at Scene of Crash Says He Saw Shocked Members of Public Who Were Filming on Mobile Phones' *The Independent*. Available at: http://www.independent.co.uk/news/uk/home-news/shoreham-airshow-medic-at-scene-of-crash-says-he-ran-past-laughing-and-gawping-members-of-public-who-10473379.html [Accessed 7 January, 2016].

Muller, D. (2013). 'Black Saturday Bushfires and the Question of Consent'. *Ethical Space*, 10(1), pp. 36–42.

Naughton, J. (2005). *Why I Have Serious Doubts About the 'Citizen Reporters'*. Available at: http://www.theguardian.com/technology/2005/jul/17/comment.mobilephones [Accessed 26 March, 2016].

Nissenbaum, H. (2004). 'Privacy as Contextual Integrity'. *Washington Law Review*, 79(1), pp.119–58.

Norquay, K. (2015). *Chris Cairns Trial: Cairns, Fitch-Holland Found not Guilty in Perjury Case*. Available at: http://www.smh.com.au/sport/cricket/chris-cairns-trial-cairns-fitchholland-found-not-guilty-in-perjury-case-20151130-glbx9j.html .[Accessed 7 January, 2016].

Organisation For Economic Co-Operation And Development (2007). *Participative Web: User-Created Content - DSTI/ICCP/IE(2006)7/FINAL 12*. OECD. Available at: http://www.oecd.org/sti/38393115.pdf [Accessed: 12 May, 2015].

Pilkington, E. (2010). *Retribution Swift and Brutal for Haiti's Looters*. Available at: http://www.guardian.co.uk/world/2010/jan/17/retribution-lynching-haiti-looters [Accessed 14 October, 2015].

Press Complaints Commission. (2009). *Mullan, Weir, Campbell v Sunday Times*. Available at: http://www.pcc.org.uk/cases/adjudicated.html?article=NTc5Mw==&type= [Accessed 15 October, 2015].

Reid, A. (2015). *BBC Launches Nepal 'Lifeline on Viber to Aid Quake Survivors*. Available at: https://www.journalism.co.uk/news/bbc-launches-nepal-lifeline-on-viber-to-aid-quake-survivors/s2/a564984/ [Accessed 4 March, 2017].

Robertson, G. and Nicol, A. (2007). *Media Law*, 5th ed. London: Sweet & Maxwell.

Ronson, J. (2015). *So You've Been Publicly Shamed*. London: Picador.

Sargent, J. (2015). *Respecting the Eyewitness; Learning Lessons from the Paris Shootings*. Available at: https://medium.com/1st-draft/respecting-the-eyewitness-learning-lessons-from-the-paris-shootings-a1391a7cbe23#.xllxvz5lc [Accessed 18 April, 2016].

Satter, R. (2015). *Witness to Paris Officer's Death Regrets Video.* Available at: http://bigstory.ap.org/article/5e1 ee93021b941629186882f03f1bb79/ap-exclusive-witness-paris-officers-death-regrets-video [Accessed 2 November, 2015].

SCC (2011). *Crookes v Newton.* [2011] SCC 47. Available at: http://scc-csc.lexum.com/scc-csc/scc-csc/ en/item/7963/index.do [Accessed 5 March, 2017].

ScotHC (2012). *British Broadcasting Corporation for Access to Crown Productions (in the case of HM Advocate v Kimberley Mary Hainey) Petitioners* High Court of Justiciary [2012] ScotHC HCJDV_10. Available at: http://www.bailii.org/scot/cases/ScotHC/2012/2012HCJAC10.html [Accessed 4 March, 2017].

SDNY (2013). Agence *France Presse v. Morel,* 934 F. Supp. 2d 547.

Tippman, S. and Powles, J. (2015). *Google Accidentally Reveals Data on 'Right to be Forgotten' Requests.* Available at: http://www.theguardian.com/technology/2015/jul/14/google-accidentally-reveals-right-to-be-forgotten-requests [Accessed 2 November, 2015].

Zimmer, M. (2010). '"But the Data Is Already Public": on the Ethics of Research in Facebook'. *Ethics and Information Technology,* 12(4), pp. 313–25.

26

ENVIRONMENT AND HUMAN RIGHTS ACTIVISM, JOURNALISM AND 'THE NEW WAR'

Libby Lester

Introduction

April 2016. Tokyo is filling with the sub-politics that precedes a gathering of the leaders of the world's richest nations. A month before the Japan-hosted G7 summit, local NGOs Fairwood Partners and Friends of the Earth Japan hire a seminar room in an office block in the city's Minato business district as well as two simultaneous translators, usually employed by the Japanese government to accompany their ministers and trade officials on overseas missions. The NGOs have invited Japanese companies that trade in and use imported timber to a seminar on due diligence and the risk of illegality in Japan's timber supply chain. Speakers include US- and Europe-based environmental and human rights activists from the groups, Global Witness and the Environmental Investigation Agency. Both groups use undercover techniques among other methods to expose the illegal timber trade and associated abuses to the rights of local communities and traditional land owners. More than 120 company officers attend the seminar, forcing a last-minute change to a larger room. Among the companies represented are Japan's giant trading corporations, which reach across the globe's resource, financing and construction sectors and provide the historic template for the global trade of today, dominated as it is by distant resource procurement and complex supply chains. Several of the country's leading environmental journalists also attend. They are here, corporate and media attendees reveal later in an interview, for a simple reason: The NGOs know more about the global timber trade, due diligence and potential corporate risk than they do.

As PowerPoint slide after PowerPoint slide suggests, the risk of buying and trading timber from the back hills of Sarawak or the virgin forests of Romania is high. Weak certification schemes or nebulous notions of 'social licence' do not protect these corporate giants from the reputational risk that can accompany buying timber illegally harvested from regions struggling with poverty, illegal land grabs and political corruption. For all the statements of concern for human rights and environmental sustainability that appear on their corporate and social responsibility websites, corporations are acutely aware of how unknowable their supply chains can be. In many cases, it is only two links back before the chain of knowing is broken, and the companies become vulnerable to misinformation provided by local suppliers or officials, or their own reluctance to investigate. Even when they are on the ground, physically in the region where the timber is logged, it can be difficult for company representatives to find their way through the fog of foreign cultural practices, language and political and corporate processes to know if the agreeable indigenous leader to whom they have been introduced by a local supplier is really a leader, or the timber stockpile they are inspecting comes from the right side of an ill-defined boundary. So they are here at the seminar, seated in rows at crowded desks, taking notes in English and Japanese, measuring the potential risks that the speakers are formally outlining and implicitly threatening, dot point by translated dot point.

This is the accessible front of the 'new war' that is following the transnational flow of information and politics concerned with natural resources, environmental harm and human rights violations. The other front is harder to access. This is where the movement of information and knowledge is curtailed, using a variety of methods but increasingly with physical violence, to prevent it appearing in the boardrooms of London, or the newsrooms of New York or a seminar room in Tokyo. Central to the new war is the 'chilling effect', which discourages others from investigating and circulating information (Mosdell 2016, 51). This new war is evidenced by the raw numbers of killings, although many more journalists and activists suffer violence and imprisonment than die. Global Witness reports that 116 environmental activists across 17 countries were killed in 2014, with 477 deaths occurring since 2002 in Brazil alone (Forte 2015; Global Witness 2015). Brazil remained the most dangerous country in 2014 with 29 killings, most of which related to conflict over the ownership, control and use of land. Here, rights to landscapes, the resources they contain and environmental futures become inseparable. Colombia was the second most dangerous country with 25 killings, with indigenous activists comprising more than half the victims. There were 15 deaths in the Philippines, mostly by paramilitary groups defending mining interests, and 12 in Honduras. Land ownership, mining, water and dams, agribusiness and logging were the issues most likely to lead to activist deaths around the world (Global Witness 2014, 2015).

Environmental journalists are also suffering increased violence. The press freedom organisation, Reporters Without Borders, lists 10 murders in 2010-2015, the majority in southeast Asia, with two in India and one in Russia (2015, 9). The four deaths in Cambodia during this period included that of Taing Try, who was shot in October 2014 after threatening to reveal illegal logging activities, and of *Vorakchun Khmer* journalist Hang Serei Oudom, whose battered body was found in his car boot in September 2012 after the publication of his story suggesting army officers were involved in timber trafficking (Reporters without Borders 2015, 10). Reporters Without Borders first noted the trend in 2009, finding that 15 per cent of the cases the group investigated involved environmental reporting (Reporters without Borders 2009; also 2010). It argued that the gathering and dissemination of information that raised environmental concerns 'complicated' development plans, and as a result environmental journalists were seen as 'an unwanted menace and even as enemies to be physically eliminated'. The report continued: 'In many countries – especially, but not only, those that are not democracies – journalists who specialise in the environment are on the front line of a new war. The violence to which they are subjected concerns us all. It reflects the new issues that have assumed an enormous political and geostrategic importance' (Reporters without Borders 2009, 1).

In this chapter, I attempt to connect the seemingly distant fronts of this new war. The chapter emerges from continuing research conducted in Australia, Japan and Malaysia that has included analysis of media texts (news, political and activist websites, corporate and social responsibility statements), direct observation and interviews with journalists, activists, trade officials and corporate executives, all of whom operate across national borders. (1) Its focus is Sarawak, one of two Malaysian states on the island of Borneo. Sarawak's timber industry is one of the world's most controversial, known for unsustainable logging practices and lack of environmental certification, unjust alienation of land from traditional owners and local communities and the close ties of major companies to politicians and their families (Straumann 2015). Six companies hold tenure over 3.7 million hectares of forests, or 30 per cent of Sarawak's total land area (Markets for Change/JATAN 2016, 11), and the UN Office on Drugs and Crime (UNODC) estimates that approximately 50 per cent of all wood products from Sarawak could be illegally harvested (Global Witness 2016, 3; UNODC 2013, 95). The stakes are high, and in June 2016, land rights activist Bill Kayong, known for his opposition to 'native customary rights' land grabbing for logging and plantations, was shot dead in traffic on his way to work.

The first part of the chapter focuses on the activism that increasingly follows transnational trade of natural resources. It argues that the political attention applied to this trade now often takes the form of revelatory, investigative information, often alleging human rights breaches or unsustainable environmental practices, and carried within and by various forms of media. The second part is concerned with the focus this places on the information suppliers and carriers, at the same time as the roles and practices of activists and journalists become increasingly blurred. Both factors potentially increase the risk of violence against the two groups. Activists carry out transnational investigations to uncover information with international NGOs providing the resources and global networks to support these activities, as traditional boundaries around 'professional journalism' continue to dissolve. Overall, the chapter asks if and how the dissolution of the distinction between journalism and activism, within the context of transnational flows of trade and information, might contribute to the 'new war'.

Transnational activism

When Ulrich Beck described NGOs as the 'entrepreneurs of the global commonwealth' (2006, 105), he was suggesting that NGOs had not only developed the ways in which global issues are categorised and understood, but had placed these issues on the political agenda, internationally and nationally. However, according to Beck, given that these 'self-declared creators of publics and interveners in foreign jurisdictions and forms of life' traded in values and information, their power was vulnerable to misinformation and dependent on the 'more or less voluntary cooperation of states and economic enterprises for the active aversion of harm' (2006, 106). Here Beck captures some of the complexities in which NGOs operate in contemporary transnational politics. Accurate information is a source of their advocatory power, but governments and industries still form a significant barrier.

How this works in practice in relation to transnational flows of politics remains poorly understood. Environmental and human rights information is often laden with images and symbols that resonate differently according to culture-specific meanings and histories (Lester & Cottle 2009). The local distorts global communicative flows, especially when it provides forests for logging or land for palm oil plantations (Kraidy & Murphy 2008) and nation states define land ownership and legality, alongside broader questions of governance under which resource industries and media systems operate (Flew & Waisbord 2015). Distant conflict over the environment and land control can be conflated or dismissed dependent on access to knowledge about local media practices, political activism or geographic detail (Waisbord 2013; Hutchins & Lester 2015). The role of language in this information flow is also not well known, but access to expert translation must be a key element in the way political knowledge is transferred transnationally (Waisbord 2016).

While the well-resourced status of many NGOs operating internationally is now recognised, their continuing reliance on local activists for highly specialised knowledge, networks and historic context is less acknowledged. Here the relationship of NGOs operating on a global stage to those activists with their feet firmly planted on the contested land is mirrored in some ways in the supply chains that link local loggers in Borneo or Tasmania to the giant trading and retail corporations headquartered in Tokyo. Within broader categories of 'industry', 'government' or 'activism', we should not presume that messages flow evenly or uncontested between actors within these groupings.

Access to public arenas where claims can be aired and negotiated has been complicated by digital media and global political networks. Claims and counterclaims, crossing platforms, languages and cultural settings, may leave only a trace of their presence in media. Even less visible is the information that never forms or is allowed to form into a transferrable media object in the first place – a self-evident statement perhaps but, given the methodological challenges it presents for research in the area in which this chapter is concerned, worth repeating (Lester & Hutchins 2012). So faced with these significant challenges in methods, how to consider the activism that increasingly follows transnational trade of natural resources, and the ways in which information is now gathered and circulated to focus political attention on this trade? How might this contribute to the 'new war'?

Information activism

Australia's first markets-focused environmental NGO, Markets for Change, describes itself as providing 'market focused research that investigates and exposes the companies and products driving environmental destruction' (Markets for Change n.d.). By distributing its research 'through Facebook, Twitter, YouTube, online forums and blogs [each tag hyperlinked]', it aims to 'drive retailers to adopt environmentally friendly procurement policies' (Markets for Change n.d.). Markets for Change's most notable victory occurred soon after its formation in 2011 when it targeted Japanese companies buying timber from Ta Ann Tasmania, a subsidiary of controversial Sarawak timber company, Ta Ann. The activist group deployed a combination of methods to publicise its claims that timber being harvested and shipped to Japan was sourced from high conservation value forests and not plantations as Japanese retailers were claiming to their customers. In Tasmania, Australia's southern island state with a long history of bitter conflict over its forests, an associate of Markets for Change began a 15-month tree sit in a threatened forest. The protester used her ample spare time to write a blog that was linked to a 'cyber action' petition aimed at the Japanese companies with contracts to buy Ta Ann Tasmania timbers.[1] A young woman living on a 60-metre-high platform in a remote eucalypt provided evidence and international awareness of the Tasmanian conflict. The existence of conflict at the procurement site was further communicated by the petition, signed by 2000 visitors to the website and automatically forwarded to key officers within the relevant Japanese companies, whose names and email addresses had been gathered and shared by local Japanese activists. Nevertheless, the turning point was face-to-face meetings in Tokyo and Osaka between Markets for Change campaigners and these corporate officers, in which the NGO provided a report detailing anomalies in Ta Ann Tasmania's claims about the source of its timber. When the report had been launched in Tasmania prior to the meetings, no journalists attended the media conference or reported the claims. In Japan, the report provided enough evidence for the companies to cancel contracts for the timber, with the sudden loss of 40 jobs in Tasmania (Lester 2014). The response of the Tasmanian government was, by Australian standards, heavy handed. Terms such as 'sabotage' and 'terrorism' were deployed to describe the campaigns (Lester 2014). The government mooted introducing mandatory jail sentences and $10,000 on-the-spot fines for protesters who interrupted workplaces – although charges laid in 2016 against forests protesters under a watered-down version of the legislation have been dismissed by courts and police as unworkable (Ikin 2016). The government also lobbied for changes to national defamation laws to encourage corporations to sue campaigners for making false or misleading claims, and proposed to revoke visas of international environmental protesters, whose participation has been key to getting campaign messages circulating internationally (Colbeck 2014). In turn, companies in Australia and Japan expressed deep concern about unwanted publicity, delays and uncertainty, placing further pressure on Australian governments to respond so as to guarantee security of supply (Interviews: June 2014). Markets for Change's follow up report 'Forest to Floor', released in 2016, provides a second example of the type of information-activism that increasingly follows the transnational trade of natural resources. Working with the Japan Tropical Forest Action Network (JATAN) and published in English and Japanese, this report focuses on the Sarawak-Japan timber trade, and specifically the 55 per cent of plywood produced from Sarawak tropical forests that is imported into Japan to be used for either concrete formwork or flooring, which in turn comprises half of all Japan's plywood imports (Markets for Change/JATAN 2016, 1). The report uses powerful images of indigenous owners and simple diagrams to trace, first, the production process from forest harvesting to shipment to Japan, and second, the companies involved in each step of the supply chain, from the Malaysian timber corporations, to major Japanese trading companies of Sarawak timber, to Japanese major flooring manufacturers, to distributors and wholesalers, to housing companies. Overall, 67 companies are identified and surveyed about their knowledge of their wood supply and issues associated with Sarawak. A total of 23 responded. The report introduces results with the following:

> Transparency is a vital component of proper ethical purchasing, but for the purposes of this report we have been unable to assess the procurement requirements and actions of companies who did not respond. They have not supplied any information that they have made efforts to address the serious human rights and environmental issues associated with Sarawak products in their supply chain The companies who did not respond are listed on the table (see overleaf).
>
> *(Markets for Change/JATAN 2016, 21)*

Company executives present themselves as reluctant partners in this form of transnational political activity, suggesting they are forced to pursue change down their supply chains on behalf of the NGOs or face public shaming through media. 'We are constantly talking to our Sarawak supplier,' said one executive in interview. 'We are aggressively asking them to report, to change their mindset. Gradually we start to change their mind. But the NGOs are not yet satisfied' (Interview: April 2016). While two companies are reported to have reduced the quantity of timber imported from Sarawak as a result of a similar Global Witness campaign in 2014, Japanese companies continue to buy – if nervously (Global Witness 2016, 3). Unlike Tasmanian eucalyptus, there are no clear alternatives to the type of timber sourced from Sarawak rainforests. Moreover, the companies claim it is not their role to pass judgement on the Sarawak timber industry. 'It is very difficult to make a judgement as a private company,' (Interview: April 2016). And so they keep buying. Here then we see campaigns targeted at the profits of a resource industry via investigating and exposing vulnerabilities within transnational supply chains that the corporations know exist. Corporations can only respond by being seen to work cooperatively with NGOs, accepting this information when it is offered and pressuring their suppliers to change their practices. It is a finely balanced relationship that has most impact on the profits, workforces and communities at the distant and often economically struggling sites of resource procurement. This is where information and its outward movement is now more than ever both a strategic weapon and a powerful threat.

Activism-journalism

While many forms of investigative journalism, not just environmental journalism, have their roots in campaign-style reporting (Neuzil 2008), environmental journalists face perceptions from colleagues and editors that they are 'anti-development', or campaigning for action on the environment in general. The dilemma this creates for journalists' professional self-representation is evident in these comments from an Australian environment editor:

> There has been an expectation that this was a campaigning round. We often ask ourselves: Are we simply reporting on all aspects of environmental issues and taking a neutral position or are we pushing for better outcomes for the environment. I'm not sure that's been resolved … But our job, like all journalism, is to report and expose the truth in areas of public interest and I guess we still take the point of view that we report strongly on areas where there are environmental problems that need to be addressed; where expert opinion and scientific evidence tells us there are problems that need addressing.
>
> *(Interview: February 2012, cited in Lester 2013)*

Compare this comment with the statement below from an investigative campaigner on the shift in activist practices towards journalism to find evidence of the increasing blurring of the distinction between the roles and practices of journalists and activists:

> We are focussed on data and data processing, data analysis and portraying the data and using the data to tell a story, and over the past year we're getting much more into the world of data link journalism in the US, and there is some international investigative reporters and different groups that do trainings.
>
> *(Interview: April 2016)*

The slogan of Global Witness, the NGO based in London and Washington and founded in 1993, provides further evidence: 'We find the facts, we uncover the story, we change the system.' Since 2013, Global Witness has produced three major reports on the role of Japan's construction industry in driving rainforest destruction in Sarawak, using among other techniques satellite photography to identify illegal logging. Its latest report, released in 2016 prior to the G7 summit, identifies seven major timber importers in Japan who dominate the plywood trade from Sarawak, claiming that all seven importers do business with Sarawak logging companies that have been a) found to be illegally logging, and b) involved in legal disputes with indigenous communities who claim their human rights have been violated (Global Witness 2016, 3). Four of the seven companies, according to the report, admitted that did not fully know where the timber they imported was sourced in Sarawak nor had they inspected their suppliers logging operations. These are investigative facts, easily cited and circulated – and highly reportable. A second relevant international NGO, also with offices in the US and UK, is the Environmental Investigation Agency. Funded by public donations, it works under the slogan 'Protecting the environment with intelligence' and includes among its methods 'undercover investigations' and 'rigorous research'. It aims to understand where the industry's pressure points are, while working with industry to lower its resistance to change.

In an interview, activists working within these groups are clear on their goals:

> [T]hey know who we are, they know what our game is, they know what our objectives are and we just stick to that plan. So we're very transparent… They know if they don't do something, we're going to do an expose, but they can expect that. So we can have

that dialogue with them and say look, like this is how it is, this is how it's going to be, you know these are our goals, these are our objectives, this is what we want.

(Interview: April 2016)

Activism and journalism – and the threat of violence to both – are spoken of in tandem, such as in this example from an investigative campaigner discussing a piece of journalism from a local reporter:

[T]hey've done five stories in the past five years about this company's illegal logging as in the most recent video, a 45-minute piece basically looking at one aspect of this company's supply chain. It's one case of going into the forest, talking to a truck driver, talking to people who used to work for the company… In that there was a scene where he's in the forest, a guy comes out with a baseball bat…

(Interview: April 2016)

The blurring of the distinction between the work of activists and journalists raises a set of questions around professional practices that pertain to both roles. How, for example, should sources embedded within local conflicts be protected by international NGOs? How are locals used and protected as 'fixers'? Here, an activist addresses NGO practices in relation to local contacts, using language that could as easily be deployed by a foreign correspondent (Murrell 2014):

We're very, very concerned with keeping them out of trouble and keeping them healthy and able to continue their campaigns and their work and everything … I mean for us we always trust our local partners to understand the situation but at the same time we're just very aware in each case to make sure that we are not in any way pressuring them.

(Interview: April 2016)

Environmental journalists have long faced accusations of 'campaigning' or being 'anti-development' both from within and outside newsrooms. Since the inception of the specialisation in newsrooms in the late 1960s, journalists reporting and researching the environment and associated human rights abuses have faced a high level of scrutiny and negative feedback or 'flak' on their stories (Neuzil 2008). Journalists claim this 'flak' has had an insidious impact on their capacity to research and investigate environmental issues – a chilling effect (Lester 2013). There has always been a fine line between what is perceived as investigation and what is perceived as campaigning, and how the two activities are framed in terms of their civic contributions (Olesen 2008). That the line is now blurred in the world of human rights and environmental politics and international trade is evident not only from the comments above by activists and journalists, but most clearly in a 2013 speech to the State Assembly by Abdul Taib Mahmud, who was Chief Minister of Sarawak from 1981 until 2014 and was regularly accused of corruption in relation to the forest industries and land grabs. According to local news reports:

KUCHING (May 29): Facing numerous land grab and corruption allegations both locally and internationally, Sarawak Chief Minister Tan Sri Abdul Taib Mahmud today hit out at these 'external forces' for spreading malicious allegations…

He said he was accountable to the august House and the people of Sarawak who have repeatedly given him the mandate to lead since 1981, but not accountable to foreign NGOs or foreign reporters or broadcasters, including Sarawak Report, Bruno Manser Fund and Radio Free Sarawak.

'To respond or react to what they wrote about me would be to acknowledge that they have a right to interfere in or participate in the affairs of this country.'

(The Edge 2013)

Conclusion

In their 2016 book analysing rising violence against journalists, Simon Cottle, Richard Sambrook and Nick Mosdell highlight the 'elastic conceptualisation of who and what exactly counts as a journalist and journalism' (2016, 10). They ask 'what happens when the definition extends from full-time paid professionals, to part-time amateurs as well as to so-called citizen journalists and social activists, or even belligerents and, on occasion, states when all are seeking to get their particular message across and/or further their cause?' We can add further questions. What happens when the environment and control of land are the subjects of investigation? What happens when not only nation states but transnational corporations and every link in their complex supply chains are also seeking to further their various causes? What happens when this is achieved more easily by keeping information contained rather than by circulating messages and providing counterarguments? And can mediated data-driven politics, without journalism's traditional requirement to provide space for counter-arguments, provide publics with access to the knowledge they require to negotiate a shared and just future? These are important questions with significant environmental and political consequences that we are a long way from answering. The case presented here suggests that the practices and representation of international campaigning and investigative reporting are becoming conflated as they target the newsrooms and webpages of global media and politics, and the board rooms and seminars of global trade. Local journalists, campaigners and their communities who are already marginalised politically, economically and professionally will be exposed to further harm if violence is allowed to continue as an effective way to contain information and prevent it reaching these distant and powerful audiences.

Notes

Fifteen interviews were conducted in Tokyo in April 2016 and June 2014 with executives from Japanese trading and forestry companies, environmental journalists, trade officials and campaigners from Japan, US and Australia.

My data is drawn from a larger Australian Research Council-funded project, (DP150103454) 'Transnational Environmental Campaigns in the Australia-Asian Region'. The research was supported by a period as a Visiting Scholar at the Policy Research Center of the National Graduate Institute for Policy Studies in Tokyo. Thank you to Janine Mikosza for research assistance.

1   See https://observertree.org/about/; also Hutchins and Lester 2013.

References

Beck, U. (2006). *Cosmopolitan Vision*. Cambridge: Polity Press.

Colbeck, R. (2014). *Warning to Fly-in Forestry Protesters*. Media release, 10 January. Available at: http://www.richardcolbeck.com.au/2014_media_releases/warning_to_flyin_forestry_protesters [Accessed 14 Aug. 2014].

Cottle, S., Sambrook, R., and Mosdell, N. (2016). *Reporting Dangerously: Journalist Killings, Intimidation and Security*. London: Palgrave Macmillan.

Flew, T., and Waisbord, S. (2015). 'The Ongoing Significance of National Media Systems in the Context of Media Globalization'. *Media, Culture & Society*, 37(4), pp. 620–36.

Forte, J. (2015). Brazil Ranks Highest in Killing of Land and Environmental Activists. *The Rio Times*, 21 April. Available at: http://riotimesonline.com/brazil-news/rio-politics/brazil-ranks-highest-in-killing-of-land-and-environmental-activists/#sthash.UJL6A4s8.dpuf [Accessed 17 June, 2016].

Global Witness (2014). How Many More? 2014's Deadly Environment: the Killing and Intimidation of Environmental and Land Activists, with a Spotlight on Honduras. Available at: https://www.globalwitness.org/en/campaigns/environmental-activists/how-many-more/ [Accessed 17 June, 2016].

Global Witness (2015). Deadly Environment: The Dramatic Rise in Killings of Environmental and Land Defenders. Available at: https://www.globalwitness.org/en/campaigns/environmental-activists/deadly-environment/ [Accessed 17 June, 2016].

Global Witness (2016). Willful Ignorance: How Japan's Voluntary Approach is Failing to Stop the Trade in Illegal Timber. A Global Witness briefing. Available at: https://www.globalwitness.org/en/reports/wilful-ignorance/ [Accessed 2 March, 2017].

Hutchins, B. and Lester, L. (2013). 'Tree-sitting in the Network Society'. In: L. Lester and B. Hutchins, eds., *Environmental Conflict and the Media*. New York: Peter Lang, pp. 1–17.

Hutchins, B. and Lester, L. (2015). 'Theorizing the Enactment of Mediatized Environmental Conflict'. *International Communication Gazette*, 77(4), pp. 337–58.

Ikin, S. (2016). 'Bob Brown: Charges Dropped over Lapoinya Forest Anti-logging Protest'. *ABC News*, 18 May. Available at: http://www.abc.net.au/news/2016-05-17/bob-brown-over-lapoinya-protest-charges-dropped/7423444 [Accessed 17 June, 2016].

Kraidy, M. M. and Murphy, P. D. (2008). 'Shifting Geertz: Toward a Theory of Translocalism in Global Communication Studies'. *Communication Theory*, 18, pp. 335–55.

Lester, L. (2013). 'On Flak, Balance and Activism: The Ups and Downs of Environmental Journalism'. In S. Tanner and N. Richardson, eds., *Journalism Research and Investigation in a Digital World*, Melbourne: Oxford University Press.

Lester, L. (2014). 'Transnational Publics and Environmental Conflict in the Asian Century', *Media International Australia*, 150, pp. 67–78.

Lester, L. and Cottle, S. (2009). 'Visualising Climate Change: TV News and Ecological Citizenship', *International Journal of Communication*, 3, pp. 920–36.

Lester, L. and Hutchins, B. (2012). 'The Power of the Unseen: Environmental Conflict, the Media and Invisibility'. *Media, Culture & Society*, 34(7), pp. 832–46.

Markets for Change (n.d.). *Markets for Change*. Available at http://www.marketsforchange.org [Accessed 2 March, 2017].

Markets for Change/JATAN (2016). Forest to Floor: How Japan's Housing Construction Is Driving Forest Destruction and the Dispossession of Indigenous People in Sarawak. Available at: http://www.marketsforchange.org/forest-to-floor/ [Accessed 2 March, 2017].

Mosdell, N. (2016). 'Mapping the Parameters of Peril'. In: S. Cottle, R. Sambrook and N. Mosdell, eds., *Reporting Dangerously: Journalist Killings, Intimidation and Security*. New York: Springer. pp. 36–60.

Murrell, C. (2014). *Foreign Correspondents and International Newsgathering: The Role of Fixers*, Vol. 9. London: Palgrave Macmillan.

Neuzil, M. (2008). *The Environment and the Press: From Adventure Writing to Advocacy*. Evanston, Illinois: Northwestern University Press.

Olesen, T. (2008). 'ACTIVIST JOURNALISM? The Danish Cheminova Debates, 1997 and 2006', *Journalism Practice*, 2(2), pp. 245–63.

Reporters without Borders (2009). The Dangers for Journalists who Expose Environmental Issues. Available at: http://www.iucn.org/content/dangers-journalists-who-expose-environmental-issues [Accessed 17 June, 2016].

Reporters without Borders (2010). High-risk Subjects: Deforestation and Pollution. Available at: https://rsf.org/en/reports/deforestation-and-pollution-high-risk-subjects [Accessed 17 June, 2016].

Reporters without Borders (2015). *Hostile Climate for Environmental Journalists*. Available at: https://rsf.org/sites/default/files/rapport_environnement_en.pdf

Straumann, L. (2014). *Money Logging: On the Trail of the Asian Timber Mafia*. Basel: Bergli Books.

The Edge Malaysia (2013). 'Taib Hits Out at Foreign NGOs in Dewan', 29 May. Available at: https://sg.finance.yahoo.com/news/taib-hits-foreign-ngos-dewan-124504411.html [Accessed 27 June, 2016].

UNODC [United Nations Office on Drugs and Crime] (2013). *Transnational Organized Crime in East Asia and the Pacific: A Threat Assessment*. Available at:www.unodc.org/documents/data-and analysis/Studies/TOCTA_EAP_web.pdf [Accessed 17 June, 2016].

Waisbord, S. (2013). 'Contesting Extractivism: Media and Environmental Citizenship in Latin America'. In: L. Lester and B. Hutchins, eds., *Environmental Conflict and the Media*. New York: Peter Lang, pp. 105–24.

Waisbord, S. (2016). 'Communication Studies Without Frontiers? Translation and Cosmopolitanism Across Academic Cultures'. *International Journal of Communication*, 10, pp. 868–U552.

PART IV

Digital activism, witnessing and human rights

27

SOCIAL MEDIA AND HUMAN RIGHTS ADVOCACY

Ella McPherson

Introduction

The rise of social media has seen its concomitant celebration as a 'liberation technology,' namely a technology that supports social, political and economic freedoms (Diamond 2010). Though most notably manifest in the media fervour around the Twitter and Facebook 'revolutions' of the Arab Spring, techno-optimism about social media's potential for human rights persists in both the popular and academic consciousness. This chapter provides a framework for understanding how the use of social media intersects with the practice of human rights advocacy at NGOs. This framework is not to deny the disruptive possibility of human rights advocacy conducted over social media, but rather to ground related techno-optimism in the broad and complex terrain that influences this potential (Madianou 2013; Youmans & York 2012).

Social media liberates advocacy by disrupting its traditional pathway to visibility – at least, this is the largely untested idea that has fuelled a spate of experimentation and innovation among those practicing human rights (Thrall et al. 2014). Specifically, the hope is that social media allows advocates to bypass the gatekeeper mainstream media – whose newsworthiness decisions can seem inscrutable and captured by elites – to instead communicate direct-to-citizen and direct-to-policymaker (e.g. Auger 2013). Furthermore, as any digitally literate actor can publish on social media, this is complemented by the perspective that social media may be a leveller in terms of the equality of visibility (e.g. Nah & Saxton 2013). These views, however, rests on an incomplete conception of visibility, one which focuses on the production of communication and overlooks the corresponding reception of that communication necessary for visibility to take place (Hindman 2010). Furthermore, production and reception are not correlated; rather, communication is mediated by the fields it crosses between producer and recipient.

In the case of human rights advocacy over social media, then, there is no direct-to-anyone. The visibility of this advocacy depends on the logics of the social media field, the target audience fields and the political field(s) in which the communication takes place. This chapter overviews this field theory approach to communication before outlining in broad strokes what we know about each of these logics. Equally important, however, is what we don't know. For different reasons, each of these logics is somewhat inscrutable – that of the social media field because of its novelty, mutability and proprietary secrecy; those of target audience fields because social media advocacy effects are both hard to isolate and under-researched; and those of political fields because surveillance tactics are often covert. All of this inscrutability creates risk, and risk, as we shall see, is anathema to visibility. One of the benefits of the field approach is its concern with inequality (Bourdieu 1993). As an actor's ability to mitigate risk corresponds to his or her resources, it may be that – instead of being a leveller – social media advocacy is exacerbating inequalities of visibility within the human rights field (Beck 1992; Mejias 2012; Thrall et al. 2014). The chapter concludes by sketching a research agenda for the use of social media in human rights work.

Social media advocacy as communicating across fields

Building loosely on the approach developed by Bourdieu (e.g. 1993), we can view the practice of social media advocacy as communicating across fields. Participants in a field adhere to a shared logic (or logics) – the explicit and implicit rules that govern success in a particular field and thus shape the practices in that field (Thompson 2010). Actors are positioned hierarchically within each field according to their relative distributions of the forms of capital valued in that field. These can include financial capital, social capital, cultural capital or knowledge, and symbolic capital or reputation (Bourdieu 1986). Conceptualizing a field's participants as occupying relative positions based on their relative wealth naturally turns a lens concerned with inequality on that field.

Fields that trade in information are often, in Bourdieu's (1993) term, heteronomous to the logics of other fields which are producing or receiving their information. This is particularly the case for fields, like journalism or human rights NGOs, where success depends on attracting the attention of those outside of the field. Whether this concern for other logics is deleterious or beneficial to these fields' own logics, it is unavoidable (McPherson 2016). This heteronomy is a theme in the small but growing literature on NGO journalism, focused in particular on how NGOs are adjusting their information logics to the information logics of the mainstream media through which they traditionally reached their target audiences – and still do today (e.g. Cottle & Nolan 2007; Fenton 2010; McPherson 2016; Powers 2014; Waisbord 2011).

This approach is a useful starting point for understanding how the field of social media platforms may be inflecting the visibility of advocacy – in part through inflecting the other fields relevant to the human rights advocacy communication chain. This chapter overviews each field in turn, though this overview is necessarily a simplification, as each field can contain a variety of logics, and these interact within and across fields with much complexity (van Dijck & Poell 2013; Waisbord 2011). During this overview, it is worth keeping in mind that an actor's ability to understand and to match external logics is itself correlated with resources (Gandy 1982; McPherson 2016). Conversely, an inability to understand external logics can create risk, and risk can stymie visibility (McPherson Forthcoming).

The logic of the human rights NGO field

Though human rights NGOs are by no means the only entities that practice human rights, I focus on their field in particular because of NGOs' relative influence in the human rights space and because of their relatively consolidated practices around communication (Krause 2014; Nash 2015). A key aim of their dominant logic is to speak truth to power through advocacy, a communication practice focused on visibility with and persuasion of target audiences to impel change. In the human rights context, these target audiences are usually policy makers – sometimes human rights violators themselves but usually those who can exert pressure on the violators; the advocacy is often amplified through media coverage and by raising public moral outrage; and the change sought is the adoption of human rights frameworks as well as the mitigation of cases or trends of violations (Keck & Sikkink 1999).

Advocacy about human rights violations may be a 'weapon of the weak,' but its potency is evidenced by accused violators' efforts to counterclaim the accusations and discredit human rights organizations – efforts that can jeopardise human rights advocates' security and correspondingly silence their advocacy (Brysk 2013). This potency stems from other aspects of human rights NGOs' logic that work to enhance the visibility of their communications, including the pursuit of social capital within the 'transnational advocacy networks' in which they usually operate and the pursuit of symbolic capital, namely credibility (Keck & Sikkink 1999; McPherson 2016). This credibility is fundamental to NGOs' work: Credibility in the eyes of political audiences is key to persuasion, credibility with publics is important for mobilizing outrage, while credibility with journalists gets media coverage and with volunteers and donors gets resources (Cottle & Nolan 2007; Land 2009). While credibility is a source of strength for human rights NGOs, it is also their Achilles' heel, as it is a precarious reputational resource that can easily be lost through poor performance, bad associations and the discrediting discourses of opponents (McPherson 2016; Thompson 2000).

The rise of social media as a communication channel has implications for these established practices through, on the one hand, promise for advocacy, and, on the other, effects on security and resources not fully understood by human rights practitioners. That said, advocates are certainly experimenting with, knowledge exchanging on and dedicating resources to social media communication strategies – even if more cautiously than one might expect (Powers 2016). These strategies include mobilizing supporters, directly and publicly targeting policy makers and influencing journalists (McPherson 2015b). A handful of social media campaigns, such as Invisible Children's viral video *Kony 2012*, which called for the capture of Ugandan warlord Joseph Kony, and Plan's 2014 campaign, which highlighted the plight of child brides through a fake blog by a 12-year-old Norwegian girl about her impending marriage to a 37-year-old, are renowned for their extraordinary visibility. Still, the adoption of social media introduces a new and, for many human rights advocates, unknown or under-known logic – that of the field of social media platforms. This logic raises many questions about how it intersects with the human rights NGO logic, as well as with other relevant logics, not least those of target audience fields and of the broader political field(s) in which advocacy takes place.

The logic of the social media field

Social media are of interest to human rights advocates because, among other potentialities, their platforms afford visibility. Thinking about social media in terms of affordances, or what they enable users to do, is a common practice in the literature – in part because it allows conclusions to be drawn across platforms and to outlast platform obsolescence. Yet, this view of affordances may place too much agency in the hands of the user through obscuring the influence of the technology designers as well as of the decisions in technology-user interaction increasingly made by the technology itself (Nagy & Neff 2015). As explored in this section, both the logic behind social media's design, which is predominantly commercial, and the design itself, which involves an inscrutable combination of algorithmic and human decisions, have significant impacts on social media visibility.

Similarly, the literature on advocacy and activism too often treats social media platforms as 'tabula rasae' for communication when, instead, scholars and practitioners should approach them the same way as they have traditionally approached the mainstream media (Madianou 2013). Namely, these are mediators following their own logic, which may coincide with the logics of communicators but often do not – and this coincidence is not necessarily predictable. Human rights advocates who seek visibility via social media, just like those who seek visibility via the mainstream media, need to understand platform logics and decide to what extent they wish to shape their communications to meet these logics.

The field of social media platforms has tended towards conglomeration and monopsony, and the resulting social media behemoths are, at their cores, commercial institutions (Mejias 2012). The profit-motivated drive for users and thus advertisers shapes many aspects of social media platforms' orthodox logic. These include the promotion of popular content and the suppression of problematic content in order to maximize user engagement – and thus eyeballs for advertisements (van Dijck & Poell 2013; Youmans & York 2012). The popularity of content – rewarded with visibility on social media platforms and, at the extreme, with virality – is determined by a complex interplay of user activity, including designing content and building networks, as well as algorithmic and human decision making (van Dijck & Poell 2013; Tufekci 2015). Problematic content is handled with a content moderation system. Users first report content as offensive or inappropriate, triggering a review by a content moderator who assesses the content's compatibility with the platform's community guidelines. Relevant to human rights content are policies about gratuitous violence, which a graphic video of a human rights violation might contravene – unless posted with sufficient explanatory notes highlighting its documentary and news value (Bair 2014).

Though social media platforms therefore act as information gatekeepers, they do not do so in exactly the same way or with the same consequences as news outlets: Their decisions are both less transparent and less accountable (Tufekci 2015). For example, social media algorithms are considered proprietary trade secrets and may be programmed to evolve via machine learning, making them unpredictable even to their creators. Their decisions are customised to individual users, and they are tweaked often – almost once a week in the case of Facebook's news feed (Tufekci 2015).

Though clearly humans are doing this tweaking, the human judgment – and, indeed, bias – behind algorithms is obscured. Rather, algorithms' automation imparts a veneer of objectivity and technology-enabled neutrality, as does social media's discursive positioning as platforms rather than as publishers (Gillespie 2010; van Dijck & Poell 2013). It is perhaps not surprising, then, that more than half of Facebook users interviewed in a recent study were unaware that their News Feed is filtered by an algorithm (Eslami et al. 2015). Content moderation also is meant to appears automatic, but is actually performed invisibly by low-wage labourers around the world who spend their workdays reviewing potentially disturbing and upsetting content (Roberts Forthcoming). Recent uproars about social media platforms' gatekeeping have shed little light on the process, as when commentators queried why *#Ferguson* news was appearing in their Twitter feeds but not in their Facebook feeds, or when a former Facebook contractor made the allegation, subsequently denied by Facebook, that he and other 'news curators' consistently manipulated Facebook's trending topics list (Nunez 2016; Tufekci 2015).

The upshot is that the logic of social media platforms can be profoundly unknowable, at least with respect to being able to predict visibility. Strategies do exist, however, for gaining certainty about visibility. As explained by Facebook on its new 'facebook for nonprofits' site, money buys visibility. Non-profits can pay to boost their posts among their existing followers or to reach out to new, targeted audiences, among other advertising strategies (Facebook 2016b). Another strategy, as with news outlets, is for non-profits to conform their content to their mediator's expectation of audience interest. In addition to suggesting non-profits strive for 'authenticity' in their posts and include visuals, Facebook (2016a) recommends the following in terms of 'voice':

> Facebook is a place where people connect with friends and communicate in a personal, casual way. Organizations tend to succeed when they also use a conversational,

authentic style. Overly formal language can feel out of place. When writing a message, whether it's funny or serious, think about how you'd write it to a friend. Posts that evoke emotion often stand out in News Feed. Inspiring, solutions-oriented messages are often the most engaging. Placing blame or otherwise alienating others can be offensive and typically doesn't lead to high engagement.

This is quite a departure from the traditional discursive register of human rights reports, which tend to be lengthy, legalistic and illustrated by statistics and testimonials (Moon 2012). Echoing earlier criticisms of the logics of the mass media field, scholars have raised the concern that the logic of the social media field is inflecting the logics of other fields (van Dijck & Poell 2013). In this case, this includes the fields of target audiences and the political field in relation to the human rights advocacy in question.

The logics of target audience fields

As the communication strategies of human rights advocates depend on inflecting the beliefs and behaviours of their target audiences, they traditionally have been very attuned to these audiences and their information logics. For example, Human Rights Watch contracted research on United Nations and European Union policymakers, finding out that they tend to get their news from the *New York Times* and the BBC (Powers 2016). Human rights advocates in Mexico know that their politicians are very switched on to coverage related to them in newspapers, as these newspapers are their gateways to the electorate (McPherson 2016). Advocates correspondingly focus their communication efforts on the mediating news outlets to which their target audiences pay attention and have developed relationships with their journalists in order to secure visibility (McPherson 2016; Powers 2016).

Many policy makers now have their own social media accounts, which in theory creates another channel for human rights advocates to attract their attention. Opportunities for visibility may have increased, but so has the competition, while attention has an upper limit (Mejias 2012; Thrall et al. 2014). Directing resources towards social media communications generally means redirecting them from somewhere else, and it is not necessarily clear to human rights advocates that this investment is worth it. Some reported that they have little understanding of how much attention target policy makers pay to social media (Powers 2016). Others are nervous about how the content exigencies of social media logic, like those outlined by Facebook above, line up with the information logics of their target audiences (McPherson [forthcoming]). Conversely, might the emphasis on the visual in social media communications support the emotional appeal of human rights communication and expand audiences through transcending literacy and linguistic divides (Brysk 2013)? We may have seen this with the 2015 viral image of the Syrian refugee child, Alan Kurdi, whose body washed up on a Turkish beach. These are still open questions for human rights advocates and are further complicated by the logics of the broader political fields addressed by advocacy.

The logics of political fields

Human rights advocacy about violations inevitably presents a threat to the government actors identified as perpetrators. An unfortunate consequence, neither uncommon nor diminishing, is the retaliation of these actors through discrediting discourses, physical threats or attacks to silence their critics. Though the history of information wars between human rights advocates and their opponents is a long one, the digital space is a new battleground (Hankey & Ó Clunaigh 2013).

Whether or not social media is beneficial for human rights advocacy, then, also depends on the logic of the contextual political field vis-à-vis critics (Aouragh & Alexander 2011; Pearce & Kendzior 2012).

To some extent, this battle has been characterized by an arms race, with early adopters in the human rights community able to leverage social media to surface information and exert pressure on governments. These opportunities have, however, become risks as states scrambled to catch up, propelled by their vast advantages of resources and legislative power and by knowledge exchange between regimes (Diamond 2010; McPherson 2015b). These advantages have allowed states to engage cutting edge tactics and technologies, including building websites to dupe Syrian activists into downloading malware by purporting to provide security tools; engaging bots, or automated Twitter accounts, to sabotage activist hashtags such as the ones protesting the 2014 disappearance of 43 students in Mexico; and reporting activist content during the Arab Spring as a contravention of social media platform community standards (Scott-Railton & Marquis-Boire 2013; Finley 2015; Youmans & York 2012). States' legislative power can also force the complicity of social media companies, including compelling them to hand over user profile information. The collection of user profile information is one area where the logics of social media platforms and states overlap, as corporate surveillance for the purposes of selling user data to advertisers tracks many data points, such as name and location, useful to governments bent on identifying dissidents.

A political context in which states use the digital footprints of human rights advocates against them has a double-bind dampening effect on their social media visibility. On the one hand, if advocates do not anticipate their adversaries' tactics, they may inadvertently jeopardize their security. On the other, advocates may very well know of these tactics because government actors are using them to create a chilling effect on the public sphere, as was the recent case in Azerbaijan (Pearce & Kendzior 2012). As sketched above, it is clear the visibility of social media advocacy goes far beyond whether or not human rights advocates use it, but depends also on the logics of various intersecting fields. These logics do not, however, have blanket effects on human rights NGOs; rather, these effects are variegated according to the respective resources of NGOs.

Risk, visibility and inequality

As we have seen, the rise of social media creates a host of uncertainties for human rights advocates. Uncertainty begets a certain kind of risk – the perception of hazards combined with the impossibility of knowing their likelihoods (Lupton 2013). The risks felt by human rights advocates about social media use are in line with the broader 'digital risk society' in which risks are particularly 'lively' and increasingly unknowable given the rapid evolution and growing penetration of technology (Lupton 2016, 302). The inscrutability of social media logic leads to a variety of risks, including the risk of expending precious resources on social media advocacy only to have visibility stymied by opaque algorithms. The uncertain compatibility of social media content with target audiences' information logics means that even if human rights NGOs master social media logics, their advocacy may fall on deaf ears – again, a waste of time and money. Whether or not their social media advocacy received attention from target audience fields, adversary actors in broader political fields may be sharply attuned to NGOs' digital activity. The possibility or probability of this surveillance creates security risks for human rights advocates. It is not hard to see that these risks can have a dampening effect on the production of social media advocacy, while their accompanying hazards can have a dampening effect on both its production and its reception.

These risks are not experienced universally by all actors in the field of human rights NGOs. Rather, the ability to mitigate differential risks is associated with access to resources, and resources vary across actors in the human rights NGO field, just as they do across all fields (Beck 1992; Giddens 1991, p. 126). Financial capital, for example, can buy visibility in the form of social media advertisements and can pay for target audience research. Offline social capital can translate into online social media networks as well as into cultural capital through knowledge exchange. Cultural capital in terms of social media literacy allows advocates to construct popular content, to evade reports of problematic content and to minimize the risk of mistakes and miscalculations detrimental to NGOs' hard-won symbolic capital (McPherson Forthcoming). Cultural capital in terms of digital security – too meagre among members of the human rights community – reduces exposure (Hankey & Ó Clunaigh 2013).

A recent study made only too clear how the distribution of resources within the human rights NGO field translates into social media visibility. Of 257 human rights NGOs, 92 percent of the group's total Twitter followers, 90 per cent of YouTube views, and 81 per cent of Facebook likes belonged to only 10 percent of the NGOs, which were also those with the most financial resources (Thrall et al. 2014). This is in line with other research that has shown that inequalities of visibility are, if anything, amplified online (e.g. Hindman 2010). Though the distribution of social media visibility within the field of human rights NGOs is of concern in and of itself, it also has implications for the individual victims and witnesses of violations on whose behalf these organizations are advocating (McPherson 2016). Violations that are the subject of advocacy at less-resourced organizations face the social media visibility barriers confronting those NGOs. Those taken up by better-resourced organizations will fare better – but only if they are represented in line with the logics of the fields across which these organizations are communicating.

Conclusion

In sum, it is clear that unpicking how communication is mediated by the fields it traverses tempers the techno-optimistic view that conducting advocacy on social media will result in greater visibility for human rights. Though, undoubtedly, social media has enabled visibility and participation in particular cases, for many others, it has heightened uncertainty and inequality (Hindman 2010; Mejias 2012; Thrall et al. 2014). The rise of the social media logic has inflected the logics of other fields, from that of human rights NGOs, to target audiences and the political field (van Dijck & Poell 2013). The social media logic, which is commercial and centres on promoting popular content and eliminating problematic content, is notoriously opaque in its mechanics due to proprietary algorithms and a lack of clarity around human versus machine decisions. The intersection of social media logics with the logics governing the attention of target audiences is also opaque, and human rights advocates are not sure how these audiences will respond to content tailored for social media visibility – if it is visible to them at all. State adversaries, whose logics with respect to human rights critics have often involved repression, have used advocates' social media communications covertly or overtly against them. It is likely that better-resourced actors in the human rights NGO field are more able to understand social media logics and the opportunities and risks they create for advocates – while the less-resourced are potentially left further and further behind.

The techno-optimist view of social media advocacy rightfully points out the medium's potential for providing new channels of not just visibility, but also accountability, mobilization, and other benefits for social, political and economic freedom (Diamond 2010). Yet, in stopping there, this view also has many shortcomings – not least the oversight of inequalities outlined in this chapter. Additional shortcomings include an amnesia about how past liberation technologies have been used for *and* against freedom as well as a myopia about how much progress is actually due to offline rather than online activity (Diamond 2010; Mejias 2012; Shapiro 2015).

Furthermore, by celebrating the emancipatory potential of social media platforms, this view elides their commercial logics and thereby becomes a discourse that plays into the hands of social media companies wishing to benefit from association with democratic projects. In so doing, this perspective falls into line with the long-standing discourse, renewed with each ICT invention, that technology creates progress (Fuchs 2012; Mansell 2010; Waisbord 2015).

Though techno-optimism has no doubt waned as social media spaces become more commercial, opaque and surveilled, empirical research counterbalancing this perspective remains sorely needed. The framework outlined here – focused on visibility, advocacy and NGOs – provides a good starting point for examining the intersection of social media and human rights. Future research should, however, also stretch beyond this to consider other metrics such as representation, other practices such as fact finding and other participants such as the amateurs whose labour is increasingly incorporated, via technology, into previously professional human rights practices (e.g. Bair 2014; Land 2016; McPherson 2015a). Other methods, less familiar for scholars of human rights and of media and communications, may also be in order – such as reverse-engineering algorithms and conducting social network analysis. Beyond benefiting the literature, this research will also support human rights defenders, for whom the logic of social media and its impacts on their own practices and those of relevant other fields remain opaque. This opacity creates risk, and risk can be silencing. Clarity, therefore, can support human rights visibility.

References

Aouragh, M. and Alexander, A. (2011). The Egyptian Experience: Sense and Nonsense of the Internet Revolution. *International Journal of Communication* 5, pp. 1344–58.

Auger, G. A. (2013). 'Fostering Democracy through Social Media: Evaluating Diametrically Opposed Nonprofit Advocacy Organizations' Use of Facebook, Twitter, and YouTube'. *Public Relations Review* 39, pp. 369–76.

Bair, M. (2014). 'Navigating the Ethics of Citizen Video: The Case of a Sexual Assault in Egypt'. *Arab Media & Society* 19, pp. 1–7.

Beck, U. (1992). *Risk Society: Towards a New Modernity*. London: SAGE Publications.

Bourdieu, P. (1986). 'The Forms of Capital'. In: J. E. Richardson, ed., *Handbook of Theory and Research for the Sociology of Education*. New York, NY: Greenwood Press, pp. 241–58.

Bourdieu, P. (1993). *The Field of Cultural Production: Essays on Art and Literature*, New York: Columbia University Press.

Brysk, A. (2013). *Speaking Rights to Power: Constructing Political Will*. Oxford: Oxford University Press.

Cottle, S. and Nolan, D. (2007). 'Global Humanitarianism and the Changing Aid-Media Field: Everyone was Dying for Footage'. *Journalism Studies* 8(6), pp. 862–78.

Diamond, L. (2010). 'Liberation Technology'. *Journal of Democracy* 21(3), pp. 69–83.

Eslami, M. et al. (2015). '"I Always Assumed that I Wasn't Really that Close to [Her]": Reasoning About Invisible Algorithms in the News Feed'. In: *CHI 2015 - Proceedings of the 33rd Annual CHI Conference on Human Factors in Computing Systems: Crossings*. Vol. 2015-April, Association for Computing Machinery, pp. 153-162, 33rd Annual CHI Conference on Human Factors in Computing Systems, CHI 2015, Seoul, Republic of Korea.

Facebook (2016a). 'Grab People's Attention'. *Facebook for nonprofits*. Available at: https://nonprofits.fb.com/topic/grab-peoples-attention [Accessed 8 Aug. 2016].

Facebook (2016b). 'Reach New People with Ads'. *Facebook for nonprofits*. Available at: https://nonprofits.fb.com/topic/reach-new-people-with-ads [Accessed 8 Aug. 2016].

Fenton, N. (2010). 'NGOs, New Media and the Mainstream News: News from Everywhere'. In: N. Fenton, ed., *New Media, Old News: Journalism & Democracy in the Digital Age*. London: SAGE Publications Ltd, pp. 153–68.

Finley, K. (2015). 'Pro-Government Twitter Bots Try to Hush Mexican Activists'. *WIRED*. Available at: https://www.wired.com/2015/08/pro-government-twitter-bots-try-hush-mexican-activists/ [Accessed 8 Aug. 2016].

Fuchs, C. (2012). 'Social Media, Riots, and Revolutions'. *Capital & Class* 36(3), pp. 383–91.

Gandy, O. H. (1982). *Beyond Agenda Setting: Information Subsidies and Public Policy*, Norwood, NJ: Ablex Pub. Co.

Giddens, A. (1991). *The Consequences of Modernity.* Stanford, CA: Stanford University Press.

Gillespie, T. (2010). 'The Politics of "Platforms"'. *New Media & Society* 12(3), pp. 347–64.

Hankey, S. and Ó Clunaigh, D. (2013). 'Rethinking Risk and Security of Human Rights Defenders in the Digital Age'. *Journal of Human Rights Practice* 5(3), pp. 535–47.

Hindman, M. (2010). *The Myth of Digital Democracy*. Princeton, NJ: Princeton University Press.

Keck, M. E. and Sikkink, K. (1999). 'Transnational Advocacy Networks in International and Regional Politics'. *International Social Science Journal* 51(159), pp. 89–101.

Krause, M. (2014). *The Good Project: Humanitarian Relief NGOs and the Fragmentation of Reason*. Chicago, IL: University of Chicago Press.

Land, M. (2009). 'Networked Activism'. *Harvard Human Rights Journal* 22(2), pp. 205–43.

Land, M. (2016). 'Democratizing Human Rights Fact-Finding'. In: P. Alston and S. Knuckey, eds., *The Transformation of Human Rights Fact-Finding*. Oxford: Oxford University Press, pp. 399–424.

Lupton, D. (2016). 'Digital Risk Society'. In: A. Burgess, A. Alemanno, and J. O. Zinn, eds., *The Routledge Handbook of Risk Studies*. London: Routledge, pp. 301–09.

Lupton, D. (2013). *Risk*, 2nd ed. London: Routledge.

Madianou, M. (2013). 'Humanitarian Campaigns in Social Media'. *Journalism Studies* 14(2), pp. 249–66.

Mansell, R. (2010). 'The Life and Times of the Information Society'. *Prometheus* 28(2), pp. 165–86.

McPherson, E. (2015a). 'Digital Human Rights Reporting by Civilian Witnesses: Surmounting the Verification Barrier'. In: R. A. Lind, ed., *Produsing Theory in a Digital World 2.0: The Intersection of Audiences and Production in Contemporary Theory*. New York: Peter Lang Publishing, pp. 193–209.

McPherson, E. (2015b). *ICTs and Human Rights Practice: A Report Prepared for the UN Special Rapporteur on extrajudicial, summary, or arbitrary executions*. Cambridge: University of Cambridge Centre of Governance and Human Rights.

McPherson, E. (Forthcoming). 'Risk and Digital Human Rights Reporting'. In: M. K. Land and J. D. Aronson, eds., *The Promise and Peril of Human Rights Technology*. Cambridge: Cambridge University Press.

McPherson, E. (2016). 'Source Credibility as "Information Subsidy": Strategies for Successful NGO Journalism at Mexican Human Rights NGOs'. *Journal of Human Rights*, 15(3), pp. 330–346.

Mejias, U. A. (2012). 'Liberation Technology and the Arab Spring: From Utopia to Atopia and Beyond'. *The Fibreculture Journal* (20), pp. 204–17.

Moon, C. (2012). 'What One Sees and How One Files Seeing: Human Rights Reporting, Representation and Action'. *Sociology* 46(5), pp. 876–90.

Nagy, P. and Neff, G. (2015). 'Imagined Affordance: Reconstructing a Keyword for Communication Theory'. *Social Media + Society* 1(2), pp. 1–9.

Nah, S. and Saxton, G. D. (2013). 'Modeling the Adoption and Use of Social Media by Nonprofit Organizations'. *New Media & Society*, 15(2), pp. 294–313.

Nash, K. (2015). *The Political Sociology of Human Rights*, Cambridge: Cambridge University Press.

Nunez, M. (2016). 'Former Facebook Workers: We Routinely Suppressed Conservative News'. *Gizmodo*. Available at: http://gizmodo.com/former-facebook-workers-we-routinely-suppressed-conser-177546 1006 [Accessed July 26, 2016].

Pearce, K. E. and Kendzior, S. (2012). 'Networked Authoritarianism and Social Media in Azerbaijan'. *Journal of Communication* 62(2), pp. 283–98.

Powers, M. (2014). 'The Structural Organization of NGO Publicity Work: Explaining Divergent Publicity Strategies at Humanitarian and Human Rights Organizations'. *International Journal of Communication* 8, pp. 90–107.

Powers, M. (2016). 'NGO Publicity and Reinforcing Path Dependencies: Explaining the Persistence of Media-Centered Publicity Strategies'. *The International Journal of Press/Politics*, pp. 1–18.

Roberts, S. T. (Forthcoming). 'Commercial Content Moderation: Digital Laborers' Dirty Work'. In: S. U. Noble and B. M. Tynes, eds., *The Intersectional Internet: Race, Sex, Class, and Culture Online*. New York: Peter Lang Publishing.

Scott-Railton, J. and Marquis-Boire, M. (2013). 'A Call to Harm: New Malware Attacks Target the Syrian Opposition'. *The Citizen Lab*. Available at: https://citizenlab.org/2013/06/a-call-to-harm/ [Accessed 1 Jan. 2015].

Shapiro, R. (2015). 'Rhetorics of Hope: Complicating Western Narratives of a "Social Media Revolution"'. *Literacy in Composition Studies* 3(1), pp. 156–174.

Thompson, J. B. (2010). *Merchants of Culture*. Cambridge: Polity.

Thompson, J. B. (2000). *Political Scandal: Power and Visibility in the Media Age*, Cambridge: Polity Press.

Thrall, A. T., Stecula, D. and Sweet, D. (2014). 'May We Have Your Attention Please? Human-Rights NGOs and the Problem of Global Communication'. *The International Journal of Press/Politics*, 19(2), pp. 135–59.

Tufekci, Z. (2015). 'Algorithmic Harms Beyond Facebook and Google: Emergent Challenges of Computational Agency'. *J. on Telecomm. & High Tech. L.* 203, pp. 203–18.

van Dijck, J. and Poell, T. (2013). 'Understanding Social Media Logic'. *Media and Communication*, 1(1), pp. 2–14.

Waisbord, S. (2011). 'Can NGOs Change the News?' *International Journal of Communication* 5, pp. 142–65.

Waisbord, S. (2015). 'El Optimismo Digi-Activista y sus Problemas'. In: A. Amado and O. Rincón, eds., *La Comunicación en Mutación*. Bogotá: Fundación Ebert, pp. 75–86.

Youmans, W. L. and York, J. C. (2012). 'Social Media and the Activist Toolkit: User Agreements, Corporate Interests, and the Information Infrastructure of Modern Social Movements'. *Journal of Communication* 62(2), pp. 315–29.

28

ALL THE WORLD'S A STAGE

The rise of transnational celebrity advocacy for human rights

Trevor Thrall and Dominik Stecula

The role of celebrities in promoting human rights causes has grown steadily over the past 30 years. Thanks to the rise of entertainment news, the fragmentation of the mass audience and the increasing diffusion of digital communications, celebrities have become important new gatekeepers of a transformed global public sphere. Their dominant position on social media platforms and the Web, in particular, gives celebrities greater potential for generating exposure for political issues than ever before. At the same time, globalization and the redistribution of power since the end of the Cold War have disrupted traditional diplomatic strategies and invigorated efforts by individuals, groups and movements to play critical roles in transnational agenda setting and persuasion. The literature on celebrity humanitarianism is relatively young but diverse and expanding rapidly (Jon 2014). Important contributions have been made from scholars working in history, critical studies, anthropology, geography, as well as political science. As with any new field of inquiry, especially an interdisciplinary one, the literature on humanitarian celebrity advocacy is somewhat disjointed and lacks systematic empirical grounding, especially when it comes to quantitative studies. Nonetheless, we can readily identify four important areas of focus in the existing literature and our essay is organized accordingly. The following section describes the emergence and evolution of humanitarian celebrity advocacy as well as its institutionalization among NGOs. We then examine how NGOs help celebrities transform into credible humanitarian advocates and harness their 'star power'. The third section reviews research on the impact of celebrity advocacy. We conclude with an assessment of the vigorous debate over the consequences of celebrity advocacy for democratic politics.

The rise and institutionalization of humanitarian celebrity advocacy

The evolution of humanitarian celebrity advocacy has seen celebrities move from occasional props used by the United Nations, to fully institutionalized elements of UN and NGO strategies, to the emergence of a small group of entrepreneurial celebrities who have become powerful advocates in their own rights. At this point most scholars agree that celebrity advocates have become central figures in transnational advocacy networks in the human rights arena and beyond (Marsh, 't Hart and Tindall 2010).

Most scholars mark the start of modern humanitarian celebrity advocacy in 1953 when the United Nations asked the American actor Danny Kaye to become the first Goodwill Ambassador of the UN. 'Mr. UNICEF', as Kaye came to be known, made two very popular documentaries that highlighted the role of UNICEF in improving the health and welfare of children in many of the poorest countries of the world. Kaye received a special Academy Award for the first, which reached an estimated 100 million people (Cooper 2008; Wilson 2014).

Two fundamental trends in the late 1960s and 1970s helped drive the rise of celebrity humanitarian advocacy. The first was the evolution of the public sphere. By elevating the role of the image and through its vast reach, television helped position celebrities as potentially important political resources. By fragmenting the media market, the Internet made generating attention an ever more difficult task, but by enabling inexpensive new ways to reach global audiences without going through traditional gatekeepers, the Internet also made possible new celebrity-fueled strategies for capturing global attention and winning support from the public (Boorstin 2012; McLagen 2003).

The second critical trend was the explosive growth in the human rights arena, which led to the establishment of hundreds of new NGOs around the world and the rapid expansion of existing NGOs such as Amnesty International and Oxfam. With more attention to human rights came more competition for funding and attention. The competition, along with emerging technologies, in turn spurred NGOs to adopt new communication and campaign strategies including a greater reliance on celebrities (Cmiel 1999; Goodman and Barnes 2011).

Thanks to these forces the use of celebrities emerged as a consistent organizational strategy in the 1980s. This period is typically demarcated by the Live Aid concert in 1985 ('the day the music changed the world'), organized by Bob Geldof and Midge Ure to raise funds for Ethiopian famine relief. The event, held simultaneously in the United States and in England, involved dozens of musicians and other celebrities and was viewed by almost two billion people on television in 150 nations, raising millions of dollars in donations (Cooper 2008). As the first effort of its kind, Live Aid established a template for large-scale celebrity advocacy on global issues that persists today, visible through mega concerts like Live Earth in 2007 and Hope for Haiti Now in 2010.

After several decades of somewhat irregular efforts to make use of its Goodwill Ambassadors program, the United Nations took organized celebrity advocacy to new levels in the late 1990s. UN Secretary General Kofi Annan took office in 1997 with a strong desire to revive the UN's image, which had been battered by polarising fights over UN action (and inaction) in Somalia, Rwanda and the Balkans. Annan led a massive expansion of the Goodwill Ambassador program. Soon 15 different UN agencies had named roughly 400 celebrity Goodwill Ambassadors (Alleyne 2005; Wheeler 2011; Lim 2014). The United Nations was not alone in its efforts to harness the power of the stars. By the early 21st century a majority of the largest human rights NGOs were partnering with celebrities in a variety of ways, with groups like Oxfam and Amnesty International going so far as to create celebrity liaison offices to manage such efforts (Goodman and Barnes 2011).

Most recently we have seen the emergence of the entrepreneurial celebrity advocate. Tsaliki, Frangonikolopoulos and Huliaris (2011) note that globalization has radically altered the distribution of power in the international arena, shifting power away from nation states towards non-state actors, leading to what Thomas Friedman (2002) has called 'super-empowered individuals'. In Friedman's words, 'Some of these super-empowered individuals are quite angry, some of them quite wonderful – but all of them are now able to act much more directly and much more powerfully on the world stage'. The most famous celebrity humanitarians certainly fall into this category. Bono, Angelina Jolie and George Clooney, for example, have each leveraged their fame and wealth to launch new organizations in response to their concerns and priorities, mobilizing significant transnational collective action outside their partnerships with existing NGOs (Busby 2007; Cooper 2008).

Though few studies exist to document the growth of celebrity involvement in political advocacy over time, scholars are in consensus about its rapid expansion. The data we do have indeed suggest that celebrity advocacy is widespread and has become more common over time (Thrall et al 2008). To provide a bit more context we have gathered some new data for this essay that illuminates the breadth and growth of celebrity humanitarianism. As Figure 28.1 indicates, the website *Look to the Stars*, which tracks celebrity advocacy, currently identifies 3626 celebrities active on a vast array of issues, supporting an average of five NGOs, while each of the 2095 non-profit organizations identified by the site is associated with an average of 8.6 celebrity supporters. Some of the largest organizations work with hundreds of celebrities; 298 celebrities support UNICEF, for example, and 246 support the Red Cross.

Meanwhile, as Figure 28.2 illustrates, a majority of the most-followed celebrities on Twitter[1] promote the organizations in their tweets.[2] That engagement, however, varies significantly from person to person. Most celebrities mention NGOs very infrequently and 14 per cent have not mentioned a single NGO in their previous 3200 tweets.[3] Finally, Figure 28.3 shows that the rise of celebrity humanitarianism – at least on behalf of the United Nations and in the United States, has led to increased attention to these issues over time. Here we measure the number of stories mentioning human rights appearing each year in *People* Magazine, a leading soft news outlet focused on celebrity news,[4] and the number of stories that mention both celebrities and human rights in the *New York Times*, a leading hard news outlet.[5] Taken together these figures, though merely suggestive, support the general argument that celebrities play a bigger and more visible role in the global politics of human rights than ever before.

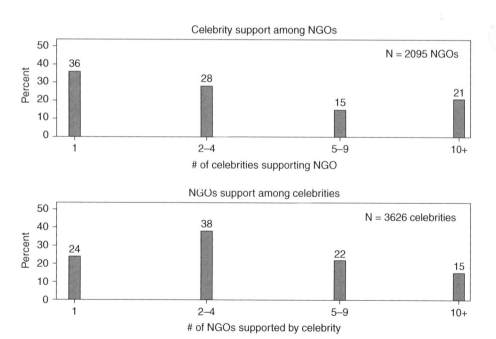

Figure 28.1   Celebrity support of NGOs and NGO use of celebrity advocates

Data retrieved from looktothestars.org

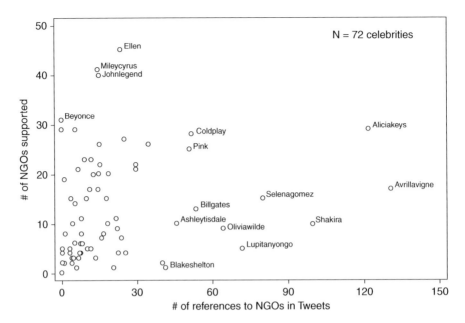

Figure 28.2 Celebrity human rights advocacy on Twitter

Data retrieved from looktothestars.org and twitter.com

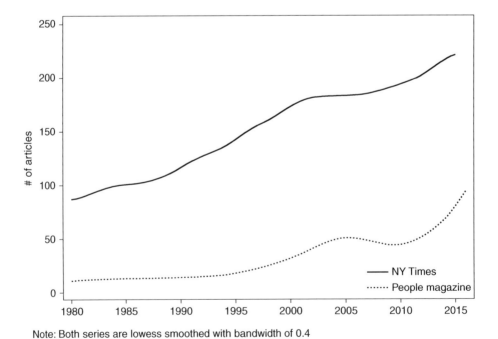

Note: Both series are lowess smoothed with bandwidth of 0.4

Figure 28.3 Media visibility of celebrity humanitarianism, 1980–2015

Data retrieved from Lexis/Nexis and the People magazine online archive

Creating and harnessing star power

Scholars have spent a great deal of time trying to explain how celebrities with no background in politics or policy can become effective champions of human rights causes. The consistent theme of this work confirms the wisdom that 'stars are not born; they are made'. As the broader literature on celebrities has documented, a great number of institutional structures and processes are at work to construct and maintain celebrity status (Marshall 1997; Cooper 2008; Van Zoonen 2005). With respect to political advocacy, as Meyer and Gamson (1995) first noted, since celebrities are neither elected officials nor subject matter experts they lack the authority to speak credibly on social and political issues. As such, most celebrities rely on NGOs to structure and support their advocacy efforts (Huliaris and Tzifakis 2015).

Thus, in order to make the most of a celebrity's star power, human rights NGOs must first help celebrities burnish their humanitarian credentials (Cooper 2008; Chouliakri 2013). As Chris Martin, the lead singer of Coldplay, admitted at the beginning of his visit to Haiti, 'I felt like a fourth-rate Bono. Later on I felt like a third-rate Bono, and hopefully it'll escalate until I feel like a full-on Bono' (Goodman and Barnes 2011, 79). A rare few celebrities like Bono do wind up investing the time and energy necessary to become experts on policy (Busby 2007). More typically, however, celebrities develop humanitarian credentials by creating what Goodman and Barnes (2011, 76) call 'materialities of authenticity' as they engage with the targets of their advocacy. The effort begins by associating with well-known and trusted NGOs and traveling to meet with the poor and needy, but it depends most critically on documenting those visits through photos, videos, diaries and other personal testimonials and then circulating them through various media. In so doing celebrities are able to illustrate their own personal growth and education about the issue, to document their efforts to understand and bear witness to the suffering of others, and to 'seem genuinely concerned and knowledgeable about the cause they are promoting' (Goodman and Barnes 2011, 80).

The case study literature has grown rapidly in recent years, documenting important examples of celebrity advocacy and revealing that NGOs use celebrities in a wide number of roles. NGOs have, of course, relied on celebrities to put a famous face on a campaign, as seen in the cases of Danny Kaye and Audrey Hepburn working with UNICEF, or to gain national and global attention as in the cases of the Live 8 concert or the International Year of Tibet (McLagen 2002; Alleyne 2005; Cooper 2008; Nash 2008; Marsh, t' Hart and Tindall 2010; Wheeler 2011; Wilson 2011; Street 2012). Celebrities often provide support as fundraisers, as in the aftermath of the earthquakes in Haiti and Japan or the tsunami in Asia (Huliaris and Tzifakis 2011). NGOs have also used celebrities as pitchmen for new consumer goods, as in the cases of Bono's Product (RED) campaign, or the Fair Trade movement (Brockington 2008; Richey and Ponte 2008, 2011; Goodman and Barnes 2011). But celebrities have also operated in the role of diplomats and lobbyists; Bono, Clooney and Angelina Jolie to name a few have helped NGOs to gain access to and put pressure on world leaders, both in the West and in nations where human rights violations are occurring (Alleyne 2005; Avlon 2011). Finally, NGOs have used celebrities to help change people's minds, whether in support of specific arguments, such as Mia Farrow's effort to recast the Beijing Olympics as the 'Genocide Games' (Huliaris and Tzifakis 2012; Budabin 2009) or as part of efforts to change people's thinking about the world more broadly as in the case of Bono's efforts in Africa or the Make Poverty History campaign (West 2008).

Sound and fury signifying…? Measuring humanitarian celebrity impact

The literature to date has made very clear that there is a good deal of celebrity engagement in human rights campaigns. There is less evidence so far, however, about the nature and extent of celebrity advocacy's impact.

Most writing on celebrity advocacy starts from the central assumption that celebrity advocacy helps issues, victims and NGOs get attention (e.g. West and Orman 2003). As deeply entrenched as this conventional wisdom is, there is surprisingly little data beyond anecdotes to support it. And though there are certainly some individual examples where celebrities were able to make themselves heard, the existing quantitative research suggests that those vivid cases are the exception. Thrall et al (2008), for example, studied the advocacy efforts and outcomes of hundreds of celebrities and found that in fact the overwhelming majority of celebrities do not appear in mainstream news media at all in their advocacy capacity, despite the fact that many of them enjoyed very high levels of news coverage of their entertainment, music or sports-related endeavours. Virgil Hawkins (2011) studied news coverage of celebrity advocates in the cases of Darfur and the Democratic Republic of the Congo and concluded similarly that '…the impact of celebrities in drawing attention to foreign conflicts is not as powerful as is often assumed' (101).

But just because celebrities' ability to make mainstream news may have been oversold does not mean that celebrities cannot generate attention for their causes. Work to date suggests that celebrity advocacy likely has its greatest impact elsewhere in the evolving global public sphere such as social media (e.g. where celebrities account for 76 of the top 100 Twitter accounts), partisan media (NGO web sites, blogs), entertainment media (daytime television shows, concerts, sporting events) and commercial media (advertising campaigns, corporate marketing) (Baum and Jamison 2006; Nash 2008; Thrall et al 2008; Huliaris and Tzifakis 2010; Click, Lee and Holladay 2015).

Getting people's attention, of course, is just a first step. The next goal is to convince people to think in new ways about human rights and other issues in order to build public support for change. On this score, celebrity humanitarian advocacy shares a fundamental assumption with corporate marketing efforts: that a celebrity will be able to change how people think about a given product or cause simply by being associated with it and approving of it (Jackson and Darrow 2005). Writing about celebrity diplomacy, Cooper argues that (2008, 7) 'Celebrities have the power to frame issues in a manner that attracts visibility and new channels of communication at the mass as well as the elite levels'.

Evidence from experiments in the United States and Canada illustrates that celebrity messages and endorsements exercise at least some influence over intentions to vote, vote choice, candidate appraisals and support for causes (Jackson 2008; Jackson and Darrow 2005; Austin et al 2008; Pease and Brewer 2008; Garthwaite and Moore 2008; Lindenberg, Joly, and Stapel 2011; Becker 2013). Fowler (2008) even found evidence to support Stephen Colbert's claims that candidates who appeared on the The Colbert Show received a 'Colbert bump'. Relying on in-depth interviews with young people in the UK, Inthorn and Street (2011) argue that celebrities can help the public identify with causes, but that this influence depends heavily on people's perception of the authenticity of the celebrities doing the selling. Similarly, Becker (2013) finds that celebrity endorsements are effective but that they are seen by the public as more appropriate when restricted to less important issues. Survey data from Couldry and Markham (2007) and Brockington and Henson (2014), on the other hand, suggest two factors that may significantly limit the influence of celebrity messages. First, people do not tend to think about celebrities when they think about politics very often. Second, the people who follow celebrities most closely are also the least likely to be engaged in the political realm. Finally, scholars have also described the ways in which celebrity advocacy is shaping public behaviour, especially in the realm of humanitarian-oriented consumption (Richey and Ponte 2008). Thanks to the emergence of the 'celebrity-compassion-consumption complex', Goodman and Barnes (2011, 81) conclude that, 'Marketing and selling development and relief aid has never been easier through the rise and spread of the development celebrity'.

Substituting spectacle for substance? The implications of humanitarian celebrity advocacy

For optimistic observers, rising celebrity engagement is mostly a good thing, reflecting a new sort of pluralism adapted to the politics of postmodern democracies in which celebrities are uniquely positioned to operate as 'moral entrepreneurs' (Street 2004; Huliaris and Tzifakis 2008; Budabin 2015). From this perspective, humanitarian celebrity advocacy represents a relatively healthy – even necessary – response to the rise of the Internet and the other major trends affecting global politics in the 21st century.

Some scholars believe that, thanks to their more personal and emotional approach to human rights issues, celebrities operate effectively as interpreters and intermediaries between their audiences and distant victims and tragedies (de Waal 2008; Chouliakri 2013). Further, by virtue of the fact that they are not politicians and generally do not take overtly ideological positions, celebrities may reach and mobilize a broader audience than traditional party politics does (Street 2004; Littler 2008; Wheeler 2012, 2013; Brockington and Henson 2014). Finally, because they are not confined by traditional roles or positions, celebrities are free to experiment with innovative approaches to human rights. Efforts like Live Aid, Product (RED), Make Poverty History and the Save Darfur Coalition, for example, all provide evidence of the ability of celebrities to create new forms of humanitarian activism.

At the global level, many argue that in their role as highly visible and charismatic faces of various issues and campaigns, celebrities are now critical elements of the broader transnational advocacy networks (Cooper 2008; Hawkins 2011; Stohl, Stohl, and Stohl 2011; Njoroge 2011). Celebrities are also able to take action and have impact when traditional modes of diplomacy hit a wall. As Wheeler (2005, 10) writes, '…celebrity diplomacy should be understood as an increasingly important form of intervention that can transcend the traditional roles of state-centric power'. Celebrities, as scholars have also noted, are clearly central to the financial strategies of NGOs. As Huliaris and Tzifakis (2011, 39) report, for example, after George Clooney's appearance on Oprah Winfrey's show to talk about his trip to Africa, donations to UNICEF spiked by 20 per cent. In that camp we must also include mega events such as Live Aid, Band Aid, Farm Aid, Live Earth and the like, each of which raised millions of dollars thanks to massive celebrity engagement.

More sceptical observers, on the other hand, provide a wide range of critiques of the optimists' position. For starters, many critics question whether celebrities, unelected and untrained elites of society, should be the ones deciding which human rights issues get attention and which do not (Drezner 2007; Dieter and Kumar 2008). Additionally, some wonder about the extent to which celebrities' choices to engage issues reflect their constant concerns about their own status, reputation and image, rather than the severity of the issues involved (Brockington 2009; Tsaliki, Frangonikolopoulos, Huliaris 2011). On this view, rather than reflecting robust pluralism celebrity advocacy reflects yet another way for the rich to shape politics and influence the masses (Littler 2008).

Beyond this, many argue that celebrity advocacy does more to obscure and oversimplify than to illuminate the issues involved (Weiskel 2005; Kellner 2009; 2010). As West and Orman (2003, 118) complain, 'Serious political issues become trivialised in the attempt to elevate celebrities to philosopher-celebrities'. Though this criticism is certainly not uniquely applicable to celebrities, the typical celebrity's lack of knowledge and experience with the issues may come with a price. As many scholars have observed, with celebrities there is always the danger that the spectacle of their personal stories and drama will divert the story from the issues they are attempting to champion (Kellner 2009). As a result, some have concluded, building on the arguments of Daniel Boorstin (2012) and Neil Postman (2006), that the celebritisation of politics represents a sad triumph of style over substance (West and Orman 2003; Wheeler 2012).

A third, and even more fundamental criticism, is that rather than producing real social change, celebrity advocacy is in fact turning human rights into a shopping experience. As Goodman (2010; 3) argues, for example, 'The growing celebritization of environment and development has reached an almost fever pitch in the UK's fair trade movement'. Celebrities like Bono, thanks to their popularity and privileged ability to endorse consumption goods, have played a significant role in creating what Richey and Ponte (2008; 2011) have called 'Brand Aid' and what Goodman and Barnes (2011) have insightfully called the compassion-consumption-celebrity complex. The danger, critics say, is that such a strategy lulls people into thinking their responsibility ends at the cash register. As long as we buy our fair trade coffee and stay away from conflict diamonds, everything will be just fine (Boykoff and Goodman 2009; Tait 2011; Chouliakri 2013). Meanwhile, critics argue, celebrity advocacy has done little to address the underlying causes of human rights issues (Richey and Ponte 2011; Goodman 2010; Huliaris and Tzifakis 2011; Tait 2011; Richey 2016). Some go as far as to conclude that celebrity advocacy in the form of efforts like Bono's Project (RED) is making things worse (Easterly 2006; Moyo 2009). Dieter and Kumar (2008, 259), for example, argue 'While these remedies may look seductive, unfortunately the reality is far more complex…Grand ideas for development are a dangerous recipe and may in fact worsen the situation of the poor'. In the long run, as scholars like Yrjola (2011) and Kapoor (2012) argue, celebrity advocacy simply reinforces the hierarchy between the North and the South rather than alleviating it.

Conclusion

Like them or not, celebrity humanitarians are clearly a vital and growing part of global human rights networks. Given this, research should press ahead in three critical areas. First, though there has been a great deal of case study work outlining the various ways NGOs have attempted to engage celebrities, there has been much less work attempting to provide a systematic accounting of the scope and scale of such efforts. There are thousands of human rights NGOs and thousands of celebrities worldwide, but we lack to date a sufficient accounting of how many of each are engaged with the other, especially outside the United States and the United Kingdom, where most of the research has focused. Without such an effort, all attempts to develop theory are ultimately built on a foundation of sand. Second, and relatedly, researchers must continue to develop empirical work – both qualitative and quantitative – to describe and explain the impact that celebrity advocacy has at various levels (individual, organizational, national, global). Finally, despite a few notable exceptions (e.g. Street 2004; Goodman and Barnes 2011, Chouliaraki 2013), the literature on humanitarian celebrity advocacy relies too heavily on single case studies and remains under-theorised. There is clearly room for future work that combines theory and empirical work in ways that provides rigorous tests of rival claims about the roles and impacts of celebrity advocacy and helps us create generalisable arguments about this important phenomenon.

Notes

1   These are made up of the most followed Twitter celebrity non-politicians, according to twittercounter. com, supplemented by the celebrities most recognized for their charity work in the recent years as Celebs Gone Good by dosomething.org.
2   These are the top 100 organizations with most celebrity supporters according to looktothestars website.
3   Tweets were extracted by Talha Oz using the Twitter API. Tweets were downloaded on January 31, 2016. The maximum number allowed (3200) was requested, though the number retrieved varied

depending on the celebrity. Some, such as Beyonce, barely tweet, which results in a number of tweets fewer than 3200 for those inactive celebrities.

4   *People* magazine has a print circulation of 3.5 million and 12.3 million unique users visit people.com each month.

5   For *People* we used the search terms 'human rights' 'goodwill ambassador' and 'United Nations' and for the *New York Times* the term was 'United Nations' AND (celebrity OR celebrities OR actor OR actress OR athlete OR singer OR entertainer).

References

Alleyne, M. D. (2005). 'The United Nations' Celebrity Diplomacy'. *SAIS review*, 25(1), pp. 175–85.

Austin, E. W., Vord, R. V. D., Pinkleton, B. E. and Epstein, E. (2008). 'Celebrity Endorsements and Their Potential to Motivate Young Voters'. *Mass Communication and Society*, 11(4), pp. 420–36.

Avlon, J. (2011). 'A 21st Century Statesman'. *Newsweek*. February 20. [Online] Available at: http://www.newsweek.com/2011/02/20/a-21st-century-statesman.html [Accessed 1 March, 2016].

Baum, M. A. and Jamison, A. S. (2006). 'The Oprah Effect: How Soft News Helps Inattentive Citizens Vote Consistently'. *Journal of Politics*, 68(4), pp. 946–59.

Becker, A. B. (2013). 'Star Power? Advocacy, Receptivity, and Viewpoints on Celebrity Involvement in Issue Politics'. *Atlantic Journal of Communication*, 21(1), pp. 1–16.

Boorstin, D. J. (2012). *The Image: A Guide to Pseudo-events in America*. Vintage.

Boykoff, M. T. and Goodman, M. K. (2009). Conspicuous Redemption? Reflections on the Promises and Perils of the 'Celebritization' of Climate Change. *Geoforum*, 40(3), pp. 395–406.

Brockington, D. (2008). 'Powerful Environmentalisms: Conservation, Celebrity and Capitalism'. *Media, Culture, and Society*, 30(4), p. 551.

Brockington, D. (2009). *Celebrity and the Environment*. London: Zed.

Brockington, D. and Henson, S. (2014). 'Signifying the Public: Celebrity Advocacy and Post-democratic Politics'. *International Journal of Cultural Studies*, pp. 1–18.

Budabin, A. C. (2009). 'Genocide Olympics: the Campaign to Pressure China over the Darfur Conflict'. *CEU Political Science Journal*, 4(4), pp. 520–65.

Busby, J. W. (2007). 'Bono Made Jesse Helms Cry: Jubilee 2000, Debt Relief, and Moral Action in International Politics'. *International Studies Quarterly*, 51(2), pp. 247–75.

Chouliaraki, L. (2013). *The Ironic Spectator: Solidarity in the Age of Post-Humanitarianism*. John Cambridge: Wiley & Sons.

Click, M. A., Lee, H. and Holladay, H. W. (2016). '"You're Born to Be Brave": Lady Gaga's Use of Social Media to Inspire Fans' Political Awareness'. *International Journal of Cultural Studies*, pp. 1–17.

Cmiel, K. (1999). The Emergence of Human Rights Politics in the United States'. *The Journal of American History*, 86(3), pp. 1231–50.

Cooper, A. F. (2008). *Celebrity Diplomacy*. London: Routledge.

Couldry, N. and Markham, T. (2007). 'Celebrity Culture and Public Connection: Bridge or Chasm?'. *International Journal of Cultural Studies*, 10(4), pp. 403–21.

De Waal, A. (2008). 'The Humanitarian Carnival: a Celebrity Vogue'. *World Affairs*, 171(2), pp. 43–55.

Dieter, H. and Kumar, R. (2008). 'The Downside of Celebrity Diplomacy: The Neglected Complexity of Development'. *Global Governance. A Review of Multilateralism and International Organizations*, 14(3), pp. 259–64.

Drezner, D. W. (2007). 'Foreign Policy Goes Glam'. *The National Interest*, (92), pp. 22–8.

Easterly, W. R. (2006). *The White Man's Burden: Why the West's Efforts to Aid the Rest Have Done So Much Ill and So Little Good*. New York: Penguin.

Fowler, J. H. (2008). 'The Colbert Bump in Campaign Donations: More Truthful Than Truthy'. *PS: Political Science & Politics*, 41(3), pp. 533–9.

Friedman, T. L. (2002). *Longitudes and Attitudes: Exploring the World after September 11*. New York: Macmillan.

Garthwaite, C. and Moore, T. (2013). 'Can Celebrity Endorsements Affect Political Outcomes? Evidence form the 2008 US Democratic Presidential Primary'. *The Journal of Law, Economics & Organization*, 29(2), pp. 355–384.

Goodman, M. K. (2010). 'The Mirror of Consumption: Celebritization, Developmental Consumption and the Shifting Cultural Politics of Fair Trade'. *Geoforum*, 41(1), pp. 104–16.

Goodman, M. K. and Barnes, C. (2011). 'Star/poverty Space: the Making of the "Development Celebrity"'. *Celebrity Studies*, 2(1), pp. 69–85.

Hawkins, V. (2011). Creating a Groundswell or Getting on the Bandwagon? Celebrities, the Media and Distant Conflict. In: L. Tsaliki, C. A. Frangonikolopoulos and A. Huliaras, eds., *Transnational Celebrity Activism in Global Politics: Changing the World*, pp. 85–104.

Huliaris, A. and Tzifakis, N. (2008). 'The Dynamics of Celebrity Activism: Mia Farrow and the "Genocide Olympics" Campaign'. *Karamanlis Working Papers in Hellenic and European Studies*, 7(July), pp. 1–26.

Huliaris, A. and Tzifakis, N. (2010). 'Celebrity Activism in International Relations: In Search of a Framework for Analysis'. *Global Society*, 24(2), pp. 255–74.

Huliaris, A. and Tzifakis, N. (2011). Bringing the Individuals Back In? Celebrities as Transnational Activists':. In L. Tsaliki, C. A. Frangonikolopoulos and A. Huliaras, eds., *Transnational Celebrity Activism in Global Politics: Changing the World*, pp. 29–43.

Huliaris, A. and Tzifakis, N. (2012). 'The Fallacy of the Autonomous Celebrity Activist in International Politics: George Clooney and Mia Farrow in Darfur'. *Cambridge Review of International Affairs*, 25(3), pp. 417–31.

Huliaris, A. and Tzifakis, N. (2015). 'Personal Connections, Unexpected Journeys: U2 and Angelina Jolie in Bosnia'. *Celebrity Studies*, 6(4), pp. 443–56.

Inthorn, S. and Street, J. (2011). 'Simon Cowell for Prime Minister'? Young Citizens' Attitudes Towards Celebrity Politics'. *Media Culture and Society*, 33(3), p. 479.

Jackson, D. J. and Darrow, T. I. (2005). 'The Influence of Celebrity Endorsements on Young Adults' Political Opinions'. *The Harvard International Journal of Press/Politics*, 10(3), pp. 80–98.

Jackson, D. J. (2008). Selling Politics: The Impact of Celebrities' Political Beliefs on Young Americans'. *Journal of Political Marketing*, 6(4), pp. 67–83.

Jon, H. (2014). 'Human Rights and Celebrities'. In: A. Mihr and M. Gibney, eds., *The SAGE Handbook of Human Rights: Two Volume Set*. Thousand Oakes: Sage.

Kapoor, I. (2012). *Celebrity Humanitarianism: The Ideology of Global Charity*. London: Routledge.

Kellner, D. (2009). 'Barack Obama and Celebrity Spectacle'. *International Journal of Communication*, 3, p. 27.

Kellner, D. (2010). Celebrity Diplomacy, Spectacle and Barack Obama. *Celebrity sSudies*, 1(1), pp. 121–3.

Lim, Y. J. (2014). 'Promoting the Image of the United Nations'. *Journalism History*, 40(3), pp. 187–96.

Lindenberg, S., Joly, J. F. and Stapel, D. A. (2011). 'The Norm-Activating Power of Celebrity The Dynamics of Success and Influence'. *Social Psychology Quarterly*, 74(1), pp. 98–120.

Littler, J. (2008). '"I Feel Your Pain": Cosmopolitan Charity and the Public Fashioning of the Celebrity Soul'. *Social Semiotics*, 18(2), pp. 237–51.

Marsh, D., t'Hart, P. and Tindall, K. (2010). 'Celebrity Politics: The Politics of the Late Modernity?' *Political Studies Review*, 8(3), pp. 322–40.

Marshall, P. D. (1997). *Celebrity and Power: Fame in Contemporary Culture*. Minneapolis: University of Minnesota Press.

McLagan, M. (2002). 'Spectacles of Difference: Cultural Activism and the Mass Mediation of Tibet'. *Media Worlds: Anthropology on New Terrain*, pp. 90–111.

McLagan, M. (2003). 'Principles, Publicity, and Politics: Notes on Human Rights Media'. *American Anthropologist*, 105(3), pp. 605–12.

Meyer, D. S., Gamson, J. (1995). 'The Challenge of Cultural Elites: Celebrities and Social Movements'. *Sociological Inquiry*, 65(2), pp. 181–206.

Moyo, D. (2009). *Dead Aid: Why Aid Is Not Working and How There Is a Better Way for Africa*. New York: Macmillan.

Nash, K. (2008). 'Global Citizenship as Showbusiness: the Cultural Politics of Make Poverty History'. *Media, Culture and Society*, 30(2), pp. 167–81.

Njoroge, D. (2011). 'Calling a New Tune for Africa? Analysing a celebrity-led campaign to Redefine the Debate on Africa'. *Transnational Celebrity Activism in gGobal Politics: Changing the World*, pp. 231–48.

Pease, A. and Brewer, P. R. (2008). 'The Oprah Factor: The Effects of a Celebrity Endorsement in a Presidential Primary Campaign'. *The International Journal of Press/Politics*.

Postman, N. (2006). *Amusing Ourselves to Death: Public Discourse in the Age of Show Business*. New York: Penguin.

Richey, L. A. and Ponte, S. (2008). 'Better (Red)™ than Dead? Celebrities, Consumption and International Aid'. *Third World Quarterly*, 29(4), pp. 711–29.

Richey, L. A. and Ponte, S. (2011). *Brand Aid: Shopping Well to Save the World*. Minneapolis: University of Minnesota Press.

Richey, L. A., ed. (2016). *Celebrity Humanitarianism and North-South Relations*. London: Routledge.

Stohl, M., Stohl, C. and Stohl, R. (2011). 'Linking Small Arms, Child Soldiers, NGOs and Celebrity Activism: Nicolas Cage and the Lord of War'. In: Tsaliki, Frangonikolopoulos, and Huliaris, eds., *Transnational Celebrity Activism in Global Politics: Changing the World*, pp. 213–230.

Street, J. (2004). Celebrity Politicians: Popular Culture and Political Representation. *The British Journal of Politics & International Relations*, 6(4), pp. 435–52.

Street, J. (2012). 'Do Celebrity Politics and Celebrity Politicians Matter?'. *The British Journal of Politics & International Relations*, 14(3), pp. 346–56.

Tait, S. (2011). 'Consuming Ethics: Conflict Diamonds, the Entertainment Industry and Celebrity Activism'. *Transnational Celebrity Activism in Global Politics: Changing the World*, pp. 157–4.

Thrall, A. Trevor, et al. (2008). 'Star Power: Celebrity Advocacy and the Evolution of the Public Sphere.' *The International Journal of Press/Politics*, 13(4), pp. 362–85.

Tsaliki, L., Frangonikolopoulos, C. A. and Huliaras, A. eds. (2011). 'Transnational Celebrity Activism in Global Politics: Changing the World?' Chicago: Intellect Books.

Van Zoonen, L. (2005). *Entertaining the Citizen: When Politics and Popular Culture Converge*. Lanham: Rowman & Littlefield.

Weiskel, T. C. (2005). 'From Sidekick to Sideshow—Celebrity, Entertainment, and the Politics of Distraction Why Americans Are "Sleepwalking Toward the End of the Earth"'. *American Behavioral Scientist*, 49(3), pp. 393–409.

West, D. M. and Orman, J. M. (2003). *Celebrity Politics*. Upper Saddle River: Prentice Hall.

West, D. M. (2008). 'Angelina, Mia, and Bono: Celebrities and International Development'. *Global Development*, 2, pp. 74–84.

Wheeler, M. (2011). Celebrity Diplomacy: United Nations' Goodwill Ambassadors and Messengers of Peace'. *Celebrity Studies*, 2(1), pp. 6–18.

Wheeler, M. (2012). The Democratic Worth of Celebrity Politics in an Era of Late Modernity'. *The British Journal of Politics & International Relations*, 14(3), pp. 407–22.

Wheeler, M. (2013). *Celebrity Politics*. Cambridge, UK: Polity.

Wilson, J. (2011). 'A New Kind of Star Is Born: Audrey Hepburn and the Global Governmentalisation of Female Stardom'. *Celebrity Studies*, 2(1), pp. 56–68.

Wilson, J. (2014). 'Stardom, Sentimental Education, and the Shaping of Global Citizens'. *Cinema Journal*, 53(2), pp. 27–49.

Yrjola, R. (2011). The Global Politics of Celebrity Humanitarianism'. In: L. Tsaliki, C. A. Frangonikolopoulosand A. Huliaras, eds., *Transnational Celebrity Activism in Global Politics: Changing the World?* Intellect Books, pp. 175–92.

29

SOCIAL MEDIA REINVIGORATES DISABILITY RIGHTS ACTIVISM GLOBALLY

Beth A. Haller

In the 1990s, media and disability scholar Jack Nelson (1994, 1999, 2000) wrote often about the technology he felt would change the lives of many people with disabilities. In particular, he saw the Internet as a game changer, with its ability to allow people with disabilities to better access the social world without leaving their home computer. In the late 20th century, the Internet was heralded as a new 'liberating technology' that allowed people with disabilities to be less isolated, as well as a way for them to interact with others with fewer barriers (Sussman 1994, 85). In 1985, Cal State Northridge began a conference on technology and disability that continues today and features more than 350 general session workshops and more than 130 exhibitors displaying the latest technologies for persons with disabilities (CSUN 2016).

But what Nelson was looking at specifically was the Internet's power to transform lives. However, in the early 1990s, when Nelson was making his predictions, only email, basic Web pages, bulletin boards and real-time online chats existed. But for all its promise, the Web 1.0 days of the Internet only provided 'liberation' for a few tech-savvy disabled people, rather than the whole community en masse. Web 2.0 and social media with their ability to support proper social networking is now transforming disability rights activism worldwide.

In addition to technology shifting the global experiences of disabled people, the United Nations pushed disability rights into an international human rights framework through the United Nations Convention on the Rights of Persons with Disabilities (CRPD). Drafted between 2002 and 2006, 'the Convention does not create any new rights. It does, however, highlight the accessibility and inclusion angle of all human rights' (Schulze 2009, 6). As of June 2016, 164 countries had ratified the CRPD (UN 2016). Because human rights for disabled people sometimes means structural changes to a society, the CRPD's focus on making sure countries embrace efforts towards inclusion and accessibility are unique. 'The Convention on the Rights of Persons with Disabilities spells out clearly and unconditionally that persons with disabilities have equal access and a right to full and effective enjoyment of all human rights – the removal of barriers explicitly termed as a condition for access and the enjoyment of equality' (Schulze 2009, 10).

However, many countries still struggle to develop human rights policies that embrace the CRPD. Rwandan Bahati Satir, who is blind, says even in countries that have ratified the United Nations Convention on the Rights of Persons with Disabilities, much more is needed for disabled people: 'In Rwanda, it is very difficult for people with disabilities to get the services they need. Many children with disabilities have to travel great distances to attend special schools, and young people with disabilities often have to beg on streets in order to survive. Rwanda ratified the United Nations Convention on the Rights of Persons with Disabilities but there are huge gaps in implementation. When will we see the effects of this UN Convention here in my community?' (Satir 2012). The ratification of the CRPD shined attention on disability rights as human rights around the world, but as Bahati Satir says, laws that support more civil rights, better access and criminalise disability discrimination need to happen.

In light of the CRPD bringing awareness to human rights for disabled people, this chapter analyses disability activism worldwide through case studies investigating social media use by disability rights activists in the US and Serbia, as well as the social media training initiative for the African Youth with Disabilities Network. In addition to social media, mobile phone technology and its social media applications have combined to truly bring together the global disability community for activism, information exchange and enjoyable social interaction (Dobbs 2009). This chapter explores how disability activists are pushing forth a disability and human rights agenda through their vigorous use of social media, with the added benefit of driving traditional journalists to cover their rights issues.

Also, some social networking activities provide added accessibility for people with disabilities to participate in human rights activism in virtual spaces. For example, New York disability activist Mike Volkman (2009) says Facebook creates a kind of 'open space' for the disability rights community – 'an unregulated, un-programmed time and place where free-flowing ideas can spring up out of nowhere' (Volkman 2009).

The case studies in this chapter illustrate how social media has reinvigorated disability rights activism, as well as fostering more interaction within the international disability rights community regardless of age, ethnicity, gender, disability or geography. Social media allow disability activists to use vast global networks of friends or followers to better promote the human rights issues or events important to them.

Social media and disability access

One thing that is unique about social media such as Facebook, YouTube, Instagram and Twitter is that they are relatively simple to use. In the past, anyone wanting to have a Web presence had to own a computer and know some basic html or how to use Web design software. But the pre-set templates used in social media mean that in a couple of minutes, anyone with some basic computer/tablet/smartphone knowledge can be online with a Facebook page or Twitter account. They are easier to use than even basic blogger software. And if a person has a disability affecting their hands or ability to type lengthy content, Facebook and Twitter are designed primarily for brief posts or re-posts/re-tweets.

However, social media platforms do have some accessibility problems, especially for people with visual impairments, intellectual disabilities (Fairweather and Trewin 2010) or who use screen readers. But most social media companies are aware of this issue and are working on better access for disabled people. For example, Facebook began an accessibility initiative in 2011 and recruited Matt King, a blind engineer, to work on ramping up better access to Facebook through things like artificial intelligence that will identify something in a photo and audio describe it to a blind person (Guynn 2016). Facebook's platform can make communication easier for people with hearing loss or speech disabilities. Many platforms are more accessible depending on a person's specific disability. For instance, in Baltimore, an aphasia centre is teaching people who have lost verbal speech due to a stroke to use picture-based Pinterest on a smartphone or tablet to communicate when they are out in the community (Alper and Haller 2016).

Activism

The power of social media for activism comes down to several aspects – the ease of sharing information through posting links and pictures and thoughts and the ease of having that same information sent to the networks of many other people. And for YouTube, the ease of putting information in a visual format that makes it more accessible to many people worldwide.

Those who write about technology and activism explain the unique structure of activism that uses social media. Canadian technology writer Noorin Ladhani says: 'Online social activism through social media should not even be compared to the physical act of social activism. Instead, it needs to be considered and evaluated as a vehicle for free speech, information sharing, and online organising' (2011, 57). She adds that Facebook makes it much easier to organize people rather than using the email or phone lists of the past. Those who watch political advocacy say 'in today's social media age, any issue advocacy or public affairs campaign that relies solely on traditional media and paid advertising will simply not succeed' (Lawrence 2010).

In the area of disability rights activism, the uses of social media are many, and disabled people come together to form their own 'networked public' (Boyd 2011, 39) that has become a collective of disabled people interacting on social media and focused on fighting for their rights. For example, in 2011, British pensioners and disabled people used social media to organize a protest against government cuts to disability living allowances; the protest brought London traffic to a halt for an hour and also gathered support from non-disabled onlookers. 'I'm not protesting for my own benefit but for all the disabled people who will be affected,' [a wheelchair user said]. Protesters said they had been brought together by communicating on social media' (BBC News 2011). Disabled people as a unique 'public' fit easily with Livingstone's definition of people who have 'a common understanding of the world, a shared identity, a claim to inclusiveness, a consensus regarding the collective interest' (Livingstone 2005, 9).

US disability activist and writer Laura Hershey, who died in 2010, explained how social media like Facebook fosters ongoing connections between disability rights advocates from around the world. Hershey, who had spinal muscular atrophy, explained, 'it's not so much about meeting new people as staying connected with long-time fellow advocates: 'When you see people once or twice a year, or even less often, it's hard to keep up with them. Facebook lets us stay in contact, even see each other's photos of home, families, local actions, travels, etc." (Dobbs 2009). British research showed that for disabled people, social media 'can foster a sense of social connection for those who can frequently feel isolated, which is important to psychological wellbeing' (Quinn 2011).

New Mobility, a US magazine for wheelchair users, reported in 2009 that 'social networking can, in many cases, propel [disabled] people into additional civic involvement when attending every meeting or demonstration is unrealistic' (Dobbs 2009). Basically social networking provides some added accessibility for people with disabilities to participate in activism. 'Participating in quasi-political action through Facebook is easy', says power wheelchair user T. K. Small, a Brooklyn, New York attorney, disability radio show co-host and disability advocate, who is also a member of numerous Facebook activism groups (Dobbs 2009). New York disability activist Mike Volkman (2009) says it was worth trading anonymity for advocacy through social media like Facebook. After he joined Facebook, he said the largest group he interacted with there were members of the disability rights community. About a third of his Facebook friends 'are what [US disability rights leader] Justin Dart referred to as "colleagues in justice,"' Volkman says.

For Volkman, Facebook allows barriers of time and distance for activism to recede: 'We have people in every corner of the country, and we have new friends from far-flung places like Great Britain and even Mongolia who want to be a big part of what we are doing' (Volkman 2009).

US disability rights activism

Most American disability rights organizations now use social media to steer people across the Internet to their activities and advocate for civil rights for disabled people. Two national organizations analysed for this chapter, National ADAPT and the Disability Rights Education Defence Fund (DREDF), illustrate the multifaceted ways social media enhance activism. ADAPT is a grassroots disability rights organization that has been around since the 1970s when it successfully got wheelchair accessible buses in Denver through nonviolent protests and civil disobedience (Shapiro 1993). It also has local chapters in 30 states. National ADAPT's Twitter feed with more than 11,000 followers, and its Facebook page with more than 3,500 likes in 2016, has become a repository for much of what is going with ADAPT nationally and locally, as well as connecting to other disability rights initiatives by posting links, pictures and videos.

When ADAPT protested proposed Medicaid changes in Washington, D.C. in May 2011, it illustrated how a disability rights organization could harness social media for activism. When a number of ADAPT activists tried to occupy Rep. Paul Ryan's office to protest his budget proposal that would cut Medicaid funding by billions and shift control of the program to the states (Hulse 2011).

ADAPT live tweeted much of its protest activities, including the arrest of about 100 disability activists. Its Twitter feed included:

- Pictures from ADAPT protestors and others and information about those arrested.
- It gave links to any media coverage.
- It gave information so someone who wanted to participate but couldn't be in DC could follow along.
- People not in DC could even become active by calling Rep. Paul Ryan via the phone number ADAPT tweeted.

The tweets built a cross-disability community. A 3 May, 2011 tweet said: 'Remember that ADAPT fights for all disabilities: physical, dd, psychiatric, blind, deaf, autism, MCS, everyone. That is why we are here'. And National ADAPT's Facebook page became a repository for protestors' pictures as National ADAPT was tagged in many of the activists' photos. Later in May 2011, local ADAPT groups held protests in Chicago, Philadelphia and Minnesota and the live tweeting continued with updates, photos and videos from those actions.

A Minnesota disability group demonstrated at the Minnesota Senate gallery, saying 'the cuts that the Republican leaders have proposed to Health and Human Services will send us to expensive and unhealthy nursing homes and institutions, keep us from work & community life and cost the state more money' (Sorem 2011). A video of their demonstration was uploaded on a citizen journalism site, The Uptake, and was headlined, 'I'd rather go to jail than die in a nursing home' (Sorem 2011). This tweet went out across ADAPT social networks: 'Check out awesome raw video from @uptakemn http://bit.ly/jgenn7 -- really captured passion/support + security professionalism'.

Because the Disability Rights Education & Defence Fund (DREDF) is a civil rights and policy centre in Berkeley, California, its activism takes place in the courtroom and through lobbying and public policy development primarily. However, the organization, founded in 1979, has long embraced social media for both activism and to educate people with disabilities and the parents of disabled children about their rights. It began its YouTube channel in 2009. Much of its work is focused on the federal law, Individuals with Disabilities Education Act (IDEA) that mandates that eligible students with disabilities have their educational needs met by their schools.

It regularly tweets about disability rights and access cases in the news, government policy changes, and its own advocacy work. For example, in April 2011, it tweeted about the Facebook page it set up as an Action Alert for people to call/email Congress to co-sponsor the IDEA Fairness Restoration Act on Wednesday, 4 May, 2011. This bill would allow parents to recover expert witness fees when they prevail in due process hearings and court actions under the IDEA. DREDF also links its online newsletter to its social media presence. For instance, in January 2016 it gave ongoing reports about its work in support of its partnership with disability rights activists in Kenya called RightsNow! Kenya (DREDF 2016, January). Through Facebook, Twitter and blogging, DREDF is reaching out to people with disabilities and their families about significant disability human rights issues.

DREDF's YouTube channel features training videos such as those helping parents understand the special education process and how to advocate for their disabled child. In addition, it has posted its short documentary (formerly a VHS tape), 'The Power of 504': 'Award-winning 18-minute documentary video, which captures the drama and emotions of the historic civil rights demonstration of people with disabilities in 1977, resulting in the signing of the 504 Regulations, the first Federal Civil Rights Law protecting people with disabilities. Includes contemporary news footage and news interviews with participants and demonstration leaders' (DREDF 2010). As a historic document of disability rights in the US, the documentary was also shown to activists who are part of RightsNow! in Kenya. DREDF reports that the 'viewing of *The Power of 504* breaks preconceived notions that disability rights in the US were given on a silver platter' (DREDF 2016 January).

African Youth with Disabilities Network

It is not unusual for a California-based disability justice organization like DREDF to be collaborating with a Kenyan disability rights organization because of the ways in which social media breaks down barriers of geography for activism. Long before Botswana writer Siyanda Mohutsiwa brought together young African voices on Twitter in 2015 (Mohutsiwa 2016), African young people with disabilities saw that leveraging social media would be a good way to bring attention to the discrimination, stigma and lack of access disabled people face in many African countries. In 2011, near Nairobi, Kenya, 40 young disabled people from 13 African countries formed the African Youth with Disabilities Network (O'Haver 2011). With meetings and conferences funded through the Open Society Foundations' Initiative for Eastern Africa, Disability Rights Initiative, and the Youth Initiative, the African Youth with Disabilities Network took part in a social media training conference in 2012. Liberian Daintowon Pay-bayee says social media is a way for young African disabled people to get their messages into an international forum with no geographic boundaries: 'Disability is not inability. To fight discrimination and change public perceptions, we need to begin talking about youth with disabilities in our homes, our neighbourhoods, and on the national and international stage' (Pay-bayee 2012). The six-day meeting familiarised the young people with Facebook, Twitter and shooting video for YouTube. In her YouTube video, Ugandan Sofia Aujo says, 'We have learned how to talk for ourselves. We have learned how to fight for our own rights. And we have learned how to monitor which activities are being carried out in our own countries. It has inspired us, we have grown strong voices' (Aujo 2012). Another young woman with a disability who participated explained: 'When you think new media training, you probably think I do all the sexy stuff like using infographics to make your website interactive or how to have a dancing or a fancy AVI on Twitter. No, think basics on how to set up a Facebook page, why it is important, why you should be on Twitter, looking for other people in your country on Twitter and seeing why they have so many followers and why or what you should do to get followers' (Haiku 2012). Although the African Youth with Disabilities Network has become inactive as a group by 2016, individuals are still working to get the message out about the stronger human rights initiatives needed for disabled people in Africa. Some disabled Africans have become citizen journalists covering more than disability rights topics. A double arm amputee in Sierra Leone helped cover the elections there in 2012 (Marshall 2012). And the first leader of the African Youth with Disabilities Network, Seray Banugra, wrote for news outlets about general topics with a disability rights slant. His *Guardian* article in 2012 says, 'Disability rights have taken a step back, with Sierra Leone also failing to include deaf and immobile people in election planning' (Banugra & Powell 2012).

Serbia's Centre Living Upright (CZU)

In Serbia, one of its main disability rights organization, the Novi Sad-based Centre Living Upright was founded in the early 2000s in an effort to get personal attendant services to disabled people who needed them (Ruzicic 2011). Its mission expanded to include 'to make change and say enough! Enough of discrimination, enough of inequality, enough of humiliation among disabled people' and to implement the UN CRPD (CZU Facebook page video 2014). In 2013, Centre Living Upright joined with the Novi Sad Journalism School to participate in a program that strengthened their social media skills for disability activism. Through Mobility International's EMPOWER program, which is funded by the US State Department, Centre Living Upright and journalism school representatives went to United States and worked with media and disability scholar Beth Haller at Towson University in Maryland and with the director of the Hussman Centre for Adults with Autism at Towson University (Lucas 2013). The project used social media training to empower disability advocates in Serbia to tell their own stories about disability rights. The project was innovative with its inclusion of students and faculty from the Novi Sad Journalism School in Serbia. The Serbian journalism students received a well-rounded education in the rights and access issues that face people with disabilities, as well as learning how to report effectively on disability topics (Novi Sad Journalism School 2013). The hope was that the disability rights content on social media would also educate the Serbian news media about disability issues. Although Centre Living Upright has struggled financially in recent years, social media has provided a low- to no-cost way of promoting its work. It no longer has an active website but has a vibrant Facebook presence instead. Its founder Milica Mima Ruzicic-Novkovic, who has cerebral palsy, also promotes CZU on her personal Facebook page, as well as issues related to disability rights. For example, in November 2015, she posted 11 photos celebrating her 15 years of having personal attendant services. She says, 'These are photos of me with my current and previous personal assistants who were with me in various life events in relation to the family, work, education, etc. It was actually the start of PA service in Novi Sad, which I wasn't aware of then. Grateful to life for this experience and opportunity to meet them all!' (Ruzicic-Novkovic 2015).

The CZU Facebook page, which is titled in both Serbian and English, posts at least 6–12 times weekly in mostly Serbian but also posts links about disability rights from around the world, often in English. Links in English come from organizations like the European Network on Independent Living, which is based in Belgium and has a website and Facebook page in English (ENIL 2016).

Though the business world doesn't usually recommend substituting a Facebook page for website, in the world of disability rights, it works well. The sharing and visual aspect of Facebook allows disability rights activists around the world to see activities of those who are doing similar work, and even if they don't speak that language, the photos might draw them to a page that can be translated. For instance, CZU's Facebook page posted several pictures of its director signing a memorandum of understanding about the importance of personnel attendant services in Novi Sad in 2016 (CZU Facebook page 2016, March 25).

Conclusions

The case studies in this chapter are just a few of the thousands of examples of disability organizations, disability activists, and individuals with disabilities using social media to further the cause of disability human rights. The power of social media for activism is still growing in strength. As technology watcher Noorin Ladhani says, social media should be evaluated as a tool for change, not as the tool that will change the world. Disability activist Mike Volkman says, 'What we are doing now with Facebook really shows the true potential of what the Internet can do to transform our society. We are seeing changes that rival historically the invention of the printing press' (Volkman 2009).

The late US disability rights leader Justin Dart pre-dated social media, but his focus on building a disability rights community in the United States after he saw disabled children being left to die in Vietnam connects to how social media is being used globally (*Ability Magazine* 2002). He spoke of the disability community 'rededicating itself to united advocacy' (United Advocacy 2010), and platforms like Facebook, Twitter and YouTube contribute to and bolster that united spirit of disability rights activists worldwide. Known as the godfather of the Americans with Disabilities Act (ADA), Dart explained how attitudes change when disabled people gain basic human rights: 'We are so proud to have passed the ADA built on the 504. And that attitudes of all Americans have changed about people with disabilities. We are real human beings in the human race. That's different than it used to be. However, now we have to get out and get our rights enforced. While no minority has all their rights enforced, we have to do it, because nobody ever gave rights away. We have to get out of life as usual and become fully 24 hour a day, 365 days a year passionate single-minded advocates for disability rights' (Smith 2014). The ADA is considered one of the inspirations for the CRPD, but the USA has yet to ratify it (National Association of the Deaf 2012). However, the fact that Justin Dart's reason for pursuing disability rights in the USA came from seeing human rights violations and the death of disabled people in Vietnam illustrates an interesting interconnection with the CRPD's current push towards inclusion and accessibility as human rights issues worldwide.

Dart knew that fighting for disability rights meant taking on established institutions, like the media: 'Empowerment is when we say no to the primitive illusion that society, government, the free market, the public media are some sort of paternalistic super gods that give us truth, equality and prosperity' (Dart 1996). He proposed a revolution of empowerment, and this chapter argues that social media platforms now aid disability rights activists in getting that message of empowerment and human rights out to the world. As Dart explained to the disability rights community, 'Together, we shall overcome' (United Advocacy 2010). With social media, the Internet truly has become a form of 'liberating technology' that was promised for disabled people around the world.

References

Ability Magazine (2002). 'Justin Dart Remembered'. *Ability Magazine*. Available at: http://abilitymagazine. com/JustinDart_remembered.html [2 June, 2015].
Alper, M. and Haller, B. (2016). 'Social Media and Mediated Sociality as Communication: Augmentations and Alternatives to Speech in the Digital Age'. In: K. Ellis and M. Kent, eds., *Social Media and Disability: Global Perspectives.* London: Ashgate.

Aujo, S. (2012). *AYWDN: Sofia Aujo, Uganda*. Available at: https://www.youtube.com/watch?v=i9FlSPWD Tnw&list=PL407C8373BB7BE5C3&index=2 [2 June, 2015].

Banugra, S. and Powell, L. (2012). "Sierra Leone Scraps Tactile Voting System for Elections," *The Guardian* (November 2016). Available at: http://www.theguardian.com/global-development/2012/nov/16/sierra-leone-tactile-voting-elections [14 June, 2015].

BBC News (2011). 'London Pensioner and Disabled Protest Disrupts Traffic'. *BBC News*, 26 May. http://www.bbc.co.uk/news/uk-england-london-13565111 [18 June, 2015].

Boyd, D. (2011). 'Social Networks as Networked Publics. Affordances, Dynamics and Implications'. In: Z. Papacharissi, ed., *A Networked Self. Identity, Community and Culture on Social Network Sites*. London: Routledge.

California State University Northridge (2016). Conference to Feature Latest Assistive Technology for People with Disabilities [press release] (March 1). Available at: http://csunshinetoday.csun.edu/media-releases/conference-to-feature-latest-assistive-technology-for-people-with-disabilities/ [20 March, 2016].

Centar Živeti Uspravno/ Centre Living Upright (2014). Facebook page video. Available at: https://www.facebook.com/zivetiuspravno/?fref=ts [14 June, 2015].

Centar Živeti Uspravno/ Centre Living Upright (2016). Facebook page (March 25). Available at: https://www.facebook.com/zivetiuspravno/?fref=ts [14 June, 2015].

Dart, J. (1996). Remarks at National Summit on Disability Policy, April 27, Dallas, Texas. Available at: https://www.ncd.gov/progress_reports/July1996 [18 June, 2015].

Dobbs, J. (2009). 'Why Does Facebook Matter?' *New Mobility*, August. Available at: http://www.newmobility.com/2009/08/why-does-facebook-matter/ [18 June, 2015].

DREDF YouTube channel (2010). 'The Power of 504' (full version, open caption, English and Spanish). Available at: https://www.youtube.com/watch?v=SyWcCuVta7M [18 June, 2015].

DREDF The Blog (2016). Tag: RightsNow! (January). Available at: http://dredf.org/web-log/tag/rightsnow/ [Accessed 3 February, 2016].

European Network on Independent Living (2016). Website. Available at: http://www.enil.eu/

Fairweather, P. and Trewin, S. (2010). 'Cognitive Impairments and Web 2.0'. *Universal Access in the Information Society* (June), pp. 137–46.

Guynn, J. (2016). 'For People with Disabilities, Surfing the Web a Daily Struggle'. *USA Today*, (24 March), p. 3B.

Haiku, H. (2012). 'Africa: Social Media Skills for Africans with Disabilities'. *Global Voices*, 12 July. Available at: https://globalvoices.org/2012/07/12/africa-social-media-skills-for-african-youth-with-disabilities/ [Accessed 8 August, 2012].

Hulse, C. (2011). 'House Republicans Propose $4 trillion in Cuts Over Decade'. *The NY Times*, 3 April. Avaialble at: http://www.nytimes.com/2011/04/04/us/politics/04spend.html?_r=0 [18 June, 2015].

Ladhani, N. (2011). 'The Organizing Impact of Social Networking'. *Social Policy*, 40(4), p. 57.

Lawrence, D. (2010). 'How Political Activists are Making the Most of Social Media'. *Forbes*. Available at: http://www.forbes.com/2010/07/15/social-media-social-activism-facebook-twitter-leadership-citizenship-burson.html [18 June, 2015].

Livingstone, S. (2005). *Audiences and Publics: When Cultural Engagement Matters for the Public Sphere*. Portland, OR: Intellect.

Lucas, J. (2013). 'Towson, U.S. State Department Partner to Bolster Disability Rights in Serbia'. News (16 October). Towson University website. Available at: http://tunews.towson.edu/2013/10/16/towson-u-s-department-of-state-partner-to-bolster-disability-rights-in-serbia/ [7 June, 2015].

Marshall, S. (2012). 'Citizen Journalists Report Sierra Leone Elections by SMS,' Journalism.co.uk website,, 20 Nov. Available at: https://www.journalism.co.uk/news/citizen-journalists-report-sierra-leone-elections-by-sms-/s2/a551240/ [7 June, 2015].

Mohutsiwa, S. (2016). 'How Young Africans Found a Voice on Twitter'. TED Talk, February. Available at: https://www.ted.com/talks/siyanda_mohutsiwa_how_young_africans_found_a_voice_on_twitter [7 June, 2015].

National Association of the Deaf (2012). UN Convention on the Rights of Persons with Disabilities. Available at: https://nad.org/issues/international-advocacy/crpd [Accessed 1 June, 2015].

Nelson, J. (2000). 'The Media Role in Building the Disability Community'. *Journal of Mass Media Ethics*, 15(3), p. 180.

Nelson, J. (1999). 'The Media's Role in Building the Disability Community'. Paper presented at the Association for Education in Journalism and Mass Communication, August.

Nelson, J. (1994). 'The Virtual Community: A Place for the No-Longer-Disabled'. Paper presented at the Association for Education in Journalism and Mass Communication. Atlanta, GA.

Novi Sad Journalism School (2013). 'The Novi Sad Journalism School Selected to Participate in U.S. Department of State Sponsored Professional Fellows Empower Program'. website, http://www.novi-narska-skola.org.rs/sr/?p=1838&lang=en [Accessed 1 June, 2015].

O'Haver, K. (2011). 'Young People with Disabilities in Africa Challenge the Status Quo' Open Society Foundations website (Dec. 5). Available at: https://www.opensocietyfoundations.org/voices/young-people-disabilities-africa-challenge-status-quo [Accessed 1 June, 2015].

Pay-bayee, D. (2012). 'Why We Need to Talk About Youth With Disabilities'. Open Society Foundations website (3 July). Available at: https://www.opensocietyfoundations.org/voices/why-we-need-talk-about-youth-disabilities [Accessed 1 June, 2015].

Quinn, B. (2011). 'Social Network Users Have Twice as Many Friends Online as in Real Life," *The Guardian* (8 May). Available at: http://www.theguardian.com/media/2011/may/09/social-network-users-friends-online?& [Accessed 1 June, 2011].

Ruzicic, M. M. (2011). Report from Mima Ruzicic, Novi Sad, Serbia and Montenegro, about the Situation of Personal Assistance Users and Students with Disabilities. Independent Living Institute website. Available at: http://www.independentliving.org/docs7/ruzicic200504.html [Accessed 1 June, 2015].

Ruzicic-Novkovic, M. M. (2015). '15 years of PA Services'. Facebook Photo Album. Available at: https://www.facebook.com/media/set/?set=a.1659432507665503.1073741832.1579078792367542&type=3 [Accessed 1 June, 2015].

Satir, B. (2012). 'Shattering Stereotypes in Rwanda'. Open Society Foundations website, July 3. Available at: https://www.opensocietyfoundations.org/voices/shattering-stereotypes-rwanda [Accessed 1 June, 2015].

Schulze, M. (2009). *Understanding the UN Convention on the Rights of Persons with Disabilities*. Lyon, France: Handicap International.

Shapiro, J. (1993). *No Pity. People with Disabilities Forging a New Civil Rights Movement.* NY Times Books/Random House.

Smith, G. (2014). *Remembering Justin Dart on this Birthday.* The Strength Coach blog, 29 August. Avalable at: http://www.thestrengthcoach.com/remembering-justin-dart-birthday/ [Accessed 1 June, 2015].

Sorem, B. (2011). '"I'd Rather Go To Jail Than Die In A Nursing Home" - Handicap Protest Budget Cuts'. *The Uptake.* Available at: http://www.theuptake.org/2011/05/11/protesters-disrupt-debate-on-mn-anti-gay-constitutional-amendment/ [Accessed 7 June, 2011].

Sussman, V. (1994). *Opening Doors to an Inaccessible World* U.S. News & World Report, 85.

United Advocacy (2010). *Justin Dart. From One Came Much. Continuing the Revolution of Empowerment.* Available at: http://www.unitedadvocacy.org/ [Accessed 1 June, 2011].

United Nations (2016). Finland Ratifies CRPD (Total: 164). Available at: https://www.un.org/development/desa/disabilities/news/dspd/finland-ratifies-crpd-total-164.html [Accessed 18 June, 2016].

United Nations Treaty Collection (2016). *15. Convention on the Rights of Persons with Disabilities'.* Available at: https://treaties.un.org/Pages/ViewDetails.aspx?src=IND&mtdsg_no=IV-15&chapter=4&lang=en [Accessed 18 June, 2016].

Volkman, M. (2009). 'Trading Anonymity for Advocacy'. *New Mobility*, http://www.newmobility.com/articleViewIE.cfm?id=11499. [Accessed 18 June, 2011].

30

MEDIA AND LGBT ADVOCACY

Visibility and transnationalism in a digital age

Eve Ng

Media and public visibility for LGBT political action

Historically, public visibility has been pursued by many LGBT[1] groups in the West, and included using different kinds of media. At the same time, visibility is fraught for various reasons, and its pursuit as a part of LGBT advocacy is therefore neither politically obvious nor straightforward.

Taking the US as an illustrative example, gays and lesbians before the 1960s rarely pursued public visibility. The mid-century homophile groups – the Mattachine Society for gay men and Daughters of Bilitis for lesbians (founded in 1950 and 1955 respectively) – deliberately stayed under the radar at a time when homosexuality was subject to both legal and social sanctions. The intersections of gay rights advocacy with the civil rights and feminist movements in the 1960s were associated with shifts towards more public demonstrations and demands, with the call for gays and lesbians to 'come out (of the closet)' argued to be crucial not just for the well-being of the individuals involved, but also for strengthening the gay and lesbian community to lobby for sociopolitical acceptance and rights.

In the strategic communication literature, using media for increasing visibility is still considered a key goal, with researchers identifying ways that LGBT groups can effectively use media for communicating with the public or to empower LGBT communities (e.g. see Tindall and Waters 2013). However, the concept of coming out has been problematised in critical social approaches, particularly queer theory, for reinscribing a problematic, hierarchical binary of interiority/exteriority and oversimplifying complex realities of being 'both inside and outside at the same time' (Fuss 1991, 4), not accounting for how discourses of being 'out' produce specific kinds of LGBT subjects (e.g. Sedgwick 1990), inadequately challenging other social hierarchies such as class and age (Barnhurst 2007) and failing to productively rethink the politics of queer marginalisations (e.g. Warner 1999).

The issue has also been addressed with respect to the impact of visibility on LGBT-identified persons. As Barnhurst (2007) commented, the US gay press noted a grim correlation between prominent media coverage of LGBT rights (such as Supreme Court rulings) and increased physical attacks on queer people. Indeed, visibility in contexts of significant homophobia and state repression has been argued to be not just dangerous, but counterproductive to progress for LGBT rights.

The effects of visibility, in other words, for LGBT subjects as well as for larger publics, always have social, cultural and political specificities. This point bears consideration in examining the significance of various forms of media for LGBT advocacy. The next section discusses print, radio, television and film, followed by a review of new media uses.

Print, radio, television and film

Print media were especially important to early LGBT rights movements. Miller (2000) catalogued over 7,000 lesbian and gay periodicals worldwide from the 1890s to 2000, the majority published from the mid-20th century onwards. While not all of these explicitly addressed LGBT rights, many were key to the kinds of community-building that facilitated advocacy efforts (e.g. see Streitmatter 1995), even as commercial interests also began to shape the content of gay media (Sender 2004). Notable US examples include *The Ladder* newsletter, published by the Daughters of Bilitis from 1956–72, the Boston-based *Gay Community News* (1973–92), and the *Advocate*, which began as the *Los Angeles Advocate* newspaper in 1967 (see Garber 1999). Also important were visual images, including cover images on gay newsletters or newspapers such as journalistic photographs or homoerotic art, as well as posters produced by the Gay Liberation Front, which have often been overlooked as sites of contestation over sexual and political expression (Meyer 2006).

In film, there have been various documentaries of LGBT activism, including those about the fight against AIDS (e.g. *How To Survive A Plague*, 2012; *We Were Here*, 2011), the US gay rights movement (e.g. *Before Stonewall*, 1995; *Stonewall Uprising*, 2010) and LGBT activism in the global South (e.g. *Queer China, 'Comrade' China*, 2013; *Call Me Kuchu*, 2012, and *God Loves Uganda*, 2013, both about Uganda; and *The Abominable Crime*, 2013, about Jamaica). Scholarly work highlighting the importance of documentary includes Bluck's (2007) discussion of films about transsexual identity in Iran and Harvey's (2007) study of educational films about AIDS in Sub-Saharan Africa.

While pre-Stonewall, the mainstream US media was fairly conservative regarding LGBT issues, news and talk show programs on alternative radio and television stations offered gays and lesbians the opportunity to air their experiences and advocate for sociopolitical change as early as the 1950s, with several of these programs being summarised or transcribed in print publications such as the Mattachine Society's *Mattachine Review* or the Daughters of Bilitis's *The Ladder* newsletters (Alwood 2007; Capsuto 2000).

Although this chapter is primarily concerned with how media is used for LGBT rights advocacy, the large body of media effects work that addresses how media, particularly news content,[2] can inform public thinking warrants acknowledgement. Much of this research uses agenda setting and framing theory (e.g. see Scheufele and Tewksbury 2007) to examine how LGBT issues are framed in public discourse, often drawing from psychological models about underlying knowledge and beliefs to explain the relationship to viewers' attitudes (e.g. see Brewer 2003; Craig et al. 2005; Johnson 2012). While some of this research traces progressive changes in the presentation of LGBT issues, mainstream media continues to be associated with homophobic or heteronormative frames, as Landau (2009) argued in relation to representations of same-sex parents and their children in much US news. Also, given that multiple agents may be involved in framing – including different groups of news professionals, LGBT rights advocates and anti-LGBT groups – situations of competing frames frequently emerge (Pan et al. 2010; Baisley 2015).

A related strand of research, on the effects of particular framings for LGBT individuals and advocacy groups themselves, suggests a mixture of positive and negative outcomes. Examining media releases from GLAAD (the Gay and Lesbian Association Against Defamation), Cabosky (2014) argued that the organization's focus on the vulnerability of LGBT people and the promotion of celebrities at media events are problematic, even as social media provides ordinary LGBT individuals a channel for some input. In an account of the US's Queer Nation, Gray (2009) identified how competing interests and press coverage complexly shaped the trajectory of the organization, which had seeds for an intersectional approach to social justice that did not ultimately develop. And addressing same-sex marriage, Moscowitz (2013) examined content from major news outlets and interviewed LGBT activists on how they sought to use media, finding that commercial media coverage was both productive and detrimental to the LGBT cause.

Taken collectively, the research here highlights the significance of how LGBT issues are presented in both mainstream and LGBT media. Social movement actors themselves, of course, also seek to shape the terms of the discussion, and, as the next section discusses, digital media provide LGBT activists various options for using media for their own purposes, even as online domains present their own challenges.

Digital media and LGBT activism

Digital media have become key to contemporary movements for social and political change (e.g. see Castells 2012; Vissers and Stolle 2014), even as disagreement remains about the efficacy of online-based activism and the relationship between online and offline practices. New media have various characteristics that lend themselves to activism, including offering greater anonymity, the ability for social movement actors to communicate and coordinate across geographic separation, and the use of digital platforms for advocacy actions, such as funding drives, email campaigns, and online petitions.

These apply also to LGBT advocacy, but the relationship between LGBT identity and activism has its particularities. The Internet has facilitated the construction of shared identities and communities amongst LGBT users (even as these commonalities remain partial and contested) that have political import in themselves, but not all who claim such identities are involved in LGBT activism per se. However, given the relationship between collective affinities and organized political action, the significance of digital media for LGBT advocacy is a dual one – 'offering a "free space" where individuals express their identities, which can be politicized for the purposes of [a] movement' (Ayoub and Brzezińska 2015, 226). Here, I refrain from reviewing scholarship on digital media and LGBT identity (e.g. see O'Riordan and Phillips, 2007; Pullen and Cooper, 2010; Taylor, Falconer and Snowdon 2014), and focus on research that explicitly addresses LGBT advocacy.

LGBT advocacy in digital domains has been discussed in multiple contexts globally, and includes the use of listservs, email lists, and online groups, which were precursors to contemporary message boards; news sites; portal sites; websites maintained by individuals (often as blogs) or organizations; and of course, social media. Examples include email campaigns in China to address homophobic search engine results (Chase 2012); message boards for transgender people in South Africa (Prinsloo, McLean and Moletsane 2011); personal blogs in China (Chase 2012) and India (Bhattacharjya and Ganesh 2011); organizational websites of queer feminist activists in Lebanon (Moawad and Qiblaw 2011) and Argentina, Brazil, Chile, Mexico, and Peru (Friedman 2007); and portal sites such as the US-based Gay.com (Campbell 2007) and Fridae in Southeast Asia (Yue 2012). As for social media, the focus has been on the most popular platforms, particularly Facebook and Twitter, but LGBT activists have also used other platforms, such as Orkut and Leskut in Brazil (Corrêa et al. 2011) and Weibo in China (Chase 2012).

One of the most high-profile instances of LGBT advocacy through digital media has been the It Gets Better project. American author Dan Savage and his partner Terry Miller made the first video in 2010 in the wake of several suicides in the US by young people who did not conform to normative sexuality or gender expression. After being posted to YouTube, the video went viral and thousands of people, including celebrities and politicians, made and circulated their own It Gets Better clips. The momentum of these videos also generated an *It Gets Better* book by Savage and Miller, published in 2011, as well as a musical performed by the L.A. Gay Men's Chorus, which tours the country by invitation.[3]

Despite such prominent achievements, various caveats about digital media for LGBT advocacy have been raised. One major strand, echoed for other kinds of activism, is the limits of online actions and therefore the need to simultaneously enact offline strategies. For example, Mwangi (2014) noted that LGBT-friendly political candidates in Kenya who seemed popular online failed to even secure party nominations during the 2013 elections, so that even as digital media can 'give agency to subaltern queer voices' (109), it is important to work towards economic and political changes through actions in the material world. In a similar vein, Chase (2012) argued that in Korea and China, online activism has not been sufficiently effective for marshalling public support for the legalization of same-sex marriage, and only those LGBT advocates who were already well-known through traditional media succeeded in reaching significant numbers of people online.

Another issue concerns the safety sometimes assumed to characterize digital spaces, which has drawn many LGBT activists. For example, Chua (2014) discussed the emergence of LGBT cyberactivism using email lists and online forums in Singapore in the 1990s, given how offline activities were subject to state surveillance and threats of sanctions against participants. However, online spaces can also be regulated and surveilled. Policies such as mandatory blogger registration or the required use of real names online – the latter in place in South Korea until being struck down by courts in 2012 – can thwart anonymity for at least some platforms. Furthermore, the Internet is not truly anonymous for the vast majority of users, and facilitates both targeted and mass surveillance. The Arab Spring, for example, illustrated government efforts to track activists through their social media use (see Hussain 2013), and recently, there have been reports about authorities tapping social and mobile platforms to specifically entrap LGBT users (Culzac 2014).

Other state encounters have to do with the censorship of LGBT content, sometimes on the basis of being considered pornographic or harmful to minors. Distinguishing between sexual content that is abusive or exploitative on the one hand and disturbing to some viewers because it is non-normative on the other has been contested ground for regulators, feminists, and other interested parties. Corrêa et al. (2011) discussed such tensions concerning the regulation of online content in Brazil, where discourses around 'child protection' shape attitudes towards LGBT sites. And while overt censorship has decreased in many Western countries, institutions such as libraries and schools still routinely block search terms or websites deemed inappropriate on sexual grounds, especially for youthful users, making some LGBT-related content inaccessible (Echols and Ditmore 2011).

State regulation of LGBT content, as well as the practices of search engines, has not gone uncontested. For example, Korean gay and lesbian groups have campaigned against both the government ratings system for online content, which, among other things, restricts access to gay and lesbian websites by user age, and against Korea's major search engines for shutting down some gay and lesbian sites and labelling others as harmful to youthful users, and for categorising LGBT search terms such as 'homosexual' and 'gay' as adult-only (Bong 2008). In China, the activist group Smile4Gay has campaigned against Baidu, both a portal site and China's largest search engine, for having advertisements for 'treating' homosexuality appear if LGBT-related search terms are entered, as well as demanding the removal of homophobic content hosted by Baidu and the removal of blocks placed on certain gay websites (Chase 2012).

Digital media also provide opportunities for anti-LGBT expression. In fact, Mwangi (2014) found that in Kenya, homophobic content was more copious and virulent in various online spaces than on traditional media, even though mainstream media discourses about homosexuality are already quite negative. And based on the tracking of online hate speech in Poland, Ayoub and Brzezińska (2015) noted that while 'transnational counter-[LGBT-]movement ties are weaker than those of LGBT groups in Europe' (237), it is clear that the Internet has also facilitated the transnationalisation of these counter-mobilizations.

Finally, counter to seeing digital media as offering LGBT subjects spaces for increased expression, some scholars have argued that the Internet can function as a 'digital closet' – a domain to which users who are not out in the offline world are confined. For example, Gorkemli (2010) argued that given the reluctance of many LGBT people in Turkey to come out, the Internet has become 'more than just a means of communication or a tool for activism' but also 'a symbol of homosexual oppression for lesbian and gay activists in Turkey' (79). As Barnhurst (2007) commented, while queers conversant with new media technologies expect digital modes of freedom, they may simultaneously remain at risk of assault and discrimination in the physical world.

Transnational dynamics of media and LGBT rights

The transnationalization of human rights advocacy and of social movements more generally has attracted much commentary, about both its positive and negative implications. While moving beyond national boundaries has sometimes allowed social movement actors to better bypass state circumscription and to voice dissent via transnational coalitions or globally recognized bodies (e.g. see Keck and Sikkink 1998), there are various concerns around global North/ South or regional disparities, including insufficiently acknowledged colonial histories as well as contemporary asymmetries tied to neoliberalism and neoimperialist expansions. For media and LGBT advocacy, these asymmetries play out in several ways, including differential access to ICTs, Orientalist and anti-Islamist discourses that thread through much transnational LGBT activism, and LGBT rights perceived as tied to Western values, whether therefore to be emulated as modern or resisted as encroachment upon local cultures.

Access to media technologies has increased globally, but remains differentiated by region, as well as by class, gender, race, ethnicity and other socioeconomic dimensions of inequality. This is true for LGBT media users as well; for example, those who blog have disproportionately higher levels of income and education, as Mitra and Gajjala (2008) found for India. For LGBT advocacy via digital media, then, privileged segments of LGBT communities are more likely to shape the agendas.

Additionally, there are more complex phenomena that inform the transnational contours of LGBT advocacy. Puar's (2007) work has generated one important line of critique, arguing that mainstream gay rights discourses in the West rely crucially upon the construction of non-Western subjects othered along multiple axes of nationality, sexuality, and religion, with queer Islamic subjects in the South positioned as especially subordinated (see also Massad 2007). At a moment when the conditional recognition of some homosexual subjects functions as 'representational currency' (4) for the moral high ground of a state such as the US, other populations are subjugated by economic and military means.

Drawing from Puar, the charge of 'pinkwashing' has been levelled against the Israeli government's promotion of Israel as welcoming to gays and lesbians, both for its own citizens to serve in the Israeli military and for tourists seeking a gay-friendly travel destination, with critics arguing that the intertwining of gay rights and nationalist discourses 'conceal[s] the continuing violations of Palestinians' human rights behind an image of modernity signified by Israeli gay life' (Schulman 2011).[4] In this vein, Ritchie (2010) argued that pinkwashing involves not just the state, but also Israeli LGBT activists and journalists who highlight narratives about queer Palestinians seeking escape from their homophobic culture by turning to a gay-friendly Israel. In another example, Rastegar (2013) discussed how the execution of two youths in Iran was widely reported online and became understood in the West as an instance of homophobic barbarism because it appealed to a 'liberal, secular imagination' that contrasts 'a violently intolerant Islam and a progressively more tolerant West' (8).

In a related transnational dynamic, the export of conservative Christian rhetoric and politics to the global South has played a key role in heightening anti-gay sentiment in countries such as Uganda and Nigeria, with same-sex relations and LGBT rights now commonly understood there as a Western phenomenon. The paradox that current laws against homosexuality are a colonial legacy[5] rather than reflective of indigenous cultures or practices is generally unacknowledged. Yet Western appeals to a universal human rights framework to condemn homophobia in the global South have also been argued to be counterproductive. A prominent case involved responses to U.K. Prime Minister David Cameron's threats in September 2011 to cut development aid to countries where homosexuality is illegal, with a number of African-based activists arguing that the assertion of Western economic control tied in this manner to 'human rights' would heighten antipathy to LGBT activists and communities (e.g. Sokari 2014), although some activists based in Africa have disputed the harms attributed to Western support (Stewart 2015).

Gunkel (2013) addressed these issues in a critical consideration of online petitions and campaigns originating in the global North against phenomena such as the 'corrective rape' of lesbians in South Africa. While such actions make use of digital media's transnational reach, they draw on and reproduce discourses about the uncivilised character of non-Western regions and fail to recognize the complexities of the postcolonial context. In addition, recent efforts to link Western aid to improved LGBT rights 'ha[ve] the effect of turning postcolonial homophobia into a position of protest against neocolonial politics and a demonstration of African sovereignty' (74) to the detriment of efforts by local activists.

These challenges notwithstanding, transnational collaborations do not only reinscribe problematic discourses or give rise to North/South frictions. Indeed, Gunkel (2013) argued against a wholly negative critique of globally oriented LGBT activism, pointing out that politically nuanced alliances do emerge out of even problematic campaigns. Furthermore, LGBT subjects in the global South exercise agency in various ways in and through media. One avenue is language use, despite the dominance of English online. For example, He (2007) discussed how LGBT users in Taiwan often choose pseudonyms in either another language, such as Japanese or a Chinese-English blend, both of which can be understood as hybridisations particular to Taiwanese history and culture, thus functioning as statements of local identities even in the global domains of the Internet. Examining the Indian LGBT blogosphere, Mitra and Gajjala (2008) noted that the prevalence of English – associated not just with contemporary geopolitics but with India's colonial history – has not simply overwritten local cultures in any simple way, citing blog content that recognizes the complex place of English for Indians and the potential to subvert its power, and arguing that even English-language blogs reflect what Boellstorff (2003) called the phenomenon of 'dubbing cultures' rather than simple reproduction.

Conclusion

Media are key elements in LGBT advocacy. While this is partly due to how media content informs public discourses about LGBT rights, new media provide LGBT activists with a variety of ways to advance their goals. However, digital domains have their own limitations and challenges, including the fact that they are subject to surveillance and may be spaces of anti-LGBT expression or censorship.

The use of media in social movements has frequently involved seeking to increase visibility for the pertinent issues. However, at both the theoretical and political levels, visibility has complex implications for LGBT advocacy; being 'out' cannot be assumed to be an unproblematic, universal goal. Furthermore, from a transnational perspective, economic and political asymmetries partially produce LGBT rights as a mode of re-asserting the supremacy of the West, and can contribute to anti-LGBT mobilizations that position themselves as resisting imperialist encroachment. These issues deserve additional attention from scholars and activists, even as recent events such as the US Supreme Court 2015 *Obergefell v. Hodges* same-sex marriage decision are hailed as unprecedented progress. Scholarship continues to be focused on the global North, but additional research elsewhere should better account for local and regional specificities, and address the complex relationships between media and LGBT advocacy in the contemporary global context.

Notes

1   No cover term is unproblematically applicable, especially when used outside the contexts in which they originated. However, following common practice by both scholars and activists, I use 'LGBT' to refer to individuals whose sexual practices and/or identities are something other than cis-gendered and heterosexual, and to groups/organizations that advocate for non-normative sexual and gender expression. I use 'gay', 'lesbian', and 'queer' in contexts where subjects self-identified as such, or when scholars of non-Western cultures found these terms to be the most appropriate English terms. I also use 'queer' when referring to academic perspectives that draw on queer theory. Finally, I use 'same-sex' in discussing legal statutes pertaining to sexual practices between individuals understood to be of the same sex.
2   I do not discuss scripted television or film, as research on these forms mainly considers LGBT characters with respect to their complexity and roundedness (e.g. Gross 2001; Russo 1987). Therefore little in this literature directly addresses media and LGBT rights per se.
3   Some queer theorists have critiqued the project for advancing a narrative that depends on embracing an individualist meritocracy 'premised on a dubious narrative of progress' that ignores gender, racial, and religious disparities (Krutzsch 2014: 1246), although others see both promises and limitations (Goltz 2013).
4   In response, a number of Israeli and American Jewish LGBT activists have argued that pinkwashing critics have overstated their complicity with the Israeli government, and noted that many of them support an independent Palestinian state (e.g. Beyer 2016).
5   British colonial law left many nations with versions of Section 377, which prohibits 'carnal intercourse against the order of nature with any man, woman or animal.' Although the section refers to heterosexual relations and bestiality, in practice it has generally been used to circumscribe male-male sex acts.

References

Alwood, E. (2007). 'A Gift of Gab: How Independent Broadcasters Gave Gay Rights Pioneers a Chance to be Heard'. In: K. Barnhurst, ed. *Media/Queered: Visibility and its Discontents*. New York: Peter Lang, pp. 27–44.

Ayoub, P. and Brzezińska, O. (2015). 'Caught in a Web? The Internet and Deterritorialization of LGBT Activism'. In: D. Paternotte and M. Tremblay, eds., *The Ashgate Research Companion to Lesbian and Gay Activism*. Surrey: Ashgate, pp. 225–41.

Baisley, E. (2015). 'Framing the Ghanaian LGBT Rights Debate: Competing Decolonisation and Human Rights Frames'. *Canadian Journal of African Studies*, 49(2), pp. 383–402.

Barnhurst, K. (2007). 'Visibility as Paradox: Representation and Simultaneous Contrast'. In: K. Barnhurst, ed. *Media/Queered: Visibility and its Discontents*. New York: Peter Lang, pp. 1–20.

Beyer, D. (2016). 'We Are Not Your Enemies – Pinklying, Pinkwashing and the Decline of the LGBTQ Left'. *Huffington Post* (January 31). Available at: http://www.huffingtonpost.com/dana-beyer/we-are-not-your-enemies_b_9128730.html [Accessed 1 March, 2017].

Bhattacharjya, M. and Ganesh, M. I. (2011). 'Negotiating Intimacy and Harm: Female Internet Users in Mumbai'. In: J. sm Kee, ed., *EROTICS: Sex, Rights and the Internet*. Association for Progressive Communications, pp. 66–108. Available at: http://www.apc.org/en/system/files/EROTICS.pdf [Accessed 1 March, 2017].

Bluck, S. (2007). 'Transsexual in Iran: a Fatwa for Freedom?' In: C. Pullen, ed. *LGBT Transnational Identity and the Media*. New York: Palgrave MacMillan, pp. 59–66.

Boellstorff, T. (2003). 'Dubbing Culture: Indonesian Gay and Lesbian Subjectivities and Ethnography in an Already Globalized World'. *American Ethnologist*, 30(2), pp. 225–42.

Bong, Y. D. (2008). 'The Gay Rights Movement in Democratizing Korea'. *Korean Studies*, 32, pp. 86 -103.

Brewer, P. (2003). 'Values, Political Knowledge, and Public Opinion About Gay Rights: A Framing-based Account'. *Public Opinion Quarterly*, 67(2), pp. 173–201.

Cabosky, J. (2014). 'Framing an LGBT Organization and a Movement: A Critical Qualitative Analysis of GLAAD's Media Releases'. *Public Relations Inquiry*, 3(1), pp. 69–89.

Campbell, J. (2007). 'Virtual Citizens or Dream Consumers: Looking for Civic Community on Gay.com'. In: K. O'Riordan and D. Phillips, eds., *Queer Online: Media Technology & Sexuality*. New York: Peter Lang, pp. 197–216.

Capsuto, S. (2000). *Alternate Channels: The Uncensored Story of Gay and Lesbian Images on Radio and Television, 1930s to the Present*. New York: Ballantine Books.

Castells, M. (2012). *Networks of Outrage and Hope: Social Movements in the Internet Age*. Cambridge: Polity Press.

Chase, T. (2012). 'Problems of Publicity: Online Activism and Discussion of Same-sex Sexuality in South Korea and China'. *Asian Studies Review*, 36(2), pp. 151–70.

Chua, L. (2014). *Mobilizing Gay Singapore: Rights and Resistance in an Authoritarian State*. Philadelphia: Temple University Press.

Corrêa, S., Maria, M., Queiroz, J., Zilli, B. D., and Sívori, H. F. (2011). 'Internet Regulation and Sexual Politics in Brazil'. In: J. sm Kee, ed., *EROTICS: Sex, Rights and the Internet*. Association for Progressive Communications, pp. 19–65. Available at: http://www.apc.org/en/system/files/EROTICS.pdf [Accessed 1 March, 2017].

Craig, S., Martinez, M., Kane, J., and Gainous, J. (2005). 'Core Values, Value Conflict, and Citizens' Ambivalence about Gay Rights'. *Political Research Quarterly*, 58(1), pp. 5–17.

Culzac, N. (2014). 'Egypt's Police "Using Social Media and Apps like Grindr to Trap Gay People"'. *The Independent*, 17 September. Available at: http://www.independent.co.uk/news/world/africa/egypts-police-using-social-media-and-apps-like-grindr-to-trap-gay-people-9738515.html [Accessed 1 March, 2017].

Echols, K. and Ditmore, M. (2011). Restricted Access to Information: Youth and Sexuality. In: J. sm Kee, ed., *EROTICS: Sex, Rights and the Internet*. Association for Progressive Communications, pp. 176–200. Available at: http://www.apc.org/en/system/files/EROTICS.pdf [Accessed 1 March, 2017].

Friedman, E. J. (2007). 'Lesbians in (Cyber)space: The Politics of the Internet in Latin American On- and Off-line Communities.' *Media, Culture & Society*, 29(5), pp. 790–811.

Fuss, D. (1991). *Inside/Out: Lesbian Theories, Gay Theories*. New York: Routledge.

Garber, L. (1999). 'Periodicals'. In: G. Haggerty, ed., *Encyclopedia of Lesbian and Gay Histories and Cultures, Vol. 1*. New York: Routledge, pp. 580–83.

Goltz, D. B. (2013). 'It Gets Better: Queer Futures, Critical Frustrations, and Radical Potentials'. *Critical Studies in Media Communication*, 30(2), pp. 135–51.

Gorkemli, S. (2012). '"Coming Out of the Internet": Lesbian and Gay Activism and the Internet as a "Digital Closet" in Turkey'. *Journal of Middle East Women's Studies*, 8(3), pp. 63–88.

Gray, M. (2009). '"Queer Nation is Dead/Long live Queer Nation": The Politics and Poetics of Social Movement and Media Representation'. *Critical Studies in Media Communication*, 26(3), pp. 212–36.

Gross, L. (2001). *Up from Invisibility: Lesbians, Gay Men, and the Media in America*. New York: Columbia University Press.

Gunkel, H. (2013). 'Some Reflections on Postcolonial Homophobia, Local Interventions, and LGBTI Solidarity Online: The Politics of Global Petitions'. *African Studies Review*, 56(2), pp. 67–81.

Harvey, D. O. (2007). 'Sub-Saharan African Sexualities, Transnational HIV/AIDS Educational Film and the Question of Queerness'. In: C. Pullen, ed., *LGBT Transnational Identity and the Media*. New York: Palgrave MacMillan, pp. 67–83.

He, T. (2007). 'Cyberqueers in Taiwan: Locating Histories of the Margins'. *Journal of International Women's Studies*, 8(2), pp. 55–73.

Hussain, H. (2013). 'The Rise of Social Media Surveillance and Censorship in the Middle East'. *Hera Hussain*, 10 March. Available at: https://herahussain.wordpress.com/2013/03/10/smsurveillance/ [Accessed 1 March, 2017].

Johnson, T. (2012). 'Equality, Morality, and the Impact of Media Framing: Explaining Opposition to Same-sex Marriage and Civil Unions'. *Politics and Policy*, 40(6), pp. 1053–80.

Keck, M. and Sikkink, K. (1998). *Activists Beyond Borders: Advocacy Networks in International Politics*. Ithaca, NY: Cornell University Press.

Krutzsch, B. (2014). 'It Gets Better as a Teleological Prophecy: A Universal Promise of Progress Through Assimilation'. *The Journal of Popular Culture*, 47(6), pp. 1245–55.

Landau, J. (2009). 'Straightening Out (the Politics of) Same-sex Parenting: Representing Gay Families in US Print News Stories and Photographs'. *Critical Studies in Media Communication*, 26(1), pp. 80–100.

Massad, J. (2007). *Desiring Arabs*. Chicago: University of Chicago Press.

Meyer, R. (2006). 'Gay Power Circa 1970: Visual Strategies for Sexual Revolution'. *GLQ*, 12(3), pp. 441–64.

Miller, A. V. (2000). 'Our Own Voices: A Directory of Lesbian and Gay Periodicals, 1890s -2000s'. *The Canadian Lesbian and Gay Archives*. Available at: http://www.clga.ca/Material/PeriodicalsLGBT/inven/oov/oovint.htm [Accessed 1 March, 2017].

Mitra, R. and Gajjala, R. (2008). 'Queer Blogging in Indian Digital Diasporas: a Dialogic Encounter'. *Journal of Communication Inquiry*, 32(4), pp. 400–23.

Moawad, N. and Qiblaw, T. (2011). 'Who's Afraid of the Big Bad Internet?' In: J. sm Kee, ed. *EROTICS: Sex, Rights and the Internet*. Association for Progressive Communications, pp. 109–34. Available at: http://www.apc.org/en/system/files/EROTICS.pdf [Accessed 1 March, 2017].

Moscowitz, L. (2013). *The Battle Over Marriage: Gay Rights Activism Through the Media*. Urbana, IL: University of Illinois Press.

Mwangi, E. (2014). 'Queer Agency in Kenya's Digital Media'. *African Studies Review*, 57(2), pp. 93–113.

O'Riordan, K. and Phillips, D., eds. (2007). *Queer Online: Media Technology and Sexuality*. New York: Peter Lang.

Pan, P. L., Meng, J., and Zhou, S. (2010). 'Morality or Equality? Ideological Framing in News Coverage of Gay Marriage Legitimization'. *The Social Science Journal*, 47(3), pp. 630–45.

Prinsloo, J., McLean, N. C., and Moletsane, R. (2011). 'The Internet and Sexual Identities: Exploring Transgender and Lesbian Use of the Internet in South Africa'. In: J. sm Kee, ed. *EROTICS: Sex, Rights and the Internet*. Association for Progressive Communications, pp. 135–75. Available at: http://www.apc.org/en/system/files/EROTICS.pdf [Accessed 1 March, 2017].

Pullen, C. and Cooper, M., eds. (2010). *LGBT Identity and Online New Media*. New York: Routledge.

Puar, J. (2007). 'Abu Ghraib and U.S. Sexual Exceptionalism'. In: *Terrorist Assemblages: Homonationalism in Queer Times*. Durham, NC: Duke University Press, pp. 79–113.

Rastegar, M. (2013). 'Emotional Attachments and Secular Imaginings: Western LGBTQ Activism on Iran'. *GLQ*, 19(1), pp. 1–29.

Ritchie, J. (2010). 'How Do You Say "Come Out of the Closet" in Arabic?': Queer Activism and the Politics of Visibility in Israel-Palestine'. *GLQ*, 16(4), pp. 557–76.

Russo, V. (1987). *The Celluloid Closet: Homosexuality in the Movies*. New York: Harper.

Scheufele, D. and Tewksbury, D. (2007). 'Framing, Agenda Setting, and Priming: The Evolution of Three Media Effects Models. *Journal of Communication*, 57(1), pp. 9–20.

Schulman, S. (2011). 'Israel and "Pinkwashing"'. *New York Times* (22 November). Available at: http://www.nytimes.com/2011/11/23/opinion/pinkwashing-and-israels-use-of-gays-as-a-messaging-tool.html [Accessed 1 March, 2017].

Sender, K. (2004). *Business, not Politics: The Making of the Gay Market*. New York: Columbia University Press.

Sedgwick, E. (1990). *Epistemology of the Closet*. Berkeley, CA: University of California Press.

Sokari. (2014). 'Africa LGBTIQ–Aid Conditionality & LGBT Rights'. *Black Looks* (5 March) Available at: http://www.blacklooks.org/2014/03/africa-lgbtiq-an-important-piece-on-aid-conditionality/ [Accessed 1 March, 2017].

Stewart, C. (2015). 'Nigerian Activists Protest Harmful, Flawed N.Y. Times Coverage'. *Erasing 76 Crimes* (24 December). Available at: http://76crimes.com/2015/12/24/nigerian-activists-protest-harmful-flawed-n-y-times-coverage/ [Accessed 1 March, 2017].

Streitmatter, R. (1995). *Unspeakable: The Rise of the Gay and Lesbian Press in America*. Boston: Faber and Faber.

Taylor, Y., Falconer, E., and Snowdon, R. (2014). 'Queer Youth, Facebook and Faith: Facebook Methodologies and Online Identities'. *New Media & Society*, 16(7), pp. 1138–53.

Tindall, N. T. and Waters, R. W., eds. (2013). *Coming Out of the Closet: Exploring LGBT Issues in Strategic Communication with Theory and Research*. New York: Peter Lang.

Vissers, S. and Stolle, D. (2014). 'The Internet and New Modes of Political Participation: Online Versus Offline Participation'. *Information, Communication & Society*, 17(8), pp. 937–55.

Warner, M. (1999). *The Trouble with Normal: Sex, Politics, and the Ethics of Queer Life*. New York: Free Press.

Yue, A. (2012). '"We're the Gay Company, as Gay as it Gets": The Social Enterprise of Fridae'. In: A. Yue and J. Zubillaga-Pow, eds., *Queer Singapore: Illiberal Citizenship and Mediated Cultures*. Hong Kong: Hong Kong University Press, pp. 197–212.

31

LIVE-WITNESSING, SLACKTIVISM AND SURVEILLANCE

Understanding the opportunities, challenges and risks of human rights activism in a digital era

Summer Harlow

On 31 March, 1991, George Holliday grabbed his Sony HandyCam analog video recorder and began filming the Los Angeles police beating of Rodney King. The video aired on local news that night, and within a week was broadcast by news outlets across the country. Now, more than 25 years later, anyone can be George Holliday. Armed with smartphones and the ability to instantaneously distribute footage around the world via online social media, people who were not even born when Holliday shot his now infamous video can use the latest digital technologies to carry on the Holliday legacy of citizen witnessing and reporting. While Holliday's video was not enough to convince jurors to convict the police officers accused of beating King, today's viral videos, although not always enough to provide the necessary evidence for conviction in human rights abuse cases, have gone a long way in changing the conversation, raising awareness and mobilizing supporters in the field of human rights.

Whether pushing back against police brutality towards people of colour, or advocating for indigenous, women, immigrants or other marginalised groups, digital tools increasingly are transforming the global fight for justice and human rights by giving voice to the voiceless, and offering new models for documentation, community building, awareness raising, civic and political engagement, mobilization and reconciliation and access to justice. With the opportunities brought on by new technologies, however, come obstacles and even potential threats. This chapter explores the possibilities, benefits, challenges and risks of using online social media to advocate for human rights.

Amplifying voices

Activists traditionally have found themselves in an adversarial role when it comes to mainstream media, which 'privilege dominant, mainstream positions' (Gurevitch & Blumler 1990, 33) and ignore ordinary citizen voices, especially when those voices are seen to oppose hegemonic power structures (Downing 2001; Rodriguez 2001). Numerous studies point to a pattern of media coverage, referred to as the 'protest paradigm' (Chan & Lee 1984; McLeod & Hertog 1999), which serves to delegitimise protesters and their causes, and support the status quo (McLeod 2007; McLeod & Hertog 1992). According to this paradigm, news stories are framed to focus on the violence and spectacle of protests, rather than their underlying causes, and official sources are quoted and protesters' views ignored or belittled, thus demonising and marginalising demonstrators (McLeod & Hertog 1999; McLeod 2007). Similarly, Chouliaraki (2008) noted that coverage of human rights abuses often is reduced to 'adventure news'.

To counter such negative portrayals common to the mainstream media, activists, dissidents and other marginalized sectors of society historically have created their own alternative media, whether leaflets and newsletters, community radio or, more recently, blogs and other digital media content (Downing 2001). Scholars define alternative media as oppositional media representing and serving the interests of groups marginalized by the mainstream media. Downing (2001) characterized alternative media as counter-hegemonic 'radical' media, interdependent with social movements. Rodríguez (2001) builds on Downing's (2001) conception of radical alternative media, proffering the notion of 'citizens' media', wherein the production and consumption of media changes or validates the individual's concept of the 'self'. Ordinary citizens participate in the mediascape, contesting hegemonic power structures through the very process of intervention in the media.

For producers and consumers of alternative media, the Internet represents an opening in power hierarchies – an alternative space where information and counter-information can easily and cheaply circulate, uninhibited by the gatekeepers of the traditional press (Bennett, 2004). For example, Harlow and Johnson's (2011) study of the media portrayal of protesters during the Egyptian uprising found that online 'alternative' media opened new possibilities for covering demonstrations. Twitter and the online citizen journalism site Global Voices, unlike the mainstream *The New York Times*, broke free of the protest paradigm by legitimising protesters and serving as commentators, even actors, in the unfolding events. Scholars tout the Internet for its creation of new spaces for public discourse, or what Fraser (1990) referred to as counter public spheres. In her critique of Habermas' (1989 [1962]) original romanticised notion of a public sphere, Fraser (1990) suggested that the exclusion of marginalized groups from the male- and elite-dominated universal public sphere leads to the creation of multiple, subaltern counter-public spheres in which excluded groups can articulate their own identities and debate ideas. Scholars link alternative media with the creation of multiple, counterhegemonic discursive spheres that allow normally marginalized voices to express themselves and participate in citizenship (Couldry 2006; Harcup 2011). New digital tools, whether mobile phones or social media sites, open alternative public spheres, allowing for horizontal communication that overcomes not just geographic and temporal boundaries (Castells 2001; Kellner 2000), but also limitations imposed by society's power hierarchies.

Thus, for those involved in the field of human rights, whether as advocates, activists or victims, digital technologies offer the possibility of voice; the ability to contribute to public discourse without a filter imposed by mainstream media. As Carty (2015) noted, digital media users can create and distribute their own unique messages without oversight or approval by mainstream media, political or business elites, or military and police. Human rights organizations, whether through Facebook, Twitter or their own websites, can communicate and engage directly with the communities they serve. Community members also have greater access to the organizations, as social media lower the barriers for communication and participation, allowing ordinary citizens and historically marginalized groups, including victims, to share their own stories.

The supersized effects of digital media, including increased speed and reach (Earl et al. 2010) thus have broadened the traditional public sphere (Castells 2001) and created counter public spheres (Fraser 1990), giving 'movements and activists the power of mass communication' (Postmes & Brunsting 2002, 294). Salter (2013, 226) pointed to the importance of new technologies for opening a counter public sphere where girls and women can make extrajudicial claims of sexual violence and abuse, and discuss and act upon these allegations in 'ways contrary to established social and legal norms'. One such example Salter cited was the Tumblr blog 'Predditors' that identified men who had posted photos of girls and women online without their consent. In 2012, Predditor activists gave to police information gathered on the blog about a male high school teacher – subsequently fired – who had surreptitiously taken photos of his female students and posted them online. Salter concluded that online social media can be used to empower women to seek justice: Online platforms not only amplified their voices, but provided them a space for support and validation that they might not find offline.

Documentation

Going hand-in-hand with the notion that new technologies allow marginalized groups to raise their voices is the way digital tools can be used for monitoring, documenting and reporting human rights abuses. Brough and Li's (2013, 284) examination of user-generated content during the 2007 Burmese 'Saffron Revolution' and the development of a human rights online video portal identified four uses for online video in human rights (HR) campaigns: 'increasing symbolic power (shaping and circulating public representations of HR issues and influencing subsequent action); the cultivation and shaping of a *collective identity* of a movement; the *mobilization of resources* (e.g. public support and funding); and *seizing opportunities to effect policy change* (e.g. lobbying governments)'.

Mobile phones and social media, particularly smart phones with cameras that allow images to be instantaneously uploaded to YouTube or other video-sharing platforms, are powerful tools that let citizens, and not just human rights organizations or mainstream media, report human rights abuses. For example, the international non-profit organization WITNESS trains citizens and activists to use video to document human rights abuses and fight for human rights. The group focuses on the power of personal stories and user-generated videos created with safe and ethical strategies. These videos then are curated and promoted to bring awareness to under-reported issues. The videos also have served as testimonial evidence in efforts to bring human rights violators to justice. Similarly, Columbia University's Voix des Kivus ('Voice of the Kivus') project allowed Congolese to use their mobile phones to send SMS messages documenting any human rights violations, as did an SMS hotline of the UN Mission for Côte d'Ivoire. In fact, information from these citizens' messages was used as part of the evidence to issue indictments (Herzberg & Steinberg 2012). Citizen eyewitness tweets during the Arab Spring also were crucial for monitoring government responses to protests (Joseph 2012). As Herzberg and Steinberg (2012) noted, digital media offer real-time, first-hand reports about what is happening on the ground, often serving as the only communication channel when journalistic or NGO access is limited. The need for such citizen monitoring, documentation and reporting is made manifest in Mexico's drug war and narco-terrorism, where 'traditional ways to inform and protect the public have shut down' (Herzberg & Steinberg 2012, 506). Further, such citizen reporting also proves essential for NGOs and other organizations and institutions charged with monitoring human rights. For example, during the Libyan conflict NATO used social media to recruit citizen volunteers to help track the movements of armed forces (Herzberg & Steinberg, 2012).

Community building and awareness raising

Beyond serving as first responders collecting evidence, citizen documentation, especially live-streaming videos, can create 'distant witnesses' (Gregory 2015) that help generate empathy and solidarity, leading to a sense of community and the raising of awareness. The ability to see events happening to other people around the world, and to be able to interact with them via social media platforms, helps engender empathy and a sense of community that, perhaps, not only raises awareness about issues, but also encourages action. Gregory's (2015, 1379) examination of live streaming during Brazilian protests and forced evictions showed how 'co-presence' technologies helped create 'shared experience at a distance'. Live-streaming video platforms, where an individual is 'present in time but removed in space' (Peters 2009, 39), can evoke empathy and a normative responsibility to act, thus potentially building community by expanding a cause's reach to new supporters. Allan et al. (2007, 373) noted the way digital tools can create 'discursive spaces for empathetic engagement' as people around the world, via Internet technologies, can be made aware of the plight of marginalized groups that otherwise they would never have known about.

One benefit of creating an online sense of solidarity is the ability of human rights organizations to call on that community for help. For example, Herzberg and Steinberg (2012) cited the importance of crowdsourcing, or turning to a crowd of people online to perform a certain task. Amnesty International regularly crowdsources information (Koettl 2013) to monitor human rights situations, verify data and uncover inaccuracies. NGOs also rely on citizen crowdsourced mapping, such as of human rights violations or corruption, as an alternative to often biased 'official' data. In fact, the Ushahidi ('testimony' in Swahili) platform, created in 2008 to map post-election violence in Kenya, has become a global leader in crowdsourcing solutions. Crowdsourced maps not only call attention to a problem, potentially prompting public outrage, but they also have been used as evidence in indictments (Herzberg & Steinberg 2012). The importance of crowdsourced maps in the fight for justice is made evident by the fact that a term has been coined to describe it: 'maptivism', or using maps for activism.

Civic and political engagement and mobilization

Just as online platforms change how human rights situations are monitored and documented, they also are transforming advocacy itself. Studies indicate that online social networking sites are important for helping mobilize protest activity throughout the world (Bennett & Segerberg, 2012; Valenzuela et al., 2012). Research increasingly suggests that online social media have a positive mobilizing impact on civic and political participation (Macafee & De Simone 2012; Pasek et al. 2009; Tufekci & Wilson 2012). For example, Lim (2012) found protesters used Facebook to create online and offline networks that facilitated mobilization in Egypt during the Arab Spring. In Latin America, studies show that Facebook played a central role in numerous protest movements, such as in Guatemala (Harlow 2012) and Colombia (Neumayer & Raffl 2008). Comparative studies of the United States and Latin America also show social networking sites to be integral to activists for both online and offline activism (Harlow & Harp 2012).

Reconciliation and access to justice

Another area within the field of human rights undergoing change is that of reconciliation and access to justice. Scholars agree that the media are crucial for any truth and reconciliation plan for a community or country emerging from conflict. Community dialogue, and the ability for individuals to voice their own stories, also are critical components for healing. Digital technologies, in particular 'rich digital media' like platforms designed to share user-generated content (such as YouTube), are facilitating post-conflict reconciliation (Best et al. 2011). Best and colleagues' (2011) study of the role of digital tools in post-conflict Liberia found that the use of such media increased Liberians' sense of self efficacy, which they argued is fundamental for reconciliation and healing.

Research also indicates that new technologies are improving marginalized groups' access to justice. For example, the Indigo Trust Foundation in Nigeria made the country's constitution, a legal directory and forums available via a mobile phone app (Herbert 2015). Further, Robertson (2012) suggested that, at least in the United States, social media platforms like Facebook are disrupting the traditional justice system by providing citizens – litigants – with more information about their legal rights. The connectivity these platforms offer, including the ability to crowdsource legal advice, as well as easier access to evidence, also are changing how individuals participate in the legal system (Robertson 2012). Additionally, as noted earlier, digital tools are providing evidence used in court cases to issue indictments and bring perpetrators to justice (Herzberg & Steinberg 2012).

Challenges and risks

Much of the research examining the role of digital media in activism and justice tends to be technologically deterministic, leaning towards either a utopian or dystopian perspective. As such, this chapter, while highlighting the potential benefits of incorporating digital technologies into the fight for social justice, would be remiss if it did not also assess the potential challenges and risks associated with using new technologies.

One major challenge for using digital tools in human rights advocacy is that of verification. Citizens' documentation and reporting of human rights abuses raises concerns over reliability and authenticity, as often sources on social media are unverifiable or anonymous. Further, misinformation spreads rapidly on social media, and is difficult to control, especially since corrections might not spread as fast or in the same manner as the misinformation. As a result, many users might never see the corrected information. Additionally, NGOs and other human rights advocates might not have the resources to verify whether information is false.

Difficulties also come with trying to use citizen-generated content as evidence in a court of law (Ellis 2015). Questions of admissibility and authenticity – such as who shot the video, where and when was it shot, was the source biased, can the information be independently tested or verified, was the chain of custody intact – all must be addressed. To help solve these concerns, the International Bar Association in 2015 launched the eyeWitness to Atrocities camera app for Android phones. The free app is meant to document human rights abuses in a secure and verifiable way, so that photo and video evidence can be used in a court of law (Ellis 2015). The app automatically collects GPS coordinates, date and time, and other data, including chain of custody information, which can be used to show the photo or video was not altered. The user then can send the footage directly to the eyeWitness organization, where it is stored until it is needed for legal proceedings.

Still, despite the availability of such technology, there remains the challenge of teaching citizens what to document, such as the need to film insignias on military uniforms to link perpetrators to human rights abuses, instead of simply documenting evidence of another atrocity (Gregory 2015). Furthermore, citizens need to be aware that their documentation could result in their long-term involvement as a witness in a criminal investigation. What's more, the possibility exists for such episodic citizen documentation to detach the event from its historical context, so that it is only 'understood via episodic crisis, rather than longer term structural human violations' (Gregory 2015, 1389).

Another challenge related to using digital tools for social justice is that of 'clicktivism,' or 'slacktivism'. Online activist campaigns often are dismissed for being less valuable or less able to provoke real-world change (Christensen 2011). Critics contend that online actions, such as joining a Facebook group or changing one's profile picture to support a cause, could be substituting offline political participation (Fenton & Barassi 2011). The KONY2012 campaign often is cited as the quintessential example of slacktivism: Social media users shared video clips and other information online, bringing attention to the abuses of the Lord's Resistance Army (LRA) during the armed conflict in Uganda, but little actual action occurred offline. The video campaign went viral, but Joseph Kony, leader of the LRA militia, was not captured. In their study of immigrant rights activists and advocates, Harlow and Guo (2014) suggested that while social media were good for raising awareness, they also might pacify people into thinking they had made more of a difference than they truly had. Still, the authors noted the potential power that comes with an online army of slacktivists, or 'baby activists', that one day could mature into 'adult' or 'real' activists. Similarly, Penney (2015), in his study of Facebook users who switched their profile pictures to a red equals sign to support gay marriage, found that symbolic online actions allowed political organizations to expand their support base, offering a way for less-committed individuals to get involved.

The use of digital technologies also brings threats, as the same tools that allow activists and citizens to document and expose human rights abuses also pose privacy and security concerns. Morozov (2011) called attention to the 'dark side' of the Internet because of its government and corporate surveillance. These fears were solidified when Edward Snowden's leak of National Security Administration documents exposed the United States' surveillance program and collection of citizen data. Other countries also monitor citizens' online activity. Turkey in 2008 instituted a nearly three-year ban on YouTube, and blocked thousands of Internet sites that referenced Kurdish or Armenian minorities (Toksabay 2010). Twitter also cooperated with the Turkish government, agreeing to some censorship to avoid being blocked altogether (Irak 2015). Howard and colleagues (2011) found that both democracies and authoritarian regimes cut off access to social networking sites when national security is a concern, and authoritarian regimes block access in order to deter so-called propaganda on social media. Pearce and Kendzior (2012) showed that in Azerbaijan, the government manipulated social media against citizens, instead of shutting it down entirely. Rather than risk politicizing typically apathetic citizens by cutting off access to their entertainment, the government instead demonised social media users and jailed dissident bloggers, effectively dissuading citizens from wanting to use social media for political ends (Pearce & Kendzior 2012).

Governments around the world have used activists' electronic footprints to identify protesters (Gregory 2010). For example, crowdmapping could identify citizens and their location, potentially placing them at risk by making them easy-to-track targets. While social media platforms might offer increased visibility and reach, activists can lose control over their privacy and message. Salter (2013) noted how girls and women who used the Internet to identify the men who had sexually assaulted them were left vulnerable to online hate speech and verbal attacks. People of colour and other marginalized groups also are regularly subjected to online attacks. Online tools also make some kinds of human rights abuses easier, like child pornography or human trafficking.

What's more, most social media platforms are commercial sites not originally designed for advocacy, complicating their use in human rights campaigns. As noted above, Twitter agreed to cooperate with the Turkish government to avoid a complete shutdown in that country. Additionally, Google and YouTube regularly take down websites and videos at the request of governments and police. Facebook's policy requiring users to use real names rather than pseudonyms also could make it difficult for human rights activists or victims to feel comfortable speaking out. Moreover, Facebook has been known to remove or stifle the pages of activists who target companies that advertise on that platform (Mathews 2013). The secret algorithms of social media companies, combined with flat-out censoring in some countries, also mean that certain content gets promoted while other content – specifically counter-hegemonic content – could be relegated to the background or disappear entirely. As such, Gehl (2015) pointed to the need for 'alternative' social media to serve as an antidote to 'corporate' social media and their lack of social responsibility or accountability. While a few such sites exist, such as Lorea, GNU social and Diaspora, as of yet they do not have the reach, visibility or influence of corporate sites like Facebook and Twitter, thus potentially making them less attractive to human rights activists looking to raise awareness in the population at large.

This chapter thus shows the way digital technologies, including online social media, are transforming human rights activism/advocacy and the fight for social justice. The widespread availability of digital media tools potentially can turn anyone armed with a mobile phone into a human rights activist or witness, creating an army of modern-day George Hollidays. Digital technologies are useful for amplifying marginalized groups' voices; raising awareness and creating community and a sense of shared solidarity; monitoring, documenting and reporting human rights abuses; enhancing civic and political participation; facilitating mobilization; and increasing access to justice. Despite these potential benefits, however, challenges and risks remain. For example, advocates must continue to find ways to translate online attention into offline action, such as ensuring that viral videos documenting human rights abuses can be used as evidence to bring perpetrators to justice. Also, just as digital tools can be used in the fight for justice, so, too, can they be used in repressive ways by governments, police, corporations and even citizens, abrogating rather than supporting human rights.

Still, as technologies continue to evolve and become ever more ubiquitous, human rights activists and advocates must seek out best practices for adopting and adapting them into their repertoires while minimizing any risks. Further, they must recognize that incorporation of the latest digital tools in the fight for human rights must come with training in order to be able to use citizens' digitally recorded evidence in a court of law. 'Clicktivists' should also not be dismissed out of hand, but rather appreciated for their contribution to awareness raising and solidarity building, and cultivated so as to strengthen their level of commitment and participation. Lastly, considering the corporate nature of most technology platforms, human rights activists and advocates must weigh the costs and benefits of using a tool designed more for making money than for fighting for social justice. Ultimately, this chapter suggests there is no denying the potential for new digital technologies to continue changing human rights advocacy; the challenge is determining how advocates can best leverage these tools to maximize meaningful solidarity, engagement, and witnessing.

References

Allan, S., Sonwalkar, P. and Carter, C. (2007). 'Bearing Witness: Citizen Journalism and Human Rights Issues'. *Globalisation, Societies and Education*, 5(3), pp. 373–89.

Bennett, W. L. (2004). 'Communicating Global Activism: Strengths and Vulnerabilities of Networked Politics'. In: W. van de Donk, B. D Loader, P. G. Nixon, and D. Rucht, eds., *Cyberprotest: New Media, Citizens and Social Movements*. London: Routledge, pp. 123–46.

Bennett, W. L. and Segerberg, A. (2012). 'The Logic of Connective Action: Digital Media and the Personalization of Contentious Politics'. *Information, Communication & Society*, 15(5), pp. 739–68.

Best, M. L., Long, W. J., Etherton, J. and Smyth, T. (2011). 'Rich Digital Media as a Tool in Post-conflict Truth and Reconciliation'. *Media, War & Conflict*, 4(3), pp. 231–49.

Brough, M. and Li, Z. (2013). 'Media Systems Dependency, Symbolic Power, and Human Rights Online Video: Learning from Burma's "Saffron Revolution" and WITNESS's Hub'. *International Journal of Communication (19328036)*, 7, pp. 281–04.

Carty, V. (2015). *Social Movements and New Technology*. Boulder, CO: Westview.

Castells, M. (2001). *The Internet Galaxy: Reflections on the Internet, Business and Society*. Oxford: Oxford University Press.

Chan, J. M., & Lee, C. C. (1984). 'The Journalistic Paradigm on Civil Protests: A Case Study of Hong Kong'. In: Arno, A. & Dissanayake, W., eds., *The News Media in National and International Conflict*. Boulder, CO: Westview, pp. 183–202.

Chouliaraki, L. (2008). 'The Mediation of Suffering and the Vision of a Cosmopolitan Public'. *Television & New Media*, 9(4), pp. 371–91.

Christensen, H. S. (2011). 'Political Activities on the Internet: Slacktivism or Political Participation by Other Means?'. *First Monday*, 16(2). Available at: http://firstmonday.org/ojs/index.php/fm/article/view/3336/2767 [Accessed 1 March, 2017].

Couldry, N. (2006). 'Culture and Citizenship The Missing Link?'. *European Journal of Cultural Studies*, 9(3), pp. 321–39.

Downing, J. (2001). *Radical Media: Rebellious Communication and Social Movements*. Thousand Oaks: Sage Publications.

Earl, J., Kimport, K., Prieto, G., Rush, C. and Reynoso, K. (2010). 'Changing the world one webpage at a time: Conceptualizing and explaining Internet activism'. *Mobilization: An International Journal, 15*, 425–46.

Ellis, M. S. (2015). 'Shifting the Paradigm-Bringing to Justice Those Who Commit Human Rights Atrocities'. *Case Western Reserve Journal of International Law*, 47, pp. 265–82.

Fenton, N. and Barassi, V. (2011). Alternative Media and Social Networking Sites: The Politics of Individuation and Political Participation. *The Communication Review*, 14(3), pp. 179–96.

Fraser, N. (1990). Rethinking the Public Sphere: A Contribution to the Critique of Actually Existing Democracy. *Social Text*, (25/26), pp. 56–80.

Gehl, R. W. (2015). 'The Case for Alternative Social Media'. *Social Media + Society*, 1(2), pp. 1–12.

Gregory, S. (2010). Cameras Everywhere: Ubiquitous Video Documentation of Human Rights, New Forms of Video Advocacy and Considerations of Safety, Security, Dignity and Consent'. *Journal of Human Rights Practice*, 2(2), pp. 191–207.

Gregory, S. (2015). 'Ubiquitous Witnesses: Who Creates the Evidence and the Live (d) Experience of Human Rights Violations?'. *Information, Communication & Society*, 18(11), pp. 1378–92.

Gurevitch, M., and Blumler, J. (1990). 'Political Communication Systems and Democratic Values'. In: Graber, D. ed., *Media Power in Politics*. Washington, DC: Congressional Quarterly Press, pp. 24–35.

Habermas, J. (1989 [1962]). *The structural transformation of the public sphere* (T. Burger, Trans.). Cambridge, MA: MIT Press.

Harcup, T. (2011). 'Alternative Journalism as Active Citizenship'. *Journalism*, 12(1), pp. 15–31.

Harlow, S. (2012). 'Social Media and Social Movements: Facebook and an Online Guatemalan Justice Movement that Moved Offline'. *New Media & Society*, 14(2), pp. 225–43.

Harlow, S. and Guo, L. (2014). 'Will the Revolution be Tweeted or Facebooked? Using Digital Communication Tools in Immigrant Activism'. *Journal of Computer Mediated Communication*, 19(3), pp. 463–78.

Harlow, S. and Harp, D. (2012). 'Collective Action on the Web: A Cross-cultural Study of Social Networking Sites and Online and Offline Activism in the United States and Latin America'. *Information, Communication & Society*, 15(2), pp. 196–16.

Harlow, S. and Johnson, T. J. (2011). 'Overthrowing the Protest Paradigm? How the New York Times, Global Voices and Twitter Covered the Egyptian Revolution'. *International Journal of Communication*, 5, pp. 1359–74.

Herbert, S. (2015). *Improving Access to Justice Through Information and Communication Technologies*. Available at: http://www.gsdrc.org/docs/open/hdq1201.pdf

Herzberg, A. and Steinberg, G. M. (2012). 'IHL 2.0: Is There a Role for Social Media in Monitoring and Enforcement?'. *Israel Law Review*, 45(03), pp. 493–536.

Howard, P. N., Agarwal, S. D. and Hussain, M. M. (2011). When Do States Disconnect Their Digital Networks? Regime Responses to the Political Uses of Social Media'. *The Communication Review*, 14(3), pp. 216–32.

Irak, D. (2015). *Turkey's Internet Bans and the Vicious Cycle of Techno-optimism*. Available at: http://researchturkey.org/turkeys-internet-bans-and-the-vicious-cycle-of-techno-optimism/

Joseph, S. (2012). 'Social Media, Political Change, and Human Rights'. *Boston College International & Comparative Law Review*, 35, p. 145.

Kellner, D. M. (2000). 'Habermas, the Public Sphere and Democracy: A Critical Intervention'. In: Hahn, L. (ed.) *Perspectives on Habermas*. Peru, IL: Open Court, pp. 259–87.

Koettl, C. (2013). *Twitter to the Rescue? How Social Media is Transforming Human Rights Monitoring*. Amnesty International (20 February). Available at: http://blog.amnestyusa.org/middle-east/twitter-to-the-rescue-how-social-media-is-transforming-human-rights-monitoring/

Lim, M. (2012). 'Clicks, Cabs, and Coffee Houses: Social Media and Oppositional Movements in Egypt, 2004–2011'. *Journal of Communication*, 62(2), pp. 231–48.

Macafee, T. and De Simone, J. J. (2012). 'Killing the Bill Online? Pathways to Young People's Protest Engagement via Social Media'. *Cyberpsychology, Behavior, and Social Networking*, 15(11), pp. 579–84.

Mathews, K. (2013). *How Facebook May Secretly Foil Your Activist Plans*. Care2. Available at: http://www.care2.com/causes/how-facebook-may-secretly-foil-your-activist-plans.html

McLeod, D. M. (2007). 'News Coverage and Social Protest: How the Media's Protect Paradigm Exacerbates Social Conflict'. *Journal of Dispute Resolution*, pp. 185–94.

McLeod, D. M. and Hertog, J. K. (1999). 'Social Control, Social Change and the Mass Media's Role in the Regulation of Protest Groups'. In: D. Demers and K. Viswanath eds., *Mass Media, Social Control and Social Change: A Macrosocial Perspective*. Ames, IA: Iowa State University Press, pp. 305–30.

McLeod, D. M. and Hertog, J. K. (1992). 'The Manufacture of Public Opinion by Reporters: Informal Cues for Public Perceptions of Protest Groups'. *Discourse & Society*, 3(3), pp. 259–75.

Morozov, E. (2011). *The Net Delusion: The Dark Side of Internet Freedom*. New York: PublicAffairs.

Neumayer, C. and Raffl, C. (2008). 'Facebook for Protest? The Value of Social Software for Political Activism in the Anti-FARC Rallies'. *DigiActive Research Series*. Available at: http://www.digiactive.org/wp-content/uploads/research1_neumayerraffl.pdf [Accessed 15 August, 2009].

Pasek, J., More, E. and Romer, D. (2009). 'Realizing the Social Internet? Online Social Networking Meets Offline Civic Engagement'. *Journal of Information Technology & Politics*, 6(3–4), pp. 197215.

Pearce, K. E. and Kendzior, S. (2012). 'Networked Authoritarianism and Social Media in Azerbaijan'. *Journal of Communication*, 62(2), pp. 283–98.

Penney, J. (2015). 'Social Media and Symbolic Action: Exploring Participation in the Facebook Red Equal Sign Profile Picture Campaign'. *Journal of Computer Mediated Communication*, 20(1), pp. 52–66.

Peters, J. D. (2009). 'Witnessing'. In: Frosh, P. and Pinchevski, A. eds. *Media Witnessing: Testimony in the Age of Mass Communication*. New York: Palgrave MacMillan, pp. 23–41.

Postmes, T. and Brunsting, S. (2002). Collective Action in the Age of the Internet Mass Communication and Online Mobilization. *Social Science Computer Review*, 20(3), pp. 290–301.

Robertson, C. B. (2012). 'Facebook Disruption: How Social Media May Transform Civil Litigation and Facilitate Access to Justice'. *The Arkansas Law Review*, 65, pp. 75–97.

Rodriguez, C. (2001). *Fissures in the Mediascape*. Cresskill, NJ: Hampton Press.

Salter, M. (2013). 'Justice and Revenge in Online Counter-publics: Emerging Responses to Sexual Violence in the Age of Social Media'. *Crime, Media, Culture*, pp. 225–42.

Toksabay, E. (2010). Nov. 3. 'Turkey Reinstates YouTube Ban'. *Reuters*. Available at: http://www.reuters.com/article/us-turkey-youtube-idUSTRE6A227C20101103

Tufekci, Z. and Wilson, C. (2012). 'Social Media and the Decision to Participate in Political Protest: Observations from Tahrir Square'. *Journal of Communication*, 62(2), pp. 363–79.

Valenzuela, S., Arriagada, A. and Scherman, A. (2012). 'The Social Media Basis of Youth Protest Behavior: The Case of Chile'. *Journal of Communication*, 62(2), pp. 299–314.

32

HUMAN RIGHTS AND THE MEDIA/PROTEST ASSEMBLAGE

Stefania Milan

The 2014 football World Cup, held in Brazil, was met by widespread popular protest, both on social media and in the streets. Protestors opposed the escalating expenditure of public money, which, they believed, should instead have been employed to address the many social problems of the country (Parkin 2014). Countering the governmental repression of the protests, the freedom of expression non-governmental organization (NGO) Article 19 created the digital platform Protestos.org, in order 'to protect the rights of privacy and freedom of expression of citizens in the streets and on the network, raising awareness and empowering activists against increased surveillance and rights violations'. An accompanying guidebook suggested tech solutions to protect activists against human rights violations and censorship.

Protestos.org illustrates the close ties between protest activism, communication and media technology. These ties have become even more apparent with the diffusion of digital technologies, and mobile technology in particular: they have multiplied the opportunities for activism but also increased the risks of privacy violation, monitoring and repression of political action. This chapter adopts a human rights perspective to explore protest and activism as they meet media technology and communicative action (or the deliberate act of engaging in communication processes, oriented towards fellow activists and potential audiences).[1] Building on concepts and approaches in media studies and political sociology, the chapter has a two-fold aim. On the one hand, it takes the use of media and technology for protest and activism as a human right, pertaining in particular to the sphere of freedom of expression, freedom of association and privacy protection. On the other hand, it looks at how social movements put media and technology at the service of human rights and other related struggles. Here the use of media for protest and activism is articulated in relation to the manifold ways in which technology shapes how the human rights discourse[2] is presented in the 'networked public sphere' (Benkler 2013), and articulated across the variety of platforms available today. The chapter is illustrated with examples from fieldwork in a variety of countries in Latin America and Europe.

The chapter is organized as follows. First, it explores the theoretical tenets of the analysis, reflecting on media practice as an instance of enactment of active citizenship. Then, it moves to analyze media/protest as a right in itself, portraying the trajectory that connects the UDHR to recent, expansive notions of rights as they relate to communicative action, including communication rights. Next, it investigates how social movements put media and technology at the service of human rights advocacy, reflecting on the impact of technology and its materiality into contemporary forms of protest activism.

Media practice as enactment of citizenship

When in the 1940s miners in rural Bolivia began to strike, their disruptive action was backed by a network of self-organized radio stations. Founded by union leaders, in the everyday the stations supported the miners' campaigning for better wages, while in times of social turmoil they functioned as a means of resistance (Gumucio-Dagron 2001). Lately, 'transmedia organizing' empowered the face-to-face mobilizing of the US immigrant rights movement (Costanza-Chock 2014); individuals and groups at the margins of the European labour market gained recognition in the political sphere only through creative media practice (Mattoni 2012). Today activism is increasingly embedded in communication processes of various kinds (Cammaerts, Mattoni & McCurdy 2013), often combining the attempt to dialogue with traditional news media with avid exploitation of social media (Gerbaudo 2012), video activism (Askanius & Uldam 2011), and self-organized media production (Downing 2001). Specific 'social movement media cultures' (Costanza-Chock 2012) empower protesters to articulate their claims and enable campaigns to go transnational.

Protest activism is a 'system of relationships' (Melucci 1996, 25) which results in a 'site of cooperation, competitions and creative transformation' (Clemens & Minkoff 2004, 167). As such, it is inherently communicative in nature. Communicative action, in turn, is deeply interwoven with the 'interactive process of constructing meaning' (Gamson 1992, xii), or meaning work, enacted by social actors in building and reproducing organized collective action.

We can approach the special connection between protest and communicative action (and the supporting media technology) as a sociotechnical assemblage. To start with, referring to an assemblage rather than discrete units of analysis allows us to foreground the social dynamics behind the activists' engagement with technology. Further, it acknowledges the intricate joining of components (media technology, infrastructure, devices, verbal and visual communication…) and social processes (interpersonal communication, awareness raising, issue framing, protesting, mobilizing…) that constitute the core of what we observe in this chapter.[3]

Following Couldry, who suggested to address media as practice, this chapter explores the media/protest assemblage looking at the 'vast domain of practice, that, like all practices, are social at a basic level through the very acts that stabilise them as practices and distinguish specific practices from each other' (2012, 44). It takes a sociological perspective in asking, for instance, '*what are people* (individuals, groups, institutions) *doing in relation to media* across a whole range of situations and contexts? How is people's media-related practice related, in turn, to their wider agency?' (2012, 37, original italics). The focus is no longer on media as such or media practices taken in isolation, but on the *social processes* enacted by individuals and groups in and through their engagement with media and communicative action. Further, most of said practices are positioned in the radical domain, because they tend to 'express an alternative vision to hegemonic politics, priorities, and perspectives' (Downing 2001, v).

Talking of practice entails foregrounding the idea that patterns of meaning production, as they relate to the collective exercise of making sense of alternative or antagonist visions of the world typical of protest activism, intersect the dynamics of technical production. The latter, in turn, is in large part determined by the respective features of the media technology adopted by activists from time to time – from radio to social media. The media/protest assemblage, then, consists in the articulation of these various meanings as they are shaped by the materiality of media infrastructure itself. In sum, embedded practices of media production point to a special relationship between meaning production, communicative action *and its material support*, which has consequences on the meanings that are produced and transmitted.

Most importantly, the media/protest assemblage enables the articulation of a new political subject, whereby not only do individuals become collectives, but they also translate into practice their democratic agency. Adopting a feminist perspective and following Rodriguez (2001), we take the re-appropriation of mediated communication typical of activist media production as a vehicle for the emergence of new political subjectivities. Rodriguez, evoking Mouffe's radical democracy perspective (1992), argues that engagement with what she calls 'citizens' media' represents the enactment of citizenship on a daily basis, and a form of first-person empowerment. This entails

> [F]irst that a collectivity is *enacting* its citizenship by actively intervening and transforming the established mediascape; second, that these media are contesting social codes, legitimized identities, and institutionalized social relations; and third, that these communication practices are empowering the community involved, to the point where these transformations and changes are possible'.

> *(Rodriguez 2001, 20)*

This holds true in particular when activists engage in media production (as opposed to the mere production of messages). In this case, not only are individuals transformed into active citizens by/through media practice; media practice itself, or the first-hand engagement with media production, contributes to create the conditions *for* the enactment of citizenship. This embodiment 'activate[s] communication processes' (2011, 25) able to shape collectivities and their social fabric. We can think of this process as empowerment, which allows individuals and groups to take control over their media technologies and messages by participating in actions that reshape their communicative present. It is an exercise of active control over technology that empowers people, including non-experts (see, e.g. Milan 2013; Dunbar-Hester, 2014).

What's more, engaging with the media/protest assemblage brings about a sort of *politicisation* of the everyday, whereby the interpretive work of media activists multiplies the instances/occasions of activation of citizenship Rodriguez theorised. 'These practices and strategies of resistance constitute the politics of the quotidian', she wrote (2011, 21). They expand and multiply spaces for political action, which is no longer merely confined in institutional spaces or pre-inscribed, top-down processes of participation (e.g. voting), but embedded in day-to-day social life.

Next, we move to analyse the media/protest assemblage as a right in itself.

Media/protest between freedom of expression and communication rights

In 1932, German dramaturgist Bertold Brecht wrote that 'radio is one-sided when it should be two […] if it knew how to receive as well as to transmit, how to let the listener speak as well as hear, how to bring him into a relationship instead of isolating him. [Radio] must strive to combat that lack of consequences….' In Brecht's view, a radio with consequences would allow citizens to talk back to power. It would constitute an instrument to express opinions, rather than just receiving them. Since 1989, Radio La Tribu, originally a pirate station operated by communication students, has been a 'radio with consequences. With witnesses, declarations and dialogues. A radio that reports the reality to be able to transform it'. Its slogan is a testimony to its commitment to freedom of expression and freedom of association: *'Apaga La Tribu, hace tu radio'* ('Switch off La Tribu, create your own station') (Milan 2013).

The use of media and technology for protest activism is intimately connected to the exercise of human rights, in particular to freedom of expression (UDHR Article 19), freedom of association (Article 20) and the right to participation in cultural life (Article 27). It also connects to the right to privacy (Article 12), especially in times of widespread monitoring of online dissent (see, among others, Lyon 2015; Uldam 2016), and to due process. The relation between communication and media and individual freedoms, however, has a long history, which criss-crosses but also outgrows the long march of human rights.

It was 1969 when the notion of the 'right to communicate' was proposed by Jean D'Arcy, then director of the United Nations (UN) Radio and Visual Services Division. In an article entitled 'Direct Satellite Broadcasting and the Right to Communicate' (1969), D'Arcy forecasted that eventually the UDHR 'will have to encompass a more extensive right than man's right to information, first laid down twenty-one years ago in Article 19. This is the right of man to communicate. It is the angle from which the future development of communications will have to be considered if it is to be fully understood'. Similar ideas were set forth in the late 1970s by a group of developing countries that promoted a debate on the New World Information and Communication Order (NWICO). Echoing the New World Economic Order, concerned with international trade issues, NWICO pointed to the imbalances in global communication flows, for instance in the allocation of satellite space. NWICO found resonance within the United Nations Educational, Scientific and Cultural Organization (UNESCO), which in 1980 appointed an International Commission for the Study of Communication Problems, chaired by Seán MacBride. The MacBride Commission was tasked with a critical analysis of the contemporary global communications scenario, in view of proposing solutions to further human development through communication (Vincent, Nordenstreng & Traber 1999). It filed a report entitled 'Many Voices, One World', identifying communication as a human right and supporting the recognition of the 'right to communicate':

> Communication needs in a democratic society should be met by the extension of specific rights such as the right to be informed, the right to inform, the right to privacy, the right to participate in public communication – all elements of a new concept, the right to communicate. In developing what might be called a new era of social rights, we suggest all the implications of the right to communicate to be further explored.
>
> *(UNESCO Recommendation 54/1980, 265)*

The recommendation, however, never found implementation in official UN documents; the NWICO itself suffered from the withdrawal of the United States of America and the United Kingdom from UNESCO, and quickly disappeared from the international agenda at the dawn of the 1980s. Its ideas, however, survived outside institutional arenas, as progressive media professionals and academics regrouped annually around the MacBride Roundtable, an advocacy group that was active since 1989 for about a decade (Milan & Padovani 2014).

In 1993, a coalition of NGOs and progressive individuals launched the People's Communication Charter: its 18 articles maintained that communication systems should be at the service of 'human needs and rights'. Learning from NWICO failure, the Charter proponents tried to build support amongst international networks of grassroots organizations, rather than solely institutions, preaching cooperation between the two. By the end of the 1990s, new coalitions for the democratization of communication emerged at the fringes of the institutional debate, which prompted some observers to celebrate a 'new NWICO in the making which sees itself as a network of networks based in civil society' (Vincent et al. 1999, x).

In the 2000s, the debate on communication as a human right re-emerged thanks to the first ever UN World Summit on the Information Society (WSIS), celebrated in Geneva (2003) and Tunis (2005). In the run-up to the WSIS, the Communication Rights in the Information Society (CRIS) campaign was launched by a coalition of civil society organizations (Thomas 2006). CRIS served as an umbrella group to represent civil society values and interests at the summit; it mobilized a vast collection of national and international NGOs as well as individual members (see also Calabrese 2004). Although civil society was invited to participate on equal footing to governments and the industry, advocates felt that the final documents only partially acknowledged human rights. In response to the WSIS Declaration of Principles (2003), then, civil society representatives put forward their own document:

> We reaffirm that communication is a fundamental social process, a basic human need and a foundation of all social organisation. […] every person must have access to the means of communication and must be able to exercise their right to freedom of opinion and expression […] the right to privacy, the right to access public information and the public domain of knowledge, and many other universal human rights of specific relevance to information and communication processes, must also be upheld. Together with access, all these communication rights and freedoms must be actively guaranteed for all in clearly written national laws and enforced with adequate technical requirements.
>
> *(WSIS Civil Society Plenary 2003)*

Fast-forwarding to today, human rights have returned to the centre of the civil society agenda on communications, and have occasionally entered the institutional agenda. The diffusion of digital technologies offers new opportunities to protest activism; yet, it has 'also significantly enhanced the ability of governments to infringe and potentially violate human rights in protests' (Article 19 2014). Back in 2011, the UN Special Rapporteur on Freedom of Expression Frank La Rue expressed concern about

> [A]ctions taken by States against individuals communicating via the Internet […] While such ends can be legitimate under international human rights law, surveillance often takes place for political, rather than security reasons in an arbitrary and covert manner. For example, States have used popular social networking sites, such as Facebook, to identify and to track the activities of human rights defenders and opposition members.
>
> *(Human Rights Council 2011)*

The Snowden leaks (2013) contributed to revitalize the global debate on media/technology and human rights, by introducing an emphasis on the right to privacy but also the right to dissent. Article 19 compiled twenty principles on the right to protest, on account that protest fulfils crucial functions in contemporary democracy, including the exercise of human rights and democratic participation. The principles 'represent a progressive interpretation of international human rights standards', and offer 'a set of minimum standards for the respect, protection and fulfilment of the right to protest'.[4]

The debate reached the UN, too. In 2012, the Human Rights Council published a seminal report (A/HRC/RES/20/8) stating that 'the same rights that people have offline must also be protected online' (Human Rights Council 2012). 'The right to safety of citizens of one country can never be guaranteed by violating fundamental human rights of citizens of another country', said the then Brazilian President Dilma Rousseff addressing the UN General Assembly in the aftermath of the Snowden scandal. She spoke to the need of protecting 'freedom of expression, privacy of the individual and respect for human rights' (Borger 2013). In 2014, the UN High

Commissioner for Human Rights published a report on the right to privacy in the digital age, denouncing the 'lack of adequate national legislation and/or enforcement, weak procedural safeguards, and ineffective oversight […and] of governmental transparency' affecting state surveillance practices, contributing to 'a lack of accountability for arbitrary or unlawful interference in the right to privacy' (UN High Commissioner for Human Rights 2014).

Following, we turn our attention to media and technology as a means to promote, defend and exercise human rights.

Making the impossible real: Media and the promotion and exercise of human rights

The history of social movements is awash with examples of how these have appropriated (or tried to hijack) media discourses, notwithstanding the power asymmetries between media organizations and grassroots activism (see, e.g. Gamson & Wolfsfeld 1993; Ryan, 1991). Protesters have also created independent media to support popular struggles, and efforts in this sense have multiplied with the diffusion of the Internet and the availability of media production skills: think about the Independent Media Centre, or Indymedia, the global information network of the alter-globalization movement at the turn of the last century (Kidd, 2010; Milan, 2010). If we are to understand the relevance of communicative action for human rights advocacy and other related struggles, it is worth reflecting on the role of media in the long-term process of norm change, but also in the development of a critical consciousness.

'Freedom is acquired by conquest, not by gift. It must be pursued constantly and responsibly. Freedom is not an ideal located outside of man', wrote Brazilian educator Paulo Freire in his *Pedagogy of the Oppressed* (1968). Freedom is rather the result of a process of 'conscientisation', which seeks to perceive and expose socio-political injustice and take action against oppressive elements. In this perspective, democracy is not just a goal but a method, and informed action is at its core. Inspired to Freire's ideals, Brazilian dramaturgist Augusto Boal created the method known as 'theatre of the oppressed': with injustice being represented on stage, the audience is invited to intervene in the play to the point of potentially changing its course. Audience members are empowered to both imagine *and* practice change, reflecting collectively and thus generating social action (Boal 1979). Both Freire's critical pedagogy and Boal's theatre of the oppressed are approaches that are deeply entrenched in communicative action. Although they mostly concern face-to-face interactions, the empowerment mechanisms they purport have influenced generations of community radio stations and other experiments of bottom-up communication in Latin America and beyond. Emphasizing two-way communication flows and interpersonal exchange as empowerment, they connect progressive ideals and values to informed action, or praxis. Communication becomes a way of consciously shaping the world as well as the individual and her community – first by imagining and verbally articulating what constitutes change, then by acting upon these transformed visions.

The power to imagine change and act upon it resonates with the idea of norm change, widely studied in social movements research, especially by scholars of symbolic interactionism. Norm change is oftentimes included in the analysis of action repertoires, alongside with disruptive protest, advocacy and resistance. Action repertoires are 'sites of contestation in which bodies, symbols, identities, practices, and discourses are used to pursue or prevent changes in institutionalized power relations' (Taylor & Van Dyke, 2004, 268). Most importantly, they 'make the impossible real' (Tarrow 1987, 59). Movements are often seen as producers and bearers of emergent normative definitions, particularly when existing systems of meaning are perceived as no longer holding true. New norms might, for example, contribute to define a situation as unjust, providing a justification for action (Turner and Killian 1987, cited in della Porta & Diani 2006). Intense moments of norm re-definition function as 'moral shocks' (Jasper 1997, 33) – catalysing moments for movement emergence. Protest provides a 'moral voice', whereby protesters 'articulate, elaborate, alter, or affirm one's moral sensibilities, principles, and allegiances' (1997, 15).

Providing activists with the opportunity to enact their citizenship as well as transform existing norms, the media/protest assemblage is a site of intense meaning work, one that has the potential to lead to discursive change. But 'technology is not neutral. […] We're living in a world of connections – and it matters which ones get made and unmade', to say it with cultural theorist Donna Haraway (1991). In other words, the technological support where meaning work takes place *matters*. In what follows, we review, in an abridged fashion, the main media in which protest activism unfolds, from the print to airwaves to the digital, in view of assessing the social affordances the various technologies bear.

The printed press has supported the human rights struggle since the early days, contributing to create 'alternative public realms' (Downing 1988). Posters, too, with the unique immediacy of 'street media' (Gerbaudo 2014), but also graffiti (Ley & Cybrinsky 1974) and zines (Atton 2002), have encountered the favour of activists worldwide. However, typically only few people, usually the so-called movement entrepreneurs (McCarthy & Zald 1977), held control over the normative production of a group or coalition, deciding what got printed and distributed.

Low-power radio is historically linked with human rights advocacy (see, among others, Berrigan 1979; Hollander & Stappers 1992; Lewis 1993; M. D'Arcy 1996; Englund 2011; Dunbar-Hester 2014; Gumucio-Dagron 2001), with community and low-power television following at a distance (see, among others, Halleck 2002; Berardi, Jacquemet & Vitali 2003; Rennie 2006). Radio is cheap, easily accessible also to the non-literates, while television typically requires a more elaborate infrastructure to operate. Both tend to support projects that are experienced collectively by participants. 'Community' does not include exclusively the practitioners but also the community of reference: the emphasis is on control of the production process by the 'enlarged community' around the station (see Milan 2013, Chapter 3). A practitioner once praised 'the possibility to offer microphones to people and let them speak. […] having the radio gave me power, the power of letting the others speak, speaking myself just a little' (2013, 54). The community station thus becomes an 'open channel' – although often the 'others' evoked by practitioners are limited to likeminded individuals and groups.

The advent of the Internet, in turn, supported a different type of collectivity, and a distinct mode of engagement. Consider blogs: by eliminating the middleman, they gave everybody the chance to express himself or herself online. Indymedia, 'the mother of all blogs' (Milan, 2010), is a case in point: for the first time in history, thanks to a open source software supporting 'open publishing', activists could report directly from the streets, bypassing the bottlenecks of mainstream media. However, 'media activists' performed an important canalising function throughout the 1990s: bearers of the specialized skills of media production, they tended to be in charge of the media production of the movement.

Lastly, social media champion yet another style of engagement. Observers claim they enable a new form of 'connective action' (Bennett & Segerberg, 2013), whereby they function 'as organizing agents', supporting leaderless organizing dynamics. The communicative practices they reinforce are said to 'choreograph' collective action (Gerbaudo 2012). However, they impose specific 'strategies, mechanisms, and economies' (van Dijck & Poell 2013, 3) on their social affordances. We have called this emerging mobilizing dynamic 'cloud protesting', precisely to foreground the materiality of social media arrangements and the related policy economy (Milan 2015). The 'cloud' identified by social and mobile media becomes the platform where the cultural and symbolic production of a movement unfolds through the input of many individuals acting independently from each other. Think of the collective blog 'We Are the 99 Percent' on Tumblr: in the run-up to the Occupy Wall Street protests, individuals pictured themselves holding a placard stating their grievances. This way, everyone could contribute to build the collective narrative. In doing so, the cloud gives voice and visibility to personalised yet universal narratives, which are flexible, real-time and crowd-controlled, connecting individual stories into a broader context that gives them meaning.

Conclusions

This chapter explored the media/protest assemblage from a human rights perspective. Following Couldry, we considered media as practice, looking at the sociological processes triggered by engagement with communicative action, and their ability to nurture political subjectivity, empowerment and agency, and to promote conscientization, the capability to image change and act upon it, as well as discursive/norm change.

First, we considered the political use of media as a human right in itself, illustrating the trajectory that, building on human rights as enshrined in the UDHR, expanded to include communication-specific rights, such as the right to communicate, community rights or the right to privacy and due process that has been brought under the spotlight by surveillance on social media. Second, we looked at how social groups and individuals put media and technology at the service of human rights and other related struggles, reflecting on how different media technology shapes how the human right discourse is articulated in the networked public sphere, and the extent to which the enactment of citizenship is influenced by the roles assigned by technology.

It remains to the seen how the human rights discourse will unfold in the near future in relation to the protest/media assemblage, as citizens will become progressively more aware of the threats to privacy inscribed in the technology they carry in their pockets.

Notes

1 Like in Habermas' conceptualization (1984), communicative action here involves cooperation amongst individuals; however, unlike Habermas, we do not assume the rationality of social actors, nor see deliberation and argumentation as the sole goals of communication processes. Rather, we foreground the ideological and emotional aspects typical of social movements and the way they communicate (see, among others, Gamson, 1992; Jasper, 1997; Goodwin, Jasper, & Polletta, 2001).
2 Human rights here embrace the Universal Declaration of Human Rights (UDHR, 1948), but also subsequent complementary texts like the International Covenant on Economic, Social and Cultural Rights and the International Covenant on Civil and Political Rights (1966).
3 Although the notion of assemblage is inspired to Science and Technology Studies, and the writings of Latour (2005) and DeLanda (2006) in particular, here it assumes a purely instrumental role, devoid of additional connections to the discipline.
4 https://right-to-protest.org/

References

Article 19 (2014). *Why the Right to Protest?* Available at: https://right-to-protest.org/debate-protest-rights/why-the-right-to-protest/
Askanius, T., and Uldam, J. (2011). 'Online Social Media for Radical Politics: Climate Change Activism on YouTube'. *International Journal of Electronic Governance*, 4(1–2), pp.69–84.
Atton, C. (2002). *Alternative Media*. London and Thousand Oaks, CA: Sage.
Benkler, Y. (2013). 'WikiLeaks and the Networked Fourth Estate'. In: B. Brevini, A. Hintz, and P. McCurdy, eds., *Beyond WikiLeaks: Implications for the Future of Communications, Journalism and Society*. Basingstoke, UK: Palgrave Macmillan, pp. 11–34.

Bennett, L. W., & Segerberg, A. (2013). The Logic of Connective Action Digital Media and the Personalization of Contentious Politics. Cambridge, UK: Cambridge University Press.

Berardi, F., Jacquemet, M., and Vitali, G. (2003). *Telestreet. Macchina immaginativa non omologata.* Milan: Dalai Editore.

Berrigan, F. J. (1979). *Community Communication: The Role of Community Media in Development.* Paris: UNESCO.

Boal, A. (1979). *Theatre of the Oppressed.* London: Pluto Press.

Borger, J. (2013). Brazilian president: US surveillance a "breach of international law." *The Guardian,* 24 September. Availableat:https://www.theguardian.com/world/2013/sep/24/brazil-president-un-speech-nsa-surveillance

Calabrese, A. (2004). 'The Promise of a Civil Society: A Global Movement for Communication Rights'. *Continuum: Journal of Media & Cultural Studies,* 18(3), pp. 317–29.

Cammaerts, B., Mattoni, A., and McCurdy, P., eds. (2013). *Mediation and Protest Movements.* London: Intellect.

Clemens, E. S. and Minkoff, D. C. (2004). 'Beyond the Iron Law: Rethinking the Place of Organizations in Social Movements Research'. In: D. A. Snow, S. A. Soule, and H. Kriesi, eds., *The Blackwell Companion to Social Movements.* Oxford: Blackwell, pp. 155–70.

Costanza-Chock, S. (2012). 'Mic Check! Media Cultures and the Occupy Movement'. *Social Movement Studies: Journal of Social, Cultural and Political Protest,* 11(3–4), pp. 375–85.

Costanza-Chock, S. (2014). *Out of the Shadows, Into the Streets! Transmedia Organizing and the Immigrant Rights Movement.* Cambridge: MIT Press.

Couldry, N. (2012). *Media, Society, World: Social Theory and Digital Media Practice.* Malden, MA: Polity Press.

D'Arcy, J. (1969). Direct Broadcast Satellites and the Right of Man to Communicate. *EBU Review,* 118, pp. 14–18.

D'Arcy, M. (1996). *Galways' Pirate Women. A Global Trawl.* Galway: Women's Pirate Press.

DeLanda, M. (2006). *A New Philosophy of Society: Assemblage Theory and Social Complexity.* London and New York: Continuum.

della Porta, D., and Diani, M. (2006). *Social Movements. An Introduction,* 2nd ed. Oxford: Blackwell.

Downing, J. D. H. (1988). 'The Alternative Public Realm: The Organization of the 1980s Anti-nuclear Press in West Germany and Britain'. *Media, Culture & Society,* 10, pp. 163–181.

Downing, J. D. H. (2001). *Radical Media: Rebellious Communication and Social Movements.* Thousands Oaks, CA: Sage.

Dunbar-Hester, C. (2014). 'Producing "Participation"? The Pleasures and Perils of Technical Engagement in Radio Activism'. *Public Culture,* 26(1 72), pp. 25–50.

Englund, H. (2011). *Human Rights and African Airwaves: Mediating Equality on the Chichewa Radio.* Bloomington and Indianapolis: Indiana University Press.

Freire, P. (1968). *Pedagogy of the Oppressed.* New York: Continuum.

Gamson, W. A. (1992). *Talking Politics.* Cambridge, MA: Cambridge University Press.

Gamson, W. A., and Wolfsfeld, G. (1993). Movements and Media as Interacting Systems. *The Annals of the American Academy of Political and Social Science,* pp. 114–25.

Gerbaudo, P. (2012). *Tweets and the Streets Social Media and Contemporary Activism.* London: Pluto Press.

Gerbaudo, P. (2014). Spikey Posters: Street Media and Territoriality in Urban Activist Scenes. *Space and Culture,* 17(30), pp. 239–50.

Goodwin, J., Jasper, J. M., and Polletta, F., eds. (2001). *Passionate Politics: Emotions and Social Movements.* Chicago: University of Chicago Press.

Gumucio-Dagron, A. (2001). *Making Waves. Stories of Participatory Communication for Social Change: A Report to the Rockefeller Foundation.* New York: Rockefeller Foundation.

Habermas, J. (1984). *The Theory of Communicative Action.* Boston: Beacon Press.

Halleck, D. (2002). *Hand-held Visions. The Impossible Possibilities of Community Media.* New York: Fordham University Press.

Haraway, D. (1991). *Simians, Cyborgs, and Women: The Reinvention of Nature.* London: Free Association Books, pp. 149–81.

Hollander, E., and Stappers, J. (1992). 'Community Media and Community Communication'. In: N. W. Jankowski, O. Prehn, and J. Stappers, eds., *The People's Voice: Local Radio and Television in Europe.* London: John Libbey, pp. 17–27.

Human Rights Council (2011). *Report of the Special Rapporteur on the Promotion and Protection of the Right to Freedom of Opinion and Expression, Frank La Rue.* United Nations General Assembly. Available at: http://www2.ohchr.org/english/bodies/hrcouncil/docs/17session/A.HRC.17.27_en.pdf

Human Rights Council (2012). *The Promotion, Protection and Enjoyment of Human Rights on the Internet.* United Nations General Assembly. Available at: https://documents-dds-ny.un.org/doc/RESOLUTION/GEN/G12/153/25/PDF/G1215325.pdf?OpenElement

Jasper, J. M. (1997). *The Art of Moral Protest: Culture, Biography, and Creativity in Social Movements*. Chicago: Chicago University Press.

Kidd, D. (2010). Indymedia (The Independent Media Center). In: J. D. H. Downing, ed., *Encyclopedia of Social Movement Media* (pp. 267–70). Los Angeles and London: Sage Publications, Inc.

Latour, B. (2005). *Reassembling the Social: An Introduction to Actor-network-theory*. Oxford: Oxford University Press. Available at: http://dss-edit.com/plu/Latour_Reassembling.pdf

Lewis, P. M., ed. (1993). 'Alternative Media: Linking Global and Local'. In: *UNESCO Reports and Papers in Mass Communication No. 107*. Paris: UNESCO.

Ley, D., and Cybrinsky, R. (1974). 'Graffiti as Territorial Markers'. *Annals of the Association of American Geographers*, 64, pp. 491–505.

Lyon, D. (2015). *Surveillance After Snowden*. Cambridge and Malden. MA: Polity Press.

Mattoni, A. (2012). *Media Practices and Protest Politics. How Precarious Workers Mobilise*. Farnham, UK: Ashgate.

McCarthy, J. D., and Zald, M. N. (1977). 'Resource Mobilization and Social Movements: A Partial Theory'. *American Journal of Sociology*, 82, pp. 1212–41.

Melucci, A. (1996). *Challenging Codes. Collective Action in the Information Age*. Cambridge, UK: Cambridge University Press.

Milan, S. (2010). 'The Way Is the Goal: Interview with Maqui, Indymedia London / IMC-UK Network Activist'. *International Journal of E-Politics*, 1(1), pp. 88–91.

Milan, S. (2013). *Social Movements and Their Technologies: Wiring Social Change*. Palgrave Macmillan.

Milan, S. (2015). 'When Algorithms Shape Collective Action: Social Media and the Dynamics of Cloud Protesting'. *Social Media and Society*, July–December, pp. 1–10.

Milan, S., and Padovani, C. (2014). 'Communication Rights and Media Justice Between Political and Discursive Opportunities: A Historical Perspective'. In: C. Padovani and A. Calabrese, eds., *Communication Rights and Social Justice: Historical Accounts of Transnational Mobilizations*. London: Palgrave Macmillan, pp. 29–54.

Mouffe, C., ed. (1992). *Dimensions of Radical Democracy*. London: Verso.

Parkin, B. (2014, June 15). #NaoVaiTerCopa: From Social Media to the Streets. Retrieved from http://www.rioonwatch.org/?p=15996

Rennie, E. (2006). *Community Media. A Global Introduction*. Lanham, MA: Rowman & Littlefield.

Rodriguez, C. (2001). *Fissures in the Mediascape. An International Study of Citizens' Media*. Cresskill, NJ: Hampton Press.

Rodriguez, C. (2011). *Citizens' Media Against Armed Conflict: Disrupting Violence in Colombia*. Minneapolis: University of Minnesota Press.

Ryan, C. (1991). *Prime Time Activism: Media Strategies for Grassroots Organizing*. Boston: South End Press.

Tarrow, S. (1987). *Democracy and Disorder. Protest and Politics in Italy 1965-1975*. Oxford: Clarendon Press.

Taylor, V., and Van Dyke, N. (2004). '"Get up, Stand up": Tactical Repertoires of Social Movements'. In: D. A. Snow, S. A. Soule, and H. Kriesi, eds., *The Blackwell Companion to Social Movements*. Malden, MA and Oxford: Blackwell, pp. 262–93.

Thomas, P. N. (2006). 'The Communication Rights in the Information Society (CRIS) Campaign. Applying Social Movement Theories to an Analysis of Global Media Reform'. *The International Communication Gazzette*, 68(4), pp. 291–312.

Uldam, J. (2016). 'Corporate Management of Visibility and the Fantasy of the Postpolitical: Social Media and Surveillance'. *New Media & Society*, 18(2), pp. 201–19.

UN High Commissioner for Human Rights. (2014). *The Right to Privacy in the Digital Age* (Report A/HRC/27/37). United Nations. Available at: http://www.ohchr.org/EN/HRBodies/HRC/RegularSessions/Session27/Documents/A.HRC.27.37_en.pdf

van Dijck, J., and Poell, T. (2013). Understanding Social Media Logic. *Media and Communication*, 1(1), pp. 2–14.

Vincent, R. C., Nordenstreng, K., and Traber, M., eds. (1999). *Towards Equity in Global Communication: MacBride Update*. Cresskill, NJ: Hampton Press.

World Summit on the Information Society (2003). *Declaration of Principles: Building the Information Society: a Global Challenge in the new Millennium*. United Nations. Available at: http://www.itu.int/net/wsis/docs/geneva/official/dop.html

WSIS Civil Society Plenary (2003). 'Shaping Information Societies for Human Needs'. Civil Society Declaration to the World Summit on the Information Society. Avaialable at: http://www.itu.int/wsis/docs/geneva/civil-societydeclaration.pdf

33

IMAGING HUMAN RIGHTS

On the ethical and political implications of picturing pain

Kari Andén-Papadopoulos

In a time of great visibility for human rights crises around the world, when digital and mobile cameras are deemed not only a political advantage in activist theatres across the globe but a prerequisite, scholars have brought increased attention to the visual politics of spectacle and empathy that create and constrain human rights discourse today. Throughout the 20th century and into the 21st, camera-mediated imagery have played a key role in justice campaigns. Rights activists have recognized and strategically tried to employ the power of photography and video to further their cause. Also, by bringing spectators into a painful proximity to distant injustice and suffering, as Sharon Sliwinski (2011) famously argues, visuals have been central to fostering the very idea and development of what we call universal human rights. She contends that the mass circulation of images of traumatic events, including the 1755 Lisbon earthquake and the Holocaust, more than the abstract notion of rights, has been instrumental in forging an international community of spectators and creating a sense of shared humanity. At the same time, since Susan Sontag's (1978) scathing critique of the photographic image's ability to provoke a meaningful ethical and political response, critics in chorus have rehearsed the denunciation of the idea that (audio)visual proof of injustice and human suffering can transform the viewer into a moral witness or effect political change. Invoking the long-standing iconophobic trope of suspicion and anxiety towards the power exerted by images, this critical discourse voices a drastic disbelief in the effectiveness and ethics of traumatic images and the ways in which we share them.

This chapter aims to delineate and advance current critical debates about the possibilities and limitations of camera-mediated imagery to re/create political and moral imagination and contribute to struggles against injustice. Given the contemporary context of both human rights practitioners and scholars that often move too easily past the ethical complexities and challenges of making and watching images of suffering others, I revisit some key critical positions in the significant body of cultural theory and criticism devoted to the problems of picturing pain in order to better evaluate the political work and promise of image activism today. First, I engage with the post-Holocaust discourse of not looking, not aestheticising. Importantly, this work forces us to appraise the ethical problems arising when making and viewing images of vulnerable others may prolong injury and injustice. Yet, it leaves us locked into the intractable 'looking/not looking dilemma' (Möller 2009). I then open up for critical consideration existent theories on how to generate a *counter*-politics of visuality, given the perceived bankruptcy of common documentary human rights imagery and its failure to account for the violence involved in the act of rendering visible. While this approach is valuable in its insistence on the political importance of the aesthetic dimension of images – commonly neglected in discussions about human rights images as 'visible evidence' – the exclusive focus on artistic image practices renders its wider political relevance unproven. In distinction, as the next section explicates, there is an emerging view that recognizes photojournalism as a key component of political culture. In appreciating the formative role that documentary imagery of pain can play in political life, and in the visual construction of the public sphere, this literature speaks to the redeeming potential of Western spectatorship on distant others. In conclusion, however, I argue that the deeper political promise of photography and video for human rights might be found in the performative practices of making, mobilizing and viewing such imagery in the (non-Western) contexts where the injustice or violence occur.

The crisis of witnessing

When humanitarian organizations and human rights activists cast witnessing as one of their governing principles in the 1960's and 1970's, this commitment was inextricably linked to the long-standing *doxa* about the power of visuals to provide visible evidence and create witnessing publics. As Leshu Torchin (2012, 4) concludes, camera-mediated imagery (photography, film, video) has invariably been 'burdened with transformative expectations: revelation contributes to recognition, recognition demands action, and representations throughout transform audiences into witnesses and publics'.

Yet, the rise of the imperative to bear witness and render atrocity visible exists in tension with the emergence of the post-Holocaust desire not to look, not to aestheticise. As Susie Linfield shows in *The Cruel Radiance* (2010), academics and critics are quite ambivalent about the ethical and political potency of the documentary image and have been since the introduction of photography in the early 1800s. Particularly in the post-World War II period, the centuries-old suspicion and anxiety towards the power exerted by images gained renewed currency in the tradition of iconophobia governing visual representations of the Holocaust. In this view, every realistic rendering of trauma betrays reality and the shattering experience of those who lived through what they themselves often call unimaginable. The discursive insistence on not looking is thus founded on the belief that the vulnerability of victims cannot be given a mimetic representation without violating their basic dignity and humanity. The post-Holocaust discourse of the inescapable inauthenticity of mimetic representations of trauma has cast a long shadow, manifest in the aniconism that continuously slips into the theoretical discussion about the problems of picturing pain.

The ethics of the image

One major line of argument poses that the imaging of extreme trauma always involves an ethical crisis of representation, including most centrally the charges of aestheticisation, objectification and the idea that such images are implicated in the violence they depict. The aestheticization critique, found in the seminal work of both Walter Benjamin and Susan Sontag, claims that photographic representations of people in pain obfuscate the reality of suffering because they inevitably subject this suffering to aesthetic form and, thereby, to the possibility that pleasure can be derived from it (Reinhardt 2012; Möller 2012). Aestheticization is also charged with causing de-politicization, by directing the viewer's attention from the suffering of those pictured to the quality of the image itself and the mastery of the image maker, thus catering to the feel-good needs of spectators or their voyeurism (e.g Berger 1980).

The idea that images objectify photographed subjects is a further staple topic in critical discourses on atrocity images. The claim is that the very making of images is in itself degrading: the suffering of victims cannot be given mimetic representation without violating their dignity because 'each photograph pins the human to its helplessness and vulnerability before the eyes of all others' (Bernstein 2012, xii). Anxieties about what is seen as the violent and conquering nature of the photographic gesture form a third prominent theme. Susan Sontag's (1978) assertion that to photograph people is a form of metaphoric 'murder', that the camera is a "sublimation of the gun" established a core association between camera imagery and violent appropriation that has held sway over decades of photographic criticism. The consensus here is that the camera itself repeats the violence perpetrated on the victims, rendering them doubly exposed in their vulnerability and humiliation and enabling the endless replay of anguish. This is also to suggest that the making of such images is in itself an aggression, an integral part of the mechanisms of violence that destroyed the visual subject in the first place. The act of documenting and rendering suffering visible is thus held to be forever fraught with the risk of both enacting and extending injury and domination.

Without dismissing the possibility of the act of making images as being repressive, it is easy to contest the notion that picture taking by definition destroys the subject's dignity or that the circulation of the image inevitably prolongs the humiliation of the pictured. First, as Carolyn J. Dean (2015) explicates, the pervasive assumption that the integrity of a suffering subject is violated simply because she is pictured relies on a normative – and thus debatable – perception of human dignity as incommensurate with weakness, despair and powerlessness. Wrenched by anxiety about the exposure of injured and defenceless bodies and the shame it provokes, many critics resort to an idealised picture of humanity whereby dignity is understood as the heroic agency of 'upright and whole subjects capable of using their last ounce of strength to fight oppression'(Dean 2015, 257). Drawing on Judith Butler's (2003) critique of the symbolic equation of invulnerability with humanity, Dean bespeaks the possibility of an alternative framework of recognition, within which subjects can possess an inherent dignity simply by virtue of being human, even – or especially – when they are weak, pained and powerless. Vulnerability, on this account, might form the very basis for humanity and human solidarity, since 'all sentient being is subject to injury and thus intrinsically and equally worthy based on this vulnerability' (Dean 2015, 252). This account aligns with Sharon Sliwinski's claim that atrocity images – as simultaneously a record of inalienable human dignity and proof of its radical frailty – are 'a significant part of the way human subjects have come to imagine the ties that bind them' (2011, 4). Likewise, in making a case for the unique capacity of the camera to make us '*see* cruelty', Susie Linfield asserts that the vulnerable subject always exceeds its normative representation: 'Every image of barbarism [...] embraces its opposite, though sometimes unknowingly' (2010, 82).

This notion that the humanity of the victim recurs even in the most undignified of (imaged) conditions leads into a second critical point to be made: namely, that the repressive reading of photography in relations of power between photographer and subject radically fails to account for the complex social interactions that operate within and beyond the image. Because the photographer lacks the capacity to seal off the effect of the image and determine its sole meaning, atrocity images, even when intended to oppress or shame their subjects, always testify in other ways. The meaning and significance of any given image vary substantially depending on complex matters of context – not only on the photographer's action and relations of viewing and display but also on the victim depicted. The most interesting work to have addressed this issue goes beyond the binary focus on photographers and spectators to recognize the agency of the *represented* in relations that muster through the photograph. Ariella Azoulay's theory of 'a civil contract of photography' (2008) is significant in this regard precisely because it proposes the idea of a productive exchange of gazes between the *all* the parties involved in the image event: the photographed, the photographer and the spectator. On Azolay's terms, the political promise of photography lies in the fertile exchange of gazes in cases where the subject stakes a claim by directing the camera lens directly, thus actively addressing a spectator whose viewing in turn animates the image, turning it into 'theater stage on which what has been frozen in the photograph comes to life' (2008, 169). It is because of this perceived mode of direct communication between the spectator and the photographed subject, which also poses the photograph as an ongoing event extending beyond the photographic frame, that Azolay identifies in photography a political space in which the subject's right to have rights can be recognized and restored. Yet, as Gil Z. Hochberg (2015) argues, Azolay's is an idealistic account that primarily banks on the act of spectatorship and, in the context of the Israeli occupation, on the ability and willingness of the (Israeli) spectator to ethically and politically respond the demand presented by the pictured Palestinian human rights victim. Given the extreme inequality of visual rights – that is, who can record and look at whom – between the Israeli occupiers and Palestinian occupied, the limitations or impossibility of any such prospect of restorative exchange are indeed blatant (Hochberg 2015, 102–6).

The ethics of looking

The second major line of argument about images of agony poses the impossibility of responding adequately to such images. First, because of the idea that such recordings implicate the viewer directly or indirectly in the violence pictured – stressing our complicity or failure to intervene – and, second, because of the notion that painful images might assault the viewer's own integrity. The fear of complicity is linked with anxieties about the documentary image's perpetuation of injury and injustice. To look at images that shame or oppress their subjects is seen as a form of collusion, a continuation of victimisation and a recreation of the original crime (Möller 2009; 2012). Mieke Bal, in considering how people in pain are often denied the right to self-determination as to the taking and use of their own image, and how their exposure usually becomes 'somebody else's merchandize', argues that viewers partake in the commodification and 'theft of their subjectivity': 'Looking at their pain is, in this sense, a secondary exploitation' (2007, 95).

A recurring argument is also that the viewer cannot assimilate the traumatic effects of violent recordings: renderings of unimaginable brutality risk becoming an offense, an aggression that arises such strong defences so as to disrupt all viewing relations (e.g Hirsch 2001). The sight of human beings reduced to bare life – such as the terrible tangle of corpses in the Nazi death camps or, more recently, ISIL's savage staging of beheadings, shootings and caged prisoners being burnt alive in Syria (and beyond) – is difficult to behold, let alone digest. Hence, some critics contend that visualisations of excessive inhumanity do not help produce understanding but rather feelings of repulsion and disgust that threaten to overwhelm the viewer and, ultimately, engender a breach in consciousness itself.

The redistribution of the visible

Taken together, these critical anxieties about the act of making and looking at painful images suggest a double bind not only for the photographer's subject but also the spectator. Whereas the suffering subject faces the no-choice between exploitative exposure or political erasure, the viewer is locked into what Frank Möller (2009) terms 'the looking/not looking dilemma'. On the one hand, we should not look at images of agony because to do so might be a form of complicity, a continuation of the injury done to the victim. On the other, we are obliged to look at them because by refusing to do so we remove ourselves from public struggles over the meaning and significance of such images – struggles that, arguably, play so significant a role in shaping contemporary political life (Hariman and Lucaites 2007).

The only strategy to move beyond this dilemma, some critics contend, is to shun photo-journalism and to seek redemption in artistic image practises. Möller (2009), among others, dispenses entirely with the need to resolve the issues posed by explicit photojournalistic images of suffering by commending artworks that instead use forms of allusive or distanced realism. There are ways of picturing atrocity, Möller suggests, that sidestep both horns of the dilemma by using implication or artifice (with reference to Alfredo Jaar) or ironic fabrications (as in the case of Jeff Wall), inviting the viewer to engage in questions of human suffering without repeating the injury done to the victim. Along similar lines, some critics propose an aesthetics of *opacity*, explicated by critics such as T. J. Demos (2013), which is staked on a strategic 'refusal to represent'. In a moment when the gesture of 'giving visibility' has proven itself not only radically failing to the task of enacting justice for human rights victims but also, in its predominant forms, seemingly performative of the very injustice it seeks to undo, what the world needs is presumably not *more* images, *more* seeing, but an interruption and reworking of dominant ways of looking and being seen. In her important book *Visual Occupations* (2015), Gil S. Hochberg explores the political importance of various artistic attempts to challenge the extreme inequity of visual rights within the Israeli/Palestinian conflict. Palestinians under occupation are hypervisible, given the emergence of the 'human rights industry' and the oppressive presence of global media in Palestine. Yet, Hochberg underlines, they are seen through a fetishised visual frame of destruction, violence and loss that drastically minimizes their political agency. Hence, the question here is not so much how the 'visible' can be expanded, but rather how we might undo the dominant visual regimes that currently limits our common understanding of the conflict. The artworks Hochberg discusses thus refuse to provide the typical visual evidence of Israeli violence and Palestinian suffering, pursuing instead the opposition force of opacity: a realm of visuality that relies not on transparency but on obscurity, ambiguity, uncertainty. They deliberately seek to throw the conventions of traditional documentary filmmaking and sensationalist media into crisis in order to implicate the viewer in new ways, to unsettle us, to 'significantly alter the realm of what can be seen, who can be seen, how and from what position' (Hochberg 2015, 7). Building on Jacques Rancière's idea that the aesthetic prefigures the political – that the 'redistribution of the sensible' is one of the crucial ways in which political change can be initiated – Hochberg contends that an effective political act necessitates the undoing of any dominant visual order, and that creating new ways of seeing is the precondition for confronting (geo)political conflicts. Picturing differently – in this case, to defy direct representation and its pretense of transparency – is a way of foregrounding the necessary gap between image and event, compelling us to actively re-imagine, rather than passively consume, the scene of suffering. The oblique approach traffics in traces, gaps and failures, and thus directs attention to the limits of representation – to that which is not shown, something that might have been there but escaped the final frame. Hence, it challenges spectators not only to engage more intensely with the scene of suffering – to sense our way into a new and more complex understanding of injustices that basically defy simple imaging – but also, as part of that engagement, to question our own operation of looking: it is an invitation to self-reflection and, ultimately, 'to look closely at one's own failure to see' (Hochberg, 2015, 162).

Yet, the embrace of opacity as a strategy of resistance apparently runs the risk of obscuring the scene of suffering and thus to participate in the desires of some to deny that the suffering took place at all. Demos admit as much by rhetorically asking if the oblique approach might not 'end up unintentionally silencing the other, as the unforeseen mimicry of political erasure reenacts the very effect of colonization?' (2015, 87). Also, the projection of the hope for a just redistribution of the visible onto the (relatively) secluded art world might reveal a bias towards intellectual elitism and even obscurantism: surely it excludes publics that want the symbolic capital presumably required for appreciating the engagement with artistic practices complexly aimed at producing 'unknowability'.

The spectatorial turn

In distinction, there is an emerging view that recognizes photojournalism as a key component of political culture, arguing that it has a decisive role to play in the process of engaging the audience in facing up to injustices. In a critical contribution to the amounting scholarship that ponders how political space is shaped by forms and practices of image making, Robert Hariman and John Louis Lucaites (2007) demonstrate that photojournalistic images and their circulation are a premier means for constituting liberal-democratic citizenship. In the visual public sphere, they contend, 'there need not be a harsh divide between critical reason and spectatorship' (2008: 296). Rather, at their best, documentary and news images become powerful symbolic resources to think about and with: focal points for intelligent civic deliberations over important questions in public life. Their book joins pioneering work by leading scholars such as Jacques Ranciere (2009), Ariella Azoulay (2008), Susie Linfield (2010), Sharon Sliwinski (2011) and George Didi-Huberman (2008) that crucially attends to the central position of the spectator in human rights discourse. This 'spectatorial turn' in critical thinking about the problem of picturing pain marks a decisive break with the idea that viewing is the opposite of knowing and that the public is locked into to passive spectatorship rather than engaged participation. In Rancière's (2009) view, the emancipation of the spectator might begin with the recognition that what she sees, feels and understands in the aesthetic encounter is by no means dictated by the image itself or by the intentions of its maker: rather, viewing is a creative practice that actively transforms and interprets its objects.

There are, to be sure, considerabe differences among these writers, but in recognizing the precariousness of spectatorship they all imagine the productive possibilities of photojournalism as a mode of political engegament and contestation and as a site of ethical engagement. In their view, such imagery has the capacity to create a form of constructive instability: one that does not necessarily generate numbness or disregard for the image's subjects but, following Dean (2015, 253), 'a more productive undoing of the self that generates grief, loss, and mourning for the damage wrought'. Didi-Huberman (2008) poses photography as an ongoing event that extends beyond the photographic frame: atrocity images, he insists, 'look at us' from the painful situation, 'the heart of hell', to which they bear witness, thus obliging us to acknowledge a debt to those whose lives were sacrificed. Their injurous gaze is an injunction that we must imagine for ourselves (*s'imaginer*) to 'see that of which they are survivors' (182). On Linfield's (2010) account, photographs, more than any other kind of journalism, allow us to *see*, in the deep sense of knowing, and to 'feel in our guts' the injustices they track. Viewing images of political violence, she argues, can fulfil a profound civic responsibility: if we hope to redress human rights abuses, we must first truly understand them – and to do that, we must begin to look. Linfield's argument speaks to ways in which viewing atrocity photographs can foster ideas of human connection and create a range of responses – not only of pity, but also solidarity and recognition. On a similar note, Sliwinski features 'the great diversity of affective responses' (2011, 33) that takes place on the aesthetic scenes of human rights. She provides a history of ambivalent looking practices that encompasses both positive cases of reflective judgement and political responsiveness but also, importantly, *refused* reception: critical instances – such as the genocides in the former Yugoslavia and Rwanda – where Western spectators reportedly shuddered and turned away. Despite their political potential, Sliwinski contends, the long history of visual recordings as a tool of human rights advocacy has yet to secure the transformative effects they are asked to perform. Yet, Sliwinski asks: what can we take from the failure of atrocity images to stop violence? She concludes that failure, rather than a point of resignation, can be politically productive: marred visual encounters with genocidal acts of violence oblige us to rethink or question the limit of our ability to respond to others and the world. Aesthetic meetings that enact a confrontation with moral failure can themselves foster an ethics of recognition, Sliwinski argues, not only of the other as human but also of the complicities of our own gaze.

The question becomes whether the spectator is able and willing to take on the exercise of reflexivity and empathetic unsettlement posed by the moral route that has commanded the shifting perspective of ethics move from the image (and its maker) to the spectator. This route pertains not only to current theoretical discussions about how photographs make human rights appeals in a Kantian aesthetic tradition, as referenced above, but also to recent studies of how Western humanitarian and news media shape responses to the suffering of distant others. Lilie Chouliaraki (2014) and Wendy S. Hesford (2011) both emphasize the failure of the contemporary humanitarian imaginary to push Western publics beyond narcissistic and increasingly corporate discourses of solidarity. Hesford provides a critical account of 'spectacular rhetorics' in Western human rights imaginary, arguing that there is a visual economy here that (unknowingly) reproduces hierarchies of suffering and relationships of power between the Global North and the Global South. On a similarly gloomy note, Chouliaraki argues that contemporary humanitarian communication has increasingly turned Western publics into ironic spectators caring more about doing good for themselves than for others. Yet, both authors ascribe the promise of a redemptive humanitarian imaginary precisely to the act of reflexive spectatorship, to the ability of Western viewers to disrupt the spectacle's repetition by practicing critical self-awareness. This keen focus on the spectator's potentiality to translate the (compromised) mediated encounter with vulnerable others into a redemptive political imagination in a sense downplays the power of dominant 'distributions of the sensible' to greatly limit any such interventions. Surely the exercise of reflexivity can only take us so far in complicating the normative Western spectacles of suffering that shapes human rights discourses. And surely the willingness/ability of the spectator to undergo the painful labour of attempting to recognize and respond to suffering others is not only a function of representation or mediation, but always complicated by the underlying cultural, moral and political affects held to by particular audiences.

This is also to say that the 'spectatorial turn' in the study of human rights would benefit from a greater interrogation of the ways in which dynamics of spectatorship and representation may play out in a broader range of places, beyond the West, or in the contexts where the injustice or violence occur. Insofar as our perception of photojournalism's political potential primarily relies on the troubling dichotomy of aspirational Western saviours who do the looking versus 'distant sufferers' who are looked at, then such a shift of focus to include the latters *own* practices of creating, mobilizing and looking at images might prompt us to think anew about the vexed relationship between atrocity images and struggles for human rights. Critically, such a reassessment is still more urgent given the emergence of a new digital media environment where networked cameras are opening up radically new ways for human rights subjects to envision and be envisioned. If we are to understand the political significance of the embrace of digital (mobile) cameras as the perhaps most power-shifting device for local activists and citizens defending their rights, I argue in conclusion, we need to flip the focus from the image and its reception (by distant publics) to the embodied practices of producing human rights imagery and making it move.

Resistance by recording

Not the least remarkable point about recent mobilizations in Arab, European and North-American countries is the embrace of the camera (phone) as a mandatory device not only for documenting and communicating but also, arguably, for *enacting* dissent and resistance (Andén-Papadopoulos 2014). When used in a context of war or political conflict, the camera can not be understood as a flat recording device but is transformed into an instrument of engagement, acting variously as a witness, deterrent or provocation to (further) exercises of violence (Lebow 2012). In the context of the Arab uprisings for instance, the urge to record the revolutions specifically spoke back to the authoritarian regimes' denial of power to represent to their citizens. On Lina Khatib's (2013) account, the production and distribution of images was thus used as a means to reclaim the notion of political agency for Arab citizens. Yet the question of the politics embodied in current street-level practices of filming and circulating human rights imagery is a largely over-looked and under-theorised one in media studies and beyond. Recent scholarship increasingly poses the power of conflict imagery as a function of its performativity and viral mobility and mutability across a wide range of contexts and publics (cf. Parry 2010). Yet, what is often lacking in the current rhetoric about image flows, spreadability, connectivity and networks is a recognition of the diverse and often *frictional* processes of translation involved not only in the reception but, crucially, in the (high-risk) efforts by activists to create politically potent images and make them move (Andén-Papadopoulos and Westmoreland 2014). Arguably, any account of how grassroots activist imagery now participates in producing and contesting political power needs to address not only the front but also the *back end* of these productions. First, the extensive cast of actors and powers (including NGO's and news organisations) typically involved in producing – or channelling – this imagery is deserving of more critical attention. The organisation of labour around image activism is far from simple: in Syria, for instance, groups of anti-regime activists at home and abroad have created highly organized networks to strategically gather and disseminate video of critical events. Yet, whether shot in Syria or, for instance, on the West Bank, activist and citizen recordings are certainly not warranted public visibility: they are often delivered by hand, and must travel complex, laborious and often dangerous routes before being publicised (cf. Stein 2013).

Second, we must qualify the notion of 'frictionless sharing' by considering how the performative structures of social media platforms themselves not simply facilitate but heavily steer user navigation and content flows (van Dijck 2013). To what extent, and in what ways, human rights activists have both appropriated and become dependent on these restricted formats form an extremely important theme of investigation. As activists now increasingly turn to online platforms, most notably YouTube, it is key that we try grasp the mutual shaping forces of radical activist practices and commercial platform strategies. That is, while the infrastructure of YouTube (and other platforms) might infiltrate the forms and practices of contemporary video activism, it is *itself*, as Peter Snowdon (2014) argues, deeply entangled in the everyday experiences, and desires of activist groups and their followers. Snowdon thus proposes that the people who performed the Arab revolutions, through the massive aggregation of video from the uprisings, are seeking to redefine YouTube as a space for embodying a new political subjectivity.

Third, we must bring a more sustained analytical lens on the perhaps most neglected aspect of image activism today, namely the agency of the image makers themselves. It is indeed curious how this agency, the multiple practices, motivations and desires of the individuals who actually stood up in a dangerous situation and wielded a camera, often risking their life doing so, seems to be forgotten once an image or video clip crosses international wires. Yet, we cannot fully appreciate the political promise of the 'crowdsourced' video revolution if we place all the weight of criticism and analysis on the images themselves, or on their perception and use by distant (Western) audiences. Rather, a further better question is how activist image practices can be understood as performances that are meaningful in themselves; actions that should be evaluated for what they accomplish, not only in terms of their image outcome and its impact on people outside of the conflict but for the activists themselves and their own communities. Livia Hinegardner (2009), for instance, shows how activists in Mexico conceived of making human rights films as a direct form of political action and social organization in its own right. Contra literature on human rights video that focuses on its usefulness in creating political pressure through shaming perpetrators of abuses (Gregory 2006; Keck and Sikkink 1998; McLagan 2003, 2006), Hinegardner poses video making as a valuable act in itself that, without ever inciting an 'outside' audience to act, create and reshape fields of action in locally contested social and political fields.

This is also to suggest that we need to go beyond a realist understanding of image activism for human rights as a means of producing visual evidence and attend also to video production as a subjective process, in which citizens and activists engage the powers of imaging and affect to re/create themselves as political subjects. Following Maple Razsa (2012) and Peter Snowdon (2014), we must conceive of current citizen and activist image practices as a means not only for speaking truth to power, but for cultivating new and unruly forms of political agency, subjectivity and collectivity within grassroots struggles to expose and resist human rights abuses around the world.

References

Andén-Papadopoulos, K. (2014). 'Citizen Camera-witnessing: Embodied Political Dissent in the Age of 'Mediated Mass Self-communication'. *New Media & Society* 16(5), pp. 753–69.

Andén-Papadopoulos, K. and Westmoreland, M. (2014). 'Resistance-by-recording: The Visuality and Visibility of Contentious Politics in Egypt, Palestine and Syria'. Research project plan (unpublished).

Azoulay, A. (2008). *The Civil Contract of Photography*. New York: Zone Books.

Bal, M. (2007). 'The Pain of Images'. In: M. Reinhardt, H. Edwards, and E. Duganne, eds., Beautiful Suffering: Photography and the Traffic in Pain Williamstown/Chicago: Williams College Museum of Art/The University of Chicago Press.

Berger, J. (1980). *About Looking*. New York: Vintage.

Bernstein, J. M. (2012). 'Preface'. In: A. Grönstad and H. Gustafsson, eds., *Ethics and Images of Pain*. London: Routledge. pp. xi–xiv.

Butler, J. (2010). *Frames of War: When Is Life Grievable?* London: Verso.

Chouliaraki, L. (2013). *The Ironic Spectator. Solidarity in the Age of Post-Humanitarianism*. Cambridge, UK: Polity.

Dean, C. J. (2015). 'Atrocity Photographs, Dignity, and Human Vulnerability. Humanity: An International Journal of Human Rights'. *Humanitarianism, and Development*, 6(2), pp. 239–64.

Demos, T. J. (2013). *The Migrant Image: The Art and Politics of Documentary during Global Crisis*. Durham: Duke University Press.

Didi-Huberman, G. (2008). *Images In Spite of All: Four Photographs from Auschwitz*, trans. Shane B. Lillis. Chicago: University of Chicago Press.

Gregory, S. (2006). 'Transnational Storytelling: Human Rights, WITNESS, and Video Advocacy'. *American Anthropologist*, 108(1), pp. 195–204.

Hariman, R. and Lucaites, J. L. (2007). *No Caption Needed: Iconic Photographs, Public Culture, and Liberal Democracy*. Chicago: The University of Chicago Press.

Hesford, W. S. (2011). *Spectacular Rhetorics. Human Rights Visions, Recognitions, Feminisms*. Durham: Duke University Press.

Hinegardner, L. (2009). 'Action, Organization and Documentary Film: Beyond a Communications Model of Human Rights Videos'. Visual Anthropology Review, 25(2), pp. 172–85.

Hirsch, M. (2001). *Surviving Images: Holocaust Photographs and the Work of Postmemory. In Visual Culture and the Holocaust*, ed. Barbie Zelizer. New Brunswick: Rutgers University Press.

Hochberg, G. Z. (2015). *Visual Occupations. Violence and Visibility in a Conflict Zone.* Durham: Duke University Press.

Keck, M. E. and Sikkink, K. (1998). *Activists Beyond Borders: Advocacy Networks in International Politics.* New York: Cornell University Press.

Khatib, L. (2013). *Image Politics in the Middle East: The Role of the Visual in Political Struggle.* London: I. B. Tauris.

Lebow, A. (2012). 'Shooting with Intent'. In: J. ten Brink and J. Oppenheimer, eds. *Killer Images Documentary Film, Memory and the Performance of Violence.* New York: Wallflower Press/Columbia University Press.

Linfield, S. (2010). *The Cruel Radiance: Photography and Political Violence.* Chicago: The University of Chicago Press.

McLagan, M. *(*2003). 'Principles, Publicity, and Politics: *Notes on Human Rights Media'. American Anthropologist* 105 (3), pp. 605–12.

McLagan, M. (2006). 'Introduction: Making Human Rights Claims Public'. *American Anthropologist*, 108(1), pp. 191–95.

Möller, F. (2009). 'The Looking/not Looking Dilemma'. *Review of International Studies*, 35, pp. 781–94.

Möller, F. (2012). 'Associates in Crime and Guilt'. In: A. Grönstad and H. Gustafsson, H., eds., *Ethics and Images of Pain.* London: Routledge, pp. 15-32.

Parry, K. (2010). 'Media Visualisation of Conflict: Studying News Imagery in 21st Century Wars'. *Sociology Compass*, 4(7), pp. 417–29.

Rancière, J. (2009). *The Emancipated Spectator.* London and New York: Verso.

Reinhardt, M. (2012). 'Painful Photographs: From the Ethics of Spectatorship to Visual Politics'. In: A. Grönstad and H. Gustafsson, H., eds., *Ethics and Images of Pain.* London: Routledge., pp. 33–56.

Razsa, M. J. (2013). 'Beyond "Riot Porn": Protest Video and the Production of Unruly Subjects'. *Ethnos* (April 8), pp. 1–29.

Sliwinski, S. (2011). *Human Rights In Camera.* Chicago: The University of Chicago Press.

Snowdon, P. (2014). The Revolution Will be Uploaded: Vernacular Video and the Arab Spring. Culture Unbound, 6(21), pp. 401–29.

Sontag, S. (1978). *On Photography.* London: Penguin.

Stein, R.L. (2013). *Viral Occupation Cameras and Networked Human Rights in the West Bank.* Middle East Research and Information Project. Available at: http://www.merip.org/mero/mero032013?utm_source= twitterfe

Torchin, L. (2012). *Creating the Witness: Documenting Genocide on Film, Video, and the Internet.* Minneapolis: University of Minnesota Press.

van Dijck, J. (2013). *The Culture of Connectivity: A Critical History of Social Media.* Oxford/New York: Oxford University Press.

34

CITIZEN WITNESSING OF HUMAN RIGHTS ABUSES

Stuart Allan

Today's global mediascape recurrently brings to light incidents where one of the most vital of human rights, the right to bear witness, becomes a site of political contestation. Time and again ordinary individuals have found themselves suddenly asserting this right, most likely generating precipitous forms of crisis reportage using a mobile camera – such as a smartphone – on their person. In the absence of professional journalists on the scene, some are compelled to document, best they are able, what they see, hear and feel for the benefit of distant others. 'The amount of bystander footage shared online has skyrocketed, becoming a critical aspect of news and human rights reporting', Madeleine Bair (2016) of WITNESS points out. 'And yet it seems like every day we are faced with a new dilemma concerning the ethics of watching and sharing footage that is often intimate, horrific, or decontextualized'. She proceeds to pose several questions, which together pinpoint pressing challenges for organisations undertaking to mediate the significance of diverse types of visible evidence:

> Does sharing videos by extremist organizations aid their goals of provoking fear and glamorizing violence, or is it a necessary part of reporting? Should eyewitnesses be asked permission before their videos are broadcast by news media, or would that hinder the reporting process? How can investigators and advocates report on abuse caught on camera without violating the privacy or impacting the security of those seen on video?
>
> *(Bair 2016)*

Pragmatic answers to these and related questions often prove frustratingly elusive under intense time-pressure, prompting considerable debate – not least amongst news editors, crisis responders and human rights investigators – regarding how best to recast traditional protocols and codes of conduct to handle citizen reportage (or, as some prefer to label it, 'user-generated content' or 'UGC', 'amateur footage', 'open-source video', and the like) produced from those on the ground.

To consider several of the implications at stake for this *Companion*'s research agendas, this chapter proceeds to elucidate several key issues through the conceptual lens of what I have termed 'citizen witnessing' elsewhere (Allan 2013). Citizen witnesses, whether they are survivors, bystanders, activists, emergency responders, or even combatants, feel personally motivated to visually document the harrowing nature of crisis events, notwithstanding attendant risks, threats and dangers (Allan 2015; Chouliaraki 2016; Cottle 2013; Mortensen 2015; Pantti and Sirén 2015; Wardle,

347

et al. 2014). Professional witnesses such as photojournalists, Daniel Joyce (2010) observes, increasingly find their work displaced by images 'which are unauthorised, which spread virally online and are taken by amateurs, perpetrators and victims, who now have the means to document (and sometimes thereby to extend the damage caused by) human rights abuses themselves' (2010, 234–5). Few of those involved are likely to self-identify as citizen journalists, however, let alone self-reflexively reaffirm conventionalised norms, values and priorities of witnessing (Kross 2016; Thorsen and Allan 2014). It is precisely at this critical juncture that several NGOs have sought to play a vital contributory role, one informed by an ethical commitment to advancing human rights causes by equipping citizens in crisis situations with cameras, and the training to use them, so that they might forge alternative strategies for documenting abuses and violations.

In striving to bring to the fore certain ethical, journalistic and strategic tensions at the heart of video advocacy, this chapter will explore how the performative right to bear witness is consolidating amongst diverse communities of interest mobilising across globalising communicative networks. In the first instance, we consider several pertinent conceptual insights to help frame our discussion, particularly those provided by Susie Linfield (2010) and Ariella Azoulay (2008, 2012), respectively, regarding human rights imagery. Next, our focus turns to WITNESS, an international non-profit organisation widely perceived to be a leader in a global movement to create change by developing citizen-centred approaches to human rights reportage. Launched in 1992 by a small group led by the pop-star Peter Gabriel (2014), its current website declares its aim to empower 'human rights defenders to use video to fight injustice, and to transform personal stories of abuse into powerful tools that can pressure those in power or with power to act'. Its initial strategy, namely to provide 'people who chose to be in the wrong place at the right time' with cameras so as to help them document violations and abuses in the field, has evolved to prioritise both activists' and ordinary citizens' engagement in personal reportage with a view to its evidential importance for the advancement of human rights causes. To date, WITNESS has partnered with more than 360 human rights groups in 97 countries, devoting particular effort to supporting the inclusion of citizen video as a 'democratic tool' in human rights campaigns seen by millions of people around the world.

Making violence visible

In undertaking an enquiry into the importance of citizen witnessing for human rights imagery, we may briefly draw upon enquiries into the gradual evolution of the eyewitness as a distinctive figure. Close scrutiny of *The Oxford English Dictionary*'s principal definition – 'The action of bearing witness or giving testimony (in witnessing of, as a witness to; to bear witnessing, to bear witness)' – reveals aspects of how its etymological lineage interweaves religious, literary and juridical conceptions over the span of centuries. Histories of visual culture recurrently privilege the ways in which codified rules of authentication and verification give shape to testimonies of witnessing within what Foucault (1980) termed 'regimes of truth' within a given society. Nicholas Mirzoeff's (2011) historiography, for example, illuminates the ways in which diverse modes of visuality have contributed to the normalisation of power relations underpinning state authority over what can be seen, where, when and by whom – constituting, in effect, a contest between visuality and counter-visuality. 'The right to look claims autonomy from this authority, refuses to be segregated, and spontaneously invents new forms', he writes. In other words, the right to look is 'the claim to a right to the real', which necessarily places witnessing on the terrain of human rights, and, as such, makes it a site of political struggle (2011, 4).

Relevant initiatives in theory-building have sought to think through typically tacit assumptions concerning the capacity of imagery to draw us into a community of compassionate witnesses. In offering a critical assessment of related enquiries, Susie Linfield (2010) emphasises the value of photography as documentary testimony, proceeding to discern the 'devastating paradox' at the 'heart of the photograph of suffering' (2010, xv, 33). In her view, there can be no doubt 'photography has, more than any other twentieth-century medium, exposed violence – made violence *visible* – to millions of people all over the globe', and yet 'the history of photography also shows just how limited and inadequate such exposure is'. In other words, she adds, 'seeing does not necessarily translate into believing, caring, or acting' (2010, 33). Clarifying photography's role in furthering human rights, it follows, demands greater recognition of its capacity as a 'medium to mirror the lacunae at the heart of human rights-ideals', which is to say, it is very good at 'making us *see* cruelty' (2010, 33, 39). Documentary photographs, Linfield elaborates, 'bring home to us the reality of physical suffering', revealing to us 'how easily the body can be maimed, starved, splintered, beaten, burnt, torn, and crushed'. It is this vulnerability, she adds, 'that every human being shares; the cruelty is something that shatters our very sense of what it means to be human' (2010, 39).

There is an intimate connection, Linfield contends, between atrocity imagery and what she terms an international human rights consciousness. Such imagery offers the prospect of making connections with this suffering of others, and in so doing underscores the extent to which the camera works to 'globalise our consciences', effectively making it impossible to claim, 'I did not know' (2010, 46). For Linfield, then, the camera – whether still, film or video – 'has become a key tool – perhaps *the* key tool – in enabling such emphatic leaps' (2010, 47). It is the moral duty of the photographer to focus attention on those denied their basic human rights, and thereby contest the terms by which perpetrators strive to conceal their crimes. The depiction of suffering, she points out, 'has been central to fostering the idea, if not yet the reality, that barbarous assaults are no longer the private property of the states that commit them' (2010, 47). At the same time, however, the capacity of such imagery to conjure deep emotion is both a great strength and a danger, she cautions, inviting the risk of misinterpretation or, even worse, misleading viewers in the absence of adequate explanation. Hence the necessity of looking beyond the frame of such imagery to grapple with painful realities in all of their complexities. 'Like human rights themselves', Linfield argues, 'this expansive kind of vision is not particularly natural but, rather, is something we must consciously create' (2010, 51).

It is precisely this theme Ariella Azoulay (2008, 2012) elaborates in her efforts to address questions of visual truth, in part by bringing together discourses of civil contracts with those of photography in the service of human rights projects. 'Photography, at times, is the only civic refuge at the disposal of those robbed of citizenship', she writes, and as such its capacity to provide visual evidence of discriminatory oppression is vital. Here she takes issue with those who insist that 'photography lies' and so cannot be trusted, who are dismissive of its enduring power as a medium of truth documenting what was present before the lens. In her words,

> Photography's critics tend to forget that despite the fact that photography speaks falsely, it *also* speaks the truth. A photograph does in fact attest to what 'was there,' although its evidence is partial, and only in this sense is it false. What was there is *never* only what is visible in the photograph, but is also contained in the very photographic situation, in which photographer and photographed interact around a camera. That is, a photograph is evidence of the social relations which made it possible, and these cannot be removed from the visible 'sense' that it discloses to spectators who can agree or disagree on its actual content. The social relation that 'was there,' to which a photograph attests, is an expression of a mutual guarantee, or its infringement.
>
> (*Azoulay, 2008, 126–7; emphasis in original*)

Inundated with a surfeit of images, certain theorists have fallen prey to what they liken to 'image fatigue', Azoulay contends, which has meant they have effectively stopped looking. 'The world filled up with images of horrors', she writes, 'and they loudly proclaimed that viewers' eyes had grown unseeing, proceeding to unburden themselves of the responsibility to hold onto the elementary gesture of looking at what is presented to one's gaze' (2008, 11).

This burden of responsibility must be borne, however emotionally difficult it may prove to endure at times. 'Photography is one of the instruments which has enabled the modern citizen to establish her liberal rights', Azoulay points out, 'including freedom of movement and of information, as well as her right to take photographs and to be photographed, to see what others see and would like to show through photographs' (2008, 125). That said, however, neither the photographer nor the photographed persons can determine how their meaning will be inscribed in the ensuing image, she contends, namely because the photograph 'exceeds any presumption of ownership or monopoly and any attempt at being exhaustive' (2008, 11–12). Prospects for alternative readings of a depicted event will be there, the social relations enabling the photograph's production and subsequent interpretation never being entirely fixed around a singular, stable meaning. In principle at least, anyone 'can pull at one of its threads and trace it in such a way as to reopen the image and renegotiate what it shows, possibly even completely over-turning what was seen in it before' (2008, 13). These negotiations necessitate a civic skill being utilised by the spectator, one that amounts to more than aesthetic appreciation. This is particularly apparent, she argues, where the event rendered concerns human suffering, with such readings being alert to the harm being perpetrated. Indeed, the spectator has a duty to employ this skill under such circumstances, she maintains, 'an obligation to others to struggle against injuries inflicted on those others' (2008, 14).

In striving to theorise spectatorship in relation to this civic duty, this belief that individuals' tacit commitment to one another should be first and foremost – rather than towards the ruling power – is of crucial import. The very nature of the photographic act in this regard, it follows, 'presumes the existence of a civil space in which photographers, photographed subjects, and spectators share a recognition that what they are witnessing is intolerable' (2008, 18). Linfield and Azoulay's respective conceptual interventions have helped to throw into sharper relief several tensions besetting efforts to theorise the moral value of imagery for human rights projects (see also Hariman 2014; Hesford 2011; Joyce 2010; Thrall, et al. 2014). In the next section, we turn to a practical, collaborative response to this pressing demand for strategic counter-visuality.

'See it. Film it. Change it.'

'Let human-rights advocates around the world take heart. They will soon receive powerful new arms with which to wage their struggles against repression: hand-held video cameras, computers and fax machines', Marvine Howe (1992) of *The New York Times* reported on March 20 1992. Pointing to the launch of WITNESS set to take place the following Monday, she quoted Michael Posner of the New York–based Lawyers Committee for Human Rights (LCHR) stating: 'This program comes in response to requests from many local rights groups who say they need equipment to get their message out'. In the ensuing press coverage of the launch, Posner explained the rationale behind the intervention. 'Timely, accurate and impartial information is the most powerful weapon individuals and groups have to ensure that governments everywhere protect and promote the fundamental human rights of their citizens', he declared. 'It's time for us, the human rights movement, to better use the communications revolution to expose abuses and galvanise public opinion to stop them' (WITNESS 1992; see also Allan, 2015).

By 1995, WITNESS had distributed video equipment to more than sixty organisations. With the repercussions of the King moment still reverberating, videotaped documentation of police brutality in places such as Guatemala, Egypt, and Nigeria provided evidential support for victims' claims. Still, persuading the international media – such as the BBC or CNN – to use the material was frequently difficult, whether purposely shot by trained activists or by 'accidental observers', or even to follow up on the story with their own correspondents. Compounding matters, as WITNESS director Sam Gregory (2008) pointed out in an interview discussing the early days, the news media often focused on 'episodic framing' emphasising 'individual actions, victims, and perpetrators', being 'less interested in structural violence, systemic challenges, or the ongoing problems that characterize many of the most pernicious abuses, especially violations of economic, social, and cultural rights'. WITNESS Network spokeswoman Barbara Becker acknowledged in a press interview that the perceived credibility of the footage was key. Journalists were 'concerned with many things including timeliness, newsworthiness and authenticity', she stated. 'We are working on these things, so hopefully the constant media attention we anticipated may come' (cited in Cobb 1995). Equally encouraging, related positive outcomes were coming to light, including local activists' use of their videos as organising tools for meetings and public education workshops, as well as for fundraising initiatives for community projects. Repurposing camera equipment for training programmes similarly met with success, such as Becker's example of how the Centre for Victims of Torture in Nepal taped its psychology trainees counselling torture victims in order to assess their skills, and then passing along the footage to share good practice with others.

Indications of WITNESS's growing public profile during the first phase of its development included the television music channel VH1's tribute to the project with a star-studded concert broadcast live in the US (and subsequently on MTV) for its annual award ceremony in April 1996. By then WITNESS was being credited with numerous breakthroughs where its videotaped footage cast a spotlight on alleged violations eluding media attention, the visual impact of which helped to focus public pressure for change. 'It's hard for people to deny what is happening when they see it for themselves', Gabriel insisted at the time. 'With text journalism, it is a lot easier to put off any emotional attachment. It's harder to explain away responsibility when it is in your face' (cited in Atwood 1996). Moreover, as WITNESS coordinator Sukanya Pillay later pointed out, cameras in the right hands – by 'coincidence, luck or planning' – sometimes helped to reduce tensions, such as when WITNESS dispatched video monitors to Northern Ireland during its annual marching season in 1997. 'The kids were running up and throwing rocks and bottles at them, and they are going back and forth', she told CNN the following year. 'And I felt strongly that our presence there stopped anything from happening beyond just this cat-and-mouse sort of game. And so it does show that a camera can be used as a deterrent' (CNN 1998).

Further examples of video monitoring by organisations using cameras and training from WITNESS ranged from refugee camps in Rwanda (as well as recording the exhumation of genocide victims) to mental hospitals in the United States, to documenting the trafficking of women from the former Soviet Union forced to work as prostitutes, to massacres in Guatemala, military abduction in India, and the plight of children turned into soldiers in Sudan and northern Uganda (see also Farrell and Allan 2015). In pointing to these and related examples, Michael Pollak (1999) of the *New York Times* observed that it took a 'strong stomach' to watch the footage made available on the WITNESS website. 'Armed with light and sound in places where there may be no electric power or paved roads, the organizations, many of them impoverished and officially shunned, are documenting atrocities that would otherwise become dry reports to be dismissed by the authorities', he wrote. In so doing, he added, they 'are turning them into riveting evidence of evil'. At the same time, some detractors were contending that WITNESS's forging of a 'new relation between aesthetics, commerce, and politics' was putting 'a "humane" corporate face on human rights issues' that contradicted 'the resistant identities of human rights victims', thereby exacerbating the risk that suffering would turn into a 'web-surfer spectacle' (Schaffer and Smith 2004, 39). New tactics continued to evolve, including with regard as to how best incorporate video footage of human rights cases into on-the-ground campaigns. The limits of documentation would have to stretch, in other words, to encompass possible solutions as well.

By the time it was marking its ten-year anniversary in 2002, WITNESS had evolved into a 'full service' organisation for its growing range of 'campaign partners'. In addition to distributing cameras – including in India, Romania, Gambia, the Philippines, and Palestinian communities of the West Bank, the Gaza Strip, and East Jerusalem that year alone – it was providing 'training and assistance in editing footage and in creating game plans for getting it seen, whether in a full-blown TV documentary or as streaming video on the Witness Web site' (Hornaday 2002). The website was attracting hits from 37,000 visitors a month by then (helped, in part, by celebrity supporters introducing the videos, such as film stars Susan Sarandon and Tim Robbins or musicians like Lou Reed and Laurie Anderson), confirming expectations that cyberspace would prove to be a key component of new strategies to extend the reach of video advocacy. 'This kind of catalytic work that Witness is doing is really erasing a lot of the boundaries', filmmaker Peter Wintonick observed, convinced that a paradigm shift in distribution was underway. 'Witness is at the forefront of this revolution of micro-documentaries, as I call them, or digi-documentaries', he explained, which entailed 'putting documentaries up on the Net, so they're not only available to the North American community of activists, but in theory to anybody who wants to log on' (cited in Hornaday 2002). Indeed, with the promise of broadband and wireless communications technology on the horizon, WITNESS was confident its partners in the field soon would be able to cut their own films using laptop editing systems (and relay them using proxy-servers to help protect their identity), rather than relying on the New York–based editors. Further training revolved around how to craft content to convey complex messages in a personal way for selected audiences ('smart narrowcasting' aimed at 'people who will act'), together with practical issues, such as handling mapping technology, the use of tools to blur or pixelate faces (or alter voices) to protect identities, archiving testimonies and related resources, as well as respecting privacy, copyright, and other intellectual-property rights, amongst other concerns.

Witnessing imperatives

What does success look like? 'Well, it's put cameras out in many countries all over the world, and armed human rights activists with a new tool', Gabriel stated when asked by ABC News to reflect on WITNESS's achievements in 2006. 'And I think both in changing laws, in getting their case heard around the world, in helping people not to feel isolated, desperate and forgotten, it's done a lot', he continued (ABC News 2006). Conceding that it was 'the tip of the iceberg', with 'a huge amount that needs doing', he nevertheless expressed his optimism that WITNESS was becoming ever-more effective in realising its aims. New, progressive opportunities were emerging to recast 'the original mission to get cameras out to the world', not least by striving to make the most of camera technologies in cell or mobile telephones. The growing ubiquity of these relatively inexpensive devices meant that George Orwell's vision in the dystopian novel *1984*, where those in power control the population through observation, was set to 'flip . . . on its head', Gabriel believed. 'If we get cameras out everywhere, perhaps through observation, the small guy, the little guy can keep an eye on those in power' (ABC News 2006). The 'internet revolution' signalled 'a real point of transition', in his view, opening up new ways to hold governments accountable for violations of human rights.

A case in point was the launch of a video-sharing site, simply called 'the Hub', on Human Rights Day, 10 December 2007. As WITNESS's Meg McLagan (2007) wrote at the time, it was intended to foster participatory possibilities by 'acting as a facilitator in making, aggregating, organizing and disseminating human-rights videos', and thereby help to summon into action 'a globally networked human-rights community' (p. 325). Envisioned as a 'central clearinghouse' for activists sharing visual material (raw footage as well as finished advocacy videos) and information resources, including anonymously when necessary for security reasons, the Hub was designed to be an open alternative to commercial video-sharing sites, such as YouTube. Material posted on the latter type of site sometimes encountered difficulties, the main concern being that it was difficult to find in the first place. Even then, it was 'often mischaracterised or mis-tagged and may even, at times, be the brunt of jokes', Caldwell explained in a press interview, 'which is very disturbing to people who are placing their lives at risk to get it on there' (cited in Wallace 2007; see also Caldwell and Federlein 2008; Thijm 2010). Furthermore, videos viewed without an adequate explanatory context risked promoting misconceptions – accidental and otherwise – as messages were actively shared, remixed or re-inscribed within alternative interpretive frameworks.

Refashioning what Caldwell and Federlein (2008) termed 'the vernacular language of human rights advocacy' in order to raise awareness and inspire action demanded fresh thinking about the strategic framing of harsh realities within the narrative conventions of digital storytelling. 'Obviously abuses being captured in the moment are incredibly powerful and can go a long way in changing a situation, but those moments are rare', Jenni Wolfson of WITNESS pointed out where the Hub was concerned. 'A lot of the video that we work on with our partners are personal testimonies of people who have survived abuses. It's those personal stories that really help people to connect to the issues' (cited in Wallace 2007). Her colleague Sam Gregory concurred. 'In a lot of cases (video documentation) can be the tipping point', he told *The Gazette* in Montreal. 'The power ... of someone speaking directly to you saying, "This is what is happening to me, this is what I want you to do"' was rapidly increasing, in his perception, as 'we move into a more video-literate culture' (cited in Valiante 2008; see also Gregory 2008, 2014a, b, 2015).

The evolving conventions of social media made platforms – not least Twitter, Facebook and YouTube – have opened-up new conditions of possibility for WITNESS. In 2012 it announced its partnership with Storyful, a private company that, in its website's words, works 'to discover, verify, acquire and deliver the most valuable real-time content the social web has to offer', and thereby bridge the gap between social media content and professional news media (see Storyful 2015). The two announced they were joining forces to launch a Human Rights Channel (HRC) on YouTube, the aim being 'to tell breaking stories through the lenses of citizen journalists that will change the way we view, share and engage human rights video' (WITNESS 2012). Storyful's expertise in corroborating video authenticity (using local sources, regional experts, and 'pioneering algorithms') complemented WITNESS's proficiency in curating footage into compelling, evidence-driven narratives of direct interest to specific audiences. 'The greatest challenge for our work is scaling it up to properly educate the millions of people who now have cameras in their pockets and are willing to use them to document human rights abuses', WITNESS's Chris Michael explained. 'This is creating enormous opportunities for video advocates to create, curate, and share stories that we may never have seen or heard previously' (cited in Romanelli 2013).

Moreover, to the extent citizen witnesses are empowered to foster a collective identity on these terms – as ad hoc members of 'witnessing publics' aligned with distributed network campaigns – human rights violations, it follows, will be all the more difficult to perpetrate. In short, through its website and YouTube channel, the HRC's self-described 'mission' is to 'curate and analyse eyewitness videos of human rights abuse, and work with peers to ensure that these sorts of videos are seen by those who can make a difference' (Human Rights Channel 2015). That it has a 'mission' sets the organisation apart from the codified strictures of journalistic objectivity; that is, rather than presenting witness footage in an ostensibly detached fashion, it does so in accordance with a specific protocol intended to support activists in their efforts to stop human rights abuses and hold perpetrators accountable. Moreover, WITNESS also offers links to training workshops and free online teaching materials via the HRC website, including guidance about the ethics and safety of filming human rights abuses as well as practical information and advice concerning video production strategies. Further links afford access to resources offered through the 'video4change' network of NGOs, including the 'Rights-Based Approach to Participatory Video' toolkit, created by the 'community development organisation' InsightShare (2015). A 'rights-based approach' seeks to align documentary filmmaking with a normative agenda, situating human rights at the heart of the partners' documentary video projects (see also Farrell and Allan 2015).

Expanding visual boundaries

Longstanding criticisms of visual advocacy, typically revolving around questions of implied causation, obscured relationships, inadequate context, and the like, were readily apparent to members of WITNESS from the outset. The hard, day-to-day grind to realise the mission's ideals routinely confronted challenges regarding how best to compel news organisations to cover such violations with sufficient depth and ethical integrity. Despite the absence of straightforward answers, WITNESS has steadily worked to prise open the visual boundaries of reportage. More than two decades since its launch, this problem has been further exacerbated by factors constitutive of the wider crisis in international journalism, yet there is scope for cautious optimism that Peter Gabriel's initial vision – as strategic as it was 'simplistic' – is gaining a critical purchase in emergent participatory cultures of video advocacy occurring in unlikely places around the globe. While few would deny that the disconnect between visible evidence and social justice can be profound, WITNESS's citizen-centred ethos promises to continue to instantiate innovative forms of reportage to help narrow this gap.

Where the news media are concerned, the ever-growing demand for visual material compels editors to refashion their commissioning practices, fostering points of engagement with a diverse array of prospective sources with an eye to ad hoc communities of interest, if not impromptu coalition building. Garnering positive news media coverage has been a key campaign element for WITNESS, but recent years have seen it become primarily focused on niche audiences; that is, what Gregory (2014a) calls 'smart narrow-casting' with the emphasis placed on mainstream media working as multipliers, as opposed to a more traditional, broadcasting-centred approach. Corresponding strategic shifts seek to combine global campaigns on selected issues (such as gender-based violence and forced evictions) with expanded training programmes (the renamed video4change network of like-minded practitioners and trainers), as well as a 'cameras everywhere' initiative revolving around video as evidence, facilitated by further engagement with supportive technology companies (see also Gregory 2015). WITNESS's citizen videos have proven increasingly important as resources (effectively an 'information subsidy', to varying degrees) for alternative types of reportage realised through professional-amateur co-operation and, even better, collaboration. As we have seen above, they bring to bear first-hand perspectives from places difficult, even at times impossible for journalists to reach, relaying insights not only into exceptional crises when violence suddenly erupts, but also more routine instances of human rights abuse.

'So as much as we celebrate the possibilities of accountability in a "cameras everywhere" world', Gregory (2015) maintains, 'we also must recognize the dangers of what this drives us to watch, share, prioritize and also what is excluded'. Advocacy videos deployed to advantage bring to light the experiences of those otherwise likely to be ignored, marginalised or trivialised in media representations, enabling news stories to secure an evidential basis that may be otherwise too dangerous – or, indeed, prohibitively expensive – to cover with sufficient rigour and depth. In addition to addressing ethical obligations to those being represented, such reportage often succeeds in rendering problematic ethnocentric assumptions underlying familiar relations of othering endemic to so much 'us' and 'them' coverage (see also Allan and Peters 2015; Bair 2016; Chouliaraki 2016; Hoskins and O'Loughlin 2015; Thrall et al. 2014). In marked contrast, these videos can help to provide the interpretive context often lacking from event-centred news reports, thereby facilitating deeper understanding of the structural imperatives shaping crises and the corresponding politics of othering that typically ensues. WITNESS's citizen reportage exemplifies this potential, and in so doing poses searching questions regarding the re-mediation of the power of visual imagery in the service of human rights and social justice.

References

ABC News (2006). Peter Gabriel Talks About the Documentary 'Witness'. Transcript, *The Charlie Rose Show*.

Allan, S. (2013). *Citizen Witnessing: Revisioning Journalism in Times of Crisis*. Cambridge: Polity.

Allan, S. (2015). 'Visualising Human Rights: The Video Advocacy of WITNESS'. In: S. Cottle and G. Cooper, eds. *Humanitarianism, Communications and Change*. New York: Peter Lang, pp. 197–210.

Allan, S. and Peters, C. (2015). 'Visual Truths of Citizen Reportage: Four Research Problematics', *Information, Communication & Society*. DOI:10.1080/1369118X.2015.1061576.

Atwood, B. (1996). 'VH1 Honors' to benefit Witness. *Billboard* (12 March).

Azoulay, A. (2008). *The Civil Contract of Photography*. New York: Zone Books.

Azoulay, A. (2012). *Civil Imagination: A Political Ontology of Photography*. London: Verso.

Bair, M. (2016). *'Announcing WITNESS' Ethical Guidelines for Using Eyewitness Footage in Human Rights*, WITNESS.org. Available at: https://blog.witness.org/ 2015/10/announcing-witness-ethical-guidelines-for-using-eyewitness-footage-in-human-rights

Caldwell, G., and Federlein, S. (2008). 'Moving Images: From Vision to Action, From Action to Transformation'. *Innovations*, 3(2), pp. 37–50.

Chouliaraki, L. (2016). The Securitization of Citizen Reporting in Post-Arab Spring Conflicts. In: M. Baker and B. B. Blaagaard, eds., *Citizen Media and Public Spaces*. London and New York: Routledge, pp. 189–207.

CNN (1998). Transcript, *CNN Newsroom Worldview*, Davin Hutchins interviewer.

Cobb, C. (1995). 'New Eye on the News'. *The Ottawa Citizen* (25 February).

Cottle, S. (2013). 'Journalists Witnessing Disasters: From the Calculus of Death to the Injunction to Care'. *Journalism Studies*, 14(2), pp. 232–48.

Farrell, N. and Allan, S. (2015). 'Redrawing Boundaries: WITNESS and the Politics of Citizen Videos', *Global Media and Communication*. DOI:10.1177/1742766515606291

Foucault, M. (1980). *Power/Knowledge: Selected interviews and other writings 1972–1977*. New York: Vintage.

Gabriel, P. (2014). Peter Gabriel RNR HOF Speech 4–10–14 Rock and Roll Hall of Fame. Available at: http://youtu.be/yZpTj9YT-IQ

Gregory, S. (2008). Interview with H. Jenkins, *From Rodney King to Burma: An Interview with Witness's Sam Gregory (Part One)*. MIT Center for Civic Media Blog. Available at: http://henryjenkins.org/ 2008/03/from_rodney_king_to_burma_an_i.html

Gregory S. (2014a). *Images of Horror: Whose Rules and What Responsibilities?* WITNESS.org, https://blog.witness.org/2014/09/sharing-images-horror-roles-responsibilities/

Gregory S. (2014b). Personal correspondence (10 November).

Gregory S. (2015). 'Ubiquitous Witnesses: Who Creates the Evidence and the Live(d) Experience of Human Rights Violations?' *Information, Communication & Society*. DOI:10.1080/1369118X. 2015.1070891

Hariman, R. (2014). 'Watching War Evolve'. In: L. Kennedy and C. Patrick, eds., *The Violence of the Image: Photography and International Conflict*. London and New York: I.B. Taurus, pp. 137–63.

Hesford, W. S. (2011). *Spectacular Rhetorics: Human Rights Visions, Recognitions, Feminisms*. Durham: Duke University Press.

Hornaday, A. (2002). 'A Lens on the World'. *The Washington Post* (21 November).

Hoskins, A. and O'Loughlin, B. (2015). 'Arrested War: The Third Phase of Mediatization'. *Information, Communication & Society*. DOI:10.1080/1369118X. 2015.1068350

Howe, M. (1992). 'Chronicle'. *The New York Times* (20 March).

Human Rights Channel (2015). *About*. Available at: http://hrc.witness.org/ [Accessed April 2015].

Joyce, D. (2010). 'Photography and the Image-making of International Justice,' *Law and Humanities*, 4(2), pp. 229–49.

Kross, C. (2016). 'Memory, Guardianship and the Witnessing Amateur in the Emergence of Citizen Journalism'. In M. Baker and B. B. Blaagaard, eds., *Citizen Media and Public Spaces*. London and New York: Routledge, pp. 225–38.

Linfield, S. (2010). *The Cruel Radiance: Photography and Political Violence*. Chicago: University of Chicago Press.

McLagan, M. (2007). The Architecture of Strategic Communication. In: M. Feher, G. Krikorian and Y. McKee, eds., *Nongovernmental Politics*. New York: Zone, pp. 318–25.

Mirzoeff, N. (2011). *Right to Look: A Counterhistory of Visuality*. Durham, NC: Duke University Press.

Mortensen, M. (2015). *Journalism and Eyewitness Images*. London: Routledge.

Pantti, M. and Sirén, S. (2015). 'The Fragility of Photo-truth: Verification of Amateur Images in Finnish Newsrooms'. *Digital Journalism*, 3(4). Available at: http://www.tandfonline.com/doi/full/10.1080/216 70811.2015.1034518

Pollak, M. (1999). 'Screen Grab: Vivid Documents of Human Atrocities'. *The New York Times* (11 November).

Romanelli, S. (2013). Q&A: 'Video Puts the Human into Human Rights'. *Inter Press Service* (20 May).

Schaffer, K. and Smith, S. (2004). *Human Rights and Narrated Lives*. London: Palgrave.

Storyful (2015). *We Are Storyful*. Available at: http://storyful.com/about/

Thijm, Y. A. (2010). *Update on The Hub and WITNESS' New Online Strategy*. Blog.witness.org. http://blog. witness.org/ 2010/08/update-on-the-hub-and-witness-new-online-strategy/

Thorsen, E. and Allan, S. (eds) (2014). *Citizen Journalism: Global Perspectives, Vol. 2*. New York: Peter Lang.

Thrall, A. T., Stecula, D. and Sweet, D. (2014). 'May We Have Your Attention Please? Human–rights NGOs and the Problem of Global Communication'. *The International Journal of Press/Politics*, 19(2), pp. 135–59.

Valiante, G. (2008). 'Telling It Like It Shoots'. *The Gazette* (20 July) (Montreal).

Wallace, N. (2007). 'Calling the World as Witness'. *The Chronicle of Philanthropy*, 20(3), p. 28.

Wardle, C., Dubberley, S. and Brown, P. (2014). *Amateur Footage: A Global Study of User-generated Content in TV and Online-news Output*. Tow Center for Digital Journalism, A Tow/Knight Report. Available at: http:// usergeneratednews.towcenter.org/wp-content/uploads/2014/05/Tow-Center-UGC-Report.pdf

WITNESS (2012). 'WITNESS and Storyful Launch New Global Channel for Human Rights Video'. *WITNESS News Release* (24 May). Available at: http://www3.witness.org/ar/node/3280 [Accessed April 2015].

WITNESS (1992). 'New Program Announced to Help the Worldwide Human Rights Movement Join the Communications Revolution'. *PR Newswire*, 23 Mar.

35

VIDEO AND WITNESSING AT THE INTERNATIONAL CRIMINAL TRIBUNAL FOR THE FORMER YUGOSLAVIA

Sandra Ristovska

Visual imagery has long facilitated the act of bearing witness as the backbone of humanitarian and human rights communication. Many examples exist. Humanitarian activism in the 1870s in response to Ottoman atrocities in the Balkans and famine in Southern India rested on images (Twomey 2012). The campaign to end colonial brutalities in Congo at the turn of the 20th century first used the term 'crimes against humanity', utilizing photographs as indispensable evidentiary materials (Sliwinski 2011). The campaign to raise awareness about and provide relief to the survivors of the Armenian genocide was organized around screenings of a film titled *Ravished Armenia* (Torchin 2012). The Universal Declaration of Human Rights (UDHR) was drafted in 1948 in the echo of the mass circulation of photographs depicting the Holocaust. A year later, UNESCO organized a traveling Human Rights Exhibition that relied upon images to communicate the significance of the UDHR. Needless to say, this longstanding practice continues to present day.

The centrality of visual media to how human rights advocates have operationalised witnessing as a pathway towards social change has drawn, in large part, from the early religious origins of witnessing that place emphasis on moral responsibility (e.g. Hopgood 2006; Torchin 2012). Although it has been taking new shapes, bearing witness through images in this context has served as a mechanism to mobilize publics that can assume moral responsibility for the portrayed suffering and subsequently create political pressure to end human rights abuses. As a communicative practice, though, witnessing also relates to the legal tradition. Religion and the law are, indeed, 'the two interconnected historical roots underlying ... witnessing' as a cultural form of communication (Thomas 2009, 89) that informs human rights work.

Yet, the law, as a key institution that safeguards human rights as legally enforceable entitlements, has had a conflicting relationship with images. The various trials related to the Holocaust, for example, both contested and legitimized the witnessing status of visual media. The International Military Tribunal at Nuremberg made extensive use of films (e.g. Delage 2014; Douglas 2001), but the evidentiary value of photography was dismissed in the Papon trial in France (Rousso 2013). In tune with the broader legal culture that has seen cameras as a disruptive presence in the courtroom (e.g. Schwartz 2009; Youm 2012), the production crew had to hide the cameras from view in order to obtain broadcast authorisation for the Eichmann trial. Contrary to the wider culture, where witnessing as seeing has been understood as a crucial moral act that sustains human rights discourses, the courtroom has sidelined the legal witnessing potential of visual records.

Today, however, visual media not only continue to shape humanitarian and human rights work, but they are also entering prominently into human rights courtrooms. In the words of one human rights attorney, 'whether you're talking about domestic criminal prosecution or international criminal prosecution, video and photographic evidence have become standard features of those cases' (A. Whiting, pers. comm., 1 Oct. 2015). This chapter interrogates the relationship between visual media and legal witnessing by mapping the uses of video at the International Criminal Tribunal for the former Yugoslavia (ICTY) in The Hague, The Netherlands. As a first court of its kind and one that standardised the use of video materials, the case of the ICTY generates fruitful opportunities to trace how, when and why contemporary human rights courtrooms put the witnessing potential of video to work. The ICTY is an international ad-hoc court established via a resolution of the United Nations Security Council in May 1993 to prosecute serious violations of international humanitarian law in the territory of the former Yugoslavia. The jurisdiction of this Tribunal is to investigate crimes that have occurred since the beginning of the armed conflicts in 1991 and to indict their perpetrators. To unpack how video is centrally implicated within the witnessing acts in human rights courts, this chapter looks at (1) how the ICTY uses video to record and broadcast its trial proceedings, (2) how it utilizes video as evidence, proving examples from the trial of Radovan Karadzic and (3) how the ICTY Outreach Office employs video. The chapter argues that witnessing in human rights trials is becoming entangled in audiovisual meaning making.

Video coverage of the ICTY proceedings

The ICTY has recorded and broadcast every trial hearing since its first trial on May 7, 1996. According to Rob Barsony (pers. comm., 17 Apr. 2015), Supervisor for Audiovisual Courtroom Production at this court, 'video facilitates justice'. The understanding is that the video coverage assists the Tribunal's mission to deliver efficient and transparent international justice. The decision to provide audiovisual broadcast of the ICTY proceedings was threefold: 'to make sure that justice would be seen to be done, to dispel any misunderstandings that might otherwise arise as to the role and the nature of the Tribunal proceedings and to fulfil the educational task of the Tribunal' (Mason 2000, para. 9). In other words, video has been burdened both with a legitimizing and a pedagogical function. It is supposed to help generate international endorsement and approval of the workings of the court – whose existence has been vastly contested, especially by the defence counsel in the early trials – and to initiate a responsible memory-making process that will set the historical record straight about the human rights crimes in the former Yugoslavia. Implicit in both functions is video's ability to create witnessing publics to the legal process, thus extending the spaces for legal, ethical and historical recognition of the human rights crimes outside of the courtroom.

The ICTY's Audiovisual Unit is in charge of the recording and broadcasting of the trial proceedings. The trials take place in three courtrooms equipped with remotely controlled cameras. Courtroom 1 and 3 have six cameras: one for the judges who are in the centre of the room, one for the prosecution (to the right), another for the witness (at the opposite end of the judges), two for the defence (to the left) and one overhead camera behind the prosecution. The second camera for the defence was added when the court merged trials with multiple individuals accused of similar indictments into one mega trial. Courtroom 2 is smaller and has four cameras, one for each party. The video booth, where audiovisual staff manages the recording process, is behind the defence. The trial proceedings are edited live and available online on the ICTY website with a 30-minute delay to ensure that no sensitive information gets accidentally disclosed (e.g. details that could jeopardize the safety of a witness testifying under protection).

The video coverage is supposed to balance between the right of the public to see justice proceed and the need to maintain the legal decorum (R. Barsony, pers. comm., 17 April, 2015). The audiovisual staff puts this mission to work by selecting and editing together shots deemed respective of the legal process. When the judges speak, for example, the camera focuses on them, except in long judgment readings when it is considered appropriate to intercut with shots of the prosecution or the defence. Balancing camera time is a priority. When there is a trial with multiple accused individuals, the camera shows each of them for equal amount of time.

Staff members differentiate between commercial and court broadcasting. Barsony (pers. comm., 17 April, 2015) insists that 'the cameras in the courtroom are not telling a story; they are following a story'. The key presumed difference is in the editing. In commercial production, for example, it is a common practice to edit together an establishing shot of the courtroom with medium or close-ups of those who speak along with some reaction shots. The courtroom production, by contrast, seeks to minimize any shots that could convey unnecessary action. In this sense, Barsony believes that his team should not show an attorney who seems distracted or likely to interrupt the hearing. That attorney may not do anything in the end, but the close-up would create a dramatic moment that could be later misinterpreted. Therefore, the camera should focus only on the main action in court. The understanding is that the ICTY must maintain control over the coverage.

What is now seen as a conventional way to record the proceedings was often learned via trial and error. Early coverage sometimes used split screen, which was later abandoned as a practice and thought to be inappropriate for courtroom broadcasting. Visually, witness protection meant obscuring only the face, but now the ICTY pixelates the full image of the witness. The Tribunal has also advised other human rights courts on ways to provide trial coverage. The Special Tribunal for Lebanon, for example, consulted the ICTY about the courtroom plan and camera placements (R. Barsony, pers. comm., 17 April, 2015).

The audiovisual coverage of the ICTY proceedings suggests that human rights courtrooms are naturalizing video as a technology that is now considered to support and expand the court's mission. Cameras are no longer 'an alien, disruptive element in the courtroom' (Schwartz 2009, 15); they are becoming a standard feature of human rights trials. Furthermore, the attempts to separate internal courtroom production from commercial broadcasting illustrates how human rights courts like the ICTY are extending the professional legal logic to accommodate for the perceived importance of video to the workings of the court. Therefore, there is a level of professionalization on the part of the audiovisual staff that drives what courts see as an appropriate legal way of broadcasting human rights trials. The ICTY's stance is that, 'the use of cameras in legal proceedings, provided that they are operated under strict guidelines, has a positive effect on the administration of justice, and helps international justice to be seen to be done' (Mason 2000, para. 3). The need to create witnessing publics, then, is implicated in the specialisation around video at the ICTY. The trial coverage is constructed in ways that the Tribunal sees capable of creating an accessible historical record and of providing a legal tool that communicates the legitimacy of the court to the wider public.

Video evidence

Although 'the infrastructures of legal knowledge have been generally unreceptive to pictures' (Feigenson 2014, 13), courts are now becoming more accustomed to the evidentiary potential of video. Typically, the law has placed images in a supportive role to words, using them for their demonstrative qualities and disregarding their unique witnessing functions. Legal doctrines have indeed long indicated that images need words to anchor their evidentiary meaning (e.g. Mnookin 1998). Legal practice, however, is increasingly tapping into the witnessing potential of visual materials. It is not so surprising, then, that video evidence has become an important component of the evidentiary display at the ICTY trials.

Thousands of hours of video footage have been shown during trials in the form of direct or contextual evidence, so-called victim impact video or recording of testimonies and investigations. Both news footage and eyewitness videos – shot by civilians, military and paramilitary members – have been presented in court. In 2004, for example, the evidence records by the Office of the Prosecution (OTP) alone included 5,500 videotapes (Schuppli 2014). At that time, the well-publicized trial against former Serbian President Slobodan Milosevic was still ongoing while Ratko Mladic and Radovan Karadzic, other high-ranking officials indicted for crimes against humanity and genocide, were fugitives.

To better understand the role of video as evidence at the ICTY, this section looks at a few examples from the trial of Radovan Karadzic, the former President of Republika Srpska (an administrative entity in Bosnia and Herzegovina). He was charged on counts of genocide, crimes against humanity and violations of the laws or customs of war and sentenced to a 40-year-imprisonment in March of 2016. The judgment on Karadzic was characterized as 'one of the most anticipated war crime trial verdicts in Europe since Nuremberg' (Borger 2016, para. 1). For the chief ICTY prosecutor Serge Brammertz, this verdict was important because it would end impunity for high-ranking officials guilty of human rights crimes. The prominent case against Karadzic illustrates how human rights courts no longer steer away from visual materials even in trials where the legal stakes are high. It thus serves as a reminder how human rights law needs to be considered not only in relation to documents, deliberations and legislations but also in terms of visual exhibits in court.

The Prosecution's Opening Statement in this trial included a total of 23 video clips or compilations that raised the importance of seeing when rendering the human rights abuses legally meaningful. Alan Tieger, a prosecuting attorney giving the opening statement at the ICTY, invoked the evidentiary value of video to communicate the consequences of the sniping and shelling attacks in Sarajevo that killed innocent civilians.

> MR. TIEGER: Despite their efforts to take precautions, despite their efforts to avoid the shelling and sniping, many civilians were nevertheless wounded or killed carrying out their everyday activities. Mothers walking their children were shot. On the 18th of November, 1994, a boy named Nermin Divovic, 7 years old, was walking beside his mother on a street in the centre of Sarajevo, just another daily activity in most days. His 8-year-old sister was walking ahead. As they crossed the street, a Bosnian Serb sniper shot at them. The bullet passed through his mother's stomach and killed Nermin instantly. And you'll see him sprawling on the zebra crossing in this video.[1]
>
> (*The Prosecutor v. Karadzic, No. IT-95-5/18, 27 October 2009, 600–1*)

The video begins with an image of a boy laying on the ground with a pile of blood next to his head. The camera zooms in on the helmet of an officer who kneels on the ground next to the boy. Then, it immediately cuts to three men who witness the scene and a distressed woman who tries to look away. The next shot depicts two officers turning the body, which reveals that the boy's face is covered in blood. Handheld camera and loud gunshots suggest that the video depicts the incident as the sniping attack unfolds. This is further emphasized by a close-up shot of two women and a little girl who cry as they seek refuge behind a car. This video exceeds the factual dimension of legal witnessing and the demonstrative role assigned to images in court. Although Tieger's brief introduction to the video helps contextualize the footage, the material does not depict the crime scene as narrated. Instead, it provides a glimpse into the emotional state of those who have witnessed the attacks. The video's relational logic, particularly emphasized by the editing choices, and its sensory richness are both mobilized to portray the magnitude of the crimes as experienced on the ground. This case, then, suggests that the assumed sensory features of video materials – their ability to portray the emotional layers of war experiences – make video an exceptional tool that facilitates the process of bearing witness in the courtroom by which people are supposed to come to grips with past atrocities.

As a visual medium, video navigates emotional and evidentiary terrains simultaneously. Unlike photography, though, video's witnessing potential is amplified by its ability to also capture sound. It is therefore well positioned to help sustain the emotional dimensions embedded in the acts of witnessing, which are often implicitly invoked in human rights trials. In the case against Karadzic, video was utilized repeatedly to portray the sense of terror that the civilians in Sarajevo experienced. In the words of Tieger,

> The combined effect of the indiscriminate random shelling and the sniping of civilians was terror, the ever-present fear of being the next one hit or killed. Between April 1992 and November 1995, a citizen of Sarajevo really couldn't be sure whether his or her last step would not be their last. Daily life in this effective death lottery was unpredictable. A civilian on a tram was just as much at risk of death or injury as was a civilian from being killed or maimed by an air bomb in another part of town. Small stretches of peace were suddenly interrupted by another round of shelling – you'll see some of that in the videos we will show you – and other times, the bombardment never seemed to end. For 44 months, the civilian population lived under a pervasive sense of terror; exactly what was intended.
>
> (*The Prosecutor v. Karadzic, No. IT-95-5/18, 27 October 2009, 597*)

The video clips screened in court depict life in Sarajevo during the attacks. Handheld camera shows civilians running and hiding as loud gunshots are heard in the background. It is this combination of sound and image that is thought to create an immersive witnessing experience that could trigger a meaningful engagement with the crime in the courtroom.

The prosecution also used video materials in connection to the examination of witnesses in court. In one case, a prosecuting attorney questioned a witness after showing a video about the shelling of the Markale Market in Sarajevo.

> MR. GAYNOR: I'd now like to move to a video which has already been admitted in evidence as P1450, and I'll be playing some extracts from that. Initially, I'd like to play the first minute of this video, please.
>
> [Video-clip played]
>
> MR. GAYNOR: We stopped at 48 seconds.
>
> Q. Mr. Besic, it's been repeatedly asserted in this court that many of the bodies at the Markale I and Markale II incidents were brought from the front-line, that the bodies were already dead. I want to ask you if you can comment on that assertion.
>
> A. It's difficult to comment. We can see, with our own eyes, everything that happened. All sorts of stories circulated, that bodies were brought there and planted there. However, we've seen what's going on. If dead bodies had been brought here, then

the wounded people here would not be acting this way. You see the man without his lower leg. If you look at the other photographs and recordings, you will see parts of extremities. There were all sorts of stories and guesses, but the facts are here.

(The Prosecutor v. Karadzic, No. IT-95-5/18, 8 December 2010, 9427)

The video clip used in this trial session starts with a wide-shot of dead and injured bodies on the street. As cars pass by, people move the bodies to the side. Sirens and painful screaming accompany the sights of blood and death. The camera situates the viewer in the midst of the incident. Although the video does not show actual evidence of who has killed the people or how the bodies have found themselves there, the presumed linkage between the shelling attack and the immediate panic on the street is what granted this video an evidentiary status in the trial of Karadzic.

The witness's response to this footage further iterates the importance of seeing. The screening of the video and the subsequent examination of the witness shed light on the interplay between seeing and legal witnessing in human rights trials. The video was framed as an undeniable testament to the horrors in Sarajevo, capable of dismissing any false allegations. Although the law still grapples how to develop practices and doctrines that can accommodate the evolving modes of visual evidence, the case of the ICTY suggests that video is becoming the standard response to concerns raised decades ago at the Nuremberg Trials to find 'credible evidence to establish incredible events' (Delage 2014, 67). What is noteworthy about this reliance on video materials is how it exceeds the primary purpose of legal witnessing as a presumed mode of factual information relay. The legal roles played by evidentiary video exhibits at the ICTY illustrate that today's human rights trials are also tapping prominently into the emotional dimensions of witnessing long dismissed by courts. Legal recognitions of human rights violations, therefore, move away from the primacy of written and verbal records, adopting visual modes of evidence as more than just demonstrative tools.

Video outreach

The ICTY Outreach Programme was set up in 1999 to help the court communicate its judgments and findings in the countries of the former Yugoslavia. Although the law insists that the judgments should speak for themselves, human rights courts are burdened with an extra-legal function. This has been the case with the ICTY, a court whose mandate requires that it contributes to peace and reconciliation in the region. Hence, the Outreach Office has taken on a variety of activities, such as conferences, lecture and discussion series in the region as well as youth exhibitions, essay-writing competitions and publications in journals and newspapers.

Driven by the vision to make the judgments resonate beyond the courtroom in order to contribute towards sustainable peace in the former Yugoslavia, the ICTY has also produced six documentaries since 2010. When commenting on the decision to produce these documentaries, Nenad Golcevski (2016 n.p.), Head of the Outreach Programme, stated:

> Trials before the Tribunal last for years. They involve hundreds of witnesses. They involve thousands of pieces of evidence. The judgments are written on anything between 1,000 to 2,000 pages of a thick legal discourse. So apart from the people who professionally follow the ICTY, nobody really reads those judgments. And no one can follow an entire course of a trial. So we wanted to create a product, which would be easily and quickly consumable, which could educate people, tackle misinformation and denial and help disseminate the stories of victims and survivors heard in the courtroom.

Video, then, is employed as a tool of both information relay and advocacy. It documents the trials and the judgments, but it also advocates for reconciliation in the region by seeking to shape lasting understanding of the crimes. And it does so seemingly more efficiently than other mechanisms that help facilitate justice.

The ICTY documentaries portray the workings of the Tribunal, examine some of the most horrific crimes committed during the war, particularly in Central Bosnia, Prijedor and Visegrad, and look closely at the judgments related to the conception of sexual violence as a human rights violation. Another documentary, *Through their Eyes – Witnesses to Justice*, depicts the stories of five men and women who survived the war and testified in court. All documentaries combine footage from the trial coverage, excerpts from the video and photographic materials used as evidence in the various trials as well as interviews with witnesses and legal staff conducted specifically for the documentaries. The six films are available online for free and have been screened at various events both in the region and internationally.

The perceived importance of video to the ICTY's mandate is also implicated in the Outreach Programme's mission 'to put into practice the principle of open justice: for justice to be truly done, it must be seen to be done'. Bearing witness to the legal process through the act of seeing is considered central to the administration of international human rights justice. By producing documentaries, the ICTY Outreach Office seeks to create a lasting witnessing record of its work and accomplishments in addition to triggering a meaningful engagement with the stories of human rights abuses. In other words, the ICTY places video at the heart of the witnessing work it deems necessary for its contribution towards transitional justice in the region.

Conclusion

This chapter has shown how visual media are shaping acts of witnessing in and outside of human rights courtrooms. The video coverage of the trial proceedings summons up witnessing publics beyond the courthouse, serving legitimizing and pedagogical functions. The use of video as evidence raises the importance of witnessing as seeing, shedding light on how the interplay between information and emotion steers legal engagement with human rights atrocities. Lastly, the video documentaries produced by the ICTY Outreach Programme provide an enduring witnessing record both of the crimes in the former Yugoslavia and of the trial proceedings, assisting the court to fulfil its extra-legal mandates. This entanglement of video with deliberation, judgment, testimony and memory means that audiovisual meaning making undergirds the legal human rights process. Video is thus attaining a high degree of recognition as a technology that is crucial to the various acts of witnessing that facilitate the work of human rights courts.

Any act of witnessing assumes an absence or indeterminacy that needs to be eliminated. The purpose of witnessing, therefore, is to contribute to the creation of knowledge (e.g. Laub 1992). The ways in which the ICTY utilizes video exemplify how audiovisual modes of information relay are helping produce knowledge about human rights crimes. Video can capture and disseminate vital information about human rights violations from the difficult scenes of their unfolding differently from written and verbal records. It can also mediate the work and accomplishments of human rights courts to wider audiences. As a result, the ICTY has standardized the utilisation of video, professionalising around courtroom broadcasting, making extensive use of audiovisual evidence and developing practices for video outreach. In doing so, this Tribunal has also diversified the traditional notion of legal witnessing, highlighting the kinds of witnessing acts that not only facilitate the court's determination of wrongdoing, but also serve ethical, historical and pedagogical functions. The employment of video to perform these roles shows how the wider cultural significance of witnessing is entering into the law. It also signals that visuals are helping shape which human rights abuses get recognized, redeemed and remembered even in a legal context.

The ICTY is not an isolated example. The International Criminal Tribunal for Rwanda (ICTR) also broadcast its trial proceedings and used video evidence. The Special Tribunal for Lebanon consulted the ICTY on how to accommodate video technology in its courtrooms. The New York-based human rights group WITNESS incorporated the lessons learned at the ICTY trials for its recently established video evidence program that trains attorneys and activists how to use and record video documentation of human rights violations that meet legal standards. The International Bar Association developed a smart phone-based application called the eyeWitness App to help human rights defenders collect verifiable video evidence. The United Nations Commission of Inquiry relied on video evidence in its reports documenting human rights violations in Syria (e.g. Independent International Commission of Inquiry on the Syrian Arab Republic 2015). Indeed, since the Yugoslav wars of the 1990s, video has become such a ubiquitous form of human rights documentation that even the International Criminal Court (ICC) formed the Scientific Advisory Board in June 2014 to guide the judiciary on new technologies and forms of evidence, among which video is a more prominent example. These cases speak both to the increasingly porous boundaries between the legal and cultural significance of witnessing and to the growing relevance of audiovisual modes of information relay – that courts have traditionally sidelined – to contemporary human rights work. They thus urge us to pay closer attention to the entanglement between video and human rights knowledge.

Note

1   All passages from the trial transcripts are presented verbatim as officially released on the website of the ICTY. Linguistic errors are not corrected.

Bibliography

Borger, J. (2016). 'Radovan Karadzic Faces Verdicts in War Crimes Trial at The Hague'. *The Guardian* (24 March). Available at: https://www.theguardian.com/world/2016/mar/23/radovan-karadzic-expects-icty-acquittal-genocide-bosnian-war-verdict

Delage, C. (2014). *Caught on Camera: Film in the Courtroom from the Nuremberg Trials to the Trials of Khmer Rouge*. Philadelphia, PA: University of Pennsylvania Press.

Douglas, L. (2001). *The Memory of Judgment: Making Law and History in the Trials of the Holocaust*. New Haven, CT: Yale University Press.

Feigenson, N. (2014). 'The Visual in Law: Some Problems for Legal Theory'. *Law, Culture and the Humanities*, 10(1), pp. 13–23.

Golcevski, N. (2016). *Communicating Justice Through Visuals: The Limitations of an Unlimited Field*. Paper Presented at Honing the Visual: Evolving Practices in Human Rights Work, University of Pennsylvania, Philadelphia.

Hopgood, S. (2006). *Keepers of the Flame: Understanding Amnesty International*. Ithaca, NY: Cornell University Press.

Independent International Commission of Inquiry on the Syrian Arab Republic (2015). *10ʰ Report of Commission of Inquiry on Syria* (Report No. A/HRC/30/48). New York: United Nations Human Rights Office of the High Commissioner.

Laub, D. (1992). 'Bearing Witness or the Vicissitudes of Listening'. In: Felman, S. and D. Laub, eds., *Testimony: Crises of Witnessing in History, Literature and Psychoanalysis*. New York, NY: Routledge, pp. 57–74.

Mason, P. (2000). *A Report on the Audiovisual Coverage of the ICTY's Proceedings Finds that Cameras Contribute to a Proper Administration of Justice*. Available at: http://www.icty.org/en/press/report-audiovisual-coverage-ictys-proceedings-finds-cameras-contribute-proper-administration

Mnookin, J. L. (1998). 'The Image of Truth: Photographic Evidence and the Power of Analogy'. *Yale Journal of Law & the Humanities*, 10(1), pp. 1–74.

Rousso, H. (2013). Competitive Narratives: An Incident at the Papon Trial. In: C. Delage and P. Goodrich, eds., *The Scene of the Mass Crime: History, Film, and International Tribunals*. Oxon, UK: Routledge, pp. 41–56.

Schuppli, S. (2014). 'Entering Evidence: Cross Examining the Court Records of the ICTY'. In Forensic Architecture, ed., *Forensis: The Architecture of Public Truth*. Berlin, DE: Sternberg Press, pp. 279–314.

Schwartz, L. G. (2009). *Mechanical Witness: A History of Motion Picture Evidence in U.S. Courts*. New York: Oxford University Press.

Sliwinski, S. (2011). *Human Rights in Camera*. Chicago, IL: University of Chicago Press.

The Prosecutor v. Karadzic. ICTY, The Netherlands. No. IT-95-5/18. (2009, October 27).

The Prosecutor v. Karadzic. ICTY, The Netherlands. No. IT-95-5/18. (2010, December 8).

Thomas, G. (2009). Witness as a Cultural Form of Communication: Historical Roots, Structural Dynamics and Current Appearances. In: Frosh, P. and Pinchevski, A. eds., *Media Witnessing*. Hampshire: Palgrave Macmillan, pp. 89–111.

Torchin, L. (2012). *Creating the Witness: Documenting Genocide on Film, Video, and the Internet*. Minneapolis, MN: University of Minnesota Press.

Twomey, C. (2012). 'Framing Atrocity: Photography and Humanitarianism'. *History of Photography*, 36(3), pp. 255–64.

Youm, K. H. (2012). 'Cameras in the Courtroom in the Twenty-First Century: The U.S. Supreme Court Learning from Abroad?' *BYU Law Review*, 6, 1989–2031.

36

MEDIA, HUMAN RIGHTS AND FORENSIC SCIENCE

Steven Livingston

Human rights organizations turn to a variety of digital tools and scientific methods when investigating potential abuses; they including crowdsourcing on digital networks (McPherson 2015), commercial remote sensing satellites (Livingston 2016), and forensic science (Melton 2014). In this chapter, I argue that digital technology and techniques used by forensic scientists help create public accounts of war crimes and abuse. Most importantly, in their absence, such accounts, conveyed as news stories, would be impossible, leaving abuses and crimes obscured and undiscovered. Secondly, I argue that the scientific nature of the information presented by forensic scientists reinforces claims made by rights groups concerning the circumstances of the death and disappearance of victims. In the face of vociferous pushback and denials from states, groups, and political leaders, claims made by human rights groups are bolstered by science and technology. In the language used in the communication research theory relied on here, in framing contests between the accusers and the accused, scientifically derived evidence is more difficult – though not impossible – to ignore and refute.

I turn first to a review of relevant aspects of news framing theory. I then outline key aspects of forensic science technology, explaining how they affect human rights news framing. That is followed by a brief case illustration and my conclusion.

Forensic science and news frames

In the face of strongly-stated denials, human rights organizations sometimes find themselves defending the veracity of their reports concerning war crimes and human rights abuses. Much of the back and forth recriminations take place in the news media. Political communication scholars call struggles over the meaning of a particular situation or event 'framing contests' (Entman 2004, 628–69). Framing involves selecting and highlighting some facets of events or issues and 'making connections among them so as to *promote a particular interpretation, evaluation, and/or solution*' (Entman 2004, 95–6, emphasis added). Carragee and Roefs remind us that framing processes ought to be examined within the contexts of the distribution of political and social power (Carragee and Roefs 2004, 214). 'Distribution of power in society—in terms of resources and authority—affects the mass media's framing of a public policy issues' (Carragee and Roefs 2004, 215). Similarly, Entman argues that the 'ability to promote the spread of frames is stratified; some actors have more power than others to push ideas along to the news and then to the public' (Entman 2004, 138–41).

My argument here is that the scientific and technical tools now available to human rights organizations address at least some of the imbalance that often exists between powerful sovereigns and non-state actors. The resources and claims to authority at play now in human rights framing contests involve access to scientific and technical expertise and information. Put another way, my argument is that forensic science alters framing contests between human rights advocates and those suspected of violating human rights and committing war crimes. In most cases, states and powerful political figures have far greater framing capacity than do less prominent figures and organizations, such as human rights organizations. When successful, human rights organizations, with the help of forensic scientists, establish the occurance of an abuse or a war crime and construct a scientifically-grounded narrative as to what happened.

I structure my argument around what Entman calls a 'substantive frame'. A news frame of this type has the following characteristics:

1.   Defines particular effects or conditions as problematic.
2.   Attributes causal responsibility for the problem.
3.   Reaches a moral judgment according to the answers given to steps one and two.
4.   Points to particular remedies or improvements according to the first three steps.

(Entman, 2004, 96–7)

Forensic science affects each element of Entman's substantive frame, especially the first two. Let's consider each in turn. The first element concerns contestation over the status of a particular condition or circumstance as a genuine problem (Cobb and Elder 1971; Edelman 1988). Much of politics involves conflict over the definition of a situation. Does a problem – a condition warranting sustained public attention and calls for redress – actually exist? Is global warming, for example, understood properly as a *problem*? Some argue that it is not, a view championed by think tanks funded by the fossil fuels industry (Oreskes and Conway 2010). Similarly, for the George W. Bush administration, the physical pain visited upon captives at Abu Ghraib and other similar prisons was not defined as torture, which, according to international convention, is a serious problem. It was instead 'enhanced interrogation techniques' (Bennett, Lawrence and Livingston 2006). Political scientists have referred to a 'second face of power' (Bachrach and Baratz 1962) when describing the ability of some groups and organizations to block a particular consideration of an issue or condition by, essentially, defining it out of existence. This chapter looks at the role of forensic science in undermining a state, group, or leader's *ability to block* consideration of a potential human rights abuse or war crime.

Those who violate human rights and commit war crimes often deny the existence of dead bodies, and therefore of the crime. If bodies are recovered, they then deny responsibility for the deaths. The objective is to deny problem status to the matters at hand, and if that fails, they deny a connection to the problem. The Argentine military junta, for example, sometimes claimed that missing relatives were in fact on holiday or that he or she had left town with a lover. When Radislav Krstić, the former deputy commander and chief of staff of the Drina Corps of the army of the Republika Srpska, was on trial at the International Criminal Tribunal for the former Yugoslavia for aiding and abetting genocide, his defence attorney suggested that some of those in a mass grave had actually committed suicide. Given the fact that the victims' arms had been tied behind their backs and that many had died of multiple gunshots, this was not a particularly effective framing gambit (Rosenblatt 2015, 41).

More extreme efforts to obfuscate the existence of a war crimes and abuse (a problem in terms of a substantive frame) come in the form of the obliteration of the victim's remains. In Afghanistan in 2001, forces allied with Gen. Abdul Rashid Dostum, an Afghan warlord allied with the US, murdered approximately 2,000 suspected Taliban and al-Qaeda prisoners. Confined to shipping containers, the prisoners either suffocated in the extreme desert heat or were killed when Dostum's men raked the containers with automatic weapons fire. The bodies were eventually buried in mass graves. Several years later, during a period of political uncertainty, Dostum ordered his men to exhume the graves with bulldozers and dump the remains in a nearby river. (Lasseter 2008).

Similarly, after Serbian nationalist forces massacred 8,000 men and boys in Srebrenica in July 1995, they returned to the graves several months later with bulldozers to dig them up, mix the remains and rebury the disassociated remains in secondary mass graves (BBC 2005). If the bodies cannot be found, or if they cannot be pieced together and identified, the existence of a 'problem' remains in doubt. Without individual identities, without personal stories of how each person was once a living father, mother, brother, sister and son or daughter, their stories remain obscure and incomplete. Through DNA analysis, however, matches between living family members and the smallest fragment of bone or tooth allow scientists to establish a missing person's identity. Science, in such cases, is an instrument of resistance against efforts to obliterate the existence of a once living human being.

According to Entman's definition of a substantive frame, if a social condition is understood as a problem, the next step involves a struggle over the correct *attribution of responsibility*. What has caused the problem at hand? Are the dead the merely the unfortunate victims of circumstance, perhaps killed by a third party, or perhaps even killed by their own hands, as Krstić defence attorney claimed was the case with the dead in Srebrenica? Or were they perhaps armed combatants, the preferred explanation of the Argentinian military junta. When the bodies of the disappeared were exhumed, Argentine authorities demanded that families sign declarations stating that their loved ones had died in gun battles with security forces. If the families did not sign the declaration they could not reclaim their loved one's remains (Rosenblatt 2015, 96). Forensic science, though, is at least sometimes able to clarify the cause and circumstances of death, thus undermining the abuser's attempt to hide their crimes.

According to Entman, how the first two questions of a substantive frame are answered leads to conclusions about the remaining two: moral judgments and an embrace of remedies that emerge from the particular logic of an assumed source or cause of the established problem. If one is an armed subversive killed in a firefight with legitimate police authorities, one is not a victim of abuse, if one is a victim at all. Yet if one has been detained, tortured, and killed for being a student, union leader, social worker, or professor, an entirely different interpretation emerges. *Forensic science constructs counterframes to the given official versions of reality.* When forensic Anthropologist Clyde Snow offered an accounting of the 'NN' cases – the anonymous 'no name' burials – during the height of the military repression in Argentina, he found that a disproportionate number occurred in proximity to a handful of detention and torture centres, rather than scattered about more randomly as one would expect with the military's death-by-firefight frame. Even simple empirical evidence can deflate some exculpatory frames.

In the balance of this chapter I describe the emergence of forensic science in human rights investigations and reporting. I then segue to a slightly technical discussion of the more powerful technologies used to identify human remains. Finally, I offer a brief illustration of forensic science in a framing contest in a case found in Mexico beginning in 2014.

Forensic science and human rights

The emergence of forensic science as a tool for human rights investigations can be traced back to two seminal periods in the second half of the 20th century. The first was the campaign of terror in the 1970s and 80s at the hands of right-wing dictatorships in South America; the second was the aftermath the civil wars in Yugoslavia. Inspired by the Nazi program of Nacht und Nebel (Night and Fog), 'disappearing' someone was a favoured tool of repression among the South American dictatorships in the 1970s and 80s (*Night and Fog* 2016). The intention was to remove someone as a fact of history. In Argentina, the so-called Dirty War got underway in 1974 – even before the military coup in 1976 – and cut a bloody trail of terror across the country until 1983. During the war, military forces and right-wing death squads killed an estimated 30,000 people, many of them executed en masse. Their bodies were either dumped into unidentified graves or dropped from planes into the River Plate or the Atlantic Ocean (Lewis 2002).

In 1983, when the military junta collapsed following Argentina's defeat in the Falklands War, the stage was set for the emergence of forensic science as a tool for human rights investigations. Even before the collapse of the junta, early steps were taken for the emergence of a scientific basis for human rights investigations. In 1982, La Asociación Civil Abuelas de Plaza de Mayo – Grandmothers of the Plaza de Mayo, or simply the Abuelas – began exploring the feasibility of using genetic testing to find their missing grandchildren (Haberman 2015). Several key events occurred over the course of the 1980s, leading to the emergence of forensic science as an important part of human rights investigations.

Following the restoration of democracy in Argentina, fragile though it was, judges investigating crimes committed by the military junta began ordering the exhumation of graves in search of victims. Argentina also created the National Commission on the Disappearance of Persons (CONADEP) to oversee the work of identifying the disappeared. Despite these steps, it became clear that more was needed. The exhumations were too often done incompetently, and sometimes by those with a greater motivation to destroy evidence than to collect it. In 1984, CONADEP and the Grandmothers of Plaza de Mayo contacted the American Association for the Advancement of Science (AAAS) in Washington, DC for technical expertise and advice. At the time, Eric Stover was the director of AAAS's program in Science and Human Rights (Joyce and Stover 1991; Rosenblatt 2015). Without experience in forensics, Stover contacted the American Academy of Forensic Sciences which then put him in touch with Clyde Snow, an already legendary forensic anthropologist.

Forensic anthropologists like Snow have an expertise in 'reading bones' – looking for tell-tale signs left on the bones that provide clues to identity and the manner of death. When ante mortem medical records exist, they can be compared with recovered bones and teeth. When records do not exist, surviving relatives or friends of the dead can provide important clues. Signs of previously broken bones, missing teeth or dental crowns, and even wear patterns on bones can suggest an identity. The approximate date of death can be determined by the condition of the remains and the state of the vegetation and soil surrounding it. These and many other techniques of forensic anthropology were brought to the exhumation of the graves in Argentina. As noted by Adam Rosennblatt, 'The Abuelas knew that scientifically sound exhumations could provide evidence for eventual trials against the torturers, murderers, rapists, and kidnappers' (Rosenblatt 2015, 4).

At about the same time that Stover and Snow were developing the use of forensic anthropology for human rights investigations, geneticist and epidemiologist Mary-Claire King travelled to Argentina to develop what would become known as the 'grandparentage index'. Her work introduced microbiology to the work of forensic science in human rights investigations. King relied on leukocyte antigen (HLA) compatibility testing to link grandparents to their grandchildren. HLAs are proteins located on the surface of white blood cells and on other tissues in the body. When two people share the same HLA, their tissues are immunologically compatible. This allowed for an inferred relationship between grandparents and grandchildren, even without the presence of the missing intermediating links, the parents. Though not as precise as the genetic tests that would follow, immunological compatibility was an important step in the development of biology in the service of human rights.

The development of local institutional capacity is also an important part of the story. In June 1984, Stover led a delegation to Argentina that included Snow and other experts in post-mortem investigations. The experience left Snow deeply moved. Inspired to do more, he recruited members of what would become the storied Equipo Argentino de Antropología Forense (EAAF) – the Argentinian Forensic Anthropology Team. EAAF developed into one of the most well-respected forensic science organizations in the world. From EAAF, other forensic anthropology teams soon emerged, including the Guatemalan Forensic Anthropology Foundation (FAFG) and the Peruvian Forensic Anthropology Team (EPAF).

Additional steps were taken in Argentina to address immediate local needs and to develop techniques that would eventually affect forensic science human rights investigations around the world. Building on Mary-Claire King's initial efforts a few years earlier, Argentina created the Nation Genetic Data Bank in 1987 with the goal to collect DNA samples from hundreds of family members related to a known or suspected missing grandchild (Stern [undated]; Steadman and Haglund 2005). This allowed for the use of a more sophisticated and precise mitochondrial DNA analysis.

> The collaboration between the Abuelas and forensic experts would lead to a small scientific revolution, spurring the development of methods of DNA testing that would later be used to identify missing people in many different settings, from genocides and other conflicts to natural disasters such as the 2004 Indian Ocean tsunami and Hurricane Katrina in 2005.
>
> *(Rosenblatt 2015, 4)*

A second historical context for the emergence of forensic science – and especially DNA sequencing for human rights investigations – were the 1991–2001 Yugoslav civil wars (*Transitional Justice*, 2009). Ethnic cleansing, rape, mass detention and executions were common practices of the Yugoslav Wars. In November 1995, the General Framework Agreement for Peace in Bosnia and Herzegovina was reached at Wright-Patterson Air Force Base in Ohio and formally signed in Paris in December 1995. Afterward, the International Commission on Missing Persons (ICMP) was created at the urging of President Bill Clinton (Wagner 2008). In the years since, ICMP has become one of the leading centres for forensic science research and operations. It even provided support for the United States following the 11 September, 2001 attacks and after Hurricane Katrina in 2005 (Rosenblatt 2015, Wagner 2008).

ICMP received initial assistance from forensic experts at the Physicians for Human Rights (PHR), a major human rights organization founded in 1986. Once again playing a key role in the development of human rights forensics, Eric Stover served as PHR's Executive Director and worked on forensic missions to examine mass gravesites in the former Yugoslavia. As noted by Sarah Wagner, PHR,

> faced a gruesome and enormous task: to piece together partial remains scattered on the surface of the forest and lying within the primary grave, as well as to disentangle and then re-associate the commingled bones from the secondary and tertiary graves.
>
> *(Wagner 2008, 98)*

As noted a moment ago, in an effort to frustrate exhumation efforts, Bosnian Serbs returned to the mass graves several months after the massacre with earthmoving equipment to dig up, mix together, and rebury the remains in several other pits. Identification efforts were also hindered by the fact that the victim's jewellery and documents had been removed before their execution (Stover and Shigekane 2004). The condition of the remains simply overwhelmed the capacity of conventional forensic anthropology. A systematic matching of genetic profiles was the only viable solution to sorting out the thousands of fragments and disarticulated skeletal remains (Wagner 2008, 102). Once an identification was made, classical forensic methods 'would again enter into the the identification process, typically confirming or augmenting the statistical evidence of the DNA profile match' (Wagner 2008, 102). Standard anthropological methods and digital DNA sequencing technology are now frequently used by human rights organizations to construct narratives about the identities and deaths of 'disappeared' persons, even when remains are damaged and disassociated. Practically, this means that the news agenda now *includes stories about human rights abuses that would simple not be possible* – beyond a fleeting news account of the discovery of a mass grave filled with unidentified victims. Forensic science empowers human rights investigators to, figuratively, reanimate massacre victims and the disappeared, to reconstitute the narratives of their demise and make it central to an ongoing struggle with forces that had attempted to extirpate them from history.

Forensic science and human rights reporting

The development of forensic science as an important tool of human rights investigations and reporting is told by the evolution of methods used to decode DNA molecules. Information encoded in DNA informs the construction of proteins and the specification of inheritance of traits from one generation to the next. DNA is a long molecule made of two strands of code that coil together, forming the double helix described by James Watson and Francis Crick in 1953. One strand contains four different chemicals: adenine, thymine, guanine, and cytosine, abbreviated A, T, G, and C. These DNA 'bases' occur along the strand in any order. The second strand of DNA carries a sequence of chemicals that 'matches' the first strand: A on one strand always pairs with T on the other strand and G always pairs with C. So for example, AAGCTG pairs with TTCGAC. The total of all our genetic information is made up of several billion base pairs.

Developed by Frederick Sanger in 1977, the so-called Sanger method constituted a major breakthrough in biology. Although an Internet search will reveal many basic descriptions of the Sanger method of DNA sequencing, suffice it to say here that it is limited by low throughput and is unable to use some sample sources. With the creation of specially designed microprocessing chips, Next-Generation Sequencing (NGS) largely replaced the Sanger method by the turn of the century By the late 1980s, a bio-electronics firm called Applied Biosystems introduced the first automated sequencing instruments. Though regarded as high throughput machines in their time, in 2005 a new generation of technology emerged that took sequencing runs from 84 kilobase per run to 1 gigabase per run (Illumnina). From 2005, data output from NGS instruments was even outpacing Moore's Law. The costs of sequencing runs dropped dramatically while the throughput rates rose in near equal proportion. Desktop instruments, such as the Illumina MiSeq/HiSeq, Life Technologies Ion Torrent PGM, or Roche GS Junior/454, perform massively parallel sequencing on thousands of DNA sequence clusters. Parallel processing allows for the production of massive amounts of data, even from smaller amounts of sample material. Instruments such as these provide human rights and war crimes investigators with unparalleled tools for countering the exculpatory frames offered by the possible sources of abuse. Furthermore, they offer scientifically sound information that is used to hold human rights abusers to public account.

The political and press significance of advances in NGS technology can be illustrated by the case of 42 missing students from Iguala, Guerrero, Mexico. On 26 September, 2014, students from the Ayotzinapa Iguala Rural Teachers' College disappeared in Iguala, Guerrero, Mexico. According to initial accounts offered by federal authorities, the students commandeered local school buses to take them to Mexico City for the commemorative anniversary of the 1968 Tlatelolco Square Massacre. After local police intercepted the buses, the students were, according to official accounts, handed over by local police officials to the 'United Warriors', a drug gang. Federal authorities claimed it was the drug gang that killed the students and burned their bodies in a local dump.

Although EAAF, the Argentinian forensic anthropology team founded by Clyde Snow, discovered the remains of 19 people at the dump, DNA analysis revealed that none of the 19 discovered bodies belonged to the missing students. Eventually, at least 129 *other* human remains were found at the dump (Lakhani, 2015). Finally, in November 2014, Mexican officials announced that several plastic bags containing badly damaged and fragmentary human remains had been found near a river in Cocula, Guerrero. It seemed that there was little to go on in putting together an account of the victim's identity.

Perhaps of greatest importance to human rights investigations is the ability of NGS to successfully analyse small and damaged samples. As a senior research scientist at the Armed Forces DNA Identification Laboratory (AFDIL), notes, 'for specific applications at AFDIL, NGS is currently the only way to get sequencing information from DNA that is degraded to less than 100 base pairs, since Sanger sequencing is not easily amenable to such small fragments' (Melton, 2014). In 2016, researchers at the Institute of Legal Medicine, Medical University of Innsbruck adapted a DNA sequencing technology known as Primer Extension Capture Massively Parallel Sequencing (PEC MPS) to sequence some of the severely damaged DNA recovered near the river in Cocula, Guerrero. 'The scientists demonstrated that this method enables identification of biological material that is too damaged for conventional forensic DNA analysis' (*Successful DNA Analyses*, 2016). In fact, the genetic material was, according to the scientifically coached language of the lead scientist, 'at least 1 billion times more likely to be observed under the scenario that the unidentified remains originated from a biological son of the father' (identified in the document by an anonymous serial number), 'as compared to the unidentified remains originating from an unrelated individual' (Scheithauer, R., 2014). In other words, despite attempts to obliterate the remains and to create an official narrative fingering local police and the drug gang, NGS told a different story. The official story was unravelling. In April 2016, an international panel of experts, initially invited to Mexico by federal authorities to investigate the disappearance of the students,

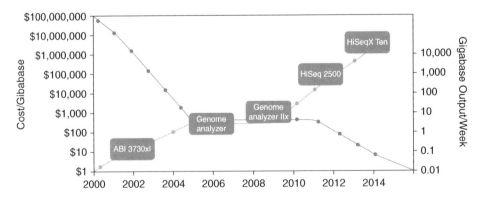

Figure 36.1 Sequencing cost and data output since 2000
Source: Illumina

said that it had been subjected to a sustained campaign of harassment and intimidation following the publication of an initial report that contradicted the federal government narrative (Ahmed and Villegas, 2016). Despite the harassment, the investigators' findings pointed to involvement of Mexican *federal*, intelligence and military authorities in the massacre of the students (Semple 2016). Despite efforts to obstruct their investigations, human rights organizations were able to put together an evidence-based counternarrative concerning the student's fates. In Entman's terms, human rights investigators offered compelling, scientifically grounded counterframes to the official account of events. News reports of human rights abuses often rely on the findings of advocacy groups such as Amnesty International and expert human rights practitioners such as EAAF. Forensic science empowers organizations like these to gather data and challenge official accounts of abuse. Often, perpetrators of abuse try to destroy evidence, and with it the story, or they attempt to deflect responsibility for events. Using Entman's substantive frame concept, I have argued that forensic science, especially NGS, undermines the ability of human rights abusers and war criminals to obfuscate and deny the existence of abuse (the problem in Entman's lexicon) or evade responsibility. In 'framing contests' between alleged abusers of human rights and advocacy groups, forensic science strengthens the arguments made by rights groups.

References

Ahmed, A. and Villegas, P. (2016). 'Investigators Say Mexico Has Thwarted Efforts to Solve Students' Disappearance', *The New York Times* (22 April). Available at: http://www.nytimes.com/2016/04/23/world/americas/investigators-say-mexico-has-thwarted-efforts-to-solve-students-disappearance.html?hp&action=click&pgtype=Homepage&clickSource=story-heading&module=first-column-region&region=top-news&WT.nav=top-news

Bachrach, P. and Baratz, M. S. (1962). 'Two Faces of Power'. *The American Political Science Review*, 56(4), pp. 947–952.

BBC (2005). 'New Srebrenica Mass Grave Found'. *BBC* (October 17). Available at: http://news.bbc.co.uk/2/hi/europe/4350840.stm

Bennett, L. W., Lawrence, R. and Livingston S. (2006). 'None Dare Call It Torture: Indexing and the Limits of Press Independence in the Abu Ghraib Scandal'. *Journal of Communication*, 56, pp. 467–85.

Carragee, K. M., and Roefs, W. (2004). 'The Neglect of Power in Recent Framing Research'. *Journal of Communication*, 54(2), pp. 214–233.

Cobb, C. R. and Elder, C. D. (1971). 'The Politics of Agenda-Building: An Alternative Perspective for Modern Democratic Theory'. *The Journal of Politics*, 33(4), pp. 892–915.

Edelman, M. (1988). *Constructing the Political Spectacle*. Chicago: University of Chicago Press.

Entman, R. M. (2004). *Projections of Power: Framing News, Public Opinion, and U.S. Foreign Policy*. Chicago: University of Chicago Press.

Haberman, C. (2015). 'Children of Argentina's 'Disappeared' Reclaim Past, With Help', *The New York Times* (11 October). Available at: http://www.nytimes.com/2015/10/12/us/children-of-argentinas-disappeared-reclaim-past-with-help.html?_r=0

Illumina. *An Introduction to Next-Generation Sequencing Technology*. Available at: www.illumina.com/technology/next-generation-sequencing.html. [Accessed 2016].

Institut für Gerichtliche Medizin, Medizinische Universität Innsbruck (2016). *Successful DNA Analyses on Missing Mexican Remains*. Available at: http://gerichtsmedizin.at/successful-dna-analyses-mexican-remains.html

International Center for Transitional Justice (2009). *Transitional Justice in the Former Yugoslavia*. Available at: https://www.ictj.org/publication/transitional-justice-former-yugoslavia

Joyce, C. and Stover, E. (1991). *Witness from the Grave*. New York: Little Brown & Co.

Lakhani, N. (2015). 'Search for Missing Mexican Students Turns up 129 Bodies Unrelated to Case', *The Guardian* (July 27). Available at: http://www.theguardian.com/world/2015/jul/27/mexico-search-missing-students-129-bodies

Lasseter, T. (2008). 'As Possible Afghan War-Crimes Evidence Removed, U.S. Silent' *McClatchey DC*, Dec. 11. Available at: http://www.mcclatchydc.com/news/nation-world/world/article24514951.html

Lewis, P. H. (2002). *Geurrillas and Generals: The Dirty War in Argentina*. Westport, CN: Praeger Publishers.

Livingston, S. (2016). 'Digital Affordances and Human Rights Advocacy', *Collaborative Research Center (SFB) 700 Governance in Areas of Limited Statehood*. Available at: http://www.sfb-governance.de/en/publika-tionen/working_papers/wp69/index.html

McPherson, E. (2015). *ICTs and Human Rights Practice: A Report Prepared for the UN Special Rapporteur on Extrajudicial, Summary, or Arbitrary Executions*, University of Cambridge Centre of Governance and Human Rights. Available at: https://www.academia.edu/16318040/ICTs_and_Human_Rights_Practice

Melton, T. (2014). 'Digging Deep: Next Generation Sequencing for Mitrochondrial DNA Forensics', *Forensic Magazine*, (4 January). Available at: http://www.forensicmag.com/article/2014/01/digging-deep-next-generation-sequencing-mitochondrial-dna-forensics

Oreskes, N. and Conway, E. (2010). *Merchants of Doubt*. New York: Bloomsbury Press.

Rosenblatt, A. (2015). *Digging for the Disappeared: Forensic Science after Atrocity*. Stanford: Stanford University Press, p. 2.

Scheithauer, R. (2014). *Expert Opinion on DNA Analyses*. Gerichtsärzte am Institut für Gerichtliche Medizin der Medizinischen Universität-Innsbruck, Austria.

Semple, K. (2016). 'Missing Mexican Students Suffered a Night of "Terror," Investigators Say', *The New York Times* (24 April). Available at: http://www.nytimes.com/2016/04/25/world/americas/missing-mex-ican-students-suffered-a-night-of-terror-investigators-say.html?hp&action=click&pgtype=Homepage&clickSource=story-heading&module=first-column-region&region=top-news&WT.nav=top-news

Steadman, D. W. and Haglund, W. D. (2005). 'The Scope of Anthropological Contributions to Human Rights Investigations', *Journal of Forensic Science,* 50(1), pp. 23–30.

Stern, A. (undated). 'Science in the Service of Human Rights: Argentina 37 Years After the Coup', *The Global Post* (28 May). Available at: http://www.huffingtonpost.com/alex-stern/argentina-dirty-war-dna_b_2941724.html

Stover, E. and Shigekane, R. (2004). 'Exhumation of Mass Graves: Balancing Legal and Humanitarian Needs'. In: *My Neighbor, My Enemy: Justice and Community in the Aftermath of Mass Atrocity*. Cambridge: Cambridge University Press, p. 92.

Wagner, S. E. (2008). *To Know Where He Lies: DNA Technology and the Search for Srebrenica's Missing*. Berkeley: University of California Press, pp. 96.

PART V

Media representation of human rights

Cultural, social and political

37

MEDIA, CULTURE AND HUMAN RIGHTS

Towards an intercultural communication and human rights journalism nexus

Ibrahim Seaga Shaw

In the space of three months – between December 2014 and February 14 2015 – three shocking incidents, which quickly turned out to be terrorist attacks, unfolded on the heels of each other. The first happened on Monday December 15 2014 just after the morning rush when a gunman, Man Harun Monis, took 16 hostages in a downtown Sydney Café Lindt, and by the time the siege ended following a protracted standoff with armed police, three people, including the gun man, had been shot dead. The second came on January 7 2015 when two masked gunmen stormed the main Paris offices of satirical French newsmagazine *Charlie Hebdo* and shot dead 12 people, including 8 journalists, among them the magazine's editor, whose life had earlier been threatened for reproducing the Danish cartoons that ridiculed Prophet Mohamed. The two killers, and a third gunman who took five hostages in a Parisian supermarket, were also shot dead following protracted standoff with armed police bringing the total number of dead to 15. The final incident came on 14 February when unknown armed men opened fire on a Copenhagen café then hosting a debate on Islam, blasphemy and free speech killing one man and injuring two other people but apparently missed their target, controversial Swedish cartoonist Lars Vilks who had also received death threats for portraying Prophet Mohammed in a negative light.

These three incidents, despite happening in three different countries, have three things in common. First, all three came as reprisal or revenge attacks against those perceived to be insulting Islam although this was largely invisible in the media. Second, all resulted from a clash of Western values of free speech and the right of Muslims to practice without harassment. Finally, all happened because of the failure of intercultural communication within the contexts of peace and human rights. The second parallel echoes Samuel Huntington's (1996) idea of 'clash of civilizations' between the West and Islam, in that the Islamic world, which is now perceived as a target, and not helper, in 'the war on terror', has since the end of the Cold War, and in particular after 9/11, replaced the former Soviet Union' as the new 'uncivilised' enemy of the 'civilised' western world (Shaw 2012a, 510). But what Huntington appeared to have ignored is the fact that both freedom of expression and freedom of religion are part of the universal human rights doctrine albeit they are often considered as Western Liberal values. Yet, Huntington's prediction in his 1996 seminal study that 'culture' is replacing 'ideology' as the new battle ground for global conflicts was all but ignored until the 9/11 terrorist attacks on the US and many others in London, Madrid, Mumbai, Nairobi, Sydney, Copenhagen and Paris (the last three being those referred to previously). Following the attacks in Paris in November 2015 which claimed about 129 lives, Pope Francis described this new war as the 'Third World War', which has claimed yet another 38 lives in the most recent terrorist attacks in Brussels on 22 March 2016. However, although this new war is underpinned by the clash of cultures, very little attention has been paid to the role of culture and human rights in understanding and addressing what Galtung (2004) called 'cultural violence'. Perhaps the few exceptions include studies by Shaw (2012a, 2016) focusing on the media framing of the London 7/7 bombings and the murder of British soldier Lee Rigby in 2013 and constructing a nexus between intercultural communication and human rights journalism, which Shaw (2012b, 46) refers to as 'journalism without borders—a journalism based on human rights and global justice'. This chapter will expand these debates by going beyond Huntington's claim of a 'clash of cultures' involving Islamophobia and comparing it with others involving gender, race and ethnicity, and argue that it is not enough to blame the increasing extremism and terrorism on the clash of cultures between the West and Islam alone, and that the contradictions in the Universal Human Rights where the right balance is hardly struck between the enjoyment of these rights are also to blame. The principal aim of this chapter is therefore to provide a critical and nuanced theoretical overview of the intersections between culture, media and human rights drawing on this expanded scope of a 'clash of civilisations'. This chapter is structured into two main sections: first, it explores the intersections between culture, media and human rights in the context of radicalisation, extremism and terrorism; second, it critically compares the clash of cultures involving the West versus Islam with others involving gender, race and ethnicity.

The culture, media and human rights nexus

I draw on cultural studies and critical theory perspectives (Weerakkody 2009); Hall's theory (1997) of 'othering' in news discourse; Galtung's idea of indirect cultural violence (1996, 2004); and intercultural communication informed by Shaw's theory of human rights journalism (2012) in exploring the intersections between culture, media and human rights. Recent research by Shaw, 2012a; Khiabany and Williamson 2012; Ogan et al., 2014; Kundnani 2009; Roy and Ross 2011; Yusha'u 2011; Musa and Fergusson 2013; Richardson 2010; Saeed 2007; Schwedler 2001) shows that the perception of people across cultures is often shaped by the way in which different cultures are represented in the mainstream media. Yet, while these studies relate mostly to cultural representation involving Islamophobia, earlier research (Hall 1997; Ward 2002; Bailey and Harrindranath 2005; Shapiro 1989; Kaye 2001; Volkmer 1999; Tomasi 1993; Brosius and Eps 1995; Coleman 1995; Clarke 1998; Ali and Gibb 1999; Van Dijk 1991, 2000; Glasgow Media Group 1997; Kundnani 2001; Ross 2005; Naylor 2001; Carter and Weaver 2003; Kitzinger 2004; Liebler and Smith 1997 took a particular look at cultural representation involving race, ethnicity and gender. As we can see, only very few works for example by Edward Said (1997), Chris Allen (1997), Samuel Huntington, 1996) and Al-Azmeh (1993) looked at Islamophobia in the decade before the 9/11 terrorist attacks on the US. But the cultural representation landscape dramatically changed since then as it came to be defined by the newly declared 'war on terror' binary of US (the West) and *them* (Islam). However, despite the increasing spate of studies on Islamophobia since 9/11, we are yet to see one that has taken a comparative study of 'clash of cultures' involving religion (West Vs Islam), and others involving race, ethnicity and gender. It is the main aim of this chapter to address this gap in scholarship. I want to first look at the links between media and culture before exploring how both are related to human rights. Simply put, culture is a way of life, a belief, or value system, while media represents the platforms that transmit messages about these cultural practices and/or events. However, critical media theorists of the Frankfurt School such as Adorno and Horkheimer (1948) argue that the media, or the culture industries do not only transmit messages about culture but they do in fact directly persuade or influence the public to think and behave in ways that serve capitalism. This means that media have effects that can manipulate the public, and according to the critical media theorists, can be constraining or negative to the extent of obscuring reality. But cultural studies theorists such as French sociologists, for example Bernard Miege disagree by saying that not all members of the public lack agency to resist the manipulation of the cultural industries (Hesmondalph 2012). These cultural studies theorists therefore dismiss the persuasive, or manipulative, role of the cultural industries as grossly exaggerated. However, since the pioneering work of McCombs and Shaw (1972) on agenda setting which point to the power of the media to make the public think and behave in certain ways, more or less building on earlier works by Lippmann (1922) and those by the Frankfurt school of scholars, a maze of scholarly works (Entman 1993 2004; Brinson and Stohl 2012; Cooper 2009 to name a few); has confirmed that media framing – the inclusion or exclusion of issues or events – has an important influence on the public's perception of news content. Writing on the media effects model, Gauntlett (1998) argues that the media has a direct impact on people's behaviour and that anti-social behaviour, which often manifests in extremism and terrorism, is usually a consequence of the consumption of negative media contents.

Agenda-setting, framing and media effects are relevant to understanding Stuart Hall's concept of 'othering' which manifests in the 'us' and 'them' binary. Hall (1982) has argued that the media gives meanings to things through actively selecting, presenting, structuring and shaping events. For Hall, representation works through marking a difference with the 'other', whether the difference is on the basis of 'gender', 'sexuality', 'race' or nationality (1997). This implies that 'difference is constructed both through language, by way of binary oppositions such as man/woman, black/white, legal/illegal, British/foreigner, and also through 'symbolic boundaries': 'marking "difference" leads us, symbolically, to close ranks, shore up culture and to stigmatise and expel anything which is defined as impure, abnormal' (Hall 1997, 237). What Hall's 'othering' calculus tells us is that there is a need to go beyond Huntington's West Vs Islam contextualisation of it and see how this compares to others involving gender, race, and ethnicity, which this chapter is doing.

The world has witnessed numerous terror attacks since 9/11 and counting, and the media has been central in each of these attacks. 'These attacks have undoubtedly reinforced hostile perceptions and attitudes towards 'other' cultures and the peoples that live in some distant countries' (Shaw 2012b, 510). Huntington (1996) argued that Islam has replaced the Soviet Union as the new 'uncivilized' enemy of the 'civilized' western world (Shaw 2012b, 510). Media representation on the war on terror has encompassed processes of 'othering', which present the 'others' as 'radical, oppressive, fanatical, irrational' enemies of 'civilized' western values and beliefs which are often presented as normal and devoid of any politics or ideology (Roy and Ross 2011). This essay now looks at human rights drawing on Galtung's idea of cultural violence (2004). News media discourses of human rights mostly relate to when any or more of these rights are denied or violated. There are overlaps between the concepts of conflict, peace, and human right, and in how they relate to media and culture. The othering of cultural values, for example West Vs Islam, is in itself conflictual, at least going by the simple definition of conflict as being a struggle between opposing interests and outlooks. Chris Mitchell defines conflict as 'a relationship between two or more parties (individuals or groups) who have, or think they have, incompatible goals, needs and interests' (1981). Some conflicts are rooted in economic contradictions and political structures, while others are located within social attitudes or cultural outlooks. The problem of communicating cultural differences resonates with what founder of peace research,

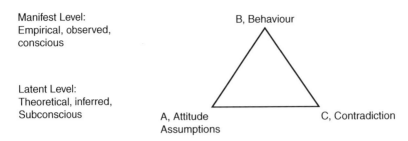

Figure 37.1   ABC (Attitude, Behaviour and Contradictions) Conflict Triangle

Johann Galtung, called 'cultural violence', and which he categorized as 'Attitude in his ABC *(Attitude, Behaviour and Contradictions)* Conflict Triangle'(See Figure 37.1). *Attitude'* (cultural violence) is represented at the bottom left of the Conflict Triangle for example 'hate speech, persecution complex, myths and legends of war heroes, religious justification for war, discrimination on the basis of skin colour, gender, religion, sex etc. 'choseness'/being the chosen people', civilisational arrogance (Galtung 2004; see also Shaw 2012a, 12 and Lynch & McGoldrick 2005, 38). Galtung believes in Lisa Schirch's theory of justpeace (Schirch, 2002) – sustainable positive peace – which can only be achieved by ensuring justice for all. Galtung (1996) argues that peace goes beyond the absence of direct violence (Behaviour) such as war, and develops the alternative concept of positive peace such as avoiding or addressing indirect cultural (Attitude) or structural (contradiction) as the 'best protection against violence' (Galtung, 1996, 32). Galtung therefore has a holistic approach to peace in that what actually happens at the manifest level (direct violence) depends on what happens at the latent level (indirect violence). It is important to recognise the resonance between Galtung's holistic peace approach with the idea of a holistic human rights approach that sees all rights – be they negative civil and political rights (first generation rights); positive economic, social and cultural rights (second generation rights), both enshrined in the 1966 Twin Covenants of the UN, or group rights (third generation rights) such as those adopted in the 1993 Vienna World Conference as universal, indivisible, interdependent and interrelated. The Twin Covenants, together with the Universal Declaration of Human Rights and the UN Charter of 1948 combined to form the foundation of the International Bill of Rights. The Twin Covenants also encompass the right to equality and non-discrimination and the rights of minority groups such as children and women, although these rights, recognised as the Third Generation Rights, were not strictly speaking recognised by most nations until the Vienna World Conference in 1993 (Nowak, 2005). While it is assumed (Cottle, 2008) that the mainstream media have taken a critical stance in reporting issues and events of risk and conflict, there is a plethora of studies (Allan and Zelizer 2004; Carruthers 2004; Shaw 2012a 2012b, 2016; Lynch and McGoldrick 2005) that have pointed to the media's subservience to the voices, views and values of powerful institutions and authorities in the framing of risk and conflict. Moreover, invisible cultural violence stories are often less dramatic and so therefore attract less media attention. Such stories only become dramatic, and so attract media attention when they move from the latent (invisible) level, for example discrimination, to the manifest (visible) level for example radicalization, extremism and terrorism. Terrorism and the media are entangled in a kind of symbiotic relationship (Miller 1982). As Shaw (2012: 12–13) argues 'Communicating a message can serve both as a means and as an end to the promotion of human rights and peace'. When you take part in a communication exercise, you are essentially contributing to the creation of peace, which can also be central to the promotion and protection of human rights. Yet, as we can see in this chapter, it is not just the lack of the human right to communicate that can lead to indirect forms of cultural or structural violence, or direct forms of physical violence, but also the failure to strike the right balance between this right and the right of others to enjoy their right of association without being subjected to discrimination and hate attacks. Klyukanov (2005) defines culture as a system of values and beliefs associated with groups based on gender, religion, nationality or physical ability/disability. He defines communication as 'the practice of creating meanings or symbolic resources' (Klyukanov 2005, 10). On the basis of this culture-communication symbiosis, Klyukanov defines intercultural communication (IC) as a 'process of interaction between groups of people with different systems of symbolic resources'. Intercultural communication, which is based on 'constructive boundary lines' that endorse and value indi-viduals for what they are, and use supportive language when referring to them, is very similar to peace journalism(PJ) and human rights journalism (HRJ), because these two models, like IC, encourage a win–win approach to constructive dialogue, demonstrate empathy for all cultures and peoples, and are orientated towards truth and solutions instead of propaganda (lies) and problems (conflicts). Lynch and McGoldrick (2005, 5) define PJ as 'a set of tools, both concep-tual and practical, intended to equip journalists to offer a better public service' and provide the society at large with opportunities 'to consider and value non-violent responses to conflict'. Shaw (2012b, 46) defines HRJ as 'a diagnostic style of reporting, which gives a critical reflection on the experiences and needs of the victims and perpetrators of human rights violations of all types – physical as well as cultural and structural – in order to stimulate understanding of the reasons for these violations and to prevent or solve them in ways that would not produce more human rights imbalances or violations in the future'. It is a journalism based on human rights and global justice, a form of journalism that challenges political, economic, social and cultural imbalances of society at both local and global levels. In fact Shaw (2016, 33) argues that 'HRJ goes one step further than Peace Journalism in resonating with intercultural communication in that it moves beyond the double win, that is win-win involving the cultural groups engaged in the cultural exchange, to a triple win, that is win-win involving not only the groups engaged in the cultural exchange but also third-party bystanders who are not directly involved'. Moreover, HRJ supports intercultural communication further by being more proactive in challenging indirect structural (contradictions) and cultural (attitude) imbalances of society as cold conflicts, instead of waiting until they manifest into direct political violence as hot conflicts.

Clash of cultures: A critical comparative look at religion, gender, race and ethnicity

As we have seen in Galtung's categorization of cultural violence, in his ABC Conflict Triangle (2004) previously discussed, the problem of communicating cultural differences – which, if not avoided or managed, can lead to direct political violence such as the terrorist incidents mentioned earlier – is not only evident in the clash of cultures involving religion, for example the West versus Islam. The rest of this section compares this and other challenging issues of discrimination involving gender, race and ethnicity where such acts of extremism and terrorism have manifested.

Religion: The West vs Islam

The juxtaposing of the West and Islam in binary terms could be considered problematic but far from strange, since it has survived many historical experiences since the emergence of Islam as a formidable and late challenger to Christianity. This binary has since 9/11 assumed a new urgency in the world. But why is it that it is the West, and not Christianity, that is pitted against Islam. In Edward Said's view, this is because it is assumed that 'whereas "the West" is greater than and has surpassed the stage of Christianity, its principal religion, the world of Islam—its varied societies, histories, and languages notwithstanding—is still mired in religion, primitivity, and backwardness' (Said 1997, 10). In his study of the coverage of the 7/7 terrorist bombings in the British press, Shaw (2012a) found the dominant use of stereotypes and clichés depicting Islam in 'hateful' light, which he argued threatened to incite hostility towards all believers of Islam on the one hand, and provoke Islamic radicalisation, extremism and terrorism on the other. In his most recent study of the coverage of the Woolwich murder of British soldier Drummer Lee Rigby by six British newspapers, Shaw (2016) found that the acts of extremism and terrorism carried out by the two Muslims who murdered the British soldier, and the rantings of Muslim hate preachers were foregrounded far above those carried out by far–right-wing fascist activists against Muslims and Islamic centres of worship and education. The attention focused on the extremism by Muslims 'is of a completely different kind to that focused on, say, right-wing extremism, which is taken to be no more than a public order threat' (Kundnani 2009, 40). Yet, in the context of IC informed by HRJ, all acts of extremism and terrorism, be it by Muslims or non-Muslims, must be presented and condemned as such, without any form of discrimination. Thus these differences in the framing of extremism and terrorism clearly reinforce the clash of cultures, and perhaps the cliché that 'one man's terrorist is another's freedom fighter. For instance, Saddam Hussain, Osama Bin Laden and the Taliban, were recently framed as terrorists, while they were framed as friends of the West and 'liberators' in the past. Since 9/11, the definitions of these two concepts in terms of Islam vs Islamophobia vary according to which of the two binary values, or sides, you find yourself: 'Western culture' (the us) and 'Islamic culture' (the *them*). Said (1997, 11) has consistently criticised the Western media for its 'exaggerated stereotyping and belligerent hostility' towards Islam. Moreover, Galtung's idea of indirect cultural violence is important in analysing how the stereotypical frames in the media about acts of extremism and radicalization by a few individuals may have a spill-over effect of blanket condemnation of the whole group to which these few individuals belong. This may slowly become institutionalized violence against the perceived 'enemies' leading to more members from the 'condemned' group coming out to engage in more acts of extremism in protest. The risk of such negative group stereotyping is that the blame and potential backlash of one human wrong committed by one member of a religious or political community are shared by all members of that community (Shaw 2016) resulting to more strained relations and fall-out between and among the two groups. It is this problematic group stereotyping that has come to define concepts such as Islamophobia, which the 1997 Rennymede Report called 'anti-Islam' or 'fear of Islam type of behaviour' (Shaw 2016, 32), although the concept itself is sometimes confused with 'Islamic or Muslim extremism and terrorism' (Ogan et al. 2014). It is also important to note that it is not only in the West that the media is found complicit in Islamophobia. In their study of the reporting of the 2009 Jos sectarian violence, Musa and Fergusson (2013) found that Nigerian newspapers used enemy images and stereotypes that reinforced prejudice and violence against the 'other' who were mostly Muslims from the North of Nigeria. Nigerian newspapers have also been found wanting in communitarian cultural logic as Mercy Ette's study of the framing of the Nigerian Detroit bomber Abdul Mutallab found that the Nigerian newspapers only blamed Western and Arabic institutions for his radicalisation and in that way obscured the role of Nigeria and its policies in the equation (Ette 2012), apparently in the name of national interest.

Race: White vs black

Race has since the era of the Slave Trade provided a space where ideological and cultural differences are contested in 'us' versus 'them' binary terms, especially in times of crisis such as riots, demonstrations, civil conflicts, and humanitarian disasters. Ideologically, while whites are perceived as having conservative ideas of reinforcing the existing power structures in their favour, blacks are perceived to have liberal ones to change them. Culturally, while whites are perceived to be 'civilised' or 'advanced', blacks are perceived to be 'primitive' or 'backward'. Thus, while whites are presented as stable and friendly, blacks are presented as resentful and hateful. This combined ideological and cultural white versus black othering was largely used to justify the plundering of North America and the 'extermination' of 'hostile' natives and for the 'enslavement' of Africans (Rhodes 2005, 30). This led to the emergence of a public discourse that sought to reinforce the idea that non-whites were inferior, unable to govern themselves, unlikely to be assimilated into mainstream American society, and therefore a threat to national stability' (Rhodes 2005, 31). There is a growing body of research that confirms the dominant white/black cultural framing of crisis situations. For instance a research led by the Guardian and the London School of Economics found out that police racism against blacks was the principal cause of the 2011 London riots sparked by the shooting of black youth, Mark Dugan, by police in Tottenham. Yet, despite the fact that many non-blacks who joined the riots partook in the massive looting that ensured because of other reasons such as poverty, exclusion from school and jobs, an increase in tuition fees, the closure of social services etc. found in the research, media reports were awash with images of blacks looting and ravaging shops. The media was accused of similar racism in the coverage of the victims of Hurricane Katrina. An AP picture caption of a black man presented him as wading through flooded water 'after looting a grocery store' while an AFP picture caption of a white couple presented them as 'two residents wade through chest deep water after finding bread and water from a local grocery store after Hurricane Katrina'(Finnegan 2007, 149). The black man and the white couple were in a similar desperate situation; however, while the act of the former was presented as abnormal (looting) that of the latter was presented as normal (finding). CNN's Wolf Blitzer reinforced this negative stereotyping of the black victims of Katrina by saying: 'You simply get chills every time you see these poor individuals … many of these people, almost all of them that we see are so poor and they are so black, and this is going to raise lots of questions as this story unfolds'. Here again like the reporting of the 2011 London riots, the focus on racial stereotyping obscures the reality of the problem of class caused largely by the inequality embedded in the neoliberal capitalist system.

Ethnicity: British vs immigrants

Cultural forms of stereotyping are also evident in the reporting of ethnicity, especially when it comes to forced immigrants such as refugees and asylum seekers. They are simply represented as the 'other' and therefore not worthy of being part of the 'chosen people' (Shaw 2012a, 202). Shaw's (2012a) study of the myths and facts about asylum seekers found the consistent use of the word 'bogus' in the media to refer to refugees where as the fact is ' a refugee is an asylum seeker who has been granted refugee status according to the 1951 Geneva Convention. Most earlier studies (Tomasi 1993; Brossuis and Eps 1995; Coleman 1995; Clark 1998; Ali and Gibb 1993 etc.) found consistency in the British press representation of asylum seekers and refugees as either a 'problem' or 'invisible'. They are presented 'in terms of suspicion and deterrence: can we trust them and how do we keep them out?' (Kundnani 2001 cited in Bailey and Harindranath, 279).

Gender: Men vs women

Cultural violence can also take the form of patriarchy and gender discrimination. Take for example the shooting incident in 1989 in Montreal by a young man which left 14 young women dead where the burning issue of discrimination against women appeared to be the root cause. The killer entered the classroom and separated the students into two groups: one men and the other women, and then opened fire on the women shouting: 'You 're all a bunch of feminists. I hate feminists' (Raboy 1992). This might have largely sounded at the time like the act of a lunatic acting alone but it is highly likely that he was influenced by the invisible crisis of everyday life associated with the idea of the growing empowerment of women in a society that was, and perhaps is, still largely characterized by patriarchy and gender discrimination. For all you know, this shooting incident may not be very different from the many cases of rape and domestic violence, albeit being less dramatic, most of which are rarely reported, or when reported it is often with little or no context. The recent kidnapping of two hundred young girls from a secondary school in Nigeria by Boko Haram should also be seen in this context of patriarchy and gender discrimination, although very little of this was reflected in the mainstream Nigerian press.

Conclusion: Towards intercultural communication and human rights journalism

This chapter has expanded the IC and HRJ debates by going beyond Huntington's idea of a clash of cultures involving the West versus Islam by looking at similar clashes of culture involving race, ethnicity and gender, and above all making the argument that the blame for the direct (visible) violence resulting from each of these clashes or cultural differences should not only be put on the indirect cultural (invisible) violence but also on the contradictions in the universal human rights principle. Moreover, in thinking through this chapter it was found that the mainstream media too have played a major role in the cultural violence and hence failure of intercultural communication in each of the clashes of cultures discussed.

But research by Shoemaker and Rees (1996), Gans (1979) and the cultural proximity news value (Galtung and Ruge 1965) suggest that there are structures, including the cultural environment in which journalists work, which influence the selection and cultural framing of what constitutes an 'extremist' or 'terrorist' act. It means journalists' framing of news involving cultural violence is largely influenced by which side of the cultural divide they find themselves. Yet this communitarian or nationalist cultural logic contradicts the universal human rights principle founded on the idea of the 'human community' (the cosmopolitan logic) where every human being or every life is important, and hence worth protecting (Anderson-Gold 2001). It is also worth noting that it is Article 19 of this human rights principle that provides for 'freedom of expression' which informs the liberal theory of the media. However, there is a provision against the use of 'hate speech' embedded in this Article 19 that is almost always roundly flouted by the mainstream media with impunity when it comes to the reporting of the West versus Islam, whites versus blacks, British/Americans/Europeans versus immigrants and men versus women, as confirmed by the research cited in this chapter. There is, therefore, an even more serious contradiction in the human rights principle in that while journalists enjoy protection in 'using' or 'abusing' Article 19, Muslims, blacks, immigrants and women who are victims of 'hate media' fail to be protected by Article 18 which provides all with the freedom to practice the faith of their choice without any attack or harassment, or to enjoy a peaceful life irrespective of their race, ethnic background or gender. Moreover, the consistent use of 'hate media' also contributes to distorting, or obscuring, the reality of the 'invisible violence' of everyday life responsible for these clashes of cultures. This chapter therefore argues that an intercultural communication approach informed by human rights journalism is needed in reporting cultural differences if the clash of cultures such as those in the case studies discussed here are to be avoided or minimised. This is because the HRJ model is informed by the holistic human rights principle enshrined in the 1966 twin covenants of the first generation (political and civil), second generation (economic, social and cultural), and the third generation (group) rights adopted at the 1993 Vienna conference – as universal, indivisible, interdependent and interrelated.

References

Adorno, T. and Horkheimer, M. (1948). *The Dialectic of Enlightenment*. London: Edward Arnolds.

Al-Azmeh, A. (1993). *Islams and Modernities*. London: Verso.

Ali, Y. and Gibb, P. (1999). 'Le Racisme, le droit d'asile et la presse britannique'. *Migrations Societe*, 11(62), pp. 123–34.

Allan, S. and Zelizer, B. (2004). 'Rules of Engagement: Journalism and War', in Stuart Allan and Berbie Zelizer (eds.) *Reporting War: Journalism in War Time*. London: Routledge.

Allen, C. (1997). *Islamophobia: 10 Years of the Runnymede Trust Report 'Islamophobia: A Challenge for Us All'*. London: Runnymede Trust.

Anderson-Gold, S. (2001). *Cosmopolitanism and Human Rights*. Cardiff: University of Wales Press.

Bailey, O.G and Harindranath, R. (2005). 'Racialized "Othering": The Representation of Asylum Seekers in the News Media'. In S. Allan, ed., *Journalism: Critical Issues*. Berkshire, UK: Open University Press.

Brinson, M. E. and Stohl, M. (2012). 'Media Framing of Terrorism: Implications for Public Opinion, Civil Liberties, and Counterterrorism Policies'. *Journal of International and Intercultural Communication*, 5 (4), 270–90.

Brosius, H.B and Ebs, P. (1995). 'Prototyping through Key Events: News Selection in the Case of Violence against Aliens and Asylum Seekers in Germany'. *European Journal of Communication*, 10(3), pp. 391–412.

Carruthers, S. (2004). 'Tribalism and Tribulation: Media Constructions of "African Savagery" and Western Humanitarianism in the 1990s', in Stuart Allan and Berbie Zelizer (eds.) *Reporting War: Journalism in War Time*. London: Routledge.

Carter, C. and Weaver, C. K. (2003). *Violence and the Media*. Basingstoke: Open University Press.

Clarke, C. (1998). 'Counting Backwards: The Roma "Numbers Game" in Central and Eastern Europe', *Radical Statistics*, 69, pp. 35–46.

Coleman, P. (1995). 'Survey of Asylum Coverage in the National Daily Press', *The Runnymede Bulletin*, 291, pp. 6–7.

Cooper, S. D. (2009). 'The Oppositional Framing of Bloggers', in Paul D'Angelo and Jim Kuypers (eds.) *Doing News Framing Analysis: Empirical and Theoretical Perspectives*. New York: Routledge, pp. 135–55.

Entman, R. (1993). Framing: Towards Clarification of a Fractured Paradigm, *Journal of Communication*, 43(4), pp. 51–8.

Entman, R. (2004). *Projections of Power*. Chicago, IL: University of Chicago Press.

Ette, M. (2012). '"Nigeria as a Country of Interest in Terrorism": Newspaper Framing of Farouk Abdulmutallab, the Underwear Bomber'. *Journal of African Media Studies*. Intellect, 4(1) pp. 45–59.

Finnegan, L. (2007). *No Questions Asked: Journalism Since 9/11*. London: Praeger.

Galtung, J. (1996). Peace by Peaceful Means – Peace and Conflict, Development and Civilization, PRIO – International Peace Research Institute, Oslo, London: Sage Publications.

Galtung, J. (2004). *Violence, War, and their Impact: On Visible and Invisible Effects of Violence*. Available at: them. polylog.org/5/fgj-en.htm

Galtung, J. and Ruge, M. (1965). 'Structuring and Presenting News', S. Cohen and J. Young (eds.) *The Manufacture of News: Social Problems, Deviance and the Mass Media*. London: Constable, pp. 62–72.

Gans, H. (1979). *Deciding What Is News: A Study of CBS Evening News, NBC Nightly News, Newsweek, and Time*. New York: Pantheon Books.

Gauntlett, D. (1998). 'Ten things wrong with the media effects model'. Available at: http://www.theory.org. uk/david/effects.htm (accessed 20 February 2016).

Glasgow Media Group (1997). *Race, Migration and Media*. Glasgow: GMG.

Hall, S. (1982). 'The Rediscovery of Ideology : Return of the Repressed in Media Studies', in M. Gurevitch, T. Bennett, J. Curran and J. Woollacott (eds.) *Culture, Society, and the Media*. London: Routledge.

Hall, S. (1997). The Spectacle of the 'Other'. In S. Hall, ed., *Representation: Cultural Representations and Signifying Practices*. London: Sage.

Hesmondalph, D. (2012). *The Cultural Industries*, 3rd ed., California, London: Sage.

Huntington, S. (1996). *The Clash of Civilisations and the Remaking of the World Order*. London: Simon and Schuster.

Kaye, R. (2001). 'Blaming the Victim', in R. King and N. Wood (eds), *Media and Migration*. London: Routledge.

Khiabany, G. and Williamson, M. (2012). 'Terror, Culture and Anti-Muslim Racism'. In: D. Freedman and D. K. Thussu, eds., *Media and Terrorism: Global Perspectives*. London: Sage.

Kitzinger, J. (2004). 'Media Coverage of Sexual Violence Against Women and Children', In: K. Ross and C. Byerly, eds., *Women and Media: International Perspectives*. Oxford: Blackwell Publishing.

Klyukanov, I. E. (2005). *Principles of Intercultural Communication*. Boston, MA: Pearson Education Inc.

Kundnani, K. (2009). *Spooked! How Not to Prevent Violent Extremism*. London: Institute of Race Relations.

Kundnani, K. (2001). 'In a Foreign Land: The New Popular Racism', *Race and Class*, 43, pp. 41–60.

Liebler, C. and Smith, S. (1997). 'Tracking Gender Differences: A Comparative Analysis of Network Correspondents and their Sources'. *Journal of Broadcasting and Electronic Media*, 41 (Winter): 58–68.

Lippmann W. (1922). *Public Opinion*. New York: Harcourt-Brace.

Lynch J. and McGoldrick A. (2005). *Peace Journalism*. Stroud: Hawthorn Press.

McCombs, M. E. and Shaw, D. L. (1972). 'The Agenda-setting Function of Mass Media', *Public Opinion Quarterly*, 36, pp. 176–85.

Musa, A. O and Fergusson, N. (2013). 'Enemy Framing and the Politics of Reporting Religious Conflicts in the Nigerian Press'. *Media, Conflict, and War*. Sage. 6(1), pp. 7–20.

Naylor, B. (2001). 'Reporting Violence in the British Print Media: Gendered Stories', *Howard Journal of Criminal Justice*, 40(2), pp. 180–94.

Nowak, M. (2005). 'The International Covenants on Civil and Political Rights and on Economic, Social and Cultural Rights', in Rhona Smith and Christien Van den Anker (eds.) *Essentials of Human Rights*. London: Hodder Arnold.

Ogan, C., Wilnat, L., Pennington, R. and Bashir, M. (2014). 'The Rise of Anti-Muslim Prejudice: Media and Islamophobia in Europe and the United States'. *The International Communication Gazette*, 76(1), pp. 27–46.

Raboy, M. (1992). 'Media and the Invisible Crisis of Everyday Life'. In: M. Raboy, and Bernard Dagenais, eds., *Media, Crisis and Democracy: Mass Communication and the Disruption of Social Order*. London: Sage, pp. 133–143.

Rhodes, J. (2005). 'Race, Ideology and Journalism: Black Power and Television News'. In : S. Allan, ed., *Journalism: Critical Issues*. Maidenhead: Open University Press.

Richardson, J. E. (2010). 'Get Shot of the Lot of Them': Election Reporting of Muslims in British Newspapers'. *Patterns of Prejudice*, 43(3), pp. 355–77.

Ross, K. (2005). Women in the Boyzone: Gender, News and Herstory'. In: S. Allan, ed., *Journalism: Critical Issues*. Berkshire, UK: Open University Press.

Roy, S. and Ross, S. D. (2011). The Circle of Terror: Strategic Localizations of Global Media Terror Meta-discourses in the U.S., India and Scotland'. *Media, War and Conflict*, 4(3), pp. 1–15.

Saeed, A. (2007). 'Media, Racism and Islamophobia: The Representation of Islam and Muslims in the Media'. *Sociology Compass*, 1(2), pp. 443–62.

Said, E. (1997). *Covering Islam: How the Media and the Experts Determine How We See the Rest of the World*. New York: Vintage Books.

Schirch, L. (2002). 'Human Rights and Peacebuilding: Towards Justpeace'. Paper presented to the 43rd Annual International Studies Association. New Orleans, Louisiana, 24–7 March, 2002.

Schwedler J. (2001). 'Islamic Identity: Myth, Menace, or Mobiliser?' *SAIS Review*, 21(2), pp. 1–17.

Shapiro, L. (1989). 'Textualising Global Politics', in M. Wetherell, S. Taylor, and S. Yates (eds), *Discourse Theory and Practice. A Reader*. London: Sage.

Shaw, I. S. (2012b). *Human Rights Journalism: Advances in Reporting Distant Humanitarian Interventions*. Basingstoke, Hampshire: Palgrave Macmillan.

Shaw, I. S (2012a). 'Stereotypical Representations of Muslims and Islam Following the 7/7 Terrorist Attacks in London: Implications for Intercultural Communication and Terrorism Prevention'. *International Communication Gazette* (SAGE), Vol. 13, 74(6), pp. 509–24.

Shaw, I. S (2016). 'Reporting the Lee Rigby Murder and Anti-Muslim Hostilities in the UK IN 2013: The Cultural Clash Communication and Human Wrongs Journalism Nexus'. In: S. Roy and I. S. Shaw, eds., *Communicating Differences: Culture, Media, Peace and Conflict Negotiation*. Hampshire, UK: Palgrave McMillan.

Shoemaker, P. J. and Reese, S. D. (1996). *Mediating the Message: Theories of Influences on Mass Media Content* (Second Edition). White Plains, New York: Longman.

Tomasi, S. (1993). 'Today's Refugees and the Media'. *Migration World*, 20 (5): 21–3.

Van Dijk, T. A. (2000). New(s) *Racism and the Press*. London: Routledge.

Van Dijk, T. A. (1991). *Racism and the Press*. London: Routledge.

Volkmer, I. (1999). *News in the Global Sphere: A study of CNN and its impact on Global Communication*. Bedfordshire: University of Luton Press.

Ward, I. (2002). '*The Tampa*, Wedge Politics, and a Lesson for Political Journalism'. *Australian Journalism Review*, 24 (1): 454.

Weerakkody, N. (2009). *Research Methods: For Media and Communication*. London: Oxford University Press.

Yusha'u, M. J. (2012). 'News Framing of the "Detroit Bomber" in the Nigerian Press.' *Global Media and Communication*, SAGE, 7(3), pp. 281–88.

38

MEDIA AND WOMEN'S HUMAN RIGHTS

Barbara M. Freeman

Women's rights in the news media are very much a human rights issue, one that the United Nations and other international bodies have emphasized in their reports on the importance of freedom of expression and the right to communicate for women and minorities. Yet news media around the world still ignore, downplay or misrepresent women and their concerns, relaying very mixed messages about their rights to equality, security and their socio-political place in society (LaRue et al. 2010; Global Media Monitoring Project 2015). Much of the emphasis in the academic research has stemmed from the concerns and goals of women's movements in a number of countries and how well, or not, the media have reported on them. The literature includes media coverage of the movement itself; the absence or misrepresentation of women in the news, especially those exercising their right as citizens to hold public office; the right of women and girls to safety from sexual and other forms of violence in both war and peacetime; and, to a lesser extent, the right to freedom from the gender, religious, racial and other forms of discrimination that contribute to female poverty, ill health and death. This chapter will discuss academic studies that are primarily engaged in posing feminist questions related to the news media and women's rights, whether they are a matter of law, policy or practice, including different forms of news on the Internet. Most of these studies involve substantial primary and secondary research in journalism studies or take an interdisciplinary approach, combining those fields with others, such as sociology, political science or international relations. Others noted are helpful literature reviews. For reasons of focus and space, they are representative of the current English-language scholarship on women, their rights and the news media, and do not cover all the many human rights violations against the female sex.

Most of the journalism studies cited here apply agenda-setting and framing theories, and/or emphasize the importance of discourse or rhetoric as analytical tools. Some scholars embrace, critique or build on a number of theories that originated in different academic specialties, including Habermas's understanding of communication in the public sphere (Byerly and Hill 2012), Bourdieu's field theory (Mady 2016), Foucault's analysis of power (Morrissey 2013) and post-colonial theory (Holmes 2014). Most usefully, more researchers have been using the concept of 'intersectionality' to examine diversity of all kinds (Meyers 2013; Morrissey 2013; Jiwani 2014). Meyers defines intersectionality as 'the complex and varied ways that gender, race, class and other markers of social identity are inextricably linked within a hierarchy of dominance'

(2013, 2), thereby shaping how African-American women and their issues, for example, are depicted in the news media.

A number of scholars, adopting critical approaches from political economy and critical communication, have blamed the absence or misrepresentation of women in the news on the ongoing masculine domination of media ownership and journalism culture that is still prevalent in this era of globalization (Byerly 2014; Gallagher 2014; 2010). Other media scholars, whose approach is essentially liberal, are more interested in seeing women attain equality within the capitalist system, which they regard as their right as citizens. Consequently, much of that research deals with the status of women in the professions and public life, such as journalists and politicians, and the interplay among them (Evanbach 2013; Barker-Plummer 2010). One related area centres on the lack of female representation, such as quoted experts and authoritative sources, in the news and other media forms (Armstrong 2013). Technically the absence of female voices, including those of media workers, may not be a human rights issue in the legislative sense, except perhaps in government-regulated broadcasting. However, it does speak to lack of recognition of women, their abilities, their concerns and their contributions as citizens, which in turn 'diminishes democracy' in those countries that espouse it (Ross and Carter 2011, 1148). Lack of female representation in the news also has a detrimental effect on women living in countries under political systems other than democracy. In Uganda, for example, a recent study demonstrated that female farmers come third after men and anonymous sources in two major newspapers citing authoritative voices on climate change, an essentially dismissive attitude that ignores these women's expertise and well-being (Semujju 2015).

Major differences in international cultures have a definite impact on female journalists in their own countries and the kinds of women's rights stories they can cover (Byerly 2013a; International Women's Media Foundation 2011). In Lebanon, for example, the media system is tied to fundamental political-religious divisions, so that even the most skilled women must negotiate their place as news anchors, reporters and senior editors, and carry out their assignments carefully, within those parameters. Despite the fact that they now cover most of the stories that men do – including bombings – they are still working within a society that allows women few legal or policy protections from gender discrimination (Melki and Mallat 2016; Mady 2016).

The media's portrayal and interpretation of women's rights activism as a social movement, and the interactions between feminist advocates and female journalists have inspired a great deal of academic scrutiny (Dow 2014; Evenbach 2013; Byerly 2013b; Minić 2013, 2014; Freeman 2011). Mendes (2011), for example, uses critical discourse and content analyses from a socialist feminist perspective to examine the British and American press coverage of the mid-20th century 'second wave' and the more recent 'third wave' of the women's movement in those countries. Her case study demonstrates that the news was more positive than one might assume, but was also contained within the parameters of liberal feminism and traditional journalism practice. Mendes argued that more radical media critiques of gender discrimination are needed to bring about far-reaching, systemic reforms. Some of the most promising research combines analysis of traditional and online media of such international protests as the anti-rape, SlutWalk movement in which young feminist activists took to the streets to insist on their right to be safe from sexual assault and from 'slut-shaming', regardless of what they chose to wear (Mendes 2015; Dow and Wood 2014).

Media coverage of 'third wave' feminism and its variants, including the highly-debated and varied meanings of 'post-feminism', has thus become another area of academic scrutiny and with good reason. As Scharff, Smith-Prei and Stehle (2016) explain in their introduction to a special issue of *Feminist Media Studies* on German feminists and digital media: 'Queer studies, intersectionality, and theories of feminists of colour have shaped discourses about gender and inequality and have disrupted white, hetero-centric, and often Western and middle-class feminism that sometimes fits all too neatly into neoliberal discourses of self-realisation, freedom, and success' (3). In Europe, a recent study shifted the focus to offline and online feminist alternative media, the ways they are organized and the gender rights topics they discuss, specifically their scope, stances and actions. The authors, Elke Zobl and Rosa Reitsamer (2014), conducted online surveys with audience members as well as interviews with a number of the media producers. They found that although the reach of these media is more global than that of their feminist press predecessors, and they prefer the term 'do it yourself' (DIY) to 'third wave' feminism, they present a 'discursive, interventionist space that is constantly renegotiated, reinvented and re-appropriated under neo-liberal social, cultural and economic circumstances' (242).

Historically and currently, women's rights movements have encouraged women around the world to take a more active role in public life, which has spurred many quantitative and qualitative studies of sexism in mainstream media coverage of the most prominent ones, especially politicians, who are exercising their equal rights to run for public office. In the US, even some of the most conservative female politicians are co-opting the term 'feminist', twisting it to suit their individual perspectives rather than acknowledge it as a social movement made up of many different variants of feminist thought (Loke, Bachmann and Harp 2015). Regardless of one's politics, being a female leader leaves one open to enhanced media scrutiny. In Australia, several examples of long form journalism; that is, essays and books, illustrate just how much the Opposition, the media and the public engaged in outright misogyny to attack the first female Prime Minister of that country, Julia Gillard of the Labour Party (S. Joseph 2015). In North America and the UK, media analysts see some improvements in media coverage of female politicians, but more subtle stereotypes or other forms of discrimination can still undermine them, even after they are elected, especially as politics become more personalized and political communication techniques advance (Ross 2014; Goodyear-Grant 2013; O'Neill, Savigny and Cann 2016; Campus 2013). Some crucial gender differences surface when academic studies compare media coverage of male and female politicians (Bystrom and Hennings 2013; Trimble et al. 2013; Ross and Comrie 2012; Valenzuala and Correa 2009), including those of minority backgrounds (Trimble et al. 2015). There is also a growing literature on media representations of female leaders in African countries, such as Nigeria, where journalists pay little attention to women and their issues, discouraging them from participating in the political process and running for public office (Omojola 2014).

Another critical area of research seeks to remedy colonialist assumptions about prominent and unknown Muslim women. Much of the western academic attention to date has focused on media representations of immigrants or 'foreigners' who are treated as threats to feminist and democratic values because they wear burkhas, hijabs or niqabs or, alternatively, don't fit the stereotype of the 'passive' victim at all (Posetti 2008; Jiwani 2010; Samie and Sertaç 2015). In nations, such as Turkey, that are engaged in a struggle between religious and secular values affecting all women, including media workers, the media image of a veiled woman can reinforce conservative government attitudes (Özcan 2015). In *Arab women in Arab News*, the authors ask what 'active' and 'passive' women look like in the context of Arabic media and culture (Al-Malki et al. 2012). 'We began to wonder what it might mean to call an Arab woman `active' when Western feminism was no longer the standard of judgment. And we began to wonder what it might mean to call an Arab woman `passive' when there was no Western myth in the background of a dark woman who is veiled, withdrawn, and silent' (xvii). Their findings are based on quantitative and qualitative analysis of English translations of print articles from mideast.wire.com – specifically from four, liberal pan-Arab publications. They found a spectrum of differences between elite, educated Arab women and the mostly silenced ones who still struggle against poverty and other ills. Aside from their media analysis, the latest research on gender and human rights helped the authors arrive at the subtleties of more precise representations of Arab women and assess the way forward for women's rights activists in their own countries and globally.

Moreover, in several Arab countries, feminist activists have related in interviews how they have taken to cyber-feminist media to champion women's rights. According to Khamis (2014), the gender-specific issues there concern 'women's struggle to gain political and social gains despite many challenges, such as reactionary social forces, the rise of political Islam, the imposition of a top-down *cosmetic feminism*, which only serves those in power, and an *unsafe public space,* which poses the risk of rape, humiliation and harassment' (Khamis' emphases, 565).

A great deal of scholarly effort has been dedicated to another one of the other key concerns of the women's movement worldwide: sexual and other forms of violence against women and girls, with the exception of genital cutting, as the media have paid little attention to the practice overall, despite the United Nations' policies against it (Sobel 2015b). Media analysis of assault has become a sub-field in itself, and is gradually expanding to examine 'gender' rather than 'women', as well as intersections of race and class, in the murder, battering, rape, sexual harassment and sex trafficking of women, including trans-women, and girls. In most cases, the news media treat these assaults as sensational crimes and indulge in various forms of victim-blaming rather than investigate the responsibilities of the men who attack and violate women – the exception being convicted criminals (Meyers 2013; Cuklanz 2014; Cuklantz and Moorti 2009; Johnson, Frieman and Shafer 2014; Sela-Shayovitz 2015; Barnett 2016; Sobel 2015a; Jiwani 2014). Since the time when Helen Benedict (1992) proposed ethical reporting guidelines for reporters covering sex crimes, some scholars have introduced a general concept of an 'ethic of care' that Steiner and Okrusch (2006) once argued 'is less about radically changing journalists' behaviour than revising journalism mythology in ways that give them permission and validation to do what they, as human beings, already may want to do and even try to do—to care about problems and to acknowledge that they care that their work has impact, and produces caring responses and actions' (115). So, in cases of assault, reporters could use such an ethic of care when covering the crime and the court proceedings, fostering better outcomes for the complainant, the accused and their communities (Freeman 2016; Fullerton and Patterson 2016; 2006). Similarly, posing 'ethic of care' research questions could help journalism studies scholars assess media coverage of crimes against women and girls to determine how well journalists respected the rights of both complainant and defendant, and the role the community played in this process.

While sexual assault is still a danger for women everywhere, they can be especially vulnerable when their appearance and behaviour, while technically legal, is counter to heterosexual community norms. Then the crime becomes a 'weapon of hate', according to Morrissey (2013, 88), who has explored how media rhetoric plays into community rationales for the rapes of Black lesbians in South Africa. Morrissey provides a short list of available news and opinion articles, human rights reports and a documentary film to illustrate her case. Judging from the relative dearth of her empirical evidence from the mainstream media, journalists have virtually ignored this devastating practice in a country where LGBT people supposedly have legal civil rights, but are targeted by rapists if they are a Black and a lesbian to 'correct' their sexual orientation. This study suggests that reporters should pay more attention to these crimes, and, I would add, avoid using the term 'corrective' rape without quotation marks because that phrase implies that lesbian sexuality is deviant, thereby contributing to the problematic semantics that seemingly justify the assaults in the first place. Scholars should similarly be wary of adopting such loaded expressions in their media analyses without questioning them.

Internationally, sex trafficking is a major human rights issue that affects mostly women and girls. In North America, according to Johnston, Friedman and Sobel (2015), the media still frame sex trafficking as a crime first, and then as a legislative or public policy issue, both domestically and abroad. When media framing focuses on human rights instead, it more often includes the perspectives of survivors, many of them minors, and their advocates who want to put an end to the practice. As these authors argue, 'Human rights are legal rights but are also viewed more as natural and universal, which greatly differ from crime and legislative focuses. For this reason, human rights frames may arguably promote shared responsibility for an issue' and more closely pinpoint related causes of sex trafficking such as the economic downside of globalization or the disruptive effects of war and natural disasters (Johnston, Friedman and Sobel 2015, 250). Another research area relating to violence against women is the situation of those in countries at war, during which the human rights for most people are suspended in the first place. Now we are beginning to see more interdisciplinary studies that give the women in war-torn countries a great deal of agency in how they deal with violence and death even as they suffer from them. Holmes' (2014) study of media coverage of the women of Rwanda and eastern Democratic Republic of Congo, and the ways in which political and local female actors tried to influence it, is a case in point. Using textual and verbal discourse analysis, Holmes examined BBC news and documentary programming between 1994–2010 that, she argued, presented these African women as silent and passive victims of violence, including rape, and murder. She also analysed extremist Hutu propaganda leading up to the 1994 murder of the Tutsis in Rwanda, British and American media coverage of the systematic rapes in the Congo and the war propaganda produced there and in Rwanda at the time. These rapes, she argues, were so disruptive to the community and to the health of the women that they constituted 'genocide by attrition' (222–26). To put her findings into further context, Holmes interviewed 34 individuals, including media workers, government officials and workers with human rights groups, NGOs and African women's organizations. Her study not only challenges western media coverage of African women but media researchers who tend to miscast them solely as victims rather than as women who used what little agency they had at the time to become resistance leaders, or perpetrators of violence, or both. It is a tough-minded study, but one that suggests that some feminist media analyses of women in war can also be simplistic or misguided in their quest to castigate patriarchal and colonialist western media without addressing the perspectives, experiences and actions of the women who have tried to survive these wars.

Denying women their basic human rights in war or in peacetime to the point where they suffer, not just from physical, emotional and sexual abuse, but from ill health, poverty and other dangers is another form of violence against them. In their ground-breaking analysis of media coverage of women's rights in India, A. Joseph and Sharma (2006) explored how English and regional Indian language newspapers, periodicals and magazines covered contentious practices that have a major impact on women's lives: dowry deaths, rape, spousal maintenance after divorce, women's rights under religious and personal laws, fetal sex selection and the officially outlawed practice of *sati*; that is, the deaths of widows on their husband's funeral pyres. Through an analysis of the content and placement of these stories, the authors concluded that coverage of women's issues in India was improving, partly through the efforts of the women's movement, and there was less blatant sexism in the language of the news. The future for mainstream coverage of women's issues became less promising, however, due to increased commercialization of the media, the growing reluctance of female journalists to be identified as feminists, and fewer women's movement campaigns in favour of contentious, events-oriented issues (A. Joseph and Sharma 2006, postscript, 348–57; A. Joseph 2014).

But again, social media may make some difference in how women's issues are kept in the spotlight, depending on access to it. In the aftermath of the 2012 New Delhi gang rape and murder of a young woman on a bus, which made headlines around the world, Poell and

Rajagopalan (2015) analysed Twitter feeds from a base of over a million tweets in national and international media and interviewed 15 participants (272–73). They found that Twitter is an important platform that helped journalists, women's groups and activists from India and other countries connect with each other, keeping the crime in the news longer than in conventional media. Its overall effect was diminished, however, because Internet use in India is limited, and it is mostly male, middle-class, urban and English-speaking users who have access to Twitter (Poell and Rajagopalan, 730).

Despite the appreciable scholarship on women's human rights in journalism studies, there are still a number of research gaps and more expansive ways to approach them. More intersectional, comparative, global scholarship is needed on any number of women's issues, but with harder questions challenging the established theories and the standard, methodological ways of gathering historical and contemporary evidence. The strengths of the studies cited here aside, there is far too much reliance on a limited number of mainstream media, especially the most prominent publications and broadcasters that do not necessarily reflect the concerns or diversity of the women throughout the country, or the world. A new direction will entail venturing well beyond the mainstream media whose news archives are fairly accessible, to regional publications, alternative media or other sources that might still be on microfilm or in a box in an archive, rather than on the Internet, or simply a little more difficult to find. In fact, one of the reasons western journalism studies tend to focus on middle-class women and their issues in the news is that those are the stories that mainstream journalists cover and therefore, the media research sources that come most easily to hand. The same is true of studies from other countries as well, even though they are now paying attention to media disseminated in the different languages of those regions, rather than the somewhat elite English language press, a welcome sign that the field has become less westernised and more diverse.

There are also a number of unanswered research questions about women's human rights in journalism studies and more expansive ways to approach them, particularly through intersectional theories, a research ethic of care and an appreciation of the agency of women as media subjects; for example: the role of unions and professional associations in hindering or helping women journalists in all their diversity to attain newsroom equality; the importance of political communication strategies in how the media cover female political leaders and their human rights goals; more attention to the advocacy roles of the women who work with NGOs everywhere and their relationships with journalists; and media coverage, or lack of it, of indigenous women and others worldwide who have suffered poverty, ill health and death because of discrimination based on gender, race, religion, class and caste among other reasons. In the meantime, researchers should continue to monitor and report on the global media (Global Media Monitoring Project 2015) because lack of attention to women's human rights cannot be rectified without a concerted effort, including activists' interventions. In Canada, for example, a feminist organization, Informed Opinions, is conducting its own research to impress upon the media the importance of using women as primary news sources and as commentators, and to persuade knowledgeable women that their expertise is valuable to journalists ((http://www.informedopinions.org/; Morris 2016). After all, our role is to challenge the news media as well as study it when it comes to human rights for women around the world.

References

Al-Malki, A., Kaufer, D., Ishizaki, S. and Dreher, K. (2012). *Arab Women in Arab News: Old Stereotypes and New Media*. London: Bloomsbury Academic.

Armstrong, C. L. ed. (2013). *Media Disparity: A Gender Battleground*. Lanham: Lexington Books.

Barker-Plummer, B. (2010). 'News and Feminism: A Historic Dialog'. *Journalism and Communication Monographs.* Association for Education in Journalism and Mass Communication.

Barnett, B. (2016). 'Dividing Women: The Framing of Trafficking for Sexual Exploitation in Magazines'. *Feminist Media Studies*, 16(2), pp. 205–22.

Benedict, H. (1992). *Virgin or Vamp? How the Media Cover Sex Crimes.* New York: Oxford University Press.

Byerly, C. M. (2014). 'Women and Media Control: Feminist Interrogation at the Macro-level'. In: C. Carter, L. Steiner and L. McLaughlin, eds., *The Routledge Companion to Media and Gender*, pp. 105–15.

Byerly, C. M. (2013a). 'Factor Affecting the Status of Journalists: A Structural Analysis'. In: C. M. Byerly, ed., *The Palgrave International Handbook of Women and Journalism*, pp. 11–23.

Byerly, C. M. (2013b). 'Media and Public Discourse: the Limits of Feminist Influence'. In: C. L. Armstrong, ed., *Media Disparity*, pp. 207–16.

Byerly, C. M. and Hill, M. (2012). Reformulation Theory: Gauging Feminist Impact on News of Violence against Women'. *Journal of Research on Women and Gender*, 3(2), pp. 1–20. Available at: https://digital.library.txstate.edu/handle/10877/4494 [Accessed 9 Mar. 2016].

Bystrom, D. G. and Hennings, V. M. (2013). 'Newspaper Coverage of Women Running for the US Senate in 2012: Evidence of an Increasingly Level Playing Field?' In: C. L. Armstrong, ed., *Media Disparity*, pp. 55–70.

Campus, D. (2013). *Women Political Leaders and the Media.* Hampshire, UK: Palgrave MacMillan.

Carter, C., Steiner, L. and McLaughlin, L. eds.(2014). The Routledge Companion to Media and Gender. London: Routledge eBook Collection (EBSCOhost), EBSCO*host*, viewed 10 Feb., 2016.

Cuklanz, L. (2014). 'Mass Media Representation of Gendered Violence'. In: C. Carter, L. Steiner and L. McLaughlin, eds., *The Routledge Companion to Media and Gender*, pp. 86–98.

Cuklanz, L. and Moorti, S. eds. (2009). *Local Violence, Global Media: Feminist Analyses of Gendered Representations.* New York: Peter Lang.

Dow, B. J. (2014). *Watching Women's Liberation 1970: Feminism's Pivotal Year on the Network News.* Urbana, Chicago and Springfield: University of Illinois Press.

Dow, B. J. and Wood, J. T. (2014). 'Repeating History and Learning From It: What Can SlutWalks Teach Us About Feminism?' *Women's Studies in Communication*, 37(1), pp. 22–43.

Everbach, T. (2013). 'Women's (Mis)Representation in News Media'. In: C. L. Armstrong, ed., *Media Disparity*, pp. 15–26.

Freeman, B. M. (2016). '"Did She Consent to *This* Sex Act with T*his* Accused?" The News Media, Sexual Assault Myths and the Complainant's Private Records in Court Testimony'. In: C. Richardson and R. Fullerton, eds., *Covering Canadian Crime: What Journalists Should Know and the Public Should Question.* Toronto: University of Toronto Press, pp. 156–181.

Freeman, B. M. (2011). *Beyond Bylines: Media Workers and Women's Rights in Canada.* Kitchener-Waterloo, ON: Wilfrid Laurier University Press.

Fullerton, R. and Patterson, M. (2016). 'Not Naming Names? Crime-Coverage in Canada, Sweden and the Netherlands'. In: C. Richardson and R. Fullerton, eds., *Covering Canadian Crime: What Journalists Should Know and the Public Should Question.* Toronto: University of Toronto Press, pp. 70–99.

Fullerton, R. and Patterson, M. (2006). 'Murder in Our Midst: Expanding Coverage to Include Care and Responsibility'. *Journal of Mass Media Ethics*, 21(4), pp. 304–21.

Gallagher, M. (2014). 'Media and the Representation of Gender'. In: C. Carter, L. Steiner and L. McLaughlin, eds., *The Routledge Companion to Media and Gender*, pp. 73–85.

Gallagher, M. (2010). Foreword. *Who Makes the News? Global Media Monitoring Project.* World Association for Christian Communication. Available at http://pages.cmns.sfu.ca/kathleen-cross/files/2010/11/GMMP-global.pdf. [Accessed 5 Feb. 2016].

Global Media Monitoring Project (GMMP) (2015). *Who Makes the News?* World Association for Christian Communication. Available at http://whomakesthenews.org/gmmp/gmmp-reports/gmmp-2015-reports. [Accessed 5 Feb. 2016].

Global Media Monitoring Project (GMMP), 2010. *Who Makes the News?* World Association for Christian Communication. Available at http://pages.cmns.sfu.ca/kathleen-cross/files/2010/11/GMMP-global.pdf. [Accessed 5 Feb. 2016].

Goodyear-Grant, E. (2013). *Gendered News: Media Coverage and Electoral Politics in Canada.* Vancouver: UBC Press.

Harp, D., Loke, J. and Bachmann, I. (2011). 'More of the Same Old Story? Women, War and News in *Time* Magazine'. *Women's Studies in Communication*, 34(2), pp. 202–121.

Holmes, G. (2014). *Women and War in Rwanda. Gender, Media and the Representation of Genocide.* New York: I.B. Tauris & Co.

International Women's Media Foundation (2011). *Global Report on the Status of Women in the News Media.* Washington, D.C. Carolyn M. Byerly, principal investigator. Retrieved from: http://iwmf.org/pdfs/ IWMF-Global-Report-Summary.pdf. [Accessed 5 Feb. 2016].

Jiwani,Y. (2014). 'Rape and Race in the Canadian Press: Reproducing the Moral Order'. *Arts and Social Science Journal*, Special Issue, S:1:1–9. Available at: http://astonjournals.com/manuscripts/Vol_5_2014/ASSJ_ S1_2014_rape-and-race-in-the-canadian-press-reproducing-the-moral-order-2151-6200-S1-009.pdf [Accessed 8 Mar. 2016].

Jiwani, Y. (2010). 'Doubling Discourses and the Veiled Other: Mediations of Race and Gender in Canadian Media'. In: S. Razack, M. Smith and S. Thobani, eds., *States of Race.* Toronto: Between the Lines Press, pp. 59–86.

Johnston, A., Friedman, B. and Sobel, M. (2015). 'Framing an Emerging Issue: How US Print and Broadcast News Media Covered Sex Trafficking, 2008-2012.' *Journal of Human Trafficking*, 1(3), pp. 235–54.

Johnston, A., Friedman, B. and Shafer, A. (2014). 'Framing the Problem of Sex Trafficking: Whose Problem? What Remedy?' *Feminist Media Studies*, 14(3), pp. 419–36.

Joseph, A. (2013). 'India: What You See Is Not What You Get'. In: C.M. Byerly, ed., *The Palgrave International Handbook of Women and Journalism*, pp. 384–403.

Joseph, A. and Sharma, K. (2006). *Whose News? The Media and Women's Issues*, 2nd ed. Palgrave: New Delhi/Thousand Oaks/London.

Joseph, S. (2015). 'Australia's First Female Prime Minister and Gender Politics'. *Journalism Practice*, 9(2), pp. 250–64, doi:10.1080/17512786.2014.924732

Khamis, S. (2014). 'Arab Women Journalists/Activists, "Cyberfeminists"' and the Sociopolitical Revolution'. In: C. Carter, L. Steiner and L. McLaughlin, eds. *The Routledge Companion to Media and Gender*, pp. 565–75.

LaRue, F., Haraszti, M., Botero, C. and Tlakula, F. P. (2010). *Tenth Anniversary Joint Declaration: Ten Key Challenges to Freedom of Expression in the Next Decade.* Available at: http://www.article19.org/pdfs/stand-ards/tenth-anniversary-joint-declaration-ten-key-challenges-to-freedom-of-express.pdf. [Accessed 5 Feb. 2016].

Loke, J., Bachmann, I. and Harp, D. (2015). 'Co-opting Feminism: Media Discourses on Political Women and the Definition of a (new) Feminist Identity'. *Media, Culture & Society*, 24 Sept. DOI:10.1177/0163443715604890 Available at: https://www.researchgate.net/publication/282414975_ Co-opting_feminism_media_discourses_on_political_women_and_the_definition_of_a_new_feminist_ identity. [Accessed 3 Feb. 2016].

Mady, C. (2016). *The Status of Women News Journalists in Lebanese Television: A Field-Gender Approach.* Unpublished Ph.D. dissertation, Carleton University, Ottawa, Canada.

Melki, J. and Mallat, S. (2016). 'Block Her Entry, Keep Her Down and Push Her Out: Gender Discrimi-nation and Women Journalists in the Arab World'. *Journalism Studies*, 17(1), pp. 57–79.

Mendes, K. (2011). *Feminism in the News: Representations of the Women's Movement Since the 1960s.* New York: Palgrave MacMillan.

Mendes, K. (2015). *SlutWalk: Feminism, Activism and Media.* New York: Palgrave MacMillan.

Meyers. M. (2013). *African American Women in the News: Gender, Race and Class in Journalism.* New York: Routledge Taylor and Francis.

Minić, D. (2014). 'Feminist Publicist Strategies: Women's NGOs' Media Activism and Television Journalism in Serbia and Croatia'. *Media, Culture and Society*, 36(2), pp. 133–49.

Minić, D. (2013). 'Between Politics and Profession: The Scope of Feminist Journalism in Serbia and Croatia'. *Journalism Practice*, 7(5), pp. 620–35.

Morris, M. (2016). *Gender of Sources Used in Major Canadian Media.* Ottawa, Canada: Informed Opinions. Available at http://www.informedopinions.org. [Accessed Mar. 2016.]

Morrissey, M. E. (2013). 'Rape as a Weapon of Hate: Discursive Constructions and Material Consequences of Black Lesbianism in South Africa'. *Women's Studies in Communication*, 36(1), pp. 72–91.

Omojola, O. ed. (2014). *Women's Political Visibility and Media Access: the Case of Nigeria.* Newcastle upon Tyne, UK: Cambridge Scholars Publishing.

O'Neill, D., Savigny, S. and Cann, V. (2016). 'Women Politicians in the UK Press: Not Seen and Not Heard?' *Feminist Media Studies*, 16(2), pp. 293–307.

Özcan, E. (2015). 'Women's Headscarves in News Photographs: A Comparison Between the Secular and Islamic Press during the AKP Government in Turkey'. *European Journal of Communication*, 30(6), pp. 698–713.

Poell, T. and Rajagopalan, S. (2015). 'Connecting Activists and Journalists: Twitter in the Aftermath of the 2012 New Delhi Rape'. *Journalism Studies*, 16(5), pp. 719–33.

Posetti, J. (2008). 'Unveiling Radio Coverage of Muslim Women'. *The Radio Journal – International Studies in Broadcast and Audio Media*, 6(2–3): pp. 161–77.

Richardson, C. and Fullerton, R. eds. (2016). *Covering Canadian Crime: What Journalists Should Know and the Public Should Question*. Toronto: University of Toronto Press.

Ross, K. (2014). 'A Nice Bit of Skirt and the Talking Head: Sex, Politics and News'. In: C. Carter, L. Steiner and L. McLaughlin, eds., *The Routledge Companion to Media and Gender*, pp. 290–99.

Ross, K. and Comrie, M. (2012). 'The Rules of the Leadership Game: Gender, Politics and News'. *Journalism*, 13(8), pp. 969–84.

Ross, K. and Carter, C. (2011). 'Women and News: A Long and Winding Road'. *Media Culture and Society*, 33(8), pp. 1146–65.

Samie, S. F. and Sertaç, S. (2015). 'Strange, Incompetent and Out-Of-Place: Media, Muslim Sportswomen and London 2012'. *Feminist Media Studies*, 15(3), pp. 363–81.

Scharff, C., Smith-Prei, C. and Stehle, M. (2016). 'Digital Feminism: Transnational Activism in German Protest Cultures'. *Feminist Media Studies*, 16(1), pp. 1–16.

Sela-Shayovitz, R. (2015). '"They Are All Good Boys." The Role of the Israeli Media in the Social Construction of Gang Rape'. *Feminist Media Studies*, 15(3), pp. 411–28.

Semujju, B. (2015). 'Frontline Farmers, Backline Sources: Women as a Tertiary Voice in Climate Change Coverage'. *Feminist Media Studies*, 15(4), pp. 658–74.

Sobel, M. (2015a). 'Confronting Sex Trafficking: Gender Depictions in Newspaper Coverage from the Former Soviet Republics and the Baltic States'. *European Journal of Communication* (29 October), pp. 1–17. Available at: http://ejc.sagepub.com/content/early/recent [Accessed 5 Mar. 2016].

Sobel, M. (2015b). 'Female Genital Cutting in the News Media: A Content Analysis'. *International Communication Gazette*, 77(4), pp. 384–405.

Steiner, L. and Okrusch, C. (2006). 'Care as a Virtue for Journalists'. *Journal Of Mass Media Ethics*, 21(2/3), pp. 102–22.

Trimble, L., Raphael. D., Sampert, S., Wagner, A. and Gerrits, B. (2013). 'Is It Personal? Gendered Mediation in Newspaper Coverage of the Canadian National Party Leadership Contests, 1975-2012'. *The International Journal of Press/Politics*, 18(4), pp. 462–81.

Trimble, L., Raphael. D., Sampert, S., and Wagner, A. (2015). 'Politicizing Bodies: Hegemonic Masculinity, Heteronormativity. and Racism in News Representations of Canadian Political Party Leadership Candidates'. *Women's Studies in Communication*, 38(3), pp. 314–30.

Valenzuala, S. and Correa, T. (2009). 'Press Coverage and Public Opinion on Women Candidates: The Case of Chile's Michelle Bachelet'. *International Communications Gazette*, 71(3), pp. 203–23.

Zobl, E. and Reitsamer, R. (2014). 'Gender and Media Activism: Alternative Feminist Media in Europe'. In: C. Carter, L. Steiner and L. McLaughlin, eds., *The Routledge Companion to Media and Gender*, London and New York: Routledge, pp. 233–44.

39

NEWS COVERAGE OF FEMALE GENITAL CUTTING

A seven country comparative study

Meghan Sobel

Female genital cutting (FGC), also referred to as 'female genital mutilation' or 'female circumcision', is a practice believed to occur in 29 African countries, various middle-eastern nations, India, Indonesia, Malaysia, Pakistan, Sri Lanka, certain communities in South America and various diaspora populations around the globe (UNFPA 2015). FGC, the 'partial or total removal of the external female genitalia' (UNFPA 2015), is estimated to have been performed on more than 100 million girls (Wade 2011). Such procedures can be 'permanent, sometimes extensive, and often debilitating' (WHO 2013). FGC procedures are typically, though not always, performed at or before puberty, giving the girl minimal ability to consent (Wade 2011). Additionally, severe health consequences have been reported as a result of the procedure, specifically when performed in unhygienic environments, with contaminated tools and/or by an unskilled practitioner (often a village elder) (Wade 2011).

Public health, legal, human rights and international development scholars have analysed where, how and why FGC occurs, as well as an array of eradication campaigns and legislation (Banasik 2015; Cloward 2015; Morris 2006). However, relatively little scholarly attention has been given to news media representations of the issue, despite the pervasiveness of the issue and the array of critics who claim that media outlets have overlooked or sensationalised the issue (Khazaleh 2010). Given the documented ability for media to mold public discourse and impact foreign policy decisions (Gilboa 2003; Piers 2002), the time is ripe to analyse how news media frame FGC.

Female genital cutting

Before diving into the relationship between news media and FGC, it is worthwhile to discuss what FGC is and why it occurs. The topic of FGC is controversial, with debate surrounding the scope of the issue, how best to stop it, and whether to stop it at all. Even the terminology of the practice has been a topic of debate. Some believe that the phrase 'female circumcision' most accurately depicts the process, but others argue that such diction is inadequate and should be replaced with 'female mutilation' to more accurately portray the brutal human rights violation that is occurring (Wade 2011). Yet, others contend that using the term 'mutilation' is ethnocentric and imperialist (Wade 2011). This chapter will use the term female genital cutting (FGC) to refer to the physical act of cutting.

FGC is largely considered a cultural ritual, and in many communities where it is practiced, it is seen as the gateway into womanhood and marriage (WHO 2013). While FGC is not explicitly proclaimed in any religious script, advocates of the practice often state that it is rooted in religious customs (WHO 2013). FGC is frequently driven by local beliefs regarding proper sexual behaviour. FGC is believed to reduce a woman's libido, in turn, reducing her desire for sexual activity and ensuring premarital virginity and loyalty to her husband (WHO 2013).

Literature on FGC largely focuses on two key positions: one that views FGC as a feminist issue and a human rights abuse, and the other that views FGC as a misunderstood and improperly criticised cultural practice. Those that view FGC as a feminist and human rights issue claim that the act is another example of how women across the world are united by patriarchy (Morgan 1984). Advocates of this position began using the term 'female genital mutilation' to describe what they understood as the embodiment of gendered oppression (Boyle 2002; Wade 2011). On the other hand, advocates of the second position claim that understanding FGC as gendered oppression and a human rights abuse are Western culturally imperialist narratives that negatively characterize people in communities that practice FGC (Njambi 2004). Supporters of this cause posit that anti-FGC laws and eradication campaigns reproduce ideas of US superiority and do little to actually protect vulnerable girls (rather, they are shamed and punished) (Piot 2007). It is argued, that such narratives oversimplify the social, cultural and economic causes that surround FGC and highlight the most extreme cases and health consequences instead of attempting to understand the multitude of complexities surrounding the practice (Obiora 2005).

Despite the two distinct positions on the issue, international organizations have increasingly turned their attention to combatting FGC. Following the 2000 United Nations Millennium Summit and the adoption of the United Nations Millennium Declaration, eight international development goals were created with the aim of being achieved by 2015, named the Millennium Development Goals (MDGs): eradicate extreme poverty and hunger; achieve universal primary education; promote gender equality and empower women; reduce child mortality rates; improve maternal health; combat HIV/AIDS, malaria, and other diseases; ensure environmental sustainability; and develop a global partnership for development (United Nations 2000). Scholars argued that the practice of FGC was a threat to the achievement of multiple MDGs (Tall 2007). In 2015, achievement of the MDGs was uneven, which resulted in the creation of a new set of 17 Sustainable Development Goals (SDGs), which continue the aims of the MDGs (UNDP 2015). Possibly as a result of the increase in international attention directed at FGC, media coverage of the topic has received heavy criticism.

Media coverage of FGC

Media representations of FGC are accused of gross embellishment, serving the function of titillating Western audiences with grisly stories about African men's sexual domination over women (Njamb, 2004; Walley 1997). While it is difficult to speak to the accuracy of such criticisms because scholarly attention to media coverage of FGC is in its infancy, two studies empirically analysed media representations of the issue.

Wade (2009) analysed newspaper coverage of FGC in the context of representations of traditional versus modern women and determined that newspapers used the issue to trivialise the oppressions of US women and simultaneously denigrate non-Western cultures. More recently, a 2015 content analysis of 15 years of newspaper coverage of FGC in the US, Ghana, The Gambia and Kenya revealed that while coverage is minimal, it tends to frame the issue thematically and portrays it as a negative, cultural ritual (Sobel 2015). Both of these studies reveal media representations that perpetuate an anti-FGC narrative, which is consistent with the feminist/ human rights position previously discussed.

Framing

Media content is created and 'framed' in certain ways, so when aiming to understand the ways in which news stories about FGC support one position or another, it is worthwhile to examine how such stories are framed. Essentially, framing theory states that media focus an audience members' attention on certain aspects or events and place them within a field of meaning (McCombs & Shaw 1993). In doing so, the way in which the information is presented (the way that it is framed) influences the judgments and reactions that someone has to the content (Scheufele 2000).

Framing can be especially important in the context of social problems, as the media can define what are important issues. Entman (1993) suggests that frames have four key functions in regards to social problems: define the problem, diagnose causes, make moral judgments and suggest remedies. Based on how each story is framed, the public and policymakers can interpret and respond to the problem differently (Gilboa 2003; Piers 2002; Wiley 1997).

Given this power of media framing, the purpose of this study is to expand previous research examining how news stories frame the issue of FGC. Specifically, this study replicates Sobel's (2015) work, and takes it further by increasing the number of countries included and the time-frame analysed in order to answer the following questions:

RQ1: How has the amount of newspaper coverage of FGC changed over time with the increase in laws and initiatives combatting the practice?

RQ2: How does the framing of FGC in newspaper coverage vary by country with differing FGC ideologies and prevalence levels?

Method

Sample

This study expands on previous research that examined news media representations of FGC in nations where it is practiced at different prevalence levels and with diverse laws/guidelines regarding the practice. This study used quantitative content analysis to compare newspaper coverage of FGC in seven countries, focusing on the *New York Times* (United States), the *Ghanaian Chronicle* (Ghana), the *Daily Observer* (The Gambia), the *Daily Nation* (Kenya), *Daily News Egypt* (Egypt), *The Nigerian Tribune* (Nigeria) and *New Vision* (Uganda). The MDGs were among the first comprehensive anti-FGC initiatives, which placed the issue in a human rights framework. The timeframe for this study will, therefore, be 1 January, 1998, two years before the creation of the MDGs, through 31 December, 2015 to understand how news media representations of FGC changed throughout the lifecycle of the MDGs and into the 2015 creation of the SDGs.

Archives for the *Chronicle* and the *Daily Nation* were accessed through AllAfrica and all other archives were accessed through LexisNexis, using the search terms 'female circumcision', 'infibulation', 'excision', 'clitor(id)ectomy', or 'female genital' -'mutilation', -'cutting', - 'surgery', or -'operation.' Letters to the editor, opinion columns and book/ movie reviews were discarded, to leave only news stories remaining. Additionally, articles that only mentioned FGC briefly, rather than featuring it as the main focus of the story, were discarded. This resulted in 351 articles being analysed: 55 from *The New York Times,* 61 from the *Chronicle,* 68 from the *Daily Observer,* 103 from the *Daily Nation,* 30 from *Daily News,* 2 from *The Tribune* and 32 from *New Vision.*

This study design allows for conclusions to be drawn regarding how the prevalence level of FGC impacts coverage of the issue. All analysed countries have been categorized as a high, medium or low FGC prevalence country. The Gambia and Egypt represent countries with high prevalence levels of FGC, with 76–100 per cent of women 15–49 years old having been cut in each country (UNICEF 2013). Kenya and Nigeria have medium prevalence levels, with an estimated 27 per cent of women cut in both countries (UNICEF 2013). Ghana and Uganda each have low prevalence levels, with approximately 4 per cent and 1 per cent of women having been cut, respectively (UNICEF 2013). There are occasional occurrences of FGC in the US, albeit largely limited to immigrant populations, so it could be classified as a very low prevalence country, but it is included in this study largely for comparative purposes.

Each newspaper selected represents the most well established English-language newspaper with reliable archives in the respective country. Levels of press freedom and government censorship, as well as media ownership and journalistic functions, vary a great deal across these seven nations. Additionally, the histories and circulations of each paper vary. For example, The *Chronicle* has a circulation of more than 45,000, making it the largest private newspaper in Ghana ('Press reference: Ghana' 2010) yet the *Daily Nation* has a circulation of 205,000, making it not only the largest newspaper in Kenya, but also the largest in East Africa ('Daily Nation (Kenya)' 2011). However, despite the differences, each outlet represents a prominent English-language newspaper capable of informing citizens and policymakers about the issue of FGC in its respective country.

Variables

All articles were coded in accordance with Sobel's (2015) FGC study and Entman's (1993) four-part typology for classifying the functions of frames to determine how FGC was defined, what causes were suggested to explain why it occurs, where blame was placed and what remedies were suggested for bringing an end to the practice.

In order to first determine how the problem was defined, all articles were coded for the date of publication, name of publication, article headline and the presence of each of the following frames: a frame portraying FGC as a health problem, human rights abuse, cultural/societal ritual, an individual women's choice, or other frame. Additionally, articles were analysed for whether they directly mentioned the MDGs or SDGs, whether they portrayed FGC negatively, and whether they portrayed FGC as an isolated incident or recurring problem.

Second, all stories were analysed for whether any contributing factors (causes) for FGC occurring were present, and if so, whether those causes were social/cultural, an individual's choice/desire, pressure from family/significant other, government policy, and/or other. Next, all stories were coded for whether the article placed blame for the FGC occurring, and if so, whether the blame was placed on the local society/culture, the lack of protective legislation, the individual girl/woman, the family of the girl/woman, the person doing the cutting and/or elsewhere. Lastly, all stories were analysed for the presence of a remedy to end or lessen the practice, and if so, whether that remedy was increased punishments for the person doing the cutting, increased punishments for the family of the girl/woman, increased punishments for the girl/woman, policy changes, informational/awareness raising campaigns, promoting NGOs and social services, and/or other remedies.

Reliability

According to guidelines by Riffe, Lacy and Fico (2013), at 95 per cent agreement, inter-coder reliability was conducted between two trained coders on a randomly selected sample of

49 content units. Using Krippendorff's Alpha, intercoder reliability was achieved for each variable ranging from .82 to 1.0.

Findings

RQ1 asked how much coverage there was of FGC. A notable initial finding was that FGC is rarely reported on in any of the seven newspapers. The *Tribune* only featured two articles about FGC in the 18 years of coverage analysed and the *Nation* had the most articles with 103. Despite the *Nation* having the most FGC-focused stories, all seven newspapers featured small amounts of coverage given the 18-year timeframe. As Figure 39.1. demonstrates, FGC-focused articles in each publication were inconsistent across years. *New Vision* had a notable spike in coverage in 2010 and the *Chronicle,* the *Nation* and the *Observer* all featured sporadic increases throughout the analysed timeframe, however, none at the same time. Interestingly, *The New York Times* featured its highest level of FGC coverage in 1999 and since declined.

RQ2 asks about the framing of FGC-focused news stories. FGC was overwhelmingly reported on as a problem or negative/harmful practice, and, as such, lends support to the side of the debate that focuses on FGC as a human rights abuse. The *Daily Observer,* the *Chronicle, Daily News* and the *Tribune* all reported on it as a problem in 100 per cent of articles. Overall, 95.4 per cent of all articles discussed it as a problem. *The Nation* from Kenya most commonly reported on FGC positively, in 8.7 per cent of articles. The MDGs and SDGs were both rarely mentioned in the text. The *Nation* and the *Daily Observer* each mentioned the MDGs in one article and the *Chronicle* directly talked about them in four articles; the remaining three newspapers

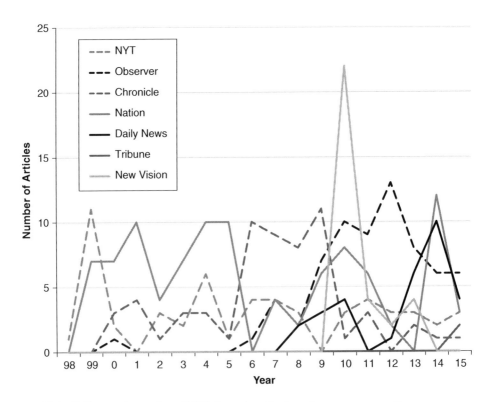

Figure 39.1   Differences in number of FGC-focused articles in each newspaper, over time

never mentioned the MDGs. The SDGs were only mentioned in one article from *Daily News*. In other words, while stories conveyed a human rights-based message by framing the issue negatively, formal human rights terminology (in terms of the MDGs and SDGs) was not used.

Next, FGC was dominantly reported on as a recurring incident, with 89.2 per cent of all analysed articles describing it as a practice that happens to multiple girls, occurs in different regions, and/or continually happens over time. The *Tribune* and the *Daily Observer* both exclusively reportedly on FGC as recurring. On the other hand, 23.3 per cent of *Daily News* and 18.2 per cent of *New York Times* articles presented FGC as an isolated incident. The other three news outlets featured between 1.6 and 15.5 per cent of articles depicting the practice as a one-time event.

Furthermore, as Table 39.1 data demonstrate, cultural practice was the most commonly used frame in the FGC coverage analysed. More than 50 per cent of articles used a cultural practice frame, compared with 22.8 per cent using a health concern frame, 29.6 featuring a human rights violation frame, 2.6 per cent demonstrating an individual choice frame and 5.4 per cent of "other" frames.

When considering the dominant topic frames present in coverage, between-paper differences emerged. *Daily News* featured a higher per centage of health concern frames than any other frame and the *Chronicle* featured almost equivalent amounts of human rights and cultural practice frames. Interestingly, the *Tribune* had exactly the same amount of stories with health concern, human rights and cultural practice frames, all of which lend themselves to anti-FGC perspectives. *New Vision* used individual choice frames more than any of the other papers, and it did so in almost 10 per cent of articles, followed closely by the *New York Times*. The presence of individual choice frames would likely be at odds with an anti-FGC position. Table 39.2

Table 39.1 Differences in presence of frames, by publication (%)

	NYT	Observer	Chronicle	Nation	Daily News	Tribune	New Vision	Total
	N = 55	N = 68	N = 61	N = 103	N = 30	N = 2	N = 32	N = 351
Differences in presence of health concern frame by publication (%). $X^2 = 20.34, 6\ d.f., p < 0.01$								
Presence	23.6	36.8	24.6	13.6	33.3	50	6.3	22.8
Differences in presence of human rights violation frame by publication (%). $X^2 = 9.51, 6\ d.f., n.s.$								
Presence	36.4	20.6	39.3	24.3	26.7	50	37.5	29.6
Differences in presence of cultural practice frame by publication (%). $X^2 = 41.24, 6\ d.f., p < .01$								
Presence	58.2	50	41	76.7	23.3	50	37.5	54.1
Differences in presence of individual choice frame by publication (%). $X^2 = 20.87, 6\ d.f., p < .01$								
Presence	9.1	0	1.6	0.0	0.0	0.0	9.4	2.6
Differences in presence of "other" frame by publication (%). $X^2 = 24.41, 6\ d.f., p < .01$								
Presence	1.8	2.9	0.0	4.9	16.7	0.0	18.8	5.4

Note: Columns do not sum to 100 as articles could feature more than one type of frame.

Table 39.2 Differences in presence of suggested cause, by publication (%)

	NYT	Observer	Chronicle	Nation	Daily News	Tribune	New Vision	Total
	N = 55	N = 68	N = 61	N = 103	N = 30	N = 2	N = 32	N = 351
Differences in presence of cause by publication (%). $X^2 = 29.29, 6\ d.f., p < 0.01$								
Presence	78.2	55.9	49.2	73.8	43.3	0.0	43.8	61
Differences in presence of cultural cause by publication (%). $X^2 = 36.284, 6\ d.f., p < 0.01$								
Presence	76.4	51.5	44.3	68.9	26.7	0.0	40.6	55.8
Differences in presence of individual desire cause by publication (%). $X^2 = 30.16, 6\ d.f., p < 0.01$								
Presence	0.0	0.0	0.0	0.0	0.0	0.0	9.4	0.9
Differences in presence of family cause by publication (%). $X^2 = 21.26, 6\ d.f., p < 0.01$								
Presence	10.9	8.8	1.6	21.4	13.3	0.0	0.0	11.1
Differences in presence of policy/legislation cause by publication (%). $X^2 = 10.42, 6\ d.f., n.s.$								
Presence	7.3	0.0	3.3	1	0.0	0.0	6.3	2.6

Note: Two articles reported other causes, and were not statistically significant.

demonstrates that approximately two-thirds of all articles mentioned a cause. The *New York Times* mentioned causes the most, in 78 per cent of articles. The *Daily Observer*, the *Chronicle*, *Daily News* and *New Vision* each discussed causes in approximately half of the stories; the *Tribune* did not discuss causes in either of its articles. Of the stories that did mention a cause, all newspapers overwhelmingly reported the causes of FGM to be cultural rituals, with the *New York Times* doing so most commonly in more than three-quarters of articles. Family causes were the next most frequently mentioned, followed by policy/legislation causes, but both were used much less regularly than cultural causes. As shown in Table 39.3, overall, less than 40 per cent of all stories placed any blame for the FGM occurring. However, clear differences emerged between newspapers. The *Nation* placed blame in more than 70 per cent of articles and the *New York Times* did so in almost half, compared to the other five newspapers which each only placed blame in 0 to 20 per cent of stories. The *New York Times* and the *Nation* both placed blame on cultural rituals the most. Neither *Daily News* nor the *Tribune* featured any articles that placed the blame on cultural traditions. The *Daily Observer* and the *Chronicle* featured more articles placing blame on the immediate family of the girls. Interestingly, *New Vision* and *Daily News* both blamed cutter more than anyone or anything else. When considering the remedies that were presented, 69.2 per cent of all articles suggested some remedy to eliminate or reduce the prevalence of FGC. The *Nation*, *Tribune* and the *New York Times* most commonly suggested remedies, in 73.8, 100 and 78.2 per cent of articles, respectively. *New Vision* and *Daily News* did so the least, in 59.4 and 53.3 per cent of stories, respectively. Of articles that did suggest a remedy, the most proposed remedy overall

Table 39.3 Differences in presence of blame placed, by publication (%)

	NYT	Observer	Chronicle	Nation	Daily News	Tribune	New Vision	Total
	$N = 55$	$N = 68$	$N = 61$	$N = 103$	$N = 30$	$N = 2$	$N = 32$	$N = 351$
Differences in presence of blame by publication (%). $X^2 = 77.28, 6\ d.f., p < 0.01$								
Presence	49.1	19.1	19.7	70.9	36.7	0.0	12.5	39.9
Differences in presence of cultural blame by publication (%). $X^2 = 61.44, 6\ d.f., p < 0.01$								
Presence	34.5	7.4	9.8	42.7	0.0	0.0	3.1	21.4
Differences in presence of legislation blame by publication (%). $X^2 = 10.07, 6\ d.f., n.s.$								
Presence	7.3	2.9	0.0	8.7	0.0	0.0	3.1	4.6
Differences in presence of individual blame by publication (%). $X^2 = 4.36, 6\ d.f., n.s.$								
Presence	3.6	2.9	0.0	4.9	0.0	0.0	3.1	2.8
Differences in presence of family blame by publication (%). $X^2 = 17.48, 6\ d.f., p < 0.01$								
Presence	21.8	11.8	13.1	28.2	10.0	0.0	3.1	17.4
Differences in presence of cutter blame by publication (%). $X^2 = 32.09, 6\ d.f., p < 0.01$								
Presence	7.3	1.5	3.3	1.9	26.7	0.0	6.3	5.4
Differences in presence of other blame by publication (%). $X^2 = 24.78, 6\ d.f., p < 0.01$								
Presence	0.0	0.0	0.0	9.7	0.0	0.0	0.0	2.8

was informational campaigns to raise awareness of the potential harms of FGC, in 35 per cent of stories, followed by policy changes in 23.9 per cent of stories. Again, however, between-paper differences were observed. The *New York Times, Daily News, Tribune* and *New Vision* all suggested policy changes more frequently than informational campaigns. The *Nation, Tribune* and the *New York Times* each suggested a number of other remedies, in 25.2 per cent, 50 per cent and 23.6 per cent of articles, respectively. The *New York Times* largely suggested asylum in the US for girls having undergone or at risk of being forced to undergo FGC. The *Tribune* and the *Nation* recommended training doctors to properly conduct the cut or stop doing it, providing alternative jobs for cutters or creating new, more modern rites of passage. No article from any newspaper suggested punishing the individual girl.

Discussion

As a whole, this study indicates that FGC is perceived as an equally salient (or, as the case appears, not salient) issue in all seven newspapers. The rate of FGC in each country does not determine the issue salience for amount of news coverage. In fact, some of the countries with the lowest FGC prevalence rates, Ghana, the US and Kenya, saw the most FGC coverage. However, given the 18-year timeframe, the number of articles about FGM is very small, suggesting that the topic is, for the most part, not considered newsworthy. This also indicates that the amount of coverage given to a specific human rights abuse depends on the type of right and FGC may not be considered the most severe abuse.

However, despite the lack of coverage, anti-FGC advocates would likely find aspects of the coverage, particularly the thematic framing, to be positive as it enables audiences to more fully understand the context and complexity of the issue and can result in more collective notions of responsibility (Iyengar 1994). However, those that believe FGC is overstated, such as Obiora (2005), may find problems in such thematic reporting. Similarly, consistently reporting on FGC as a negative practice, and not as an individual girl's choice, enables FGC to uniformly be defined as a problem. Advocates of the position that FGC is gendered oppression and a human rights abuse (Boyle 2002; Morgan 1984) may view such coverage as being representative of the problem. But, again, those on the other end of the debate (Njambi 2004) could interpret this as imperialist or misunderstanding the nature of the practice, especially given that prominence of frames depicting FGC as a cultural tradition.

Four newspapers, the *Chronicle, Daily News, Tribune* and *New Vision*, each mentioned causes in fewer than half of stories, making it difficult for audiences to have enough context to identify the driving forces behind the issue (Entman 1993). Causes are largely portrayed as cultural factors in all newspapers; however, consistent with Sobel's (2015) study, the *New York Times* featured the highest per centage of articles discussing the cause of FGC to be cultural. This brings into question the validity of Njambi's (2004) critique regarding Western ideologies not accounting for the cultural importance of the practice.

When considering where blame was placed, in turn, suggesting to audiences where responsibility for the issue should fall, most newspapers did not specify. The *Nation* and the *New York Times* were the only newspapers to notably place blame, and both did so mostly on cultural factors. *Daily News* stuck out as largely placing blame on the individual doing the cutting, and the *New York Times* followed suit with a smaller but still notable per centage. The *New York Times* and *Daily News* function similarly with regard to blaming the cutter, which is interesting given that these two news outlets come from countries on opposite ends of the FGC prevalence spectrum. However, as a whole, with less than 40 per cent of all stories placing blame, audiences may be left with uncertainty concerning responsibility.

This heavy focus on cultural causes and blame suggests that local traditions play an important role in how journalists and their sources approach FGC. However, given that prominent differences were not regularly observed between newspapers, it does not appear that varying eradication campaigns and legislation in each country play an important role in how each media outlet covers the issue.

Similarly, the country of publication, and the accompanying level of existing anti-FGC policies and programs, does not appear to severely change the proposed remedies. Sobel (2015) found that the *New York Times* recommended policy changes more than any of the other papers, suggesting a possible Western view of oversimplifying the solution, while the other newspapers all proposed raising awareness of the dangers. However, this study found a similar focus on policy changes in the *New York Times* as well as the *Tribune, Daily News* and *New Vision*, indicating that this is not merely a Western misunderstanding of the local complexities as suggested by Piot (2007) given that a policy focus was seen in coverage from high, medium and low prevalence countries. As such, it does not appear that pervasiveness of the practice impacts the suggestion of local versus national/international solutions.

In sum, while minor between-paper differences were seen, as a whole, coverage from all seven countries functioned similarly, indicating that country-to-country differences in FGC prevalence level and government responses do not drastically change the way(s) that news media frame the topic. FGC was predominantly reported on as a cultural practice with negative/harmful implications, which furthers the argument put forth by anti-FGC advocates that view the practice as mutilation and a barbaric human rights abuse (Wade 2011). It is likely that advocates of the opposing position would maintain their criticism that coverage perpetuates narratives which oversimplify the array of complexities that accompany the practice and the cultures within which it occurs (Obiora 2005).

While revealing important findings, the research suffers from many of the broader weaknesses inherent in cross-cultural studies. The study only examined English-language newspapers, which provide insights into the news being covered in each country, but are often targeted at the educated elite or foreigners, and may not be representative of coverage in varying languages and dialects. Hence, the conclusions should not be thought of as representative of all news coverage from each country. Additionally, this study analysed the change in amount of coverage by looking at the number of articles. This does not take into account the size or content of the article. Further, this study cannot prove a causal link between FGC prevalence in a country and media representation, rather, it describes the similarities and differences across countries with varying levels of FGC.

Despite the limitations, this study builds on initial understandings of news media representations of FGC and provides a platform for additional research. Future research should continue this line of inquiry by analysing content from others newspapers, social media, broadcast news outlets and/or from other countries. Additionally, future research should dive deeper into understanding the linkages between FGC and news-making actors including the commitment level of journalists to FGC and other rights abuses, internal and external influences on newsmakers when reporting on the topic and how coverage of FGC is similar and different to that of other types of human rights issues.

References

Banasik, K. (2015). 'Female Genital Mutilation in Light of Polish Criminal Law'. *Progress In Health Sciences*, 5(2), pp. 216–28.

Boyle, E. (2002). *Female Genital Cutting: Culture Conflict in the Global Community*. The Johns Hopkins University Press, Baltimore.

Cloward, K. (2015). 'Elites, Exit Options, and Social Barriers to Norm Change: The Complex Case of Female Genital Mutilation'. *Studies in Comparative International Development*, 50(3), pp. 378–407.

Daily Nation (Kenya) (2011). Available from: http://www.kenya-advisor.com/daily-nation-kenya.html [26 Jan. 2016].

Entman, R. (1993). 'Framing: Toward Clarification of a Fractured Paradigm'. *Journal of Communication*, 41(4), pp. 51–56.

Gilboa, E. (2003). 'Television News and US Foreign Policy: Constraints of Real Time Coverage'. *Harvard International Journal of Press/Politics*, 8, pp. 97–113.

Iyengar, S. (1994). *Is Anyone Responsible? How Television Frames Political Issues*. Chicago: University of Chicago Press.

Khazaleh, L. (2010). *Yes to Female Circumcision?* Antropologi.info Social Cultural Anthropology in the News, Blog, Feb. 15. Available from: http://www.antropologi.info/blog/anthropology/2010/female-circumcision [2 December 2015.]

McCombs, M. and Shaw, D. (1993). 'The Evolution of Agenda-setting Research: Twenty-five Years in the Marketplace of Ideas'. *Journal of Communication*, 43(2), pp. 58–67.

Morgan, R. (1984). *Sisterhood Is Global: the International Women's Movement Anthology*. New York: Anchor Books/Doubleday.

Morris, K. (2006). 'Issues on Female Genital Mutilation/Cutting-progress and Parallels'. *Lancet*, 368, pp. 64–67.

Njambi, W. (2004). 'Dualism and Female Bodies in Representations of African Female Circumcision: A Feminist Critique'. *Feminist Theory*, 5(3), pp. 281–303.

Obiora, L.A. (2005). '*Female Circumcision and the Politics of Knowledge: African Women in Imperialist Discourses.* Westport: Praegar.

Piers, R. (2002). *The CNN Effect: The Myth of News Media, Foreign Policy and Intervention.* New York: Routledge.

Piot, C. (2007). 'Representing Africa and the Kasinga Asylum Case'. In: *Transcultural Bodies: Female Genital Cutting in Global Context*, eds. Y. Hernlund and B. Shell-Duncan. . London: Rutgers University Press, New Brunswick.

Press Reference (2010). Ghana Press, Media, TV, Radio and Newspapers. Available from: http://www.pressreference.com/Fa-Gu/Ghana.htl [18 Jan. 2016].

Riffe, D, Lacy, S and Fico, F. (2013). *Analyzing Media Messages: Using Quantitative Content Analysis in Research*, 3rd ed. London: Routledge.

Scheufele, D. (2000). 'Agenda-setting, Priming, and Framing Revisited: Another Look at Cognitive Effects of Political Communication'. *Mass Communication & Society*, 3(2–3), pp. 297–316.

Sobel, M. (2015). 'Female Genital Cutting in the News Media: A Content Analysis'. *International Communication Gazette*, 77(4), pp. 384–405.

Tall, S. (2007). 'FGM/C A Threat to Human Rights and to the Achievement of Millennium Development Goals'. Available at: https://www.unfpa.org/sites/default/files/pub-pdf/fgm_2008.pdf [6 Jan. 2016]

UNFPA (2015). Female Genital Mutilation (FGM) Frequently Asked Questions. Available at: http://www.unpfa.org/resources/female-genital-mutilation-fgm-frequently-asked-questions#sthash.VjtbmEHT.dpuf [18 Feb. 2016]

UNICEF (2013). Female Genital Mutilation/Cutting: A Statistical Overview and Exploration of the Dynamics of Change. Available at: http://www.unicef.org/media/files/UNICEF_FGM_report_July_2013_Hi_res.pdf [6 Jan. 2016].

UNPD (2015). World Leaders Adopt Sustainable Development Goals. Available at: http://www.undp.org/content/unpd/en/home/presscenter/pressrelease/2015/09/24/unpd-welcomes-adoption-of-sustainable-development-goals-by-world-leaders.html [18 Feb. 2016].

United Nations (2000). United Nations Millennium Development Goals. Available at: http://www.un.org/millenniumgoals/ [1 Mar. 2016].

Wade, L. (2009). 'Defining Gendered Oppression in U.S. Newspapers: The Strategic Value of "Female Genital Mutilation"'. *Gender & Society*, 23(3), pp.293–314, doi:10.1177/0891243209334938

Wade, L. (2011). 'Learning from "Female Genital Mutilation": Lessons from 30 Years of Academic Discourse', *Ethnicities*, 12(1), pp. 26–49, doi:10.1177/1468796811419603

Walley, C. (1997). 'Searching for 'Voices': Feminism, Anthropology and the Global Debate over Female Genital Operation,' *Cultural Anthropology*, 12(3), pp. 4053–58.

Wiley, D. (1997). 'Academic Analysis and U.S. Policy-making on Africa: Reflections and Conclusions'. *ISSUE: A Journal of Opinion*, 19(2), pp. 38–48.

World Health Organization (2013). *Female Genital Mutilation.* Available at: http://www.who.int/mediacentre/factsheets/fs241/en/ [Accessed 21 Dec.].

40

MEDIA, HUMAN RIGHTS AND RELIGION

Jolyon Mitchell and Joshua Rey

This chapter brings religion into the conversation between media and human rights. Its central contention is the need for the development of religious literacy in and through different media. This need partly stems from the unique relationship between religion and human rights. To understand this relationship we explore the interwoven history of the two discourses. We will see that this history has meant that human rights and religion often offer competing frames for various interpretations of events through different media. Because of the turn history has taken in the last hundred years, however, the human rights frame often predominates in a way that may lead to the over-simplifying of religious issues.

A news story can be like a mirror, reflecting the presuppositions of journalists and editors. It can be like an oil painting: highly coloured and stylised. Or it can be like a window which, though it limits what can be seen, does appear to allow the reality to be viewed more or less directly. Even though the three metaphors of the picture frame (as distinct from the painting itself), the window and the mirror have 'dominated film theory' (Sobchack 1991, 14), when adapted they can also be useful for reflecting on the role and relations of other kinds of media (Manovich 2001, 80). Just as mirrors, windows and paintings tend to have different kinds of frames, so too do different kinds of media. Frames are variously understood: from frames created by media producers, to media consumers' own frames of reference (Mitchell 2007).

These different perspectives shed light on what we analyse in the pages that follow: the recurring tension between what can be described as human rights frames and religion frames.

Increasingly, scholars underline how dynamic and creative media users now inhabit what Henry Jenkins describes as 'participatory culture' (Jenkins 2006, 3), creating their own mediated frames. Active audiences, with access to multiple digital platforms, have extraordinary freedom, some might say the right, to create their own frames of both media and religion. They do so regularly and in many different settings (Hoover 2006, 147–232). To explore the complex interrelation of human rights and religion, as well as the media that can be used to frame both of them, it will be helpful to begin with a couple of concrete examples that foreground the peculiar quality of religion as it relates to human rights.

The joker in the pack

When the so-called Islamic State took control in 2014, life changed for residents of Mosul. Among many new rules, IS forced women to wear a two-layered black veil with a black cloak, to hide every part of the body, including the eyes, rather than the lighter head scarf, or hijab. The rules were enforced by the Hisbah, the religious police. *The Guardian* quoted a thirty-six-year-old paediatrician, Maha Saleh:

> They forced women of all ages to wear a veil, even though the majority of the women in Mosul wear a hijab … The Hisbah would hit a woman on her head with a stick if she was not wearing a veil. At the beginning, some female doctors refused to wear veils and went on a strike by staying at home. Hisbah took ambulances and went to their houses and brought them by force to the hospital.
>
> *(Mahmood 2015)*

The same year, *The Guardian* told the story of Meryem Belmokhtar, a language graduate who had turned to running a halal confectionery business from her sitting room. Why had she, and several other Muslim women, resorted to working at home? Because the European Court of Human Rights had upheld the ban on the full-face veil, which the government of France, where Ms Belmokhtar lives, had brought in. These women are thus faced a choice: stay home, or, in going out of the house unveiled, cease to practise their religion as they understood it (Zerouala 2014). The French ban had been contested by a woman who remained anonymous:

> The woman, who was born in France in 1990 and identified only as S.A.S. in court documents, said that she wore the veils voluntarily, without any pressure from her husband and family, and that they allowed her to manifest her faith. She argued the French ban violated her religious freedom.
>
> *(Steinhauser and Landauro 2014; see also Brems 2014)*

These two stories say something interesting about the unique way religion relates to human rights and media. Think about the *other* headings in this section: Prisoners. Refugees. Surveillance. Slavery. From a human rights perspective, you probably know which side they're on. Slavery infringes human rights. Refugees may be denied their rights. Slaves and refugees, in a human rights story, feature as victims. On the other hand we don't read of prison governors or National Security Agency directors having their rights abused: if they feature in a human rights story it is in the role of the abuser.

Religion is not so clear cut. Maha Saleh and Meryem Belmokhtar are both Muslim women wearing full-face veils. Meryem Belmokhtar is prevented by the state where she lives from exercising her religion. Maha Saleh is prevented from dressing how she chooses by people exercising their religion where *she* lives. Two human rights stories about Muslim women wearing full face veils: in one, religion is the right being curtailed; in the other religion is the force curtailing rights.

Religion is the joker in the pack of human rights. And there are some really interesting reasons why: reasons rooted deep in history. One thing we will find as we explore this history is that human rights and religion are closely related. We will also see how elements of news media have come to have something of a religious 'blind spot' (Marshall, Gilbert and Green 2009) It is, however, striking, even 'troubling that the time of greatest need for religious literacy has coincided with the time at which religious literacy in the media is at a low ebb' (Wakelin and Spencer 2015, 227–36). We turn first to some examples of the ways human rights, media and religion overlap with one another.

Framing the news frame

Frames of reference are like belly buttons. Everybody has one. Each of us has a different way of looking at things. People notice what concerns them and tune out what doesn't. Moreover, if they don't reflect, then as Erving Goffman puts it in his book on *Frame Analysis*, they 'actively project their frames of reference into the world immediately around them' (Goffman 1974, 39). Simply to call a news event a 'story' is to frame it: A story has a structure, heroes and villains, a beginning and an end – unlike real life. The story has been *mediated* and is therefore not imme-diate: It leaves things out; it has a point of view. In other words a frame includes and excludes. Media always involves 'persistent emphasis, selection, and exclusion' which enables journalists 'to process large amounts of information quickly and routinely' and relay it efficiently to their audiences (Gitlin 1980, 7).

This is not to criticise journalists. News would be unintelligible without frames. Consumers of media draw on their own frames of reference to interpret, interact with and even challenge the news frame they are offered. Examining how news is framed shows how different perspec-tives interact. Sometimes a story is framed one way, but might have been framed in another way (Mitchell 2007, 64–114). In a digitised communicative environment more and more mediated frames are created by consumers. Where this happens a lot, something interesting may be going on. Religion and human rights are two frames that do often compete for dominance in this way.

Human rights stories in religious frames

Many news events framed as stories about religion might fairly have been framed as about human rights. One example is the mass suicide by members of the 'Peoples Temple' in Guyana on 18 November, 1978. The Peoples Temple is usually called a religious group, and the poison-ing of around 900 members at the instigation of its leader, Jim Jones, is usually reported as a religious event. *The Guardian*, for example, framed it by reference to religious mass suicides from antiquity and the middle ages (Adamson 1978). By 1978, however, the Peoples Temple was essentially a political organisation – described in a US Congressional report as a 'socio-political movement'. The supposed mass suicide could be as well understood as an abuse of the rights of group members. Jim Jones derives considerable advantages from this ambiguity: 'The issue of People's Temple's status as a "church" is also significant in connection with First Amendment protections it sought and received' (US House of Representatives 1979, 20).

It is also instructive to read early reports of the Afghan Taliban, in the period in 1995 when they first appeared in Western media, as they made rapid territorial gains in post-Soviet Afghanistan. Looking back through the filter of ISIS and al-Qaeda, it is salutary to see how in these early weeks Western media often portrayed the Taliban positively. Their 'success in drawing together people from factions whose enmities have made Afghanistan ungovernable for so long' is contrasted with the self-indulgent excesses of the armed bands they oppose, such as 'a group known as "the Gucci muj" because of the expensive tastes of its leader' (Burns 1995).

Other articles had a negative take, but also couched in secular terms, such as that headlined 'Women Being Forced From UN Workplaces in Afghanistan'. The article quotes a UN official who had told the Taliban that 'women's rights were human rights' (Crossette 1995). Positive or negative, though, the story is framed in terms of human rights and other secular concerns. Some reportage, though, even well-disposed to the Taliban, does put religion centre stage. One article quotes a hotel owner in Southern Afghanistan as saying the Taliban are 'a source of great happiness'; the article is headlined 'Travelling down the road of the Islamic enforcers' (Rouard 1995).

What we see here is the process of framing by selection, foregrounding and backgrounding, but at an early stage, before a consensus has emerged about what the frame is. By 2002, after the 9/11 terrorist attacks in the US, the frame has hardened. Now the Taliban are taken to share the universalising Wahhabist doctrines of Osama bin Laden: Their story has been framed as a story of religious militancy. The alternative frame, of the Taliban as an Afghan cultural and political movement (whose ideology is inextricably mingled with a geographically specific Islam), has been lost. For many this is not a human rights story; it is a religion story.

Religious stories in human rights frames

Likewise there are many examples of events framed as human rights stories, which could have been framed as religious narratives. In November 2012 the Synod of the Church of England narrowly voted not to permit women to become Bishops. This was framed squarely as a human rights story. The *Daily Express* illustrated double-page spread was headlined 'From exclusive golf clubs to Morris dancing, we reveal why it's not just the church that unfairly bans the fairer sex' (*Daily Express* Staff 2012). The *Daily Mirror* reported that remarks by the Prime Minister had 'raise[d] the possibility of equality laws being used to force the Church to change'. Strikingly though, the story acknowledged that 'Downing Street ... said there were no plans to compel it to comply with laws barring discrimination on the basis of gender' (*Daily Mirror* Staff 2012). But this could have been a story about a Prime Minister's commitment to the integrity of the Established church in which he was brought up.

Few reports described the event in religious terms, or set out the theological motivations claimed by participants, or the religiously grounded preference for consensus which led to a decision being made contrary to the views of the majority. One rare article that saw a religious dimension, framed the story with a parallel between the church of England and the Taliban, whereas the issues had very different scriptural and creedal roots from those of 'the sexism' of the Taliban (Finnigan 2012). The *Irish Times* editorial framed the vote as 'a public relations disaster' (Irish Times Editorial Staff 2012), which, though not untrue, put the religious aspects of the story in the background.

The Israel/Palestine conflict is a much longer running event with fundamental religious features which has in recent years been framed largely in human rights terms. Victims of rights abuses by the State of Israel are usually identified as Arabs, rather than Muslims or Christians. Those favourable to Israel contrast its parliamentary democracy with the authoritarian structures of neighbouring countries. While this frame is legitimate one, and the issues it foregrounds are real, given where and why this conflict is going on, there is little religiously framed reportage, and religion is often misinterpreted and misunderstood (Philo and Berry 2004, 2007). Religion features as an ethnic dividing line and a source of rhetoric; the religious conceptions of human life and God's purposes are seldom part of the frame.

A fortiori these events are never framed as episodes in the continuing story of God working out his purposes for his people. Such metaphysical framing would indeed call for explanation or even justification. The result is that even the cultural and historical weight of Jerusalem's religious inheritance (Sebag Montefiore 2011, 501–22) (let alone any possibility of Divine existence and action) is underplayed. Perhaps the only paper that (almost) takes the religious frame seriously is the satirical magazine *Private Eye*, which frames the conflict in a parody of the Old Testament, perhaps capturing something that other frames lose:

So Ehud sent forth a mighty army and tanks, even an hundred-fold, to carry out the next round of smiting that would finally bring lasting peace to the land of Israel.[20] Just as it hath done so many times before.[21] And, lo, the war continued, even unto the twenty-second day… [22] Then said Ehud, son of Olmert, 'let us now declare an cease-fire.[24] For, lo, we have achieved our object. [25] Which was to get a quick war in before Obama cometh.[26] For Barack, son of Obama, may not looketh so kindly on our smiting as did Dubya, that is called the Burning Bush.[27]

(Hislop 2009)

Religion and human rights

Boundaries between religion and human rights, then, are fluid and contested. These boundaries can be blurred or amplified by different kinds of media framing. We now consider situations where the two discourses conflict or otherwise overlap.

Religion conflicts with human rights in the case of abortion. Most religious traditions seek to curtail the right of a woman to obtain an abortion. Some countries have a clear link between religious heritage and the curtailment of this right. This curtailment of one set of rights is sometimes framed as the defence of the rights of the unborn child. Laws against suicide also have religious roots. Much opposition to assisted suicide is religiously motivated, and the increased acceptance of assisted suicide parallels a decline in religious commitment. (Duncan and Parmelee 2006, Gallup 2015) Human rights and religion have also been opposed over laws governing marriage and divorce.

On the other hand some of the most strenuous defenders of human rights have been motivated by religion. William Wilberforce (1759–1833) and other campaigners against the slave trade, saw this campaign as the outworking of their Evangelical Christian faith. They made use of a wide range of contemporary media, such as newspapers, billboards, tracts and pamphlets, to frame the issue of slavery. Liberation Theology catalysed opposition to totalitarian regimes in Latin America in the late twentieth century, using local radio stations such as in El Salvador, where Salvadorians owned around 1.5 million radios (Mitchell and Kidwell 2016, 419–31). The Jubilee 2000 campaign for the remission of Third World Debt, drew on religious themes. Each movement made use of diverse media and attracted considerable media attention.

Human rights doctrine can support a religious agenda. The Universal Declaration of Human Rights and the European Convention on Human Rights both assert the right of everyone to 'manifest his [*sic*] religion' (United Nations Organisation 1948: *Article 18*, Council of Europe 1950: *Article 9*). Most rights-based actions, however, protect religious groups which are also coterminous with ethnic or national groups, and quite often protect them against other such groups. The 1999 NATO intervention in Kosovo aimed to secure the rights of Muslims in Kosovo but this was not a defence of religious freedoms, but a defence of all freedoms of a group demarcated by religion. In the same year the headquarters of the Radio Television Serbia in Belgrade, broadcasting nationalistic propaganda, was hit by a Nato air strike, killing sixteen employees (Krieger, 2001, 349–52), leading to condemnation of the attack several years later by Amnesty International (2009) and Human Rights Watch (2014).

Media, human rights and religion

Various media are often involved too. There can be tension between religion and the freedoms of individuals and groups to express themselves. Religious book burning is surprisingly rare in history and is usually a sideshow to a conflict *between* religions. Destruction of books on purely religious grounds is usually the province of religious eccentrics, such as Savonarola's destruction of supposedly pornographic books in Florence in 1497. In modern times the murder of nine members of staff and three other people at the French satirical magazine *Charlie Hebdo* by Saïd and Chérif Kouachi on 7 January 2015 stands out as an example of this kind of conflict. The Kouachi brothers did not represent mainstream Shi'a or Sunni Islam; but implicit in their action was the idea that the claims of religion trump the claims of human rights. And even very moderate people are willing to argue that freedom of expression must be balanced by respect for religion (Tryhorn 2006).

An even more complex collision between media, human rights and religion was triggered by the decision in September 2005 by the Danish newspaper *Jyllands-Posten* to publish cartoons depicting Muhammad (Veninga 2014). They took the view that freedom of the media was more important than religious considerations: others, not just Muslims, took the contrary view (Klausen 2009 – controversially, the publisher chose not to include the cartoons themselves in this book).

The religion of human rights

It is now time to consider the historical roots of this ambiguous relation between religion and human rights. This will help understand in turn why some media framing of religion is so often problematic.

Simply put, human rights discourse and religion are both potentially ways of life. A religion involves a universal vision of how to live, of what matters, of why we do what we do. Unlike the other 'rights' in this section, religion is what Charles Taylor calls a 'hypergood' (Taylor 1989, 63) – not just something good, but a standard by which the competing claims of other goods are arbitrated. Hence the strange relationship, sometimes conflictual, sometimes symbiotic, between religion and human rights. For this is also, of course, what the doctrine human rights is. In sociological terms human rights discourse functions in many ways like a religion, albeit a religion without God, the supernatural or the afterlife; it has been referred to as 'the Religion of the UN' (Appleby 2015).

One of the most significant historical events of the last two hundred years has been the movement of human rights doctrine into the space religion has always occupied. Thus, as many have noted, human rights either has to reach an alliance with religion, or the two will conflict. John Witte, a legal historian and human rights theorist argues that 'the struggle for human rights cannot be won' without such alliances. Scott Appleby observes that religious communities have often resisted the spread of a universal (and UN-supported) vision of human rights, seeing it as a quasi-colonial imposition of a specifically Western way of thinking (Appleby 2000). Appleby himself, for all that he is sympathetic to religion, tends to see its main value as being in support of a human rights agenda: he refers to the principles of religions as 'culturally determined' – whereas adherents of religions may frequently consider the principles of their religion to be of divine origin.

Media, human rights and religions, plural

If religion is not just a right but a way of life, the detail of *which* religion is in question becomes very important. There is no generic religious outlook. Christianity, Islam and Buddhism are all globalising ways of life but they are *different* ways of life, each with their own histories, traditions and ways of embracing different media. They indeed contain multiple competing ways of life. Michael Griffin, who murdered Dr David Gunn, a Florida abortion practitioner, was a Christian, not a generically religious person. Saïd and Chérif Kouachi, who murdered the Charlie Hebdo cartoonists, were Muslims, not generically religious people.

Media runs the risk of misinterpretation if it ignores this specificity. Yet this can be uncomfortable, at least for Western liberal media. To say, for example, that Religion A is more prone to promote violence than Religion B, feels like something close to racism. Scott Appleby notes that participants in debates on religion and conflict commonly take one of two points of view: Either that all religion is anti-progressive, 'threatening a return to the Dark Ages'; or that all religion upholds the sanctity of human life and those who do acts of violence in the name of religion are not true to their faith. (Appleby 2000, 10) This simplistic dualism is no less a feature of media treatments. Interestingly, Appleby's preferred approach is to say that all religions have within them the 'ambiguity of the sacred', both the seeds of violence and oppression *and* the resources to value life and peace, which again elides structural differences between different religions that make some more compatible with a human rights perspective and some less so.

For human rights doctrine itself has its roots in one particular religion. The doctrine of human rights, as it crystallised in the eighteenth century, was articulated by people often hostile to religion. But their starting point was the dominant ideology of their time and place: a continent formed over fifteen hundred years by one particular religion, namely Western Catholic Christianity and its Protestant progeny. This long history is explored by Larry Siedentop (Siedentop 2014) whose argument informs the following paragraphs. A claim expressed through a range of medieval and modern Christian media, and embodied in the founding texts, is that the value of a human being stems from 'being made in the image of God' (Genesis 1.27) and his or her likeness to Jesus Christ, who is both human (so that other human beings can be like him) and also God. Visually and verbally the claim is made that everyone is born with the capacity to know and to resemble God: so each life is of infinite value. In the liberal climate that still dominates many parts of the Western world in the 21st Century this does not sound a radical doctrine, even if such Christian beliefs are no longer the dominant world view. But the Classical world, which understood human societies as inherently hierarchical, would have thought it absurd. The reason equality seems obvious today is because the typical reader of academic books written in English inhabits a culture steeped in the Christian tradition. The modern concept of rights was first articulated in an intra-church debate in the 14th century over whether a Christian could own property. The concept of a secular realm was a byproduct of the eleventh-century development of a church government that enforced a distinction between spiritual and temporal power.

By the time of the Enlightenment these concepts (equality, rights, a secular sphere for the free exercise of conscience) were taken for granted, and could form the basis for a revolt against the church in which they had developed. But the religious element is ineradicable. Perhaps the most influential document in the development of secular human rights discourse is the American Declaration of Independence. Its starting point is religious: 'We hold these truths to be self-evident, that all men are created equal, that they are endowed by their Creator with certain unalienable Rights…' (Gwinnett et al. 1776)

None of this should be taken as suggesting Christians, or other religious groups, are superior in human rights terms. As Larry Siedentop says, human rights doctrine 'developed against fierce resistance of the … churches.' (Siedentop 2014, 333) Christians have perpetrated more than their share of human rights abuses. Charles Villa-Vicencio argues 'For hundreds of years the Christian Church actively promoted religious intolerance' (Villa-Vicencio 1999). Nevertheless, the historical roots of human rights doctrine in Western Christianity are hard to deny, even if they are now commonly excluded from most news frames and related interpretations of different media. These roots may help explain the suspicion of human rights often felt by those from a different religious background. Appleby records the opposition of Asian leaders, at a 1993 conference, to a universal regime of human rights, which they felt reflected 'an excessive penchant for personal autonomy – a value given little priority in Asian cultures'; and the leader of the Sudanese National Islamic Front, urging others not 'to force Muslims to conform to alien values' (Appleby 2000, 248–9). Perhaps what lies behind this is a recognition that human rights is not a universal doctrine, but the descendant of one particular religion.

Conclusion: Media and religious literacy

Understanding this history, and the specificity of religions, is key to addressing the 'religious blindspot' (Marshall, Gilbert and Green 2009) to be found in much Western news media. Often the portrayal of human rights and religion fails to grasp that this is a multilateral relationship between several distinct worldviews, including the human rights vision itself. Though there are many points of commonality, each perspective, Christian, Confucian, Hindu, Human Rights, Jewish, Muslim, has unique doctrines, scriptures and practices, in terms of which it relates to all the others. To say that one religion sits more comfortably with a human rights agenda than another is not to praise the first and criticise the second. It is simply to notice what is going on, just as one would notice that Islam and Christianity have more in common with one another than either has with Shintoism. Religious literacy calls for media practitioners and participants to learn to articulate these differences without implying (or being afraid of seeming to imply) value judgements between religions. Social media debates and news media treatment of the relationship between human rights and religion can only be enriched by this recognition that religion is more than just one of a number of different rights. Understanding that religions and human rights offer competing, sometimes overlapping, visions of how to live, will widen the media frame to show us what is really going on. Presenting religions as specific, not generic, will respect the uniqueness of their doctrines and history. Lastly, if contemporary news and social media is to portray, frame and debate with insight the relationships between the great religions of the world and that secular religion, human rights, it will be very helpful to understand the genealogy of human rights doctrine in one of those world religions.

References

Adamson, L. (1978). 'The Short-circuit Logic that Can Lead to Mass Suicide'. *The Guardian*, 21 Nov.
Appleby, S. (2000). *The Ambivalence of the Sacred*. Oxford: Rowman & Littlefield.
Appleby, S. (2015). Remarks at a public event on *Changing the Conversation about Religion: Partnerships for Global Development*. London, 13 Nov.
Brems, E., ed. (2014). *The Experiences of Face Veil Wearers in Europe and the Law*, Cambridge: Cambridge University Press.
Burns, J. (1995) 'New Afghan Force Takes Hold, Turning to Peace'. *The New York Times*, 16 Feb.
Council of Europe (1950). *European Convention on Human Rights*. Available at: www.echr.coe.int/Documents/Convention_ENG.pdf [Accessed 10 Apr. 2016].
Crossette, B. (1995) 'Women Being Forced From U.N. Workplaces in Afghanistan'. *The New York Times*, 11 Oct.
Daily Express Staff (2012). 'NO WOMEN ALLOWED!'. *Daily Express*, 22 Nov.
Daily Mirror Staff (2012). 'OUT-OF-TOUCH CHURCH NEEDS A SHARP PROD'. *Daily Mirror* 22 Nov.
Duncan, O. and Parmelee, L. (2006). 'Trends in Public Approval of Euthanasia and Suicide in the US, 1947–2003'. *Journal of Medical Ethics*, 32(5), pp. 266–72.
Finnigan, J. (2012). 'Richard & Judy'. *Daily Express*, 22 Nov.
Gallup (2015). '1948–2015 Time Series Data on "What is your religious preference?"'. Available at: www.gallup.com/poll/1690/religion.aspx [Accessed 25 Apr. 2016].
Gitlin, T. (1980). *The Whole World Is Watching: Mass Media in the Making and Unmaking of the New Left*. Berkeley, CA: University of California Press.

Goffman, E. (1974). *Frame Analysis: An Essay on the Organisation of Experience.* London: Harper Row.

Gwinnett, B. et al. (1776). *Declaration of Independence.* Available at:www.archives.gov/exhibits/charters/declaration_transcript.html [Accessed 14 Apr. 2016].

Hislop, I., ed. (2009). *Private Eye Annual.* London: Private Eye Productions Ltd.

Hoover, S. (2006). *Religion in the Media Age.* London and New York: Routledge.

Irish Times Editorial Staff (2012). 'Bad Move on Bishops'. *The Irish Times*, 23 Nov.

Jenkins, H. (2006). *Convergence Culture: Where Old and New Media Collide.* New York and London: New York University.

Klausen, J. (2009). *The Cartoons that Shook the World.* New Haven: Yale University Press.

Krieger, H., ed. (2001). *The Kosovo Conflict and International Law: An Analytical Documentation 1974-1999.* Cambridge: Cambridge University Press.

Mahmood, M. (2015). 'Double-layered Veils and Despair: Women Describe Life Under Isis'. The Guardian (17 February). Available at: www.theguardian.com/world/2015/feb/17/isis-orders-women-iraq-syria-veils-gloves [Accessed 23 Apr. 2016].

Manovich L. (2001). *The Language of New Media.* Cambridge, MA: MIT Press.

Marshall, P., Gilbert, L., and Green, R. (2009). *Blind Spot: When Journalists Don't Get Religion.* Oxford: University Press.

Mitchell, J. (2007). *Media Violence and Christian Ethics.* Cambridge: Cambridge University Press.

Mitchell, J. and Kidwell, J. (2016). 'Changing Uses of Old and New Media in World Christianity.' In: S. Lamin and M. McClymond, eds., *The Wiley-Blackwell Companion to World Christianity.* Oxford: Wiley Blackwell.

Philo, G. and Berry, M. (2004). *Bad News from Israel.* London: Pluto Press.

Philo, G. and Berry, M. (2007). *More Bad News from Israel.* London: Pluto Press.

Rouard, D. (1995) 'Travelling Down the Road of the Islamic Enforcers'. *The Guardian* (10 March).

Sebag Montefiore, S. (2011). *Jerusalem.* London: Weidenfeld & Nicolson.

Siedentop, L. (2014). *Inventing the Individual.* London: Allen Lane.

Sobchack, V. (1991). *The Address of the Eye: A Phenomenology of Film Experience*, Princeton: Princeton University Press.

Steinhauser, G. and Landauro, I. (2014). 'European Human Rights Court Upholds France's Burqa Ban'. Wall Street Journal (1 September). Available at: www.wsj.com/articles/european-human-rights-court-upholds-frances-burqa-ban-1404210496 [Accessed 23 Apr.].

Taylor, C. (1989). *Sources of the Self.* Cambridge: University Press.

Tryhorn, C. (2006). 'Jack Straw Praises UK Media's "Sensitivity" Over Cartoons'. *The Guardian*, 2 Feb.

United Nations Organisation (1948). *The Universal Declaration of Human Rights* (www.un.org/en/universal-declaration-human-rights [Accessed 10 Apr.].

US House of Representatives (1979). *The Assassination Of Representative Leo J. Ryan And The Jonestown, Guyana Tragedy: Report Of A Staff Investigative Group To The Committee On Foreign Affairs U.S. House Of Representatives* (Washington, DC: Houses of Congress).

Veninga, J. (2014). *Secularism, Theology and Islam: The Danish Social Imaginary and the Cartoon Crisis of 2005-6.* London: Bloomsbury.

Villa-Vicencio, C. (1999). 'Christianity and Human Rights'. *Journal of Law and Religion* 14(2) pp. 579–600.

Wakelin, M. and Spencer, N. (2015). 'Religious Literacy and the Media: The Case of the BBC'. In: A. Dinham and M. Francis, eds., *Religious Literacy in Policy and Practice.* Bristol: University of Bristol Press.

Zerouala, F. (2014). 'Headscarf Ban Turns France"s Muslim Women Towards Homeworking'. *The Guardian* 3 Oct. Available at: www.theguardian.com/world/2014/oct/03/france-muslim-women-home-working [Accessed 30 Apr. 2016].

41

THE ROLE OF NEWS MEDIA IN FOSTERING CHILDREN'S DEMOCRATIC CITIZENSHIP

Cynthia Carter

Introduction

The news media are central to the advancement of children's civic inclusion in democratic societies. They have an informal responsibility to each new generation to help establish, from a young age, a sense of public belonging as well as individual and collective political responsibility. News organisations also have formal duties towards children such as those related to specific Articles in the *UN Convention on the Rights of the Child* (UNICEF 1989), ensuring, for instance, that children have 'freedom to seek, receive and impart information and ideas of all kinds, regardless of frontiers, either orally, in writing or in print, in the form of art, or through any other media of the child's choice and empowerment' (Article 13). Additionally, Article 17 obliges that signatories 'recognize the important function performed by the mass media and shall ensure that the child has access to information and material from a diversity of national and international sources [...]'. To realise this latter aim, mass media need to 'disseminate information and material of social and cultural benefit to the child' through international cooperation to produce and disseminate a wide variety of cultural forms, take into account different linguistic and minority group cultural needs, and development of guidelines to protect children from information and material which might cause them harm.

Likewise, Article 24 (1) of the *Charter of Fundamental Rights of the European Union* (European Convention 2000) declares that children should be given the opportunity to 'express their views freely. Such views shall be taken into consideration on matters which concern them in accordance with their age and maturity'. This point is reconfirmed in the *An EU Agenda for the Rights of the Child* that states 'Full recognition of the rights of the child means that children must be given a chance to voice their opinions and participate in the making of decisions that affect them' (European Commission 2011, 13).

Children were rarely seen or heard in the news in the run up to the UK's Referendum on membership of the European Union held on 23 June 2016 (Stalford 2016). Although a bill was tabled in the House of Commons in 2015 to extend the poll to 16 and 17 year olds, as had been the case in the Scottish Independence Referendum of 2014, The House of Lords, succumbing to pressure from the Commons, defeated it. Around 1.2 million young people thus had no say in a plebiscite that would fundamentally shape their future. Shadow Foreign Office minister, Lady Morgan, reflected that 'Today's 16- to 17-year-olds are the most informed in history, having undertaken citizenship classes at school and having information … at their thumb tips with their constant tapping of their mobile phones' (cited in Wintour 2015). When citizens are given political franchise from the age of 16, she claimed, they are more likely to become and remain politically active throughout their lives.

The news media have an unquestionable obligation to support children's civic rights and engagement to ensure their informed voices are included in public debates. Indeed, as David Oswell (2013, 252) suggests, 'an important aspect of the globalisation of children's human rights has not only been legal and state-governmental discourse, but also mass media discourses and vehicles'. Although not specifically addressing the child citizen, Kate Nash reminds us that it is the duty of journalism in democratic states not only to inform and educate but also to be the 'voice of the people' and act as 'the peoples' protectors and advocates' (2009, 55). It is perhaps surprising, then, that news research on children has had little to say about their access, opportunity and voice, instead tending to focus on socialisation to political norms and values or upon monitoring and exposing negative effects of news on children's emotions. Whilst such studies have yielded important results, they nevertheless tend to reinforce adult power around monitoring and controlling children's relationships to news. This chapter connects insights drawn from these areas of research with a critical news research agenda centred on children's information and communication rights to explore how a rights centred approach might highlight ways to enhance children's civic inclusion. Before doing so, I will briefly outline the conceptual foundations underpinning political socialisation and effects news research before considering a critical, social constructionist perspective informed by sociology of childhood studies.

Defining childhood

Who is a 'child' and what does 'childhood' represent in democratic societies? Chris Jenks (1992), a prominent sociology of childhood researcher, argues there is a belief that childhood represents a time of both difference and particularity. Adults have accounted for children's difference by integrating them into a broad framework of social order, which adults define and shape for children.

For example, in the field of developmental psychology, childhood is marked by a series of psychological and physical developments or 'stages', outlined in the pioneering work of developmental psychologist Jean Piaget (1969). As Lemish (2007) notes, 'the key to stage theories is the understanding of "stage" as a unique period of development, with each stage typified by its own special behavioural and cognitive characteristics' (2007, 38). Each of us passes through similar stages of development from childhood to adulthood in roughly the same order. Moreover, these stages are 'also perceived to be both hierarchical, as well as, integrative' (Lemish 2007, 38). As individual cognitive skills develop, children become more rational. Although the social context through which individuals progress in each life stage is acknowledged, stages are perceived to be universal (Walkerdine 2004). Developmental theories have been widely adopted by media researchers, although primarily used to examine entertainment genres. Childhood is presumed to be a period of innocence and vulnerability where lack of worldly experience makes children susceptible to corruption (by 'bad' adults and harmful media) so it becomes the responsibility of adults ('good' ones and child friendly media) to protect and guide them. These assumptions also underpin much of the limited research on children and news, assuming that exposure to news must be carefully handled to inculcate normative social and political values or to protect children from emotional harm. For other researchers, childhood is regarded as a social construction and therefore an arbitrary, provisional, and changing category (Ariés 1962; Jenks 1992). Over-emphasis on understanding childhood in terms of cognitive and physical (brain) developments, they argue, has meant there has been little focus on the importance of the social, economic, cultural and political contexts of childhood. Social constructionists maintain that dominant ideas about childhood tend to be ahistorical, universalistic and unable to account for differences amongst children. Of central importance is the ground breaking research of historian Philippe Ariés, who examined western European historical records related to childhood dating back to medieval times, when the idea of childhood as separate from adulthood did not exist. That is why, Ariés has suggested, 'as soon as the child could live without constant solicitude of his mother, his nanny or his cradle-rocker, he [sic] belonged to adult society' (1962, 125). News media habitually portray children as vulnerable and in need of adult protection (Archard 2004, 61). I would not wish to argue the opposite, but instead draw attention to the ideologies reinforcing such assumptions and how they have shaped news research. Even though the work of Ariés and others has led to important advances in thinking about childhood, they still largely lack the voices of children, and as long as this is so, our historical understanding will remain incomplete (Hendrick 1992).

Researching children and news

Children's researchers have typically sought to understand how children might be incrementally socialised into society, in line with their cognitive development, so that as adults they will have reproduced its norms and values. This research forms a broad framework upon which scholars have examined the role of the news in this process. Others have been more concerned with negative emotional effects of news violence on children. Critical news scholarship has explored how the news relates (or does not) to children as citizens. In the next section, each of these approaches is briefly outlined and considered in relation to children's citizenship and communication rights.

News and political socialisation

Early research on the relationship between children and news in the US sought to understand how they best learn and internalise accepted political norms and values of the prevailing system. Appropriate socialisation was regarded as important for the future health of democratic political structures (Deth, Abendschön and Vollmar 2011). Families, schools and news media were to be the 'conduits in transmitting to the neophyte citizens [children] what mature citizens knew and practiced' (McLeod 2000, 46). In this process, children were largely perceived to be passive recipients of information passed on by authoritative, adult sources. By the 1970s, researchers began moving away from this conception to one where children were encouraged to express their views as a way of becoming more politically active. Contemporary approaches tend to assume children are citizens in the making and should be active participants in society amid increasing concern over declining political participation and civic knowledge (Banaji and Buckingham 2013; Pascal and Bertram 2009). Political socialisation theory now highlights the importance of democratic deliberation – social stability is achieved not through reproducing dominant views but instead through active discussion of diverse points of view. The notion of politics has also expanded to include young people's volunteer work and community involvement as markers of civic engagement.

Tolley's (1973) study of US children's political socialisation to international conflict (Vietnam war) is an engaging example of the earliest research focus. At the time, there was public concern that children were getting distorted, anti-war messages from news or that it was desensitising them to human suffering. His survey of 2,677 children between the ages of 7–15 refuted these claims. Children acquired a broad knowledge and understanding of war from television news and it was an important influence in their maturation as citizens. Surveying 760 10–12 year olds, Conway et al.'s (1981) study also gauged the impact of news media on children's political attitudes and opinions. Frequent news consumption establishes a greater knowledge of societal norms – those of political processes, parties and support for the electoral system – than schools or parents provide. 'In short', concluded the authors, 'news media use, alone and in conjunction with knowledge of the American political process, is a significant determinant of children's political attitudes and patterns of political participation' (1981, 175).

Active citizenship, argued McLeod, is 'largely indirect result of contextualised knowledge and cognitive skills learned from news media use, interpersonal communication and active participation in school and community volunteer activities' (2000, 45). Given that voter turnout in the US has been steadily decreasing over several decades, urgent action was required to develop 'intervention programs and strategies that would stimulate and depend the level of civic engagement among youth' (2000, 45). The need for a stable society came to be regarded as deficient as it 'failed to recognize both the diversity and conflict in our own society' (2000, 46). Past approaches downplayed the importance of deliberation to the health of democracy. In a similar vein, a Canadian Newspaper Association online survey with 1,500 14–34 year olds (Cobb 2010) concluded that young newspaper readers make good citizens. Regular readers are more likely than occasional ones to vote, volunteer their time and help out in their communities. Since such habits are formed in childhood, it is vitally important to expose them to news at home and in schools.

Negative news media effects

In contrast to those who emphasise the importance of news in children's political socialisation, others caution care is needed when exposing children to news. Yet, as Valkenburg (2004) notes, given the thousands of studies undertaken on children's behavioural and emotional responses to entertainment media, it is surprising how few scholars have investigated the effects of news on children (2004, 68). Those who have undertaken such research have tended to focus on news violence, concluding that exposure may lead to short and long term psychological trauma and negative emotional effects (Cantor and Nathanson 1996; Hoffner and Haefner 1993; van der Molen 2004). Cantor and Nathanson's (1996) study on the negative effects of television news on children is widely regarded as significant in setting the terms of debate. In an extensive survey with parents of US children aged 5–12, over one third claimed their children were sometimes frightened by the news. The topics most frightening, parents claimed, were violence between strangers, war and famine, and natural disasters (1996, 144). Because of the potential for emotional harm, 'parents would be well advised to be aware of their children's exposure to news and to avoid exposure to the most sensational programs while young children are present' (1996, 151). That doesn't mean children shouldn't follow the news; what is required is limited exposure to 'the diversity and variety of tragedies and disasters currently presented to the public on a regular basis' (1996, 151). Children's developmental abilities should inform decisions about exposure to difficult news content bearing in mind that 'the informed child must not necessarily be a traumatised child' (1996, 152). Other researchers have suggested that exposure to frightening news may also 'strengthen the accessibility and availability of cognitive structures that govern how children react to threats and dangers in real life' (Smith, Pieper and Moyer-Gusé 2011, 229). More news studies are needed, especially in light of the growing number of online news sites, to understand the negative and positive ways it is shaping children's conceptions of the world.

Various strategies for coping with news have emerged from this field of study. These include not permitting young children to follow news, minimising discussion of traumatic events (giving bare facts) and reassuring children they are ok. It is assumed negative news will almost always cause children harm as they tend internalise frightening stories, leading to fears that bad things will happen to them (Moyer-Gusé and Smith 2007). Without protection, children may perceive the world to be a 'confusing, threatening, or unfriendly place'. A recommended therapeutic response is to give 'calm, unequivocal, but limited information' that tells children the facts 'but only as much truth as a child needs to know' (Gavin 2011).

Critical news research

Critical researchers tend to regard children's relationship to news as underpinned by the assumption they are citizens with particular legal rights to information, communication and to have their voices heard. Whilst it is often argued children are not really interested in news, there is a growing body of research examining children's civic engagement challenging this view, regarding it as a self-fulfilling prophecy if children's citizenship rights remain restrained (Lister 2007). What should be done to engage children in the public sphere? Educators, according to Buckingham (2000, 223), need to enable children to build connections between the personal and political to prepare them for participatory forms of citizenship. The news media have a critical role to play in providing children with opportunities to express themselves publicly, see their interests reflected and to be taken seriously. In this way, politics may be understood in a broader sense, including traditional party politics as well as issues and events that affect children indirectly or directly as citizens of global and local communities (Banaji and Buckingham 2013). In the next section, I examine the role of news media in supporting or undermining children's civic belonging, first turning to research on children's representation in news, followed by studies of the child news audience, and, finally, those looking at children's relationship to news production.

Representing children

Historically, children have had little control over their representation and have largely been constructed as news objects rather than subjects. 'Their voices', claims Holland, 'have had only limited access to the channels that produce public meanings, and even then the tools that are available to them have been inevitably honed by adults. Like all groups without power, they suffer the indignity of being unable to present themselves as they would want to be seen or, indeed, of even considering how they might want to be seen' (2006, 20).

Children are frequently used to symbolise the brutality of war, famine and genocide in adult news to arouse sympathy and humanise events (Carter and Messenger Davies 2005, 229; McKee 2003; Messenger Davies 2004; Seu 2015). For example, a 2003 *Guardian* story reported on the 11-year-old Iraqi boy, Ali Ismaeel Abbas's, loss of both arms and 14 family members in a bomb attack on Baghdad. As Carter and Messenger Davies suggest, 'Compounding this representation of Ali as a symbol of the suffering child was the absence of his voice telling us what had happened to him. Like the majority of children used to illustrate news stories about war and disaster, Ali was not interviewed or quoted in the article; he was not allowed to tell his own "story"' (2005, 230). On a related note, Aqtashi, Seif and Seif's (2004) comparative research on the Intifada examining news in the US, UK, Israel and Qatar found few stories about children. 'Palestinian children and their suffering and experiences', argued the authors, 'have a precarious place on the periphery of the dominant news narrative' (2004, 404). When children do show up in the news, they tend to be framed within discourses of violence and conflict; in discursive terms they do not exist outside these frames.

In Jakens's (2008) review of the UK charity Barnardo's study into public perceptions of childhood 'over 50% of the respondents believed that children were "beginning to behave like animals" and that children were responsible for "up to half of all crime" when, in fact, they are responsible for only around 12%' (Jakens 2008). The significance of these views is considerable, for as Davis and Bourhill (1997, 29) note they are often used as the basis for public policies restricting children's lives. Adult news reinforces its power over children through the use of 'simplistic generalisations with children represented as objects of concern or as threats to adult order' (1997, 31).

One of the strengths of children's news is that it emphasises understanding and context in the stories reported (Buckingham 2000, 45). However, often assumptions are made about children's news interests, knowledge and cognitive abilities, regarded as different and less developed than adults'. In Israel, children's news has developed because it is believed children need age-appropriate news to cope with the ongoing conflict (Alon-Tirosh 2012). Nevertheless, they are also discursively constructed as vulnerable citizens so content must be 'presented in a gentle, balanced manner that will not cause unbearable emotional load. Including soothing, reassuring (at times even optimistic) aspects is viewed as vital' (2012, v). In the US, *Nick News* tends to frame children as active 'consumer citizens' rather than political citizens (Banet-Weiser 2007). The aim is to encourage children to become discriminating actors in consumer culture. Children's information and communication needs are thus constructed as commercial, individual and apolitical rather than social, structural and political.

The child news audience

Lemish's (1998) research with kindergarten-aged children in the US and Israel found their interest in adult news is related to sociopolitical context and parental mediation. In Israel, children are encouraged to follow news since it provides important information about the ongoing conflict needed to stay informed and safe. They also discuss news with family and have high levels of news engagement (1998, 502). In the US, children tend to be protected from news for fear it will cause emotional harm. They rarely discuss news with family and have low levels of news engagement (1998, 501). In each country children are 'socialised into very different sets of expectations towards their news media and its role in a democratic society'. This point is confirmed by Seiter's (2007) study of US children's responses to the 2003 Iraq War, where she concluded that protection from news did not allay fears precisely because children had an insufficient grasp of facts needed to weigh up possible risks.

Nikken and Götz's (2007) investigation of children's postings about the Iraq war on children's news websites in the Netherlands and Germany regard them as important avenues through which children are enabled to share opinions. Most opposed the war and were concerned about its impact on ordinary people, but were not more fearful as a result of viewing news. 'Children', argued the authors, 'should also be given the opportunity to participate in contemporary debates. By writing to a children's channel or program, children can become politically active and very much involved in their own society' (2007, 117). Similarly, Carter (2007) examined children's message board postings on the *Newsround* website during the Iraq war and after the London bombings in 2005. On Iraq, some supported the war whilst others challenged its legality and morality. Certain children were upset that adults viewed their participation in anti-war marches as ill informed (various newspapers suggesting most were participating in order to bunk off school). 'Young people repeatedly state that they want to be accepted as citizens who possess legitimate points of views and rights' (2007, 132). In July 2005, some posters talked about a possible link between the London bombings and Britain's support for the Iraq war. Such message boards are valuable for children's development as citizens 'where many must feel they are being listened to and their views are valued' (2007, 138). Similarly, Carter et al.'s *Newsround* study (2009) established that whilst several expressed anger over exclusion from the news, others offered explanations. 'I think all children's ideas are important, just as important as adults, they just don't let us say anything because they think that adults' ideas are more sensible than children's' (Nat, Bournemouth, aged 9) (2009, 26; Mendes, Carter and Messenger Davies 2011).

News production

Early news production research sought to understand how children are drawn to newspaper reading so that they might develop the habit of reading a daily paper and become lifelong readers (Fendrick 1941). Such habits, it was argued, are central to the health of democracy. Several concerns shaped these studies: First, part of the responsibility of citizens is to ensure they keep informed about what is happening in the world in order to make informed contributions to public discussion and elect politicians who will represent their views. Thus, studies have typically focused on how news can be made to appeal to children (Clarke 1965). One idea was that a weekly comics section might lure young readers to newspapers (Schramm, Lyle and Parker 1960). Others have concentrated on understanding how much children recall from news to ensure the best medium is used to attract them and enhance civic knowledge (van der Molen and van der Voort 2000). A related interest has been economic, where news organisations seek to maximise existing audiences and build new ones to ensure long-term commercial viability (Molnar 2004)..

Scholars have also examined the production of news for children. Most have focused on television news, partly because it is regarded as the most child friendly (not requiring reading skills). Historically, few commercial broadcasters have produced children's news since it rarely returns a profit. The dearth of these programmes is partly due to high costs of production compared to dramas, cartoons and other entertainment genres that can be sold, resold and endlessly repeated worldwide. Additionally, advertisers prefer promotional slots next to 'fun' rather than 'serious' content. This has meant that few children's television news programmes have been produced, particularly daily bulletins, anywhere in the world (Hirst 2002). In most countries it is public service broadcasters who create children's news because of formal commitments to fostering children's citizenship. What sorts of programming do they produce and to what extent does it support children's civic needs and rights? Matthews's (2008) study of *Newsround* found that to maintain audiences, producers typically choose to highlight 'entertaining' stories over 'serious ones', and emotional reactions over reasoned ones (2008, 269–72). Moreover, stories tend to be simplified and events de-contextualised, making them more 'palatable' rather than 'intelligible' (2008, 274). Producers tend to view most children as too emotionally immature to handle serious news and are therefore acting in children's best interest by not routinely including them. Children are rarely challenged by difficult or upsetting stories that might encourage them to ask questions, think about the world differently, and mature as citizens. *Newsround* also tends to exaggerate children's participation in the world, creating a false impression of their contribution to civic life (Matthews 2008).

In their comparative study of the German children's news programme *logo!* and its Dutch counterpart *Jeugdjournaal*, Nikken and van der Molen (2007) found that in covering the 2003 Iraq war producers in the two countries took different presentational approaches. Reporters for *logo!* openly expressed anti-war sentiments whilst at *Jeugdjournaal* they were broadly supportive of the war. *logo!* was more cautious in its reports (using graphics, animations) than *Jeugdjournaal* which incorporated images of American prisoners. Both used pictures of George Bush to represent the 'good guys' and Saddam Hussein the 'bad guys' to simplify the war.

That said, producers in both countries felt it was important to cover the war and spent a great deal of time on the issues. Children's news has a vital role to play, the authors argue, 'in developing the political awareness and empowerment of children, and that broadcasters at all times should budget enough air time for these informational programmes' (2007, 196).

Conclusion

A focus on children's information and communication rights offers a vital starting point for future research on the importance of news to children's citizenship. If children feel politically alienated and disenfranchised, it is partly because their rights and responsibilities as citizens have been undermined by a failure to live up to legally enshrined commitments to encourage, value and take seriously their contributions to public discussion (Buckingham 2000; Carter et al. 2009). As a result, their civic rights and obligations have been diminished, often by those who unwittingly do so under a problematic assumption that children are in need of broad protection from the harsh realities of contemporary life. When the desire to protect diminishes their knowledge, understanding and empathy for the world around them, it diminishes everyone's social responsibility. As Seaton passionately contends, 'We worry about the damage violent media may do to them, but hardly show any concern for what might be valuable. We are very fearful for our children when what we ought to worry about is how to help them to thrive' (2005, 133).

References

Alon-Tirosh, M. (2012). *Children's News in Israel: Texts, Creators and Audiences*. Unpublished PhD dissertation, Tel Aviv University.

Archard, D. (2004). *Children: Rights and Childhood*, 2nd ed. London: Routledge.

Ariés, P. (1962). *Centuries of Childhood*. New York: Vintage.

Aqtashi, N. A., Seif, A. and Seif, A. (2004). 'Media Coverage of Palestinian Children and the Intifada.' *Gazette: The International Journal for Communication Studies*, 65(5), pp. 383–409.

Banaji, S. and Buckingham, D. (2013). *The Civic Web: Young People, the Internet, and Civic Participation*. Cambridge: The MIT Press.

Banet-Weiser, S. (2007). *Kids Rule! Nickelodeon and Consumer Citizenship*. Durham: Duke University Press.

Buckingham, D. (2000). *The Making of Citizens: The Role of News Media in Fostering Children's Information and Communication Rights Young People, News and Politics*. London: Routledge.

Cantor, J. and Nathanson, A. (1996). 'Children's Fright Reactions to Television News'. *Journal of Communication*, 46, pp. 139–52.

Carter, C. (2007). 'Talking about My Generation: A Critical Examination of Children's BBC *Newsround* Web Site Discussions about War, Conflict and Terrorism'. In: D. Lemish and M. Götz, eds., *Children and Media in Times of War and Conflict*. Creskill: Hampton Press, pp. 121–42.

Carter, C., Messenger Davies, M., Allan, S., Mendes, K., Milani, R. and Wass, L. (2009). What Do Children Want from the BBC? Children's Content and Participatory Environments in an Age of Citizen Media. Available at: http://www.bbc.co.uk/blogs/knowledgeexchange/cardifftwo.pdf [Accessed 8 July, 2016].

Carter, C. and Messenger Davies, M. (2005). '"A Fresh Peach Is Easier to Bruise": Children, Young People and the News'. In: S. Allan, ed., *Journalism: Critical Issues*. Maidenhead: Open University Press, pp. 224–38.

Clarke, P. (1965). 'Parental Socialization Values and Children's Newspaper Reading'. *Journalism & Mass Communication Quarterly*, 42(4), pp. 539–46.

Cobb, C. (2010). *Reading Newspapers May Spark Youth to Turn a Civic Leaf*. Available at: http://www.nationalpost.com/story.html?id1⁄476586c85-0db5-492f-8092-48ffdb2b2640 [Accessed 6 June, 2010].

Conway, J. J., Wyckoff, M. O., Feldbaum, E. and Ahern, D. (1981). "The News Media in Children's Political Socialization." *Public Opinion Quarterly*, 25(2), pp. 164–78.

Davis, H. and Bourhill, M. (1997). "'Crisis': The Demonization of Children and Young People." In: P. Scraton, ed., *'Childhood' in Crisis*, London: UCL, pp. 28–57.

Deth, J. W. van, Abendschön, S. and Vollmar, M. (2011). 'Children and Politics: An Empirical Reassessment of Early Political Socialization'. *Political Psychology* 32(1), pp. 147–74.

European Commission (2011). *An EU Agenda for the Rights of the Child.* Available at: http://eur-lex.europa. eu/legal-content/EN/TXT/PDF/?uri=CELEX:52011DC0060&from=en [Accessed 4 July, 2016].

European Convention (2000). *Charter of Fundamental Rights of the European Union*, Brussels. Available at: http://www.europarl.europa.eu/charter/pdf/text_en.pdf [Accessed 4 July, 2016].

Fendrick, P. (1941). 'Newspaper Reading Interests of High School and College Students'. *The Journal of Educational Research*, 34(7), pp. 522–30.

Gavin, M. L. (2011). 'How to Talk to Your Child About the News'. *KidsHealth.* Available at: http://kidshealth.org/ parent/positive/talk/news.html# [Accessed 2 Apr. 2012].

Hendrick, H. (1992). 'Children and Childhood'. *Refresh: Recent Findings of Research in Economic & Social History*, 15, pp. 1–4.

Hirst, C. (2002). 'Watch Out John Craven, Here's Jimmy Neutron: Why Isn't Commercial TV Interested in News Programmes for Children?' *The Independent* (8 February). Available at: http://www. independent. co.uk/news/media/watch-out-john-craven-heres-jimmy-neutron-641552.html [Accessed 8 July, 2016].

Hoffner, C. and Haefner, M. (1993). "Children's Affective Responses to News Coverage of the War." In: B. S. Greenberg and W. Gantz, eds., *Desert Storm and the Mass Media*. Cresskill: Hampton Press, pp. 364–80.

Holland, P. (2006). *Picturing Childhood: The Myth of the Child in Popular Imagery*. London: I.B. Taurus.

Jakens, F. (2008). 'Media Stereotypes Are Alienating a Whole Generation Argues Felix Jakens'. *Compass: Direction for the Democratic Left*. http://www.compassonline.org.uk/news/item. asp?n1⁄43473 [Accessed 16 July, 2011].

Jenks, C. (1992). *The Sociology of Childhood*. Aldershot: Ashgate.

Lemish, D. (2007). *Children and Television: A Global Perspective.* Oxford: Blackwell.

Lemish, D. (1998). 'What Is News? A Cross-Cultural Examination of Kindergartners' Understanding of News.' *Communication: European Journal of Communication Research*, 23, pp. 491–504.

Lister, R. (2007). 'Why Citizenship: Were, When and How Children?' *Theoretical Inquiries in Law*, 8(2), pp. 693–718.

Matthews, J. (2008). 'A Missing Link? The Imagined Audience, News Practices and the Production of Children's News'. *Journalism Practice*, 2(2), pp. 264–79.

McKee, K. B. (2003). "The Child as Image: Media Stereotypes of Children." In: P. M. Lester and S. D. Ross, eds., *Images that Injure: Pictorial Stereotypes in the Media*, 2nd ed. London: Praeger, pp. 159–66.

McLeod, J. M. (2000). 'Media and Civic Socialization of Youth'. *Journal of Adolescent Health*, 27, pp. 45–51.

Mendes, K., Carter, C., and Messenger Davies, M. (2011). "Young Citizens and the News." In: S. Allan, ed., *Routledge Companion to News and Journalism*. London: Routledge, pp. 450–59.

Messenger Davies, M. (2004). 'Innocent Victims, Active Citizens'. *Mediactive*, 3, pp. 55–66.

Molnar, A. (2004). *Virtually Everywhere: Marketing to Children in America's Schools. The Seventh Annual Report on Schoolhouse Commercialism Trends, 2003–2004.* Education Policy Studies Laboratory, Arizona State University College of Education. http://nepc.colorado.edu/files/EPSL-0409-103-CERU.pdf

Moyer-Gusé, E. and Smith, S. L. (2007). "TV News and Coping: Parents' Use of Strategies for Reducing Children's News-Induced Fears." In: D. Lemish and M. Götz, eds., *Children and Media in Times of War and Conflict*. Cresskill: Hampton Press, pp. 267–86.

Nash, K. (2009). *The Cultural Politics of Human Rights: Comparing the US and the UK*. Cambridge: Cambridge University Press.

Nikken, P. and Götz, M. (2007). 'Children's Writings on the Internet about the War in Iraq: A Comparison of Dutch and German Submissions to Guestbooks on Children's TV News programs.' In: D. Lemish and M. Götz, eds., *Children and Media in Times of War and Conflict*, Cresskill: Hampton Press, pp. 99–120.

Nikken, P. and van der Molen, J. H. (2007). 'Operation Iraqi Freedom' in the Children's News: A Comparison of Consolation Strategies Used by Dutch and German News Producers'. In: D. Lemish and M. Götz, eds., *Children and Media in Times of War and Conflict*, Cresskill: Hampton, pp. 177–99.

Oswell, D. (2013). *The Agency of Children: From Family to Global Human Rights*. Cambridge: Cambridge University Press.

Pascal, C. and Bertram, T. (2009). 'Listening to Young Citizens: The Struggle to Make a Real Participatory Paradigm in Research with Young Children'. *European Early Childhood Education Research Journal*, 17(2), pp. 249–62.

Piaget, J. (1969). *The Origins of Intelligence in the Child*. New York: International University Press.

Schramm, W., Lyle, J. and Parker, E. B. (1960). 'Patterns in Children's Reading of Newspapers'. *Journalism & Mass Communication Quarterly*, 37(1), pp. 35–40.

Seaton, J. (2005). "Little Citizens: Children, the Media and Politics." *The Political Quarterly*, 76, pp. 124–5.

Seiter, E. (2007). 'U.S. Children Negotiating the Protective Silence of Parents and Teachers on the War in Iraq'. In: D. Lemish and M. Götz, eds., *Children and Media in Times of War and Conflict*, Creskill: Hampton Press, pp. 37–56.

Seu, I. B. (2015). 'Appealing Children: UK Audience Responses to the Use of Children in Humanitarian Communications'. *The International Communication Gazette*, 77(7), pp. 654–67.

Smith, S. L., Pieper, K. M. and Moyer-Gusé, E. J. (2011). 'News, Reality Shows, and Children's Fears: Examining Content Patterns, Theories, and Negative Effects'. In: S. L. Calvert and B. J. Wilson, eds., *The Handbook of Children, Media and Development*, Oxford: Blackwell, pp. 214–34.

Stalford, H. (2016). *Not Seen, Not Heard: The Implications of Brexit for Children* (8 June). Available at: https://www.opendemocracy.net/brexitdivisions/helen-stalford/not-seen-not-heard-implications-of-brexit-for-children [Accessed 4 July, 2016].

Tolley, H., Jr. (1973). *Children and War: Political Socialization to International Conflict*. New York: Teachers College Press.

UNICEF (1989). *United Nations Convention on the Rights of the Child*. Available at: http://www.unicef.org.uk/Documents/Publication-pdfs/UNCRC_PRESS200910web.pdf [Accessed 4 July, 2016].

Valkenberg, P. M. (2004). *Children's Responses to the Screen: A Media Psychological Approach*. Mahwah: Lawrence Erlbaum.

van der Molen, J. W. (2004). 'Violence and Suffering in Television News: Toward a Broader Conception of Harmful Television Content for Children'. *Paediatrics*, 112(6), pp. 1771–75.

van der Molen, J. H. and van der Voort, T. H. A. (2000). 'The Impact of Television, Print, and Audio on Children's Recall of the News: A Study of Three Alternative Explanations for Dual-Coding Hypothesis'. *Human Communication Research*, 26(1), pp. 3–26.

Walkerdine, V. (2004). 'Developmental Psychology and the Study of Childhood'. In: M.J. Kehily ed., *An Introduction to Childhood Studies*, Maidenhead: Open University Press, pp. 96–107.

Wintour, P. (2015). 'Lords Reject Attempt to lower EU Referendum Voting Age to 16'. *The Guardian* (14 December). Available at: http://www.theguardian.com/politics/2015/dec/14/lords-reject--lower-eu-referendum-voting-age-16 [Accessed 8 July, 2016].

42

NEWS LANGUAGE AND HUMAN RIGHTS

Audiences and outsiders

Martin Conboy

Introduction

This chapter will assess how the language of the news can act to exclude vulnerable outsider communities as part of the process of media audience construction.

Despite journalism's long-articulated claims to contribute to an Enlightenment tradition of scrutinising the activities of politicians and other powerful figures in society, the construction of outsiders has long been a familiar strategy in newspapers, fitting within another less-heralded pattern of representation that comprises calls to insider communities of language and national identification. Particularly, but not exclusively, within the still politically potent British popular tabloid press, the maintenance of a core readership founded on insider and often reactionary communality is nowhere better illustrated than in dealing with the issue of 'human rights'. This phrase is often deployed to make an implicit claim that Britain is losing control of its borders, sovereignty, national integrity, courts and that it is assailed from the outside by alien cultures and authority figures.

News media and outsiders

It is a well-established point of departure that the news media are central to the representation and recycling of negative images of outsiders. This hostility can be expressed during times of war overseas or of social or political unrest at home. One of the most powerful articulations of the direct role that journalists play in reinforcing the declared positions of both the state and the military during armed conflict was Knightley's *First Casualty* (1975). A specifically linguistic analysis focusing on the first Iraq war included an assessment of the construction of Us/Them that invited engagement from readers in these terms (Hodge and Kress 1993). Such media coverage demonstrates a continuing pattern according to which the news media fall in line with the prevailing political preferences at any point of crisis when called upon to do so (Raboy and Dagenais 1992).

There has been a keen interest in the media representation of human rights issues in the last decade or so, notably with summative work such as Hamelink (2001) and Tomaselli and Young (2001). This work underlines the fact that from our Western perspective human rights are most often framed in terms of outsiders (e.g. China or Saudi Arabia) particularly when countries such as these are seen to evade international law on account of their political or financial influence. This sort of coverage strongly implies accusations of hypocrisy towards Western governments and companies who trade with countries with poor human rights records. The issue of human rights is equally framed in relation to or in terms of abuse of outsiders by our own government or its allies: torture during the Iraq war; Guantanamo Bay; Western complicity with corrupt regimes overseas; sales of weapons to military dictatorships. More recently we have seen specific explorations of human rights in specific circumstances such as the media's representation of human rights during the financial crisis (Chalabi 2010); the role of newspapers in addressing readers on human rights (Clark 2012); geopolitical case studies such as Anglo-American media representations of human rights in Latin America (Hafner-Burton and Ron 2013) or even, closer to our own topic under investigation, the security ramifications of human rights (Gordon 2014). Less often do we see human rights as an issue that looks inwards; human rights as a 'script' (Hall 1978) that triggers feelings of hostility to those who are perceived to be upholding a bogus or exploited version of these rights as a threat to the stability and security of the national community.

Audience construction

It could be claimed that one of the functions of news, beyond the simple provision of information, is to create a form of information that can consistently map onto audience expectations of insider/outsider groups. Research into news values across the decades has asserted that such tendencies are indeed characteristic of the press, particularly in its modern commercial manifestation (Galtung and Ruge 1965, Harcup and O'Neil 2001; Brighton and Foy 2007).

When viewed simply in market terms the construction of audiences might appear a benign and even necessary process in maintaining a consistent connection with consumers of a particular news product; 'stylin' the audience' as Bell has phrased it (1991). Capel (2008) and Martin and White (2005) have developed this work further emphasizing the bonding with audiences that the language of the media enables.

However, there are issues here beyond the commercial appeal of maintaining a close link with the target audience as was highlighted in the work of Cohen and Young (1981) which demonstrates the role of the press in constructing and reinforcing negative stereotypes of outsiders. The problem comes when insider identification comes at the cost of empathy to outsider groups and the extent to which news media act explicitly in the construction and marginalisation of those groups from the inside.

Even in terms of the 'imagined communities' of Benedict Anderson (1983) we can see a largely positive view of the impact of news media on the identification of an insider audience as a national grouping. Nevertheless, as Billig (1995) has pointed out, virulent forms of extreme nationalism can only be sustained by the routine flagging of banal, everyday versions and the press is an ideal conduit for such daily representations of the nation as an insider group. For all the differences between the language of the elite press and the popular tabloids (Jucker 1992; Conboy 2006; Bednarek 2006a) there is a commonality in representing outsiders as outside the national community across newspapers. For the purposes of this chapter, we can see in the work of Bednarek (2006b) how Europe is evaluated in the British press building on work by Anderson and Weymouth (1999) and Mautner (2000) on how the British press routinely calls upon the idea of an insider national community under attack from the hostile and intrusive forces of the European Union; Anderson and Weymouth go so far as to claim that this misinformation is nothing more than the press 'insulting the public'.

Despite journalism's long-articulated claims to contribute to an Enlightenment tradition of scrutinizing the activities of politicians and other powerful figures in society, the construction of outsiders for core communities of readers has long been a familiar strategy in newspapers particularly, but not exclusively, within the still politically potent British popular tabloid press. The maintenance of a core readership founded on insider and often reactionary communality is nowhere better illustrated than in dealing with the issue of 'human rights'. This phrase in itself often acts as a 'script' to be exploited as demonstrating that Britain is losing control of its borders, sovereignty, national integrity, courts and that it is assailed by alien cultures and outsider authority figures. In terms of human rights issues it is of note that this discourse can shift relatively easily to construct demon images of 'evil' insiders. The linguistic aspect of this process is key:

> [A]n audience is called into being by a particular discourse....Does it speak to us directly? Does it use a language we recognize as ours? Do we feel included in the world view and attitudes articulated by the text?
>
> *(Fulton 2005, 5)*

Building upon this, Wodak's work (2009, 2015) has consistently emphasized the vital link that the language of the media plays in establishing and maintaining national identities. This particular media language 'inscribes' (Conboy 2006, 15) the reader into a national narrative that has both exclusivity and exclusion at its heart. A key component in this process is the evaluative stance which, amplified through emotivity, ensures that it is 'in line with readers...' (Bednarek 2006a 206). This chapter will briefly identify the mechanisms that appear to predetermine the ways in which newspaper language is deployed to maintain reader identification in terms of constructing human rights as a threat to national sovereignty and security.

News narratives associated with human rights

In researching this chapter, I was interested in exploring whether, in an era increasingly characterized by more insular views of the outside world, the issue of human rights which has been so often associated with a representation of a superior benevolent attitude to the issues faced by non-Western political and economic cultures had shifted to being a discourse more associated with an introspective view of Britain as a country whose sovereignty is being challenged. I conducted an initial search for articles in the UK daily press on the Nexis database that contained the term 'human rights' over a period of three months from October to December 2015. This sample was then searched for items that dealt with human rights as an issue of internal concern for the UK. I should emphasize that this was not a quantitative survey and nor did it claim to provide an exhaustive account of the representation of human rights in the British press. It is rather intended as a qualitative assessment of some of the strategies used by the press in the UK to incorporate discussion of human rights into a more inward-looking set of political and cultural agendas and how this representation is mapped onto longer narratives that have appealed to British readers. The brief longitudinal survey, having shown a certain consistency in issues related to audience identification, was then supplemented by a selection of extracts from the press in early 2016 that confirm the clustering of ideas in the representation of human rights. In effect, this could be considered an exercise in extended pilot study exploring how the British press is shaping the language of representation of human rights to fit with insider identification with their targeted readerships.

An initial example of the conflation of human rights with people identified as social outsiders there is an online piece in the *Daily Mirror* that makes the association between human rights and prisoners serving sentences for violent crime. In a television panel discussion of the news, a celebrity panelist is reported as expressing the view that the Yorkshire Ripper should be denied any human rights, in an example of somebody undeserving of human rights because of his conviction for the murder of thirteen women. This is combined with the script of the taxpayer who is presented in the panelist's opinion as the funder of these 'rights' (Corner 2015).

Human rights when associated with overseas regimes considered implicitly or explicitly as inferior to the UK can be used as a means of political point scoring as here in the Conservative-supporting *Mail on Sunday* under the headline: 'Labour Law Chief's £2M Human Rights Hypocrisy'. The newspaper is quick to point out that the same shadow cabinet minster, Lord Falconer, who is representing the Republic of Djibouti in a human rights case was the same man who spoke with pride at the Labour Party conference only a month previously of his pride that it was a Labour government that passed the Human Rights Act which is now so criticized by the current Conservative government for its infringement of British sovereignty (*Mail on Sunday* 11 October 2015). In the body of the article we have a clear exposition of the sorts of human rights issues that are frequently associated with the 'uncivilized' outside states in implicit contrast to the UK's presumed civilized status.

On 12 October the provides a story from a liberal perspective, linking potential human rights violations with the government's proposed immigration bill; an example of an insider liberal readership being addressed in the coupling of an assessment of the Conservative government's policies running counter to the profile of a liberal constituency proud of its record on human rights at home:

> New fast-track eviction powers could breach human rights, warns watchdog:
> Measures in government's proposed immigration bill could violate protections if families and children are made destitute as a result of being made homeless
> Government proposals to legally require landlords to check the immigration status of their tenants risk a serious breach of human rights, an official has warned.
> (Guardian *12 October 2015*)

As the discussion on the Human Rights Act evolves, the Conservative-supporting *Daily Telegraph* launches one of its columnists into a deeply ironic tirade against film and television personalities who have expressed their views on the migration crisis. Using the rhetorical strategy of direct address and direct questioning of the reader, with a typographical emphasis in the capitalisation of 'REALLY' the headline reads:

'You know what would improve this country? I mean REALLY make Britain a better place to live?' The piece continues, positing 'luvvies and lawyers' against the presupposed interests of 'ordinary people' in a binary discussion which links human rights to Syrian migrants. (*Telegraph* online 12 October 2015).

The next day, we can read another contribution to this tradition of acerbic commentary in the *Daily Mail* by commentator Max Hastings whose article is headlined in a rude, imperative address to a caricatured judiciary: 'KEEP YOUR NOSES OUT M'LUDS'

It begins by asserting a clearly held and explicit hostility to the European Court of Human Rights, referring to it as: 'That pernicious body'. While criticising a judiciary that is out of touch and safely distanced from any actual contact with the realities of experiencing the migrants personally, the piece reinforces the status of Britain as a constituent of the 'civilized and peaceful Western world' which enjoys the privileges of human rights (*Daily Mail* 13 October 2015).

Amidst this heated discussion of the implications of human rights on home issues, the consideration of the human rights record of outsider communities to Britain is not ignored totally. In the left-leaning *Daily Mirror* we can see a good example of how the visit of Chinese President

Xi is exploited in a popular and humorous fashion. A core British culinary reference to fish and chips is developed in a series of punning gambits. The President has 'skip the human rights' inserted into his order and it is assumed he does not expect to be 'battered' over China's human rights record. A reference to Britain's implicit superiority is touched upon when it is explained that only the British tradition of 'good manners' will prevent the President being embarrassed:

I'll have fish and chips please… but skip the human rights:
China president's menu for British visit
China's president does not expect to be battered over his human rights record during his land-mark visit to Britain.
Xi Jinping, who cannot wait to sample fish and chips on the four-day trip, hopes another of our traditions – good manners – will prevent Labour leader Jeremy Corbyn from tackling him over the appalling abuses.
(Daily Mirror *19 October 2015*)

Several newspapers in the period under review pick up on the story that there has been an increase in claims against British military personnel in the courts under the general heading of human rights abuses. A piece in *Daily Mail* dealing with the subject on 19 October 2015 by Tamara Cohen, the newspaper's political correspondent, provides a useful illustration of modality and metaphorical vernacular so characteristic of the tabloid genre and concluding with a reductive journalistic script in the context of the real-life complexity of military targets: 'Britain could ditch Human Rights Law for Troops in Battle' (*Daily Mail* 19 October 2015). This piece stresses the communality of the 'taxpayers' (Conboy 2006) who are being asked to pay for the law suits against British troops who are fighting 'suspected Taliban and bomb-makers'.

On the front page of the *Sunday Times* on 8 November 2015 we see a presupposition (Conboy 2007, 69–70; Richardson, 2007, 62–4) of abuses of human rights flowing from the existing Human Rights laws shared with Europe and the highlighting of the British traditions enshrined in the alternative that is being considered by British judges:

Human rights law to be axed; British bill of rights revealed
Plans to end the abuse of human rights laws and stamp out the courtroom compensation culture can be revealed today… judges will be told they will not have to follow rulings of the European Court of Human Rights in Strasbourg slavishly.
Instead they would be able to rely on common law – the body of judicial rulings built up in Britain over centuries – or rulings in courts in other Commonwealth countries such as Australia and Canada, when making their judgments.
(Sunday Times *8 November 2015*)

The European Court of Human Rights is regularly articulated as a crossroads of competing narratives on British identity, British exceptionalism, the sovereignty of the British parliament, the ability of the Armed Forces to function effectively. These all fit within the patterns of European representation identified by Anderson and Weymouth (1999) and Mautner (2000) in the British press.

To answer, in part, this constant flow of stories demonizing the European Court of Human Rights, a more liberally inclined newspaper, the *Daily Mirror*, provides another characteristically humorous account that links the release of a very popular British television sitcom *Dad's Army* as a film with Cameron's attempts to negotiate an improved deal for Britain within the EU. The headline is a play on the first line of the title song of the sitcom which runs: 'Who do you think you are kidding, Mr Hitler?' The ready reference to such television programmes is facilitated in part by the regularity with which they are referenced in the tabloid press (Conboy 2006, 35–7). The piece draws for different purposes on the use of direct questions to the readership and, in highlighting the genesis of the Human Rights Act out of the sacrifices of World War Two stresses the figure of Winston Churchill so often an iconic figure for right-wing, patriotic rhetoric but here exploited for very different liberal purposes and concludes by paraphrasing part of one of his most famous speeches.

> Who do you think you are kidding Cam?
>
> Seventy years after the end of the Second World War, Herr Hitler would crack a wry smile if he saw Britain today...
>
> Remember human rights? Hundreds of thousands gave their lives to protect them. And after we conquered Nazism, Britain helped establish the European Convention on Human Rights.
>
> Many have said these enshrined rights, this moral code, has helped stop more world wars.
>
> Now Cameron wants to leave it, to rip up our own Human Rights Act and stand alone...
>
> Churchill must be spinning in his grave. We may have fought them on the beaches but soon they'll be beating us in the courts.

By the end of the year, the papers are returning to the story of the European Court's perspective on the status of the Armed Forces in relation to human rights. One particular account is framed within the broader context of human rights as a cornerstone of the superiority of the West over 'despotic enemies' but also provides an equally strong assertion of Britain's 'common sense' on this issue.

> Britain's soldiers need the legal freedom to fight.
>
> The Government is right to review the impact of human rights law on the Armed Forces.
>
> ... Human rights are critical: the West's recognition of civil liberties not only protects us from abuse by the state but gives the democratic nations a moral edge over their despotic enemies ... The Government's reassertion of common sense is most welcome. Britain's servicemen and women need to know that justice won't let them down.
>
> (Sunday Telegraph *December 27 2015)*

As an editorial contrast we can read a very different view in the *Daily Mirror* which, much more sympathetic to the Human Rights Act which is the substance of the report, chooses to select a quotation from Liberal Democrat leader Tim Farron who takes on Michael Fallon's reductive and highly memorable sound bite on 'ambulance-chasing lawyers' dismissing his statement as 'jingoistic rubbish'. It reverses the arguments made in the right-wing press, asserting the role of human rights in protecting all of our liberties, including the soldiers who have fought to protect those same rights:

> Our soldiers are currently fighting extremism to protect values like freedom, democracy and civil liberties – the very human rights that others seek to extinguish.
>
> We do not win by joining such terrorists in the gutter by diminishing our own commitment to human rights. We win by being more tolerant, open and decent,' he said.

Our soldiers fought to protect our liberties, now some politicians are trying to hide behind them to strip us of our human rights.

(Mirror *online 27 December 2015*)

Inscribing an audience for human rights issues

At the start of 2016, several running news stories became a catalyst for human rights issues, related to fears of intrusions into Britain territorial and judicial space. The two most prominent stories are associated with the refugee crisis that is deepening by the day and the impending referendum on Britain's place in the EU. As these have been long-running opportunities for the right-wing press to express concerns about British sovereignty and control of borders, it is no surprise to see that they emerge most often attached to news that fits within audience expectations. Such stories are not restricted to the popular tabloids as a news item on the first page of the broadsheet *Daily Telegraph* demonstrates. The headline here compresses the story into a metaphor that implies that the court judgment has provided an easy passage to Britain for some of the refugees in Calais. The story prefers to stress that it is a 'victory for migrants' although it could more easily be considered such a victory if it were narrated with a more positive perspective on human rights themselves. The story continues with modal verbs 'must' and 'could' that highlight the possibility of further migrants being encouraged to try to enter Britain through this route but which contrast with the certainty of the headline, designed to draw the reader into a *fait accompli*. The choice of phrasing 'court orders' presents the reader with a verbal expression that highlights the action of the court, acting under the jurisdiction of the European Convention of Human Rights, that appears to diminish the ability of the British courts to legislate on their own terms and indeed this is a common thread within the right-wing newspapers' agenda:

> Human rights ticket to Britain
> Victory for migrants as judges rule that young men in Calais 'Jungle' can join siblings in UK…. Right to a family life
> 'Jungle' residents must be allowed into Britain to be with siblings, court orders
> Human rights ruling could set precedent allowing more refugees to join families living in UK.

(Daily Telegraph *21 January 2016*)

A similar approach is taken on the same story in the popular tabloid the *Sun* where the abbreviation of the headline is once again deployed to present the decision as a victory for the refugees. The impersonal construction, 'It sparked fears' avoids stating who has these fears, so it becomes a statement of undisputed but undemonstrated fact. This leads in the same sentence to the modal assertion that it 'could open the floodgate into Britain,' drawing upon a familiar reference to the metaphorical domain of water so potent in the imaginary of an island nation:

> Syrians win right to UK
> Four Syrian refugees living in the Calais 'Jungle' camp can come to the UK, a court has ruled.
> It sparked fears the landmark decision could open the floodgate into Britain.

(Sun *21 January, 2016*)

A final example, also prominently displayed on a front page comes from a different right-wing popular tabloid, the *Daily Mail*. This piece is illustrative of a direct implication that the paper is talking to a knowing readership, fully aware of and supportive of the newspaper's stand on this issue and equally aware of the supposed failings of claims which rest on the human rights of suspected criminals. The phrase 'human rights' is presented in inverted commas, once again implying an insider gesture towards scepticism. This is further underlined by the phrasing of the opening sentence where the paper reports that 'you guessed' that the reason the police have to keep details of suspected criminals secret is because of their human rights. This allusion to the readership being one step ahead of the game here suggests that the script of human rights has a sense of inevitability built into to it, encouraging a sense of cynical resignation among the readership. The presupposition of this assertion, 'you guessed,' links with the targeted readership's understanding as presented in the paper and also the further expectations of impotence in the face of bureaucracy. This aside flatters the readership that they have already figured out why this is the case because implicitly a) they share the same perspective as the newspaper and b) they are capable of following the implications of an issue which is of great interest to them:

POLICE: WE WON'T NAME FUGITIVES
Identities of suspected killers and rapists on run are kept secret and, you guessed, it's because of human rights.

(Daily Mail *13 February, 2016*)

Conclusion

This chapter has considered how the subject of human rights is addressed in the British press as a theme that incorporates more complex identifications of the insider-outsider dynamics of newspaper readerships. It has considered various linguistic devices that newspapers from left and right of the political spectrum regularly deploy in substantiating their support or opposition to contemporary legislation regarding human rights. No newspapers, it should be noted, express the opinion that human rights should be discarded or ignored. All newspapers consider themselves and the British squarely within a discourse of Western superiority on the issue of human rights but different newspapers qualify their support depending on where they stand on broader issues. These issues in the press from late 2015 to early 2016 are aligned very clearly with political debate about the status and power of the EU and its proxy on human rights the European Court of Human Rights.

References

Anderson, B. (1983). *Imagined Communities*. London: Verso.

Anderson, Peter, J. and Weymouth, T. (1999). *Insulting the Public: The British Press and the European Union*. London: Routledge.

Anon (2015). 'Britain's soldiers need the legal freedom to fight'. *Sunday Telegraph* (27 December). Available at: http://www.telegraph.co.uk/comment/telegraph-view/12070047/Britains-soldiers-need-the-legal-freedom-to-fight.html [Accessed 31 Mar. 2016].

Anon (2015). 'Who do you think you are kidding, Cam?' *Daily Mirror* (15 November), p. 14.

Anon (2015). 'You cannot have human rights on the battlefield'. *Daily Express* (19 October), p. 12.

Baker, P.; Gabrielatos, C.; KhosraviNik, M.: Krzyzanowski, M.; McEnery, T.; Wodak, R. (2008). 'Useful Methodological Synergy? Combining Critical Discourse Analysis and Corpus Linguistics to Examine Discourses of Refugees and Asylum Seekers in the UK Press'. *Discourse and Society*, 19(3), pp. 273–306.

Barrett, D. (2015). 'Britain Wins Ground in Prisoner Voting Row'. *Daily Telegraph*, 11 Dec., p. 16.

Beal, J. (2016). 'Syrians Win Right to UK'. *Sun*, 21 Jan., p. 2.

Bednarek, M. (2006a). *Evaluation in Media Discourse: Analysis of a Newspaper Corpus*. London: Continuum.

Bednarek, M. (2006b). 'Evaluating Europe: parameters of evaluation in the British press' in C. Leung and J. Jenkins (eds.) *Reconfiguring Europe: The Contribution of Applied Linguistics* (British Studies in Applied Linguistics 20). London: BAAL/Equinox, pp. 137–56.

Bednarek, M. and Caple, H. (2012). *News Discourse*. London: Continuum.

Bell, A. (1991). *The Language of News Media* Oxford: Blackwell.

Billig, M. (1995). *Banal Nationalism*. London: Sage.

Brighton, P. and Foy, D. (2007). *News Values.* London: Sage.

Capel, H. (2008). 'Intermodal Relations in Image-nuclear Stories'. In: L. Unsworth ed., *Multimodal Semiotiocs: Functional Analysis in Contexts of Education*. London: Continuum, pp. 125–38.

Chalabi, M. O. (2010). 'The Media's Presentation of Human Rights During the Financial Crisis: Framing the "Issues"', *Journal of Global Ethics*, 6(3), pp. 255–72.

Clark, R. (2012). 'Bringing the Media In: Newspaper Readership and Human Rights'. *Sociological Inquiry*, 82(4), pp. 532–56.

Cohen, S. (1976). *Folk Devils and Moral Panics: The Creation of Mods and Rockers*. London: Paladin Press.

Cohen, S.Y. and Young, J. (1981) eds. *The Manufacture of News: Deviance, Social Problems and the Mass Media*. London: Sage.

Cohen, T. (2015). 'Britain Could Ditch Human Rights Law for Troops in Battle'. *Daily Mail* (19 October), p. 13.

Conboy, M. (2006). *Tabloid Britain*: *Constructing a Community Through Language*. London: Routledge.

Conboy, M. (2007). *The Language of the News.* London: Routledge.

Conboy, M (2015). 'Locating Critiques of Normativity: Geo-historical Perspectives.' *African Journalism Studies*, 36(1), pp. 78–84.

Corner, N. (2015). 'Angry Coleen Nolan says Yorkshire Ripper should be "denied human rights" for taking lives of 13 women'. *Daily Mirror online* (October 5). Available at: http:// www.mirror.co.uk/tv/ tv-news/angry-coleen-nolan-says-yorkshire-6576852 [Accessed 23 April 2017].

Dominiczak, P.; Barrett, D. and Holehouse, M. (2016). 'Human Rights Ticket to Britain'. *Daily Telegraph* (21 January), p. 1.

Fulton, H. (2005). 'Introduction: The Power of Narrative', In: H. Fulton, R. Huisman, J. Murphet and A. Dunn eds., *Narrative and Media*. Cambridge: Cambridge University Press, pp. 1–7.

Gabrielatos, C. and Baker, P. (2008). Fleeing, Sneaking, Flooding: a Corpus Analysis of Discursive Constructions of Refugees and Asylum Seekers in the UK Press, 1996-2005'. *Journal of English Linguistics*, 36(1), pp. 5–38.

Gallagher, I. (2015). 'Labour Law Chief's £2M Human Rights Hypocrisy'. *Mail on Sunday* (11 October), p. 14.

Galtung, J. and Ruge, M. (1965). 'The Structure of Foreign News: The Presentation of the Congo, Cuba and Cyprus Crises in Four Norwegian Newspapers'. *Journal of International Peace Research*, 1, pp. 64–91.

Glaze, B. (2015). 'I'll Have Fish and Chips Please… But Skip the Human Rights' *Daily Mirror*, 19 Oct., p. 23.

Gordon, N. (2014). 'Human Rights as a Security Threat: Lawfare and the Campaign against Human Rights NGOs'. *Law & Society Review*, 48(2), pp. 311–44.

Greenslade, R. (2005). *Seeking Scapegoats: The Coverage of Asylum in the UK Press*. London: Institute for Public Policy Research.

Hafner-Burton, E. and James R. (2013). 'The Latin Bias: Regions, the Anglo-American Media, and Human Rights'. *International Studies Quarterly*, 57, pp. 474–491.

Hall, S. (1978). 'The Social Production of News'. Hall, S., Critcher, C., Jefferson, T., Clark J. and Roberts, B. *Policing the Crisis*. London: Macmillan.

Hamelink, C. J. (2001). 'Introduction Human Rights and the Media' *Critical Arts*, 15(1–2), pp. 3–11.

Harcup, T. and O'Neill, D. (2001). 'What is News? Galtung and Ruge Revisited'. *Journalism Studies,* 2 (2), pp. 261–80.

Hartley-Brewer, J. (2015). 'Luvvies and Lawyers Should Shut-up about the Syrian Refugee Crisis'. *Telegraph.* (October 12). Available at: http://www.telegraph.co.uk/news/worldnews/middleeast/ syria/11926192/Luvvies-and-lawyers-should-shut-up-about-the-Syrian-refugee-crisis.html [Accessed 31 Mar., 2016].

Hastings, M. (2015). 'Keep Your Noses Out M'luds', *Daily Mail* (13 October), p. 18.

Hodge, R. and Kress, G. (1993). *Language as Ideology*. Routledge: London.

Horsti, K. (2007). 'Asylum Seekers in the News: Frames of Illegality and Control'. *Observatorio*. 1(1), pp. 145–61.

Jucker, A. (1992). *Social Stylistics: Syntactic Variation in British Newspapers*. Berlin/New York: Mouton de Gruyter.

KhosraviNik, M. (2010). 'The Representation of Refugees, Asylum Seekers and Immigrants in British Newspapers: A Critical Discourse Analysis'. *Journal of Language and Politics*, 9(1), pp. 1–28.

Knightley, P. (1975). *The First Casualty: The War Correspondent as Hero, Propagandist and Myth Maker from the Crimea to Vietnam.* New York: Harcourt Brace Jovanovich.

Martin, A. (2016). 'Police: We Won't Name Fugitives'. *Daily Mail* (13 February).

Martin, J. R. and White, P. R. R. (2005). *The Language of Evaluation: Appraisal in English.* Basingstoke: Palgrave Macmillan.

Matthews, J. and Brown, A. R. (2011). 'Negatively shaping the asylum agenda? The representational strategy and impact of a tabloid news campaign'. *Journalism: Theory, Practice and Criticism,* 13(6), pp 802–17.

Mautner, G. (2000). *Der britische Europa-Diskurs. Methodenreflexion und Fallstudium zur Berichterstattung in der Tagespresse.* Wien: Passagen Verlag.

Ovsiovitch, J. S. (1993). 'News Coverage of Human Rights'. *Political Research Quarterly*, 46(3) pp. 671–89.

Raboy, M. and Dagenais, B. (1992). *Media, Crisis and Democracy: Mass Communication and the Disruption of Social Order.* London: Sage.

Reisigl, M. and Wodak, R. (2014). 'The Discourse-Historical Approach'. In: R. Wodak and Meyer, eds., *Methods of Critical Discourse Analysis*, 3rd ed. London: Sage, pp. 23-61.

Richardson, J. E. (2007). *Analysing Newspapers: An Approach from Critical Discourse Analysis.* Houndmills: Palgrave.

Shipman, T. (2015). 'Human Rights Law to be Axed'. *Sunday Times* (8 November), pp. 1, 8.

Smith, M. (2015). '"Suspend Human Rights Act so Soldiers Don't Have to Worry about Being Sued", says Michael Fallon'. *Mirrror,* 27 Dec. Available at: http://www.mirror.co.uk/news/uk-news/suspend-human-rights-act-soldiers-7078149 [Accessed 31 Mar. 2016].

Swerling, G. (2015). 'Racist Killer Wins Human Rights Case'. *Times* (1 October). 2015, p.13.

Tomaselli, K. & Young, M. (2001). 'Revisiting Media and Human Rights', *Critical Arts*, 15(1–2), pp. 1–2.

Travis, A. (2015). 'New Fast-track Eviction Powers Could Breach Human Rights, Warns Watchdog'. *Guardian*, 12 Oct. Available at: http://www.theguardian.com/uk-news/2015/oct/12/new-fast-track-eviction-powers-could-breach-human-rights-warns-watchdog [Accessed 31 Mar. 2016].

Van Dijk, T. (1993). *Elite Discourse and Racism.* London: Sage.

Van Meeren, F. H. and Grootendorst, R. (1992). *Argumentation, Communication and Fallacies: A Pragma-Dialectical Perspective.* Hillsdale, NJ: Lawrence Erlbaum.

Wodak, R. (2015). *The Politics of Fear: What Right-Wing Populist Discourses Mean.* London: Sage.

Wodak, R., De Cilla, R., Reisigl, M., Liebhart, K. (2009). *The Discursive Construction of National Identity.* Edinburgh: Edinburgh University Press.

43

MEDIA, HUMAN RIGHTS AND POLITICAL DISCOURSE

Lisa Brooten

This chapter examines the intersection of human rights, media and political discourse. It provides an overview of the politics of rights as they emerged and as they relate to communication, representations of human rights issues in media and the impact on political discourse as a result of the increasing pervasiveness of rights. Drawing on critical rights scholarship, the chapter analyses the limitations of rights discourse in addressing political problems, in particular the focus on civil and political rights characteristic of globally dominant approaches to human rights. Human rights discourse has come to dominate discussions on vital issues of concern globally, yet in some cases is also avoided in media coverage, with significant political impact. The focus on civil and political rights often displaces attention to key political interests and elides key structural issues central to efforts for change, issues that would be unavoidable with attention to social, economic and cultural rights. The chapter will analyse the efficacy of human rights discourse as a tool for addressing fundamental global problems, with attention to its impact on immigration and citizenship, war and humanitarian disasters, and media reform.

The politics of human rights

The political nature of modern human rights debates and norms has been clear from their emergence, and divergent accounts of the origins of the modern human rights system provide insight into the different interests at stake. The various 'generations' of rights and the attention they receive is further evidence of the political nature of human rights concepts. The marginalization of calls for a broader set of communication rights beyond press freedom demonstrates these distinctions in play in the field of communication. We begin with debates about the origins of the modern human rights system.

The emergence of rights

The most common framing of the origins of modern international human rights norms is that they emerged in reaction to the atrocities of World War II and the Holocaust. This version, if it mentions colonialism at all, generally notes that colonial oppression was a causal factor, along with calls for minority rights and the right to a homeland. Yet critical historians such as Samuel Moyn (2010) and Randall Williams (2010) argue that human rights emerged not as a utopian ideal or normative goal but as a way to depoliticise popular post-war anti-colonial struggles. Moyn (2010) argues that this celebratory, 'most universally repeated myth' misrepresents these origins, which were actually regarded as a 'consolation prize' for 'what many around the world wanted, the collective entitlement to self-determination' (44–5). This more critical version, then, attributes the rise of human rights to the efforts of powerful nations to displace revolutionary nationalism and anti-colonialism, despite the role of rights as perhaps 'the most inspiring mass utopianism Westerners have had before them in recent decades' (Moyn 2010, 9; Williams 2010).

During the 1960s, almost no non-governmental organizations (NGOs) promoted human rights as a goal, yet within a decade, this had changed, and since the 1970s, human rights have risen in prominence, arguably through 'the moral displacement of politics' (Moyn 2010, 43). Williams (2010) argues that 'it is precisely here, in a post-Cold-War context marked by an unprecedented militarisation of the world by a singular hegemonic power, that human rights emerged as the privileged epistemic form for political violence' (xx). In this era of advanced global capitalism, the state has found in human rights discourse as advanced by NGOs 'a default ally', he maintains, by 'rejecting out-of-hand any and all claims to the right of armed resistance regardless of conditions, past or present' (Williams 2010, xxii).

As the language of criticism internationally, human rights are established by national and international laws defining and protecting them, and 'the securing of rights is a profoundly *political* process' (Crawford 2010, 94, emphasis in original) in which the concept of human rights concepts often displace politics through commodification or co-optation by dominant interests. Human rights developed in the UK, for example, as an alternative to the collective securement of rights, as through trade unions (Bell and Cemlyn 2014). In Ghana, a high degree of NGO intervention in efforts to promote rights focuses primarily on rights education, rather than on the mobilization and networking needed to demand rights from local government officials, who have more accountability to the President than to the people they ostensibly serve (Crawford 2010). Since September 11, 2001, anti-terrorism laws have been passed in many countries worldwide, extending counterterrorism legislation and restrictions to a broader range of groups and forms of protest than previously targeted, becoming in many cases a pretext for repression of political rights and the right to freedom of expression (Balabanova 2015).

Three 'generations' of rights

Human rights are commonly classified into three 'generations' or 'tiers'. The best known are the 'first generation' civil and political (CP) rights, which arose during the eighteenth century, and the 'second generation' social, economic and cultural (SEC) rights, which emerged during the late nineteenth and early twentieth centuries. The third is a set of group-oriented rights such as the right to self-determination, the right to development, and the right to peaceful coexistence, which arose during the late twentieth century (Yokota 1999). First generation rights are considered negative, requiring restrictions on action, usually from the state, and are immediately enforceable. Second generation rights are considered positive, requiring governments to act by providing resources for their progressive realization over time, especially in poorer countries with few resources (Crawford 2010). The 'third generation' rights are framed as people's rights or group rights, as their realization is collective in nature, a controversial notion that raises questions about their categorization as 'human rights', widely understood as protections for individuals (Yokota 1999).

CP rights are protected under the International Covenant on Civil and Political Rights (ICCPR), one of two fundamental global human rights treaties adopted by the UN General Assembly. SEC rights are guaranteed by the other, the International Covenant on Economic,

Social and Cultural Rights (ICESCR). Both came into force in 1976. The ICCPR guarantees the right to freedom of belief, speech, association and the press. The ICESCR focuses on basic human needs, and in terms of communication and media includes the right to self-determination, public participation in cultural life, education and academic freedom, and protection from discrimination. While very few developed nations have pursued the advancement of SEC rights, or the mechanisms to enforce them (Bernier 2010), the United States is the only major industrialised democracy that has not ratified the ICESCR, despite signing it in 1979.

SEC rights generally are not as clearly defined or established as CP rights, were established later, are still evolving, and have yet to be taken up and in many cases supported or even accepted within domestic legislative and judicial systems. Thus in many countries, remedies to redress their violation are often unavailable, inadequate or ineffective (Alexander 2004; Yokota 1999). The literature on human rights emphasizes the interdependence and indivisibility of the various rights, yet also widely acknowledges the global emphasis on individual CP rights at the expense of SEC rights (Ajei 2015; Alexander, 2004; Bell & Cemlyn 2014; Yokota 1999). As a result, SEC rights often 'remain as nominal rights without any force', generating scepticism about the sincerity of the human rights movement, especially given the magnitude of deprivation globally, the ambiguity of rights language, and its inability to express people's most urgent needs (Alexander 2004, 463).

Communication rights

The issue of how rights relate to media and political discourse involves not only media content but also the longstanding debate over the concept of 'communication rights', which mirrors concerns regarding the globally dominant focus on CP rights and how and in whose interests this functions. The debate arose during calls for a New World Information and Communication Order (NWICO) during the 1970s and 1980s from critics in many newly independent nations of the global south, who decried 'a continuation of imperialism by other means: patterns of information flows clearly still mirrored a centre-periphery power relationship concerning content as well as infrastructure' (Hamelink and Hoffman 2008, 2). To promote greater access to the means of expression for marginalized peoples and for the least powerful nations, they called for a 'right to communicate' (R2C) that would help people worldwide access media not only to *receive* a diverse set of viewpoints but also to speak and *be heard*. R2C would be both an individual and a social right, and would democratise communication. Recognition of the R2C might require journalists to work to better include marginalized people's perspectives and participation, and policymakers to prioritize a community media sector, thus increasing people's ability to participate in the political process.

The US and its allies, however, pushed instead for the 'free flow of information' doctrine, arguing that the R2C would sideline individual rights and strengthen state intervention in people's lives. The R2C 'became the victim of ferocious ideological disputes, mutual distrust and incidental uprisings of paranoia which eventually made it impossible to consider the merits of all arguments in a rational manner' (Hamelink and Hoffman 2008, 3). In 1984, the US, the UK and Singapore withdrew their membership in UNESCO, effectively ending the debate over NWICO and the R2C, which became a taboo topic at UNESCO. The push for R2C remains frustrated, exemplified by the marginalization of public service and community media around the world.

Nevertheless, the call for communication rights continues, including at the United-Nations-sponsored World Summit on the Information Society (WSIS), convened in Geneva, Switzerland in 2003 and in Tunis, Tunisia in 2005, and in follow-up meetings since. The R2C again became the focus of intense debate, with critics such as the World Press Freedom Committee arguing that it would muzzle press freedom. The final summit documents do not include discussion of the R2C, or the digital divide, a problem that has come to be framed not in terms of communication rights, but in terms of development.

Framing development, the market and human rights

Rights-based approaches to development have often been considered too political or controversial, yet have recently been incorporated by prominent international development agencies, UN agencies, bilateral agencies, NGOs and people's movements (Alexander 2004; Crawford 2010; Mokhiber 2001). Aid has largely become contingent on human rights conditions and assumptions of liberal development goals, the market economy, and participative democracy (Nascimento, 2015). Yet policy generally frames CP rights disproportionately in relationship to democracy, while SEC rights have been reframed from rights to trade and aid using the rhetoric of the free market, which positions citizens as indebted recipients of aid and charity. This 'reverses the moral obligation, placing its recipients in a position of moral if not legal obligation toward 'democracy donors'" (Teti 2015, 16). Those with the most influence over which human rights get prioritized are 'powerful market actors', and Bernier (2010) argues that

> [T]he real importance given to the universal values enshrined in international human rights treaties mainly depends on their compatibility with the overall purposes of the market. This way, the fact that socio-economic human rights violations are often caused by powerful market forces is not addressed in the dominant human rights discourse. This can bring people to wrongly believe in a just world where human rights are valued and respected when, in reality, many suffer from serious deprivation.
>
> *(263–4)*

The solution to securing SEC rights is often framed discursively as continued liberalization and privatization, and 'market efficiency… is the main factor used to assess policy initiatives' (Bernier 2010, 263; Brooten at al. 2015). Many countries claim their SEC rights obligations are being met through trade and development initiatives, but loans are often made contingent upon participation in international trade, usually involving cuts in the social sector. Human rights stories tend to focus on abuses within communities, rather than on the state's limitations in providing for its inhabitants, and then only some states become the focus of attention and repeated popular tropes. Also, a focus on the state as the arbiter of human rights elides examination of the 'very real inequalities between states' stemming from the military and economic dominance of the most powerful countries (Bernier 2010, 265). In Mexico, for example, the national and state human rights commissions were established during negotiations for the North America Free Trade Agreement, 'largely as a way to allay US concerns about the Mexican government's human rights record' (McPherson 2102, 98). As a result, 'the critical lens is focused closely on the behavior of the Mexican state toward its citizenry, rather than aimed abroad' (McPherson 2012, 98). Similarly, although human rights agencies in Cambodia's political transition claim to be supportive of civil society, Hughes (2007) finds that they have undermined collective interests, atomising political participation by focusing on monitoring abuses, advocacy with the government, and training, largely discouraging protests and undermining contentious political action. The media play a key role in this process, for example, by discouraging representations of militant workers as champions of the oppressed (Hughes 2007).

These findings challenge the notion that 'global civil society' exists in tension with networks of global capital or alliances of states, demonstrating how INGOs can be 'the handmaidens of multilateral institutions…. empowering the industrialized north at the expense of the South' (Hughes 2007, 837). An elite consensus has emerged 'around a notion of liberal peace, which incorporates the promotion by force of globalized market democracy at the expense of genuinely redistributive agendas' (Hughes 2007, 837). Bernier (2010) argues similarly that 'one of the biggest problems with socioeconomic rights is the powerful interest lying at the core of existing political and economic institutions that undermine their realization" (266). Human rights discourse has been used to justify contemporary imperialist interventions, with the communications industries playing a key role as media texts often erase detrimental forms of US involvement while 'figuring the West… as humanitarian saviour' (Williams 2010, xxv).

Media coverage and political impact

Media are vital in the formation of public opinion and dominant discourses, yet a great deal of human rights news 'never reaches a public because it is not witnessed, it is not considered newsworthy, or it contraindicates the media's editorial line aims' (McPherson 2012, 119; Borer, 2012a; Cottle, 2009). This includes information concerning groups that do not make up a significant portion of the readership, or stories that do not involve bloodshed, such as health and education rights. Discussing the right to healthcare, for example, Bernier (2010) finds that the 'international socio-economic human rights [legal] system… as it currently operates, is incompatible with a global distributive justice framework in health' (246). And while the UN and other international agencies often critique countries for their civil and political rights record, they generally fail to hold nations and institutions equally responsible for violations of economic rights (Alexander 2004; Yokota 1999). These news 'silences' can have just as much of an impact on public opinion, public discourse and policymaking as those human rights stories that do appear in the news (McPherson 2012).

Since the 1990s, the visibility and media coverage of human rights has increased dramatically, yet tends to be negative and focused on repressive countries, while for audiences in the developed countries, 'human rights violations and the resultant suffering are often things that happen to people far away and on a massive scale' (Balabanova 2015, 13; Cole, 2010; McPherson, 2012). This was Cole's (2010) major conclusion in his analysis of the prevalence and nature of human rights discourse in the *New York Times* and *Washington Post*. He found that as a country's level of respect for human rights increased, it was mentioned fewer times in proximity to the term 'human rights', and vice versa. His conclusion echoed others' findings that 'democracy trumps repression with respect to media coverage: journalists overlook acts of repression in democratic countries' (Cole 2010, 315).

News of human rights violations often does sell, especially for middle- and upper-class readers, and it can contribute to a media outlet's credibility. Yet an outlet's desire to increase its audience among certain populations, such as women or youth, means its selection criteria may privilege human rights news regarding these populations. As McPherson (2012) notes, 'this tactic… may also limit other sorts, such as coverage of violations committed against other vulnerable populations less likely to buy newspapers, including the elderly or indigenous' (113–14). For popular sensationalistic media, for example Mexico's *nota roja* papers, which employ disturbingly graphic and often horrific news, specific kinds of abuses are pursued, which potentially excludes non-violent violations of SEC rights and affects political discussions and policy decisions (114). The use of high-profile celebrities as human rights mediators can sell human rights news, but can also function as an obstacle to lasting political change. Celebrities potentially 'drown out alternative voices from the global South and the anti-globalization voices from the North' or 'defuse, drain or stifle more radical forms of protests and political mobilization' (Borer 2012a, 27).

Coverage of human rights abuses can desensitise or overwhelm audiences, provoke calls for revenge, or 'turn viewers into voyeurs of exoticised and objectified victims in an almost pornographic way', and commonly reproduces 'a dichotomous "us" versus "them" sentiment' (Borer 2012a, 4, 12; Brooten et al, 2015). This can lead to compassion fatigue, whereby the more suffering we see, the less we feel; psychic numbing, in which people are unable to feel for large numbers of distant victims; and difficulties in creating 'a global citizenry or a sense of cosmopolitan solidarity' (Borer 2012a, 11). These consequences all undermine political pressure to change the status quo.

The resulting impact on political discourse is at least in part a result of 'rote journalism, and looking-over-your-shoulder reporting' and the production processes of news and other media (Borer 2012a, 14). The framing of global crises generally reflects national interests and identities, or focuses on human interest stories about the involvement of 'our' nationals in the crisis (Borer, 2012a; Cottle, 2009). Simplistic, formulaic coverage is commonplace, highly repetitive and often criminalizes victims. Coverage also needs to align with the interests of the outlet's editorial stance and advertisers (Borer, 2012a). Generally, to be newsworthy, stories must involve violations, with most coverage of human rights focusing on negative rights such as freedom of expression or freedom from violence and abuse rather than positive SEC rights (Balabanova, 2015).

In global media images, suffering becomes spectacle in the name of profit, replicating what some have called the 'iconography of famine' in which 'starvation itself is portrayed in simple terms, more akin to natural disasters such as earthquakes than as a calculated political strategy' (Borer 2012a, 34–5). Shock media coverage of rights abuses is often co-opted for political purposes, and tends to perpetuate the common tropes of 'their' barbaric and illiberal behaviour and 'our' advanced and civilized behaviour. This cultural focus and accompanying graphic, violent images divert attention from the deeply rooted causes of violence and how 'the West is highly complicit in the suffering' by supporting undemocratic regimes that foment coups, dictatorships and civil wars (Borer 2012b, 159–60). Shock media primarily focus on abuses of CP rights, and as a result, violations of SEC rights are generally ignored, as are shocking images of rights violations in the West (Borer, 2012b). This rhetorical diversion reinforces the common trope of the West as more developed and as saviour figure for the problematic 'other', making it easier to co-opt rights violations for political agendas (Borer, 2012b; Brooten et al., 2015), as can be seen in the discourse on immigration and citizenship rights.

Immigration and citizenship

Politically important for most states, immigration and citizenship issues provoke debate involving human rights concerns implied rather than explicit in media coverage, which tends to leave undiscussed the political context and causes for migration (Balabanova, 2015). Many governments perpetuate recurrent myths through 'alarmist discourses on asylum abuse' and 'the "threats" posed by so-called "bogus"... as opposed to "genuine" asylum seekers' (Da Lomba 2006, 83). Such narratives help to justify strict policies, anti-immigrant legislation and restrictions in the provision of SEC rights for asylum seekers 'too often perceived and portrayed as undeserving recipients of State benefits and assistance' (Da Lomba 2006, 83; Balabanova, 2015). Research has found consistently hostile coverage involving inaccuracies, exaggeration of numbers, confusion over terminology, a lack of contextualisation, inclusion of few migrant or refugee voices and reliance on a few official sources (Balabanova, 2015).

Anti-terrorism and anti-trafficking policies and the criminalization of migrants have increased the power of the state, yet efforts to expand the rights of migrants have garnered very little public or political attention (Balabanova, 2015). In the post 9/11 period, the discourse of 'security' has superseded that of 'rights' as immigration and asylum are increasingly represented as security-related matters, contributing to a hostile climate for asylum seekers and to the argument that human rights norms threaten state sovereignty (Balabanova 2015; Da Lomba 2006). The call for states to be 'tough' on immigration and asylum 'presents a direct challenge for any approach to the subject that is based on human rights' (Balabanova 2015, 112).

War and humanitarian disasters

In recent decades, humanitarian interests have become increasingly allied with military and state objectives and justified discursively in ways that often elide the political interests at stake. Terms such as 'humanitarian war', 'liberal peace', 'human security' and the 'responsibility to protect', increasingly frame Western military intervention as humanitarian (Cottle 2009, 496–7). Beginning in the 1990s, a more political conception, dubbed 'new humanitarianism', introduced longer-term objectives such as peace building and human rights protection (Nascimento 2015). The rhetoric of humanitarianism has increasingly become an instrument of foreign policy and large donors, reflecting 'the growing politicisation of humanitarian assistance.... no longer aimed at responding above all to the victim's needs and suffering, but instead to stimulate more political and social processes'(Nascimento 2015, 4). 'New humanitarianism' in practice often means ignoring human rights in pursuit of political and economic objectives, harming those suffering the most and creating 'a moral hierarchy of victims who do or do not deserve assistance' (Nascimento 2015, 8). The hostility of donor countries towards the Taliban regime in Afghanistan in the late 1990s, for example, 'contributed to a clear marginalization of the civilian victims of the humanitarian crisis in the country', prolonging the crisis and its resultant human rights abuses (Nascimento 2015, 6).

Global media coverage can politicise major disasters as opportunities for elites 'to capitalise on the 'disaster shock' of catastrophic events... ritualised moments of national and international unity and solidarity, or occasions that give vent to voices of dissent' (Cottle 2009, 503). Crises can become opportunities for states to 'militarise disaster zones and increase their control of affected populations, and occasionally... tip over into political contention' (Cottle 2009, 504). In the aftermath of Hurricane Katrina, for example, news coverage perpetuated a number of disaster myths with political consequences (Tierney et al., 2006). Victims were represented as violent criminals and opportunistic looters, and images of civil unrest appeared along with comparisons of New Orleans with a war zone and the urban insurgency in Iraq. Such framing provided the justification for military and law enforcement responses, and for the argument that the military is the only body capable of effective action in response to crises (Cottle 2009; Tierney et al., 2006).

Geopolitical factors are often more important than human rights in states' decisions about intervention, and news media can play a role in worsening human rights violations. Not all disasters gain prominent news exposure, as 'the vast majority of 'uninsured lives' in the South, it seems, are not only cheap... but also unnewsworthy' (Cottle 2009, 502). In Rwanda in 1994, for example, local and global media supported official propaganda and failed to hold governments to account for the genocide against the Tutsi population. Reporting was dominated by a framing of the conflict as ethnic and tribal 'acts of primordial hatred' rather than resulting from a pre-planned and politically motivated campaign (Balabanova 2015, 97). Similarly, in the case of the genocide beginning in 2003 in Sudan, Western media 'largely failed to adequately report the scale and brutality of the ongoing human rights abuses and their underlying causes', resulting in a lack of pressure from the international community to intervene (Balabanova 2015, 98). The framing of the conflict was similar to the Rwanda coverage, repeating traditional stereotypes about African tribal warfare that deflected attention from the political roots of the violence (Balanbanova 2015).

Media reform

Media reform advocates often attempt to create broad coalitions, appealing to populism yet missing 'a whole range of political expressions' that potentially offer alternative solutions, a strategy that 'casts the net so widely as to remove politics almost entirely' (Berger 2009, 10, 11). Reform strategies often ignore the structural racism that characterizes public debate and policy issues, and prioritize formal, institutional reform 'at the expense of what is perhaps the media's greatest power: their ability to shape meaning through content' (Berger 2009, 3). The modern media reform movement in the US, for example, has been plagued by a division between media reform activists and those who prefer the term 'media justice'. Reformers have prioritised federal policy advocacy, especially ownership concentration, requiring powerful allies and attention to mainstream issues in order to get on the national political agenda (Berger 2009; Themba-Nixon 2009). This strategy prioritises engagement by middle-class whites, and leaves racial justice, class oppression, and gender justice largely off the reform agenda (Berger 2009; Themba-Nixon 2009). The media justice movement, on the other hand, focuses on structural issues as well as civil rights, equality and political representation, including opposition to denigrating content that influences racial, economic and gender justice. They also 'situate their work as part of a struggle for self-determination', arguing that reform efforts 'must include the full political, social, economic and cultural rights, desires and participation of marginalized populations' (Berger 2009, 17–18, 13).

This distinction between reform and justice is mirrored in other parts of the world. Analysis of media reform efforts in the Philippines and Myanmar (formerly Burma) demonstrates how in areas of conflict with significantly constrained political discourse, attention to the individual rights of the journalist, while necessary, deflect attention from a broader set of communication rights and the role of media as a public service (Brooten 2011). Nyamnjoh (2009) writes about the tensions in Africa between the rights of cultural or ethnic communities and 'dominant theories of journalism that demand of journalists professional independence and detachment' (8). This 'trivialises [the people's] collective experiences and memories in the guise of a socially and culturally disembedded professional ethic' that undermines 'aspirations for recognition and for a voice by the very Africans and communities [the media] target' (Nyamnjoh 2009, 13, 16).

Human rights are political

The very conception of human rights and the rights norms that have emerged have clear political impact, as evidenced by the differing versions of the origin of rights in the modern era, the different categorisations of rights, and the varying degrees of attention they receive. The categorizations themselves have political connotations. But rights discourse and its influence on media framing clearly play a key role in shaping public perceptions of political issues and influencing political and policy decisions. Human rights discourse has been used to undermine more radical political movements, and to promote a globalized market at the expense of more redistributive agendas. It has been used to divert attention from the least sensationalistic but most pernicious rights violations, such as poverty and lack of education and healthcare. Media attention to human rights news tends to be repetitive, reinforcing common tropes of the Western saviour and 'us' versus 'them' framing. These problematic uses of human rights discourse can have life altering effects on immigrants, refugees and victims of natural disasters and war. Even efforts at media reform are influenced by the political uses of human rights discourses, and advocates for more diverse and genuinely democratic media call for broadening the recognized set of communication rights as the key way to include the voices of those generally ignored or silenced.

References

Ajei, M. O. (2015). 'Human Rights in a Moderate Communitarian Political Framework'. *South African Journal of Philosophy*, 34(4), pp. 491–503. doi:10.1080/02580136.2015.1119920

Alexander, Jo. M. (2004). 'Capabilities, Human Rights and Moral Pluralism'. *International Journal of Human Rights*, 8(4), pp. 451–69.

Balabanova, E. (2015). *The Media and Human Rights: The Cosmopolitan Promise*. New York: Routledge.

Bell, K. and Cemlyn, S. (2014). Developing Public Support for Human Rights in the United Kingdom: Reasserting the Importance of Socio-economic Rights. *International Journal of Human Rights*, 18(7–8), pp. 822–41.

Berger, D. (2009). 'Defining Democracy: Coalition Politics and the Struggle for Media Reform'. *International Journal of Communication* 3, pp. 3–22.

Bernier, L. (2010). International Socio-economic Human Rights: The Key to Global Health Improvement?' *The International Journal of Human Rights*, 14(2), pp. 246–79.

Borer, T. (2012a). 'Introduction: Willful Ignorance - News Production, Audience Reception, and Response to Suffering'. In: Tristan A. B., ed., *Media, Mobilization and Human Rights* (1–41). New York: Palgrave MacMillan.

Borer, T. (2012b). 'Fresh, Wet Tears': Shock Media and Human Rights Awareness Campaigns'. In: Tristan A. B. ed., *Media, Mobilization and Human Rights*. New York: Palgrave MacMillan, pp. 143–80.

Brooten, L. (2011). 'Media, Militarization and Human Rights: Comparing Media Reform in the Philippines and Burma'. *Communication, Culture & Critique*, 4(3), pp. 312–32.

Brooten, L., Ashraf, S. I. and Akinro, N. A. (2015). 'Traumatized Victims and Mutilated Bodies: Human Rights and the "Politics of Immediation" in the Rohingya Crisis of Burma/Myanmar'. *International Communication Gazette*, 77(8), pp. 717–34.

Cole, W. M. (2010). 'No News Is Good News: Human Rights Coverage in the American Print Media, 1980–2000'. *Journal of Human Rights*, 9, pp. 303–25.

Cottle, S. (2009). 'Global Crises in the News: Staging New Wars, Disasters, and Climate Change'. *International Journal of Communication*, 3, pp. 494–516.

Crawford, G. (2010). Decentralisation and Struggles for Basic Rights in Ghana: Opportunities and Constraints'. *The International Journal of Human Rights*, 14(1), pp. 92–125, doi:10.1080/13642980902933720

Da Lomba, S. (2006). 'The Threat of Destitution as a Deterrent Against Asylum Seeking in the European Union'. *Refuge: Canada's national newsletter on refugees,* 23(1), pp. 81–93.

Hamelink, C. and Hoffman, J. (2008). 'The State of the Right to Communicate'. *Global Media Journal*, 7(13), Article No. 1. Available at: http://lass.calumet.purdue.edu/cca/gmj/fa08/gmj-fa08-hamelink-hoffman.htm [Accessed 22 Apr. 2012].

Hughes, C. (2007). 'Transnational Networks, International Organizations and Political Participation in Cambodia: Human Rights, Labour Rights and Common Rights'. *Democratization*, 14(5), pp. 834–52, doi:10.1080/13510340701635688

McPherson, E. (2012). 'How Editors Choose Which Human Rights News to cover: a Case Study of Mexican Newspapers'. In: Tristan A. B. ed., *Media, Mobilization and Human Rights* (96–121). New York: Palgrave MacMillan.

Mokhiber, C. G. (2001). 'Toward a Measure of Dignity: Indicators for Rights-based Development'. *Statistical Journal of the United Nations ECE*, 18, pp. 155–62.

Moyn, S. (2010). *The Last Utopia: Human Rights in History*. Cambridge, MA: Belknap Press of Harvard University Press.

Nascimento, D. (2015). 'One Step Forward, Two Steps Back? Humanitarian Challenges and Dilemmas in Crisis Settings'. *The Journal of Humanitarian Assistance*, February 18. Available at: http://sites.tufts.edu/jha/archives/2126 [Accessed 19 May, 2016].

Nyamnjoh, F. B. (2009). *Africa's Media: Between Professional Ethics and Cultural Belonging* (fesmedia Africa series). Windhoek, Namibia: Freidrich-Ebert23 Stiftung.

Teti, A. (2015). 'Democracy Without Social Justice: Marginalization of Social and Economic Rights in EU Democracy Assistance Policy after the Arab Uprisings'. *Middle East Critique*, 24(1), pp. 9–25, doi:10.1080/19436149.2014.1000076

Themba-Nixon, M. (2009). 'Mainstreams and Margins: A Critical Look at the Media Reform "Story."'. *International Journal of Communication,* 3, pp. 54–6.

Tierney, K., Bevc, C. and Kuligowski, E. (2006). 'Metaphors Matter: Disaster Myths, Media Frames and their Consequences in Hurricane Katrina'. *The Annals of the American Academy*, 604, pp. 57–81.

Williams, R. (2010). *The Divided World: Human Rights and its Violence*. Minneapolis: University of Minnesota Press.

Yokota, Y. (1999). Reflections on the Future of Economic, Social and Cultural Rights. In: Burns H. W. and Stephen P. M. eds., *The Future of International Human Rights*, . Ardsley, NY: Transnational Publishers, pp. 201–23.

44

MEDIA, HUMAN RIGHTS AND REFUGEES

Kerry Moore

Introduction

Despite national politicians' oft cited platitude that, 'we have a proud tradition of providing sanctuary to those who need it', regimes governing the admittance and control of asylum seekers and refugees in wealthy, 'receiving' countries have become increasingly restrictive (Moore 2012). Since at least the early 2000s, scholars have pointed to the 'securitisation of migration' across Europe, in North America and Australia (Andreas 2003; Buonfino 2004; Diez & Squire 2008; Gerard & Pickering 2013; Huysmans 2000; Huysmans & Buonfino 2008; Pickering 2004; Walters 2006). Indeed, during the current 'refugee crisis' in Europe, although concerns for better co-ordinated, humanitarian responses have clearly been evident in some national press, calls for ever-increasing security controls within and across borders continue to be heard in mainstream news media and political discourse, especially and most notably in UK right-wing tabloids (Berry et al. 2016). Such calls follow in the wake of at least a decade and a half of escalating political and media hostility towards asylum seekers and refugees (e.g. Buchanan et al. 2003; Kaye 2001; Kushner 2003; Lloyd 2003; McKay et al. 2011; Pitcher 2006; Saxton 2003; Schuster 2003; Threadgold 2009; Vas Dev 2009). Hostilities have been predicated upon fears about overwhelming numbers of newcomers and the threats they are assumed to present. Concerns about anticipated pressures on welfare, education, health and other social resources; fears about differences of cultural and religious practices or values; and suspicions associating asylum seekers with propensity towards crime, extremist politics or terrorism have led to demands for pre-emptive or deterrent policy responses. In fact, since the 1990s, most asylum seekers have, effectively, been criminalised by the closing down of legal routes to safety in Europe and ever-more restrictive interpretations of rules aimed at stamping out 'abuse' of the system (Flynn 2003; Schuster 2011). An image of illegality more generally has been encouraged by the increasing convergence between immigration and criminal systems in many liberal democratic countries (Miller 2005; Welch 2012) – a trend labelled by US criminologist Juliet Stumpf as 'crimmigration' (Stumpf 2006). Alongside the criminalisation of migrants, scholars have also highlighted the use of immigration law as a social control mechanism, with detention, deportation and deprivation of citizenship used symbolically and materially to exclude 'undesirable' individuals from the sphere of 'rights' in the name of protecting national populations (Guild 2009; Kanstroom 2005; Legomsky 2007). What critical criminologists call 'popular punitivism' has clearly established a significant foothold in the terrain of immigration control, playing a prominent role in the politics of mobility (Franko Aas & Bosworth 2013).

An important element of the negative discourse on asylum in the UK has involved reviewing how 'rights' are balanced against 'responsibilities'. An in-depth study of broadcast news coverage in the mid-2000s illustrated how stories about asylum were regularly caught in a web of news narratives connected with perceived threats to public safety (Gross et al. 2007). These narratives repeatedly positioned the extant framework of human rights law and its associated institutions as 'problematic', potentially compromising to security prerogatives, national sovereignty and the protection of UK citizens. National news media, largely uncritically, reproduced official frameworks of understanding wherein the protection of public safety was 'balanced' against human rights claims as a matter of 'common sense'. This equation was also coloured by the premise that the asylum system, and the underlying international conventions upon which it was based, were vulnerable to 'abuse'. International Human Rights Law and the UN Convention on Refugees were, ministers argued, 'anachronistic' – no longer suited for our modern age and its challenges. As Tony Blair put it in a speech to the CBI, 'It became increasingly apparent that our asylum system was being widely abused. The UN Convention on Refugees, first introduced in 1951 ... has started to show its age' (Blair 2004).

In the post-9/11 period, 'human rights' became a focus of sustained discursive struggle, enmeshed in the highly controversial, mediatised legal conflicts between the British State and figures whom the tabloids labelled 'radical Muslim clerics'. Between 2004 and 2012, Abu Hamza, imprisoned in the UK in 2007 for inciting violence and racial hatred, fought extradition in the European Court of Human Rights (ECHR) on the grounds that he would face inhuman or degrading treatment on terrorism charges in the US. Abu Qatada, repeatedly detained under terrorism charges, also resisted removal from the UK – appealing to the ECHR on grounds that evidence obtained through torture would be used against him in Jordan. Both figures, appearing to advocate violence and extremism in the name of Islam, received extensive sensationalised press attention. As their various legal battles hit the headlines from around 2003, proposals to derogate from the ECHR and overturn its incorporation into UK law – the Human Rights Act 1998 – became serious subjects of debate pursued relentlessly in the right wing press. These cases seemed to symbolise the threat to national security from 'human rights' and the unnecessary 'trouble' it created. If those whose rights were in question happened to be asylum seekers, an equivalential logic indicated 'trouble' to be self-evident. As one *Daily Mail* article had it, the Human Rights Act in 1998 hindered 'procedures involving our national security and that of our allies', since it functioned to 'prevent deportation of failed asylum seekers or even terrorists ...' (Doughty 2003). According to such commentators, the risks of defending 'human rights' were now being irresponsibly disregarded due to 'judicial activism'. International human rights law, and particularly the ECHR, were demonised as weakening the State's capacity for achieving policy aims and maintaining security. As such, repeatedly, proposals to repeal human rights law, to derogate from certain elements of the Convention or to replace it with a 'British Bill of Rights'[1] were mooted by successive governments. The Ministry of Justice proposed in 2014 to make the ECHR 'advisory only', and in October 2015 the government amended its ministerial code to remove all references to the requirement to comply with international law (Conservative Party 2014; Webber 2016). In opposition, organisations such as Liberty, Amnesty International, the British Institute of Human Rights, and commentators in the liberal press as well as celebrity advocates have consistently defended the ECHR, encouraging a sense of 'ownership' of human rights law and its protections (e.g. Susman et al. 2016).

Although international legal instruments defining the right to asylum and delineating human rights developed separately during the post-Second-World-War period, there is considerable interaction between the two and many practical consequences of human rights law for the experiences of, and conduct of states towards, asylum seekers and refugees (Chetail 2014). It should then, perhaps, come as no surprise, that in the public imagination ideas about 'human rights' and about 'refugees' might be entwined, along with the ethical/political discourses governing whether compassion, empathy, cosmopolitanism or hostility towards each prevail. Nonetheless, despite the polarised public debate on human rights, there is little convincing evidence to suggest that public opinion is clearly opposed to human rights or the Human Rights Act in particular (MCBR 2012). Similarly, although research evidence concerning public attitudes towards human rights and asylum seekers and refugees remains limited and highly fragmented (Crawley 2009; Jeong-Woo 2015), some opinion polls, both historic and recent, indicate far more positive public attitudes towards refugees than might be anticipated (Amnesty International, 2016b; IPSOS/MORI, 2002). Nonetheless, politicians repeatedly claim to be addressing intense public concern in their securitising policies, journalists, in turn to be factually reporting these concerns and policy debates. However, news media do not merely reflect 'facts' but also reproduce ideas, reiterate positions and contribute to the construction of the 'realities' on which they report. They are the productive agents through which meaningful frameworks for understanding public issues are usually encountered and through which ideas about human rights and refugees are defined and redefined. As such, migration scholars argue, the media has a key role in producing and maintaining public opinion, and *could* do more to allay fears and promote integration (Threadgold 2009; Triandafyllidou 2013).

Legitimating the denial of human rights

A discourse calling human rights and refugee rights into question continues to permeate news stories in the UK, especially when the human rights of migrants and/or fears about extremism and terrorism have been high in the news agenda (Moore 2012). A basic keyword search of UK national newspaper coverage 2001–16 in which 'refugees', 'human rights' and 'terrorism' are all mentioned indicates that this discourse may have become increasingly significant. As Figure 44.1 demonstrates, significantly more stories meeting these criteria appeared in the UK national press since 2012 – a period clearly coinciding with media reporting of the current 'refugee crisis' in Europe.

Despite the magnitude of human suffering facing asylum seekers from war torn Syria, Afghanistan and other contemporary conflict zones, the current crisis has all too often been represented as a crisis *for* Europe (Berry et al. 2016).

Policy action (and inaction) bearing serious implications for human rights, international refugee law and EU law[2] seems aimed primarily at controlling inward flows of refugees across Europe. Salient policies have included the reduction of resources to rescue sinking craft in the Mediterranean, the reluctance/refusal to accept non-Christian refugees' in Poland, Hungary, the Czech Republic and Slovakia, and the confiscation of valuables from refugees at the borders of Denmark. There have also been 'push backs' or 'hot returns' (collective expulsions) from external borders in contravention of EU law risking *refoulement*, including the highly controversial EU-Turkey agreement to forcibly return people illegally crossing the Mediterranean from March 2016. Whilst dehumanising conditions faced by refugees in detention in some EU countries has received little press attention in the UK, the so-called Jungle (informal camps in northern France) has been widely covered in print and broadcast news (Berry et al. 2016). Yet, although UK newspapers have contained humanitarian themes as an element of coverage and largely represented people to be fleeing war or persecution, human rights concerns, when

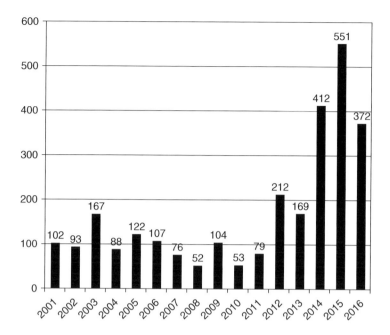

Figure 44.1 Refugees, human rights and terrorism in UK national newspaper coverage 2011–2016[3]

featured, are frequently 'balanced' against other policy challenges or priorities, such as how to manage numbers arriving or deter further attempts at entry. Moreover, UK right-wing tabloids have been especially hostile, suspicions about supposed social welfare 'pull factors' and refugees' motivations to 'do us harm' being far more evident than in other national press.

Following the global front page coverage in August 2015 of the extraordinarily symbolic, and heart-rending image on a beach of deceased three-year-old Syrian toddler, Aylan Kurdi, there seemed, for a time at least, to be a potentially transformative 'turning point' or public 'awakening' to the failures of Europe responding to a humanitarian crisis (Bhatia & Singleton 2015). Initially, a shift in focus of dominant media narratives towards the human tragedy of the crisis seemed possible, as did a softening of tough political positions on accepting refugees in the UK. Yet even in the immediate aftermath of this event, a prominent discourse premised upon differentiating those 'deserving' from 'undeserving' of sanctuary continued (Holmes & Castaneda, 2016). Following the 13 November 2015 terrorist attacks in Paris, speculation abounded across global news media about the identity of the perpetrators and, in particular, their migration backgrounds (e.g. Tharoor 2015). Although all of the known Paris attackers were found to be EU citizens, suspicions that insufficient security controls at European borders had assisted the attacks were fuelled by reports that perpetrators had visited Syria, returning unnoticed under the cover of refugee flows. Sensationalist headlines warned that Syrian refugee camps, infiltrated or controlled by ISIS, provided a base from which assaults on Europe were being planned (e.g. Austin, 2016; Blanchard 2015). News of this atrocity and that of the ongoing refugee crisis in Europe appeared, almost irresistibly, intertwined. Consequently, speculation about the end of the Schengen Agreement exacerbated the sense that the institutions and ethical discourses constituting the European Union were under severe strain (e.g. France 24 2015). Overall, the association of refugees with threats to the safety of Europe's extant citizenry further intensified, again placing refugees' rights in question.

Such a string of connections does not come about 'naturally' – the only one rational line of thinking in public discourse. Rather, these 'common sense' links are essentially unstable, constructed hegemonically as a result of multiple struggles between competing political identities and interests. Out of these struggles, an equivalent logic has been established pitting refugee and human rights against 'our' safety and security (Laclau & Mouffe, 1985). For such a discourse to prevail, it has to be maintained, reiterated, sustained and reproduced in public through the regular repetition of ideas, images, narratives and representations of subject positions – in mainstream political rhetoric and in news and other forms of media. In the remainder of this chapter, I would like to suggest as worthy of further attention, four interrelated discursive strategies delegitimising human rights commonly at work in the representation of asylum seekers and refugees: 1. It's not us, it's them! 2. It's not them, it's *them*! 3. It's not them, it's us! 4. It's them or us!

It's not us, it's them! (Or, our prejudices are reasonable)

The first legitimating strategy for denying human rights is predicated upon 'differentiating the self' – for example, proclaiming 'our' humanitarian credentials whilst delegitimising those with 'bogus' claims upon our hospitality. In the early 2000s asylum seekers were so routinely represented in the UK as a 'menace', the 'folk devils' of contemporary times, that a 'credible' discriminatory discourse emerged positioning 'our' prejudice as 'reasonable' (Lynn & Lea 2003). Migrants still rarely have a voice as primary definers within news coverage about themselves, or in ways that might humanise, legitimise or defend their positions (Thornbjornsrud & Figenschou 2014; Threadgold 2006). The kind of 'voice' migrants are afforded, some argue, may actually reinforce stereotypes, appearing in clearly sympathetic news as an exception to the norm (Crawley et al. 2015). The assumption that *they* are likely to exploit *us* in some way – either as 'criminals', 'scroungers', or neoliberal 'entrepreneurs of the self' – continues to resonate as a reasonable proposition (Moore 2013).

The conflation of asylum seekers with other categories of migrant, and with threatening, often criminalising images also serves to further legitimate the binary opposition 'us-them' (Rasinger 2010; Vicol & Allen 2014). Hungary's recent refusal to accept that current flows of migrants into Europe reflects a 'refugee' crisis at all, for example, simply side-steps discussion of what to do about humanitarian subjects' rights. Proposals to deny refugee rights as a universal ethical obligation *as such* during the current crisis have generally been based upon generalising fears about refugees as potentially 'threatening others' hidden among us. This was evident in some responses to the 2015 Paris attacks, voicing suspicion that Syrian refugees (many fleeing from ISIS) could, in fact, also be the terrorists, as one *Washington Post* article put it:

> The prospect of Islamist infiltration through the current refugee influx in Europe has spooked politicians on both sides of the Atlantic, with a slate of Republican governors and presidential candidates in the United States pointing to the terror attacks as reason to bar entry to all Syrian refugees.
>
> *(Tharoor 2015)*

Such a legitimising strategy for denying rights also relies upon ardently asserting inherent or historic human rights credentials. As reports emerged that Greece and Bulgaria were turning back refugees at their borders with Turkey in late 2013, EU migration and asylum commissioner Cecilia Malmström's spokesperson Michele Cercone reiterated in a press conference that responsibility for protection of refugee rights was integral to the identity of the EU itself:

> Nobody arriving in the EU territory and asking for asylum can be pushed back or can be denied this possibility. This is an obligation and not just stemming from

international conventions or EU legislations but also from the core values on which the European Union is built.

(Cercone 2013)

However, on Friday 18 March 2016, a European Union deal with Turkey aimed at preventing Aegean crossings agreed to return all migrants reaching EU shores, with refugees to be instead selected directly from Turkey. Amnesty International called the agreement an 'historic blow to human rights', with Director for Europe and Central Asia, John Dalhuisen noting, 'Promises to respect international and European law appear suspiciously like sugar-coating the cyanide pill that refugee protection in Europe has just been forced to swallow' (2016a), and although not widely reported, by April 1ˢᵗ, stories of forcible returns from Turkey to Syria were appearing in the international news media (e.g. BBC News 2016; Fahim 2016).

Its not them, it's *them*! (Or, the *really* undesirable 'others')

Whilst most mainstream public discourse neither refutes the existence of refugees nor entirely ignores rights, the binaries 'genuine/bogus', 'deserving/undeserving', 'desirable/undesirable' have clearly served to legitimate a form of conditional hospitality that can be endlessly deferred. In some recent UK right-wing press coverage this has been represented through the regular joint articulation of border security concerns with the spectre of a terrorist threat in ways that position refugees as potential terrorists:

ISIS recruiting refugees in TERROR TRAINING camps in Europe as it plots UK attack.

(Culbertson, 2016)

ISIS DISGUISED AS MIGRANTS: Christian refugees recognise Daesh jihadi living among them.

(Smith, 2016)

Terrorist ringleader got into EU as 'refugee': Thousands of jihadists not being monitored.

(Holehouse & Samuel, 2015)

'The refugee', as a category of subject ascribed special licence to cross borders is positioned as problematic only because *really* threatening, inauthentic groups or individuals are thought to be exploiting it as an institutional vulnerability. When identifying 'the undesirable' becomes the most vital and primary obligation, refugee rights become submerged, and at best an indefinitely postponed concern.

It's not them, it's us! (Or, our system is not fit for purpose)

The main element of this discursive strategy for rights denial is not to demonize those seeking to exercise rights, but rather to characterise the system to which they are subject as persistently lax, lenient or, 'in crisis' (Gross et al. 2007). The policy principles, border and immigration control systems policing asylum seekers' access to states and their resources are represented as incapable of identifying those 'undeserving' of sanctuary and thus abetting the potential entry of 'dangerous others'. For example, a *Daily Express* article discussing emergency proposals to bring Syrian refugees directly to the UK suggests a reckless disregard of threats to UK security and social resources:

> The migrants, many of whom are being brought here from camps in Lebanon and Jordan believed to be under the control of ISIS fanatics, will immediately be able to claim full benefits or work here even through they have not yet claimed asylum under a fast tracking scheme.
>
> *(Austin 2016)*

Within this discourse, it is unnecessary to express overt and direct racism to legitimate the fear-based exclusion of refugees from 'our' public space. Rather, it is only necessary to insist, perhaps even reluctantly, upon the need to reinvent or reinforce the state's apparatus of security and control, that we may be *sure* that *only* the 'genuine' are supported. These arguments may take little or no account of human rights: The obligation to protect rights is tempered by a perversely self-deprecating declaration of systemic weakness. A cognate version of this strategy is to argue that whilst 'we' might *prefer* to do more, to accept more refugees, to be more hospitable, the system (due to its unfortunate inadequacies) does not facilitate our preferences: There is insufficient capacity, space, funding or resources.

It's them or us! (or 'balancing' their human rights against our safety)

In this final, perhaps most clearly antagonistic of strategies, it is 'our' very existence that is represented as at stake in recognising the rights of 'the other'. The focus draws in from 'the system' to our sense of selves – a competitive struggle for our own interests in relation to those of threatening 'others' (Moore, 2012). In the multi-layered discourse of debates surrounding human rights law, it is our security and safety that is represented in jeopardy should 'the balance' of rights and responsibilities be miscalculated (Gross et al. 2007). As Charles Clarke put it when UK Home Secretary:

> I do not think derogating from the European Convention on Human Rights is a very pleasant thing to do, but I would do it if I considered it to be necessary, I certainly would, because at the bottom line my responsibility is national security and that is the number one issue'.
>
> *(Clarke 2005)*

Whilst the analytical distinctions between these four strategies may be useful, in practice in public discourse, there is considerable overlap and interchange between them. The arguments are not necessarily consistent and may even be contradictory, but the notions that 'our' prejudices are reasonable, that there are some *really* undesirable 'others' undeserving of compassion, that our system is 'not fit for purpose' and that we need to protect ourselves by 'balancing' the human rights of others against 'our' safety, act as lenses through which refugees and human rights are too often represented and defined. There are certainly further variations and alternative strategies that serve to justify curtailments of fundamental rights obligations. Similarly, although not directly discussed in this chapter, there are undoubtedly powerful counter discourses within mainstream media and politics that challenge the currently illiberal direction of dominant discourse with more global cosmopolitan or openness towards the humanitarian plight and human rights of others. These too are of crucial importance to understanding the political terrain as a whole.

In reviewing some of the key trends in news media discourse surrounding refugees and human rights in liberal democratic countries, the chapter has adopted a discourse analytical approach, but has also sought to demonstrate the value of looking across academic fields, from media and cultural studies and political theory, to critical criminology and legal studies, sociology and anthropology to more fully illuminate the complex articulations and re-articulations of political identities, ideas and shifting social imaginaries. Future interdisciplinary research exploring media in relation to refugees and human rights might seek to address the evidential gaps in understanding how and why these shifting social imaginaries are influenced, both through engaging with journalists and editors who report on these issues and by addressing how such discursive strategies actually play out with media publics.

Notes

1 The latest manifestation is the Conservative's 2015 manifesto promise, and proposal in the 2016 Queen's speech, to repeal the Human Rights Act 1998 (which incorporated the ECHR into UK law) and to replace it with a new 'British Bill of Rights'.
2 With the Treaty of Lisbon in 2009, the EU charter of fundamental rights entered into force, entrenching into EU law 'the rights and freedoms enshrined in the European Convention on Human Rights' (European Commission, 2016).
3 Data based on an unfiltered keyword search of UK national press coverage using the Nexis database and the terms: refugee! and human right! and terror! and Britain (n=2759).

References

Amnesty International. (2016a). EU-TURKEY REFUGEE DEAL A HISTORIC BLOW TO RIGHTS, *Amnesty International*, 18 Mar Available at: https://www.amnesty.org/en/press-releases/2016/03/eu-turkey-refugee-deal-a-historic-blow-to-rights/

Amnesty International. (2016b). 'Refugees Welcome Index Shows Government Refugee Policies Out of Touch with Public Opinion'. *Amnesty International*, 19 May. Available at: https://www.amnesty.org/en/latest/news/2016/05/refugees-welcome-index-shows-government-refugee-policies-out-of-touch/

Andreas, P. (2003). 'Redrawing the Line: Borders and Security in the Twenty-first Century'. *International Security*, 28(2), pp. 78–111.

Austin, J. (2016). Refugees coming from 'ISIS camps' sidestep UK asylum checks to 'get them in more quickly, *The Express*, 20 Jan.

BBC News. (2016). 'Turkey "illegally returning Syrian Refugees' - Amnesty, *BBC News*, 1 April. http://www.bbc.co.uk/news/world-europe-35941947

Berry, M., Garcia Blanco, I. and Moore, K. (2016). 'Press Coverage of the Refugee and Migrant Crisis in the EU: A Content Analysis of Five European Countries'. *Report for the Office of the United Nations High Commissioner for Refugees*. Genève, Suisse: UNHCR.

Bhatia, M., and Singleton, A. (2015). 'Turning Point for Europe: Humanity Remembered'. *Open Democracy*. Available at: https://www.opendemocracy.net/ourkingdom/monish-bhatia-ann-singleton/turning-point-for-europe-humanity-remembered [Accessed 17 July, 2016].

Blair, T. (2004). PM Speech on Migration to the CBI. *Number10.gov*, 27 Apr. Available at: http://www.number10.gov.uk/Page5708

Blanchard, J. (2015). 'Officials Warn 20,000 ISIS Jihadis "Have Infiltrated Syrian Refugee Camps"', *Daily Mirror*, 19 November.

Buchanan, S., Grillo, B., and Threadgold, T. (2003). *What's the Story?* Results from Research into Media Coverage of Refugees and Asylum Seekers in the UK: Article 19 (The Global Campaign for Free Expression).

Buonfino, A. (2004). 'Between Unity and Plurality: The Politicization and Securitization of the Discourse of Immigration in Europe.' *New Political Science*, 26(1), pp. 23–49.

Cercone, M. (2013). Statement on Behalf of the EU Migration and Asylum Commissioner. Brussels.

Chetail, V. (2014). 'Are Refugee Rights Human Rights? An Unorthodox Questioning of the Relations between Refugee Law and Human Rights Law'. In: R. Rubio-Marín, ed., *Human Rights and Immigration*. Oxford: Oxford University Press.

Clarke, C. (2005). *Oral evidence taken before the Home Affairs Committee on Tuesday 8 February 2005 (Questions 40–59).* UK Parliament. Available at: https://www.publications.parliament.uk/pa/cm200405/cmselect/cmhaff/321/5020804.htm [Accessed 17th July 2016].

Conservative Party. (2014). Protecting Human Rights in the UK: The Conservatives' Proposals for Changing Britain's Human Rights Laws.

Crawley, H. (2009). *Understanding and Changing Public Attitudes: A Review of Existing Evidence From Public Information And Communication Campaigns.* Swansea: Centre for Migration Policy Research, Swansea University.

Crawley, H., McMahon, S., and Jones, K. (2015). *Victims and Villains: Migrant Voices in the British Media.* Coventry: Centre for Trust, Peace and Social Relations, Coventry University & Open Society Foundations.

Culbertson, A. (2016). 'ISIS Recruiting Refugees in TERROR TRAINING Camps in Europe as it Plots UK Attack'. *Daily Express*, 26 Jan.

Diez, T., and Squire, V. (2008). 'Traditions of Citizenship and the Securitisation of Migration in Germany and Britain'. *Citizenship Studies*, 12(6), pp. 565–81.

Doughty, S. (2003). 'Call To End Human Rights "Passport" to the UK'. *Daily Mail*, 4th February.

European Commission (2016). *EU Charter of Fundamental Rights* (23 March). Available at: http://ec.europa.eu/justice/fundamental-rights/charter/index_en.htm

Fahim, K. (2016). 'Turkey has Forcibly Returned Thousands of Refugees to Syria, Amnesty International Says'. *New York Times* (1 April).

Flynn, D. (2003). *Tough as Old Boots'? Asylum, Immigration and the Paradox of New Labour Policy: A Discussion Paper.* London: JCWI.

France 24. (2015). Paris attack terrorists used refugee chaos to enter France, says PM Valls, *France 24*, 20 Nov. Available at: http://www.france24.com/en/20151119-paris-attackers-slip-refugee-migrant-crisis-terrorism

Franko A. K., and Bosworth, M., eds. (2013). *The Borders of Punishment: Migration, Citizenship and Social Exclusion.* Oxford: Oxford University Press.

Gerard, A., and Pickering, S. (2013). 'Crimmigration: Criminal Justice, Refugee Protection and the Securitisation of Migration'. In: H. Bersot and B. Arrigo, (eds. *The Routledge Handbook of International Crime and Justice Studies.* London: Routledge.

Gross, B., Moore, K., and Threadgold, T. (2007). *Broadcast News Coverage of Asylum April to October 2006: Caught Between Human Rights and Public Safety.* Cardiff: Cardiff School of Journalism, Media and Cultural Studies.

Guild, E. (2009). *Criminalisation of Migration in Europe: Human Rights Implications.* Strasbourg: Council of Europe Commissioner for Human Rights.

Holehouse, M., and Samuel, H. (2015). 'Terrorist Ringleader Got into EU as "Refugee": Thousands of Jihadists Not Being Monitored, *Daily* Telegraph (20 November).

Holmes, S. M., and Castaneda, H. (2016). 'Representing the "European Refugee Crisis" in Germany and Beyond: Deservingness and Difference, Life and Death'. *American Ethnologist*, 43(1), pp. 12–24.

Huysmans, J. (2000). 'The European Union and the Securitization of Migration'. *Journal of Common Market Studies*, 38(5), 751–77.

Huysmans, J., and Buonfino, A. (2008). 'Politics of Exception and Unease: Immigration, Asylum and Terrorism in Parliamentary Debates in the UK'. *Political Studies*, 56(4), 766–88.

IPSOS/MORI. (2002). Attitudes Towards Asylum Seekers for 'Refugee Week'.

Jeong-Woo, K. (2015). 'Public Opinion on Human Rights is the TrueGgauge of Progress'. *Open Democracy* (3 July). Available at: https://www.opendemocracy.net/openglobalrights/jeongwoo-koo/public-opinion-on-human-rights-is-true-gauge-of-progress

Kanstroom, D. (2005). 'Immigration Law as Social Control: How Many People Without Rights Does It Take to Make You Feel Secure'. In: C. Mele and T. Miller, eds., *Civil Penalties, Social Consequences.* New York: Routlledge, pp. 161–84.

Kaye, R. (2001). 'Blaming the Victim: An Analysis of Press Representations of Refugees and Asylum Seekers'. In: R. King and N. Wood, eds., *Media and Migration: Constructions of Mobility and Difference.* London: Routledge.

Kushner, T. (2003). 'Meaning Nothing but Good: Ethics, History and Asylum-seeker Phobia in Britain'. *Patterns of Prejudice*, 37(3), pp. 257–76.

Laclau, E., and Mouffe, C. (1985). *Hegemony and Socialist Strategy: Towards a Radical Democratic Politics.* London & New York: Verso.

Legomsky, S. H. (2007). The New Path of Immigration Law: Asymmetric Incorporation of Criminal Justice Norms. *Washington and Lee Law Review*, 64, pp. 469–528.

Lloyd, C. (2003). 'Anti-racism, Racism and Asylum-seekers in France'. *Patterns of Prejudice*, 37(3), pp. 323–40.

Lynn, N., and Lea, S. (2003). 'A Phantom Menace and the New Apartheid': the Social Construction of Asylum-Seekers in the United Kingdom. *Discourse and Society*, 14(4), pp. 425–52.

McKay, F. H., Thomas, S. L., and Warwick Blood, R. (2011). '"Any One of these Boat People Could be a Terrorist for All We Know!" Media Representations and Public Perceptions of "Boat People" Arrivals in Australia'. *Journalism*, 12(5), pp. 607–26.

Members of the Commission on a Bill of Rights (MCBR) (2012). *A UK Bill of Rights? The Choice Before Us*. London: Commission on a Bill of Rights.

Miller, T. (2005). 'Blurring the Boundaries Between Immigration and Crime Control After September 11th.' *Boston College Third World Law Journal*, 25(1), pp. 81–124.

Moore, K. (2012). '"Asylum Crisis", National Security and the Re-articulation of Human Rights'. In: K. Moore, B. Gross and T. Threadgold, eds., *Migrations and the Media*. New York: Peter Lang.

Moore, K. (2013). '"Asylum Shopping" in the Neoliberal Social Imaginary'. *Media, Culture & Society*, 35(3), pp. 348–65.

Pickering, S. (2004). 'Border Terror: Policing, Forced Migration and Terrorism'. *Global Change, Peace & Security*, 16(3), pp. 211–26.

Pitcher, B. (2006). 'Are You Thinking What We're Thinking? Immigration, Multiculturalism and the Disavowal of Racism in the Run-up to the 2005 British General Election'. *Social Semiotics*, 16(4), pp. 535–51.

Rasinger, S. M. (2010). 'Lithuanian Migrants Send Crime Rocketing': Representation of "New" Migrants'". In: Regional Print Media. *Media, Culture and Society*, 32(6), pp. 1021–30.

Saxton, A. (2003). 'I Certainly Don't Want People Like That Here: The Discursive Construction of "Asylum Seekers"'. *Media International Australia Incorporating Culture and Policy*, 109 (November), pp. 109–20.

Schuster, L. (2003). *The Use and Abuse of Political Asylum in Britain and Germany*. London: Frank Cass.

Schuster, L. (2011). 'Turning Refugees into "Illegal Migrants": Afghan Asylum Seekers in Europe'. *Ethnic and Racial Studies*, 34(8).

Smith, O. (2016). 'ISIS DISGUISED AS MIGRANTS: Christian Refugees Recognise Daesh Jihadi Living Among Them'. *Daily Express*, 24 Jan.

Stumpf, J. (2006). 'The Crimmigration Crisis: Immigrants, Crime, and Sovereign Power'. *American University Law Review*, 56, pp. 367–419.

Susman, D., Gormley, J., Wyse, P., Silverstone, T., and Riddell, J. (Producer) (2016). 'Patrick Stewart Sketch: What Has the ECHR Ever Done for Us?', *the Guardian*, 19 May. Available at: http://www.theguardian. com/culture/video/2016/apr/25/patrick-stewart-sketch-what-has-the-echr-ever-done-for-us-video

Tharoor, I. (2015). 'Were Syrian Refugees Involved in the Paris Attacks? What We Know and Don't Know, *Washington Post*, 17 Nov.

Thornbjornsrud, K., and Figenschou, T. (2014). 'Do Marginalised Sources Matter? A Comparative Analysis of Irregular Migrant Voice in Western Media'. *Journalism Studies*, 17(3), pp. 337–55.

Threadgold, T. (2006). 'Dialogism, Voice and Global Contexts.' *Australian Feminist Studies*, 21(50), pp. 223–44.

Threadgold, T. (2009). *The Media and Migration in the United Kingdom 1999-2009*. Washington DC: Migration Policy Institute.

Triandafyllidou, A. (2013). 'Migrants and the Media in the Twenty-First Century: Obstacles and Opportunities for the Media to Reflect Diversity and Promote Integration'. *Journalism Practice* 7(3), pp. 240–47.

Vas Dev, S. (2009). Accounting for State Approaches to Asylum Seekers in Australiasia and Malaysia: The Significance for National Identity and Exclusive Citizenship in the Struggle against Irregular Mobility'. *Identities*, 16(1), pp. 33–60.

Vicol, D., and Allen, W. (2014). 'Bulgarians and Romanians in the British National Press'. *COMPAS Migration Observatory Report*, 1 December 2012 - 1 December 2013. Oxford: Oxford University.

Walters, W. (2006). 'Border/Control'. *European Journal of Social Theory*, 9(2), pp. 187–203.

Webber, F. (2016). Short Cuts. *London Review of Books*, 38(7), p. 10.

Welch, M. (2012). 'Panic, Risk, Control: Conceptualising Threats in a Post-9/11 Society'. In: C. E. Kubrin, M. S. Zatz and R. Martínez (Jr.), eds., *Punishing Immigrants: Policy, Politics, and Injustice*. London and New York: New York University Press.

45

LABOUR JOURNALISM, HUMAN RIGHTS AND SOCIAL CHANGE

Anya Schiffrin and Beatrice Santa-Wood

Introduction—the role of the media in promoting human/labour rights

Labour struggles are some of the most dramatic and powerful stories that journalists cover. Suffused with human interest on a topic that readers can relate to, reporting on labour can galvanize governments, companies and the public. Indeed, throughout modern history, media coverage has been central to some of the major campaigns for labour rights around the world. Unions and human rights activists have worked closely with journalists to spread the word and create public outrage.[1]

But when does labour reporting make a difference? What conditions need to be in place for it to have an impact? In this chapter we will try to delineate some of the characteristics present in cases in which labour reporting has affected corporate or government behavior and present two case studies in support of our arguments.

First we will note the myriad ways in which media coverage can support campaigns for both labour rights and/or improved working conditions. These include the reporting and coverage of labour stories; the research done by investigative reporters can discover and bring to light new information which can then be acted upon by the public or by activists. By focusing on individual stories, labour journalism can call attention to abuses that can be fixed. By looking at deeper structural inequalities, journalists can place these broader social problems on the public agenda.

As well as providing its own research, the media can highlight and inform both the public and elite policy makers of research done by civil society organizations (CSOs) such as unions and human rights groups. Journalists often have a symbiotic relationship with CSOs such as Human Rights Watch which rely on the media to spread their messages while journalists often turn to human rights groups and unions for information.

Media reporting on human rights and labour rights can have discernible effects by galvanising people to take action. Op-eds targeted at influencers and policy makers and news articles aimed at the general public can bring about a shift in public opinion. The stories journalists tell can help persuade the public to support workers and campaigns for better conditions. This public support can pressure government and companies to change their behavior and enforce existing regulations or pass new ones.

Critical to these media effects is not just the quality of the media outlets, the coverage itself and the public response but also the larger 'media ecosystem'. Media coverage has more impact when there are already parts of civil society that are fighting for a cause, or who are at least ready to accept change and where there are mechanisms for redress. Generating an activist response is more likely when similar cases have already been written about. Because of the agenda-setting function of the media, a preponderance of coverage about, say, a labour abuse, signals to society that a problem is serious and that there is widespread worry and a desire for change. This idea that extensive media coverage of a topic or an event adds a feeling of immediacy applies even when the topic being covered is a perennial one that has existed for hundreds of years (human trafficking for example). Each time the media focuses on a single episode or a cause, it can seem to the reader or viewer as though it is urgent and even novel. For this reason, framing a case of labour abuse as a human rights problem rather than as an isolated news event, or piece of spot business news, has the potential to help create outrage that can create support for labour movements.

In this chapter we will discuss the current revival of labour reporting in the US and consider two recent labour-related stories that received substantial media coverage. We compare the Fight for 15 campaign in the US to the campaign for rights for workers building a campus for New York University located in the Middle East. We argue that the campaign for Fight for 15 had more discernible impact and we argue that the feeling of immediacy and relevance created in part by the media coverage contributed to the relative success of the campaign.

Background

Labour rights are an important part of human rights and have been enshrined in multiple conventions. But enforcement of labour laws is an ongoing problem and news media has an important role to play in calling attention to abuses, naming and shaming the perpetrators and mobilizing public outrage in order to force government regulators and employers to comply with labour laws (Dyck and Zingales 2002). The media can change how society sees and even addresses a problem partly by changing how it is 'framed' (Greenberg and Knight 2004) (Enteman 1993). By redefining the nature of a social problem the media can help pave the way for action to be taken. It can also strengthen those groups in society that are working for change (Stapenhurst 2000) (Camaj 2012).

Labour unions and advocacy groups are aware of the power of the media and have a long history of engaging with journalists by providing them with story ideas and information and helping journalists find sources in the labour community. The symbiotic relationship between journalists and labour activists meant that labour coverage in the news media has evolved over time in tandem with changes in the state of the US labour movement. When US labour unions weakened, so did labour coverage in the US (Glende 2012).

As US manufacturing supply chains moved overseas, the US media began to cover the overseas operations of US companies and human rights groups such as Human Rights Watch began to provide information to journalists about labour issues. This collabouration, however, was not always reflected in the frames that US journalists used to cover labour stories. Instead of looking at large systemic questions of human rights, journalists often reported on labour using journalistic traditions and language for example by framing questions of labour rights as a matter of conflict between workers and their employers or by describing the human cost of labour conflicts without delving deeply into underlying systemic causes (Frank 1997).

The role of the news media is generally to report on events as they happen which means reporting does not necessarily discuss broader macroeconomic pressures or structural factors that *allow* the 'unconscionable' violations of labour and human rights to which the media is drawn (Bekken 2005). A fire in a factory or the collapse of Rana Plaza in Bangladesh which killed 1,100 workers receives remarkable global coverage. And in the wake of that coverage, there is a sense that *something* is wrong. But too often, attention is drawn too narrowly: a building code violation, corruption in the inspection of the building, etc. The broader systemic issues are typically (but not always) brushed aside: how is it that workers accept working in a building that is known to be unsafe? Even when such events are seen as labour abuses, they are seldom characterized as a human rights problem (Bekken 2005). Nor do media reports generally refer to the language of human rights or conventions on labour practices. An exception, scholars have noted, is media coverage of events in China which often draws on human rights language or framing (Guo, Holton, Hsu & Jeong 2012).

The ability of journalism to motivate social change is greater when it bridges the gap between the great tragedies that draw global attention and the underlying social, economic, and political forces that allow such tragedies to happen so frequently. But because journalists often focus on the short term and the dramatic rather than on long term, systematic or incremental changes, journalists don't always see the gradual encroachment on labour rights. The less dramatic changes, in laws and how they are interpreted, or the economic transformation that happens incrementally but ultimately affect, for instance, the bargaining power of workers seldom receive the attention they deserve, even when those changes weaken workers' power to the point where there is a substantial increase in the risk of labour and human rights abuses. On its own, not being allowed to deduct union dues from a regular pay check may seem like a small thing. Over time it may cause unions to lose their funding and so impinge on the rights of workers to organize.

History of US labour reporting

Labour journalism has a long and illustrious history in the US with journalists reporting regularly on labour disputes and working conditions. In addition, labour unions often founded or funded publications and in the late 1820s and early 1830s 'some fifty labor weeklies appeared', most of them in the industrialising Northeast (Streitmatter 1999; Kabela 1960). Newspapers in the Southern part of the United States, however, tended to take an anti-labour stance (Atkins 2008).

During the 19th century, British abolitionists formed alliances with journalist crusaders such as Henry Wood Nevinson and E.D Morel and funded a number of newspapers that wrote articles against slavery (Hochschild 1998). In the period just after slavery was abolished, the search began for other forms of cheap labour, and these journalists turned their attention to the labour abuses that occurred worldwide, such as the human trafficking that supplied workers to mines in South Africa or the construction of railways (Higgs 2012).

In this rich period of activist journalism, some of the more famous coverage of labour conditions in the US included Upton Sinclair's *The Jungle* (Whitt 2008), the reporting after the Triangle Shirtwaist factory fire in 1911 and the writing of Progressive era labour reporter Eva Valesh (Faue 2002). Thomas Frank also cites the emblematic labour reporting of John Reed, Mary Heaton Vorse, Edmund Wilson, John Dos Passos, James Agee and Ruth McKenney (Frank 1997). During the turn of the century 'Progressive Era', industrialisation and the growth of labour unions gave rise to a generation of writers and journalists who promoted socialism both through writing fiction and journalism—in the mainstream press, through labour union newspapers and in publications such as like *The Awl* of Lynn Massachusetts; *The New York Call*; Milwaukee *Journal*; Socialist party journal *An Appeal to Reason)* and the Chicago labour paper *The New Majority* (Bekken 1997)

The 'labour beat' reached its peak in the 1930–50's with labour reporting integrated into mainstream media coverage, a result of industrial growth and booming union membership (Witwer 2013). Pro-labour newspapers also existed including the *New York Post* under Dorothy Schiff and *PM*, founded by Ralph Ingersoll and backed by millionaire Marshall Field (Schiffrin 1984).

The globalization of supply chains and coverage

As labour union membership began to fall in the US and the industrial supply chain moved overseas, so too did the number of dedicated labour reporters and the amount of space given to labour-related news. This trend was aggravated by attempts of many media companies, in the 1970s, to target 'upscale' readers (Martin 2008). With the explosion of business journalism in the 1980s and 1990s, business journalists often took on labour-related subjects. Coverage of labour became more focused on greater economic trends rather than a study of conflict between workers, unions and corporations (Mort 1987). Labour stories coverage continued but instead of dedicated beat reporters it was often investigative and/or business reporters who covered labour stories. (Mort 1987: Glende 2012).

The move of production overseas, especially in textile, apparel and footwear manufacturing meant journalists covered stories about labour conditions overseas when US companies were involved. In the nineties a number of reports on 'sweatshops' appeared as labour activists worked to provide journalists with information. Jeff Ballinger and the trade union federation AFL-CIO were instrumental in giving journalists information about labour disputes at the Nike subcontractor factories in Vietnam and Indonesia (Ballinger 2014). The press coverage had an impact, with the founding of the United Students Against Sweatshops in 1997 and the Workers Rights Consortium. While some called for a boycott, the USAS wanted universities to use their purchasing power to push for better conditions for workers (Featherstone 2002). US companies, such as Nike, joined the Fair Labour Association, derided by student activists as being controlled by manufacturers, and codes of conduct and verification processes were developed (Featherstone 2002). The growing interest in sweatshop labour meant it was easier to place more stories in the media. Ira Arlook, now at Fenton Communications, worked with Charlie Kernaghan to provide journalists with information about the working conditions in the garment factories producing clothes for the Kathy Lee Gifford clothing line (Arlook 2014) (Strom 1996).

Throughout the nineties, as the economic situation of the US media worsened, US newspapers cut their labour reporting positions. By the time Steve Greenhouse retired from the *New York Times* in 2014, he was one of the last reporters in the country officially on the labour beat. Of course labour stories were being written but few media outlets still had a designated labour beat. As the unions cut back on their activities, some say that fewer resources were devoted to working with journalists. In addition, having fewer labour organisers in the field meant that there were fewer union members witnessing labour abuses and bringing them to the attention of journalists (Greenhouse 2016 [author correspondence]).

Overseas NGOs were still able to highlight labour abuses and bring them to the attention of the world's media. With the help of groups like the Catholic Agency for Overseas Development and Hong Kong Labour Watch, news broke of the terrible working conditions at the Foxconn factory producing i-Pads for Apple (Chao 2012). Although the news spread from China to the UK and the US, and the *New York Times* published its own series on labour conditions at Apple stores in the US, Apple's sales were unaffected. Indeed author, Mike Daisey, who had written a theatre piece about conditions at FoxConn was held to the same standards as working journalists were and was criticized for factual mistakes in his theater piece and claims he made to public radio show *This American Life*. The backlash that ensued discredited some of his work (Peralta 2012).

Other important international labour stories published in the last decade include Cam Simpson's series for *Bloomberg Business Week* on labour conditions at the FoxConn factory in Penang, Malaysia (Simpson 2013), a *Los Angeles Times* series in 2013 about Mexican farm workers in California and coverage of the coalition of Immokalee workers the *New Yorker*. Slave labour on Thai fishing boats and in shrimp facilities covered in 2015 resulted in pressure on the Thai government (Anusonadisai 2015: Mason et al. 2015: Urbina 2015) a class action lawsuit and steps by US lawmakers to end the abuses (Urbina 2015). In 2015 the *New York Times* investigation of nail salons attracted the attention of state health officials leading to immediate action by US lawmakers and education campaigns so that nail workers would know about their rights (Robbins 2015).

The power of the recent reporting and its globalized nature have contributed to what many believe is a resurgence of labour reporting particularly in the US. The growth of cross-border journalism (evidenced in projects like *The Panama* Papers) has contributed to a renaissance of investigative reporting that naturally includes labour reporting. As well, interest in labour conditions in the US has been boosted by growing anger about economic inequality and a new generation who use social media to organize protests and spread information about their activities (Timm 2015: Uetricht 2015: Valla 2015). The media coverage of the Occupy movement also likely contributed to the prevailing climate of interest in economic inequality, putting the problem on the agenda.

Fight for 15: A Labour campaign with media coverage and impact

The agenda setting function of the media was visible in the extensive coverage in the US of the Fight for 15 campaign. The disturbing rise of inequality in the US and the wage stagnation of male workers since the 1970s provided the backdrop for this successful campaign (Democracy Now! 2015). Since 2012 the Fight for 15 campaign to raise US minimum wage to $15 has gained substantial media coverage and helped in hiking minimum wage around the US (Dixon 2014) (Strangler 2015). At the head of the campaign were fast food workers, many of them people of colour, women and migrants (Hogler, Hunt & Weiler 2014). The strikes of fast-food workers resulted from unions and political/civil society organizations working together to address the effect that labour conditions have on social and economic inequality.

The first major strike of fast-food workers occurred 29 November 2012 (Greenhouse 2016). Steven Greenhouse described that first strike as 'The biggest wave of job actions in the history of America's fast-food industry'. Several hundred workers gathered in Times Square, receiving coverage from the *New York Times* and Reuters. As Earl, Martin, McCartney and Soule (2004) noted in their study on newspaper coverage of collective action, the main determination of coverage was not the nature of the subject but factors such as the urban location, number of protesters, and proximity to parallel topics already being covered. Other determinants of coverage are the size of protests and their proximity to media outlets (Andrews and Caren 2010). Given the timing close to the US Thanksgiving holiday and location in New York City, the 29 November strike was primed for media attention. Also making it newsworthy was the ongoing parallel national conversation on racial and social inequality, which some media outlets included in their coverage (Resinkoff 2013). Indeed in 2017, the Black Lives Matter movement publicly teamed up with the Fight for 15 movement (Whack 2017).

The first strike was the result of months of work between local organizations like NYC Communities for Change, The Black Institute and United NY with the Service Employees International Union (SEIU) (Zillman 2014). Organizations like NYC Communities for Change are offshoots of the now defunct ACORN, which targeted problems of inequality and poverty, and they realized that many of those struggling were fast-food workers (Finnegan 2014). Accordingly, they decided to organize these workers.

The American labour movement as a whole has moved towards greater collaboration between unions, labour advocates and grassroots organizations (Dixon and Martin 2012). AFL–CIO and SEIU in particular work with grassroots organizations and NGOs to build larger labour campaigns (Dixon and Martin 2012). Their size and existing network and successful communications strategies helped them garner media coverage (Nike and Fight for 15, respectively) (Dixon and Martin 2012). Historically, unions led more insular campaigns, but are moving towards more cooperation with political and civic organizations to grow the labour movement (Compa 2015). As Kennedy's theory of organizational networks argues, when multiple organizations work together on an issue, there is a higher chance of the media covering the story (2008).

Organizing by fast-food workers, political/civic NGOs and the Service Employees International Union (SEIU) has led to increasing gains for the campaign making it a success (Greenhouse 2015 ['Why the Media Started Caring about the American Worker Again']; Lathrop, Sunn & Tung, 2015; Wright 2016). From 2014-2016 there have been strikes in 270 cities in the US, legislation or proposals to raise minimum wage to $15 in over twenty states and localities and yielded more than 300 newspaper headlines on Fight for 15 (Lathrop, Sunn & Tung 2015; Fight for 15 2015). By 2021 New York is poised to be the first to have statewide minimum wage of $15 for all workers (Lathrop, Sunn & Tung 2015).

Early on organizers realized the struggles of fast-food workers were closely tied to racial and social inequality, and that became a key part of the campaign (Resnikoff 2013; Compa 2016; Wright 2016). While journalists continue to focus mostly on the strikes as events, some coverage has made connections between the strikes and social inequity (Compa 2015; Wright 2016). Journalists like Ned Resnikoff, then at *MSNBC*, and Sarah Jaffe, then at *Salon*, have framed Fight for 15 in the context of economic and racial inequality (Resnikoff 2013; Jaffe 2014). Profiles of Fight for 15 leaders and workers, notably in Steven Greenhouse's ongoing coverage in the *New York Times* and the *Atlantic* and William Finnegan's 'Dignity' in the *New Yorker* (Finnegan 2014) have illustrated the human cost and deeper systemic problems tied to the strikes. While coverage of Fight for 15 still relied heavily on event-focused coverage, it is clear that some journalists took cues from the civil society organizations leading Fight for 15, addressing issues of inequality as well as the strike. Coverage helped build support for Fight for 15 and provided journalists with reporting angles on labour that tied it to human rights issues like racial, gender and political inequality.

Working conditions on Saadiyat Island: A less successful campaign

By contrast, another campaign to improve working conditions which brought together Human Rights Watch, trade unions and the press had less of a tangible impact on labour conditions. We will briefly discuss here the campaign to improve working conditions on construction sites in the United Arab Emirates. Plans by the Guggenheim and Louvre Museums and New York University to build outposts in the United Arab Emirates have been met with sharp criticism of labour conditions on the construction sites (Gulf Labour 2015).

In 2006 Human Rights Watch published a report detailing ongoing labour abuses of migrant workers in the UAE, including Saadiyat Island, and in 2009 published an investigative report on the project (2006, 2009) The report described the exploitative environment for the thousands of Southwest Asian migrant workers labouring there. Abuses included 12-hour work days in intolerable conditions, dangerous housing, and contracts that left workers indebted, unable to leave their jobs (Human Rights Watch 2009). The UAE has an estimated five million migrant workers (Human Rights Watch 2015b) and because there is no free labour market, workers take the price offered to them by recruiters in their home country. The contracts the workers sign tie them to their sponsors through the Kafala system that regulates migrant labour in the UAE and makes organizing or reporting near impossible (Sönmez, Apostopoulos, Tran & Rentrop 2011).

In their 2009 report Human Rights Watch noted, 'There is virtually no public discussion of the systemic nature of workers' rights violations. Local news media do report some violent strikes and worker deaths due to unsafe working conditions, but self-censorship appears to prevent robust media coverage of abuses of foreign workers' rights'. Human Rights Watch had worked since 2007 pressuring NYU, the Guggenheim and the Louvre to address labour abuses. Human Rights Watch said the three organizations responded with promises to enforce labour protections, including a 2009 'statement of labour values' from NYU (Human Rights Watch 2009). According to Human Rights Watch, more action was necessary to address root issues of abuse (2012).

Along with Human Rights Watch, the activist group Gulf Labour was one of the earliest groups to bring Western attention to conditions on Saadiyat Island. Gulf Labour is a group of Middle Eastern artists and activists pressuring the Guggenheim to address labour abuses in the UAE. It must be noted that the *New York Times* and other reputable media outlets have a policy of doing their own reporting and not just reprinting HRW reports verbatim. Given the current financial difficulties facing newsrooms it is difficult to send journalists out for long periods of time to do investigative reporting, especially in far-flung places that cost money to get to and require hiring translators and fixers. The newsroom climate now is different from, say, 20 years ago when a newspaper journalist at an outlet like the *Wall Street Journal* could be given a year to report a story in depth.

> 'If Saadiyat were 50 miles away from reporters on the East Coast rather than 5,000 miles away, certainly more journalists would have covered it sooner. It's not an easy story to do, and it costs a lot of money to fly there and stay there, and in this age of strained newsroom budgets, one can understand why the news media were so slow to cover it. God bless the *Guardian* and the *NYT* for finally writing about it', journalist Steve Greenhouse said
>
> *(Greenhouse 2016 [author correspondence]).*

Perhaps because of these constraints, the earliest press coverage was of a 2011 Gulf Labour protest in the *New York Times* followed up in 2012 with a *New York Times* Art Beat piece summarising a 2012 Human Rights Watch progress report on Saadiyat (Ouroussoff 2011; Cohen 2012). The first in-depth investigative journalism report was published December 2013 in the *Observer* and the *Guardian*, the result of months of work by Glen Carrick (a pseudonym used by Sean O'Driscoll) and David Batty (Schlanger 2016). The report detailed abuses and focused on the growing number of strikes and the individual human costs (Carrick and Batty 2013). The *New York Times* published a front page investigative report five months later, detailing working conditions and deportation of striking migrant workers constructing the NYU campus, with the *Independent on Sunday* publishing a similar report the same week (O'Driscoll and Kaminer 2014; Glenza 2014). According to *Newsweek*, the *Khaleej Times*, the UAE-based publishing partner of the *New York Times*, prevented the story from being published in the UAE (Schlanger 2014). After the report, NYU Public Affairs and Communications president publicly apologised stating that they would investigate and address abuses at the site (Schlanger 2014). Coverage of labour abuses on Saadiyat Island resulted from the efforts of Human Rights Watch as well as reports by Gulf Labour and ITUC. The investigative reports in the *Guardian*, the *Observer* and the *New York Times* helped uncover further abuses (Human Rights Watch 2015b). In a 2015 progress report on Saadiyat Island, Human Rights Watch reported that serious labour abuses persisted on Saadiyat Island (Human Rights Watch 2015b). The *New York Times* reported in 2015 that in the aftermath of the 2014 coverage of abuses, NYU commissioned a report investigating alleged abuse. The report confirmed many of the abuses HRW had outlined and commented on the disparity of UAE labour laws in comparison to the US and the west (Saul 2015). The UAE government declined to comment on the NYU reports. HRW said the UAE has made some progress in reforming Kafala law, though there has been limited prosecution of migrant labour abuses, and workers continue to face deportation for striking (Saul 2015; Human Rights Watch 2015a). HRW noted in their progress report, 'Implementation and enforcement remain a critical problem in ensuring that workers benefit from labour law reforms and employer-initiated codes of conduct'. (Human Rights Watch 2015a) The 2015 Human Rights Watch progress report emphasized the need for action from the Guggenheim, NYU, the Louvre, Abu Dhabi EEA (Executive Affairs Authority) and TDIC (Tourism Development and Investment Company), saying 'As project developers, those entities are subject to the UN Guiding Principles on Business and Human Rights, which require corporate actors "to prevent or mitigate adverse human rights impacts that are directly linked to their operations"' (Human Rights Watch 2015b).

Certainly the type of actor being targeted is likely to affect the impact that campaigning and press coverage can have. Without mechanisms of accountability and entities that are responsive to naming and shaming it can be difficult for journalism to have an impact. The case of the United Arab Emirates highlights some of these difficulties. As labour journalist Steve Greenhouse notes 'while it is possible to persuade big, image-conscious companies to change by embarrassing them – although McDonald's hasn't come close to accepting unionisation – it's much harder to persuade proud, sovereign nations, especially dictatorships, to budge on labour rights issues, even when you embarrass them'. (Greenhouse 2016 [author correspondence])

These two very different campaigns about labour abuses, which led to different outcomes, show the limits of what journalism can do in the fight for human rights. The campaign for better labour conditions at Saaidyat Island received publicity but has so far had little tangible effect in part because labour rights and trafficking of workers are perennial problems that are very hard to fix (Schiffrin 2016). In contrast, by targeting something narrow and achievable, Fight for 15 has apparently persuaded large sections of the public and lawmakers that wages need to rise.

Conclusion

We argue that the two cases (Fight for 15 and the New York University labour controversy) highlight essential differences in the way that labour reporting media can bring about social change. In both cases civil society organizations and journalists provided information about a social problem that needed fixing. Through social media, legacy media and opinion pieces, campaigners in both cases tried to target elite policy makers and galvanize public opinion. But Fight for 15 succeeded in bringing about lasting change with the passage of wage legislation while the labour problems in the UAE do not seem closer to resolution. At first glance it would seem that addressing exploitation on one building site would be easier than solving the problem of wages in an entire industry across multiple states. In fact, the campaign was effective partly because it targeted something closer to home that had a direct effect on the lives of many Americans and had a clear-cut solution.

By contrast, the problem of labour conditions in the Middle East felt far away, complicated, and lacked a simple solution. Moreover, Fight for 15 galvanised people at a time when there was already growing anger about inequality and wage stagnation in the US.

Even so, although the recent interest in economic inequality and the power of the 1%, as well the spread of social media has contributed to increased coverage of labour conditions, many of the labour rights topics discussed by the media are not framed as human rights questions. While media does not consistently cover labour in a human rights context, cooperation and interaction between unions and NGOs and journalists can help garner support for workers. Civil Society Organizations have long realized the benefits that media coverage has on public awareness and the success of its campaigns. (Compa 2015). The cases of Fight for 15 and Saadiyat illustrate a cautious return to labour coverage more in step with the 'labour-beat' of the past. As historian

P.W. Glende notes, newspaper coverage of labour set an early precedent for reporting that went beyond simple fact-based coverage towards writing that 'explained the news', looking at deeper inequalities and conflicts at stake in labour disputes (2012).

Questions of how the media affect the framing of a subject and the use of language as well as social media responses to media coverage are all subjects that can be easily studied now that data scraping from the Web has become widespread. The role of social media in mobilizing awareness and outrage about labour rights needs to be explored, as does the role of citizen journalists (Compton and Bendetti 2010) and impact of advocacy campaigns that use social media.

Building on the work of Matthew Powers, a further area for research is past spending by trade unions on producing labour newspapers and funding content compared to current spending by human rights groups. There is also the question of to what extent US labour coverage has become more international and whether digital technology and donor funding has spurred an increase in transnational, cross-border reporting.

But perhaps most important for human rights advocates is whether the reporting will make a difference especially in an age where low barriers to entry for media have resulted in an information deluge and NGOs find it hard to compete for attention (Thrall et al. 2014). How labour reporting will or will not succeed in generating outrage, naming and shaming companies and changing labour conditions are the key questions that ultimately will determine whether labour reporting is effective or simply descriptive.

Note

1   For space reasons, this chapter will not delve into the academic debate about the relationship between labour rights and human rights.

Acknowledgements: Thanks to our interviewees for their time: Ira Arlook, Eliza Bates, Lance Compa, Steve Greenhouse and Carter Wright. Thanks to Katherine Sullivan and Courtney Pruden for their research help, Laura Quintela and Susanna de Martino for working on the references and Joseph E. Stiglitz for reading an earlier draft of this paper.

References

Andrews, K. and Caren, N. (2010). 'Making the News: Movement Organizations, Media Attention, and the Public Agenda'. *American Sociological Review*, 75(6), pp. 841–66.

Anusonadisai, N. (2015). 'Thai Government Says It's Not Ignoring Shrimp Industry Slavery Highlighted by AP Investigation'. *US News & World Report*. Available at: http://www.usnews.com/news/world/articles/2015-12-21/thai-government-says-its-not-ignoring-shrimp-sheds-slavery [Accessed 1 Jul. 2016].

Arlook, I. (2014). 'Introduction'. In: A. Schiffrin, ed., *Global Muckraking: 100 years of Investigative Journalism from Around the World*, 1st ed. New York: New Press, pp. 49–51.

Atkins, J. (2008). *Covering for the Bosses*. Jackson: University Press of Mississippi.

Ballinger, J. (2014). 'Introduction', in: A. Schiffrin, (ed.) *Global Muckraking: 100 years of Investigative Journalism from Around the World*, 1st ed. New York: New Press, pp. 45–7.

Bekken, J. (1997). 'A Paper for Those Who Toil: The Chicago Labor Press in Transition'. *Journalism History*, 23(1), pp. 24–33.

Bekken, J. (2005). 'The Invisible Enemy: Representing Labour in a Corporate Media Order'. *Javnost - The Public*, 12(1), pp. 71–84.

Camaj, L. (2012). 'The Media's Role in Fighting Corruption: Media Effects on Governmental Accountability'. *The International Journal of Press/Politics*, 18(1), pp. 21–42.

Carrick, G. and Batty, D. (2013). In: Abu Dhabi, They Call It Happiness Island. But for the Migrant Workers, it is a Place of Misery. *The Guardian*. Available at: http://www.theguardian.com/world/2013/dec/22/abu-dhabi-happiness-island-misery [Accessed 29 June, 2016].

Chao, R. (2012). *The Impact of the Media on the Apple-Foxconn Labor Scandal*. [Unpublished paper] Columbia University.

Cohen, P. (2012). 'Report Cites Continued Problems for Workers at Abu Dhabi Cultural Site'. *New York Times*. Available at: http://artsbeat.blogs.nytimes.com/2012/03/21/report-cites-continued-problems-for-workers-at-abu-dhabi-cultural-site/ [Accessed 29 June, 2016].

Compa, L. (22 Feb. 2016). Author Correspondence.

Compton, J. and Benedetti, P. (2010). 'Labour, New Media, and the Institutional Restructuring of New Media'. *Journalism Studies*, 11(4), pp. 487–499.

Democracy Now!. (2015). *Our Economy Is Not Working: Joseph Stiglitz on Widening Income Inequality & the Fight for $15*. Available at: http://www.democracynow.org/2015/11/12/our_economy_is_not_working_joseph [Accessed 30 June, 2016].

Dixon, M. (2014). 'Union Organizing and Labor Outreach in the Contemporary United States'. *Sociology Compass*, 8(10), pp. 1183–90.

Dyck, A. and Zingales, L. (2002). 'The Corporate Governance Role of the Media'. In: R. Islam, ed., *The Right to Tell: The Role of Mass Media in Economic Development*, 1st ed. Washington, D.C.: World Bank.

Eakin, H. (2015). 'The Terrible Flight from the Killing'. *The New York Review of Books*. Available at: http://www.nybooks.com/articles/2015/10/22/terrible-flight-killing/ [Accessed 29 June, 2016].

Earl, J., Martin, A., McCarthy, J. and Soule, S. (2004). 'The Use of Newspaper Data in the Study of Collective Action'. *Annual Review of Sociology*, 30(1), pp. 65–80.

Entman, R. (1993). 'Framing: Toward Clarification of a Fractured Paradigm'. *Journal of Communication*, 43(4), pp. 51–8.

Faue, E. (2002). *Writing the Wrongs*. Ithaca NY: Cornell University Press.

Featherstone, L. (2002). *Students Against Sweatshops: the Making of a Movement*. New York: Verso Books.

Fight for $15 (2016). *Press Room - Fight for $15*. Available at: http://fightfor15.org/press-room/ [Accessed 29 June, 2016].

Finnegan, W. (2014). 'Dignity'. *The New Yorker*. Available at: http://www.newyorker.com/magazine/2014/09/15/dignity-4 [Accessed 29 June, 2016].

Frank, T. (1997). 'When Class Disappears'. *The Baffler*, (9). Available at: http://thebaffler.com/salvos/when-class-disappears. [Accessed 29 June, 2016].

Glende, P. (2012). *Labor Makes the News*. Oxford, UK: for the Business History Conference by Oxford University Press.

Glenza, J. (2014). NYU 'Will Investigate' Reports of Abu Dhabi Campus Worker Mistreatment'. *The Guardian*. Available at: https://www.theguardian.com/world/2014/may/19/nyu-abu-dhabi-investigate-worker-mistreatment [Accessed 29 June, 2016].

Greenberg, J. and Knight, G. (2004). 'Framing Sweatshops: Nike, Global Production, and the American News Media'. *Communication and Critical/Cultural Studies*, 1(2), pp. 151–75.

Greenhouse, S. (2014). 'Strong Voice in 'Fight for 15' Fast-food Wage Campaign'. *The New York Times*. Available at: http://www.nytimes.com/2014/12/05/business/in-fast-food-workers-fight-for-15-an-hour-a-strong-voice-in-terrance-wise.html?_r=1 [Accessed 29 June, 2016].

Greenhouse, S. (2015). 'On the Road to Nowhere'. *The American Prospect*. Available at: http://prospect.org/article/road-nowhere-3 [Accessed 29 June, 2016].

Greenhouse, S. (2015). 'Why the Media Started Caring about the American Worker Again'. *The Atlantic*. Available at: http://www.theatlantic.com/business/archive/2015/01/why-the-media-started-caring-about-the-american-worker-again/384287/ [Accessed 29 June, 2016].

Greenhouse, S. (2016). Author correspondence.

Greenhouse, S. (2016). 'With Day of Protests, Fast-food Workers Seek More Pay'. *The New York Times*. Available at: http://www.nytimes.com/2012/11/30/nyregion/fast-food-workers-in-new-york-city-rally-for-higher-wages.html?_r=0. [Accessed 29 June, 2016].

Greenshouse, S. (2015). 'How to Get Low-wage Workers into the Middle Class'. *The Atlantic*. Available at: http://www.theatlantic.com/business/archive/2015/08/fifteen-dollars-minimum-wage/401540/ [Accessed 29 June, 2016].

Gulflabour.org. (2015). 'Timeline | Gulf Labor Artist Coalition'. [online] Available at: http://gulflabour.org/timeline/ [Accessed 29 June, 2016].

Guo, L., Hsu, S., Holton, A. and Jeong, S. (2012). 'A Case Study of the Foxconn Suicides: An International Perspective to Framing the Sweatshop Issue'. *International Communication Gazette*, 74(5), pp. 484–503.

Higgs, C. (2012). *Chocolate Islands*. Athens: Ohio University Press.

Hochschild, A. (1998). *King Leopold's Ghost*. Boston: Houghton Mifflin.

Hogler, R., Hunt, H. and Weiler, S. (2014). 'Killing Unions with Culture: Institutions, Inequality, and the Effects of Labor's Decline in the United States'. *Employee Responsibilities and Rights Journal*, 27(1), pp. 63–79.

Human Rights Watch (2009). *The Island of Happiness: Exploitation of Migrant Workers on Saadiyat Island, Abu Dhabi*. Human Right Watch. Available at: https://www.hrw.org/report/2009/05/19/island-happiness/ exploitation-migrant-workers-saadiyat-island-abu-dhabi [Accessed 29 June, 2016].

Human Rights Watch. (2012). 'The Island of Happiness Revisited'. Human Rights Watch. Available at: https://www.hrw.org/report/2012/03/21/island-happiness-revisited/progress-report-institutional-commitments-address.

Human Rights Watch, (2006). 'Building Towers, Cheating Workers: Exploitation of Migrant Construction Workers in the United Arab Emirates'. *Human Rights Watch*. Available at: https://www.hrw.org/ report/2006/11/11/building-towers-cheating-workers/exploitation-migrant-construction-workers-united [Accessed 29 June, 2016].

Human Rights Watch (2015a). Migrant Workers' Rights on Saadiyat Island in the United Arab Emirates: 2015 Progress Report. *Human Rights Watch*. Available at: https://www.hrw.org/report/2015/02/10/migrant-workers-rights-saadiyat-island-united-arab-emirates/2015-progress-report [Accessed 29 June, 2016].

Human Rights Watch (2015b). *Gulf Countries: Bid to Protect Migrant Workers*. [online] Available at: https:// www.hrw.org/news/2015/12/22/gulf-countries-bid-protect-migrant-workers [Accessed 29 June, 2016].

Jaffe, S. (2014). Black Poverty Is State Violence, Too: Why Struggles for Criminal Justice and Living Wage are Uniting. *Salon*. Available at: http://www.salon.com/2014/12/05/black_poverty_is_state_violence_too_why_struggles_for_criminal_justice_and_living_wage_are_uniting/ [Accessed 29 June, 2016].

Kabela Jr, F. (1960). 'The Labor Press: Its History, Nature and Influence'. *Labor Law Journal*, 11(5), pp. 407–14.

Kennedy, M. (2008). 'Getting Counted: Markets, Media, and Reality'. *American Sociological Review*, 73(6), pp. 1021–21.

Lathrop, Y., Sonn, P. and Tung, I. (2015). The Growing Movement For $15. *National Employment Law Project*, Nov 04. Available at: http://www.nelp.org/publication/growing-movement-15/ [Accessed 23 March, 2016].

Martin, C. (2008). '"Upscale" News Audiences and the Transformation of Labour News'. *Journalism Studies*, 9(2), pp. 178–94.

Mason, M., McDowell, R., Mendoza, M. and Htusan, E. (2015). 'AP: Global Supermarkets Selling Shrimp Peeled by Slaves'. *ap.org*. Available at: http://bigstory.ap.org/article/0d9bad238bc24a059beeb404 1aa21435/ap-global-supermarkets-selling-shrimp-peeled-slaves [Accessed 29 June, 2016].

Mort, J. (1987). 'The Vanishing Labor Beat'. *The Nation*.

Nytimes.com. (2013). *Death and Servitude in Qatar*. Available at: http://www.nytimes.com/2013/11/02/ opinion/death-and-servitude-in-qatar.html?_r=0 [Accessed 30 June, 2016].

O'Driscoll, S. and Kaminer, A. (2014). Workers at N.Y.U.'s Abu Dhabi Site Faced Harsh Conditions. *Nytimes. com*. Available at: http://www.nytimes.com/2014/05/19/nyregion/workers-at-nyus-abu-dhabi-site-face-harsh-conditions.html?_r=1 [Accessed 29 June, 2016].

Ouroussoff, N. (2011). 'Guggenheim Threatened With Boycott Over Abu Dhabi Project'. *Nytimes.com*. Available at: http://www.nytimes.com/2011/03/17/arts/design/guggenheim-threatened-with-boy-cott-over-abu-dhabi-project.html?_r=0 [Accessed 30 June, 2016].

Peralta, E. (2012). *'This American Life' Retracts Mike Daisey's Apple Factory Story*. [online] NPR.org. Available at: http://www.npr.org/sections/thetwo-way/2012/03/16/148761812/this-american-life-retracts-mike-daiseys-apple-factory-story [Accessed 30 June, 2016].

Powers, M. (2015). 'The New Boots on the Ground: NGOs in the Changing Landscape of International News'. *Journalism*, 17(4), pp. 401–16.

Read, B. (2002). 'Students' Research Forms the Basis of a Web Site on Labor Journalism'. *The Chronicle of Higher Education*. Available at: http://chronicle.com/article/students-research-forms-the/28166 [Accessed 30 June, 2016].

Resnikoff, N. (2013). 'New York's Fast Food Workers Strike. Why now?' *MSNBC*. Available at: http://www. msnbc.com/the-ed-show/new-yorks-fast-food-workers-strike-why-now [Accessed 30 June, 2016].

Resnikoff, N. (2016). 'Historic fast food strike draws lessons from MLK's last campaign'. *MSNBC*. Available at: http://www.msnbc.com/all-in/historic-fast-food-strike-draws-lessons [Accessed 30 June, 2016].

Robbins, L. (2015). *The Scene of a Nail Salon Sweep*. NYTimes.com – Video. Available at: http://www. nytimes.com/video/nyregion/100000003866231/the-scene-of-a-nail-salon-sweep.html [Accessed 30 June, 2016].

S, P. (2016). 'To Fix the Racial Wealth Gap, We Need Solutions That Sound Radical'. [*The Nation*. Available at: http://www.thenation.com/article/to-fix-the-racial-wealth-gap-we-need-solutions-that-sound-radical/. [Accessed 30 June, 2016].

Saul, S. (2015). 'N.Y.U. Labor Guidelines Failed to Protect 10,000 Workers in Abu Dhabi, Report Says'. *Nytimes.com*. Available at: http://www.nytimes.com/2015/04/17/nyregion/nyu-labour-rules-failed-to-protect-10000-workers-in-abu-dhabi.html [Accessed 30 June, 2016].

Schiffrin, A. ed. (2014). *Global Muckraking: 100 years of Investigative Journalism from Around the World*. 1st ed. New York: New Press.

Schiffrin, A. (1984). *We Are Against People Who Push Other People Around: A Study of the Newspaper PM*. B.A. Reed College.

Schlanger, Z. (2014). UAE Halts Printing of New York Times Over Damning NYU Labor Article. *Newsweek*. Available at: http://www.newsweek.com/uae-halts-printing-new-york-times-over-damning-nyu-labour-article-251495?piano_t=1 [Accessed 30 June, 2016].

Schlanger, Z. (2015). 'Under Surveillance in Abu Dhabi: A Reporter's Saga of Being Followed, Bribed, and Recruited as a Spy'. *Newsweek*, 30 March. Available at: http://www.newsweek.com/under-surveillance-abu-dhabi-reporters-saga-being-followed-bribed-and-317627 [Accessed 12 March, 2016].

Simpson, C. (2013). 'An iPhone Tester Caught in Apple's Supply Chain'. *Bloomberg.com*. Available at: http://www.bloomberg.com/bw/articles/2013-11-07/an-iphone-tester-caught-in-apples-supply-chain#p6 [Accessed 30 June, 2016].

Sönmez, S., Apostolopoulos, Y., Tran, D. and Rentrope, S. (2011). 'Human Rights and Health Disparities for Migrant Workers in the UAE'. *Health and Human Rights*, 13(2), pp. 17–35.

Stapenhurst, R. (2000). *The Media's Role in Curbing Corruption*. [Washington, D.C.]: World Bank Institute.

Strangler, C. (2015). 'Fight For 15 Has Helped Pass Minimum Wage Hikes, But Yet To Deliver Broad-Based Pay Gains. *International Business Times*'. Available at: http://www.ibtimes.com/fight-15-has-helped-pass-minimum-wage-hikes-yet-deliver-broad-based-pay-gains-2082404 [Accessed 30 June, 2016].

Streitmatter, R. (1999). 'Origins of the American Labor Press'. *Journalism*, 25(3), pp. 99–106.

Strom, S. (1996). 'A Sweetheart Becomes Suspect: Looking Behind Those Kathie Lee Labels'. *Nytimes.com*. Available at: http://www.nytimes.com/1996/06/27/business/a-sweetheart-becomes-suspect-looking-behind-those-kathie-lee-labels.html?pagewanted=all [Accessed 30 June, 2016].

Thrall, A., Stecula, D. and Sweet, D. (2014). 'May We Have Your Attention Please? Human-Rights NGOs and the Problem of Global Communication'. *The International Journal of Press/Politics*, 19(2), pp. 135–59.

Timm, J. (2015). 'Can Millennials Save Unions?'. *The Atlantic*. Available at: http://www.theatlantic.com/business/archive/2015/09/millennials-unions/401918/ [Accessed 30 June, 2016].

Uetricht, M. (2015). 'Steven Greenhouse on Keeping the Labor Beat Alive'. *Inthesetimes.com*. Available at: http://inthesetimes.com/article/17634/keeping_the_labor_beat_alive [Accessed 30 June, 2016].

Urbina, I. (2015). 'Sea Slaves': The Human Misery That Feeds Pets and Livestock. *Nytimes.com*. Available at: http://www.nytimes.com/2015/07/27/world/outlaw-ocean-thailand-fishing-sea-slaves-pets.html [Accessed 30 June, 2016].

Urbina, I. (2015). 'Consumers and Lawmakers Take Steps to End Forced Labor in Fishing'. *Nytimes.com*. Available at: http://www.nytimes.com/2015/09/14/world/consumers-and-lawmakers-take-steps-to-end-forced-labor-in-fishing.html [Accessed 30 June, 2016].

Vallas, S. (2015). 'Covering Labor: An interview with Steven Greenhouse, long time labor reporter for The New York Times'. Work in Progress. 2 March. Retrieved from http://workinprogress.oowsection.org/2015/03/02/covering-labor-an-interview-with-steven-greenhouse-long-time-labor-reporter-for-the-new-york-times/ [Accessed on 24 March, 2016].

Whack, E. H. (2017). 'Black Lives Matter groups joining forces with wage activists'. *Associated Press*. Available at: https://apnews.com/32e040002e0243048cf560fd817c37fd/black-lives-matter-groups-joining-forces-wage-activists.

Whitt, J. (2008). 'From The Jungle to Food Lion: The history lessons of investigative journalism'. *Journalism History*, 34 (3), 170–3.

Witwer, D. (2013). 'The heyday of the labor beat'. *Labor: Studies in Working-Class History*, 10 (2), pp. 9–29.

Wright, C., Assistant Director of Communications SEIU. (01 Mar. 2016). Author Correspondence.

Zillman, C. (2014). 'Fast food workers' $15 demand: How aiming high launched a social movement'. *Fortune*. Available at: http://fortune.com/2014/12/04/fast-food-workers-15-demand-how-aiming-high-launched-a-social-movement/.

46

PUBLIC SAFETY

Sonja Wolf

Crime and violence constitute a significant social problem throughout the world, but it is in developing countries that homicides and gang activity have become apparently intractable public policy challenges. The media play a critical role in informing citizens about delinquency and violence, and the way they do so has important repercussions for people's perceptions of security concerns and the policies they require. This chapter draws on the existing research literature to examine the general trends in media coverage of public safety issues and their human rights implications. It argues that the prevalence of commercial media, with their reliance on certain news production styles and routines, results in mostly decontextualised news content that distorts the social reality of crime, helps increase audiences' fear of crime, and elicits preferences for punitive strategies. The chapter begins by discussing media depictions of public safety matters, as well as the effects and production process of crime news. Subsequently, it explores alternative approaches to covering violence and criminality before appraising the use of social media. The chapter concludes with some reflections on the possibilities for greater media diversity and more analytical reporting.

Media representations of crime and violence

Both news and entertainment media provide extensive treatment of acts of crime and violence. What information they choose to communicate and how they package it, has important consequences for people's understanding of a problem and the most appropriate response to it, particularly since most individuals lack immediate experience of criminality. Social constructivist studies show that media accounts of crime, violence and victimisation tend to offer simplistic and decontextualised explanations of complex events and issues. These portrayals often distort social reality by overstating serious and brutal incidents, leading the public to overestimate the nature and frequency of crime and violence. Narratives of victimisation foment certain myths, such as the prevalence of predators, stranger-danger and random violence (Altheide 2006). In general terms, media reports feature white victims and racial minority or juvenile offenders, and make the world seem more hostile and dangerous than statistics bear out. Research relates frequent news exposure to higher levels of crime anxiety, yet also suggests that content may be more relevant than the rate of consumption. Local and sensational stories about indiscriminate violence appear to create more fear than distant and less dramatic pieces about targeted attacks.

Youth violence is one example of how news reporting can raise the visibility of a social problem independent of its actual incidence or destructiveness. In the summer of 1993, the media in Denver provided ample and conspicuous coverage of a purported epidemic of youth violence, even though the city was seeing no striking increase in serious offenses (Colomy and Greiner 1999-2000). Concentrating on a series of atypical crimes, the stories highlighted the innocence of the victims and the boldness of the juvenile delinquents, the unprecedented and haphazard character of the violence, and its intrusion into reputable areas. The coverage terrified citizens, prompting some to alter daily routines, move to supposedly safer neighbourhoods or improve home security. Others, assuming that the coverage spotlighted a serious problem that required intervention, organised marches and wrote to public officials. These reactions fed into the media narrative and served to reaffirm the inaccurate perception that the city was facing a security crisis that required a swift crackdown.

School shootings, a type of youth violence that occurs with disproportionate regularity in the United States, are covered prominently by the country's mass media. In April 1999, Eric Harris and Dylan Klebold opened fire at Columbine High School, slaying twelve fellow students and one teacher, as well as wounding 21 others before committing suicide. The Columbine massacre is considered the nation's bloodiest school episode of the 1990s and, unlike previous school mass killings, it took place in a largely White, middle-class suburb (Birkland and Lawrence 2009). Columbine received comparatively more media attention than other student-on-student shootings and, statistics to the contrary, was taken as evidence that school violence was a growing national problem. Associating it with widespread firearms availability and an aggressive popular culture, the coverage nonetheless had little effect on public opinion and gun policy reform (ibid.). After the terrorist attacks of September 11, 2001, reporting described school shootings as terrorism, ostensibly to garner support for tougher measures against school violence. This framing served entertainment criteria and political expediency, but other than increasing the power and resources of counterterrorism agencies, it had no discernible impact on school shootings (Altheide 2009).

Conversely, the United States began legislating against stalking – the unwanted and obsessive attention by another person – once the media had applied the term to the persistent pursuit of celebrities. Spitzberg and Cadiz (2002) find that the media publicise stereotypes of stalking that can pervert perceptions of the crime and its potential victims. Often it is wrongly implied that stalking affects mostly superstars, is a gendered crime that is carried out by mentally ill strangers, and is unrelated to normal romantic relationships. Thus, individuals who fail to see beyond these inaccuracies may understand neither their own risk of victimisation and nor how to deal with stalking attempts.

Effects of crime news

While the media do not determine public opinion, they help mould perceptions of social problems, set public agendas, and shape preferences for certain policies. Through the framing of events and issues, the media disclose some things and conceal others, define problems, identify causes, and propose solutions. This framing can be either episodic – focused on individual circumstances and responsibility – or thematic – foregrounding context and societal accountability. The choice of framing impacts people's interpretation of the reality conveyed to them. Who they come to think of as answerable for a problem, can influence their inclination towards one response over another. Episodic reports, the more common ones in crime news, have been related to narrowly punitive rather than comprehensive strategies.

Audiences, reception research argues, interpret information in different ways, depending on their own characteristics (such as sex, age and race), experiences (such as victimisation) and the levels of crime in their community or city. Eschholz (1997-1998) distinguishes four approaches to understanding variation in the decoding of media messages. Substitution occurs when individuals who lack exposure to victimisation, or are at little risk thereof, replace their own experiences with those of the stories' protagonists. Resonance, by contrast, implies that a person connects with crime news because they have previously been attacked or live in an unsafe neighbourhood. Affinity suggests that someone believes themselves to be more likely to be victimised because they share the traits of frequent crime targets. Finally, vulnerability indicates that individuals who consider themselves to be susceptible to crime may be more responsive to media reports about the subject.

Mass media coverage of offences and groups scapegoated as perpetrators, such as youths, immigrants or mentally ill persons, has fed widespread anxiety of crime even in times of declining criminality. This fear is typically more acute among frequent consumers of news (particularly television broadcasts), middle-aged white women, residents in mostly black neighbourhoods, recent victims, and low-salaried workers. When reporting consistently amplifies the incidence of crime, or periodically emphasises a particular issue, this fear can even develop into a moral panic. The exaggeration of a social phenomenon can raise profits for media companies and revitalise electoral campaigns, but above all it can lead people to become distrustful, adopt avoidance behaviour, and favour greater social control (Altheide and Michalowski 1999).

McGinty, Webster and Barry (2013) explored the ways in which exposure to news media portrayal of mass shootings committed by persons with serious mental illness, and using firearms with high-capacity magazines, shapes attitudes towards that population and gun policy. The study suggests that the coverage heightened negative attitudes towards people with serious mental illness and raised support for both weapons restrictions for this group and a ban on high-capacity magazines. Stories that narrowly relate mass shootings to serious mental illness may lead audiences to view such incidents as isolated acts of certain individuals, rather than as consequences of broader problems in society. Polling data, for example, indicates most US citizens increasingly favour specific, rather than general, weapons control. A related concern is that policymakers might try to prevent seriously mentally ill persons from obtaining firearms, instead of tightening gun laws more broadly as a way of reducing gun violence. Such targeted measures, however, are considered counterproductive because most of the – in any case limited – violence carried out by this population is attributable to trauma and substance use, and may deter members of this group from seeking medical care.

Media research has also tested the effects of television shows on attitudes towards the police. News coverage of law enforcement tends to highlight police brutality and corruption. Reality TV programmes, by contrast, present actual footage or re-enactments of police operations and generally portray officers in a positive light. Media content of this kind exaggerates police success in apprehending suspects and glosses over police abuse. Among the US population, African Americans generally hold less positive attitudes towards the law enforcement than Whites, a situation that is thought to arise from racial differences in citizen-police interaction. In their study of the relationship between race and attitudes towards the police, Eschholz, Blackwell, Gertz and Chiricos (2002) found that reality TV programmes disproportionately display African Americans as offenders rather than officers, and the latter more often forcibly subduing Black, not White, suspects. Furthermore, reality police shows increase confidence in law enforcement among White, but not Black, audiences.

Crime news production

Media coverage of public safety issues, and its effects among the public and policymakers, is better understood when examining the nature and functioning of the contemporary media industry. The growing global trend from publicly to commercial and privately owned outlets has heralded an increase in the number of media, yet greater concentration of sources because ownership often spans different media segments. This concentration, particularly in cases of conglomerate ownership, makes firms more susceptible to censorious pressure by powerful economic or political actors. Since the media depend heavily on advertising, the prospect of losing valuable revenue can encourage them to soften or supress content that might offend their financial backers (Germano and Meier 2013). Media owners may manipulate media content directly but mostly do so indirectly, either by setting profit targets that affect newsroom budget and size, or by taking managerial decisions that can impact the workplace culture and views of acceptable journalistic routines. Self-censorship is considered a widely adhered to practice that moderates and slants news coverage, especially in corporately owned media (Baker 2002).

News outlets rely on certain formats, or ways of selecting, organising and presenting information to audiences. The drive towards greater commercialisation, and hence profit orientation, of the media, has seen many companies cut funding for relatively expensive forms of journalism, such as investigative and foreign news reporting. In order to attract more consumers and advertising income, the mainstream media have adapted the light-hearted entertainment format to news production. With an informal communicative style, this format privileges celebrity gossip and decontextualised news about crime, violence and corruption. Often, particularly on local television crime news, it adopts a problem frame which narrates issues as concrete, tangible and realistic, and can lead audiences to view life as perilous and fearful (Altheide 1997).

The content and nature of crime news reporting are moulded by criteria of newsworthiness as well as journalistic routines. Considering factors such as crime seriousness and special group offences (for example, child victims), the media select stories they deem interesting and emotionally relevant to their audiences. In a bid to capitalise on limited news space, the media present extreme cases as representative of a crime problem and potentially end up distorting public perceptions of it. The pressure to do so is most intense for television, the dominant medium despite the mounting influence of the Internet, which transmits technology-heavy broadcasts and caters to larger and more diverse audiences than newspapers.

Crime news production, however, is also shaped by journalistic and editorial routines as well as newsroom imperatives. Reporters, often underpaid and overworked, rely extensively on official sources and typically exclude victims, defendants and experts from their stories. Criminal justice sources, generally accepted as credible, can regularly supply journalists with information. The media can thus routinise their news production and churn out stories inexpensively, while police, prosecutors and judges can legitimate their roles, justifies budget increases, lift their image, and satisfy political aspirations (Chermak 1994).

The predilection for news routines becomes clearer when surveying the nexus between journalistic working conditions and reporting practices. The global trend towards media privatisation and the associated push for budget cutbacks has prompted more recruitment of younger, casual and low-paid staff, rather than experienced and better remunerated journalists on long-term contracts. In developing countries this situation is considered even bleaker than in the United States and Western Europe. Research comparing journalists' salaries and employment conditions in 38 countries (Cushion 2007) revealed two basic tendencies: while media concentration and external pressures by governments and advertisers result in bland news, job insecurity and low wages prompt a decline in critical, investigative and ethical reporting.

Alternative approaches to covering crime and violence

The last decade or so has witnessed the emergence, perhaps particularly in Latin America, of novel ways of covering public safety issues. One is narrative journalism, which is committed to investigating violence and inequality, telling in-depth stories and giving a voice to society's marginalised actors. Typically taking an extended format, narrative journalism has been experiencing somewhat of a boom with the growth in digital media. Four techniques characterise it: a detailed description of the setting, the reproduction of entire dialogues, a third-person viewpoint, and an account of everyday practices (Palau Sampio 2013). Its preferred genre is the chronicle, which distances itself from figures and official discourse and chooses instead an immersion in the milieu of its protagonists. The main characters are individuals who suffer hardship or violence and whose concerns and fears the journalist tries to capture and publicly condemn. Narrative journalism critiques social reality and tackles issues such as organised crime, violence, poverty, and displacement.

Founded in 1998, the Salvadoran digital newspaper *El Faro* has distinguished itself for publishing extensive reports and chronicles on issues that the country's mainstream media avoid or distort. Unafraid to expose the wrongs of those power, in 2010 the team created Sala Negra, an investigative unit focused on organised crime, gangs, violence, and corruption. Its painstakingly-researched stories have addressed subjects such as the country's security policy and extrajudicial executions by state agents, prison conditions, forced disappearances, and forced displacement. In a number of cases, these publications have achieved international recognition. Given their sensitive nature, some of these accounts have carried threats for the journalists. One example is their 2011 report on the Texis Cartel, a drug trafficking group operating in northwestern El Salvador, which revealed that this illicit network comprised entrepreneurs, gang members, politicians, police officers, judges, and prosecutors. The exposé, however, did not prod the authorities to dismantle this criminal structure. Since Internet in the country remains very limited, the stories also have limited reach. With a reduced readership it is difficult to create public outrage and mobilise citizens to demand social and institutional change. Narrative journalism can contribute to a fuller understanding of society's hidden dimensions, but it may not overcome preconceived opinions or galvanise the fight against corruption and impunity when the political class is unprepared to wage it.

A second unconventional media approach to public safety issues is peace journalism. Originally proposed by sociologist Johan Galtung, peace journalism proposes to contextualise violence and expose its structural and cultural roots. Normatively oriented, its implementation is meant to counter 'war journalism', the dominant form of reporting crime and conflict. War journalism is concerned with isolated incidents of physical violence, one-sided propaganda, the voices of elites, and the victory of one group over another. Peace journalism, by contrast, attempts to paint a more complex picture of a conflict by explaining its causes and background, supplying impartial information, giving a voice to ordinary people, and promoting conflict resolution and reconciliation (Lacasse and Forster, 2012).

Peace journalism has been pursued in contexts such as urban violence in Brazil and the drug war in Mexico. In 2009 *O Globo*, Rio de Janeiro's largest newspaper, published a special series on the Police Pacification Units that were deployed to the city's favelas the previous year to conduct community policing and buttress prevention. An analysis of this coverage (Biazoto 2011) showed that the reports relied on multiple sources and displayed awareness that the occupation of the favelas constrained the rights of their residents. Nonetheless, the pieces said little about the origins and circumstances of the violence, and extrajudicial killings went unexamined. The series dehumanised drug traffickers and implausibly implied that their removal from the communities would be welcomed by the residents, although the drug gangs must have enjoyed some level of acceptance by their neighbours in order to conduct their business.

In their comparative study of Mexican drug war coverage by local and national US newspapers, Lacasse and Forster (2012) found that local newspapers in the border region contained more peace-oriented articles than their more distant counterparts. Although they offered a more even-handed perspective of the conflict, by omitting a host of actors and experiences they failed to convey its sheer complexity. These examples indicate that a peace journalism framework can guide reporters in moving from body counts to more neutral and sensitive coverage of public safety issues. In practice, however, media profit goals and newsroom priorities make this aspiration difficult to accomplish.

Crime, violence and the social media

The growth of social media has generated greater pluralism of voices and information on public safety issues. The police use the social media to enhance public trust, enlist citizens for crime reduction, and track down suspects. In countries such as Brazil and El Salvador law enforcement officers celebrate the killings of gang members. Criminal groups share videos on YouTube or send intimidating tweets to their rivals. In Mexico organised crime has perpetrated grenade attacks on traditional news outlets and disappeared or murdered journalists. Threats and violence have encouraged self-censorship among reporters, and in some states, particularly along the country's northern border, they have effectively created news blackouts. Underreporting of the drug violence has prompted citizens to turn to blogs and the social media in order to stay informed about gunfights, roadblocks, homicides, and disappearances (Correa-Cabrera and Nava 2013).

Citizen journalism, the process whereby ordinary people collect and disseminate news and information (Antony and Thomas 2010), can help raise awareness of public safety incidents and foster accountability of state agents. One of the early examples of citizen journalism in the United States is a homemade videotape showing the brutal beating of Rodney King, a black taxi driver, by Los Angeles Police Department officers in March 1991. The footage was broadcast by a local news station, but the following year the acquittals of the officers involved sparked widespread riots in the city. Today citizen-created media content, through the use of Internet-based and wireless technologies, allows alternative discourses on crime, violence, and official misconduct to circulate through blogs as well as social networking and video sharing websites.

Police brutality has proved a central concern for citizen journalists. In January 2009, Oscar Grant, a young Black man, was fatally shot in an Oakland, California, subway station by a White Bay Area Rail Transit officer, Johannes Mehserle. Passengers recorded the event on their mobile phones and later uploaded their videos to YouTube. The recordings triggered extensive protests and were used as evidence in the ensuing trial that resulted in Mehserle's conviction for involuntary manslaughter (Antony and Thomas 2010). The episode shows that individuals can successfully challenge racialised policing and hold state agents responsible for their actions. However, YouTube has a community-flagging regulatory system whereby individuals can alert the company to sexually explicit or violent content, and the criteria for removing inappropriate videos are unclear. The social media, therefore, are very much a contested space in which some champion transparency and accountability, while others may try to bury uncomfortable truths.

Twitter has become another tool for highlighting and opposing police brutality as well as slanted media coverage of minority group victims. In August 2014 an unarmed black teenager,

Michael Brown, was lethally shot by Darren Wilson, a White police officer, in Ferguson, Missouri. Demonstrators' calls for the arrest of the officer and their violent confrontations with local law enforcement were documented and shared on Twitter. Meanwhile, the "#Ferguson" hashtag activism attempted to make police abuse visible and hold its perpetrators accountable. Although the officer involved was ultimately not indicted, the Twitter campaign revealed the systematic nature of racialised profiling and the vulnerability of African-American citizens, particularly young men, in the United States (Bonilla and Rosa 2015). By underscoring black people's humanity, the campaign also countered mainstream media narratives that ascribe danger to black bodies and blame victims for their own suffering.

The *Blog del Narco* was created in March 2010 as a citizen-based response to the previously mentioned news blackouts in Mexico's drug war. Perhaps the most prominent of such platforms, it is run anonymously and endeavours to inform the public impartially about different aspects of the drug war. Drawing on sources that include ordinary citizens, officials and even members of criminal groups, the blog offers both empirical data (such as homicides, arrests, and human rights abuse) and analyses about the conflict (Monroy-Hernández and Palacios 2014). The gruesome nature of many posts has generated controversy, and at some point complaints by the Mexican authorities led Google to limit access to the site. Despite doubts about the accuracy of some of the information, as well as reprisals against administrators and users of the blog, it continues to be widely consulted.

Conclusion

In many countries around the world, crime and violence need to be tackled not through more repressive policing and surveillance, increasingly punitive legislation, and more incarceration, but through community policing and social prevention. There is little prospect of such a turn in security policies unless citizens begin to view and think differently about public safety issues and the ways in which governments ought to handle them. Media coverage of crime and violence is often entertainment-oriented, presents events in an isolated and decontextualised manner, and asks how individuals can protect themselves rather than how society can address the roots of insecurity. The following changes in the media industry and journalism practices could open up avenues for more critical and investigative media content about public safety problems.

Ideally, news organisations would improve employment conditions for journalists, including higher pay, overall job satisfaction and greater autonomy to follow-up issues they consider of public interest. Such changes, however, are unlikely given the profit-orientation of the mainstream media. The proliferation of alternative outlets would contribute to a multiplication of voices, but in order to be sustainable these organisations would need to reduce their advertising dependence and attract other sources of income. Stepping up regulation of media ownership would go a long way towards building a non-oligopolistic, non-commercial system that would allow for a greater viewpoint diversity. Such a structural shift seems unlikely as long as politicians resist state interference in the telecommunications sector and civil society groups do not promote media reforms. Meanwhile, the growth in digital media and social media use broadens access to information, although online content is of variable quality, and in developing countries Internet access remains extremely limited.

Two strategies can help make the news treatment of public safety issues more rigorous and comprehensive. One is data journalism and would see reporters collect and use different kinds of statistics to tell more compelling stories about the nature and impact of crime and violence in society. Journalists who are unfamiliar with methods of obtaining data, for example through public information requests or digital research, or inexperienced in the use of software and production of visual aids, could work with non-governmental organisations (NGOs) that provide training in these fields.

A second strategy concerns the advocacy journalism of civil society groups. Many larger and better resourced organisations have professionalised their communications work in order to impact news reporting, public opinion and policymaking. Mostly, however, they engage the mainstream media because of their ample reach and authority in elite circles. NGO influence shifts with each policy issue and political situation, but reporters need dependable and responsive sources, opening up possibilities for civil society activism (Waisbord 2011). Whereas grassroots organisations operate in communities and can offer the perspective of ordinary people, research organisations possess technical expertise and data on specific topics. If NGOs consistently come across as credible, they can take advantage of the media demand for data to generate public debate and promote policy transformations.

References

Altheide, D. L. (1997). 'The News Media, the Problem Frame, and the Production of Fear'. *The Sociological Quarterly*, 38(4), pp. 647–68.

Altheide, D. L. (2006). 'The Mass Media, Crime and Terrorism'. *Journal of International Criminal Justice*, 4(5), pp. 982–97.

Altheide, D. L. (2009). 'The Columbine Shootings and the Discourse of Fear'. *American Behavioral Scientist*, 52(10), pp. 1354–70.

Altheide, D. L. and Michalowski, R. S. (1999). 'Fear in the News: A Discourse of Control'. *The Sociological Quarterly*, 40(3), pp. 475–503.

Antony, M. G. and Thomas, R. J., (2010). 'This is Citizen Journalism at its Finest': YouTube and the Public Sphere in the Oscar Grant Shooting Incident'. *New Media and Society*, 12(8), pp. 1280–96.

Baker, C. E. (2002). 'Media Concentration: Giving up on Democracy'. *Florida Law Review*, 54(5), pp. 839–919.

Biazoto, J. (2011). 'Peace Journalism Where There Is No War. Conflict-sensitive Reporting on Urban Violence and Public Security in Brazil and its Potential Role in Conflict Transformation'. *Conflict and Communication Online*, 10(2). Available at: http://www.cco.regener-online.de/2011_2/pdf/biazoto.pdf

Birkland, T. A. and Lawrence, R. G. (2009). 'Media Framing and Policy Change After Columbine'. *American Behavioral Scientist*, 52(10), pp. 1405–25.

Bonilla, Y. and Rosa, J. (2015). '#Ferguson: Digital Protest, Hashtag Ethnography, and the Racial Politics of Social Media in the United States'. *American Ethnologist*, 42(1), pp. 4–17.

Chermak, S. M. (1994). 'Body Count News: How Crime Is Presented in the News Media'. *Justice Quarterly*, 11(4), pp. 561–82.

Colomy, P. and Greiner, L. R, (1999–2000). 'Making Youth Violence Visible: The News Media and the Summer of Violence'. *Denver University Law Review*, 77(4), pp. 661–88.

Correa-Cabrera, G. and Nava, J. (2013). 'Drug Wars, Social Networks, and the Right to Information: Informal Media as Freedom of the Press in Northern Mexico'. In: T. Payan, K. Staudt and Z. A. Kruszewski, eds., *A War that Can't be Won: Binational Perspectives on the War on Drugs*. Tucson, AZ: University of Arizona Press. pp. 95–118.

Cushion, S. (2007). 'Rich Media, Poor Journalists'. *Journalism Practice*, 1(1), pp. 120–9.

Eschholz, S. (1997–8). 'The Media and Fear of Crime: A Survey of the Research'. *University of Florida Journal of Law and Public Policy*, 9, pp. 37–59.

Eschholz, S., Blackwell, B. S., Gertz, M. and Chiricos, T. (2002). 'Race and Attitudes Toward the Police: Assessing the Effects of Watching "Reality" Police Programs'. *Journal of Criminal Justice*, 30, pp. 327–41.

Germano, F. and Meier, M. (2013). 'Concentration and Self-censorship in Commercial Media'. *Journal of Public Economics*, 97, pp. 117–30.

Lacasse, K. and Forster, L. (2012). 'The War Next Door: Peace Journalism in US Local and Distant Newspapers' Coverage of Mexico'. *Media, War and Conflict*, 5(3), pp. 223–37.

McGinty, E. E., Webster, D. W. and Barry, C. L. (2013). 'Effects of News Media Messages About Mass Shootings on Attitudes Toward Persons With Serious Mental Illness and Public Support for Gun Control Policies'. *American Journal of Psychiatry*, 170, pp. 494–501.

Monroy-Hernández, A. and Palacios, L. D. (2014). 'Blog del Narco and the Future of Citizen Journalism'. *Georgetown Journal of International Affairs*, 15, pp. 81–92.

Palau Sampio, D. (2013). 'Los otros rostros y voces. La crónica como vehículo de compromiso social y denuncia'. *Revista Faro*, 1(17), pp. 95–112.

Spitzberg, B. H. and Cadiz, M. (2002). 'The Media Construction of Stalking Stereotypes'. *Journal of Criminal Justice and Popular Culture*, 9(3), pp. 128–49.

Waisbord, S. (2011). 'Can NGOs Change the News?' *International Journal of Communication*, 5, pp. 142–65.

47

PRISONERS, HUMAN RIGHTS AND THE MEDIA

Paul Mason

Introduction

The mainstream British media are not very interested in prisoners' rights. Or rather the manner in which prisons and prisoners are constructed makes any positive coverage unlikely. The dominant media discourse of prison and the prisoner is twofold. First, it is the representation of danger, fear and risk ('Baby Rapist' Paedophile Found Hanging in Prison Cell, *Daily Telegraph,* 19 January 2016; Five Prison Guards Taken Hostage by Inmate Wielding Twin-Bladed Weapon, *The Sun*, 12 May 2016; Belmarsh Maximum Security Jail is 'Like a Jihadi Training Camp', *Daily Mail* 17 May 2016). This partial and misleading representation often relies upon myth and notoriety surrounding a handful of prisoners, which is then applied to the prison population as a whole: the serial killer, the paedophile and the terrorist (Mason 2006a; 2006b; Machin & Mayr 2012).

The consequence of this portrayal is the presence of a second dominant media discourse. Prisoners are either constructed as undeserving of the same rights as the rest of the population, or as possessing too many rights. This is often underscored by contrasting a prisoner's claim to rights with the effect of the crime they have committed on the victim and their family. When prisoners seek to assert their (often legitimate) rights, the media report such claims as unreasonable. They are reported as demands made of the system by prisoners taking advantage of soft-touch regimes at the taxpayer's expense.

In this chapter, I aim to demonstrate how this construction of prisoners' rights in news media operates. Further, to offer some explanation why such a representation exists. I do this by looking at three contrasting stories concerning two different human rights. First, to understand the dominant discourses and textual strategies employed by the British press in such stories, I examine two recent short stories about religious freedom and prisoners. Second, I look the considerably larger issue of prisoner's rights to vote. The reporting of the debate raised wider issues beyond simply disenfranchisement, to include questions around the status and role of the detained and of punishment in modern society.

Prisoners, media and crime

The media representation of prisoners' rights is inexorably linked to the representation of crime and punishment more broadly. Since the studies on constructions of crime news in the 1970s (Chibnall

1977; Cohen 1972; Cohen and Young 1973; Hall et al. 1978; Young 1971), questions have been asked about crime reporting and the manner in which crime and punishment has been reported.

These works explored the dominant ideologies and structures in news production (for useful reviews see Kidd-Hewitt and Osborne 1995; Reiner and Greer 2007; Jewkes 2015). They noted how the state's failure to deal with social and economic inequality was glossed over by media coverage of crime, and replaced by a series of moral panics about violent youth (Cohen 1972), drug use (Young 1971) and black muggers (Hall et al. 1978). Thus, what and whom the state labelled as 'crime' and 'criminals', and how it should be punished were reinforced by media reportage. A media constructed, moral public consensus polarised the law-abiding majority from the criminal class.

As Reiner (2007) notes, the hegemonic model of crime news production has been repeatedly challenged by more recent empirical work. Research has shifted attention away from analyses of media content *per se*, towards an exploration of news production (Ericson, et al. 1987, 1989; Schlesinger and Tumber 1994; Doyle & Ericson 1996; Innes 2002). However, as Reiner also states:

> Empirical analyses of news production in action do emphasize its contingency and fluidity, but they do not fundamentally challenge the hegemonic model. While news may be a competitive arena of conflicting viewpoints, it is culturally and structurally loaded. The news media...reproduce order in the process of representing it.
>
> *(Reiner and Greer 2007, 326)*

As well as concerns about the pernicious effect of over-representing violent and sexual crime (Soothill & Walby 1991; Sparks 1992; Wykes 2001) writers have suggested that such reporting creates support for more draconian criminal justice measures (Mason 2003; Reiner 2002; Reiner et al. 2003; Carabine 2008; Jewkes 2015).

These concerns have been echoed in the media portrayal of prison and prisoners. Thomas Mathiesen (2000; 2001; 2003) has argued that media reporting magnifies violent and serious crime to the extent that prison is constructed as the only viable solution:

> In the newspapers, on television, in the whole range of media, the prison is simply not recognised as a fiasco, but as a necessary if not always fully successful method of reaching its purported goals. The prison solution is taken as paradigmatic, so that a rising crime rate is viewed as still another sign showing that prison is needed.
>
> *(Mathiesen 2000, 144)*

It is Mathiesen's contention that the media persist in creating conditions for the support of the penal system through over-reporting of crime, creating a fearful public who look to prison to protect them as the essential means of social control. As I have argued previously (Mason 2007), the mainstream media do not simply normalise prison. There is a promotion of its use and expansion through misinformation and distortion about those in prison and the conditions they are subjected to. As Ryan and Sim rightly point out, 'the prison has achieved a hegemonic status that has made it virtually impregnable to sustained ideological and material attack' (Ryan & Sim 2006). Public opinion is invoked in these and other stories by the press to support their position on prison. However, little evidence is offered to support their claim.

In this media environment, it is perhaps unsurprising that prisoners' rights are either ignored or recontextualised. They are subsumed into a construction of the prisoner as high risk, dangerous and beyond redemption. Such a dominant discourse bolsters support for government policy built upon mass incarceration, but constructs public opinion as overtly supporting it too. In stark contrast, there is an absence of reporting on the brutalising nature of prison, of overcrowding, cuts to prisoner education programmes, and the rise in prison suicides. As Machin and Mayr (2012, 171) note: 'those who were previously defined as at risk have now become the risk to be monitored, controlled and imprisoned for the sake of the law-abiding citizen'.

Prisoners' rights in the press

How does this dominant discourse operate and what does it look like? Below, I give two recent examples of how prisoners' rights are treated by the mainstream British print media. Both stories appeared a month apart in two tabloid newspapers and dealt with the same issues. They are both examples of how prisoners' rights, in this case freedom of religion, are trivialised and distorted, but also subsumed within a discourse of dangerousness.

On 3 April 2016, *The Sun* ran the following story: 'Cons' Scran Scam Ain't Kosher; Prison Farce; Lags "Convert" for Pricey Jewish Grub'. The story concerned prisoners 'pretending' to be Jewish to get more expensive (and presumably) better quality prison food. A month later, *The Daily Mail*'s headline 'Pagan Prisoners Given Wands and Tarot Cards for Their Spell Inside' reported on the recent '104 page guide entitled Faith and Pastoral Care for Prisoners'.[1] The story, contrary to the headline was about the possibility that Pagan prisoners may be permitted to use incense and to wear robes when worshipping.

On the face of it, these stories are knockabout tabloid fare. They are, at first blush trivial stories, light hearted in tone. There are the puns of 'spell inside' and the opening line of the *Daily Mail* article of 'Many a criminal facing life behind bars has wished for a bit of magic to help them escape their fate'. However, both articles are illustrative of something more important. Both construct the rights of prisoners in a particular way. They use what Conboy (2006, 9) has called 'an identifiable range of textual strategies'.

The first part of *The Sun* article reads as follows:

> PRISONERS are causing canteen chaos by pretending to be Jewish to get pricey kosher food. Around 25 cons, including killers and sex fiends, claim they need the special diet at Glenochil nick because they converted behind bars.
>
> The religiously-approved meals cost more than three times as much as standard grub because of the special way they are prepared.
>
> And sources slammed the move, which mirrors a plot in US TV prison drama Orange is the New Black. One said: 'This is just an attempt to be awkward and waste taxpayers' money'.
>
> 'These people are among the most depraved prisoners in Scotland - there's nothing holy about them at all. It started in the sex offenders' wing when one of them claimed he was now Jewish and demanded kosher food. But once word got about, loads of them began saying they had converted, too'.
>
> […]
>
> Cons who claim to have converted at the Clackmannanshire nick include cross-dressing murderer Gavin Boyd, 56, and rapist Steven Dick, 39, who is serving ten years for tricking women into sex with fake film auditions … Jail chiefs have launched a bid to crack down on the brazen scam, which is costing taxpayers £1,500 a week. A Scottish Prison Service spokesman said: 'We cater for all religious diets'.

Three strategies stand out in this piece. The first is the emphasis on the prisoners who are alleged to have taken advantage of the system. They include 'killers and sex-fiends' and are 'among the most depraved prisoners in Scotland'. The use of emotive language seeks to create fear in its readers from the very outset of the article is a theme that permeates the report. Later, two prisoners are named and labelled by their offences – 'cross dressing murderer' and 'rapist'. The article reduces those prisoners seeking to eat kosher food to those convicted of violent and sexual offences. This plays into the stereotype of the prison population as one predominantly made up of rapists, murderers and paedophiles.

The principle function of this representation of prisoners is to allow readers to pass judgment. This is the second strategy at work here. In reducing the men converting to Judaism to beasts and fiends, the article invites the public to find that they are undeserving of these or, I would argue, any rights. The underlying discourse here is that not only are these men lying about their religion to get better food, but also that they are not deserving of such food in the first place. This is underscored by the use of the phrase 'taxpayer's money'. It is a familiar method employed in prison stories. It is a further linguistic strategy, a lexical choice, which characterises the public not as a society who may have a variety of views on prisoners' rights but as an homogenous outraged mass, up in arms about the use of their hard earned money to pamper the most depraved criminals in Britain.

A similar discourse of the undeserving prisoner is used on the *Daily Mirror* story about paganism in prison. It quotes a member of the Prison Officers Association who is quoted as saying:

> They don't have to prove anything, they just have to say, 'I'm a pagan, and that's it', and then they get special privileges. It will do nothing but create uncertainty and instability and lead to more prisoner complaints that are futile and vexatious.

Once again, religious rights for prisoners are constructed as a privilege. Any attempt by them to assert their claims are characterised as vexatious and pointless. The prison-as-soft-touch discourse is front and centre. The paper's attempt at balance is a quote from a commentator on paganism and witchcraft: 'But Christina Oakley Harrington, a commentator on paganism and witchcraft who describes herself as a high priestess, said the items were incredibly important for us to make a spiritual connection'. Note here the phrase 'who describe herself as', which undercuts her authority and echoes the tone of the *Daily Mirror* article as sceptical of paganism as a proper religion at all. Further, it limits her comment to the use of the articles: wands, tarot cards and so on and not to the wider issues of religious freedom. Finally, in adding in the word 'witchcraft', the paper conflates paganism and witchcraft. The story only mentions the word once, but fails to acknowledge that the Wiccan sense of 'witchcraft' is far removed from the stereotypical representation in popular culture of pointed hats, spells, broomsticks and evil.

The treatment of the two sources in this report is telling also. It is an example of Becker's hierarchy of credibility' (Becker 1967) later developed by Hall *et al* into the idea of news sources as 'primary definers'. In what Chibnall termed the 'structured access' of news (Chibnall 1977), Hall et al. argued that the media were subordinate to elite and powerful sources, such as the police officer; the government minister; the judge and so on. Even where oppositional views are quoted, offering the appearance of balance, they are limited to the initial definition of the topic in question. It is these primary definers that set the frame of reference, giving other voices little choice but to shape their views into the pre-existing parameters defined by elite sources. Thus, in the *Mirror* story, Ms Harrington's comments on religion are reduced to a quote about the legitimacy of wands, tarot cards and so on. There is no opportunity given to her to comment on paganism as a religion, or the rights of those in prison to practise it.

The third matter that arises in these articles is the distortion of the facts. There is no evidence offered by the *Sun*'s story that any of the prisoners have not converted validly to Judaism.

The 'sources' are not names or attributed. Are they from the Scottish Prison Service? Officers? Other prisoners? The piece claims there has been a 'crack down on the brazen scam' but then appears to undercut that bald assertion with a quote from the Scottish prison service confirming that the prison caters for all religious beliefs. Further, HMP Glenochil holds 660 prisoners.[2] The number of prisoners who 'claim they need the special diet' is 25 according to *The Sun*. This equates to around 4% of the prison population at HMP Glenochil.

The *Daily Mail* article adopts a similarly distorted approach in its story about Pagan rights. The headline Pagan Prisoners Given Wands and Tarot Cards for Their Spell Inside is written in the present tense. Readers may well think it is current prison policy to hand out such artefacts. The report is entirely speculative however. It is based upon the Prison Service Instruction on faith and religion in prison. The article uses far less definitive language in the report than in its headline: '[P]risoners may be able to have incense and special dress for worship following a risk assessment ... this may be allowed under the supervision of the pagan chaplain'. I have chosen these two short, and seemingly trivial articles deliberately. The undeserving dangerous prisoner seeking to enforce their rights in a soft touch prison system is a dominant theme of prison stories in the British press. It is the normalising of this discourse in even the shortest and seemingly unimportant stories that demonstrates its prevalence. It is a discourse that was also prevalent in one of the biggest stories concerning prisoners' rights in recent years: the right to vote.

Prisoners right to vote

Under domestic law, serving prisoners do not have the right to vote. Section 3(1) of the Representation of the People Act 1983 states that

> [a] convicted person during the time that he is detained in a penal institution in pursuance of his sentence or unlawfully at large when he would otherwise be so detained is legally incapable of voting at any parliamentary or local government election.

The rationale for the position was summarised by Baroness Scotland, during a House of Lords debate in 2003:[3]

> It has been the view of successive governments that prisoners convicted of a crime serious enough to warrant imprisonment have lost the moral authority to vote ... Prisoners have a variety of ways in which they can express their views about conditions in prison, including by writing to their Member of Parliament – and many do so.
>
> Parliament has decided that the convicted prisoners have forfeited their right to have a say in the way the country is governed for the period during which they are in custody. This temporary disenfranchisement pursues a legitimate aim and is proportionate, and is considered a reasonable restriction within the terms of Article 25. It does not, in our view, affect the substance of Article 25, which is concerned with universal franchise and the free expression of the people in the choice of legislature. Long-standing precedent set by the European Court of Human Rights upholds that certain sections of society, including convicted prisoners, can be excluded from voting.

The right to vote is enshrined in international law. This includes Article 25 of the International Covenant on Civil and Political Rights, to which Baroness Scotland refers. Further, Article 3 of Protocol 1 to the European Convention On Human Rights (ECHR) states that those signed up to the Convention will 'undertake to hold free elections at reasonable intervals by secret ballot, under conditions which will ensure the free expression of the opinion of the people in the choice of the legislature'.

In 2001, three prisoners challenged the decision of the Electoral Registration Office not to register them to vote. The High Court found that the question of whether serving prisoners should have the right to vote was a matter for parliament rather than the courts.[4] One of those prisoners was John Hirst. He was well known in the prison system for his knowledge of prison law. Later, he would run a prison law advice clinic from his cell, and on his release run a blog and Twitter account called 'jailhouselawyer'. At the time of his challenge, Hirst was serving a life sentence, having pleaded guilty to manslaughter after killing his landlady in 1979.

Hirst challenged the High Court decision. The case reached the European Court of Human Rights (ECtHR) in 2004. On 30 March 2004, the ECtHR found that there had been a violation of Article 3 of Protocol 1. It held that the disenfranchisement of prisoners stripped a large group of people of the vote; that it applied automatically irrespective of the length of the sentence or the gravity of the offence; and that the results were arbitrary and anomalous, depending on the timing of elections. The UK Government appealed the decision to the ECtHR Grand Chamber. Its judgment was handed down on 6 October 2005.[5] The Grand Chamber found that

> [p]risoners generally continued to enjoy all the fundamental rights and freedoms guaranteed under the Convention, except for the right to liberty … There was, therefore, no question that prisoners forfeit their Convention rights merely because of their status as detainees following conviction … That standard of tolerance did not prevent a democratic society from taking steps to protect itself against activities intended to destroy the rights or freedoms set out in the Convention …

The *Hirst* judgment was confirmed on 22 May 2012 by the Grand Chamber in the case of *Scoppola v Italy (No 3)*.[6] However, the Court accepted that member states should have a wide discretion (what is known as 'margin of appreciation') in how they regulate a ban on prisoners voting. The ECtHR noted the UK's continuing violation of Article 3 to Protocol 1 in refusing prisoners the right to vote in the cases of *Firth and Others v UK*[7] and *McHugh and others v UK*.[8]

The decision in *Hirst v UK (No.2)* was reported in most of the daily newspapers at the time. The *Daily Mail* headline read KILLER WINS VOTE FOR PRISONERS (7 October 2005). The following day, it described Hirst as a '54-year Old Axe Killer', a phrase also used by *Daily Mirror* (8 October 2005). *The Times*, *Daily Telegraph* and *The Independent* also referred to Hirst's conviction and the murder weapon. Hirst killed his landlady with the handle of the axe, not the blade. Hirst was convicted of manslaughter, not murder. The phrase draws upon a more specific trope, reminiscent of serial killers and horror films, of using the blade rather than the handle and of seriality: committing 'axe murders' more than once. Thus, a landmark case in prisoners' rights which finally recognized the breach of human rights in the 'civic death' of prisoners under the Forfeiture Act 1870, reconstructed and reduced the narrative around a discourse of violence and fear.

A Channel Four News story, which appeared four days before the European Court's decision, followed John Hirst's case, outlining his background and legal education but also stressed the ex-prisoner's dangerousness. Newsreader Jon Snow introduced the piece, describing Hirst as a 'convicted killer' and how his case 'has brought torment to his victim's relatives'. Interviews with Hirst discussing his legal expertise were juxtaposed with an interview with Nina Burton-Harris, the victim's daughter. Early on in the film, she said, 'for me he's not changed; if anything he got worse'. Burton-Harris had no contact with Hirst since the trial in 1981, yet her unsubstantiated assertion suggests Hirst is more dangerous and still a threat to the public.

Channel Four's Home Affairs Correspondent, Simon Israel, regularly adopted aggressive language to describe Hirst's case against the government. Phrases employed such as 'waging a war', 'fighting the system' and 'law a potent weapon to beat the system with'. Legal challenges are often described in such terms, especially when they involve, a citizen against the State. However, they take on a more literally context in this case because of what the report has told us about the citizen bringing the challenge. Consequently, 'law a potent weapon to beat the system with' serves to remind the viewer of the violence used in Hirst's crime. His legal battle remains inextricably linked to offence, emphasised by Israel's comment that 'John Hirst has now forced the government to the point where it may have no choice but to give all prisoners the right to vote. But what he did in 1979 left his victim and her family with no rights'. Note here the emphasis on reluctance – the government 'may have no choice' – rather than reporting that the government's position may be untenable, illegal or unlawful. It is also inaccurate to suggest that the victim's family have surrendered all their rights. What rights are Israel referring to and what act of total forfeiture has the family suffered? The undermining of Hirst is very clear in the cuts between Hirst's journey to the ECtHR and Burton-Harris's interview.

The discourse of violence employed to cast doubt on the legitimacy of prisoners' rights was also present in most of the newspapers that carried the story on 7 October 2005. Several mentioned who wouldn't get the right to vote: 'rapists, murderers and armed robbers' (*Daily Mail*); 'killers and rapists will remain barred' (*The Times*); and Dominic Grieve, Shadow Attorney-General was quoted in the *Daily Telegraph* as saying, 'If convicted rapists and murderers are given the vote, it will bring the law into disrepute'.

The debate continued in the press, following the UK's refusal to abide by the decision in *Hirst*. There were some articles, which supported prisoners' rights, or at least offered a view on the issues but they were almost all from *The Guardian*. For example, 'Disenfranchising Democracy' (10 April 2009); Britain Urged to Allow Prisoners to Vote (12 June 2009); and Coalition in the Dock Over Prisoner Voting (21 October 2012). The majority of newspaper reporting continued to construct the issue via the dominant discourses I note above. 'Once convicts get the vote what else will they demand?' asked *The Express* (9 April 2009); 'How an Axe Killer Used 'Human Rights' to Change the Law, and Give the Government a Splitting Political Headache, punned *The Telegraph* demonstrating taste usually reserved for the tabloids. Note also the problemtising of the phrase 'human rights', suggesting (incorrectly of course) that the legal framework relied upon by Hirst was illegitimate. Hirst himself continued to be described not by his legal knowledge but by his offence: a 'vicious killer' (*The Express* 11 February 2011) and 'axe monster' (*The Sun* 11 November 2011).

The issue of prisoners' rights to vote fed into a wider debate about Europe also. There is continuing confusion in the press over the effect of ECtHR decisions on the UK. This is because there is a difference between the effect of decisions in the ECtHR on courts and its effect on parliament. The Human Rights Act 1998, which incorporated the ECHR into UK law, makes clear that courts 'must take into account' any judgment, decision, declaration or advisory opinion of the ECtHR.[9] Article 46 of the ECHR states that the UK government must 'abide by' final decisions of the ECtHR. In other words, it must follow those decisions rather than simply taken them into account as the courts are required to do.

This important difference is lost in the reporting of prisoners' rights to vote. Instead, the dominant discourse concerns Britain 'standing up' to Europe. In reporting the 2012 ECtHR decision in *Scoppola v Italy (No 3),* the *Daily Mail* asserted that 'EUROPEAN (sic) judges rode roughshod over British sovereignty yesterday by ruling that prisoners must be allowed to vote' (23 May 2012). Conservative backbencher Dominic Raab was quoted in the *Daily Telegraph* as saying 'Britain will stand firm and defend out democratic prerogatives' (29 September 2012).

It is interesting to see how politicians employed the discourse around the undeserving prisoner to make this point. Most noticeably, David Cameron stated in the House of Commons debate on prisoners rights to vote, that 'it makes me physically ill even to contemplate having to give the vote to anyone who is in prison'.[10] This was repeatedly quoted in the prisoner vote debate sometimes years after the Prime Minister said it. The notion of a physical reaction to prisoners' getting the vote operates only if prisoners are represented via the crimes for which they have been found guilty. Cameron's quote carries weight where it is reported alongside descriptions of prisoners as dangerous. For example, in *The Daily Telegraph* report on 24 October 2012, repeated the quote 'Mr Cameron stands by his comments that the prospect of giving prisoners the vote made him feel physically "sick"', then later in the piece it noted that 'the row began in 2004 when the ECHR (*sic*) ruled the blanket ban in the UK was unlawful in a case brought by convicted killer John Hirst'. Similarly, the *Daily Mail* on 11 June 2013 repeated the Cameron quote under the headline 'Thousands in Legal Aid for Man Who Raped And Killed His Niece, Seven to Fight for Right to Vote'. At the heart of the issue are the UK's legal obligations under the ECHR. It is not simply 'a row' as the *Telegraph* suggest. However, so dominant is the representation of prisoners as dangerous and undeserving, that the fundamental questions around human rights are lost, reduced to an emotive and simplified discourse about rapists and murderers getting things they aren't entitled to. As Afua Hirsch argued in *The Guardian* on 9 February 2011:

> But we all know that politicians, including those on the left, are willing to abandon human rights principles when to do so seems in accordance with public opinion … The European Court of Human Rights exists for exactly these situations – where politicians lack the vision, courage or wisdom to provide unpopular people with the level of human rights protection that is accepted as part of an emerging international standard. As history has repeatedly shown, in the end that standard tends to be bigger than the small-minded politicians of the day.

Conclusion

Perhaps one should not be surprised that the British press report prisoners and prison rights in this way. However, the manner in which prison and prisoners are constructed by the British media plays a crucial role in public comprehension of prisoners' rights. The invisibility of prisoners and regimes of punishment means the public are reliant on media reporting of prisons for their information. As I have suggested elsewhere (Mason 2007), in the space between the reality of prison and public ignorance about it, lies the media. Media discourses of prison and prisoners' rights therefore become a potent opinion shaper for the public. However, it is the relationship between press reporting and policy that is crucial. While governments must be seen to reflect public opinion, in reality that opinion is largely one constructed by, and represented in the printed press and other media. Thus, to reframe Afua Hirsch's point above, politicians are willing to abandon human rights principles when it accords with the dominant media discourse to do so. As long as prisoners remain characterised by the press as high risk, social junk draining resources from the taxpayer, any rights they seek to enforce will be assessed by the State in that context. As prison abolitionist Angela Davis has noted, prison 'functions ideologically as an abstract site into which undesirables are deposited, relieving us of the responsibility of thinking about the real issues afflicting those communities from which prisoners are drawn in such disproportionate numbers' (Davis 2003, 16).

Notes

1 The 'guide' is actually Prison Service Instruction PSI 05/2016, issued on 12 April and effective from 1st June. A PSI is a summary of prison rules and regulations relating to a particular aspect of prison. They are issued by the Ministry of Justice. Available here <https://www.justice.gov.uk/offenders/psis>, last accessed 3 June 2016.
2 Scottish Prison Service, <http://www.sps.gov.uk/Corporate/Prisons/Glenochil/HMP-Glenochil.aspx>, last accessed 6 June 2016.
3 HL Deb 20 October 2003, col WA143.
4 *R v (1) Secretary of State for the Home Department (2) Two Election Registration Officers, Ex Parte (1) Pearson (2) Martinez: Hirst v HM Attorney General* [2001] EWHC Admin 239.
5 *Hirst v UK (No.2)*, App. 74025/01, 6 October 2005.
6 *Scoppola v Italy (No 3)*, App 126/05, 22 May 2012.
7 *Firth and others v UK*, App 47784/09, 12 August 2014.
8 *McHugh and others v UK*, App 51987/08 10 February 2015.
9 In s. (2)(1)(a).
10 Hansard Official Report, 3 November 2010; Vol. 517, c. 921.

References

Becker, H. (1967). 'Whose Side Are We On?' *Social Problems*, 14(3), pp. 239–47.
Carabine, E. (2008). *Crime, Culture and the Media*. Cambridge: Polity Press.
Chibnall, S. (1977). *Law and Order News: An Analysis of Crime Reporting in the British Press*. London: Tavistock Press.
Cohen, S. (1972). *Folk Devils and Moral Panics*. Harmondsworth: Penguin.
Cohen, S. and Young, J. eds. (1973). *The Manufacture of News: Social Problems, Deviance and Mass Media*. London: Constable.
Conboy, M. (2006). *Tabloid Britain: Constructing A Community Through Language*. London: Routledge, p. 9.
Davis, A. (2003). *Are Prisons Obselete?* New York: Seven Stories.
Doyle, A. and Ericson, R. (1996). 'Breaking Into Prison: News Sources and Correctional Institutions'. *Canadian Journal of Criminology*, 38(n2): 155–90.
Ericson, R., Baranek, P. and Chan, J. (1987). *Visualising Deviance: A Study of News Organisation*. Milton Keynes: Open University Press.
Ericson, R., Baranek, P. and Chan, J. (1989). *Negotiating Control: A Study of News Sources*. Milton Keynes: Open University Press.
Hall, S., Critcher, C., Jefferson, T., Clarke, J. and Roberts, B. (1978). *Policing The Crisis: Mugging, the State and Law and Order*. London: Macmillan Press.
Innes (2002). 'Police Homicide Investigations'. *British Journal of Criminology*, 42(4), pp. 669–88.
Jewkes, Y. (2015). *Media and Crime*. London: Sage.
Kidd Hewitt, D. and Osborne, R. eds. (1995). *Crime and the Media: the Post-Modern Spectacle*. London: Pluto Press.
Machin, D. and Mayr, A. (2012). *The Language of Crime and Deviance: An Introduction to Critical Linguistic Analysis in Media and Popular Culture*. London: Continuum Books.
Mason, P. (ed.) (2003). *Criminal Visions: Media Representations of Crime and Justice*. Cullompton: Willan Publishing.
Mason, P. (2006a). *Captured By The Media: Prison Discourse in Popular Culture*. Cullompton: Willan.
Mason, P. (2006b). 'Lies, Distortion and What Doesn't Work: Monitoring Prison Stories in the British Media'. *Crime, Media, Culture*, 3(2), pp. 251–67.
Mason, P. (2007). 'Misinformation, Myth and Distortion: How the Press Support Mass Incarceration'. *Journalism Studies*, 8(3), pp. 481–96.
Mathiesen, T. (2000). *Prisons on Trial*. Winchester: Waterside Press.
Mathiesen, T. (2001). 'Television, Public Space and Prison Population: A Commentary on Mauer and Simon'. *Punishment and Society* 3, pp. 35–42.
Mathiesen, T. (2003). 'Contemporary Penal Policy - A Study in Moral Panics'. *European Committee on Crime Problems: 22nd Criminological Research Conference*. Strasbourg.

Reiner, R. (2002). 'Media Made Criminality: The Representation of Crime in the Mass Media', in M. Maguire, R. Morgan & R. Reiner (eds.) *The Oxford Handbook Of Criminology*. Oxford, UK: Oxford University Press, pp. 376–416.

Reiner, R., Livingstone, S. and Allen, J. (2003). 'From Law and Order to Lynch Mobs: Crime News Since the Second World War'. In: P. Mason (ed.), *Criminal Visions: Media Representations of Crme and Justice*. Cullompton: Willan Publishing.

Reiner, R. and Greer, C. (2007). 'Media-Made Criminality: The Representation of Crime in the Mass Media'. In: R. Reiner, M. Maguire and R. Morgan, eds., *The Oxford Handbook of Criminology*, 4th ed. Oxford: Oxford University Press, pp. 245–278.

Ryan, M. and Sim, J. (2006). 'Campaigning For and Campaigning Against Prisons: Excavating and Re-Affirming the Case for Prison Abolition'. In: Y. Jewkes ed., *Handbook On Prisons*. Cullompton: Willan Publishing.

Schlesinger, P. and Tumber, H. (1994). *Reporting Crime: The Media Politics of Criminal Justice*. Oxford: Clarendon Press.

Soothill, K. and Walby, S. (1991). *Sex Crime in the News*. London: Routledge.

Sparks, R. (1992). *Television and The Drama of Crime: Moral Tales and the Place of Crime in Public Life*. Milton Keynes: Open University.

Wykes, M. (2001). *News, Crime and Culture*. London: Pluto Press.

Young, J. (1971). *The Drug Takers*. London: Paladin.

48

CHANGES IN WAR-MAKING, MEDIA AND HUMAN RIGHTS

Revolution or repackaging?

Melissa Wall

Media coverage of human rights abuses have long been used to prompt to calls for military actions. Likewise, the waging of war itself often includes human rights violations, making the military management of media images about those abuses crucial to its execution (der Derian 2001/2009; Maltby 2012). Media are even used to incite audiences to commit human rights crimes during times of war and armed conflict (Kellow & Steeves 1998). In recent years, war, human rights and the media have separately and collectively evolved to create what some observers argue are new patterns and practices, potentially remaking their intersections in profound ways.

First, the concept of war has changed since the twentieth century with scholars such as Kaldor (2012, 1) identifying what she calls 'new war', or a hybrid form in which organized violence blurs war, organized crime and large scale human rights violations in previously unseen ways. At the same time, we have seen changes in the media's forms, speed and distribution, from the rise of networked communications to personalized, participatory media (Allan 2013; van der Haak, Park & Castells 2012). In such an environment, millions of people are constantly online and networked with others. Human rights information in such a system can be spread both by traditional information sources as well as by ordinary people. Media researchers concerned with armed conflict suggest that these changes are part of the rise of 'digital war', 'diffused war', or 'information war' (Matheson & Allan 2009, 7; Hoskins & O'Louglin 2010, 2; Tumber and Webster 2006, 6). While fewer individuals particularly in the West may actually engage in direct combat, civilians are more likely to be targeted within conflicts and more people from afar may take part vicariously through a 'massively increased media experience of information war' (Tumber & Webster 2006, 3).

At the same time, scholars studying humanitarian communication, which historically was a key genesis of human rights information and news, see similar changes. Cottle and Cooper (2015) note that human rights violations are not simply relayed by traditional news organizations today but are shaped or even staged and performed for the media. Hoskins and O'Louglin (2010) add that those involved in violent conflicts are now incorporating that knowledge strategically into their enactment of war. Ironically, the nature of discourse about war-making over the last two decades has come to invoke the same sort of motives and language of human rights defenders. Meanwhile, the mainstream news media is joined by other organizations such as

NGOs along with a multitude of amateurs potentially producing content about war through connective and seemingly ubiquitous circuits of information.

In contrast with these claims of what amounts to a paradigm shift, other observers argue that war coverage and its connection to human rights abuses continues to follow long-standing patterns (Altheide & Grimes 2011). Matheson and Allan (2009) suggest that the competition between various stakeholders involved in media coverage of war hasn't stopped so much as the forms of such information and the ways it is disseminated has transformed. Downey and Murdoch (2003/2005) go further in dismissing claims of dramatic change, noting that there is not even a new form of war involving media and that long-term patterns of power, regardless of technological revolutions, remain.

The overall contention of this chapter is that both ground-breaking technological changes along with a rise in a new array of political actors have influenced the ways human rights and the media intersect but not as profoundly as some observers might wish to believe. Thus, this chapter first reviews trends in terms of war-making, media and human rights abuses, an area of research that has historically found military-government manipulations of reporting on these issues. Following this is an examination of claims concerning more recent patterns arising from the introduction of new actors and new uses of media in terms of war-making and human rights. The chapter concludes with a look at the evolving considerations of the audience's reception and responsibilities when exposed to human rights abuse information in an age of connective media.

The unpredictable intersection of all of these phenomenon means that a critical examination of the area of war-making, human rights and media is more important than ever. At stake are the very justifications for waging war and the concomitant taking of human lives.

Overview: Human rights, media and war

Human rights as justification for war

Much of the existing research about war-making, media and human rights has focused on the interactions of media with governments and, often more specifically on the military and its increasingly sophisticated means of shaping news narratives (Allan & Zelizer 2004; Andersen 2006; Carruthers 2000/2011; Keeble 1997; Knightley 1975/2004; Tumber & Palmer 2004). This body of research consistently shows the West tends to used human rights discourses to justify military interventions as opposed to paths to avoiding conflict or supporting peace (Andersen 2006; Shaw 2012). In doing so, they manipulate traditional news media to help manufacture threats from an 'enemy state' whose leadership is presented as a gross violator of rights who must be stopped (Hammond and Herman 2000; Hammond 2000). Indeed, scholars have shown over the last two decades that US and other Western governments effectively manage the perceptions of the public which is led to believe that the armed invasion of a sovereign nation can actually be viewed as a defence of human rights (Andersen 2006; Bennett 1994; Carruthers 2000/2011; MacArthur 1992/2004). Across multiple conflicts from Bosnia to Gulf War II, Hammond (2007) suggests that media coverage of human rights during war is extraordinarily one-dimensional and distorts the complexities of conflict. Indeed, scholarly research in this area has a tendency to follow the media's performance. When there is no abundance of news media coverage of human rights issues, then, unsurprisingly, media researchers tend also to look in other directions. Thus, we know a lot about embedding and reporting pools, which have been highly visible practices, and less about human rights violations in part because the military aims to obfuscate such actions.

Military-media interactions: Human rights as information strategy

Much of the research in this area focuses specifically on the ways the military interacts with and seeks to control the ways the news media incorporate human rights stories as a key part of the military's war information strategy. A frequent aim is to facilitate the production of dubious evidence of rights violations that are accepted often with little to no critical questioning (Andersen 2006). An example of framing a military invasion as a defence of human rights is seen in justifications given for the war in Afghanistan. Said to be in retaliation for the 911 terrorist attacks, the US-led invasion was also depicted as more than revenge by deploying a human rights angle that said the incursion was to challenge the Taliban oppression of Afghani women. This lens was then uncritically adopted by many news outlets (Fahmy 2004; Stabile & Kumar 2005).

Some scholars have aimed for a broader probe of the ways war and human rights form a particular media-oriented strategy used by Western countries (Herman and Peterson 2010/2011; Hammond 2007; Thussu and Freedom 2003/2005). This critical framework creates a lens for understanding modern wars in general. For example, Hammond (2007, 38) argues that with the end of the Cold War and the rise of a postmodern society, the West experienced an existential crisis and thus sought a 'new source of meaning' in humanitarian and human rights intervention. Likewise, Der Derian (2001/2009) has made an argument that the West engages in what is labelled for the public as 'virtuous war' while in reality committing mass acts of violence. In this formulation, the West labels its violence as a rescue of victims of human rights and other abuses and at the same time focuses attention on the technology that enables such actions.

Downplaying Western abuse

A noted body of research probes the ways Western military are sometimes revealed as the perpetrators of specific human rights abuses (Butler 2009; Herman & Peterson 2010/2011). For example, human rights violations by the US troops degrading Iraqi prisoners at the Abu Ghraib prison did gain significant media coverage, but researchers suggest this amount of coverage of soldier-initiated abuses appears to be the exception (Butler 2009). Even when such events are covered by mainstream news media, they are framed by the perpetrators' government (here the US) as rare, unsanctioned incidents and not as part of the war effort (Altheide and Grimes 2011). Another tactic frequently activated by Western military and governments is what Herman and Peterson (2010/2011, 22) call 'atrocity management', controlling the ability to identify what counts as human rights abuses and what does not. As Altheide and Grimes (2011) argue, human rights crimes committed by the West are rarely a part of Western war reporting unless a scandal forces it to attention.

Even the once-celebrated claims that social media such as blogs would lead to greater transparency making public Western soldiers' human rights abuses have faded with ever-increasing sophisticated forms of military censorship and intimidation of critical voices (Wall 2009). Ultimately, questions of visibility and invisibility in which some human rights crimes come to public attention and others are either never known or quickly disappear depend on much more than the existence of media technologies (Hochberg 2015).

New actors, new media

While the initial research on war-making and human rights focused on government and militaries specifically interacting with mainstream news media, increasingly the range of influential actors involved in producing news and information from and about conflict zones has increased.

These include institutional actors as well as informal and even individual citizens participating in media making about human rights and war.

Rise of NGOs as voices for human rights

It's impossible to talk about the connections between media, human rights and war without considering the role of NGOs as key advocates for human rights (Herman and Peterson, 2002). In fact, researchers from a number of disciplines have written about the steady rise in numbers, presence and power of NGOs with an interest or focus on human rights issues, documenting their spectrum of operations from local, grassroots operations to large, international outfits with a global reach (Murdie & Peksen 2014; Ramos, Ron & Thoms 2007; Thrall, Stecula & Sweet 2014).

Some media scholars have argued that the proliferation of NGOS has contributed to heightened public awareness of human rights (Webster 2003/2005). This line of inquiry has often focused on the ways NGOs use information about human rights violations in order to try to prompt actions, identifying specific practices used to try to stop conflicts or in some cases to encourage military responses. For example, human rights groups have been shown to employ public 'naming and shaming' of rights abuse perpetrators to influence states and other actors including the news media (Hafner-Burton 2008; Murdie & Peksen 2014). While some studies suggest that certain types of abuses receive more extensive media coverage, others argue that it is based less on the crimes or those who commit them than on what human rights organizations decide to emphasize (Ramos, Ron & Thoms 2007; Thrall, Stecula & Sweet 2014). These choices are also affected by location with certain countries more likely to be identified as prolific sites for human rights abuses regardless of whether they actually commit more or not (Ramos, Ron and Thoms, 2007). Additional research suggests that NGOs' ability to call attention to abuses is not evenly exercised around the world; generally, larger, Western outfits such as Amnesty International, Human Rights Watch, etc. have the global clout to potentially influence governments and global media, while smaller, non-Western organizations rarely get noticed outside of their own countries (Ramos, Ron & Thoms 2007; Waisbord 2011).

Recently, research within media studies has probed the ways some NGOs have become media makers themselves, thus potentially lessening their reliance on mainstream news media to disseminate their information. Powers (2015) has argued that NGO media are replacing professional journalists, suggesting that they may be 'new boots on the ground', adapting journalism logics to their information production while serving as key sources for their own reporting. Such changes have clearly been enabled by economic changes (cutbacks in foreign reporting), technological innovations (increasingly easy to use equipment to produce high quality content), and social practices (new ways of carrying out not only human rights work but war itself.) However, Cottle (2015) argues that by adapting the logic of the media, such organizations may be failing in their true humanitarian mission.

Other important avenues of research have mapped the ways human rights organizations are also partnering with digitally savvy organizations and even with amateur witnesses and other citizens who might help watchdog human rights abuses in the midst of wars and armed conflicts. Farrell and Allan (2015) examined the evolution of the Witness, which was one of the first organizations in a pre-social media era to train ordinary people to collect video evidence of human rights abuses. In response to changes arising out of a more networked communications environment, Witness has partnered with Storyful, itself a relatively recent organization that was created to verify citizen content for mainstream news outlets. They collaborated to create the Human Rights Channel on YouTube that allows them to disseminate an increasingly large amount of witness video footage, providing a greater platform for activists monitoring abuses.

Farrell and Allan's work is part of an initial wave of research attempting to map these new human rights groups and media collaborations.

This is related to another growing area of research focused on the ways that social media and other forms of non-traditional news are now challenging mainstream media's primacy as sources of information about human rights (Bennett 2013; Murphy, 2015). This line of research has in particular stressed the ways that we increasingly see conflict news from non-professional sources such as amateur witnesses and activists who can capture images of violence and disseminate them through networked communication structures (Allan 2013; Andén-Papadopoulos & Pantti 2013; Hoskins & O'Loughlin 2010; Mortensen 2014; Matheson & Allan 2009). Groups such as Human Rights Watch and Witness have sought to incorporate this material into their own, creating yet another layer of complexity in the ways human rights abuses get reported today. But as Smit, Heinrich and Broersma (2015, 4) warn, while citizen video can be evidence of atrocities, such media do not appear to be 'neutral spaces in which every witness is equally heard'.

What has gotten less research attention is the rise of human rights organizations existing at the local or national level in highly volatile war zones (e.g. Syria Justice and Accountability Center, Syrian Observatory for Human Rights, etc.) Their media practices are less well understood, although we see some outlines of a research agenda in the revelations by Andén-Papadopoulos and Pantti (2013), Wiesslitz and Ashuri (2011) and others that a layer of intermediaries has become necessary to shepherd these grass-roots voices and their information towards powerful nodes in the global communication environment. Indeed, important initiatives that operate outside the mainstream-news-media-NGO nexus have received sparse research attention. Two examples of this important but under-studied phenomenon are The Iraq Body Count site, which started as an individual effort by an American trying to map the number of deaths from the US invasion of Iraq and grew into a credible source of documented evidence, and Bellingcat, the project started by a UK citizen journalist that turned a hobby of identifying weaponry in the Syria conflict into a full-blown investigative journalism site. The latter initiative has received some recent scholarly attention but more of these sorts of projects need to be analysed (Sienkiewicz 2015).

Non-human intermediaries

Other important new areas of research examine the increasingly sophisticated uses of technology as part of human rights work. In particular, researchers have focused on the production of satellite images as well as maps used to monitor and respond to human rights abuses in conflict areas in what Lisa Parks (2005) has called 'satellite witnessing' (77). Scholarly examinations tend to fall into two main camps: Those who mainly see benefits such as an extension of eyes on the ground in places difficult to get into; and b) more critical voices that call into question the compromises in making use of such tools and question the automation of human rights image collection (Burns 2015). Scholars in the former category such as Marx and Goward (2013) argue that satellite imagery should be embraced as it has become a key form of media evidence of human rights abuses. They cite the ability of remote sensing products such as Digital Globe to track destruction of civilian homes and movements of people forced to flee. When reporters or other monitors are not allowed in, satellite images may be able to provide on-site information.

More critical voices suggest a different view, arguing satellite images of human rights abuses are used in ways that make the information seem objective and 'apolitical' and, further, the increasing use of satellite imagery by human rights defenders supports the rise of global surveillance and the idea that these private tools are to be accepted unquestioningly (Parks, 2001, 2009).

Herscher (2014) calls this 'surveillant witnessing' and raises serious concerns about handing off the witnessing of human rights to machines (469). In a related argument, Ewalt (2011, 339) suggests that these technologies often contain within them

> a politicized, militarist, and capitalistic history that produces the subject behind the computer screen as simultaneously a citizen war-consumer and one who has the power of the digital divide to embody the viewing position of the colonizer in advanced capitalism.

Ethics of looking

Another growing area of research that lies at the intersection of war-making, media and human rights is a focus on how audiences receive this information. One well known line of thought was well articulated by Susan Moeller (1999/2002) who argued that audiences exposed to a plethora of images of tragedy, including rights abuses, would experience compassion fatigue. Today, millions of people have an even greater chance of being exposed to graphic and horrific images of human rights abuses committed during war-making. Such content may be collected directly at the site where events have occurred and be uploaded into a potentially global communication sphere while entirely unfiltered by journalists or other professional gatekeepers. This content may be particularly powerful because it is generally a form of visual media, which audiences tend to believe to be more truthful (Mirzoeff 2005). While such specific images may be necessary evidence for human rights groups to build their cases, researchers warn they can also feed an ever escalating audience appetite for graphic spectacles and, in that way, ultimately lead to a diminished potency (Kozol 2011).

Critical considerations in this area have been led by the work of Chouliaraki (2006, 2010) in particular. Among the questions she raises are what are the rights and responsibilities of the audience watching coverage of human rights abuses. As Cottle and Nolan (2006) argue 'The media lens is peculiarly insensitive to the distant suffering of others and, based on geopolitical outlooks and historical legacy, is apt to see through a prism of ethnocentrism and Western-led interests' (863). In this vein, Chouliaraki (2006) has written about the 'spectatorship of suffering' and asked how we can ethically view graphic content such as the recording of human rights violations during war. If human rights abuses are increasing 'staged for public consumption, spread through social media and then picked up by the mainstream news' viewing such images may in fact be aiding bad actors (Cottle 2006, 143). Indeed, in a world of 'image wars', ordinary people may watch beheadings, people being burned alive, etc. What then are our individual responsibilities as viewers of such content or how, if at all, can audiences engage in 'ethical spectatorship' (Kozol 2011, 166)? Perhaps future researchers will need to engage in developing media literacy guidelines for consuming human rights imagery.

Conclusions

Clearly, we are in a time of enormous change regarding the intersections of media, war-making and human rights. While new practices appear with regularity, these have not been thoroughly probed and, just as importantly, researchers run the risk of seeing new technologies, new actors, etc. as automatically embodying challenges to traditional powers as opposed to reinforcing them or being adopted by those who already disproportionately shape information flows and image creation. Indeed, it is important to ask if war is a disruptive period in terms of changing norms and logic in how human rights are responded to, or whether during a period of war-making elite sources of power will protect themselves more carefully than usual and thus make change even more unlikely?

The optimist may well conclude that the former is the case. The ways in which human rights information about war is created and disseminated through media has been refashioned by technologies, bringing new practices and attitudes shaped by a participatory ethos. In this view, ordinary people around the world have become increasingly aware of and committed to try to protect human rights, often using new technologies and new networked forms of communication. Here dispersed power courses through the public at large, able to highlight abuses and counter those who carry them out and those who cover them up.

More sanguine observers will suggest a different view. While new actors, often using new technologies, are bringing new voices and perspectives into the nexus of war-making, media and human rights, it remains uncertain whether these changes are indeed fundamentally altering long-standing patterns of manipulation and 'perception management', much less the balance of power (Webster, 2003/2005, 64). Even though citizens, NGOs and others may be celebrated as offering their own views, these perspective are likely to embody the values of the societies from which they originate; these are more likely to be Western and wealthier than most places on earth. In other words, the question still remains: Who is more likely to have a true platform to identify and characterize what is a human rights abuse? Second, in networked forms of communication that now are said to dominate, there is not quite the flattening of hierarchies optimists hope for. Power still accrues to those who already have it and can more easily adapt to and take advantage of such networks. In this way, the same influences may continue to disproportionately influence both what gets amplified through the most robust communication networks and what gets ignored.

Finally, there is the issue of attention. Thrall, Stecula and Sweet (2014) point out there is an increasingly competition for 'global attention' and the 'ability to gain media coverage limited to handful of [human rights] organizations' (4, 17). Thus, the rise of citizens, NGOs and others may bring more content, but contribute to a diluted focus. While there may indeed be many more voices, the range of those voices we actually hear may be actually narrowing.

References

Allan, S. (2013). *Citizen Witnessing: Revisioning Journalism in Times of Crisis*. Malden, MA: Polity Press.

Allan, S. and Zelizer, B. eds. (2004). *Reporting War: Journalism in Wartime*. New York: Routledge.

Altheide, D. and Grimes, J. N. (2011). 'War Making and Propaganda: Media Responsibility for Human Rights Communications'. In: D. Papademas, ed., *Human Rights and Media: Studies in Communication*, Vol. 6. Emerald Group Publishing Limited, pp. 59–76.

Andén-Papadopoulos, K. and Pantti, M. (2013). 'The Media Work of Syrian Diaspora Activists: Brokering Between the Protest and Mainstream Media'. *International Journal of Communication*, 7, 2185–2206.

Andersen, R. (2006). *A Century of Media, a Century of War*. New York: Peter Lang.

Bennett, D. (2013). *Digital Media and Reporting Conflict: Blogging and the BBC's Coverage of War and Terrorism*. New York: Routledge.

Bennett, W. L. (1994). 'The News About Foreign Policy'. In: W. L. Bennett and D. L. Paletz, eds., *Taken by Storm: The Media, Public Opinion, and US Foreign Policy in the Gulf War*. Chicago: University of Chicago Press, pp. 12–40.

Burns, R. (2015). 'Rethinking Big Data in Digital Humanitarianism: Practices, Epistemologies, and Social Relations'. *GeoJournal*, 80(4), pp. 477–90.

Butler, J. P. (2009). *Frames of War: When Is Life Grievable?* Brooklyn: Verso.

Carruthers, S. L. (2000/2011). *The Media at War*. New York: Palgrave Macmillan.

Chouliaraki, L. (2006). *The Spectatorship of Suffering*. Thousand Oaks: Sage.

Chouliaraki, L. (2010). 'Post-humanitarianism Humanitarian Communication Beyond a Politics of Pity'. *International Journal of Cultural Studies*, 13(2), pp. 107–26.

Cottle, S. and Nolan, D. (2007). 'Global Humanitarianism and the Changing Aid-media Field; "Everyone was dying for footage"'. *Journalism Studies*, 8(6), pp. 862–78.

Cottle, S. and Cooper, G. (2015). *Humanitarianism, Communication and Change*. New York: Peter Lang.

Cottle, S. (2015). 'Humanitarianism, Human Insecurity and Communications: What's Changing in a Globalized World?' In: Cottle, S. and Cooper, G. eds. *Humanitarianism, Communication and Change*. New York: Peter Lang, pp. 19–38.

Der Derian, J. (2001/2009). *Virtuous War: Mapping the Military-Industrial-Media-Entertainment-Network*. New York: Routledge.

Downey, J. and Murdoch, G. (2003/2005). 'The Counter-revolution in Military Affairs: Globalization of Guerrilla Warfare'. In: Thussu, D. K. and Freedman, D. eds., *War and the Media: Reporting Conflict 24/7*. Thousand Oaks: Sage, pp. 70–85.

Ewalt, J. P. (2011). 'Mapping Injustice: The World Is Witness, Place framing, and the Politics of Viewing on Google Earth'. *Communication, Culture & Critique*, 4(4), pp. 333–54.

Fahmy, S. (2004). 'Picturing Afghan Women: A Content Analysis of AP Wire Photographs during the Taliban Regime and After the Fall of the Taliban Regime'. *Gazette*, 66(2), pp. 91–112.

Farrell, N. and Allan, S. (2015). 'Redrawing Boundaries: WITNESS and the Politics of Citizen Videos'. *Global Media and Communication*, 11(3), pp. 237–53.

Hafner-Burton, E. M. (2008). 'Sticks and Stones: Naming and Shaming the Human Rights Enforcement Problem'. *International Organization*, 62(4), pp. 689–716.

Hammond, P. and Herman, E. S. (2000). 'Introduction'. In: Hammond, P. and Herman, E. eds., *Degraded Capability: The Media and the Kosovo Crisis*. London: Pluto Press, pp. 1–4.

Hammond, P. (2000). 'Reporting "Humanitarian" Warfare: Propaganda, Moralism and NATO's Kosovo War'. *Journalism Studies*, 1(3), 365–86.

Hammond, P. (2007). *Media, War and Post-modernity*. New York: Routledge.

Herscher, A. (2014). 'Surveillant Witnessing: Satellite Imagery and the Visual Politics of Human Rights'. *Public Culture*, 26(3), pp. 469–500.

Herman, E. S. and Peterson, D. (2010/2011). *The Politics of Genocide*. New York: NYU Press.

Herman, E. and Peterson, D. (2002). 'Morality's Avenging Angels; the New Humanitarian Crusaders'. In: Chandler, D., ed. *Rethinking Human Rights*. Basingstoke: Palgrave, pp. 196–216.

Hochberg, G. Z. (2015). *Visual Occupations: Violence and Visibility in a Conflict Zone*. Durham, NC: Duke University Press.

Hoskins, A. and O'Loughlin, B. (2010). *War and Media*. Malden, MA: Polity.

Kaldor, M. (2012). *New and Old Wars: Organised Violence in a Global Era*. Cambridge: Polity Press.

Keeble, R. (1997). *Secret State, Silent Press*. Luton: John Libbey.

Kellow, C. L. and Steeves, H. L. (1998). 'The Role of Radio in the Rwandan Genocide'. *Journal of Communication*, 48(3), pp. 107–28.

Knightley, P. (1975/2004). *The First Casualty: The War Correspondent as Hero and Myth-Maker from the Crimea to Iraq*. Baltimore: Johns Hopkins University Press.

Kozol, W. (2011). Complicities of Witnessing in Joe Sacco's Palestine'. In: E. S. Goldberg and A. S. Moore, eds. *Theoretical Perspectives on Human Rights and Literature*. New York: Routledge, pp. 165–79.

MacArthur, J. R. (1992/2004). *Second Front: Censorship and Propaganda in the 1991 Gulf War*. University of California Press: Berkeley.

Maltby, S. (2012). 'The Mediatization of the Military'. *Media, War & Conflict*, 5(3), pp. 255–68.

Marx, A. and Goward, S. (2013). 'Remote Sensing in Human Rights and International Humanitarian Law Monitoring: Concepts and Methods'. *Geographical Review*, 103(1), pp. 100–11.

Matheson, D. and Allan, S. (2009). *Digital War Reporting*. Malden, MA: Polity.

Mirzoeff, N. (2005). *Watching Babylon: The War in Iraq and Global Visual Culture*. New York: Routledge.

Moeller, S. D. (1999/2002). *Compassion Fatigue: How the Media Sell Disease, Famine, War and Death*. New York: Routledge.

Mortensen, M. (2014). *Journalism and Eyewitness Images: Digital Media, Participation and Conflict*. New York: Routledge.

Murdie, A. and Peksen, D. (2014). The Impact of Human Rights INGO Shaming on Humanitarian Interventions'. *The Journal of Politics*, 76(1), pp. 215–28.

Murphy, P. D. (2015). 'Voice, Visibility, and Recognition: Vertical and Horizontal Trajectories of Human Rights and Social Justice Media'. *Popular Communication*, 13(2), 101–04.

Parks, L. (2009). 'Digging into Google Earth: An Analysis of "Crisis in Darfur"'. *Geoforum*, 40(4), pp. 535–45.

Parks, L. (2001). 'Satellite Views of Srebrenica: Televisuality and the Politics of Witnessing'. *Social Identities*, 7(4), 585–611.

Parks, L. (2005). *Cultures in Orbit: Satellites and the Televisual.* Durham, NC: Duke University Press.

Powers, M. (2015). 'The New Boots on the Ground: NGOs in the Changing Landscape of International News'. *Journalism.* 17(4), pp. 401–16.

Ramos, H., Ron, J. and Thoms, O. (2007). 'Shaping the Northern Media's Human Rights Coverage, 1986-2000'. *Journal of Peace Research*, 44(4), pp. 385–406.

Shaw, I. S. (2012). *Human Rights Journalism: Advances in Reporting Distant Humanitarian Interventions.* New York: Palgrave McMillan.

Sienkiewicz, M. (2015). 'Open BUK: Digital Labor, Media Investigation and the Downing of MH17'. *Critical Studies in Media Communication*, 32(3), pp. 208–23.

Smit, R., Heinrich, A. and Broersma, M. (2017). 'Witnessing in the New Memory Ecology: Memory Construction of the Syrian Conflict on YouTube'. *New Media & Society.* 19(2), pp. 289–307.

Stabile, C. A. and Kumar, D. (2005). 'Unveiling Imperialism: Media, Gender and the War on Afghanistan'. *Media, Culture & Society*, 27(5), pp. 765–82.

Thrall, A. T., Stecula, D. and Sweet, D. (2014). 'May We Have Your Attention Please? Human-rights NGOs and the Problem of Global Communication'. *The International Journal of Press/Politics*, 19(2), pp. 135–59.

Tumber, H. and Palmer, J. (2004). *Media at War: The Iraq Crisis.* Thousand Oaks: Sage.

Tumber, H. and Webster, F. (2006). *Journalists Under Fire: Information War and Journalistic Practices.* Thousand Oaks: Sage.

Thussu, D. K. and Freedman, D. (2003/2005). 'Introduction'. In: Thussu, D. K. and Freedman, D., eds., *War and the Media: Reporting Conflict 24/7.* Thousand Oaks: Sage, pp. 1–12.

Van der Haak, B., Parks, M. and Castells, M. (2012). 'The Future of Journalism: Networked Journalism'. *International Journal of Communication*, 6, pp. 2923–38.

Waisbord, S. (2011). 'Can NGOs Change the News?' *International Journal of Communication*, 5, pp. 142–65.

Wall, M. (2009). 'The Taming of the Warblogs: Citizen Journalism and the War in Iraq'. In: Allan, S. and Thorsen, E., eds., *Citizen Journalism; Global Perspectives.* New York: Peter Lang, pp. 33–42.

Webster, F. (2003/2005). 'Information Warfare in an Age of Globalization'. In: Thussu, D. K. and Freedman, D., eds., *War and the Media: Reporting Conflict 24/7.* Thousand Oaks: Sage, pp. 57–69.

Wiesslitz, C. and Ashuri, T. (2011). 'Moral Journalists': The Emergences of New Intermediaries of News in an Age of Digital Media'. *Journalism*, 12(8), pp. 1035–51.

49

MEDIA, TERRORISM AND FREEDOM OF EXPRESSION

Brigitte L. Nacos

Everyone has the right to freedom of opinion and expression; this right includes freedom to hold opinions without interference and to seek, receive and impart information and ideas through any media and regardless of frontiers.

United Nations' Universal Declaration of Human Rights (1948)

The [United Nations] Security Council …calls upon all States to adopt such measures
as may be necessary and appropriate and in accordance with their obligations under
international law to… prohibit by law incitement to commit a terrorist act or acts…

UNSC Resolution 1624 (2005)

The contradiction between declaring free speech a fundamental human right and calling for
nation states to prohibit terrorist incitement as reflected in the above citations from United
Nations Resolutions points to the difficulties of resolving the conflict between freedom of
expression and security – in this case in the face of terrorist verbal belligerency and actual violence. The same incongruity exists between the Council of Europe's early acknowledgement
that freedom of expression is a human right and the same body's more recent directive that
provoking terrorist attacks and recruitment to terrorism ought to be criminal offenses under
domestic law.[1] However, such declarations do not address the problems of how to safeguard the
human right of free speech and the right to life and property. While liberal democracies struggle
to reconcile these rights, non-democratic governments are not faced by such dilemma; the latter
tend to intensify human rights violations, including the oppression of freedom of speech under
the guise of counterterrorism.

This chapter discusses why free speech and free press issues are central in the context of terrorism and why, when and how governments, public sentiments and terrorists interfere with the
fundamental human right to exercise these freedoms.

Background: The role of media/communication in the terrorist calculus

Censorship issues in the face of terrorist attacks and threats arise because there is a widespread
belief that terrorists want and need publicity to further their causes. However, taking stock of

relevant research in the decades before 9/11 two scholars noted that 'the bulk of the literature on the relationship between media and terrorism is dismaying' (Paletz & Boiney 1992). Since 9/11, many more books and articles on various aspects of terrorism were published, among them those focusing on linkages between terrorism and mainstream and social media. Most scholars in the field assume close relationships between terrorism and the news media (Bassiouni 1981; Wilkinson 1997; Schmid & de Graf 1982; Nacos 1994, 2016; Weimann 1990; Weimann & Winn 1993; Weimann & Hoffman 2015). Many public officials share British Prime Minister Margret Thatcher's expressed belief that publicity is the lifeblood of terrorism. As Paul Wilkinson (1997, 54) summarized,

> When one says 'terrorism' in a democratic society, one also says 'media'. For terrorism by its very nature is a psychological weapon which depends upon communicating a threat to the wider society. This, in essence, is why terrorism and the media enjoy a symbiotic relationship. The free media clearly do not represent terrorist values. Generally they tend to reflect the underlying values of the democratic society. But the media in an open society are in a fiercely competitive market for their audiences, are constantly under pressure to be first with the news and to provide more information, excitement and entertainment than their rivals.

The idea that media and terrorists need and feed off each other has been rejected by others who discount the high value of communication in the terrorist calculus (Wieviorka 1988), look at the media as part of or controlled by the power elite in governments and corporate sectors (Herman 1982; Herman & O'Sullivan 1989, Chomsky 2002, p. 30), or simply see no advantage for either terrorists or governments in pertinent media content (Schlesinger, Murdoch & Elliott 1983; Delli Carpini & Williams 1987). As one team of researchers (Paletz and Boiney 1992, 21) put it, 'Television is consistently a friend neither of insurgents nor the state'. Finally, most Western terrorism and communication scholars as well as counterterrorism communities recognize social media as potent means for terrorists to disseminate their propaganda directly to global audiences and in the process radicalise and recruit followers (Weimann & Hoffman 2015; Nacos 2015, 2016; Berger 2015; Zelin 2015). The debate about censoring direct and indirect terrorist speech heated up in the post-9/11 era, when the media centres of al-Qaeda Central, al-Qaeda in the Arabian Peninsula, ISIS or the self-proclaimed Islamic State, Al-Shabaab in Somalia, and like-minded groups unleashed sophisticated propaganda via internet sites and social media providers, such as Facebook, YouTube, Twitter, Tumblr and so on.

In the literature of terrorism and the law, First Amendment issues pale in comparison to those dealing with Fourth Amendment violations and especially the (mis)treatment and rights of terrorist detainees (Ignatiev 2004; Cole & Dempsey 2006; Pious 2006; Posner 2007; Wittes 2008). However, the following discussion focuses on efforts to curb the fundamental human right of freedom of expression and press in the name of countering terrorism by governments, by news organizations themselves; and by terrorists.

Government censorship and mainstream media

Following the Iran Hostage Crisis (1979–81), Middle East expert Gary Sick (1986, 258) observed that the incident 'was the longest running human interest story in the history of television, in living colours from the other side of the world [and] commercially [for the TV networks] a stunning success'. More important and for many observers more troubling was that during the 444 days of that crisis and subsequent hostage incidents in the 1980 the news media provided terrorists sheer unlimited access to print presses and airwaves to publicise their propaganda, whether they staged press conferences, gave interviews, provided their own film footage or released communiqués. Zbigniew Brzezinski spoke for many media critics at the time when he noted that television permitted terrorist to 'directly appeal to the American people over the head of the government for the acceptance of the[ir] demands' (Hickey 1985).

The widely respected journalist and columnist David Broder suggested that 'the essential ingredient of any effective antiterrorist policy must be the denial to the terrorist of access to mass media outlets. The way by which this denial is achieved – whether by voluntary means of those of us in press and television, self-restraint, or by government control – is a crucial question for journalists and for all other citizens who share our beliefs in civil liberties'.[2] Katharine Graham, the publisher of the Washington Post and Broder's boss, did not agree. Arguing strongly against any press restraint at all, she wrote,

> Publicity may be the oxygen of terrorists. But I say this: News is the lifeblood of liberty. If the terrorists succeed in depriving us of freedom, their victory will be far greater than they ever hoped and far worse than we ever feared.
>
> *(Szumski 1986, 81)*

Given the high value on freedom of expression and the press in liberal democracies many legal scholars and civil libertarians reject government censorship. But whereas many object to any form of restriction, there have been also suggestions for self-restrain on the part of news organizations (Bassiouni 1981; Miller 1982; O'Sullivan 1986), the establishment of guidelines within media organizations (Terrell & Ross 1988; Kupperman & Trent 1979), voluntary cooperation between press corps and counterterrorism communities (Paust 1978; Scanlon 1989) and the creation of media bodies to monitor terrorism coverage (Schmid & de Graaf 1982; Clutterbuck 1983). Because of First Amendment restrictions in the United States neither domestic terrorism by left extremists, such as the Weather Underground, nor transnational terrorism targeting Americans abroad led to anti-terrorism laws with provisions for curbing press and free speech freedoms. Comparable democracies in Europe took a different path in response to attacks by extremist separatists (i.e. in Ireland, Spain) and by Marxist groups (i.e. in Germany, Italy, France, Greece). Several countries, among them Spain, Germany and Greece outlawed the publication of statements and other material deemed to encourage or glorify terrorism. Spain went especially far when making it a crime to support and praise terrorist organizations 'or the deeds or commemorative dates of their members by publishing or broadcasting via the mass-media, articles expressing opinions, news reports, graphical illustrations, communiques and in general any other form of dissemination' (Wilkinson 2006, 156). Beginning in the early 1970s, the Irish Republic banned radio and television from using the voices of the Provisional Irish Republican Army (PIRA) and its political arm Sinn Fein in interviews. Similarly, based on the 1984 Prevention of Terrorism Act, the British government intimidated UK broadcasters 'into not allowing supporters of, or participants in, paramilitary movements to appear on the air' (Donohue 2005/6, 266). Following a PIRA attack on a high British representative in Northern Ireland in 1988 and a subsequent BBC interview with Gerry Adams, the Thatcher government implemented the ban of terrorist voices requiring UK broadcasters to not allow Sinn Fein and other PIRA members to speak in their programs., TV companies found ways to circumvent the ban based on a loophole in the 1984 law. As Laura Donohue (2005/6, 268) noted,

When it became clear that the order did not apply to the written media, broadcast authorities began subtitling interviews. They later used voice-overs to allow the views of the parties prohibited from appearing on the programs to be expressed.

No wonder that the ban ended six years after it was enacted – it was deemed utterly ineffective.

The story is different in authoritarian or pseudo-democratic systems where government censorship is justified and implemented with iron fists as counterterrorist measure. As a 2015 report by the Freedom House organization noted, 'More aggressive tactics by authoritarian regimes and an upsurge in terrorist attacks contributed to a disturbing decline in global freedom in 2014'.[3] The report documented furthermore that under the pretence of fighting terrorism and/or cybercrime authoritarian governments tightened their grip on freedom of expression: 'While a vigorous debate over how democracies should respond to terrorism at home and abroad is under way in Europe, Australia and North America, leaders elsewhere are citing the threat as they silence dissidents, shutter critical media ...'[4]

Mainstream media's self-censorship

Following a series of bloody attacks and hostage takings by the Red Army Faction (RAF) in the 1970s, the German media agreed to deny terrorists responsible for those actions access to print and broadcast outlets buying readily into the government's news management during hostage crises. After industrialist Hans Martin Schleyer was kidnapped in 1977, for example, this news management/self-censorship model worked as intended. Although the RAF managed to send more than a hundred messages with their demands and threats to the press, the news rooms ignored most of them. Moreover, news organizations agreed to government's requests to publicize false reports designed to misinform the RAF about Bonn's true counterterrorist measures. For the duration of the hostage situation there was basically a news blackout of the incident (Elter 2008, 178–81). Similarly, when Hezbollah kidnapped two German businessmen in Beirut in the 1980s in order to force Germany to release an imprisoned Hezbollah hijacker, there was little reporting besides the initial information about the hostage takings. As a result, the German hostages were far quicker released than various American captives that Hezbollah held. Whereas the US media reported frequently about the American hostages – indeed, whenever Hezbollah chose to make communications available, the German press remained mostly silent.

The British media, too, was not immune to self-censorship during the long conflict between the PIRA and the United Kingdom. One terrorism expert concluded, 'In general the British state has been largely successful in inducing the broadcasting organizations to censor themselves under the guise of "responsibility"' (Schlesinger 1981, 92).

Self-censorship seems most likely in the wake of catastrophic terrorist strikes. Take the 9/11 attacks and the US press's reluctance to discharge its responsibility as watchdog of government. Based on content analyses of the news in the years following those catastrophic strikes, a number of scholars concluded that the press had failed by buying the administration's hard sell of its hawkish counterterrorism agenda (Bennett, Lawrence and Livingston 2008; Nacos, Bloch-Elkon & Shapiro 2011) and that 'the largely complacent mainstream media were essentially covering *for* Big Brother by allowing elites to frame the issue of terrorism around individual exemplars while the pendulum swung out toward national security' (McLeod & Shah 2015, xi). Much of the self-restraint seemed to come from within the newsrooms but in some cases it came in response to government officials' prodding. For example, a month after 9/11 then President George W. Bush's National Security Adviser Condoleezza Rice called the bosses at the news divisions of the TV-networks ABC, CBS, NBC, FOX and MSNBC and requested that they omit inflammatory passages and hate speech from Osama bin Laden's videos before airing them. There was no resistance. Instead, the quick agreement was characterized by one network executive as 'patriotic decision' (Carter & Barringer 2001). This response shouldn't have come as a surprise. After all, people in newsrooms are not disconnected from the public at large but rather part of the overall societal culture in their reactions, values and prejudices (Shipler 1998, 28).

The point here is that in certain instances, in particular during hostage situation, news organizations are well advised in withholding information that is likely to endanger captives. But different judgments should be made in the face of counterterrorism policies with far-reaching consequences, such as curbs to civil liberties or massive military deployment, when the public needs to be fully informed.

Government censorship of direct terrorist speech

In response to terrorist attacks and threats by the Red Army Faction (RAF) the Federal Republic of Germany adopted a law criminalising publicity advocating offenses against the stability of the state. To this day, in Germany and several other European countries hate speech and denial of the holocaust are criminal offenses that can be and have been prosecuted with the justification that these kinds of expression incite political violence or, in other words, terrorism. The events of 9/11, major terrorist attacks in Madrid in 2004 and in London in 2005, and more recently several lethal strikes in Paris and Ottawa in 2015 led to new laws against incitement and glorification of terrorism (e.g. the 2006 Terrorism Act in the UK and the 2015 Anti-Terrorism Act in Canada) or stricter implementation of existing laws. Thus, immediately after the horrific attacks on the Paris office of the satirical magazine Charlie Hebdo in early 2015 the French government ordered prosecutors to crack down on hate speech and the glorification of terrorism. After reviewing free speech and anti-terrorism laws in Europe Barak-Erez and David Scharia (2011, 26) concluded that 'European countries have consistently acknowledged the legitimacy of anti-incitement law, subject to judicial methods of balancing the government interest in prohibiting terrorist incitement with the right of free speech, in the particular context'.

Contrary to Europe, no anti-incitement law exists in the US; there is no criminalization of hate speech or the glorification of violence. Strangely, the one legal case concerning incitement to terrorist violence in the United States is absent from pertinent scholarly work because of the selective use of the term 'terrorism' by public officials and the media. Whereas in the past left-extremist political violence was and in the post-9/11-era political violence by Muslims and/or Arabs is readily called 'terrorism', politically motivated violence by right-extremists tends to be characterized as crime – shooting, killing, murder, etc.

Yet, the case arising from the so-called Nuremberg Files – detailed data about abortion providers on a web site – was in essence about freedom of expression and incitement to terrorism. Framed by drippings of animated blood, the Nuremberg Files registry listed working 'baby butchers' (names printed in black font), 'wounded' abortion providers (names of those injured in anti-abortion actions greyed out) and 'fatalities' (names of doctors assassinated by anti-abortion terrorists struck out). In essence this was a hit list that kept score of physicians killed and injured by anti-abortion extremists. The site encouraged visitors to 'search for the office address of the baby butchers listed above' and lists the URL of the American Medical Association as a source of such information. In addition to physicians, the site showed lists with the names of clinic owners and workers, judges ('their shysters'), politicians ('their mouthpieces'), Law enforcement officials ('their bloodhounds'), and of 'miscellaneous spouses & other blood flunkies'.

A Planned Parenthood organization at the West coast sued the group responsible for the Nuremberg Files and the distribution of 'Wanted' leaflets with the pictures of abortion providers in the area. A District Court recognized the material as 'clear and present danger' to the lives of those whose names were publicized, awarded the plaintiffs one hundred million dollars in actual and punitive damage, and ordered the removal of the web site. However, a small panel of judges of 9th Circuit Court of Appeals set aside the verdict and ruled that the publication of the Nuremberg Files on the Internet fell within the constitutionally protected free speech. The court held that abortion foes could not be held responsible for the possibility that their inflammatory Internet postings and leaflets might encourage some persons to commit violence against abortion providers and clinics. 'If defendants threatened to commit violent acts, by working alone or with others, then their statements could properly support the [guilty] verdict. But if their statements merely encouraged unrelated terrorists, then their words are protected by the First Amendment. Political speech may not be punished just because it makes it more likely that someone will be harmed at some unknown time in the future by an unrelated third party'. The full Appeals Court, however, ruled in a 6–5 vote that the web site material amounted to serious threats and was not protected by the First Amendment; the Court reinstated the original verdict including the order to remove the Nuremberg Files from the Web.[5] The US Supreme Court refused to hear the case – although the 6-5 Appeals Court decision left doubts about the issues central in this case and showed the difficulty to win an incitement case against a First Amendment defence.

In the US the judiciary can and does find ways to punish persons for incitement by charging them with offenses not involving limits to First Amendment rights. In the post-9/11 era, this alternative has been successfully used against a growing number of Muslims. A case in point was that of Javed Iqbal who in 2009 was sentenced to five-and-a-half years in prison for providing material support to a terrorist organization although defence lawyers argued that First Amendment values – free speech and press freedom--were at the centre of this case. Iqbal had enabled the banned satellite broadcasts of Al Manar, a global TV-network operated by the Lebanese Hezbollah, and offered this service to customers of his small satellite programming service in New York (Weiner 2008). Both Hezbollah and Al Manar are on the US government's list of terrorist organizations. With respect to the Iqbal trial and similar cases Barak-Erez and Scharia (2011, 19) concluded, 'Although incitement to terrorism is not criminalised in the United States, its law enforcement agencies are equipped with many other tools to limit the spread of terrorist messages'. Because contemporary terrorist organizations utilize advanced communication technology and especially social media to radicalize, recruit, plan and coordinate horrific acts of terrorism, leading legal scholars in the US discussed the pro and con of limiting free speech of terrorist entities, most of all ISIS. Eric Posner (2015) writes,

> Never before in our history have enemies outside the United States been able to propagate genuinely dangerous ideas on American territory in such an effective way—and by this I mean ideas that lead directly to terrorist attacks that kill people. The novelty of this threat calls for new thinking about limits on freedom of speech.

But suggestions to reconsider the clear and present danger test with respect to most potent terrorist propaganda was rejected forcefully by others, among them David Post (2015) who warns,

> Do we really want government agents deciding which Internet sites 'glorify, express support for, or provide encouragement for ISIS'? That slope is far too slippery for me. Conspiracy to commit murder or mayhem is already a crime, and if it occurs at these sites, the government can and should take action.

While the legal community agreed that the US would stick to its strong First Amendment stance, there was also the recognition that in the face of more devastating terrorism in the homeland justices and the general public could change their minds. In the words of constitutional lawyer Geoffrey R. Stone, 'Five years from now, who knows? You can imagine a scenario in which things get so terrible that you start watering down the protections' (Eckholm 2015).

Terrorists against press freedom or hate speech?

On 7 January, 2015, Said and Cherif Kouachi shot their way into the editorial offices of the satirical weekly *Charlie Hebdo* in Paris killing 11 persons and injuring 11 more. Affiliated with al-Qaeda in the Arabian Peninsula (AQAP) the brothers 'punished' their targets for repeatedly depicting the Prophet Mohammad, a no-no in the religious precepts of certain fundamentalist Muslims. *Charlie Hebdo* editor-in-chief and cartoonist Stephane Chardonnier, one of the victims, had been on AQAP's 'Most Wanted' list for years along with three staff members of the Danish newspaper *Jyllands-Posten*: Fleming Rose, Kurt Westergaard and Carsten Juste. All four had been the targets of several terrorist attacks. Ten years before the lethal incident in Paris the three Danes had been instrumental in the publication of 12 cartoons showing the Prophet Mohammad – in the most controversial depiction with a bomb as turban. Thanks to around-the-clock police protection Rose, Westergaard and Juste were not harmed by jihadist foes.

From the American perspective, the issue surrounding these cartoons was one of media ethics not legal rights. In comparing the Danish Cartoon case with respect to American and European law Robert Post (2015, 83) emphasized,

> [In the United States] content-based restrictions on speech cannot be imposed on the ground that the speech might cause a future harm unless the speech 'is directed to inciting or producing imminent lawless action and is likely to incite or produce such action'. This severe restriction is deemed necessary because a more lax causal connection would invite the government to use the pretext of a causal connection in order to prohibit speech. Classic historical examples of this abuse were statutes prohibiting the advocacy of Communist doctrine on the ground that such speech might cause a future revolution.

But there was also criticism from some quarters that almost all American news organizations did not publish a single of the controversial Danish cartoons. William J. Bennett and Alan M. Dershowitz (2006, A19) wrote in an op-ed article, 'To put it simply, radical Islamists have won a war of intimidation. They have cowed the major news media from showing these cartoons. The mainstream press has capitulated to the Islamists – their threats more than their sensibilities'. For these critics, the news media had violated the fundamental meaning of the First Amendment, namely that 'without responsibility for the right to know carried out by courageous writers, editors, political cartoonists, and publishers, our democracy would be weaker, if not nonexistent'.

In Europe, Muslim clerics sued Jyllands-Posten and Charlie Hebdo for blasphemy and hate speech – in vein. Although many European countries ban hate speech and blasphemy, most legal scholars (Hansen 2006; Post 2015; Heyman 2008) agreed with Brenden O'Leary's (2006, 25) conclusion that publishing 'mockery of Muhammad in an outlet not noted for its Muslim consumers was well within the newspaper's rights (and indeed public manners) both under Danish law, and under the European Convention'. Eric Bleich (2012, 115) along with a few other legal experts differed in their conclusion, namely, 'that there is a very plausible case that at least *some* of these images constitute hate speech in the context of European legal developments and precedent'. Finally, there were Europeans (Modood 2006; Carens 2006) who argued that publicizing these sorts of cartoons does not come down to actionable offenses but is unethical and inappropriate.

These different viewpoints did not matter as far as millions of Muslims around the globe were concerned; they were so offended by the caricatures that riots broke out in a number of Muslim countries causing the violent deaths of more than one hundred persons.

Since the old media – newspapers, radio and television as well as their online offerings – remain for the majority of people the most important sources for public affairs information, terrorists need the mainstream media to further their propaganda objectives. While the mainstream media, simply by reporting about terrorism, unwittingly help terrorists to frame their narratives, they never satisfy fanatic extremists. That is one of the reasons why journalists, editors, cartoonists, photographers and other media personnel are put on terrorists' 'most wanted' lists.

Conclusion

When terrorists strike and kill and maim innocent people, they also attack fundamental human rights. Referring to the Bush government's post-9/11 successful appeal to US television networks not to air Osama bin Laden's video-taped messages in full length the al-Qaeda leader said gleefully, 'freedom and human rights[of free expression and press freedom] in America have been sent to the guillotine with no prospect of return' (Lawrence 2005, 113). Both transnational and domestic terrorist groups challenge liberal democracies to effectively respond to their violent deeds without abridging fundamental human rights and civil liberties, among them the right to free expression and press freedom. In reaction to public fear and anxiety even democratic governments are tempted to and actually do curb direct terrorist communications and news and social media that facilitate terrorist messages. Some terrorists target specifically members of the news media for publicizing material they deem offensive. And, finally, authoritarian rulers oppress the expression of oppositional views in the name of counterterrorism – even if those dissenting voices have nothing to do with terrorism.

Notes

1   The Council of Europe Convention on Human Rights (1950) is available at http://www.echr.coe.int/Documents/Convention_ENG.pdf; the Convention on the Prevention of Terrorism (2005) at http://app.parlamento.pt/webutils/docs/doc.pdf?path=6148523063446f764c3246795a5868774d546f334e7a67774c336470626d6c7c7561574e7059585270646d467a4c31684a4c33526c65485276637939776348 49314e5331595356387a4c6d527659773d3d&fich=ppr55-XI_3.doc&Inline=true, both accessed 21 January, 2016.
2   Broder made his remarks during a seminar on "The Media and Terrorism," sponsored by the Center for Communication, Inc., 23 October, 1985.
3   The report is available at https://freedomhouse.org/report/freedom-world/freedom-world-2015#.VQxvo-FcA89, accessed 21 March, 2015.
4   See note 4.
5   Planned Parenthood v. American Coalition of Life Activists, 41 F. Supp. 2d 1130 (D. Ore.), aff'd in part and remanded, 290 F. 3d 1058 (9th Cir. 2002).

References

Barak-Erez, D. and Scharia, D. (2011). 'Freedom of Speech, Support for Terrorism, and the Challenge of Global Constitutional Law.' *Harvard National Security Journal*, 2, pp. 1–30.

Bassiouni, M. C. (1981). 'Terrorism, Law Enforcement, and the Mass Media: Perspectives, Problems, Proposals'. *The Journal of Criminal Law and Criminology,* 72, pp. 1–51.

Bennett, W. J. and Dershowitz, A. M. (2006). 'A Failure of the Press'. *Washington Post,* 23 February, A19.

Bennett, W. L., Lawrence R. G. and Livingston, S. (2008). *When the Press Fails: Political Power and the News Media from Iraq to Katrina.* Chicago: University of Chicago Press.

Berger, J. M. (2015). 'The Metronome of Apocalyptic Time'. *Perspectives on Terrorism,* 9 (4), pp. 60–70.

Bleich, E. (2012). 'Free Speech or Hate Speech? The Danish Cartoon Controversy in the European Legal System'. In: K. Khory, ed., *Global Migration: Challenges in the Twenty-First Century.* New York: Palgrave Macmillan, pp. 113–128.

Carens, J. H. (2006). 'Free Speech and Democratic Norms in the Danish Cartoon Controversy'. In: Modood, T. et al. 2006. 'The Danish Cartoon Affair: Free Speech, Islamism, and Integration'. *International Migration Journal,* 44(5), pp. 3–62.

Carter B. and Barringer, F. (2001). 'A nation challenged: The coverage'. *New York Times,* 11 October, p. 1.

Chomsky, N. (2002). *9-11.* New York: Seven Stories Press.

Clutterbuck, R. (1983). *The Media and Political Violence,* 2nd ed. New York: Macmillan.

Cole, D. and Dempsey, J. X. (2006). *Terrorism and the Constitution: Sacrificing Civil Liberties in the Name of National Security.* New York: The New Press.

Delli Carpini, M. X. and Williams, B. A. (1987). 'Television and Terrorism: Patterns of Presentation and Occurance, 1969 to 1980'. *Western Political Quarterly,* 40(1), pp. 45–64.

Donohue, L. K. (2005-2006). 'Terrorist Speech and the Future of Free Expression'. *Cardoza Law Review,* 27(1), pp. 234–341.

Eckholm, E. (2015). 'ISIS Influence on Web Prompts Second Thoughts on First Amendment'. *New York Times,* December 27. http://www.nytimes.com/2015/12/28/us/isis-influence-on-web-prompts-sec-ond-thoughts-on-first-amendment.html?hpw&rref=us&action=click&pgtype=Homepage&module=well-region&region=bottom-well&WT.nav=bottom-well [Accessed 20 Jan., 2016].

Elter, A. (2008). *Propaganda der Tat: Die RAF und die Medien.* Frankfurt: Suhrkamp.

Freedom House (2015). 'Freedom on the Net 2015'. Available at: https://freedomhouse.org/sites/default/files/FH_FOTN_2015Report.pdf [Accessed 20 Jan. 2016].

Hansen, R. (2006). 'The Danish Cartoon Controversy: A Defense of Liberal Freedom'. In: Modood, T. et al. eds., 'The Danish Cartoon Affair: Free Speech, Islamism, and Integration'. *International Migration Journal,* 44(5), 3–62.

Herman, E. S. (1982). *The Real Terror Network: Terrorism in Fact and Propaganda.* Boston: South End.

Herman, E. S. and O'Sullivan, G. (1989). *The "Terrorism" Industry: The Experts and Institutions that Shape our View of Terror.* New York: Pantheon.

Heyman, S. J. (2008). 'Hate Speech, Public Discourse, and the First Amendment'. Paper available at Researchgate.

Hickey, N. (1985). 'The Impact on Negotiations: What the Experts Say'. *TV Guide* (21 September).

Ignatieff, M. (2004). *The Lesser Evil: Political Ethics in an Age of Terror.* Princeton, NJ: Princeton University Press.

Kupperman, R. H. and Trent, D. M. (1979). *Terrorism: Threat, Reality, Response.* Stanford, CA: Hoover Institution Press.

Lawrence, Bruce, ed. (2005). *Messages to the World: The Statements of Osama bin Laden.* New York: Verso.

Miller, A. H. (1982). *Terrorism, the Media, and the Law.* Dobbs Ferry, NY: Transnational.

Modood, T. et al. (2006). "The Danish Cartoon Affair: Free Speech, Islamism, and Integration. *International Migration* Journal, 44(5), pp. 3–62.

McLeod, D. M. and Shah, D. V. (2015). *News Frames and National Security: Covering Big Brother.* New York: Cambridge.

Nacos, B. L. (2016). *Mass-Mediated Terrorism: Mainstream and Digital Media in Terrorism and Counterterrorism.* Third Edition. New York: Routledge.

Nacos, B. L. (2015). 'Young Western Women, Fandom, and ISIS'. *E-International Relations* (May), Available at: http://www.e-ir.info/2015/05/05/young-western-women-fandom-and-isis/ [Accessed 4 January, 2016].

Nacos, B. L. (1994). *Terrorism and the Media.* New York: Columbia University Press.

Nacos, B. L., Bloch Elkon, Y., and Shapiro, R. Y. (2011). *Selling Fear: Counterterrorism, the Media, and Public Opinion.* Chicago: University of Chicago Press.

O'Leary, B. (2006). 'Liberalism, Multiculturalism, Danish Cartoons, Islamic Fraud, and the Right of the Ungodly'. Modood, T. et al.

O'Sullivan, J. (1986). 'Media Publicity Causes Terrorism'. Szumski, B. (ed.) *Terrorism: Opposing Viewpoints*. St. Paul: Greenhaven.

Paletz, D. L. and Boiney, J. (1992). 'Researchers' Perspective'. Paletz, D.L. and Schmid, A.P (eds.) *Terrorism and the Media*. Newbury Park: Sage, pp. 6–27.

Paust, J. J. (1978). 'International law and control of the media: Terror, repression, and the alternatives'. *Indiana Law Journal*, 53, pp. 621–77.

Pious, R. M. (2006). *The War on Terrorism and the Rule of Law*. Los Angeles: Roxbury.

Posner, E. (2015). 'SIS Gives Us No Choice but to Consider Limits on Speech'. *Slate.com* (15 December). http://www.slate.com/articles/news_and_politics/view_from_chicago/2015/12/isis_s_online_radicalization_efforts_present_an_unprecedented_danger.single.html [Accessed 15 Jan. 2016].

Posner, R. A. (2007). *Countering Terrorism: Blurred Focus, Halting Steps*. Lanham, MD: Rowman & Littlefield.

Post, D. 2015. 'Protecting the First Amendment in the Internet Age'. *Washington Post* (December 21), 2015 https://www.washingtonpost.com/news/volokh-conspiracy/wp/2015/12/21/protecting-the-first-amendment-in-the-internet-age/ [Accessed 24 February, 2016].

Scanlon, J. (1989). 'The Hostage Taker, the Terrorist, the Media: Partners in Public Crime'. Walters, L. M., Wilkins, L. and Walters, T. eds. *Bad Tidings: Communication and Catastrophe*. Hilldale, NJ: Lawrence Erlbaum, pp. 115–30.

Schlesinger, P. (1981). 'Terrorism, the Media, and the Liberal-Democratic State: A Critique of the Orthodoxy'. *Social Research* 48(1), pp. 74–99.

Schlesinger, P., Murdock, G. and Elliott, P. (1983). *Televising Terrorism: Political Violence in Popular Culture*. London: Comedia.

Schmid, A. P. and De Graaf, J. (1982). *Violence as Communication*, Beverly Hills: Sage.

Shipler, D. K. (1998). 'Blacks in the Newsrooms: Yes, but…' *Columbia Journalism Review* (May/June), pp. 26–32.

Sick, G. (1986). *All Fall Down: America's Tragic Encounter with Iran*. New York: Penguin Books.

Szumski, B. (ed.) (1986). *Opposing Viewpoints: Terrorism*. St. Paul: Greenhaven Press.

Terell, R. L. and Ross, K. (1988). 'Terrorism, Censorship, and the US Press Corps'. *Gazette* 42, pp. 33–51.

Weimann, G. and Hoffman, B. (2015). *Terrorism in Cyberspace: The Next Generation*. New York: Columbia University Press.

Weimann, G. and Winn, C. (1993). *The Theater of Terror*. London: Longman.

Weiner, B. (2008). 'A Guilty Plea in Providing Satellite TV for Hezbollah'. *New York Times*, December 23. Available at: http://www.nytimes.com/2008/12/24/nyregion/24plea.html [Accessed 20 Mar. 2016].

Weimann, G. (1990). 'Redefinition of Image: The Impact of Mass-Mediated Terrorism'. *International Journal of Public Opinion Research* 2, pp. 16–29.

Wieviorka, M. 1988. *The Making of Terrorism*. Chicago: The University of Chicago Press.

Wilkinson, P. (1997). "The media and terrorism: A reassessment." *Terrorism and Political Violence*, 9(2), pp. 51–64.

Wilkinson. P. (2006). *Terrorism versus Democracy: The Liberal State Response*. Second Edition. London and New York: Routledge.

Wittes, B. (2008). *Law and the Long War: The Future of Justice in the Age of Terrorism*. New York: Penguin Press.

Zelin, A.Y. (2015). 'Picture or it Didn't Happen: A Snapshot of the Islamic State's Official Media'. *Perspectives on Terrorism* 9(4), pp. 84–100.

INDEX

Note: Page numbers followed with "n" refer endnotes.